M000280091

"Finally, an anthology that places the power and rar[...] context not just of the Western tradition but also th[...] World. The essays in this collection, many of which stress the performative and normalizing function of language, invite us to mark what has gone before in the hope of moving forward into a new era of Feminist theorizing. Broad in scope and rich in information, it is the best guide available to the range and depth of Feminist theory."
Donn Welton, State University of New York at Stony Brook

"Jaggar and Young's *Companion to Feminist Philosophy* successfully introduces the uninitiated to the full scope of this rapidly burgeoning subject and, at the same time, provides a truly authoritative consolidation which will serve as an invaluable platform for further developments. Ranging across several continents and even more traditions, its three score chapters touch upon all the main branches of philosophy – language, knowledge and nature, religion, aesthetics and ethics, politics and society – showing in each case what difference is made by distinctively feminist concerns, such as subjectivity and embodiment. It is a tour de force that will impress skeptics and confirm the committed."
Robert E. Goodin, Australian National University

"Companions of this ultra-compendious kind will always be monumental in a certain way, but this one seems especially so. Its publication marks the fact that now is an exciting moment in feminist philosophy . . . This Companion captures the moment, and one would hope that anyone who consults it, whether out of special interest or simple intellectual curiosity, will be stimulated by it."

Miranda Fricker, Times Literary Supplement

Blackwell Companions to Philosophy

This outstanding student reference series offers a comprehensive and authoritative survey of philosophy as a whole. Written by today's leading philosophers, each volume provides lucid and engaging coverage of the key figures, terms, topics, and problems of the field. Taken together, the volumes provide the ideal basis for course use, representing an unparalleled work of reference for students and specialists alike.

Published

Blackwell
Companions to
Philosophy

A Companion to Feminist Philosophy

Edited by

ALISON M. JAGGAR AND
IRIS MARION YOUNG

BLACKWELL
Publishers

Copyright © Blackwell Publishers Ltd 1998, 2000

First published 1998
First published in paperback 2000
2 4 6 8 10 9 7 5 3 1

Blackwell Publishers Inc.
350 Main Street
Malden, Massachusetts 02148
USA

Blackwell Publishers Ltd
108 Cowley Road
Oxford OX4 1JF
UK

Library of Congress Cataloging-in-Publication Data

A companion to feminist philosophy / edited by Alison M. Jaggar and Iris Marion Young
p.   cm. — (Blackwell companions to philosophy)
Includes bibliographical references and index.
ISBN 1–55786–659–7 (hardback : alk. paper)
ISBN 0–631–22067–4 (paperback : alk. paper)
1. Feminist theory. I. Jaggar, Alison M. II. Young, Iris
Marion, 1949– . III. Series.
HQ1190. C665   1998
305.42'01–dc21   97–10412
                                                          CIP

British Library Cataloguing in Publication Data

A CIP catalogue record for this book is available from the British Library.

Typeset in 10.5 / 12.5 pt Photina by Pure Tech India Ltd, Pondicherry.
Printed in Great Britain by T. J. International, Cornwall.

This book is printed on acid-free paper

Contents

CONTENTS

Contributors

Rachel Adler is a Jewish theologian and ethicist who teaches at Hebrew Union College, Los Angeles. She is the author of *Engendering Judaism: A New Theology and Ethics* (1997).

Linda Martín Alcoff teaches philosophy and women's studies at Syracuse University, where she is the Meredith Professor for Teaching Excellence. She is the author of *Real Knowing: New Versions of the Coherence Theory* (1996) and co-editor of *Feminist Epistemologies* (1993). Her essays on race and gender have appeared in *Signs, Hypatia, Cultural Critique* and *Radical Philosophy*, and she is currently writing a book called *Visible Identities: Race, Gender, and the Self*.

Anita Allen is the Associate Dean for Research and Adjunct Professor of Philosophy at Georgetown University Law Center. She teaches constitutional law, legal philosophy, torts, professional responsibility and privacy law, and her research interests include ethics and law of privacy, reproductive rights and responsibility, and race relations policy. She has published dozens of articles and two books: *Uneasy Access: Privacy for Women in a Free Society* (1988) and (with co-authors) *Cases and Materials on Privacy Law* (1992).

Barbara Hilkert Andolsen is the Helen Bennett McMurray Professor of Social Ethics at Monmouth University. She is the author of several books, including *Good Work at the Video Display Terminal: A Feminist Ethical Analysis of Changes in Clerical Work* (1989).

Sandra Lee Bartky is Professor of Philosophy and Women's Studies at the University of Illinois at Chicago. She is a founding member of the now international Society for Women in Philosophy, author of *Femininity and Domination: Studies in the Phenomenology of Oppression* (1990), and co-editor of *Revaluing French Feminisms* (1992).

Katharine T. Bartlett is Professor of Law at Duke University School of Law, where she teaches gender and law, feminist legal theory, family law, and contracts. She has lectured and published extensively on topics in gender theory, employment law, theories of social change, and legal education. She is the author of two leading law casebooks, *Family Law, Cases, Text, Problems* (with Ira Ellman and Paul Kurtz) (2nd edn 1991) and *Gender and Law: Theory, Doctrine, Commentary* (1993), and a reader, *Feminist Legal Theory: Readings in Law and Gender* (1991).

Lynda Birke is a biologist, whose work focuses on feminist analyses of science, particularly biology, and on making science more accessible. She teaches women's studies and science studies in the Centre for the Study of Women and Gender at the University of Warwick, England. Her books include *Women, Feminism and Biology* (1986), and *Reinventing Biology* (with Ruth Hubbard, 1995).

Rosi Braidotti is Professor of Women's Studies in the Arts Faculty of Utrecht University and scientific director of the Netherlands Research School of Women's Studies. She coordinates the European Thematic Network of Women's Studies for the SOCRATES program of the European Union, as well as the NOISE inter-European university exchange program. Her books include *Patterns of Dissonance: A Study of Women in Contemporary Philosophy* (1991), *Nomadic Subjects: Embodiment and Sexual Difference* (1994), and (with co-authors) *Women, the Environment and Sustainable Development: Towards a Theoretical Synthesis* (1994). Her current research focuses on the concept of difference in the work of Gilles Deleuze.

Teresa Brennan's books include *History after Lacan* and *The Age of Paranoia* (forthcoming).

Tina Chanter is the author of *Ethics of Eros: Irigaray's Rewriting of the Philosophers* (1995) and articles on figures such as Derrida, Heidegger, Kristeva, Levinas, Lacan, and Merleau-Ponty.

Lorraine Code is Professor of Philosophy at York University in Toronto. The author of *What Can She Know? Feminist Theory and the Construction of Knowledge* (1991) and *Rhetorical Spaces: Essays on (Gendered) Locations* (1995), she is working on a project, "Ecology, Responsibility, and the Politics of Knowledge," which develops an ecological model for knowledge and subjectivity.

Vrinda Dalmiya teaches philosophy at the Indian Institute of Technology, Delhi, India. She has also taught at Montana State University and the University of Washington.

Natalie Dandekar publishes on topics of international justice, development ethics, and philosophy of law. Her most recent work focuses on exploring the connections between an ethics of care and the work of international humanitarian agencies.

Daša Duhaček is a Coordinator of the Belgrade Women's Studies Center. She has been teaching and writing on issues of political philosophy and feminist theory. Her publications include "Women's Time in the Former Yugoslavia" in Nanette Funk and Magda Mueller, eds, *Gender Politics and Post-Communism* (1993) and introductions to Serbian translations of Mary Wollstonecraft, Harriet Taylor and John Stuart Mill, Hannah Arendt, and others.

Ann Ferguson is Professor of Philosophy and Women's Studies and Director of Women's Studies at the University of Massachusetts at Amherst. The author of two books: *Blood at the Root: Motherhood, Sexuality and Male Dominance* (1989) and *Sexual Democracy: Women, Oppression and Revolution* (1991), she is currently working on a book on feminist ethics and politics co-edited with Bat-Ami Bar-On, and on papers on such topics as selfhood and racial, class, and gender identities; feminist utopias; risky practices as a topic in feminist ethics; and Foucault and postmodernism.

Cynthia Freeland is Associate Professor of Philosophy and former Director of Women's Studies at the University of Houston. She is co-editor of *Philosophy and Film* (1995) and editor of *Feminist Interpretations of Aristotle* (1997).

Marilyn Friedman teaches philosophy at Washington University in St Louis and works in ethics, social philosophy, and feminist theory. She is the author of *What Are Friends For? Feminist Perspectives on Personal Relationships and Moral Theory* (1993), the co-author of *Political Correctness: For and Against* (1995), the co-editor of *Mind and Morals: Essays on Ethics and Cognitive Science* (1996), and the co- editor of *Feminism and Community* (1995).

Moira Gatens is Senior Lecturer in Philosophy at the University of Sydney. She is author of *Feminism and Philosophy: Perspectives on Difference and Equality* (1991) and *Imaginary Bodies: Ethics, Power and Corporeality* (1996).

Mary Hawkesworth is Professor of Political Science and a member of the Women's Studies faculty at the University of Louisville. She is the author of *Beyond Oppression: Feminist Theory and Political Strategy* (1990). *Theoretical Issues in Policy Analysis* (1988), and editor of *The Encyclopedia of Government and Politics* (1992) and *Feminism and Public Policy* (1994).

Virginia Held is Distinguished Professor of Philosophy at Hunter College and the Graduate School of the City University of New York. Her most recent books include *Feminist Morality: Transforming Culture, Society, and Politics* (1993) and *Rights and Goods: Justifying Social Action* (1984).

Azizah Y. al-Hibri is an Associate Professor of Law, teaching corporate law and Islamic jurisprudence at the T. C. Williams School of Law. University of Richmond. Dr al-Hibri is a former professor of philosophy, a founder and the first editor of *Hypatia: A Journal of Feminist Philosophy*, founder and former president of Karamah: Muslim Women Lawyers for Human Rights. She has written numerous articles on women's rights.

Sarah Lucia Hoagland is Professor of Philosophy and Women's Studies at Northeastern Illinois University. She is author of *Lesbian Ethics* (1988) and co-editor of *For Lesbians Only: a Separatist Anthology* (1988).

Nancy Holmstrom is Associate Professor of Philosophy at Rutgers University, Newark. She has written on a number of central concepts in social philosophy, including freedom, exploitation, and human nature, and is active in movements for social justice.

Alison M. Jaggar is Professor of Philosophy and Women's Studies at the University of Colorado at Boulder. Her books include: *Feminist Frameworks*, co-edited with Paula Rothenberg (1978, 1984, 1993), *Feminist Politics and Human Nature* (1983), *Gender/Body/Knowledge: Feminist Reconstructions of Being and Knowing*, co-edited with Susan Bordo (1989), and *Living with Contradictions: Controversies in Feminist Social Ethics* (1994). Currently she is working on a book on feminist moral epistemology, tentatively entitled *Sex, Truth and Power: A Feminist Theory of Moral Justification*.

Jin Yihong is currently Director and Associate Research Fellow of the Department of Cultural Research at the Philosophy Institute of Jiangsu Provincial Academy of Social Services. Her current research in the area of Chinese women's studies focuses on the ways in which a market economy affects rural women and their families.

Catherine Keller, author of *Apocalypse Now and Then: A Feminist Guide to the End of the World* (1996) and *From a Broken Web: Separation, Sexism and the Self* (1986), is Associate Professor of Constructive Theology at the Graduate and Theological Schools of Drew University.

Elizabeth Kiss is Director of the Kenan Ethics Program and Associate Professor of the Practice of Politics and Philosophy at Duke University. Her research interests include ethics and political theory, feminist theory, and Central European politics. She is completing a book on human rights entitled *Rights as Instruments*.

Eva Feder Kittay is Professor of Philosophy at SUNY Stony Brook. She is the author of *Metaphor. Its Cognitive Force and Linguistic Structure* (1987), co-editor (with Diana T. Meyers) of *Women and Moral Theory* (1987), author of *Some Mother's Child: Essays on Equality and Dependency* (forthcoming), and founder of *Women's Committee of One Hundred*, an organization devoted to women and welfare.

Cornelia Klinger is a Permanent Fellow at the Institute for Human Sciences in Vienna, Austria, and lecturer at the University of Tübingen, Germany. She has published a wide range of articles on feminist philosophy, German Idealism, and Romanticism. Her latest book is *Flucht–Trost–Revolte: Die Moderne und ihre aesthetischen Gegenwelten* (1995).

Rhoda Hadassah Kotzin is a professor in the Department of Philosophy at Michigan State University. The areas of her teaching, research, and publication include the history of philosophy (especially Plato, Aristotle, and Kant), phenomenology, ethics, and, of course, feminist philosophy.

Sonia Kruks is the Dansforth Professor of Politics at Oberlin College, where she teaches political philosophy and feminist theory. She has written extensively on political and social aspects of phenomenology and is currently writing a book on phenomenology and feminism.

Kathleen Lennon is a senior lecturer in Philosophy at the University of Hull, England, where she also chairs the Board of Gender Studies. She is co-editor with Margaret Whitford of *Knowing the Difference: Feminist Perspectives in Epistemology* (1994).

Lin Chun teaches at the London School of Economics and Political Science and has been working closely with friends in China on various projects.

Liu Bohong is an associate professor with the Women's Studies Institute of China. She has researched and written on Chinese women's employment and recently has coordinated the Chinese Women's Health Network and the Chinese NGO Forum.

Genevieve Lloyd holds the Chair of Philosophy at the University of New South Wales, Sydney, Australia. She is the author of *The Man of Reason: "Male" and "female" in Western Philosophy*, (2nd edn 1993), *Being in Time: Selves and Narrators in Philosophy and Literature* (1993), *Part of Nature: Self-Knowledge in Spinoza's "Ethics"* (1994), and *Spinoza and the "Ethics"* (1996).

María Lugones is a feminist theorist/activist and popular educator. She teaches at the Escuela Popular Norteña, a center for popular education in New Mexico, and at the State University of New York at Binghamton.

Andrea Maihofer has studied philosophy, Germanic studies and education. In 1987, she received a doctoral degree in philosophy with the thesis *Das Recht bei Marx: Zur dialektischen Struktur von Gerechtigkeit. Menschenrechte und Recht* (*The Law in Marx: Toward a Dialectical Stucture of Justice: Human Rights and Law*). In 1995, she completed her habilitation thesis in sociology, *Geschlecht als Existenzweise: Macht, Moral, Recht und Geschlechtdifferenz* (*Gender as a Way of Existence: Power, Morality, Law and Gender Difference*). Presently, she is a lecturer in the social sciences at the University of Frankfurt.

Jane Roland Martin, Professor of Philosophy Emerita at the University of Massachusetts, Boston, as well as past president of the Philosophy of Education Society and a former Guggenheim Fellow, is the author of several books and numerous articles in the philosophy of education. For her work on gender and education she has received an honorary doctorate from Salem State College in Massachusetts and Umeâ University in Sweden.

Johanna Meehan is Associate Professor at Grinell College. She is also the editor of and contributor to *Feminists Read Habermas: Gendering the Subject of Discourse* (1995). Her research focuses on feminist theory and critical theory. Her current project is a book entitled *The Intersubjective Construction of Selfhood*.

Diana Tietjens Meyers is Professor of Philosophy at the University of Connecticut at Storrs. She is the author of *Subjection and Subjectivity: Psychoanalytic Feminism and Moral Philosophy* (1994), *Self, Society, and Personal Choice* (1989), and *Inalienable Rights: A Defense* (1985).

Michelle M. Moody-Adams is Associate Professor of Philosophy at Indiana University, Bloomington. She has published essays on a variety of topics in moral and political philosophy, and is the author of *Morality, Culture, and Philosophy: Fieldwork in Familiar Places* (forthcoming).

Herta Nagl-Docekal is Professor of Philosophy at the University of Vienna, Austria, and co-editor of the journal *Deutsche Zeitschrift für Philosophie*. Her recent books include *Jenseits der Geschlechtermoral* (co-edited with Herlinde Pauer-Studer, 1993), *Feministische Philosophie* (edited, 1994), *Politische Theorie: Differenz und Lebensqualität* (co-edited with Herlinde Pauer-Studer, 1996), *Der Sinn des Historischen* (edited, 1996).

Lynn Hankinson Nelson is Chair and Associate Professor of Philosophy at Rowan College. She is the author of *Who Knows: From Quine to a Feminist Empiricism* (1990), editor of a special issue of *Synthèse* devoted to Feminism and Science (1995), and co-editor with Jack Nelson of *Feminism, Science, and the Philosophy of Science* (1996) and *Re-Reading the Canon: Feminist Perspectives on Quine* (forthcoming).

Linda Nicholson is Professor of Educational Administration and Policy Studies and Women's Studies at The University of Albany. She has authored *Gender and History: the Limits of Social Theory in the Age of the Family* (1986), edited *Feminism/Postmodernism* (1990), *The Second Wave: Readings in Feminist Theory* (1996), coedited *Social Postmodernism* (1995) and is presently putting together a collection of her essays for publication.

Andrea Nye is Professor of Philosophy at the University of Wisconsin at Whitewater. She is the author of a number of books on feminist philosophy, including most recently *Philosophy and Feminism: At the Border* (1995).

Sophie Oluwele is a member and sometime chair of the Department of Philosophy at the University of Lagos, Nigeria, and she has also served as National President of the Nigerian Philosophy Association.

Anne Phillips is Professor of Politics at London Guildhall University. She has written extensively on issues in feminist and democratic theory, including *Engendering Democracy* (1991), *Democracy and Difference* (1993), and *The Politics of Presence* (1995).

Val Plumwood is presently an honorary Research Associate at the University of Sydney. She has wide interests in feminist and ecofeminist philosophy, social and environmental philosophy.

Sara Ruddick teaches philosophy and feminist studies at The New School for Social Research. She is the author of *Maternal Thinking: Towards a Politics of Peace* (1989).

Robin May Schott is currently Associate Professor of Philosophy at the University of Copenhagen. Her books include *Cognition and Eros: A Critique of the*

Kantian Paradigm (1988; paperback, 1993), *Reproduction, Gender, and Technology* (co-edited with Bente Rosenbeck, 1995), and *Feminist Interpretations of Kant* (1997).

Ofelia Schutte is Professor of Philosophy and Affiliate Professor of Women's Studies and Latin American Studies at the University of Florida, Gainesville. She is the author of *Beyond Nihilism: Nietzsche without Masks* (1984) and *Cultural Identity and Social Liberation in Latin American Thought* (1993). She has written on French and Latin American feminism and has guest-edited the special cluster on Spanish and Latin American Feminist Philosophy in *Hypatia* (9: 1994).

Charlene Haddock Seigfried is Professor of Philosophy at Purdue University. She is the author of *Pragmatism and Feminism* (1996), *William James's Radical Reconstruction of Philosophy* (1990) and *Chaos and Context* (1978). She also edited a special issue of *Hypatia* on pragmatism and feminism and is President of the Society for the Advancement of American Philosophy. She is the John Dewey Lecturer for 1998.

Laura Shanner is the l'Anson Assistant Professor in the Department of Philosophy and Joint Centre for Bioethics at the University of Toronto, Canada. Her work in bioethics and reproductive medicine has been conducted in the USA, Canada, Australia, and the UK, and she has served on a federal policy committee on embryo research in Canada.

Susan Sherwin is a Professor of Philosophy and Women's Studies at Dalhousie University, Halifax, Nova Scotia. She is just completing a very interesting and challenging four-year (1993-97) interdisciplinary research project on feminist health- care ethics involving eleven Canadian feminist scholars from a variety of disciplines and institutions.

Laurie Shrage is Professor of Philosophy at California State Polytechnic University, Pomona. She is the author of *Moral Dilemmas of Feminism: Prostitution, Adultery, and Abortion* (1994), as well as articles on race and gender, sex commerce, and film aesthetics.

Anita Silvers is Professor of Philosophy at San Francisco State University. She is the co-author of *Puzzles about Art*, has published over fifty essays in aesthetics, ethics and social justice, disability studies, bioethics and educational policy; and is currently completing a book on *What Lives are Worth Living?: Disability, Difference, Discrimination.* Silvers was the first recipient of the California Council for the Humanities' annual Distinguished California Humanist Award and of the California Faculty Association's Equal Rights Award.

Basharat Tayyab teaches philosophy at the University of Karachi, Pakistan. She has been a Fullbright Fellow at the University of West Virginia. Her interests include contemporary French and Islamic feminisms.

Lynne Tirrell is Associate Professor of Philosophy at the University of Massachusetts at Boston. She has published articles on philosophy of language, literature, moral theory, and feminism, and she is working on a book on derogatory terms.

Margaret Urban Walker has published essays on moral agency, epistemology, responsibility, and feminist critique of ethics. Her book *Moral Understandings* will appear in 1997.

Chris Weedon is Reader in Critical and Cultural Theory at the University of Wales, Cardiff. Her publications include *Feminist Practice and Poststructuralist Theory* (1987/1997); *Cultural Politics: Class, Gender, Race and the Postmodern World* (with Glenn Jordan, 1996) and *Feminism and the Politics of Difference* (1998).

Iris Marion Young is Professor of Public and International Affairs at the University of Pittsburgh, where she teaches ethics and political philosophy. She is author of *Justice and the Politics of Difference* (1990), as well as numerous articles in journals of philosophy and political science. Her most recent book is a collection of essays under the title *Intersecting Voices*: *Dilemmas of Gender, Political Philosophy, and Policy* (1997).

Jacqueline Zita received her Ph.D. in Philosophy from Washington University in St Louis. Currently she is Chair and Associate Professor of Women's Studies at the University of Minnesota and an executive officer in the National Women's Studies Association. Her work is focused primarily on sexuality and gender theory, corporeal philosophical, and epistemological questions concerning the interdisciplinarity and oppositional disciplinarities and pedagogical practices of Women's Studies.

Acknowledgments

This volume could not have come into existence without the help of many people. Most prominent among them were, of course, our authors who, without exception, were remarkably co-operative in following our demanding instructions and have produced some invaluable essays. In addition, we are extremely grateful to all those people who suggested either categories or authors, or who gave us expert advice about articles that we felt unprepared to evaluate. They include: Xinyan Jiang, Safro Kwame, Uma Narayan, Linda Nicholson, Sally Sedgwick, Nancy Tuana, Alison Wylie, and Li Jun Yuan. For research support, we should like to thank the Women's Studies Program at the University of Colorado at Boulder; for help with copy-editing as well as translating, we thank Christian Hunold, and for most of the nitty-gritty administrative work, as well as the daunting bibliography, we must thank Amy Kane. At Blackwell, we appreciate the contributors of Stephan Chambers, who first suggested the project, Steven Smith, who took it over from him, Mary Riso, who handled most of the adminstration, and Juanita Bullough, our long-suffering copy-editor. Finally, we are, as always, grateful to our partners, David Alexander and David Jaggar, who have supported us in this as in so many previous projects, and to our children, Morgen Alexander-Young and Dylan Jaggar, who helped us get the project into perspective at times when it seemed overwhelming.

Introduction

What is feminist philosophy?

Feminist philosophy is a body of scholarship which began in the early 1970s as one branch of the women's studies movement. Like women's studies in other disciplines, feminist philosophy started out with the somewhat modest goal of ending the invisibility of women in much disciplinary knowledge. Twenty years ago few would have predicted that this project of greater inclusion for women and women's experience in philosophical inquiry would produce the huge body of work partially documented in this volume, much of which has challenged and helped transform basic philosophical paradigms in many subfields.

Begun with the intention of using existing philosophical tools and techniques to address issues of special concern to women, primarily issues of practical ethics and politics, feminist philosophy has moved to investigating the overt and covert ways in which the devaluation of women may be inherent in the most enduring ideals, the central concepts, and the dominant theories of philosophy. Feminist philosophy is thus defined by its commitment to redressing perceived male bias in philosophy.

This commitment has appeared in a variety of ways. Feminist philosophy includes projects to recuperate the work of forgotten women philosophers excluded from the canon. It also includes direct challenges to the disparagement of women explicit in the work of many canonical philosophers; in the Western tradition, these philosophers include Aristotle, Aquinas, Rousseau, Kant, Hegel, and Sartre who, in a tradition that has invariably regarded rationality as the essential human characteristic, argued that women's capacity for reason was different from and inferior to men's. In addition, feminist philosophers have challenged moral and political theories or applications which treat women as instrumental to the interests of men or male-dominated institutions such as the family or the state; they have also sought to rectify philosophical neglect of many issues that particularly concern women. In the Western tradition, these include especially issues of sexuality and domestic life, which have been generally conceptualized as belonging to a private realm outside the domain of justice.

As well as disputing the marginalization, neglect, and even overt disparagement of women which characterize many mainstream philosophical traditions, feminist philosophers have also addressed what many perceive to be philosophy's more subtle and covert devaluation of the feminine. In the West, this feminist

1

project has often been taken to require deconstructing conceptual dichotomies such as culture/nature, transcendence/immanence, universal/particular, mind/body, reason/emotion, and public/private; by associating the more highly valued term with masculinity and the less valued with femininity, these dichotomies are charged with inscribing the cultural devaluation of women into the structure of ultimate reality. Finally, some feminist philosophers have argued that the general, though incomplete, exclusion of women from practicing philosophy has resulted in the acceptance of perspectives which reflect experiences and preoccupations that are characteristically masculine. For instance, modern Western philosophy's commitment to the centrality of such values as respect, autonomy, equality, and impartiality has been said to rest on a conception of human nature that represents individuals as essentially separate from others, insatiably appetitive, and with interests typically in conflict, a conception thought to reflect men's experience of adversarial market relations.

Conception of this volume

For the purposes of this volume, feminist philosophy does not name a particular set of propositions or methodological commitments. Although feminism certainly presupposes a substantive ethical or political commitment to opposing women's social subordination, this commitment is too indeterminate to entail specific answers to most philosophical questions. Rather than offer some general account of the scope of this term, we have left it to each author to determine what for her counts both as feminist and as philosophical. We think the result is a rich diversity of ideas and approaches to philosophical and human inquiry.

Our goal in this volume is to make more easily and widely available the range of work included under the rubric of feminist philosophy. As editors, we have worked hard to represent all those philosophical traditions, fields, and approaches in which we are aware that feminist work has been undertaken. We have included feminist scholarship on the history of Western philosophy and some non-Western traditions. Entries on twentieth-century philosophy include Anglo-American and European and, to a lesser extent, Asian, Latin American, and African philosophy.

We have tried to include chapters on all the major standard subfields of philosophy people write about today. In some cases, such as ethics, the work in feminist philosophy related to standard subfields is so extensive that we have several distinct topics within the subfield. While much feminist inquiry in philosophy has engaged with standard fields in the discipline, however, some of the originality of feminist philosophy consists in bringing subjects and modes of experience under philosophical reflection for the first time. Thus some of the topics in our table of contents, such as "body politics," "language and power," or "lesbian ethics," are exciting and important areas of feminist philosophy with no counterparts in the wider discipline.

Although we asked our authors to undertake as comprehensive a survey of feminist work on their topic as was possible in the limited space allotted, we also

2

requested them to avoid an authoritative tone that inevitably would have been misleading. Instead, we not only encouraged authors to organize their survey around themes that they found most salient, but also invited them to develop their own critical perspective on this work, emphasizing the particularity of their authorship by using the first-person singular. As a result, the volume is not only diverse in its range but also includes diversity in its authors' styles and conclusions.

Certainly the table of contents is not definitive. Other editors might have emphasized some fields more than we have, and de-emphasized or excluded others. Doubtless there are some people who will not find their particular interest well represented. Nevertheless, together, the essays in this volume offer an exciting and comprehensive collection and analysis of the main ideas in feminist philosophy to date.

Global dimensions

Academic feminist philosophy, like many other academic fields, is dominated today by Anglophone and especially US authors. The size and wealth of US society make possible the production and distribution of enormous quantities of academic writing, which often influences scholars in other parts of the world. It is not uncommon for US authors to write out of their own experience without noticing its cultural specificity.

In planning this *Companion*, we tried to mitigate the dominance of US authors, as far as was possible within the restrictions of an English-language volume. Since feminist philosophy is actively pursued today in virtually every Western European nation as well as in Canada, New Zealand, and Australia, we sought contributions from authors in several of those countries who were recognized as experts in various fields of feminist philosophy. Authors from different countries often write from somewhat different reference points or traditions, so that including voices from several Western nations adds to the range and subtlety of the ideas presented here.

We did not want to limit the volume to Western contributions, however, and so we included a section with entries on feminist philosophy in Africa, Asia, Eastern Europe, and Latin America. The irony of this gesture toward geographical inclusion is that it highlights the many respects in which Western academic philosophy, feminist philosophy, and our own editorial practice neglect or marginalize philosophical and theoretical ideas from the Eastern and Southern hemispheres. If the volume contained no such section, we suspect that its absence would be noticed by few, so that we would be able to evade the issues of exclusion and differential treatment that the section raises. Although we knew in advance that our efforts were bound to be inadequate, we decided to represent at least some ideas from the Eastern and Southern hemispheres and to confront the questions and criticisms this was bound to evoke.

A few articles invoke non-Western perspectives in the sections that are not geographically identified, but most of the articles on universalist-sounding

3

topics such as "knowledge," "ethics," and "politics" refer almost exclusively to Western and even US writers, even when many of their ideas are relevant to other cultural contexts. The main reason for this exclusivity is that most of the scholarly literature self-identified as "feminist philosophy" is written by North Americans and Western Europeans. However, interest in women's studies has developed in most academic settings in the world today and this has begun to stimulate more specialist work in feminist philosophy. We thought that the best way to document the new scholarly interest in feminist philosophy emerging in Africa, Asia, Eastern Europe, and Latin America would be to invite contributions from scholars familiar with each of those contexts.

Each author in our geographically identified section was asked to survey feminist philosophy in a continent or subcontinent. This assignment was Western-biased in several respects. Most obviously, it lacked symmetry with the other, more specifically topic-oriented, entries elsewhere in the volume. It also confronted authors with the impossible task of summarizing the diverse philosophical traditions of a vast region and explaining feminist responses to them. Thirdly, the paucity of self-identified feminist philosophy in all these regions except for Latin America often required authors to construct philosophical positions from writing that did not necessarily define itself by reference to a recognized philosophical tradition. Finally, our assignment expected authors in this section to address primarily a Western audience, requiring them to explain concepts that might be quite familiar to a non-Western audience and sometimes to compare these ideas with Western approaches.

Despite the problems inherent in this section, we think that readers will find it to be one of the most exciting in the volume. In the regrettably limited space available to them, the authors reveal aspects of the philosophical richness of ancient traditions of thought in Asia and Africa, as well as of distinct traditions of Marxism, existentialism, hermeneutics, and liberalism as these have been developed by writers in the Eastern and Southern hemispheres. The chapters in this section demonstrate that feminist challenge is at least as relevant in non-Western as it is in Western philosophical contexts but that non-Western feminist philosophy generates quite distinct problematics and conclusions.

The future of feminist philosophy

This volume demonstrates that inquiry informed by a feminist perspective is salient to virtually every field and subfield of contemporary philosophical scholarship. It also reveals that these lines of inquiry are further advanced in some fields than others. Moral, social, and political philosophy were the arenas in which Western feminist philosophers first intervened because, as noted earlier, Western feminist philosophy was originally conceptualized as applying existing philosophical tools and techniques to issues of special concern to women. When these projects encountered difficulties, feminist philosophers turned to examining the tools and techniques themselves, embarking on an extensive critical investigation of the ideals, concepts, and methods of Western moral and political philosophy. Today feminist ethics is probably the most mature field of feminist philosophy, with an especially flourishing subfield of feminist biomedical ethics. Epistemology and the philosophy of science are also terrains in which feminist inquiry has been particularly fruitful and which are currently experiencing a boom in feminist scholarship. Given that art criticism and aesthetics are often considered "softer" and more feminine topics than the supposedly "harder" questions of epistemology and philosophy of science, it is surprising that more work has not been done on investigating the possible masculinist biases of aesthetic theories and the contributions that theorizing from women's social locations or out of feminist philosophical views of self and knowledge can make to aesthetic inquiry. Feminist inquiry in logic and the philosophy of language also seems relatively underdeveloped.

Some areas of feminist philosophical investigation are undeveloped because philosophical inquiry in those areas generally is still relatively new. Theories of justice are as old as philosophy, but the philosophical issues raised by the idea of justice between peoples across the globe are only just beginning to be articulated. Philosophical reflection on the normative dimensions of social policy is also a recent development.

Although feminist philosophical work is still in its infancy in a few areas, it has proceeded in most fields through two stages and may be ready for a third. Early work in feminist philosophy established the need to interrogate both historical and contemporary philosophical scholarship from the point of view of an interest in the subordination and distinctive experience of women. Feminist philosophers revealed masculinist biases lurking in specific philosophical claims about women, sexuality, and family; in conceptions of human knowledge, reason, and passion; and in the way that the canon of philosophy had been defined. They uncovered and wrote about women philosophers and showed that feminist questions generated alternative interpretations of the texts of many male philosophers. This first stage, or perhaps aspect, of feminist philosophy consisted primarily in critiquing the existing philosophical canon.

Remedies are usually implicit in diagnoses and critiques lead naturally to reconstructions. The second stage or aspect of feminist philosophy consisted in developing new philosophical perspectives or theories, informed by the earlier critiques, and especially by philosophical reflection on the specific experience of women. This volume documents most of the new approaches to ethics, political philosophy, epistemology, and the philosophy characteristic of this stage which, in many cases, have had significant impact on the wider discipline. Since the emergence of these theories and approaches, much of feminist philosophy has been devoted to internal conversation among those developing and teaching this work, criticizing one another within shared premises, building on one another's arguments and charting further directions of inquiry within paradigms set by feminist philosophers. In this stage of "normalization," the various arenas of feminist philosophical inquiry often appear to be subspecialties within their respective fields, each with its defining problematic, its key texts and its community of specialist scholars.

Developing alternatives to established ways of thinking always requires that certain questions be closed at least temporarily to debate. This is as true in philosophy as it is in science. By holding certain premises constant, intellectual communities, such as the community of feminist philosophers, provide the intellectual space within which members are freed from pressure continually to defend their assumptions and explain their technical vocabulary. Because the feminist philosophical community has been small and many of its members known personally to each other, communication has been informal and rapid. Half-formed ideas have been tried out and sometimes even developed by members literally thinking together. In addition, the feminist philosophical community has provided support for its members in the face of attacks and ridicule from some philosophers.

The time for critique is never past and, as long as feminism generates distinct questions and perspectives, the feminist philosophical community will not become obsolete. As feminist philosophy matures, moreover, "the" feminist philosophical community naturally subdivides into further specialist sub-communities, which are also indispensable to the development of feminist philosophy. By now, however, we believe that feminist philosophy has become sufficiently mature and well established that it is time to give more emphasis to a third stage or aspect, namely, more direct engagement with philosophical work that is not self-identified as feminist. In addition to working within the now established tradition of feminist philosophy, we think it is important that feminist philosophers should intervene more regularly and vigorously in the broader philosophical conversation.

Prior to the emergence of a distinct tradition in feminist philosophy, feminist philosophers were positioned as isolated voices speaking idiosyncratically from the margin or the periphery. Today, the sophisticated level of development reached by the first two stages or aspects of feminist philosophy means that feminist scholars are now prepared to engage as equals with other philosophers. We believe that a period of intensive dialogue between feminist philosophers and those whose work is not explicitly informed by feminist perspectives will be valuable for both traditions. Entrenched assumptions on both sides will be opened to new challenges, their adequacy will be tested and they will be enriched by alternative perspectives. We intend that this volume will stimulate and facilitate such dialogue.

ALISON M. JAGGAR
IRIS MARION YOUNG

PART I
THE WESTERN CANONICAL TRADITION

1

Ancient Greek philosophy

RHODA HADASSAH KOTZIN

Where were the women?

Our access to reliable information about women thinkers who might be classified as philosophers of ancient Greece is fragmentary at best. Drawing from the texts of Herodotus, Plato, Aristotle, Diogenes Laertius, Iamblicus, Clement of Alexandria, Plutarch, Porphyry, Suidas, and many other sources, Gilles Ménage published a *History of Women Philosophers* in Latin in 1690. His aim was to refute the long-standing and widely held view that there were not and never had been any women philosophers (or at most only a very few). He attempted to classify (by "school" of thought) and cited by name about twenty Greek women thinkers who lived between about the twelfth century BCE and the death of Aristotle (322 BCE) or shortly afterward. Beatrice H. Zedler has translated Ménage's book into English (1984) and has provided a useful introduction, with helpful notes and appendices.

Some three hundred years later, several feminist philosopher–scholars are continuing Ménage's project, reclaiming, where it is justified, women philosophers of ancient Greece. Some of this recent work has involved: (1) critically examining the sources that have been handed down to us and providing a corrective to sexist (and other) biases which have distorted, trivialized, or ignored women's participation in philosophical pursuits; (2) exposing and providing a corrective to the sexist and other biases of many of the traditional nonfeminist scholars and commentators of the past century; (3) taking into account the circumstances of women's lives as a factor in their near-erasure from the history of ancient Greek thought. Recent feminist scholarship includes the following literature.

Sr Prudence Allen's compendious book, *The Concept of Woman: The Aristotelian Revolution 750 BC – AD 1250* (1985) is not principally about women philosophers but about developments and changes in concepts – that is, mainly men's concepts – of "woman." However, she discusses, among others, the poet Sappho (on the conflict between intellect and emotion), the rhetorician Aspasia of Miletus, the Diotima of Plato's *Symposium*, and a number of the women of the Pythagorean school and of the later neo-Pythagorean tradition whose letters and fragments have been preserved. Allen discusses a passage in which Diogenes Laertius lists by name a number of members of Plato's Academy and includes in this list two women, Lastheneia [Lasthenia] of Mantinea, and Axiothea of Philius [Phliasia].

Volume 1 of *A History of Women Philosophers* (edited by Mary Ellen Waite, 1987) covers the period 600 BCE to 500 CE. It includes translations of texts attributed to women thinkers as well as biographical, interpretive, and critical-analytical materials. It contains a discussion of Aspasia of Miletus, revisiting the controversial passage in Plato's dialogue *Menexenus*, in which Plato's Socrates recites a funeral oration which – he says – Aspasia taught him. Waite also devotes a chapter to Diotima. She rejects the arguments purporting to establish that the Diotima of Plato's *Symposium* is a fictitious character. Indeed, she argues in support of the thesis that the views ascribed to her in Plato's dialogue are in fact Diotima's own views.

In a long essay published in the journal *Hypatia* (1986), Kathleen Wider argues that it was not in fact a rare exception to find a woman engaged in philosophical inquiry. She emphasizes the importance of situating the work of women thinkers in the context of women's lives. She reexamines and finds sexist bias in some of the very sources of whatever information we have about women thinkers in ancient Greece. She examines the arguments supporting inter-pretations of some scholars of the twentieth century, e.g. concerning Aspasia and Diotima. She urges that arguments for maintaining that Diotima is a fictitious character seem especially weak when the underlying sexist biases are laid open.

Most of the women thinkers of ancient Greece represented in Ménage, Allen, Waite, and Wider were associated with Pythagoreanism, both earlier and later. Recent work emphasizing a "care" perspective on moral matters has stimulated a renewed interest in the thought of some women in the Pythagorean tradition, whose letters reflect a concern with virtue. These letters stress *harmonia* in the building, continuation, preservation, and enhancement of close relationships (see also Ward, in Cole and Coultrap-McQuin 1992).

Plato's Socrates talks about wise women in the dialogue *Meno*: "the speakers were among the priests and priestesses whose care it is to be able to give an account of their practices" (81a–b). However, few women were given personal recognition in their own time as making significant contributions in philosophy or, for that matter, in any area of cultural endeavor. The women whose names were recorded were "exceptional."

One noteworthy woman was Aspasia of Miletus. It is alleged that, like Anaxa-goras, Socrates, and others, she was prosecuted in Athens for impiety. Aspasia was acquitted, but even attempting to use the court system in Athens to prosec-ute a woman on a charge reserved chiefly for those engaged in the study of nature – and for teachers and other foreigners labeled as sophists – must have been remarkable. However, Aspasia was then the "mistress" of Pericles and not a married woman. Moreover, she was from Miletus and not, at the time, a citizen of Athens. The standard accounts of Aspasia credit her with intelligence but, typically, texts that suggest that she made a positive contribution of her own to rhetoric are explained away by nonfeminist historians (see, e.g., Carlson 1994). (For further discussion of the Diotima of Plato's *Symposium* see below.)

10

The lives of women in ancient Greece varied somewhat from one locale and time-period to another. In addition, we must remind ourselves that the lives of both women and men who were not full citizens of the *polis* where they resided were more restricted than those of the citizens. In particular, it should be emphasized that the lives of poor urban and rural women, women who were alien residents, and women who were slaves, were very different from the lives of middle-class and well-to-do women citizens living in urban societies. Even among these urban women citizens there were differences. The lives of Athenian women citizens, however. were typical of the lives of the wives of urban citizens. For example, during the period between Socrates and Aristotle the lives of most women citizens of Athens were restricted, by law and by custom, to living in separate women's quarters under the authority of their husbands, fathers, or other male relatives. Their activities outside the home were restricted chiefly to attending religious festivals and funerals. Women who were full citizens of Sparta, by contrast, did not live in seclusion; they may have been doing some of the very things that Plato described in the *Republic* as suitable to female members of the guardian and ruling classes in his ideal *polis*. Spartan citizen girls received a public education which included physical training. According to some sources. women stripped for certain athletic activities and engaged in these activities on a regular basis. They also competed in running races and the winners won public recognition. Women performed publicly in choirs. There were Spartan women poets mentioned by name. At the same time, however, philosophy did not flourish in Sparta as it did in Athens and elsewhere.

There is now a growing body of responsible feminist research into the contributions of women to the cultural achievements of ancient Greece. A history of philosophy which incorporates the results of this research has not yet been written.

Feminist approaches to "canonical" male philosophers: Anaximander to Aristotle

Most of the philosophy of ancient Greece was done by men, for other men, in the context of a bias against women in the general culture. For this reason alone it is important for feminist philosophers of our own time to approach these philosophers' work with caution, raising the questions: What difference did this exclusion of women make? To what extent has a thinker accepted, set aside, challenged, or overcome the anti-woman bias of his general culture? These questions are all the more important to raise in light of the fact that the work of the ancient Greek philosophers has had a profound and pervasive influence on Western philosophy (and beyond) in subsequent periods and even up to the present time. It is unsurprising, then, that many feminist philosophers of the past three decades have undertaken to "reread" the canonical works of this period – most especially the pre-Socratics, Plato, and Aristotle. Further, studying their work affords an occasion for reflecting on the antiwoman bias and exclusion of women that have been part of the Western philosophical

11

heritage and of our own philosophical training. We ask ourselves: In what ways does it remain, and remain operative, in the Western philosophical heritage? How can we remove it from our own thinking? Finally, we may ask ourselves: What is left? What can one learn, as a feminist and as a philosopher, from studying these thinkers? In the following I shall address some of these questions in connection with the pre-Socratics, Plato, and Aristotle.

Reflections on pre-Socratics

On opposites

In the *Metaphysics* Aristotle presents a Table of Opposites which he attributes to the Pythagoreans, containing ten contrast-pairs. The first-mentioned of each pair is superior to the second-mentioned. Several of these pairs pertain to the Pythagoreans' cosmological and mathematical concerns: Limit/Without limit; One/Many; Odd/Even; Straight/Crooked; Square/Oblong; and, perhaps also, Rest/Movement. The remaining contrast-pairs are: Light/Darkness, Right/Left, Good/Evil, and Male/Female. The associations of the male with right, light, and good, and of the female with left, darkness, and evil, were fairly common among prephilosophical Greeks and people in many other cultures as well. Here, however, this association received a reinforcement and – through centuries of repetition thanks to Aristotle's retelling – a pervasive influence.

Some feminist philosophers have urged that "binary" thinking necessarily divides any domain into a positive, valorized pole and a negative, denigrated pole. This way of thinking, it is proposed, inevitably valorizes the male, the masculine – especially intellectual and moral virtues associated with what men as men aspire to. What is rejected as inferior, blameworthy, or despicable is lumped together under the heading "the feminine." Taking the Pythagoreans as representative, the Table of Opposites is often cited as illustrative of the deep-seated sexism of ancient Greek philosophy.

Thinking, speaking, and writing in terms of dualisms, contrast-pairs, or polarities, and classification by dichotomous division, are not peculiar to the Pythagoreans, nor to ancient Greek thinkers. However, "opposites" have played particularly prominent roles in the views of many of the pre-Socratics. Are the Pythagoreans typical and representative?

The Milesian philosophers Anaximander and Anaximenes came before Pythagoras. The one fragment that has been preserved from the work of Anaximander of Miletus concerns opposites: "They pay the penalty and recompense one another for their injustice according to the assessment of time." Processes are, as it were, continuous reciprocal movements from pole to opposite pole and back again. Hot/cold and dry/wet are the standard oppositional pairs for many pre-Socratics. For Anaximander, on one reading, the transition from summer to winter (and back) is a process of going from dry and hot to wet and cold (and back). There is no suggestion that one member of an opposition-pair is superior to the other. In his theory of the formation of the world from the Limitless the first differentiation is a pair of "opposites" – but again there is no suggestion of a value-asymmetry. The cosmology of Anaximenes, whose "opposites" are the processes of condensation and rarefaction, does not seem to have a value-asymmetrical conception of opposites either. Perhaps each of these thinkers has succeeded in producing a cosmology with a genderless basic scheme. For Heraclitus, who came after Pythagoras, oppositional pairs have something in common or something that connects them in some way. Thus, night and day follow one another. Salt water is beneficial (for fishes of the sea) and bad for the health (of human beings). Death and life are "one." Female and male require one another. Although Heraclitean oppositional pairs do not, in most of the fragments, suggest the superiority of one over the other, Heraclitus does give preference to fire as fundamental. A wise soul is dry, as contrasted with the wet, besotted soul of a drunken man. Heraclitus also insists on contrasting being awake and wise with being asleep and ignorant or deceived.

Empedocles of Acraga includes as the basic constituents of the universe, four "elements" (fire, air, earth, and water) and two cosmic forces: Love (personified as female and divine), which brings together things that are unlike, and Hate or Strife (personified as male and divine), which separates unlike things. Love and Hate are opposite but equal in power and prerogative. During one period in cosmic history one of the two prevails. Then there is a transition to the other (opposite) world-state, where the other prevails. Then there is a transition to a state where the first prevails. And so on.

One lesson that might be drawn from a consideration of the pre-Socratic philosophers on the issue of opposites and binary thinking is that the Pythagoreans may not be representative of the (male) philosophers in Greece before Socrates, Plato, and Aristotle. I would suggest that an association of "opposites" with asymmetrical valorization of the masculine over the feminine is not inevitable after all.

Theories of sexual reproduction

When we look at various pre-Socratic views on the role of the female (and hence of the woman) in sexual reproduction, we find that for some thinkers the roles of male and female are of equal importance and for others the role of the male is more important than the role of the female. There is no evidence that any of the pre-Socratics held that the role of the female in generation is more important than that of the male.

On souls, wisdom, and virtue

Reincarnation is one view of the soul associated with Pythagoreanism. The soul of a human being is separable from the body it resides in. Since a soul may reside in a female human body in one lifetime and in a male human body in another lifetime and in the body of, say, a dog (whether male or female) in yet another, we may conclude that a soul as such is not, as it were, gendered. Nevertheless, men and women were not regarded as equals. It was the virtue of a man (as husband) to rule and the virtue of the woman (as wife) to obey him. The reason why a family relationship demands this asymmetry has not been

13

handed down to us. It would seem that, in addition to seeking wisdom (open to anyone), a major function of the soul is to rule. Each soul is to rule over its own body and in addition, it seems, the souls of some people are to exercise authority over the souls of other people. One's virtue was connected, then, not with one's soul as such nor with one's body as such, but with one's fulfilling some assigned role as determined by one's having a certain sort of body. This arrangement was not challenged by the Pythagorean women whose letters have been preserved.

In her discussion of the poem of Parmenides, Sr Prudence Allen makes the point that in the Prologue we are introduced to a female deity (Thea), who teaches Parmenides to exercise his reason by calling upon him to follow her example of inquiring and testing truth and opinion through argument. Allen calls this passage "the first example in western writing of a female philosopher on the cosmic level." Thea leads Parmenides through the Way of Truth. What is, is. There is no not-to-be, nor a combination of to-be and not-to-be, nor coming-to-be, nor alteration, nor increase, nor decrease, nor change of place. What is, is the undivided, whole, invariable, motionless, undifferentiated one. The Way of Truth leaves no room for sex difference, gender difference, or any other sort of differentiation, contrast, or opposition. It is only in the Way of Opinion that illusions of distinction and difference can arise.

Some later pre-Socratics and contemporaries of Socrates express views that stereotype women and their relation to men. It is clear that these men are writing for other men.

For Plato's Gorgias, as he is characterized in the dialogue *Meno*, one's virtues and their corresponding vices seem to be tied to one's assigned role, status, or function. Men and women, free persons and slaves, young and old, have separate virtues. The virtue of a (free) man is "to manage public affairs and in so doing to benefit his friends and harm his enemies" and the virtue of a woman is to "manage the home well, preserve its possessions, and be submissive to her husband" (71e–72a).

Antiphon asks whether marriage is worthwhile for a man. The pleasures of sexual intercourse are more than counterbalanced by the pains, toils, and worries of family responsibilities.

Democritus endorses and underlines the antiwoman bias of his culture. For him, a woman who is silent, or not very talkative, is praiseworthy. Men are warned that women have "malign thoughts." He says that for a man to be ruled by a woman is the ultimate outrage (insult).

There are nearly as many different feminist approaches to Plato and Aristotle as there are feminist philosophers approaching their works. The following can be no more than a sampling of some approaches. The reader is referred to anthologies and collections of feminist essays on Plato and Aristotle and their select bibliographies.

Some feminist approaches to Plato

Plato sometimes displays a disdain for women in his writings. For example, in *Phaedo*, Socrates' wife Xanthippe and "the women" are sent away. In one version of the doctrine of reincarnation (*Timaeus*), a person born with the body of a man in one life might be punished for cowardice or injustice by having to be associated with the body of a woman in the next incarnation. In the *Republic* Plato's Socrates says that the future guardians and rulers in his envisioned ideal society should not imitate women, slaves, or inferior sorts of men. He explains timocracy by "blaming the woman:" she is a greedy, ambitious, complaining shrew who belittles her decent, high-minded husband and turns her son into a timocrat. Also, bad things happen in a society when men spend too much money on their wives. Plato's Socrates suggests that just as women and children prefer many-colored things, so some men prefer democracy. He warns that poets bring out the "womanish" in their hearers, with the suggestion that poets encourage unseemly displays of emotion. Cowardly men are also "womanish." Elsewhere women are charged with being bad-tempered. Stealth and secretiveness are ascribed to women as a group. Again in the *Republic*, Socrates and his interlocutors agree that although many women are better than many men in many things, the male sex is superior to the female. On most readings of the text the superiority of some male(s) to all females was claimed to extend to all pursuits, including those traditionally assigned to women as indoor occupations and in which women were believed to excel, e.g. weaving, baking, and cooking vegetables.

Nevertheless, in the dialogue *Meno* Socrates is looking for that one thing, virtue (excellence), which is the same in a man as in a woman. In *Phaedo* and elsewhere the immortal soul as seeking wisdom does not seem to be tied forever to any particular human body and would be better off without any body at all. In *Republic* I the *ergon* or function or work of the soul of a person includes life, rule, care, and planning. That is the work of the soul as such. It is not characterized as a gendered soul in this passage. Indeed, in the *Republic* Socrates insists that in the ideal *polis* the philosopher–rulers (the guardians) might be women as well as men: all the women that are born sufficiently able by nature (and, I'd add, trained and educated appropriately) will share equally in all the activities of the men (*Republic* VII, 540c). Even though the discussion concerning the training and education of the guardians and of the ascent and descent of the philosopher–"king" had been conducted, from a linguistic point of view, in the third-person masculine gender, we are explicitly reminded that everything that had been said applies equally to any woman who is qualified.

Clearly Plato would not qualify as a feminist by the standards of the latter part of the twentieth century and the beginning of the twenty-first. He seems to have retained what I would call an attitudinal misogyny, while at the same time proposing a remarkably bold sketch of an ideal society in which the inborn differences in talents that were relevant to one's future role were to be judged on an individual basis. Being musical, athletic, high-spirited, and intellectually curious were inborn traits distributed among both females and males in the population. These were the significant "natures" to be developed in determining one's "place" in the society as a guardian. The areas of excellence to be inculcated – honesty, cooperation, unselfishness, courage, high-mindedness – were, simply, human virtues.

The vision of a ruling class for the ideal society includes the provisions that the guardians shall serve in the military, that they shall live in barracks and eat in a common dining hall, that they must not have private wealth, private spouses, or private children, and that their studies shall continue many years past their entrance into adulthood, while they learn to perform administrative tasks. Plato's eugenics program for improving the stock, by "mating the best with the best," involved a rigged lottery for determining the (temporary) sex partners for officially appointed "marriage" festivals. Plato says very little about regulation of sexual relations or other aspects of the daily lives and relations between men and women in the largest part of the ideal society, those for whose benefit the rulers rule but who do not share in ruling. There is no reason to suppose that the abolition of private property, private spouses, and private children applied to the lower-class citizens.

Many feminist commentators have addressed themselves to the provisions for guardians, and especially for women as guardians and rulers with the same power and authority as men as guardians and rulers. In her 1987 book *Women and the Ideal Society*, Natalie Harris Bluestone lists several types of antifemale bias in Plato scholarship from 1870 to 1970 concerning the inclusion of women in the guardian class in Plato's *Republic*. For one group of scholars, erasure of the whole issue of equality for women was effected simply by their omitting the relevant passages from their translations or not mentioning the relevant provisions in commentaries. Other scholars have translated passages in a biased and misleading manner. A number of scholars have held that Plato went wrong in making these proposals. The proposals were, for these scholars, contrary to what they thought they knew about women's true nature. Another line of rejection has been to claim that the proposals are undesirable. Not even women would welcome such so-called opportunities. Another technique has been to deflect attention from the issue of gender equality by introducing social-historical and psychoanalytic interpretations of Socrates and Plato. Other scholars, who had thought of themselves as profeminist, would approve of some measure of gender equality but warn that one can go too far with that sort of thing. Bluestone is at her best in examining the views of some Plato commentators who hold that Plato didn't really mean what he said: he did not have much faith in his own argument, or the proposal is paradoxical, or it is amusing, ironic, meant to be a joke. Bluestone, as well as Allen, Pierce, and others before her, have been instrumental in providing a corrective to bias in scholarship and interpretation.

16

Much of the feminist work done thus far on Plato's *Republic* goes well beyond correction of bias in past and present scholarship. It provides new questions and perspectives on traditional issues. Many feminist commentators have addressed themselves to the provisions for guardians, and especially for women as guardians and rulers with the same power and authority as men as guardians and rulers. Some studies have examined the relation between the abolition of private property, the abolition of private spouses, and the abolition of private children. Some have examined the eugenics program and asked whether a woman guardian has enough time to be a ruler – that is, whether it could have been rendered feasible for the same *crème de la crème* women to be reproducing most often as well as performing at the highest levels the functions of guardians and rulers. Some have examined Plato's reasons for proposing these radical changes in social and political arrangements and compared these proposals with the proposals of his later work, the *Laws*, with special attention to provisions for women in the latter work. Some have stressed the fact that Plato is not only an attitudinal misogynist; he is not concerned with the "rights" of women in the way that rights have been understood in theories of the past few hundred years and hence would not have been a "feminist" by today's standards. However, they ask, might he be considered a feminist of some sort? Space limitations permit only one example here of thinking about Plato on women as guardians.

Elizabeth V. Spelman (1988) notes an ambiguity in Plato's use of the term "woman." When he uses it in referring to women as a group, women as he stereotyped them, he seems to be talking about an inferiorized soul in a female body. When he uses it in referring to guardian women, he seems to be talking about an excellent soul in a female body that could just as well be in a male body (a "manly" soul in a female body). A "womanish" (e.g. cowardly) soul of a man is an inferiorized soul in a male body. Plato's contempt for the feminine suggests the identification of the inferiorized soul with the feminine, in both its male and female embodiments. However, as Spelman points out, "we have heard nothing about the third class of people in Plato's world, the artisans, farmers, and other producers." The equality Plato is talking about obtains only between men and women who would be guardians and philosopher–rulers. They are the ones with power and authority. She asks, "What kind of feminism is it that would gladly argue for a kind of equality between men and women of a certain class and at the same time for radical inequality between some women and some men, some women and some other women, some men and some other men?"

Some of the most interesting and provocative feminist writings on Plato have centered on the dialogue *Symposium*. There Plato's Socrates begins his long speech, saying that it is Diotima of Mantinea – a woman – from whom he learned about Love (Eros). Most of the recent work does not address the question of whether Plato's Diotima is wholly fictional or not. Interpretations vary, and with them correspondingly various feminist lessons are drawn. Sr Prudence Allen connects Plato's Diotima with the goddess Thea in the poem of Parmenides and Lady Philosophy in the later Boethius: female figures guiding men in their quest for philosophical wisdom. According to Luce Irigaray and some others (1993c), the facts that Diotima is a woman and that she herself is not a speaker in the dialogue (Socrates speaks for her) are essential to an understanding of the *Symposium*. According to Irigaray, Diotima is somehow a failure; Socrates has, as it were, stolen her voice. Andrea Nye agrees that it is essential to an understanding of the *Symposium* that Diotima is a woman. However, she disagrees with Irigaray. For Nye, Diotima is the host of the *Symposium*. She is the "spokesperson for ways of life and thought that Greek philosophy feeds on, ways of thought whose authority Plato neutralized and converted to his own purposes." According to Page duBois (1988), Socrates speaks the words of Diotima, acts her part as if he were a male actor playing the part of a woman in the theater. He shares his knowledge with the other men. "She teaches him that the philosophical intercourse, conception, pregnancy, and delivery of male lovers are superior to the corporeal acts of human women." The imagery deployed by Plato appropriates the vocabulary of female reproductive powers to the (male) philosopher.

Some feminist approaches to Aristotle

Aristotle on women

In his biological writings Aristotle treats males as superior to females. Women are, as it were, infertile men. We come to understand males by what they have and females by what they lack. Males and females play quite different roles in the generation of new individuals. The father's semen conveys motion (but not matter) to an embryo. Matter for an embryo is provided by the mother's menstrual fluid. The male, then, because of his heat, can "concoct" and contribute what the colder female cannot. If the reproductive process is completely successful the new member of the species will be a male. The female is a deformity or failure. She is a deficient or defective male.

In the *Politics* Aristotle recommended that, for citizens, girls as well as boys receive an education. He thought it would be better if girls, or women, married a bit later than was the custom, and if husband and wife were closer in age than was the custom in Athens at the time. However, he only recommended minor changes in the legal and political status of women citizens. He maintained that it was both natural and expedient that the husband rule the wife in the household.

In the family or household there are three distinctive types of association: free adult male (master) and slave; free adult male (husband) and free woman (wife); and free adult male (father) and (free) child. These relationships are irreducibly different but in each relationship the same person, the adult free male, is superior to, and rules, someone inferior. That is, these are three irreducibly different relationships between ruler and subject.

In support of his view about the superiority of the free adult male in these household relationships, Aristotle offers two sorts of analogies: (1) the relations of ruler and subject that should obtain within the soul or between the soul and the body (in the case of master/slave); and (2) political relations: the king over his subjects (= father and child), the tyrant over his subjects (= master and slave); and an arrangement in which citizens rule and are ruled in turn – except that in the case of husband and wife the ruler/subject arrangement is permanent. The only nonanalogical support is concerned with the power of deliberation. In the slave it is lacking; in the child it is present but undeveloped; in the adult free woman it is present but ineffective (*akuron*).

For Aristotle, the moral virtues of a slave were circumscribed by his obedience to the master (or the master's surrogates) and how well he performed his assigned tasks. I say "his" because Aristotle does not even discuss female slaves. A citizen's wife's virtues were also tied to her performance of her role as wife, whether in doing the tasks typically assigned to wives in households or in the moral virtues appropriate to her station. Her courage in obeying is not the same as his courage in commanding; restraint is not the same in a woman as in a man. In short, moral virtue was, for Aristotle, one thing in a man and another in a woman.

Where did Aristotle go wrong?

Some feminist philosophers have drawn attention to the oddity of claiming that about half of the members of a species are deformed or defective, arguing that Aristotle's bias in favor of males (and men) has gotten in the way of his doing good science. Others have taken Aristotle's views on sexual reproduction to be an underlying premise in his claim that women's power of deliberation is ineffective (*akuron*) and trace his views on the naturalness of the subordination of women in the household to his biology. Others again have urged that Aristotle does not make this connection explicitly and that he has two independent sets of wrongheaded views – one in biology and one in the moral and political domain.

One line of argument is that Aristotle's views about women are arbitrary and "bias-driven." They are not required by anything in Aristotle's philosophy taken as a whole nor by any of the central concepts or principles. Some make the stronger claim that Aristotle's position on women is inconsistent with some central features of his philosophy; to say that to be a woman is to have a chronic and incurable inability to make decisions and carry them out, is to say that a woman as a woman does not have a full measure of rationality. Yet to be rational is to be human, and clearly Aristotle does not want to deny that women are human. On the other hand, it has been argued that these apparent inconsistencies can be explained away. What has gone wrong, in the final analysis, is Aristotle's methodological assumption that "the norms of the society he lives in are for the most part morally sound" (Modrak, in Bar-On. 1994).

Many feminist thinkers have taken up the themes of rationality and virtue, claiming that these are "gendered" concepts in Western philosophy. The claim often goes further: gender (and gender hierarchy) are implicated in the seemingly neutral methods, concepts, and principles that are at the very center of a

19

"canonical" philosopher's work. "Our trust in a Reason that knows no sex has... been largely self-deceiving" (Lloyd 1984, 1993). Nancy Tuana claims that a canonical philosopher's views about women "cannot simply be dismissed as not being integral to his central philosophical doctrines. Philosophers' gender assumptions often affect the central categories of their system – their conceptions of rationality, their construals of the nature of morality, their visions of the public realm" (Tuana 1992). Aristotle is often cited as a case in point. What has gone wrong, then, is – everything.

Does anything remain?

What can we, as feminist philosophers, learn from Aristotle? Some recent work acknowledges that Aristotle makes notoriously derogatory and harmful statements about women and that nevertheless there is much that is worthwhile for feminist philosophers to study and take seriously. Marcia L. Homiak (in Antony and Witt 1993) claims that Aristotle's model of the rational ideal – of the value of reason and exercising one's rational faculties – is worthy of emulation by both men and women. Homiak draws a distinction between the way a value is used (e.g. to denigrate women, nonwhite men, and the uneducated) and the value itself. She argues that the life of the virtuous citizen that Aristotle admires and recommends does not require (as Aristotle himself thought it did) that those who rule must exploit menial laborers and exclude women from civic life, nor does it require the devaluation of the nonrational side of the human being. His ideal virtuous citizens would relate to one another with a type of care and concern that is fully in keeping with a feminist ideal of friendship, intimacy, and compassion that is positive and constructive. Cynthia A. Freeland (in Bar-On 1994), in a long essay entitled "Nourishing Speculation," undertakes to provide, in the spirit of Irigaray, a "feminist reading" of Aristotle's scientific activity and his conception of science. She attempts to look beyond what Aristotle actually says about females in his biology; she looks for what is "implied" in his imagery, his contradictions, his paradoxes, his silences. She finds much in Aristotle that conforms well to the notion of gender-free science advanced by many feminist thinkers. She also finds what other critics have found: that Aristotle does indeed sometimes apply "androcentric or anthropocentric criteria to justify claims about the superiority of beings he regards as best – male humans." She finds that there are tensions and does not believe that there are neat resolutions to them. Neither Freeland nor Homiak attempts to paper over Aristotle's faults. Nevertheless, a feminist philosopher does well to study him carefully.

2

Modern rationalism

MOIRA GATENS

Modern, or continental, rationalism refers to the works of the seventeenth-century philosophers René Descartes, Baruch Spinoza, and Gottfried Leibniz. While there is much to mark each philosopher off from the others, there are nevertheless several shared fundamental assumptions that warrant the common title of "rationalist." Each philosopher believed that mathematics and geometry were appropriate models on which to base philosophical methodology. Each, whilst critical of founding knowledge on mere faith – which they believed could only lead to skepticism – nevertheless relied on theological arguments at various points in their philosophies. All three philosophers share a distrust of the notion that sensation, emotion (passion), and the body are capable of providing knowledge. Reason alone, on all three philosophers' accounts, is the a priori faculty which can provide secure foundations for human knowledge. It is Descartes' philosophy that has received most critical attention from feminist theorists. Spinoza has received less attention and Leibniz is all but ignored. At the end of this article, some attempt will be made to explain this uneven treatment of the modern rationalists.

Descartes

Feminist philosophers generally agree that Descartes' philosophy has had profound effects on contemporary philosophical conceptions of women. Descartes, often described as the "father" of modern philosophy, certainly saw himself as breaking out of the medieval and scholastic paradigms. His attempt to preserve rational inquiry from the revival of skepticism was influential in deciding the role of reason, as against faith, in settling the disputes between theology and natural philosophy (science). He argued that if knowledge was to have a foundation that could resist skepticism then it must be capable of rationally demonstrating the correspondence between the truths of reason and the external world. Descartes offered this foundation in the argument of the "cogito" and in the proof for the existence of a veracious God. It is by the provision of this foundation that Descartes sought to resolve the contradictions between the theological view – which stressed the freedom of human action and its responsibility in moral matters; and the scientific view – which stressed the mechanically ordered and determined character of all nature, including human nature. In positing two distinct and mutually exclusive substances which exhaustively describe all that exists, mind and matter, Descartes endeavors to offer a worldview in which a mechanical and determined physical universe is compatible with the existence of God and moral freedom. Natural philosophy – in particular, the work of Kepler and Galileo – may well have displaced human being from the center of the physical universe, but Descartes' dual substance thesis ensures that human being remains at its intellectual and moral center. This "reconciliation" between science and theology has had important effects on modern conceptions of the self and human agency. In particular, Descartes' radical dualism entrenched the oppositions between reason and passion, freedom and bondage, and the mind and the body. As we shall see, this dualism served to sharpen and strengthen older associations between these oppositions and sexual difference.

On Descartes' conception, the human body per se is an epistemologically neutral machine. The essential self, for him, is the autonomous *res cogitans* (thinking thing). Insofar as Descartes disqualifies the body and passion from supplying any constructive content to human knowledge, he ties conceptions of the rational subject to a disembodied self. This subject is understood to contain intrinsic adequate ideas and principles of thought. Reason, on this conception, has substantive a priori content that is obscured by the intrusions of mere matter in motion. The attainment of truth and wisdom presupposes a practical mastery, or discipline, of the body and an intellectual mastery of the external world. Hence, the attainment of knowledge requires that one employ the method in order to detach one's essential self (the mind) from the body and its passions. It is this notion of detaching oneself from one's embodiment that has been identified as one of the prime means through which women have been excluded from the Cartesian ideal of reason.

Cartesian method involves subjecting all one's thoughts and beliefs to a stringent test for truth. Anything which can be doubted should be rejected (at least, provisionally). Only those things which can be clearly and distinctly perceived should be accepted as true. Any complex problem or idea should be broken down into its simplest constituent parts and each of these parts should be subjected to the test of clarity and distinctness. Only then should one proceed from clear and distinct simple ideas to deductive chains of these ideas, taking care not to move from the indubitable to the dubitable in the linking of one idea with the next. Finally, with practice, one should be able to review, in a single movement, all the clear and distinct intuitions, along with the systematic deductions which constitute true knowledge.

The method functions to discern truth, and discipline of the will is necessary in order that it give its assent only to that which is absolutely certain. A disciplined will is not only crucial to the attainment of knowledge, Descartes tells us, it is also the secret of virtue. This is because, for Descartes, good judgment involves not only knowledge but the cultivation of good habits. Irrationality, error, and ignorance may be traced to the mind's dependence on the body and sense experience. It is the health and strength of any particular body and its passions, set against the strength and discipline of the mind and will, that determine one's capacity to cultivate both reason and virtue. Hence, as several feminist critics have noted, both training and a good natural constitution appear to be prerequisite to the attainment of truth and virtue. These features of Descartes' philosophy are important to a consideration of how reason came to be associated with "maleness" in the modern period.

"The man of reason"

Genevieve Lloyd (1984) has argued that Descartes' rejection of Aristotelian souls, which contain both rational and irrational elements, in favour of a rational mind/irrational body dichotomy, has had important repercussions for our understanding of sexual stereotypes. Whereas previously, women were conceived on a continuum of rationality – as less rational than men – they now come to be conceived as having souls or minds identical to men. Sexual difference is thus located in bodily difference. However, maleness does not carry the same metaphorical or symbolic associations with body, nature, and passion. Historically, embodiment has been conceived as especially associated with women. Reason, understood as involving a transcendence of the bodily, is thus conceptually at odds with what women have come to symbolize. Moreover, insofar as reason is conceived as a technical skill requiring training in method, it becomes the attainment of a privileged few. Both Lloyd and Janna Thompson (1983) have rightly stressed that the egalitarian appearance of Descartes' philosophy recedes when one takes account of the fact that most men and all women would not have had access to the learning and practice of the method that is presented as necessary to the cultivation of truth and virtue. Given that women were symbolically associated with the body, the dualistic conception of the rational mind and the irrational body carries the further implication that differences between male and female capacities for reason now appear to arise from bodily sexual difference. The capacity for reason is sex-neutral – the mind has no sex – but since human minds are embodied minds, differences in rationality now will be explained by bodily difference. Reason thus comes to represent the transcendence of a feminized corporeality. In a recent paper, Lloyd (1993) has argued that it is the network of symbolic associations surrounding reason and sexual difference, including those introduced by Descartes, that remain elusive and which function to ensure the opposition between women and reason. The Cartesian legacy (perhaps in spite of Descartes' intentions) serves to justify a sexual division of labour in the realm of human knowledge. Abstract reason and the attainment of objective knowledge become the province of the "man of reason" whereas practical reason, necessary for the satisfaction of the needs of everyday embodied life, becomes the province of women.

The "masculinization" of thought

A rather different view of Descartes' philosophy is offered by Susan Bordo. Bordo (1987) reads Descartes' texts as cultural documents open to a psychocultural analysis. She finds in Descartes' ideals of clarity, distinctness, and objectivity, evidence of "reaction formations" to the cultural context in which uncertainty and anxiety characterized the place of the masculine subject. This "reaction formation" gives rise to the birth of the modern period – what Bordo calls a "drama of parturition" – in which masculine science struggles to free itself from the medieval and Renaissance conception of Nature as feminine and maternal. Modern philosophy, she suggests, is born out of a fear of Nature's frightening powers as well as a desire to control and dominate Nature.

Bordo draws heavily on the psychoanalytic theory of "separation–individuation" developed by theorists such as Nancy Chodorow (1978) and Carol Gilligan (1982a, 1982b). These theorists have argued that modern ideals of reason, morality, and knowledge reflect a bias toward typically masculine forms of subjectivity. Part of the development of an autonomous adult individual involves the separation of oneself from one's primary carer – typically the mother – and the development of a sense of oneself separate from the mother in particular, others in general, and from the world. In the modern period this process of separation–individuation operates differently for male and female children. A much greater degree of individuation is required from male than from female children. This is because, first, the figure with whom the male child has initially identified (the mother) is sex-inappropriate; and second, because the cultural demands upon masculinity are such that he must distinguish himself from others in order to meet the cultural ideals of reason, knowledge, and morality. The story is quite different for the female child. Her degree of separation from the mother is not so dramatic. Hence feminine subjectivity is stereotypically marked by a lack of autonomy from others and a failure to actualize the highest ideals of culture: objectivity in reason, knowledge, and morality. Women, it is argued, have a greater sense of connectedness to others and the world and so develop a style of reason, a relation to knowledge, and a sense of morality that traditionally have been seen as inferior to those of men. They are said to be immersed in the particular and partial concerns of those with whom they are connected. Embodied women are conceived as incapable of actualizing the capacity for abstract and universal reason.

Carol Gilligan (1982) and Sandra Harding (1986) have argued that feminists should revalue women's specific modes of reasoning in both the moral and the epistemological realms. Gilligan argues that women's moral sense is different rather than inferior to masculine morality. Harding and Evelyn Fox Keller (1985) have argued that women's sense of connectedness with the world generates different epistemological methods and knowledge that should be valued. Jane Flax (1983), too, has produced readings of modern philosophy which seek to explain the distinguishing features of modern thought by a psychocultural analysis of those who have produced it.

Susan Bordo focuses elements of these feminist analyses of modern philosophy on a reading of Descartes' philosophy. She claims to have shown that the seventeenth century saw a revolution in conceptions of self and world which effected a "masculinization of thought," that is, a new conception of philosophy which valued detachment from others and the world, clarity and distinctness of ideas, and the radical separation of mind and body. Body and Nature are now conceived as mere inert matter to be objectified, known, and dominated. On Bordo's reading, this transcendence of the body, Nature, and emotion entails a "flight from the feminine" to the objectivity of a newly conceived science.

Bordo characterizes the essential elements of the Cartesian worldview as follows. First, objective and certain knowledge is guaranteed by the ability of the mind to dissociate itself from the body in its quest for truth. Second, the substantial distinction between mind and body allows for their interaction but not for their merging, since they are defined in opposition to one another: mind is a thinking but unextended thing, body is an extended but unthinking thing. Subject and object are now radically distinct and Nature may be reconceived in masculine terms. Nature as pure clockwork, conceived in mechanical and geometric terms, transforms the task of the philosopher/scientist. The task of the philosopher now is to know this object and. through such knowledge, to dominate Nature. In a double movement, Descartes thus achieves the death of the universe as mother/feminine and the birth of the masculine, mechanistic worldview.

Both Lloyd and Bordo are interested in the effects, in the present, of Cartesian philosophy. Other theorists have stressed that Cartesian philosophy was used, in the seventeenth century, and later, to argue for women's equality in reason. Margaret Atherton (1993), for example, has argued that Descartes' philosophy was the basis on which Mary Astell and Damaris Lady Masham presented their arguments for women's equality. Atherton questions whether Bordo's analysis is anachronistic and overly selective. The family structures which underpin the psychoanalytic theory of separation–individuation are not timeless ones, and Descartes' rationalistic philosophy was not the only one available in the seventeenth century. In this context, Atherton mentions the empiricist philosophy of John Locke. More generally, Atherton thinks that the notion of two, and only two, forms of reason ("male" and "female") is untenable.

Ethics and the passions

Whereas English-speaking feminists have tended to focus on Descartes' account of reason and dualism, French philosophers Michèle Le Doeuff and Luce Irigaray have focused on Descartes' ethics and his theory of the passions. Like Atherton, Le Doeuff does not fail to note the significance of Descartes' female interlocutors: Princess Elizabeth of Bohemia and Queen Christina of Sweden. Le Doeuff (1989) maintains that there is a general pattern in the relation between women and philosophy, which she names the "Héloise complex." The desire of male philosophers to present their thought as complete, self-contained, and free of any unthought elements, leads them to project their own necessary lack of knowledge onto others – typically the student, or women, both of whom have a relation to philosophy that is mediated by the "Master," who presumes to know. (In this context, Le Doeuff mentions Héloise and Abelard, Descartes and Elizabeth, Sartre and de Beauvoir.) And, like Lloyd, Le Doeuff stresses that the images and symbols employed by philosophers are essential, though unacknowledged, components of philosophical thought. It is this "philosophical imaginary" which acts to discourage women from the pursuit of philosophy since such images frequently involve the objectification of women. The desire to create a complete philosophy, capable of explaining everything, is certainly present in modern rationalism. Le Doeuff (1989) shows that Descartes' desire for a complete philosophical system leads him to present a moral philosophy which his system of thought cannot justify. Le Doeuff (1991) argues that this desire for absolute knowledge results in a philosophical practice that is intrinsically unethical because it involves displacing the necessary deficiencies in knowledge onto others – typically, an image of the other as lacking. An ethical philosophical practice would be one which would not exclude women a priori but which would take responsibility for its own conditions of production, including its imaginary.

Luce Irigaray (1993) offers a reading of Descartes' theory of the passions, especially the passion of "wonder." Echoing Heidegger, Irigaray asserts that each age has one issue which it must address – and one issue only. On her view, the issue that marks our time is that of sexual difference and the absence of an ethical relation between the sexes. Irigaray's reading strategy is to rethink the Cartesian passion of wonder as the passion which should be returned to its locus – the wonder felt by each sex in the face of the irreducible difference of the other sex. Irigaray insists that the invention of a genuine ethical relation between two positively conceived sexes would amount to the overturning of Cartesianism. The creation of an ethical reciprocity between the sexes would assume that men accept responsibility for their own materiality, thus "healing" the gendered mind/body split. This, in turn, would allow women to create a home for themselves in the cultural symbolic. The reduction of all women to the maternal function would then cease.

Spinoza

Spinoza is a somewhat neglected figure in the history of philosophy. Such neglect perhaps explains why some feminists have found his monistic philosophy a suggestive counterpoint to Descartes' dual substance thesis. Spinoza argues that all that exists may be explained by reference to one substance – God or Nature. The words God *or* Nature (*Deus sive Natura*) signal that Spinoza's conception of God departs from the anthropocentric Judeo-Christian tradition. God is not separate from or transcendent to Nature but is conceived as the immanent power or force of Nature. This view has important consequences for Spinoza's conception of ontology. Body and mind, for him, enjoy a modal existence only – mind and body are understood as "expressions" or modifications of the humanly knowable attributes of substance: extension and thought. Human being, on the Spinozistic view, is thus conceived as part of a unitary, dynamic, and interconnected whole. Unlike the Cartesian body-automaton, Spinoza conceives of the human body as a relatively complex individual, which is open to, and in constant interchange with, its environment. For him, the powers of the human body are not dependent upon an intrinsic self-regulating mechanism or the intervening will of a soul-like substance. Rather, the human body expresses under the attribute of extension that which the human mind expresses under the attribute of thought. There are not two substances which make up human being, rather human being expresses itself under the parallel attributes of thought and extension – or, to paraphrase Spinoza: the human mind is the idea of an actually existing human body. This means that the reason, politics, and ethics of collective bodies – such as bodies politic – are always embodied and as such will bear the traces of past arrangements.

The problem of mind–body interaction that so plagued Cartesianism cannot arise in Spinoza's account since mind and body are expressions or modes of the attributes of a single substance. The sharp division in Cartesian thought between human and non-human life is not supported by Spinoza's ontology. Whereas Descartes viewed animals as mere self-moving machines, Spinoza draws more subtle distinctions between types of animate bodies. The complexity of any particular mind is intrinsically related to the body of which it is an idea. Hence, nonhuman animals have minds but not minds similar to human minds, since any specific animal's mind will be the idea of its body. Some feminists have found this view of Nature as one single, complex, interconnected substance useful in thinking through issues in environmental and ecological philosophy (Mathews 1991).

Embodied difference

Spinoza's ontology also allows one to rethink differences within human being in a non-dualistic way. Desire, knowledge, and ethics are embodied and express, at least in the first instance, the quality and complexity of the specificity of corporeal passions. Both Moira Gatens and Genevieve Lloyd have signalled the potential of Spinoza's philosophy for rethinking sexual difference in terms other than the Cartesian-like sex/gender distinction (Gatens 1988, Lloyd 1989). Spinozistic conceptions of reason, power, activity, and conatus (the tendency for all things to persevere in their existence) offer new ways of conceiving of old problems in philosophy, problems which feminist theorists have inherited. Spinoza offers an alternative perspective on human subjectivity that rejects the dualist ontology that has dominated modern philosophy. From this perspective it is incoherent to affirm the existence of a sexless soul which is joined to a sexed body. As Lloyd has remarked (1989), differently sexed bodies must be matched by sexually differentiated minds. If the mind is the idea of the body then female minds must, in some respects, reflect the specificity of the female body, including the embodied effects of cultural conceptions of that body. This is not to entertain an essential sexual difference, since what specific minds reflect are the pleasures, pains, and powers of specific bodies. In some instances, men and women would enjoy the same pleasures and pains; in other cases, these would differ. As Lloyd (1994) points out, the multifacetedness of bodies leaves open what the content of any particular mind will be – and for Spinoza, what a body can do cannot be known in advance. The capacities of any particular body will be dependent on the total context of that body. Human bodies always exist in human societies and the powers of any particular body will reflect the social and symbolic value of that type of body within that type of society. The exigencies of institutionalized power will differentially affect the powers of individuals formed through its structures.

Spinoza's view can also accommodate the fact that human bodies exist in the context of other, more complex, bodies: specific societies, cultures, subgroups. All these factors will play a role in determining the capacities of any given body. Individuals or groups that are singled out for discriminatory treatment, or that are excluded from contexts which are empowering, will not develop either bodies or minds that express their full capacities or powers. Spinoza's philosophy allows a way of theorizing the impact of social and political arrangements that neither posits an essential sameness between the sexes which underlies history (the sexless "soul" or mind), nor an essential sexual difference. Rather, difference is understood as the unfolding, in history, of the way in which our social and political arrangements construct specific forms of embodiment. This notion of the body as dynamic and productive defies traditional divisions between knowing and being, between ontology and epistemology, and between politics and ethics (Gatens 1996b).

Luce Irigaray (1993) offers a brief, and very different, reading of Spinoza to the one above. Rather than seeing Spinoza's monism as a potential resource for "healing" the mind/body distinction, she argues that Spinoza fails to provide any way of accounting for the reciprocal determination of flesh and thought. She presents Spinoza's all-enveloping notion of substance (God or Nature) as an instance of the philosophical appropriation of the powers of the maternal–feminine. Such appropriation leaves women without a home (or "envelope"). Man's inhabitation of women as the maternal–feminine prohibits woman from taking up a "place" of her own. She does not inhabit matter but, rather, is forced to become mere matter for man. The extent to which it is appropriate to understand this as a "reading" of Spinoza is not clear. Spinoza seems rather to be the occasion for a demonstration of the misogynistic character of Western philosophy.

Leibniz

Leibniz has not yet played a significant role in feminist appraisals of the canon of Western philosophy. Occasional allusions to his work suggest that his philosophy may offer an alternative to Cartesianism. Carolyn Merchant (1980) offered an early appraisal of Leibniz that, unfortunately, has not been developed further by contemporary feminist philosophers. Merchant points out that Leibniz's vitalistic philosophy, which stressed the intrinsic power and moral worth of nature, presents feminists with a powerful alternative to the Cartesian-inspired "death" of nature. Merchant traces the ecological disasters of the late twentieth century to the victory of the Cartesian worldview over the holism and vitalism of the Leibnizian conception of nature. Leibniz, like Spinoza, does restore to nature the notion of a "life-force" and characterizes things by their power to affect and be affected. Leibnizian monadology, while confirming the notion of an absolute separateness between beings, is nevertheless suggestive in relation to thinking genuine differences within unity. The unity and compatibility of all things is guaranteed, according to Leibniz, by the existence of a God who is both rational and benevolent. God has created the "best of all possible worlds" – a world in which progress and change result from the forces inherent to nature rather than from the domination and exploitation of nature by culture. Leibniz, along with Spinoza, may well prove fertile ground for imaginative future feminist explorations of alternative, non-dualistic ontologies.

Feminist historiography

One possible explanation for the uneven feminist treatment of the rationalists is that much feminist engagement with the history of philosophy has involved retrospective reading, looking for causes to known effects of that history. This has produced readings of the Western philosophical canon that are partial and, in some ways, inevitably distorting. This is endemic to the nature of the exercise. From a present feminist perspective, it is impossible not to be struck by the consonance between the aims of Descartes' method and the ideals of the separative, masculine subject of knowledge as described by contemporary feminist theorists. There is an ever-present danger that such readings find confirmation of precisely what it was they were looking for. This is not to deny that what we have become in the present is, in part, able to be traced to aspects of our past. But it is to deny that the past should simply be reduced to the cause of our present ills. Genevieve Lloyd (1984) has shown the extent to which masculine and feminine ideals in the present have been partially formed by past philosophical ideals. To accept this proposition is not, however, to be blinded to the rich metaphysical and ontological possibilities of the history of philosophy. As Lloyd (1994) has observed, if Descartes has helped define aspects of what we presently are, then Spinoza may provide insights into what we might have been or could yet become. In this respect, the history of philosophy is not just a means to understand how our past has formed and limited our present, but also a resource for our present and future possibilities. Much contemporary feminist philosophy is engaged in this task of rereading the canon in order to open the past to the present. One can only surmise that future appraisals of feminist approaches to modern rationalism may be very different from this one.

3

Empiricism

LYNN HANKINSON NELSON

Many of our beliefs, practices, and theories reflect the assumption that the world impinges on us via our senses and, by so doing, shapes and constrains what it is reasonable to believe. And most of us engage in the practice of justifying and judging claims about ourselves and the rest of the world by reference to experience. As much to the point of the present discussion, feminist philosophers have long insisted that the questions, methods, and theories of philosophy should reflect and be evaluated, at least in part, on the basis of women's experiences. Most of us are in these ways empiricists.

But while empiricism so understood may be nonuncontroversial and, indeed, an impetus for much of the work undertaken in feminist philosophy, the content of the notion of experience, and the nature of its relationships to knowledge and the natural and social worlds about which we theorize, are hardly obvious. Many feminists have come to doubt, for example, that experience is "spontaneous" or "passively absorbed." Further, although feminists often use women's experiences in their assessment of philosophical theories, many have come to doubt claims positing universals in those experiences. Finally, integral to the critiques post-modern feminists have leveled against the modern conception of selves – as constituting, for example, stable and unified entities – are critiques of conceptions of experience that take it to be the "origin" of knowledge, immediately accessible to its "subjects," and/or incorrigible. One source of these several kinds of doubt is feminist scholarship, which in a variety of disciplines and sciences suggests that concrete historical, sociopolitical, and material contexts both shape and constrain experience, and that women's experiences (as well as men's) differ across specific historical and cultural environments, and the social relations of class, race, and ethnicity that, along with gender, have characterized these environments (Alcoff 1988, Bordo 1987, Code 1991, Duran 1991, Harding 1986, Jaggar 1983, Longino 1990, Nelson 1990, Potter 1993, Scheman 1993a, Scott 1992).

The nature of the relationships between experience and knowledge is, then, a theoretical issue in feminist philosophy. It is in light of the specific and broad issues just noted, and those concerning the import of philosophical theories for women's lives, that feminist philosophy intersects epistemology and the philosophy of science, and the empiricist traditions that have dominated both. Feminist perspectives on philosophical empiricism, particularly approaches to knowledge and science with origins in British empiricism of the seventeenth and eighteenth centuries, are the subject of this article. One can, some feminists maintain, recognize experience as the source and checkpoint of knowledge, yet reject some or all of philosophical empiricism.

Philosophical empiricism

At its core, philosophical empiricism is a theory of evidence. As advocated by John Locke, George Berkeley, and David Hume, the central thesis of empiricism is that sensory experience constitutes all the evidence there is for knowledge (Locke 1694, Berkeley 1871, Hume 1955a, 1955b). This thesis remains the core of contemporary empiricism, the "cardinal tenet" of which, as W. V. Quine describes it, is that "whatever evidence there *is* for science *is* sensory" – here construing science broadly to include philosophy and so-called common-sense theorizing about physical objects and events, as well as the sciences proper (Quine 1969, p. 75).

So understood, philosophical empiricism incorporates far less by way of doctrines or dogmas than its advocates and critics typically attribute to it. But the connections that Locke, Berkeley, and Hume maintained between everyday and scientific knowledge on the one hand, and "ideas" and sensory experience on the other, and those connections that contemporary philosophers of science maintain between theories or models and the triggerings of exteroceptors or "phenomena," require explication. Such explication, and accounts of the scope and limits of knowledge that build on it, constitute the subject matter of empiricist theories of knowledge and of science.

The view that empiricism is fundamentally a theory of evidence will be controversial in some quarters, but there is little question that different theories of knowledge and science have been built on the empiricist account of evidence. The theories of knowledge advocated by Locke, Berkeley, and Hume differed in significant respects from one another. Contemporary empiricist epistemology is itself far from monolithic, including as it does quasi-foundationalists and coherentists, as well as advocates of both traditional and naturalized epistemology. So, too, empiricist philosophy of science includes a variety of methodological approaches (constructive empiricism and naturalized philosophy of science among them) that differ significantly from one another and, to varying degrees and in various ways, from logical positivism – the self-proclaimed heir of Hume's empiricism.

Such differences notwithstanding, "empiricism" is often used in feminist philosophy to encompass all theories of knowledge and science built on the empiricist thesis concerning evidence, in large part because these theories have shared several methodological commitments. Among these are two methodological commitments with roots in British empiricism (and in Cartesian rationalism before that): epistemological individualism – the commitment to taking individuals *qua* individuals as the primary loci of knowledge and science, and of theories about them – and the commitment to a hard and fast boundary between "noncognitive" values and knowledge.

Several distinguishable lines of analysis will be discernible in the summaries that follow of feminist perspectives on these two commitments. One line of analysis has been concerned to assess the warrant for these commitments (including the ways in which they support one another) and their implications for empiricist theories of knowledge and science. A second line of analysis, evolving apace with the efforts some have undertaken to develop distinctively feminist epistemologies and philosophies of science, has explored the obstacles these commitments pose to reconciling empiricist and feminist insights into knowledge, including the obstacles to "feminist empiricism." Feminists have also explored the ways in which theories of knowledge informed by these commitments have reflected and served to justify other theories, methodologies, and practices: liberal political theory, for example, and conceptions of scientific objectivity that have had an impact on scientific practice and served to under-write science's cognitive authority. And on the basis of these several lines of analysis, feminists have been led to explore what are aptly described as "meta-methodological" issues: among these, the empirical and normative import of philosophical methodologies, and the criteria to be used in evaluating them.

Epistemological individualism

Many feminist philosophers locate the origins of the empiricist commitment to taking individuals as the loci of knowledge and theories about it in a cluster of assumptions at work in British empiricism: the assumption that experience, and the "mental objects" ("sensations" or "impressions," and "ideas") prompted by it, are attributes or properties of individuals *qua* individuals and immediately accessible to their "subjects;" the assumption that experience is largely passive and at least in principle similar for individuals "appropriately situated"; and the assumption that knowing is itself the "mental activity of individual knowers" (Addelson and Potter 1991) – or, in more general terms, the undertaking and achievement of individuals *qua* individuals. Given these assumptions, some feminists argue, knowing would appear to have "no necessary social preconditions" (Jaggar 1983, p. 355). The individuals that constitute the domain of traditional empiricist theories of knowledge and science, like their counterparts in modern political theory, ethics, and metaphysics, are self-sufficient and autonomous (Alcoff 1988, Code 1991, Harding 1986, Jaggar 1983, Scott 1992; cf. Bordo 1987, Lloyd 1984, Scheman 1993a).

The "ideas" that figured centrally in the theories of knowledge advocated in British empiricism gave way, of course, to "sense data" in logical positivism, to "beliefs" and "propositions" in some contemporary empiricist epistemology, and to "brain states," behavior, and/or "cognitive processes" (e.g. decision making) in naturalized epistemology and naturalized philosophy of science. These objects have also been attributed to individuals *qua* individuals. And while some contemporary empiricists insist that even so-called basic sensory experiences are made possible and largely structured by bodies of current theory, feminists point to specific methods and emphases that reflect a lingering commitment to individualism. In analytic epistemology, they have argued, individualism is reflected in the emphasis placed on identifying necessary and sufficient conditions for "S" (understood to stand in for any individual knower) to know "that p" (Dalmiya and Alcoff 1993, Code 1991, Duran 1991); in post-logical-positivist philosophy of science, it is reflected in the lack of attention paid to the so-called context of discovery and in the emphasis on logical relations characterizing accounts of the so-called context of justification (Harding 1986, Longino 1990, Potter 1993); and in naturalized epistemology and naturalized philosophy of science, it is reflected in the emphasis placed on empirical psychology and cognitive science (Addelson 1993, Duran 1991, L .H. Nelson 1995).

Feminist philosophers have argued that the assumptions about mental objects and mental processes linked above to epistemological individualism have had significant consequences for empiricist theories of knowledge and science. For one thing, some point out, the result of building a theory of knowledge or science on objects and processes that are attributed to individuals *qua* individuals, is that additional assumptions are required to insure intersubjectivity, and the reliability of experience and knowledge claims.

Some of the assumptions taken to insure these things concern the epistemological "subject" or knower. Beyond its capacities for inferential reasoning and sensory experience, feminists have argued, "the knower" that figures in empiricist theories is largely featureless and contextless. It is abstracted (with the exception of its sensory receptors and brain states) from its embodiment, from its specific social and historical location (including its gender), and, at least in its cognitive activities, from its emotions, interests, and values. That is to say, none of these things has been taken to be relevant to how and what individuals know (Alcoff and Potter 1993, Bordo 1987, Code 1991, Jaggar 1983, 1989, Nelson 1990, Scott 1992; but cf. Baier 1993b). As a figure enjoying "deep background status" in modern epistemology (Addelson 1993), the knower so construed would appear to preclude some kinds of relativism (i.e. "any S" is in principle the subject of "S knows that p" statements) and, in this and other ways, to support the assumption that a comprehensive theory of knowledge, one specifying necessary and sufficient conditions for *all* knowledge claims, is possible (Alcoff and Potter 1993, Code 1991, Duran 1991).

The view of knowers as in principle interchangeable may preclude some forms of relativism, but it is not sufficient to preclude all forms of skepticism. Assumptions about what is known are also needed. One such assumption, explored in the next section, is that there is a boundary between knowledge and noncognitive values – an assumption necessitated by empiricist denials that values are subject to empirical constraint. Another assumption that has functioned to preclude relativism and skepticism is that there is a unique true theory of nature that our sensory receptors are sufficiently refined to discriminate (Addelson and Potter 1991, Nelson 1993). When argued for, this assumption functions as the conclusion of an inference to the best explanation: as the best (if not the only) explanation for intersubjectivity and successful prediction of features of the world. Feminists have criticized such arguments and linked the perceived need

33

for them to the commitment to individualism. Given this commitment, they point out, *unless* we also assume that there is one true theory and that the evidence for it is unequivocal, our allegedly individual successes in explaining and predicting experience. and the *match* between our individual experiences. are mysterious (e.g., Jaggar 1983, Nelson 1993). A third assumption with roots in British empiricism cited by feminists as functioning to preclude some kinds of skepticism (but also to fuel other kinds, including skepticism about "unobservable" objects, induction, causation, metaphysics, and values) is that allegedly "simple" observation claims constitute the basis or checkpoint for more esoteric claims (e.g. generalizations), are linked to features of the world relatively straightforwardly, and constitute paradigmatic cases of knowing (Dalmiya and Alcoff 1993, Code 1991, Jaggar 1983).

Not all contemporary empiricists presume a unique, true theory of nature, a "pretheoretic" or foundational status for "simple observation claims," or the possibility of linking individual claims to some specifiable range of stimuli. But often, feminists argue, the accounts contemporary empiricists provide of knowledge and science appear to assume that a "shared" theory of nature so substantively shapes experience, what is recognized as evidence, and theorizing more generally, that knowers are in principle interchangeable (e.g. Antony 1993, Longino 1990, Nelson 1990).

Each of the assumptions just listed has been criticized in feminist philosophy. Some have argued that the "self-sufficiency" characterizing the empiricist knower is only plausible if one ignores the interdependence dictated by human biology and the processes necessary to cognitive development (Code 1991, Duran 1991, Jaggar 1983). Sociolinguistic environments and interpersonal experience, feminists point out, are required for the postnatal development of neurobiological structures that allows for language acquisition and other cognitive capacities, and research into the effects of sensory deprivation indicates that a child's capacity for various kinds of sensory experience is dependent upon its environment, including that provided by caregivers (e.g. Code 1991, Duran 1991, Jaggar 1983). In an effort to reclaim both the subject and experience as epistemologically significant in the light of postmodern critiques, and to do so in light of postmodern insights, Linda Alcoff has advocated a view of both as positioned. and a view of "human subjectivity" as an "emergent property of historicized experience" (Alcoff 1988, p. 443). From perspectives such as those just outlined, it is questionable whether the form of introspection in which Locke, Berkeley, and Hume engaged *can* serve as the basis for a theory of knowledge. Lorraine Code has argued, for example, that these introspections are decidedly curious in "consistently bypassing the epistemic significance of early experiences with other people" (Code 1991, p. 129, Jaggar 1983; but cf. Baier 1993b). And Code and other feminists have suggested that ignoring these experiences and processes would seem to reflect specifically male experience in cultures in which women take primary responsibility for the care of children. According to this line of reasoning, the methods employed and theories advanced by Locke, Berkeley, and Hume challenge the assumption that knowers, including epistemologists, *can* be abstracted from the concrete social locations, including gender relations, in which they are situated (Bordo 1987, Code 1991, Duran 1991, Harding 1986, Scheman 1993) – an insight in keeping with Alcoff's view of selves and experience as emergent and positioned (Alcoff 1988).

In a related line of critique, some feminists have challenged the construal of beliefs and knowledge as "attributes" or "properties" of individuals. Naomi Scheman has argued, for example, that complex psychological objects such as beliefs or emotions cannot be assimilated to objects of introspection or to non-introspectable bodily states. Humans have "emotions, beliefs, abilities, and so on," Scheman maintains, "only in so far as they are embedded in a social web of interpretation that serves to give meaning to the bare data of inner experience and behavior" (Scheman 1983; cf. Jaggar 1989). Postmodern feminists, as noted above, challenge the modern conceptions of selves and experience as stable or foundational entities. Finally, feminists reflecting a range of philosophical traditions have argued that knowing, both in everyday contexts and specialized enterprises like the sciences, is an inherently social process. When we study the actual circumstances in which knowledge claims are generated and sustained, these arguments maintain, it is clear that both experience and knowledge are made possible and shaped by historically-specific standards, practices, and theories (e.g. Antony 1993, Duran 1991, Harding 1986, Longino 1990, Nelson 1990). From such perspectives, "the subject of experience, the individual, is a nexus of interpretation coming into existence at the boundary of nature and culture" (Longino 1990, p. 221), and it is a variety of social processes, no less than the world experienced, that produces experience and knowledge.

The assumption that simple observation claims constitute paradigmatic cases of knowing has also been criticized in feminist philosophy. Code argues, for example, that the contrast between the "multidimensional, multiperspectival character [of knowing other people]," and the "stark simplicity" of the claims usually granted paradigmatic status, "raises questions about the practice of granting exemplary status" to the latter (Code 1991, p. 37). Vrinda Dalmiya and Linda Alcoff have used knowledge attributed to women ("old wives' tales," for example) to challenge the assumption that all knowledge is propositional (Dalmiya and Alcoff 1993). And taking logical positivism to represent the culmination of modern empiricism, Alison Jaggar has criticized the emphasis on simple observation claims in British empiricism and what she takes to be the related commitment to reductionism in empiricist philosophy of science (Jaggar 1983).

Feminists have also argued that their own analyses of divisions in knowledge and cognitive authority based on social relations such as gender, race, and class challenge the presumed interchangeability of knowers. When such divisions and their consequences for the content of knowledge are considered, some have argued, it becomes clear that social situations both enable and set limits on what individuals experience and know (Alcoff and Potter 1993, Antony 1993, Code 1991, Harding 1986, Jaggar 1983; cf. Scott 1992). And while some feminists note that the assumption of interchangeability can be taken to represent an advance over philosophical theories that explicitly excluded women (e.g. Tuana 1992), many also maintain that the assumption functions to make actual exclusions and divisions in cognitive authority, and the relationships between knowledge and power more generally, invisible (Alcoff and Potter 1993, Code 1991, Harding 1986, Jaggar 1983, Tuana 1992).

Finally, for reasons noted or implicit in the foregoing, feminists have been critical of the understandings of experience at work in traditional and contemporary empiricist theories of knowledge and science. Viewed through the lens of feminist scholarship, women's and men's experiences appear neither "transparent" to their "owners," universal, nor incorrigible. And feminists drawing on a variety of traditions, including pragmatism and the continental tradition, have argued that the emphasis in British empiricism on "ideas" directly prompted by sensory experience, the emphasis in logical positivism on "sense data" (or "observation sentences" taken to constitute reports of sense data), and the emphasis in recent empiricism on "the triggerings of exteroceptors," behavior, and "phenomena," constitute decidedly impoverished understandings of experience (Alcoff 1988, Code 1991, Scott 1992, Seigfried 1993b).

Knowledge and values

Hume's tenet that "ought cannot be derived from is," and his more general tenet that every meaningful claim is either derivable from sense experience or statements about sense experience or is a claim about the meanings of words, have underwritten a deep skepticism about values within the empiricist tradition. In general, empiricist theories of knowledge and science have assumed or demanded a hard and fast boundary between facts and knowledge on the one hand, and noncognitive values on the other. As earlier noted, the boundary between knowledge and values has in part functioned to insure intersubjectivity and the reliability of knowledge claims. Given the assumption that values are not subject to empirical constraint or control, they appear to threaten intersubjectivity and to compromise any theorizing or theories they inform.

One important consequence of Hume's tenets, feminists have argued, is that objectivity has been linked to value-neutrality. Sandra Harding locates the source of this conception of objectivity in the reflections of Locke and Hume (and Descartes before them) on "the nature and activities of what they took to be 'disembodied' [human minds], beholden to no social commitments but the willful search for clear and certain truth" (Harding 1986, pp. 140–1; but cf. Baier 1993b, Hodge 1988). Alison Jaggar argues that the positivist conception of scientific objectivity explicitly builds on the assumption that intersubjective agreement will be impossible unless "values, interests, and emotions are prevented from directing the scientific enterprise" (Jaggar 1983, p. 356; cf. Harding 1986, Longino 1990). Indeed, even contemporary empiricists who reject key features of Humean and positivist empiricism (the analytic/synthetic distinction, for example, the possibility of coherent "pretheoretic" experience, and the tenet that individual sentences have empirical content in isolation from a body of theory), continue to demand a boundary between values and science on the grounds that values are not subject to empirical controls (see, e.g., Quine 1981).

Not all feminist philosophers reject the fact/value distinction outright, but many are critical of the skepticism about values that has characterized the empiricist tradition and of the conceptions of knowledge and objectivity to which that skepticism has contributed. Some argue that the boundary between "value-informed" claims and "empirical" claims is difficult to maintain in many arenas, including many areas of research in the sciences; and many take it to be an implication of feminist scholarship that value-neutrality is not a litmus test for "good" knowledge or science. Two lines of argument are common. One is that feminist analyses of the methods, categories, and content of everyday and professional knowledge indicate that social beliefs and values substantively shape both, and that knowledge generated in the sciences and other arenas in turn shapes social perspectives and experiences (e.g. Alcoff and Potter 1993, Code 1991, Harding 1986, Jaggar 1983, Longino 1990). Nor, according to a second line of argument, can we take the lesson of, say, feminist science scholarship to be that stricter methodological controls are needed to "filter out" social beliefs and values, for the latter motivate and inform the critiques feminist scientists and science scholars offer of various research programs and theories, and the alternatives they advocate (Harding 1986, Jaggar 1983, Longino 1990, Nelson 1990). From these perspectives, it is the notion of the intrinsic value-neutrality of knowledge, including scientific knowledge, that needs to be rethought, for it relies on "inadequate notions of experience, of inference, and of the inquiring subject" (Longino 1990, pp. 222–3; cf. *Synthèse* 104(3)).

Conclusion

The foregoing suggests considerable agreement among feminist philosophers that the two empiricist commitments considered here are problematic. But feminist perspectives on philosophical empiricism, like feminist perspectives on other philosophical traditions, are less than monolithic. It remains an open and contested issue, for example, whether empiricism can be separated from its historical commitments to individualism or to a boundary between knowledge and non-cognitive values. Some feminists have maintained a necessary connection between the empiricist thesis about evidence, these methodological commitments, and the doctrines to which they have led, and for these and other reasons advocate alternative, nonempiricist theories of knowledge and science (e.g. Harding 1986, Jaggar 1983). Others have argued that it is possible to separate empiricism from both methodological commitments, and some maintain that there are important resources for feminist theorizing about knowledge and science in traditional and contemporary empiricism: for example, in Hume's work (e.g. Baier 1993b, Hodge 1988), in that of Hesse (Potter 1993), in naturalized philosophy of science and epistemology (e.g. Addelson 1993, Antony 1993, Duran 1991, Nelson 1990), and in constructive empiricism (e.g. Campbell 1994, Longino 1990).

Nor is there consensus concerning the appropriate conceptualization, if there is one, of notions that have been central to empiricist theories of knowledge, including selves, experience, and evidence (cf., e.g., Alcoff 1988, Scott 1992).

Finally, feminists have raised questions about whether epistemology in general, and empiricist theories of knowledge and science in particular, are inherently conservative, the product and tool of those traditionally recognized as "knowledge makers" (Addelson and Potter 1991). And some maintain, partly on the basis of this issue and others we have considered, that the goal of epistemology to construct a comprehensive theory of knowledge is in principle untenable and deeply incommensurate with feminist politics (e.g. Code 1991, Fraser and Nicholson 1990, Hekman 1990, Yeatman 1990).

4

Kant

ROBIN MAY SCHOTT

Introduction

Why do feminist philosophers read Kant? Because of his misogyny and his disdain for the body, Barbara Herman has described Kant as the modern moral philosopher whom feminists find most objectionable (Herman 1993a, p. 50). But that unhappy status alone would not justify a separate entry on Kant in this volume. Immanuel Kant is the figure in modern philosophy who most clearly articulates the Enlightenment program that reason is the vehicle for humanity's progress towards emancipation from unjust authority, a program that epitomizes the self-understanding of the Western culture of modernity. Kant's paradigm of objectivity, which formalizes the universal and necessary conditions for knowledge, provides a philosophical justification for the view that cognitive and moral judgments must be disinterested and impartial. This assumption about the impartiality of knowledge is deeply entrenched in academic disciplines. The quest for objectivity undergirds prevailing methodologies in the natural and social sciences as well as in philosophy. The assumption that knowledge is impartial informs the practices of daily life as well – e.g., in how one evaluates newspaper reporting or jury decisions. Feminist philosophers seek to come to terms with these features of modernity. They debate whether Enlightenment conceptions of progress and rationality offer tools for women's emancipation and empowerment, or whether this philosophical inheritance itself has contributed to the historical subordination of women in Western society.

Kant's historical stature is also due to the scope of his work, which provides the systematic basis for modern discussions of reason, ethics, aesthetics, and politics. His philosophy has also been pivotal for contemporary postmodern discussions. Contemporary philosophers debate whether Kant's later work on aesthetics leads to a radical alteration of his views of feeling, imagination, and subjectivity presented in the *Critique of Pure Reason*. Many philosophers are inspired by the postmodern critique of the "philosophy of the subject" – of the view that there is a stable, coherent self, possessing a form of reason capable of privileged insight into its own processes and into the laws of nature. For them, Kant's *Critique of Judgment* seems to provide evidence of a more complex theory of the creative processes of the self than was evident in the first *Critique*. On the other hand, philosophers committed to the legacy of Enlightenment seek in Kant the certainty of philosophical truth, which can provide a bulwark against the unsettling winds of postmodernism. For them, Kant's analysis of the conditions of knowledge and morality in the first and second *Critiques* anchor claims for universality. In the midst of this renaissance of interest in Kant, it is especially urgent that feminist voices be heard.

In the *Critique of Pure Reason* (1787), Kant describes his philosophical revolution on analogy with Copernicus' revolution. Whereas metaphysicians had previously sought to make human knowledge conform to objects, Kant sought to make objects conform to human knowledge. Only in this way could a priori knowledge – knowledge that is prior to and independent of experience – be proven to exist. The Copernican turn places the activity of the knowing subject at the center of cognition. Kant's philosophical revolution paved the way for the further development of the concept of critique in Hegel and in the Frankfurt School of Critical Theory. Since knowledge is possible because of the activity of the knowing subject, the critique of reason is possible as a form of self-knowledge (Benhabib 1986, p. 45). This emphasis found in both Kant and in the post-Kantian tradition that human activity is the enabling condition of critique has had enormous political repercussions. Marx defined human activity as labor that constitutes material and intellectual life. Feminist philosophers informed by the tradition of critique would argue that this concept of constituting activity is the precondition for feminist critiques of gender. It is because bodies, psyches, and theoretical categories are all constructed by human activities (e.g. language, economics, sexual politics) that feminist critiques of sex and gender are possible.

Feminist strategies

The growth of philosophical feminism is a response to the history of philosophical sexism, which has identified "human" by a masculine model and defined the feminine only in relation to the masculine. As Elizabeth Grosz writes, it is urgent to engage both in the critical project of analyzing how sexism has functioned in philosophical theories, and in the constructive project of taking traditional discourses as points of departure for creating new theories, methods, and values. This constructive project takes women's experience rather than men's to select the objects and methods of investigation (Grosz 1990, pp. 60–1).

Given Kant's explicit endorsement of the subordination of wives to their husbands and the exclusion of women from intellectual and political rights, it is no surprise that many feminists consider Kant to be an exemplar of philosophical sexism. Here the tensions between Kantian philosophy and feminist theory are mutual. Kant would consider feminists to be concerned with questions of empirical import, of interest perhaps to a particular group but not relevant to universal questions about knowledge or ethics. and therefore not properly belonging to the domain of philosophy. On the other hand, many feminists seek to redefine the ground on which a sympathetic dialogue with Kant can take place. But there are certain common threads that are present in both critics and sympathizers. Both groups challenge the accepted topography of Kantian philosophy by which central philosophical concerns are defined as those that are

abstract, universal, and transcendental, whereas issues relating to bodily existence, to emotion, or to empirical identity are defined as marginal. Instead,
feminists have begun with questions founded in the politics of everyday life to
resituate Kantian questions (e.g. about the rational self, moral relations, aesthetic
judgment, and political rights and responsibilities) in the context of relations
between the sexes, races, nations, and between humans and the natural environment. Thus, although there is no one way of reading Kant from a feminist
perspective, feminist perspectives on Kant are distinguished by their resistance to
oppression and discrimination in its various forms – whether based on gender,
race, class, religion, or geographical location. Some philosophers (e.g. Barbara
Herman and Adrian Piper) explore the ways in which Kant's philosophy provides
reflective tools for resisting discrimination, whereas others (Hannelore Schroder
and Robin Schott) focus on the way Kantianism enacts discrimination.

Feminist philosophers reading Kant invoke diverse strategies. Some appropriate Kant's philosophy to positively address feminist concerns (e.g. Piper 1992–3,
p. 191, argues that Kant provides the tools necessary for a rational person to
enlarge her own experience through an openness to otherness); others explore
the internal contradictions of Kant's philosophy (e.g. Schott 1996, p. 477, shows
the contradiction between his call for universal enlightenment and his exclusion
of women and servants from enlightenment), while others use the tools of Kant's
philosophy to go beyond itself (e.g. Kneller 1997 argues that Kant's discussion of
imagination could lead to a more satisfying conception of moral subjectivity than
Kant himself gives). But there is no easy mapping of feminist readings of Kant that
fits the typical classification of feminists into radical, liberal, Marxist–socialist, or
postmodern. Radical feminists might criticize Kant as the archetype of patriarchal
misogynist thought, or they may see his comments on the objectification entailed
by sexual desire as sympathetic with radical feminist critiques of the sexual
objectification of women. (See Barbara Herman's comparison of Kant's *Lectures
on Ethics* with Andrea Dworkin's *Intercourse*, Herman 1993a, p. 56.) Liberal
feminists may seek to include women in Kant's conception of cognitive and
moral subjectivity, or they may argue that his conception of individuality cannot
account for the kind of community required in a well-functioning democratic
society. (See Annette Baier's discussion, 1993a, pp. 228–48.) Marxist–socialist
inspired feminists may view Kant as articulating the alienation and objectification of individuals in capitalist society (see Schott 1988), or argue that his
concept of the thing-in-itself retains a vision of knowledge that can transcend
the bounds of contemporary existence (see Goldmann 1971, p. 157). Postmodern feminists might view Kant as the exemplary spokesman of the "philosophy
of the subject" (see Flax 1990, p. 43), or as the philosopher who opens the door
to a more complex reading of subjectivity.

Rationality debates

Feminist discussions of Kantian rationalism should be situated in the context of
the general feminist debates about objectivity and reason. Many theorists have

been inspired by the claims of philosophers like Genevieve Lloyd, who argues that in the history of philosophy reason has had a particularly male (rather than human) face (Lloyd 1984). Hélène Cixous invokes the following polarities to illustrate that the hierarchical dualisms embedded in Western culture are related to the couple man/woman: "Activity/Passivity, Sun/Moon, Culture/Nature, Day/Night, Father/Mother, Head/Heart, Intelligible/Sensitive, Logos/Pathos" (Cixous 1986, p. 63). From her viewpoint, the very structures of reason are imbued with gender hierarchies, since reason inheres in a system that subordinates women and all that has traditionally been linked to women: passivity. nature, emotion, and bodily processes.

Feminist philosophers who read Kant have debated the question of the maleness of reason along two axes: debates about Enlightenment rationality, and debates about universality. Kant's phrase, "Have courage to use your own reason!" (Kant 1963, p. 3) has been the motto for the Enlightenment view that progress is possible through the use of reason and the advancement and spread of knowledge. Feminist theorists have a particularly embattled relation to the question of Enlightenment. Some theorists argue that the Enlightenment tradition in general, and Kant's philosophy in particular, provide a basis for individual reason, progress and freedom that is a precondition for the discourse of women's liberation and for the political gains that women have won. They argue that although historically the Enlightenment excluded women from the public exercise of reason, this historical project should now be completed by incorporating previously excluded groups (see Flax's discussion, 1990, p. 42). Other feminists point out that Kant's obvious exclusion of women from his invocation to humanity to free itself from tutelage is a clue that Enlightenment rationality is itself highly gendered, premised as it is on the exclusion of emotion from rationality, and the association of women with unruly emotion (Schott 1996, p. 478).

Debates about enlightenment are linked more generally to the status of universals in contemporary feminist debates. Some feminists argue that understanding the formal conditions for universal rational or moral agreement is a precondition not only for coherent claims about knowledge and moral judgment, but for the healthy functioning of a society built on reciprocal recognition of persons. On this view, the formalism of rationality need not imply rigidity, but can elucidate the conditions for an ability to rationally respond to and learn from new experiences, and can therefore provide the tools for countering xenophobic fears (Piper 1992–3, p. 191). Other feminists, however, point out that claims for so-called "universal" conditions of reason reflect the experience of the dominant social group in society, and thus undermine the validity of any transcendental, transhistorical claims for truth. Jane Flax writes, "What Kant's self calls its 'own' reason and the methods by which reason's contents become present or self-evident, are no freer from empirical contingency than is the so-called phenomenal self" (Flax 1990, p. 43). Moreover, Kantian objectivity may be viewed as an articulation of Western culture's commitment to a form of asceticism that requires not only the social subordination of women, but the existential and cognitive suppression of emotion and sensuousness that historically has been identified with women (Schott 1988). Finally, Kantian rationalism can be viewed as a statement of impartiality that demands a Godlike perspective outside any particular viewpoint, and thus undermines one's ability to adjudicate the specific interests or feelings in any individual perspective (Young 1990b, p. 96).

Ethical debates

Kant's ethical theory has been the focus of the largest body of feminist work on Kant. His views regarding the autonomy of rational persons is thematically close to the widespread interest among feminists in relations between persons. Some view Kantian autonomy as undermining concrete relations between persons (e.g. Robin Schott), while others view Kantian autonomy as necessary for the flourishing of such relations (e.g. Marcia Baron). Kant's categorical imperative, built on respect for the moral law, has given rise to a formalist interpretation of ethics. In the *Foundations of the Metaphysics of Morals* Kant writes, "I should never act in such a way that I could not also will that my maxim should be a universal law" (Kant 1959, p. 18). Kant's moral philosophy demands respect for persons as rational beings, warns against treating persons as means to an end, and argues against any role for emotion in ethical judgment except for the feeling of respect for the moral law.

Feminist ethicists writing on Kant have been interested primarily in two themes: debates about an "ethic of care" and debates about autonomy. "Care ethicists" have been inspired by Carol Gilligan's book, *In a Different Voice: Psychological Theory and Women's Development* (1982a). In her book, Gilligan argues not only that the prevailing psychological theories of moral development display a distinctly masculine bias, but that they focus exclusively on justice and rights and devalue the concern with care and responsibility that is so pronounced for many women. Feminists inspired by Gilligan's work focus on how moral judgments are contextual, are immersed in the details of relationships, and presuppose a "concrete other," rather than a self that is disembodied and disembedded from social relationships (Benhabib 1992, p. 159).

Feminists engaged in debates about care ethics approach Kant from divergent points of view. Some argue that the moral universalism of Kantian philosophy does not contradict the concerns of care ethics. For example, Herta Nagl-Docekal argues that the formal rule of morality should be understood as both universalist and radically individualizing, and that Kant's ethics can be an important tool in identifying the moral wrongs to which women are subjected because of their gender (Nagl-Docekal 1997). On the other hand, Sally Sedgwick argues that Kant's formalist conception of the moral law is based on a false dichotomy between reason and nature, and cannot be adequate to understanding the complexities of human life which care ethicists seek to incorporate in their accounts of morality (Sedgwick 1990a, pp. 60–79).

Other feminists are critical of the turn to a feminist ethics of care. Claudia Card argues that the values exalted by an ethics of care can cover a reality of abuse, in which women are either abused or themselves abusers, and that this ethical view may itself merely articulate the moral damage done to women through the history of their disempowerment (Card 1988, pp. 125–35). From such a perspective, feminist ethicists would be interested in understanding moral luck, individual separateness, or concepts of autonomy.

Thus, some feminist ethicists argue that patriarchal social structures historically have deprived women of autonomy, and they may look to Kant for providing insights into developing self-determination and responsibility. Alternatively, many care ethicists point out that Kant's conception of autonomy is premised on the notion of a disembodied and disembedded individual, and argue that autonomy needs to be revisioned in order to account for the concrete features of a self situated in particular relations with others (Rumsey 1997). Still other feminists argue for the need for another conceptual revolution that focuses not on autonomy but on heteronomy, on the interdependence of individuals and the moral status of collectivities (Schott 1996, p. 481). Yet other feminists use psychoanalytical tools to dissect the concept of autonomy, to analyze its component parts of lawfulness and guilt in relation to the question of sexual difference, and thus to inquire whether men and women have a different relation to the moral law (David-Ménard 1997).

Debates in aesthetics

Kant's *Critique of Judgment* has been central for the contemporary resurgence of interest in Kant. In his writing on aesthetics, Kant moves away from the mechanistic conception of nature that is dominant in the first *Critique*. In the *Critique of Judgment* Kant attempts to resituate nature in relation to subjective purposes that are omitted from the scientific analysis of nature, and to explore the free play of imagination in contrast to the lawful work of cognition. The pleasure in the experience of a beautiful object is grounded in the harmonious interplay of the imagination and the understanding, which gives rise to the experience of objects *as if* they were designed for our own purposes.

Feminists who debate Kant's aesthetics are divided between those who view Kant's third *Critique* as opening avenues for rethinking the role of feeling and embodiment in subjectivity, and those who see it as reenacting the dualisms and forms of dominance characteristic of modern Western culture. For example, Jane Kneller follows Hannah Arendt's reading of the *Critique of Judgment* to show that Kant's notion of common sense – *sensus communis* – implies that community is crucial for his understanding of autonomy. From this point of view, impartiality need not mean detachment from or indifference to particular perspectives, but an ability to think in the place of everyone else. Kneller argues, furthermore, that Kant's aesthetics open up the possibility not just of thinking with others, but of feeling with others, and thus creates a space for imagination and feeling in moral subjectivity that can be used to revise Kant's earlier account (Kneller 1997). In the same spirit, Marcia Moen reads the *Critique of Judgment* as offering an analysis of intersubjectivity – as providing a role for feeling in his account of *sensus communis* and in his turn to the body as the locus of feeling, and as opening the door to an understanding of perspective and context in narrative that moves beyond absolutist claims for truth (Moen 1997).

But other feminist philosophers have read Kant's third *Critique* as reiterating the dualistic hierarchies and power relations of Western culture. For example, Cornelia Klinger argues that the pair of the beautiful and the sublime is part of a long list of dualisms in Western culture, including the dualisms between form/matter, mind/body, reason/emotion, public/private, active/passive, transcendent/immanent. All of these oppositions are rooted in the dualism between culture and nature that have a gendered meaning in the history of Western civilization. From her point of view, the resurgence of the interest in the sublime in contemporary postmodern appropriations of Kant point to a renewal of masculinism in contemporary culture (Klinger 1995, pp. 207–24). Other feminists read Kant's aesthetics through the grid of ideology-critique – for example, analyzing how his theory of beauty, *sensus communis*, and pleasure reflects sexual, racial, or class hierarchies. For example, Kim Hall examines Kant's examples and metaphors to show the Eurocentric assumptions of Kantian aesthetics, which celebrate the colonizer who "civilizes" the "savages" (Hall 1997). Robin Schott explores the way in which the structure of pleasure in Kant's aesthetic theory is based on the notion that we experience objects "as if" they were created for our own purposes, and thus reveals the frustrated nature of pleasure in a market-based society (Schott 1988, p. 158).

Kant's views of women and nature

Kant's comments on women's nature are among the most obvious targets of feminist criticism. For example, Kant asserts woman's character, in contrast to man's, to be wholly defined by natural needs. Women's empirical nature shows their lack of self-determination, in contrast to the rational potential that inheres in their humanity. In *Anthropology from a Pragmatic Point of View* he writes, "Nature was concerned about the preservation of the embryo and implanted fear into the woman's character, a fear of physical injury and a timidity towards similar dangers. On the basis of this weakness, the woman legitimately asks for masculine protection" (Kant 1978, p. 219). Because of their natural fear and timidity, Kant views women as unsuited for scholarly work. He mockingly describes scholarly women who "use their books somewhat like a watch, that is, they wear the watch so it can be noticed that they have one, although it is usually broken or does not show the correct time" (Kant 1978, p. 221). Kant's remarks on women in the *Anthropology* echo his sentiments in *Observations on the Feeling of the Beautiful and the Sublime*. In that early work, Kant notes, "A woman who has a head full of Greek, like Mme. Dacier, or carries on fundamental controversies about mechanics, like the Marquise de Chatelet, might as well even have a beard, for perhaps that would express more obviously the mien of profundity for which she strives" (Kant 1960, p. 78). In Kant's view, women's philosophy is "not to reason, but to sense." And he adds, "I hardly believe that

45

the fair sex is capable of principles" (Kant 1960, pp. 132–3). No wonder that under these conditions the woman "makes no secret in wishing that she might rather be a man, so that she could give larger and freer latitude to her inclinations: no man. however. would want to be a woman (Kant 1978, p. 222).

Although Kant's later development of the concept of rational autonomy is increasingly at odds with his earlier depiction of women's subjective character, it would be difficult to defend Kant's views of women. Nor can his misogynist views be dismissed as merely reflections of an earlier epoch. For example, the lawyer Theodor von Hippel, mayor of Kant's city of Königsberg, contemporary and friend of Kant, was a spokesperson for equal human and civil rights for women. Thus Kant's views on women must be viewed as reactionary for his times. Hannelore Schroder argues that Kant's anthropological principle of women's natural inferiority to men is reflected in *Rechtslehre*. the first part of *The Metaphysics of Morals*, which she argues gives a justification of women's status as property of her husband in marriage (Schroder 1997). Schroder's argument is a controversial one. Although she acknowledges that Kant never defined women as property, she looks to Kant's justification of the power held by the male head of the household over his wife and daughters, and Kant's views of men's natural superiority over women, to argue that women cannot consistently be viewed as persons in Kant's account. Thus, in her view, his treatment of women makes a mockery of Kant's universal principle of respect for persons. More sympathetically, Barbara Herman interprets Kant as trying to establish through the political institution of marriage a moral framework for a sexual relationship which in itself is objectifying. Herman thus rejects the view that Kant treats the wife as the property of the husband. Such a view of marriage would reflect the assault on autonomy that is inherent in the sexual relation, rather than correct for it, as Kant sought to do. She argues that sexual relations are not private in Kant's account, but are only permissible within the juridical relation of marriage. Thus, there are no conceptual barriers in Kant's philosophy for defining and prohibiting spousal rape and battering (Herman 1993a, pp. 55–7, p. 63). In addition to the ethical and juridical perspectives, one can approach Kant's views on women from a psychoanalytical perspective. For example, Sarah Kofman argues that the nature of men's respect for women, implied in Kant's ethical writings, bears the trace of the originary relation of respect – for example, a child's respect for her/his mother. According to Kofman, this relation implies a desire to hold women at a distance in order not to be crushed by her power nor to reveal her weakness. But the price one pays for this respectful distance is the loss of sensual pleasure, which characterized Kant's own celibate life (Kofman 1982, pp. 383–404).

Although most feminists view Kant's association of women with nature and with the survival of the species as an example of patriarchal ideology, Holly Wilson argues that from an ecofeminist point of view women's association with nature is a positive correlation. She suggests that Kant's comments about women's role in the preservation of the species might be sympathetic to feminists like Nel Noddings, who take mothers' care for the preservation of their children as the source of ethics. Moreover, ecofeminists would view sympathetically Kant's account of nature as an interconnected system of purposes. His theory of nature can be aligned with the view of nature as an ecosystem of interconnected relations in which human beings are co-members in the system of nature, but not set apart as separate from and superior to nature (Wilson 1997).

Conclusion

Having summarized the general features of feminist debates in Kant – though by no means covering all feminist philosophers currently writing on Kant – I would like to pose the following questions: What do feminist interpretations of Kant contribute to Kant scholarship? What do they contribute to feminist philosophy? And what, if anything, do they contribute to social life more generally?

Feminist readers of Kant, whether sympathizers or critics, have transformed the inherited terrain of debate. Rather than dealing merely with Kant's internal philosophical criteria, as Kant scholars typically have done, feminist readers have taken concerns arising from feminist philosophy as points of departure in their analyses of Kant. In this context, questions about embodiment, emotion and imagination, community and power relations have become central in debates about Kant. Feminist interpretations of Kant are an example of the rejuvenation of philosophy that occurs when women become participants in a dialogue that historically has excluded them.

Feminist readings of Kant also make an important contribution to feminist philosophy more generally. Such readings are part of the important task of historical self-knowledge. As Elizabeth Spelman points out in *Inessential Women* (Spelman 1988, p. 6), if feminists do not know adequately the historical tradition from which they seek to distance themselves, they will repeat the premises that they ostensibly reject. Moreover, feminists engaged in reading Kant contribute to a more sophisticated and nuanced theorizing about epistemology, ethics, and aesthetics than can occur in a historical vacuum. Feminists have moved far from an earlier dismissal of Western male philosophers as patriarchal, and hence of no interest for feminist philosophy. Rather, feminist philosophers currently recognize that however much one may identify rightly a philosopher as masculinist, one still needs to engage either positively or critically with this tradition. Otherwise, feminist theorists risk staying in a realm of utopianism that leaves existing forms of thought untouched (Grosz 1990, pp. 60–1). Moreover, the diversity of feminist interpretations of Kant are a contribution to the more general theoretical recognition of the multiplicity of feminist perspectives. One can no more justify a unitary truth in feminist philosophies than one can in masculinist philosophies.

Finally, one can ask whether feminist interpretations of Kant have any larger significance beyond these particular debates. Women's access to university scholarship has led not only to the creation of women's studies and gender studies as academic disciplines, but to the revamping of previously existing fields. Although

47

in Kant's own time women were denied access to university education, this century has shown that education is crucial for women's entering what Kant calls the "public" exercise of reason, defined as the "use which a person makes of it as a scholar before the reading public" (Kant 1963, p. 5). When women become scholars, they do not grow beards (as Kant joked), but they do open paths for rethinking the contents and methods of research and teaching in the contemporary world.

5

Pragmatism

CHARLENE HADDOCK SEIGFRIED

In feminist philosophical writings "pragmatism" has two diverse meanings. The first is closely related to the everyday meaning of the pragmatic as what is useful or even expedient. The second refers to any theoretical position that closely ties theory to practice, that values practice over theory, or that tests theory by its actual effects, most notably on women or other marginalized groups. More exactly, it refers to the historically specific tradition of classical American pragmatism and its contemporary variants.

In the first, uncritical common-sense use of the term, "pragmatism" can refer to any theoretical perspective that emphasizes the practical, that subordinates theoretical to useful concerns, or that rejects theory altogether for actively changing unjust social conditions. It is also used negatively for positions that sacrifice transcendent values for expediency. All feminist theory has been claimed to be pragmatic in the positive sense insofar as it is concerned with actually changing women's conditions of exploitation. Some feminist positions, actions, or groups, on the other hand, have been criticized as being too pragmatic and not sufficiently grounded in theory.

Although many feminist theories have a practical dimension, or emphasize practice, or praxis, pragmatism as a philosophical movement began with a discussion group in Cambridge, Massachusetts in the 1870s. It was first articulated by Charles Sanders Peirce as the pragmatic principle that concepts be understood as the conceivable practical effects that follow from holding them, and reformulated by William James, who first brought it to public attention. For James theorizing begins with experience, which can only be reflectively distinguished into subjective and objective aspects by adopting a point of view that expresses interests or values (Seigfried 1990). John Dewey, as head of a pragmatist, interdisciplinary department of philosophy, psychology, and education at the University of Chicago from 1894 to 1904, worked closely with Alice Chipman Dewey, Katherine Camp Mayhew, Anna Camp Edwards, and Ella Flagg Young at the Laboratory School and with Jane Addams (1860–1935), Florence Kelley, Julia Lathrop, and other women active in the inner-city Hull House settlement. As a continuing and quite diverse historical movement, pragmatism cannot be reduced to any essentialist definition. In accordance with the pragmatist principle that nothing can be defined apart from a selective interest or end-in-view, only those features of pragmatism that are or might be of particular interest to feminists will be developed here.

Dewey rejected the quest for certainty that characterizes essentialist views of reality that he traced back to the class interests of Greek philosophers of the classical period, who were dependent on the slave labor of most men and all women and who sought absolute, unchangeable truth and good in transcendent realms unaffected by transient material conditions. He also rejected the exaggerated autonomy of the liberal individual and the absolute freedom posited by existentialists, as well as behaviorism or the determinism that follows from believing that persons are constituted by the external relations of community or trapped by inherited traditions or customs. He emphasized instead that the freedom and creativity of persons can only develop in dynamic relations with others. His post-Darwinian theory recognized that the organism and environment interaction out of which consciousness evolved includes both nature and society. As organisms who seek to thrive under adverse conditions, human understanding is interested and fallible and can only develop beyond pure speculation experimentally. The emergence of consciousness greatly enhanced the ability of human beings to learn from their experiences, but it did not guarantee a favorable outcome. Since we are "body-minds," understanding is pluralistically situated, historically, socially, and culturally. Thinking is a tool or instrument used to transform the problematic situations that arise in experience toward a satisfactory resolution. Pragmatists advocate resolutions that are subject to further revisions as their shortcomings become apparent and assert that unless such resolutions are inclusive, cooperative, and empowering, they are less than satisfactory.

Two distinct periods of pragmatist philosophy are particularly relevant for feminist theory because women actively contributed to the development of pragmatist and feminist theory in both. The first period covers the foundational years in the decades immediately preceding and following the beginning of the twentieth century and established the core of the pragmatist canon as consisting of the writings of Peirce, James, Josiah Royce, Dewey, and George Herbert Mead. But this view has recently been challenged (Seigfried 1996). Not only were there significant contributions to pragmatist theory by women and Blacks, but early pragmatist analyses of racism and of sexism were developed. The second period of interest only began in the last few decades of the twentieth century. It is challenging and expanding the traditional canon to include the voices of women and minorities and developing a second wave of pragmatist feminism.

Recovering a feminist version of pragmatism

Although the access of women and Blacks in the United States to undergraduate and graduate education in philosophy was severely limited in the late nineteenth and early twentieth centuries when pragmatism was being developed, there were some notable exceptions. Mary Whiton Calkins (1863–1930), who later became president of both the American Philosophical and the American Psychological Associations, was the first student to study *The Principles of Psychology* with James on its publication, but her own philosophy of personalist idealism owes more to Josiah Royce than to James. She performed early psychological experiments to demonstrate that there were no significant differences in women's and men's powers of association. Ethel Puffer-Howes (1872–1950), W. E. B. Du Bois, and Alain Locke all studied with the Harvard pragmatists and in their own writings deepened the pragmatist understanding of perspectivism and pluralism by showing how they were distorted by sexism and racism, in addition to classism. Christine Ladd-Franklin, who studied with Peirce at Johns Hopkins, wrote about women's issues in the *Nation*. Dewey credits Ella Flagg Young, both a student and colleague, with impressing on him the importance of testing all philosophical formulations by rephrasing them in terms of experience, particularly of what they mean when attempted in practise beyond the philosophical. Under Mead and Tufts at the University of Chicago, Jessie Taft (1882–1961) wrote what seems to be the first philosophical dissertation on the women's movement (Taft 1915), and Helen Thompson (Wooley) carried out psychological experiments undermining beliefs in the innate inferiority of women. Among educational reformers, Elsie Ripley Clapp (1882–1965) collaborated with Dewey at Columbia Teacher's College and Lucy Sprague Mitchell at both Harvard and Columbia. Pushing the boundaries beyond the academy, Charlotte Perkins Gilman (1860–1935) also drew on evolutionary theory to demonstrate the negative effects of the androcentrism of culture and institutions, and Dewey praised the importance of her work showing the economic basis of women's oppression (Gilman 1966, 1971). Addams and Dewey repeatedly acknowledged the importance of their mutual influences. Still to be determined by further research is the relevance to pragmatist theory of such prominent black feminist theorists and activists as Ida B. Wells-Barnett, known to have worked with Addams.

Pragmatism took the Darwinian revolution as marking a decisive turn from formalism, a priori thinking, essentialism, and the quest for certainty toward concrete analyses of the human condition, emergent intelligence with its inevitable limitations, pluralistic interpretations depending on ends-in-view, and experimental reconstruction. Its task was emancipatory and transformative. Pragmatist reflection begins with experience as an interactive process involving individuals and their social and natural environment, and it is therefore at odds with the epistemological turn of modern philosophy. Experience is undergone, suffered, enjoyed, transformed, hated, and loved, as well as known. Like feminist standpoint theorists, pragmatists argue that the perspectivism of such situated experiences means that those who are marginalized know the limits of the dominant interpretation of reality better than those holding the standard view. According to Dewey, "If the ruling and the oppressed elements in a population, if those who wish to maintain the *status quo* and those concerned to make changes, had, when they became articulate, the same philosophy, one might well be skeptical of its intellectual integrity" (Dewey 1968, p. 9). But unlike standpoint

51

theorists, pragmatists hold that even such perspectives must still be reflectively validated after being acted upon.

Reflecting on the role of rationality in interpreting experiences, James shows how it has at least four dimensions: intellectual, aesthetical, moral, and practical. Dewey also rejects abstract reason for engaged understanding that incorporates value and purpose in actively assessing and reorganizing disturbing experiences. The world of experience or field of consciousness comes with body as the center of vision, action, and interest. Feeling is not simply an inner, psychic fact, but is both the world as experienced and the experience of it. Situations are qualitatively pervaded throughout. They have dominant qualities which signal both a need for action and suggest possible resolutions. Such pervasive background qualities function as points of departure and regulative principles of all thinking. Felt experiences of discord or conflict set inquiry in motion, not uncertainty in general, but the unique qualities of particular situations.

The problematic situation that Jane Addams was concerned with was that of the growing ranks of the working poor, unemployed, and the social dislocations, class antagonisms, and suffering brought about by the Industrial Revolution as these were experienced by a growing number of college-educated women eager to expand their responsibilities beyond the domestic sphere. Addams's analysis of experience differs from that of the academic pragmatists in at least two ways. In the first place, she draws on a wider and more diverse range of experiences in her reflections, including those of factory and domestic workers, various ethnic groups of recent immigrants, and poor and working-class women. Secondly, she also develops a pragmatist account of experience from women's experiences as differentiated by class and ethnicity. She attributes many social ills "to the lack of imagination which prevents a realization of the experiences of other people," and therefore comes to the radical conclusion "that we are under a moral obligation in choosing our experiences, since the result of those experiences must ultimately determine our understanding of life." If, in our contempt for others, we limit the circle of our acquaintances to those we already respect, "we not only circumscribe our range of life, but limit the scope of our ethics" (Addams 1964, pp. 9–10).

Morality is developmental, experimental, and social. It aims at individual growth and empowerment through consideration of how one's decisions and acts affect others. It emerges over time both in individuals and in societies, the result of dynamic interactions between inherited cultural norms and emancipatory challenges. Pragmatist ethics rejects the dogmatism of a universal morality and recognizes the actual diversity and fallibility of moral codes, emphasizes the resolution of problems actually encountered instead of intellectual puzzles, and strives for cooperative problem-solving in which all members of society have a voice instead of submission to rule-governed imperatives, and requires that outcomes both enhance individual growth and empowerment and actually transform situations for the better. Some of the issues concerning women that the first-generation pragmatists addressed were the philosophical separation of theory and practice as arising from the class divisions in ancient Greece, which must be overcome if women are to be fully emancipated; arguing against the legal restrictions on birth control because they prevented women from intelligently controlling their own reproductive choices; arguing for the right of women workers to organize for equitable pay and to participate in decisions that concerned them and their work; backing women's right to quality education and to publicly supported child care; undermining essentialist views of women's nature while recognizing multiple solidarities of interest around specific issues, and, in general, challenging the restriction of women to the domestic sphere.

Since pragmatists reject the possibility of transparent access to reality and absolute values, some feminists have confused its contextualism, instrumentalism, and functionalism with the relativism and support of the status quo of positivist versions of functionalism or instrumentalism. But pragmatists reject the possibility of value-free pursuit of means tied to predetermined ends. Although they emphasize that the means chosen in investigations be adequate to ends that are attainable as well as desirable, they do so to avoid the very separation of abstract principle from the embodied and situated actualities of the human condition that have ignored the particular experiences of marginalized groups. They are just as concerned that the ends chosen are emancipatory as that they can actually be attained with the means available. Such ends are distinguished both from teleological determinism and from universally attractive but unattainable ends by the designation "ends-in-view." While all intelligent human interactions transform the social and natural environment according to ends-in-view, not all of them do so for ends worth pursuing. Such pragmatically valued ends do not subordinate the general welfare to private gain, nor are they predetermined or dogmatically imposed on one segment of society by another, but they support the growth and empowerment of individuals within society and the betterment of the inextricably joined natural and social conditions.

The relevant context of inquiry from a pragmatist feminist perspective is that of the care and concern required for human beings to intelligently grow and develop interactively with one another and the environment. Reflections on the developmental character of human understanding both through one's own lifetime and as an evolved species, lead pragmatists to deny both the realist position that ends are intrinsic in nature, including human nature, and the idealist position that ends are one-sidedly imposed on nature. Therefore, the determination of ends is central to pragmatist philosophizing and the pragmatic method pertains to ends at least as much as to means. Such ends-in-view must be consistent with the means at our disposal if situations are to be actually and not just imaginatively transformed for the better. These means include the usable part of inherited traditions, all the relevant findings of the natural and social sciences, and the imaginative and constructive creative perspectives and problem-solving skills of all members of the community.

That knowledge always includes values and is perspectival directly opposes belief in the transparency of knowledge and the neutrality of observation assumed in the positivism of much philosophical and scientific theory. Such scientism should be distinguished from the pragmatist appeal to science as

53

intelligence in action, as a fallible method that challenges unquestioned dogmas, as engaged in actual transformations of given conditions rather than in idle or utopian speculation, as a social effort tied to the goals of actual communities, and as revisable in light of unforeseen outcomes. The first wave of pragmatist feminists found the pragmatist version of the experimental method, with its existential origins, concrete specificity of analysis, and emancipatory goals a welcome antidote to the aridity and irrelevance of the abstract theoretical problems hallowed by the canonical tradition and driven by intellectualist debates in professional journals. It provided both the means and the justification for undermining traditional gender and racial prejudices. The emphasis on the value of shared understanding and communal problem-solving rather than forced imposition of demonstrably necessary logical conclusions appealed to women who already valued inclusiveness and community over exaggerated claims of autonomy and detachment. At the same time, it provided a means for questioning received opinions and provided a justification for linking theory and practice in activist interventions in changing the actual conditions of one's life and that of the wider community.

Situated understanding rejects the logic of general notions and abstract categories for knowledge of specific groups of individuals, actual persons, and particular institutions and historically evolved social arrangements. Too general a level of analysis supplies the apparatus for justifying the established order. This typical neglect of context is the greatest failing of philosophers and is exacerbated by narrowly disciplinary interests and forums of discourse. Since context includes the temporal and spatial background as well as selective interest, the horizon of meaning and value, its neglect too often turns into denial, which means that the intellectual and social structures that inform our perceptions are not recognized, criticized, rejected, or transformed. To recognize the operative structures of power requires knowledge of the specific conditions informing the actually problematic situations of everyday life. It requires sensitivity to the experiences and perspectives of those for whom situations are problematic and who are well situated to recognize, name, and resist its oppressive aspects and whose empowerment is necessary to develop and implement more positive conditions required for resolving the situation satisfactorily. The exposure by feminists of the many ways that gender, race, class, and sexual orientation form the unacknowledged context of social beliefs and practices is central rather than peripheral to the emancipatory emphasis of pragmatist philosophy. Without historical contextualization pragmatism too easily slides into positivist, value-free functionalism. When developed as just another variant of linguistic analysis by later philosophers influenced by pragmatism, such as W. V. O. Quine, Hilary Putnam, and even Richard Rorty, the pragmatic method is subject to the same feminist criticisms as are applied to the modernist epistemological turn in philosophy.

The moral judgment that social relations ought not to be hierarchically determined but reciprocally worked out in conditions of free and effective participation is fundamental to the pragmatist feminist position. Differences are

54

valued perspectives that open up the possibilities of reality and their inclusion ensures both maximal effectiveness of resolutions and ongoing revisions as unforeseen consequences differently affect participants. According to Dewey, philosophy's task is "to promote the capacity of peoples to profit by one another's experience and to cooperate more effectively with one another." Such sympathetic understanding and cooperative problem-solving were most explicitly linked to oppressed and marginalized groups by W. E. B. Du Bois and Addams. Du Bois not only exposed the pervasiveness of racial and sexual prejudices as barriers to such understanding, but he explicitly linked the fight for the rights of women and Blacks, as when he said that "the race question is at bottom simply a matter of ownership of women; white men want the right to own and use all women, colored and white, and they resent any intrusion of colored men into this domain." As Addams says in *Twenty Years at Hull House*, she sought, no matter how wearisome the effort, "to secure the inner consent of all concerned," particularly "the sanction of those upon whom the present situation presses so harshly," rather than imposing top-down solutions; and to "put truth to 'the ultimate test of the conduct it dictates or inspires.'" Hull House was founded "on the theory that the dependence of classes on each other is reciprocal; and that as the social relation is essentially a reciprocal relation, it gives a form of expression that has peculiar value" (Addams 1981, p. 76).

Contemporary pragmatist feminism

The status of contemporary pragmatist feminist thought is more difficult to categorize. As with many marginalized and oppressed groups before them, the post-civil rights wave of feminists became conscious that their experiences, needs, and desires were denied or distorted by the prevailing explanations, whether customary, popular, or theoretical. Since theorizing is not only motivated, but situated, the varieties of feminist theories developed out of criticisms of some dominant view that was already familiar or deliberately adopted and that already had legitimacy in academic or radical circles. Since thinking does not take place in a vacuum, they can still be found as major divisions of feminist theory, even as they are transformed and as new ones are articulated. Neither classical American pragmatism nor Rorty's neo-pragmatism were among the canonical Western theories criticized and revisioned as standard feminist theoretical alternatives in the last few decades. In hindsight, it can look as though pragmatism has a general theory of liberation, of knowledge, of value, of education, of multi-perspectivism, of embodiment, etc., that can underpin the explicit perspectives drawing on the varieties of women's experiences. But such a simple, non-historical relation of generality and specificity is untenable. It is now known that an earlier version of pragmatist feminism exists, and some tentative steps have been taken to develop a specifically pragmatist version of feminism that draws on the earlier classical pragmatist theories.

In this very recent resurgence of interest in pragmatism from a feminist perspective, Dewey's idealization of the domestic sphere has been criticized, especially in light of Gilman's and more recent discussions of the negative personal and social effects of the patriarchal home and women's economic oppression. It has also been pointed out that in striking contrast to Addams and Dewey, James's defense of pluralism, perspectivism, and celebration of otherness as a source of renewal did not extend to women, the lower classes, or other ethnic groups (Seigfried 1996, pp. 111–41). Rorty's neo-pragmatism has been criticized by both pragmatists and feminists for its sharp separation of theory and practice, strict separation of the public and private spheres, ungrounded conversation as a model of change apart from an analysis of its background conditions, including differential access to power, and without an experimental method that includes actual reconstruction of qualitative situations, all of which are more characteristic of classical liberalism than of classical pragmatism (Fraser 1989, Bickford in Seigfried 1993, pp. 104–23).

More positively, issues that have attracted recent feminist interest include pragmatism's linkage of theoretical analyses to specific social, political, and economic changes, such as progressivism, evolutionary environmentalism, women's growing numbers in higher education and in professions, and critique of the domestic sphere (Brown 1995, Sklar 1985). The role of emotions, feeling, and the aesthetic in pragmatist theories of knowledge and ethics has also been explored and so has the rejection of rationality for an interpretation of understanding as a part of "body-mind," informed by emotions, interests, and expressed in habits, not just in concepts, and interactive with nature rather than simply observing and recording it. Phyllis Rooney argues that feminists are better able to answer earlier charges that pragmatists used mere utility as a criterion of truth because – unlike many of their predecessors – they recognize and appreciate the cognitive value pragmatists give to emotion, desire, and interest (Seigfried 1993, p. 24).

Another area of interest is pragmatism's nonpositivist theory of science as a social practice that is accountable to the public. Science has the potential to free thinking from detached speculation and dogma by its method of actual transformation of natural and social conditions and willingness to revise its approach in light of outcomes. It is liberating when understood as a transaction with nature rather than a blind domination of it. Eugenie Gatens-Robinson links it with Sandra Harding's search for a new relationship between mind and nature, with Donna Haraway's call for a successor science which recognizes situated knowledge, and with Evelyn Fox Keller's notion of passionate attention to, instead of distanced manipulation of, nature (Gatens-Robinson 1991).

Dewey's logic of experience and transformative communal inquiry has been found to be more appropriate as an instrument of feminist methodology than the detached symbolic manipulation that dominates contemporary positivist logics. Timothy V. Kaufman-Osborn uses a nonessentialist pragmatist explanation of experience as a process of undergoing and doing to reflect on Adrienne Rich's exploration of the experience and institution of motherhood and to criticize Rorty's impoverished view of experience (Seigfried 1993, pp. 124–44). Marjorie C. Miller suggests that pragmatism can take feminist criticism the next step beyond the numerous criticisms of the privileging of reason by such feminists as Genevieve Lloyd, Seyla Benhabib, Alison Jaggar, and Susan R. Bordo by its replacement of the category of universal reason with that of intelligence as not only embodied but historicized and reconstructive. In Dewey's words, it is "the sum-total of impulses, habits, emotions, records, and discoveries which forecast what is desirable and undesirable in future possibilities, and which contrive ingenuously in behalf of imagined good" (Miller 1992).

Addams, Dewey, and to some extent, James, are recognized as developing pragmatist versions of an ethics of care that does not reify gender and that dynamically relates intimate concerns with democratic communities, that is, ones that are inclusive and non-hierarchical. According to Addams, democracy is a way of life in which "the identification with the common lot which is the essential idea of Democracy becomes the source and expression of social ethics" (Addams 1964, p. 11). Addams and Dewey argue that social ethics based on the actual facts of human association, beginning with the intersubjective need to care for the youngest members of society, should replace the dominant model of individualistic ethics based on an assumption of isolated individualism and the privacy of consciousness. It requires identifying and rejecting the exploitation by special interests that characterizes actually existing democratic societies. Although this pragmatist feminist approach to ethics has been little recognized by contemporary feminists, it is one worth pursuing further (Seigfried 1996, pp. 202–58).

6

Modern moral and political philosophy

HERTA NAGL-DOCEKAL

Surveys of modern thought usually distinguish between different philosophical positions, for example, "liberalism," "utilitarianism," "universalist moral philosophy," "German Idealism," "Marxism," "Critical Theory," or "communitarianism." A feminist perspective, however, reveals shared patterns of thinking: certain androcentric conceptions recur regularly, linking otherwise widely disparate philosophical approaches with each other. This article concerns these kinds of patterns. I shall discuss eight concepts that exemplify the masculine features of the philosophical tradition of modernity. At the same time, I aim to show that the feminist critique of the canon does not rely on a unified theory. Although the critics agree largely, if not entirely, on the task of revealing women's exclusion and devaluation, views differ regarding the conclusions to be drawn from this critical reading. While some authors suggest that ideas such as "the individual," "equality," or "autonomy" should be discarded entirely, others seek to develop new understandings of these concepts that fully include women. These differences of position are related to the controversies that characterize contemporary philosophy generally, particularly in connection with the objections against universalist conceptions formulated in the context of so-called "postmodern" thought and communitarianism. Since the feminist critique of the canon as a whole is so diverse, I can discuss only a few examples here.

The various forms of classical social contract theory as developed by authors like Hobbes, Locke, Rousseau, and Kant are a central topic of this critique. Feminist critics remind us, first, that these conceptions of the social contract, whatever their other disagreements, share one point: without exception, they conceptualize the contracting partners as men. A further limitation is that they deny full citizenship not only to women but also to wage-dependent men. One central aim of the feminist analysis is to demonstrate that this exclusion of women is not simply a historical contingency, to be easily repaired by a straightforward expansion of the concept. This definition of the contracting partner, it is argued, derives its central provisions from a characteristically modern image of the male. Given this pointed demarcation from the female, its domain cannot be stretched to cover both sexes without modification.

The individual

In these reflections, the concept of the individual shifts to the foreground. One of their core concerns is that contract theory imagines the contracting parties as isolated single beings. "The assumption in this case is that human individuals are ontologically prior to society" (Jaggar 1983, p. 28). A number of authors assume that the various conceptions of the contract rest on a social atomism that does not do justice to the fact that human beings must always have already grown up in a community before they can emerge as individuals. According to this view, a theory which fails to address the social ties that lie behind individuality rests on an androcentric perspective: it ignores the experiences of women, who in Western civilization traditionally carry out the tasks of primary socialization (Di Stefano 1991). For some critics, the problem of an atomist social ontology persists in contemporary conceptions of equality and justice, particularly in Rawls, Nozick, and Dworkin (Wolgast 1987, Held 1993).

It is surely legitimate to reject a conception of individuality which denies that individuals are always embedded in community contexts of some kind. We should ask, however, whether contract theorists consistently operate with such a conception. There exist suggestions for an alternative reading according to which contract theory does not claim to develop a complete conception of individuality in the first place; individuals play a role only so far as is required for a theory of the state. Consequently, authors like Charles Taylor (1989) and Will Kymlicka (1990, p. 62) warn against an ontological misunderstanding that might conceal the real point of contractarian theory, that is, to promote the rights of each individual person. What further supports this reading is that the philosophy of the Enlightenment provides a remarkably richer understanding of individuality once we consider, in addition to writings on state theory, studies in other areas including anthropology, philosophy of history, ethics, aesthetics, and philosophy of religion. At this point we should ask: if the central aim of feminist theory and practice is to reveal and overcome the numerous disadvantages women face, does this not involve promoting the rights of each individual woman? Given this perspective, the idea that the feminist concern requires a complete dismissal of the concept of the contract appears overdrawn. Rather, it is more plausible to work toward a new definition of the "citizen" that includes the rights of women in the same way as those of men. "The point... is not a rejection of Enlightenment in toto, but a critical renegotiation of its legacy" (Benhabib 1994).

Autonomy

The value the liberal tradition places on autonomy is frequently taken to be a strong indication of its masculine character (Nedelsky 1989). This concept is usually interpreted in the light of object-relations theory, particularly of the research of writers like Nancy Chodorow, who ask to what extent the early childhood socialization typical of Western civilization proceeds in a gender-differentiated fashion. The following findings in this body of research are of particular relevance here: The psychological development of boys is marked by a "double disidentification from the mother" (Greenson 1978); this is necessary, on the one hand, in order to form a separate identity at all and, on the other hand, to form a gender identity, which is different from that of the mother. Thus, there rises a tendency toward excessive separation, which eventually results in detachedness being a typically male character trait. Within this context, the term "autonomy" refers to this masculine behavior, which stands in opposition to the tendency toward identification and connectedness observed in women. We should discuss, however, whether we are justified in supposing this meaning wherever "autonomy" appears in philosophical debates. On closer inspection, there are several ways of using this term that are not identical with its psychological understanding. In the political philosophy of the Enlightenment, for instance, "autonomy" is antonymous to "heteronomy" and is thus an instrument of the critique of paternalism and oppression. This critical impulse has since generated different goals. The project of "self-legislation" aims for the equal, active participation of all individuals in the decision processes affecting the community as well as for the protection of groups from outside interventions, including state interventions. Given this meaning of the word, the thesis that we should reject the term "autonomy" because it is thoroughly masculine does not seem plausible. Rather, we must ask ourselves how it should possibly be conceivable to formulate a feminist critique of the various forms of gender hierarchy without simultaneously demanding "women's self-legislation." Is it not true, moreover, that feminist efforts, notwithstanding their different emphases, have appropriated both of the aims just mentioned? Young, for example, envisages autonomy in this dual sense when, in critically engaging the passive aspect of the distributive paradigm, she argues, on the one hand, for the active participation of all citizens and, on the other hand, for the recognition of group difference (cf. Young 1990a). We should consider, furthermore, that for Kant the term "autonomy" designates not only a legal–philosophical but also a moral–philosophical concept. We shall address the question of whether this variation of the idea is a typically masculine one below.

The public and the private

First let's return to the fact that in the "classical texts" the contracting parties are exclusively male. The background for this conception is the ideal of a division of labor between the sexes that assigns to women the tasks of the domestic sphere. This dichotomy of public/private was for a long time the chief target of the feminist critique, persisting as it does to this day in contemporary clichés concerning "women's role". Feminists began by establishing that the symmetry between the two spheres that authors like Rousseau, Kant, or Fichte insisted upon does not in fact exist: while women remain excluded from the public sphere, men are imagined as members of the public sphere as well as the family, what is more, as the family's head (cf. Bennent 1985, Jauch 1988, Clark and Lange 1979, Schroder 1992). This conception of gender roles thus places women in a relationship of dual dependency: on the one hand, they are subordinate to the male head of household; on the other hand, their living conditions are determined decisively by political and economic decision processes in which they cannot participate. The following circumstance further sharpens the problem of their dependence: insofar as liberal legal theory assigns the family primarily to the private sphere, which is defined in terms of being removed from direct state interventions, the lives of women unfold predominantly in an extra-legal space. (Current debates in many countries on "rape in marriage" laws show that repercussions of this view persist to this day. It was in regard to problems like this that the women's movement coined its slogan "the personal is the political.")

The point of the feminist analysis is to show that contract theory does not apply its central principles of justice to its reflections on marriage and the family. As Okin (1989a) has shown, this is true even of such differentiated contemporary reformulations as that of Rawls: although he uses gender-neutral language in conceiving the contracting parties as "heads of households," he nevertheless seems to envisage a hierarchical model, which points back to the traditional understanding of marriage.

The contract

Initially, feminist critics saw in Enlightenment philosophy a simultaneity of the dissimultaneous; according to this view, older patriarchal patterns of thought had persisted alongside the newly developed egalitarian political theory. For Pateman, in contrast, the problem resides in the term "contract" itself. Her thesis is that there are two different forms of contract involved. In concluding the social contract, "equal" and "free" male citizens also conclude the "sexual contract." The latter justifies their rule over women in two ways: first, it secures "men's political right over women" and, second, it guarantees "orderly access by men to women's bodies" (Pateman 1988, p. 7). The gender hierarchy thus established in the original pact determines, in Pateman's view, that the actual contracts that women conclude also have an asymmetrical character. In an analysis of Kant's observations concerning the marriage contract Pateman examines this problem more closely. She stresses that Kant denies women, on the one hand, the maturity that enables men to be citizens and enter into contracts, while he ascribes to them, on the other hand, the ability to enter into the marriage contract. She sees a further contradiction between Kant's initial characterization of the marriage contract as based on the principle of mutuality – speaking as he does of the "reciprocal use that one human being makes of the sexual organs and capacities of another" (Kant 1959, p. 24) – and his simultaneous assumption that the woman entering marriage agrees to being subordinate to her husband. In light of such inconsistencies – of which other authors too are guilty – Pateman concludes that the term "contract" should be discarded entirely; she emphasizes the "incongruous character of an alliance between feminism and contract" (p. 184). This conclusion, however, is not entirely plausible. That is to say, once we reformulate the concept of the contract with a view to assuring all individuals of equal rights and equal duties without regard to their gender and membership in a class, ethnic group, or religious community, it forms the necessary theoretical

61

basis for revealing particular injustices (Herman 1993a). Must not Pateman herself presuppose such a conception in order, for example, to plead for ending the political and sexual subordination of women? (A different problem to be distinguished from this question, however, is that formal equality alone does not suffice to eliminate all asymmetries between the sexes. Justice in the full sense requires a lot more, such as a conception of social rights (cf. Yeatman 1994, Fraser and Gordon 1994).

Equality

The debate concerning the concept of equality is similarly situated. MacKinnon (1989), for example, rightly points out that statutes which are formulated in gender-neutral language frequently disadvantage women, for the legislature regards what is typical only for the lives of men in our culture as a generally valid model; male career patterns, for example, are thus generalized in an unwarranted fashion. However, this kind of androcentrism is not, as some feminist critics appear to assume (Flax 1992), an inevitable consequence of the liberal understanding of justice. Rather, this understanding is characterized by a formal conception of equality whose point is that each individual has the right "to be treated as an equal." As Dworkin explains, this idea of equality refers to "the right to be treated with respect and consideration in the same way as everyone else" (Dworkin 1977). Thus, when feminists reject systems of legislation and jurisprudence that subsume women under a masculine model, they presuppose as the standard of criticism a formal conception of equal treatment that corresponds precisely to this liberal conception.

The family

The feminist engagement with the canon of modernity, however, is by no means confined to the various aspects of contractarian thinking. It traces, among other things, concepts of the family developed outside the liberal tradition. Of primary interest in this endeavor is the way in which Hegel distances himself from Kant's contractual definition of marriage (see above), emphasizing the relational element. Like Rousseau before him (Nagl-Docekal 1994), Hegel endows the family with compensatory qualities: while the world of politics and work is character-ized by impersonal interactions and the pressure of competition, the family constitutes a place for attending to actual individuals and their specific needs. This view of the family as a "counterworld" (Klinger 1990) to a reality disen-chanted by modernization has been reformulated repeatedly until the present, uniting otherwise rather disparate philosophical approaches such as those of the Romantics, Simmel, and Horkheimer. From a feminist perspective, however, this conception too proved to be asymmetrical: according to many male authors, the family's ability to fulfill its specific function derives from the virtues of "motherli-ness" (Rumf 1993). That is to say, women are expected unilaterally to provide loving care not only to their children but also to their husbands. In keeping with "an emotional division of labor between the sexes" (Heller 1990), women are to compensate for the hardships men experience in the public sphere (Baier 1987b, Houston 1987). Concerning the contemporary debate, a number of feminist theorists point to the danger that communitarian proposals to reevaluate traditional ways of life might once again give rise to such an asymmetry (Frazer and Lacey 1993). Other authors, in contrast, do not focus on this one-sidedness, but argue for placing a higher value on the feminine virtues inherent in the traditional image of the family and to make these virtues the foundation of a new, more adequate appraisal of moral conduct – a "care ethic" (see below).

The central concern of feminist critics is that Hegel, in spite of having distanced himself from the contractarian conception of marriage, preserves the dual dependency of women who remain confined to the sphere of the household. In addition to his reflections on the philosophy of law, his observations concerning Sophocles' *Antigone* articulated in the *Phenomenology of Spirit* are particularly revealing in this regard. In these remarks, moreover, the moral stance ascribed to women appears obsolete from a world-historical perspective. "Hegel is the gravedigger of women" is the conclusion of Benhabib's (1992b) critical reading.

Many authors explain the tenacious persistence of the conception of a division of labor between the sexes in terms of an unwarranted naturalization. From the days of the Enlightenment until today, philosophers have argued repeatedly that the activities and virtues characteristic of the domestic sphere correspond to "woman's nature." To such a view, we should reply that all conceptions of an ideal social order have a normative character, and that norms by virtue of what they are cannot derive legitimacy from an appeal to nature. The very fact that a rule is being formulated suffices to indicate that the behavior in question is not a natural inclination.

Work

Several studies observed that Marx's and Marxism's interpretation of gender relations and work were also tainted by an unwarranted naturalization. Critics first pointed to the ambiguity of the concept of "production." On the one hand, it denotes all activities "that are necessary for the reproduction of the human species, including the nursing and rearing of children as well as the production of food." On the other hand, it refers only to those activities that serve the production of goods (Benhabib and Nicholson, 1988, p. 549). The lack of clarity is rooted in Marx's and Engels's tendency to link domestic activities to female biology. In *The German Ideology*, for example, they mention "the natural division of labour in the family" (Marx and Engels, 1970, p. 52). Feminist critics made it clear that this was deeply inconsistent: concerning women's living conditions, the basic principle of "historical materialism" was not applied. Jaggar (1983, p. 72), for instance, notes, along these lines: "No Marxist theory provides a satisfactory historical account of the sexual division of labour." What is more, feminist critics showed that the customary Marxist definition of the concept of "production" in gender-neutral terms exacerbates the problem by concealing women's dual marginalization. This removes from view both that Marxist theory-building does not thoroughly investigate the tasks women perform in the domestic sphere and that it does not critically discuss the common practice that working women frequently perform tasks comparable to domestic ones, which entails income discrimination based on sex. The feminist reading made clear, moreover, that as a result of this deficit of Marxist economic analyses, "gender" was not perceived as an independent principle of social organization giving rise to a specific form of domination, up until the days of the Frankfurt School (Becker-Schmidt 1989). The gender-blind conceptualization of "work" persists, beyond the Marxist tradition, in contemporary economic theory. Thus, among other things, women in the labor market continue to be identified with little-valued work and are paid less than men (Walzer 1983, Okin 1979).

The moral law

The objection that general philosophical concepts do not address the subtext of gender also shifted to the center of debate in a wholly different area: it was also leveled against universalist moral philosophy. The real points of contention in this debate are theories for which moral conduct is characterized by an orientation toward abstract principles, particularly the "golden rule" ("Do not do unto others...") and/or the principle of noninterference. Actions thus guided by a perspective of justice, argue feminist critics, conform to a stance that in Western culture is characteristic of men, and therefore do not represent a universally valid model. Starting from Gilligan's critique of authors like Kohlberg and Piaget, numerous authors took part in the effort to prove that the problem of falsely generalizing the masculine pattern of moral perception taints all universalist conceptions of contemporary moral philosophy, and that this holds true for their theory-historical background as well, particularly for Kant. At the same time, these critics claimed that women typically solve moral conflicts in a way that differs from that of men. The perspective of care thus moved to the center of debate, that is to say, the attitude of empathetically attending to individuals in their specific situation and their particular needs. In analyzing this pattern of behavior more closely, Baier employed Hume's conception of empathy.

This is not the place to discuss whether gender differences in moral conduct can be shown in fact to exist. As far as the critique of the canon is concerned, however, it is surely legitimate to problematize the position that morality requires a distancing from actual individuals. But we must ask whether such a position does indeed govern the entire tradition of universalist moral philosophy. A closer reading of Kant's reflections on practical philosophy, for example, yields a very different picture; it reveals distinctions not considered by the feminist critique summarized here. For example, feminist critics frequently ignored the way in which Kant distinguishes between law and morality: justice is a duty which derives from the categorical imperative but which does not incorporate all of the latter's implications. While it is true that Kant's writings contain contractarian elements, including the principle of noninterference, we should note that these are part of his considerations concerning the philosophy of law. At the same time, Kant emphasizes that contractarian thinking does not suffice for a comprehensive rendering of morality. Consequently, he emphasizes that the "golden rule" and the categorical imperative are not identical (Kant 1964). From this perspective it now seems significant that the above-mentioned objections were usually made in the absence of any direct reference to Kant's moral-philosophical writings. Similarly ignored was Kant's explicit intimation that the moral law – according to which each person is to be respected as an "end in itself" – not only prohibits using others merely as a means, but also prescribes helping others as far as possible and assisting them on their self-chosen paths to happiness. In Kant's account, the categorical imperative demands least of all to abstract from the actual situations of individuals but, in stark contrast, to accommodate them as far as possible. Kant uses the term *Liebespflichten* here – why shouldn't we translate this term as "duties of care"?

Thus, it is evident that these are not only questions of philological accuracy. Rather, we should ask whether Kant's reflections provide a basis for solving a much discussed contemporary problem, that is, the question of how care-theoretical approaches might avoid the danger of relativism (Nagl-Docekal forthcoming, b). This affirms once more what the above considerations have hinted at several times before: the feminist confrontation with the canon of modernity is critique in the dual sense of this word. It exposes not only the questionable – androcentric – elements, but also those that might become relevant for a reformulation of moral philosophy and political theory that aims for symmetry between the sexes.

7

Existentialism and phenomenology

SONIA KRUKS

Existentialism and phenomenology seem, at first glance, to constitute one of those rare strands of modern Western philosophy that converges productively with feminism. They form a tradition that opposes abstract, rationalist thought and is instead committed to elucidating concrete, "lived experience," including experiences of embodiment and emotion. As such, they anticipate much "second-wave" feminist thought that criticizes abstraction, beginning from accounts of women's concrete experiences and emphasizing the importance of personal politics. However, feminists engaged with the tradition have also cautioned that the main canonical figures remained ensconced in masculinism, since their allegedly generic accounts of "human existence" were tacitly grounded in male experience. During the 1980s interest in existentialism and phenomenology waned, as notions of women's experience increasingly came under suspicion with the poststructuralist, or "postmodern," turn in feminism. But in the last few years interest has grown again, as theorists have sought insights from the tradition that might move theory beyond the impasses that postmodernism now seems to some to present.

Although often treated as a single philosophical tradition, existentialism and phenomenology are historically distinct in their origins and aims. Existentialism is generally said to originate in the nineteenth century with the work of Kierkegaard, and phenomenology effectively to begin in the early twentieth century with that of Husserl. The two strands of thought meshed only later, initially in the work of Heidegger, and then in the work of the French "existential phenomenologists." The latter, who published mainly in the 1940s and 1950s, extensively harnessed phenomenology to the endeavor of elucidating "existential" questions concerning human being and experience. Feminist engagement has been fullest with the work of members of this group, notably Merleau-Ponty, Sartre, and Beauvoir. The work of Beauvoir has been particularly important, and interpreting her has often been a site of debate among different generations of feminists, visions of feminism, and versions of feminist theory.

Kierkegaard, Husserl, and Heidegger

The work of Kierkegaard has received relatively little attention from feminists, perhaps because he operated within a religious framework that has few resonances today. But many of the themes of later existential phenomenology that are germane to feminism were already present in his work. Reacting against

66

both Hegel's grand system and the growing tide of positivism, Kierkegaard argued that there are experiential truths, particularly those concerning one's relationship to God, that cannot be captured through abstract reason. His philosophy represented a turn towards personal experience as a source of truth. In his analysis of human selfhood, his concern with inner experiences of faith and doubt, his emphasis on freedom and on our personal responsibility to make ethical choices, and his preoccupation with the anguish involved in doing so, Kierkegaard anticipated many of the central motifs of later atheistic forms of existentialism, including those of Sartre and Beauvoir.

Feminists engaged with Kierkegaard's work have criticized his texts for misogyny and sexism. Woman is frequently portrayed as man's temptress, or else as merely his adjunct. She is also depicted as, by nature, mired in immediacy and thus incapable of the self-reflection Kierkegaard deems necessary for full ethical development of the self. Howe (1994) argues that his identification of woman with immediacy precludes her capacity for full personhood such as Kierkegaard conceives it. However, others have argued that Kierkegaard's account of gender differences pertains only to the secular world, and that in the true "God relation" they are transcended. Walsh (1987) argues that Kierkegaard's vision of personhood on the highest ethical plane may be read as involving an equal blending of masculine and feminine attributes, and offers feminism a valuable androgynous ideal.

Husserl's project was radically different from Kierkegaard's, though they shared a mutual distrust of positivism and a common focus on experience. Husserl aimed above all to develop a method by which the essential characteristics of phenomena – of any kind of phenomena – could be known independently of the philosophical, scientific, or common-sense presuppositions through which we normally grasp them. This "return to the things themselves" was to be achieved through the "reduction," a process of "bracketing" assumptions so that the essence of phenomena might be revealed undistorted. Husserl's work has been criticized as idealist since it presupposes a disembodied (hence also genderless), constituting consciousness, or transcendental ego, which brings phenomena into being in an intentional relationship. However, some have suggested that the reduction is only a heuristic device designed, like much feminist critique, to cast new light on what usually appears natural, or normal. Fisher (1996) reads Husserl in this vein and argues that reading Husserl raises for feminist philosophy important questions, such as whether there are distinctly masculine and feminine ways of being conscious, or whether there are gendered forms of intentionality, that parallel gender differences in the domains of the body and experience.

With the later development of existential phenomenology, neo-Husserlian phenomenological methods were put to work to illuminate specific kinds of phenomena: those of human existence. Work shifted toward the exploration of social and ethical issues, including questions of freedom and historicity, responsibility, self–other relations, and embodiment. Heidegger elaborated a phenomenological ontology in which *Dasein*, the "being there" of human being – that unique being which alone can reflect upon its own existence – is central. There has been surprisingly little feminist discussion of Heidegger, considering that (unlike Kierkegaard or Husserl) he directly anticipates many of the central themes of feminist philosophy. His account of human existence is strongly antidualistic, privileging engagement in the world over the more distanced relationship of knowing. He also argues that "care" is a primary structure of "Being-in-the-world" and an ethical imperative of authentic human existence. This perspective leads Heidegger to develop a profound critique of modern technology which, he claims, involves an attitude of control and appropriation. From such an attitude, not only nature but human being itself comes to be disclosed as a "standing reserve," that is, as a set of objects of use stripped of all intrinsic meaning. Resemblances to recent ecofeminist critiques of modern technology are striking, as are resonances between Heidegger's account of care and discussions of care in recent feminist ethics. Although Heidegger's account of care has been analyzed through the lens of Kristeva's account of language (Graybeal 1990), and his analysis of technology has been briefly brought to bear on issues of reproductive technology (Klawiter 1990), further feminist appropriations of Heidegger are certainly needed.

Merleau-Ponty

With the work of Merleau-Ponty, existential phenomenology turned toward the human body in ways that have made it particularly germane to feminist philosophy. For Merleau-Ponty, human existence is above all the existence of a "body-subject," an embodied subjectivity for whom a tacit, sensory, and sentient knowledge is always prior to explicit, conscious knowledge. Merleau-Ponty thus rejects Husserl's notion of the detached transcendental ego, arguing that the phenomenological reduction always takes us back to embodied experience as the (usually ignored) ground that makes possible philosophical and scientific knowledge. If even abstract knowledge has its roots in embodied experience, this implies moreover that knowledge is always "situated" and that the location of the knower has a bearing on what is known. Merleau-Ponty thus anticipates, in ways that still call for fuller exploration, recent feminist arguments that claims to objective or disembodied knowledge obscure gender differences, and that theories need always to take account of the situatedness of knowers.

Merleau-Ponty's turn to embodiment also entails giving an account of how subjectivity is lived through various structures of the body. For him the human body is not simply a natural organism, but always "a historical idea" (1962, p. 170). Its structures, which include spatiality and motility, expressive capacities, and sexuality, are thus social and cultural, as well as disclosive of individual style. Aspects of Merleau-Ponty's account of the human body have been subjected to feminist critique, but also creatively appropriated.

Butler (1989) argues that the strength of Merleau-Ponty's account is that it treats the body, particularly in its sexual aspect, as above all a historical and cultural modality of existence. It treats sexuality as coextensive with existence, and not as an isolated sphere of drives, or natural givens. However, she argues, Merleau-Ponty undermines and contradicts his own position because of the misogynistic coloration of his perceptions. The account he gives of "the body" in its sexual being is actually an account of the heterosexual, male body. Merleau-Ponty claims to talk of concrete, "lived experience" but, paradoxically, he does so abstractly, without asking the necessary questions about whose bodies are being discussed. The issue here is not simply one of the omission of gender differences, Butler argues. For in giving an account of desire that is tacitly from a male, heterosexual perspective. woman is cast in the position of the object of a voyeuristic male gaze and her body is naturalized. Relations of male dominance are thus ideologically reproduced in Merleau-Ponty's text.

Merleau-Ponty's thought has also been criticized by Luce Irigaray for its masculinist privileging of vision. In his later work, Merleau-Ponty develops the notion of "flesh" as a means of characterizing ontological relations of reversibility that, he claims, overcome forms of human/world dualism. He gives as a key example the phenomenology of touching, in which one is always also touched by what one touches. However, Irigaray (1993b) argues that Merleau-Ponty's account still privileges vision, whereas in actuality vision is never independent of the tangible. The tangible is the primordial sensation – of the womb, of woman, of the maternal – Irigaray claims. But Merleau-Ponty refuses to acknowledge this debt, continuing instead to privilege the (masculine) perceiving subject.

Contrary to critiques such as those of Butler and Irigaray, Bigwood (1991) argues that the masculinist bias of Merleau-Ponty's account of the body does not hinder creative appropriation of his work. She uses Merleau-Ponty to move beyond what she regards as the excessive social constructivism of poststructuralist feminists such as Butler. Whereas Butler reads Merleau-Ponty as rendering a fully historicized account of the body, which he then undermines by unfortunate lapses into naturalism fueled by his misogyny, Bigwood reads him as a dialectical thinker, who gives an account of a "connatural" body that is both natural and cultural. Merleau-Ponty offers feminism a model in which the body is not the source of strict biological determinism, yet does remain a "weighty" and constant element: bodies proffer motivations and predispositions to ways of being, but not strict causes. For example, pregnancy, as Bigwood portrays it, is not a purely biological process; yet to experience pregnancy is to encounter in one's bodily existence certain sex-specific and natural "givens" that poststructuralists erroneously disregard.

Like Bigwood, Young (1990c) also draws on Merleau-Ponty to explore aspects of women's embodied experience. She creatively appropriates his account of motility to examine women's forms of body comportment in Western society, suggesting that women's more constrained ways of occupying space are expressive of their subordinate social status. In her treatments of "breasted experience" and of the complex experiences of the doubling and decentering of one's "self" in pregnancy, she also explores aspects of feminine embodiment that defy classification as either biological or cultural. Work such as this suggests that

69

Merleau-Ponty may well be a rich resource for feminists who wish to move beyond the distinctions of sex and gender without, in poststructuralist fashion, reducing all experience to discursivity.

Sartre

Feminist work on Sartre has mostly been highly critical. Sartre's best known work, *Being and Nothingness* (1953), has been extensively (and rightly) criticized for the overt sexism of its images and examples. Although Barnes (1990) has argued that this sexism is merely contingent, and not integral to Sartre's theory, many others have followed Collins and Pierce (1973) in arguing that masculinism is fundamentally built into the work through the central distinction Sartre makes between "being-for-itself" (as active, free, and transcendent, hence masculine being) and "being-in-itself" (as inert and passive, yet also freedom-threatening, hence feminine being). Sartre's account of interpersonal relations where, in typically masculinist fashion, he depicts antagonism as the central dynamic, arguing that each autonomous self attempts to objectify the other through the "look," has also been criticized (e.g. Kruks 1992).

But in spite of such critiques, there have also been creative uses of Sartre's work. Bartky (1990) and Murphy (1989) both begin from Sartre's account of "the look" to explore aspects of women's experience in patriarchal society. Bartky argues that shame, which Sartre describes as one possible relation to oneself in the presence of an objectifying other, often becomes a generalized condition for women in patriarchal society. Living so pervasively under hostile male scrutiny, women may create a permanent internalized other before whom they continuously experience shame. Shame then becomes a general mode of "Being-in-the-world," a disclosure of women's subordination that is itself thoroughly disempowering. Murphy also uses Sartre's account of "the look" to develop a phenomenology of women's oppression, and she additionally draws on Sartre to explore ways of overcoming women's disempowerment. In *Being and Nothingness* Sartre also develops (albeit briefly) an account of collective experiences of otherness. He describes the emergence of what he calls an "Us-object," that comes into being when a series of people discover that they are all under the same objectifying gaze of a dominating "Third." Murphy argues that such a common realization may become a basis for the positive affirmation of women's collective identity. in which they assert the value of their otherness as a way of resisting domination by a generalized patriarchal Third.

More recently attention has begun to shift to Sartre's later work, the *Critique of Dialectical Reason* (1976), particularly to address debates concerning women's identities and differences. Young (1994a) has argued that, although differences between women should not be minimized, and poststructuralist arguments that "women" do not exist notwithstanding, feminism does need to retain a concept of women that is more than merely strategic. It can do so without either essentializing women or attributing a core identity to them, she claims, by rearticulating Sartre's account of "collectives." A collective, in Sartre's terminology, means an ensemble of people who are passively unified by external conditionings and structures not of their choosing. What they have in common is that none of them can avoid acting within these conditionings, but this does not mean that they necessarily share a conscious identity or even a common purpose. What women have in common, in this account, is that they are each positioned within a collective – gender – that is constituted by such structures as enforced heterosexuality and the sexual division of labor. This approach allows us to develop a nonessentialized concept of women, but one which is adequate for forming alliances and developing strategies of resistance.

In Kruks (1995) I have also argued that Sartre's *Critique* offers an epistemological theory that can be bought to bear on problems of identity and difference between women. Feminist epistemologies that insist on the situated nature of knowers have the virtue of pointing out that women's experience is not homogeneous, and that differences in social location give rise to different perspectives and forms of knowledge. However, such epistemologies of "provenance" often present an account of knowledge as so fractured and incommensurable that the possibility of comprehension and communication across difference, on which any broad feminist politics must depend, is put into question. I draw on Sartre's account of "reciprocity," the mutual recognition by differently located selves that their apparently separate actions are interconnected because they are mediated by collective exterior conditionings, to point toward a feminist epistemology that is sensitive to differences while demonstrating how knowledge can be shared across them.

Beauvoir

The possibility of such positive uses notwithstanding, the masculinist elements of Sartre's work, especially of *Being and Nothingness*, do make it problematic for feminism. It is thus intriguing that Simone de Beauvoir's *The Second Sex* (1952), undoubtedly the classic of feminist philosophy, was developed within its ambit. Beauvoir repeatedly claimed that she was Sartre's philosophical disciple and initially most readers took her at her word. More recently, however, scholars have begun to demonstrate her considerable philosophical autonomy from Sartre (Simons 1995).

Feminist readings and evaluations of Beauvoir's work have varied markedly by place and generation. For early second-wave feminists in the USA it was Beauvoir, the person, as much as her work, who stood as a symbol of resistance to patriarchy. Her role as a public intellectual and her (apparently) free and equal relationship with Sartre stood as an ideal to many women. What made *The Second Sex* the feminist "Bible" was her detailed telling of the experience of living under patriarchy (a telling that still resonated in the 1970s, even though it drew mainly from the lives of upper-class French women of an earlier era) and her firmly egalitarian vision of a better future for women. However, although it was widely read and alluded to, there was little close theoretical engagement with *The Second Sex* until the 1980s. In Britain, by contrast, in the 1970s socialist

71

feminists engaged with the book as an important attempt to synthesize feminism with a humanistic Marxist materialism. Similarly, in France some regarded Beauvoir as the originator of a materialist feminism. But with the turn to poststructuralism in France and the development of *écriture féminine* from the late 1970s, Beauvoir was increasingly dismissed as a male-identified, phallocentric, "Enlightenment" thinker. The animosity was so intense that some have explained it in Oedipal terms, as hostility against an all-powerful mother by her daughters.

English-language (mainly US) scholarship on Beauvoir expanded dramatically in the 1980s (Pilardi 1993): that is, after the peak of second-wave activism and as feminism was becoming academicized in the context of debates about difference, poststructuralism, and the "new" French feminism. But thinkers celebrating woman's difference now criticized Beauvoir for having a vision of the liberated woman as one who enters the realm of masculine transcendence. She was criticized also for dualism and hostility to the female body, as well as her failure to value feminine qualities (e.g. Hartsock 1985). Authors who made such objections either assumed or asserted that these failings were the result of Beauvoir's adoption of a Sartrean philosophic framework.

From a poststructuralist feminist perspective Beauvoir's work was additionally found lacking on other counts: her focus on subjectivity as the locus of freedom, her "Enlightenment" faith in reason and progress, her lack of concern with issues of discourse, and the tone of moral certainty with which she evaluated women, were criticized. But more recently, others have begun to argue that such critiques tend to caricature Beauvoir's work and that close reading shows that she cannot be dismissed as a naive Enlightenment thinker. In this context, feminist scholars, in both Europe and the United States, have begun carefully to demonstrate that Beauvoir's work diverges significantly from Sartre's. These newer readings have also engaged *The Second Sex* in contemporary debates about such matters as subjectivity, embodiment, and sex/gender relations.

Beauvoir formulates the question of woman's oppression within a framework that owes a debt to Sartrean existentialism. But as Le Doeuff has suggested, she stretches it "beyond and above its means" (Le Doeuff 1991, p. 55ff.). Her project, to account for the apparently universal oppression of woman, is initially cast in Sartrean terms as the problem of woman's otherness. But, unlike Sartre, Beauvoir distinguishes self–other relations between equals, where reciprocity is possible, from those between men and women, where structural inequality results in relations of domination and oppression (Kruks 1992). While for Sartre's "man," the self–other relation is one of equals, for Beauvoir's woman, "[man] is the Subject, he is the Absolute – she is the other."

Beauvoir offers no one fundamental cause for woman's universal otherness, though she examines several monocausal explanations, including biological difference. Each has a bearing on how the oppression of woman operates but, following Sartre, Beauvoir insists that it is only through human choices that these can come to operate as real constraints on individual women. She argues that biological differences between the sexes, which require that women endure the main physical burden of the reproduction of the human species, are real. Yet it is the values that men have imposed on these differences that cause women to be alienated from their bodies and to experience bodily processes as oppressive. Unlike earlier readings, that castigated Beauvoir for her distaste at the female body and her hostility to maternity, recent interpretations have insisted that her thought is more subtle. Lundgren-Gothlin (1996) has argued that Beauvoir gives a dialectical account of embodiment, in which the body is lived as "situation," a complex dialectic of the natural and the historical; while Zerilli (1992) has argued that much of Beauvoir's apparent disgust at the female body is a deliberate rhetorical strategy to shock the reader and destabilize what appears natural. Such readings complicate our understanding of Beauvoir. They also suggest that her work cuts across current debates about the social and discursive construction of the body and the relation of sex to gender in ways that defy easy categorization, and that she points toward ways of reading women's embodiment that are neither poststructuralist nor biologistic in any straightforward sense.

Beauvoir's unfaithful reworking of Sartre's existentialism extends also to her use of phenomenology. She performs a highly original "reduction" of (male) views of woman as destined for marriage and maternity: her practice of suspending naturalistic assumptions and foregrounding experiences of enforced maternity as women live them, led to much that was original (and scandalous) in the work. She was concerned also to give an account of what she called "The Lived Experience" of woman's oppression, to apprehend it from woman's perspective, as a mode of existence. She begins this undertaking with the much cited statement, "one is not born a woman, one becomes one," in which the ambiguous notion of becoming involves a sense both of being created by externalities and of creating oneself. Beauvoir's account of the subjective experience of living one's entire life within a situation of constraint – bodily, psychological, cultural, and material – reveals how such a situation both coerces and entices women to assume and perpetuate their "femininity." In contrast to Sartre, she presents an account of a subjectivity that is not always, in the final analysis, constitutive or free.

Beauvoir's account was, however, based mainly on the experience of French upper- and middle-class women, and she has recently been criticized for her lack of sensitivity to variations in women's experience by race or class (Spelman 1988, ch. 3), and her implicit privileging of heterosexual experience (Card 1985). Since Beauvoir was writing about French women in the early twentieth century, one probably cannot have expected her to be sensitive to issues of race, but her virtual exclusion of working-class and peasant experience is troubling, and her privileging of heterosexuality does tacitly reintroduce a naturalism she otherwise contests.

Beauvoir's final portrait of the "independent woman" as a childless, unwed professional has been much criticized by those who value women's difference. But Moi has pointed out that Beauvoir's concern was not with the issue of identity – whether women are, or should be the "same" as or "different" from men – but with the possibility of freedom that escapes these very terms. Although

Beauvoir underestimated the strategic value of a politics of difference, a great virtue of her work is its utopian dimension: it reminds us that "the aim of feminism is to abolish itself" (1994, p. 213).

A question that remains is whether the strengths of Beauvoir's work stem from her rootedness in existential phenomenology, or whether they emerged in spite of it. Certainly, she pushes at the confines of Sartrean philosophy; yet her framing of the issue of women's subordination in terms of existential notions of subjecthood, embodiment, and freedom still remains remarkably powerful, as does her phenomenological account of women's experience. Beauvoir's work, along with the fruitful appropriations of existential phenomenology on the part of more recent theorists, suggests that this is a philosophic tradition with which feminists can and should continue to engage, if with caution.

8

Postmodernism

CHRIS WEEDON

For the past few decades *postmodernism* has been at the center of debates about philosophy, history, culture, and politics, including feminist theory and politics. Its theoretical rationale can be found in poststructuralist modes of social and cultural analysis and its concerns are echoed in postmodern cultural practices. The range of theories broadly described as "postmodern" includes writers as diverse as Lyotard (1924–), Baudrillard (1929–), Derrida (1930–), Lacan (1901– 81), and Foucault (1926–84). Among women theorists Julia Kristeva (1941–) and Luce Irigaray (1932–) have been particularly important.

The development of Western feminism since 1968 has been marked by a critical engagement with postmodern theory. Attempting to go beyond the liberal feminist goal of extending rights to women, postmodern feminists have sought to theorize those areas of women's experience and oppression that elude liberal theory and politics. In doing so they have mobilized the postmodern critique of the authority and status of science, truth, history, power, knowledge, and subjectivity, bringing a transformative gender dimension to postmodern theory and developing new conceptions of sexual difference.

In poststructuralist theory, meaning is not guaranteed by a world external to it. Language neither reflects nor expresses meaning but constructs it through an infinite process of what Derrida calls *différence*, that is, difference and differal. Postmodern theory offers no privileged objective position from which to ground universally valid ideas of truth and morality or the politics that follow from them. Nor does it offer a position from which to write a history that is objectively true. Knowledge and power are integrally related and, as feminist postmodernists argue, they have worked systematically to marginalize women, defining them as "other" to the patriarchal order of meaning. In Hélène Cixous's (1937–) words, women are "other in a hierarchically organized relationship in which the same rules, names, defines and assigns 'its' other" (Cixous and Clément 1986, p. 71). Postmodern theory challenges the status of both reason and the reasoning subject in the Western philosophical tradition. Far from being an objective faculty able to transcend the limitations of a particular time and place and access true knowledge, reason is partial. Moreover, the abstract individual, reasoning subject of much Western philosophy is implicitly male.

In postmodern theory subjectivity is not seen as unified, sovereign, rational consciousness but as discursively produced (Lacan 1977, Foucault 1978) and as a process (Kristeva 1984). Moreover, subjectivity encompasses unconscious as well as conscious dimensions and is embodied in bodies that are culturally gendered (Irigaray 1985, Butler 1990, 1993, Gallop 1988, Grosz 1994c, 1995a).

Universalizing theories

A key area addressed in both feminist and postmodern critique is the general, universalizing theories – *metanarratives* – that structure Western thought. Post-modernism has delegitimized the Western "grand narratives" (Lyotard) of liberalism, Marxism, philosophy, and science. Feminists have criticized them for their failure to see gender as a fundamental category constituting individuals and social relations. Metanarratives mobilized in political struggle include, for example, the Enlightenment conception of human progress, which is fundamental to liberal humanist sexual and cultural politics, Marxist theories of history and revolution, radical feminist theories of patriarchy, and black nationalist theories of race and culture.

Postmodern thought suggests that the criteria used to establish what is true or false are not universal and objective but rather internal to the structures of modern Western discourses. Moreover feminists have shown these discourses to be both androcentric and Eurocentric (Jaggar 1983, Spivak 1990, Mohanty et al. 1991). While some feminists have produced their own alternative grand narratives, for example, forms of Marxist feminism or radical feminist theories of patriarchy, postmodern feminists have sought either to elude or transform what they see as the masculine order of language (Kristeva 1986, Irigaray 1985b, Braidotti 1991) or, in the case of feminists influenced by Foucault, to develop theories that are historically and geographically located and no longer claim universal status.

Subjectivity

The subject of the Western philosophical tradition has been a "disembodied" abstract individual governed by conscious rational thought (Jaggar 1983). More-over, common-sense views of subjectivity in the West tend to reiterate humanist assumptions that we are unique, rational individuals, born with a human potential which, given the right environment, we can realize through education and personal development. We learn about the world through experience and this experience is expressed in language. This transparent relationship between the individual, experience and language allows little scope for theorizing contradictions either in our sense of ourselves or in the meanings of our experience. Postmodern feminism has sought to deconstruct the hegemonic assumption that we are whole and coherent subjects with a unified sense of identity. In this project the work of particular postmodern thinkers – Lacan, Kristeva, Irigaray, and Foucault – has been seminal.

Postmodern notions of subjectivity – both feminist and nonfeminist – go beyond conscious reason to encompass unconscious and subconscious dimensions of the self and imply contradictions, process, and change. They also stress the embodied nature of subjectivity. The sovereign subject of much Western philosophy had already been challenged by Marx (1818–83) and Freud (1856–1939). For feminists, it was psychoanalysis, with its attention to the acquisition of gendered subjectivity, which seemed to offer a way forward, particularly in its postmodern reinscription in the work of Lacan (see Article 27, PSYCHOANALYTIC FEMINISM).

In Lacanian theory, gendered subjectivity is the precarious effect of the entry of the individual into the symbolic order of language and the law. It involves the formation of the unconscious as the site of repressed meanings and desires which do not conform to the laws of the patriarchal symbolic order. Feminist rewritings of Lacan have identified the unconscious as the site of the repressed feminine which has its roots in the pre-Oedipal relationship with the mother. In order to enter the symbolic order of language, women must inhabit a patriarchal definition of themselves as lack. The process of assuming subjectivity invests the individual with a temporary sense of control and of sovereignty which evokes a "metaphysics of presence" (Derrida) in which s/he becomes the source of the meaning s/he speaks and language appears to be the expression of meaning fixed by the speaking subject. Yet, in postmodern theory, the speaker is never the author of the language within which s/he takes up a position. Language preexists and produces subjectivity. In Lacanian theory the symbolic order is necessarily patriarchal since the difference which makes meaning possible is guaranteed by a primary signifier, the phallus. For women this is a masculine-defined subjectivity. Western thought is thus both logocentric, privileging the word, and phallocentric, privileging the phallus. In postmodern feminism these two aspects are seen as integrally related. Western culture is phallologocentric. Feminist appropriations of Lacanian theory have sought to transcend the inevitability of patriarchy (Brennan 1989).

Feminist critiques of Lacanian theory have attempted to go beyond a dualistic model of difference, defined by lack, in which women are lesser men. Among the most influential feminist rereadings of Lacan is the work of Julia Kristeva. Her work is wide-ranging, addressing questions of philosophy, theology, linguistics, literature, art, and politics, but above all psychoanalysis.

Kristeva rewrites aspects of Lacanian theory of the constitution of the individual as gendered subject in the symbolic order, reinstating the importance of the feminine, yet detaching it in anything more than a gestural way from actual women. Her theory of the *subject in process* is perhaps the most influential aspect of Kristeva's work. Rather than seeing subjectivity as a fixed, humanist essence, Kristeva sees it as rooted in unconscious processes, constituted in the symbolic order and subject to the laws of that order. Language, with both its masculine and feminine dimensions, becomes a potential site for revolutionary change, an idea most fully developed in Kristeva's *Revolution in Poetic Language* (1984).

In the course of the 1970s, Kristeva's work came to focus more on psychoanalytic approaches to femininity and motherhood in the West. She argues that in the Judeo-Christian tradition "motherhood is perceived as a conspicuous sign of the *jouissance* of the female (or maternal) body, a pleasure that must at all costs be repressed: the function of procreation must be kept strictly subordinated to the rule of the Father's name" (1986, p. 138). Women's access to the symbolic order is via the father and involves the repression of the maternal body. The feminine thus becomes the unconscious of the symbolic order. Women must find a third way which allows them access to the symbolic order without embracing a masculine model of femininity.

Like other theorists whose work has been taken up as postmodern, Kristeva resists replacing existing dominant master discourses with alternative master discourses, be they socialist, feminist, or whatever. Her texts seek to disrupt monolithic power structures. To speak is to inhabit the kind of discourse permitted by the patriarchal law of the symbolic order. Even if the feminine is different or other in relation to language and meaning. it can only be thought within the symbolic. The conclusion to be drawn from this is the need to transform the symbolic order.

The transformation of the symbolic order is an idea taken up rather differently by Luce Irigaray. Irigaray's work is marked by a critique of rationality and the legacy of the Enlightenment. She writes in the context of the postmodern questioning of the primacy of conscious rational subjectivity. The idea that the speaking subject is produced within discourse effectively decenters the knowing subject of philosophy. Similarly, the postmodern critique of foundations of knowledge and its insistence that the conditions of knowledge always lie outside of the knowledge in question inform Irigaray's examination of the foundations and presuppositions of philosophy.

Drawing on Freudian and Lacanian theory, Irigaray posits a symbolic order in which reason, the liberal humanist subject, and language are male. She argues that the West is a monosexual culture in which women are seen as a lesser form of men. As she puts it in her influential text *This Sex Which is Not One* (1985), women's difference is not represented by the patriarchal symbolic order, nor are women's interests served by the laws and language of this order. The apparently objective, gender-neutral discourses of science and philosophy are, she argues, the discourses of a male subject. Moreover, the feminine in Western philosophy and culture is a masculine feminine. The male-defined nature of the symbolic order in the West, in which women figure only as lesser men, motivates Irigaray's project of creating a female symbolic, specific to women, in which separatism becomes a strategy in the struggle for a non-patriarchal society in which sexual difference is both voiced and valued (see Articles 27 and 30, PSYCHO-ANALYTIC FEMINISM and SEXUAL DIFFERENCE THEORY).

Postmodern feminist philosophy has taken up both Derridean deconstruction (Grosz 1995a) and Derrida's critique of Western philosophy. It focuses in particular on the idea that "the many discourses on the feminine" in recent philosophy are a "symptom of the crisis and malaise of the masculine subject" but also that "the symbolic absence of the feminine is the source of its strength as a counter strategy by which to destabilize the symbolic (Braidotti 1991, p. 101). Braidotti points to the need "to analyse philosophy's 'marketing of the other' as well as its 'becoming woman' in terms of their relation to the theoretical, political and affective transformations brought about in and by the women's movement" (1991, p. 9).

Postmodern feminist philosophers argue that "Patriarchy is the practice, phallologocentrism the theory; both coincide, however, in producing an economy, material as well as libidinal, where the law is upheld by a phallic symbol that operates by constructing differences and organising them hierarchically" (Braidotti 1991, p. 213). In an attempt to move beyond phallologocentrism, postmodern feminists have attempted to develop ways of seeing an embodied feminine otherness as a site of resistance and transformation (Montrelay 1978, Cixous and Clément 1987, Jardine 1985, Braidotti 1991, Gallop 1988, Grosz 1994, 1995).

This focus on resistant feminine otherness includes attempts to move beyond Lacanian models of desire which draw on the work of Deleuze. Braidotti sees Deleuze (together with Foucault) as offering the conceptual tools with which to "rethink feminist theory" along more politically productive lines (1991, p. 146). Grosz draws on Deleuze and Guattari in her attempt to refigure lesbian desire. Their work is useful "because they refuse to structure it with reference to a singular signified, the phallus, and because they enable desire to be understood not just as feeling or affect, but also as doing and making" (1995, p. 180). "Deleuze's work," she argues, "unsettles the presumptions of what it is to be a stable subject and thus problematizes any assumption that sex is in some way the center, the secret, or truth of the subject" (p. 214).

Postmodern theory, power, and the body

The other central area in which feminists have appropriated and developed postmodern theory has been in their engagement with the work of Foucault. Several key feminist concerns figure centrally in Foucault's work: the body as a site of power central to the constitution of subjectivity, the dispersed, discursive nature of power and its link with knowledge. Foucault's work takes issues with centralized models of power. For Foucault, power is not reducible to any one source, it is a relationship which inheres in material discursive practices. Discourses create embodied forms of subjectivity which are implicated in power relations. Yet power also creates resistance.

The key site in Foucault for the exercising of power is the body. Several important feminist theorists, influenced to different degrees by Foucault, Deleuze, Lacan, and Irigaray, have sought to theorize the body and its relation to difference and gendered subjectivity. Key examples are the work of Jane Gallop, Elizabeth Grosz, and Judith Butler.

Gallop (1988) challenges the culture–biology opposition as a restatement of traditionally oppressive binary oppositions in which women are placed outside of culture. She argues that it is not biology itself but rather the ideological use made of biology which is oppressive. Gallop, like Irigaray, develops a different understanding of corporeality in which the female body is a site of resistance to patriarchy, but one which is refused representation.

Elizabeth Grosz (1994c, 1995a) is critical of the tendency in much postmodern writing to analyze the representation of bodies without due attention to their materiality. The exclusion of the materiality of bodies is, she argues, the unacknowledged condition for the dominance of reason. Drawing on Foucault, Deleuze, and Irigaray, she argues that: "Sexual differences, like those of class and race, *are* bodily differences" and that "the body must be reconceived, not in opposition to culture but as its preeminent object" (1995, p. 32). Moreover, a new language is needed to articulate women's specific difference.

Judith Butler (1990, 1993) is critical of philosophy's tendency to "miss the body or, worse, write against it" (1993, p. ix). Drawing on Foucault and psychoanalysis, she attempts to theorize the materiality of the body and the ways in which "bodies are materialised as sexed" in the light of a critique of heterosexism. She wishes to go beyond the conventional limits of constructionist theories to consider "how such constraints not only produce the domain of intelligible bodies, but produce as well a domain of unthinkable, abject, unliveable bodies" (1993, p. xi).

Many postmodern feminists have taken up Foucault's work to produce analyses which start from detailed examinations of the many localized forms which gender power relations take in a particular area of discursive practice. Yet Foucault's view of power remains controversial among feminists who are skeptical toward the postmodern project. The most frequent objection to it is that it denies women a place exterior to power from which to ground transformative political action (Fraser 1989a). This lack of grounding is seen as incompatible with feminism since feminists are said to need a position outside of power from which to speak and act in order to effect change.

Postmodern feminists argue that the theory that all discursive practices and all forms of subjectivity constitute and are constituted by relations of power is only disabling if power is seen as always necessarily repressive. It is precisely such singular notions of power as repression that Foucault attempted to question in his historical studies.

Similarly, the Foucauldian assumption that subjectivity is an effect of discourse is a source of controversy among feminists. For Foucauldian feminists, subjectivity is realized in the material practices of everyday life which are also discursive practices. As Foucault argued in his case-studies of psychiatry, the prison, and sexuality, forms of subjectivity – conscious, unconscious, rational, and emotional – are produced through socially located discourses. It is the move away from any fixed or essential qualities of women or femininity, which unite all women, that disturbs feminists who are skeptical toward postmodernism.

Feminist critiques of postmodernism

The debate about the usefulness of poststructuralist theory to feminism has been underway since at least the late 1970s when, for example, in Britain, the journal

M/F (1978) aroused much hostility among feminists for what was seen as its antihumanist dissolution of the concept "woman." How, it was asked, could women organize together and develop new positive identities if there were no essence of womanhood on the basis of which women could come together in the spirit of sisterhood?

Feminist advocates of postmodern theory argue that its questioning of universals and the possibility of objectivity, and its focus on the very criteria by which claims to knowledge are legitimized, provide for theory which can avoid generalizing from the experiences of Western, white, heterosexual, middle-class women. By questioning all essences and relativizing truth claims, postmodern feminisms create a space for political perspectives and interests that have hitherto been marginalized. They also help guard against creating alternative generalizing theories.

Many feminist critics of postmodern theory claim that the Western Enlightenment discourse of emancipation is essential to feminism. They argue, among other things, that postmodernism "expresses the claims and needs" of white, privileged Western men who have had their Enlightenment and can afford to be critical (Di Stefano 1990, p. 86). Nancy Hartsock, for example, argues that:

> Somehow it seems highly suspicious that it is at the precise moment when so many groups have been engaged in "nationalisms" which involve redefinitions of the marginalized Others that suspicions emerge about the nature of the "subject", about the possibilities for a general theory which can describe the world, about historical "progress". Why is it that just at the moment when so many of us who have been silenced begin to demand the right to name ourselves, to act as subjects rather than objects of history, that just then the concept of subjecthood becomes problematic? Just when we are forming our own theories about the world, uncertainty emerges about whether the world can be theorized. Just when we are talking about the changes we want, ideas of progress and the possibility of systematically and rationally organizing human society become dubious and suspect. (1990, p. 164)

These objections to postmodernism rest on the assumption that to question the Western Enlightenment category of the subject is to undermine the possibility of subjecthood. They are shared by feminist writers who advocate the importance of identity politics. They highlight a fundamental question in postmodernism about the relationship between a deconstructive approach to subjectivity and the question of agency. While it is the case that some versions of postmodernism show no interest in the question of lived subjectivity or agency, this has not been the case in feminist appropriations of Foucault, Derrida, Deleuze, Irigaray, and Kristeva. Here agency is seen as discursively produced in the social interactions between culturally produced, contradictory subjects.

While many postmodern feminists acknowledge that there may be strategic needs for identity politics, defined by shared forms of oppression and political objectives, they argue that it is important to recognize the nature and limitations of the essentialist foundations of many forms of identity politics. They propose a theory of identity which sees it as discursively produced, necessary but always

81

contingent and strategic. Commenting on the relevance of postmodern theory to black identity politics, bell hooks suggests, for example, that, while the poststructuralist critique of subjectivity causes problems for black identity politics, it can also be liberating and enabling:

> Criticisms of directions in postmodern thinking should not obscure insights it may offer that open up our understanding of African-American experience. The critique of essentialism encouraged by postmodern thought is useful for African-Americans concerned with reformulating outmoded notions of identity. We have too long had imposed upon us from both the outside and the inside a narrow constricting notion of blackness. Postmodern critiques of essentialism which challenge notions of universality and static overdetermined identity within mass culture and mass consciousness can open up new possibilities for the construction of self and the assertion of agency. (1991, p. 28)

A positive and politically useful reading of postmodern theories of subjectivity would see it as socially constructed and contradictory rather than essential and unified.

Feminist critics of postmodernism often assume that to question metanarratives is to undermine the possibility of knowledge. Yet postmodernism can also be read as rendering both subjects and knowledges provisional and differentiated, according to the social and discursive location of the "knowing" subject. Poststructuralist feminists would ask, for example, of Enlightenment narratives of emancipation: "the emancipation of whom and from what?" They would insist on consciously limited and located narratives and struggles. As Gayatri Spivak has argued, "We cannot but narrate" but "when a narrative is constructed, something is left out. When an end is defined, other ends are rejected, and one might not know what those ends are" (1990, pp. 18–19). Thus the invoking of Western feminist theories, for example, emancipatory liberal feminism or Marxist feminism, as general theories of historical progress often leads to a denial of the specificity of black and Third World women's interests.

The assertion by critics of postmodern theory that feminism necessarily stands on Enlightenment ground is not without its political consequences. It begs the question as to whether Enlightenment metanarratives have a monopoly interest in progressive social change. It is also blind to the historically specific class and ethnic interests that structure many feminist Enlightenment narratives.

It is an often repeated criticism of postmodern thinking that it leads to pluralism, relativism, and ultimately to individualist politics. Critics argue that feminist politics are impossible from within postmodernist perspectives because "feminism itself depend[s] on a relatively unified notion of the social subject 'woman', a notion that postmodernism would attack" (Di Stefano 1990, p. 77). Without the category "woman," it is argued, we descend into a "pluralism ... [that] reduces us to being an other among others; it is not a recognition, but a reduction to difference to absolute indifference, equivalence, interchangeability" (p. 77). To avoid relativism, it is argued, women need a general theory of oppression and liberation.

Yet politically disabling relativism is not the only alternative to general theories. Postmodernism can offer partial and located theory and practice. Feminist poststructuralist analysis is neither concerned with the abandonment of theory nor of subjectivity. It does not argue for relativism, but rather the necessarily always partial, historically specific and interested nature of theory and practice. Pluralism allows for the representation of many competing and sometimes conflicting interests, for example, black feminist as well as white feminist perspectives. Yet an adequate feminism requires that the structural relations of inequality between different groups of women be recognized and addressed. Speaking of race, for example, bell hooks argues: "Postmodern theory that is not seeking simply to appropriate the experience of 'Otherness' to enhance the discourse or to be radically chic should not separate the 'politics of difference' from the politics of racism" (1991, p. 26). Indeed difference in patriarchal, racist, heterosexist, capitalist societies always involves oppressive power relations.

While postmodern feminists reject essentializing theories, they continue to use theory strategically in the interests of understanding and transforming oppressive social relations. In their work theories have no external guarantee in "truth" or "reality," but rather a strategic status. In using theories postmodern feminists look to their material effectivity in the struggle for change. They argue that feminists do not need a single metanarrative in order to develop and use theories in politically effective ways. As postmodernists, we can use categories such as "gender," "race," and "class" in social and cultural analysis but on the assumption that their meaning is plural, historically, and socially specific. The effects of using such categories will depend on both how they are defined and on the social context in which they are used.

The need for narratives that are non-universalizing, do not have foundationalist status and allow for cultural and historical specificity is clear from "Third World" appropriations of postmodern theory. "Third World feminism" as it has developed in the United States brings together women from the so-called "Third World" and minority peoples and peoples of colour living in "first world" countries. It has a dual focus: deconstructing the Eurocentrism of much writing about women in the "Third World" and giving adequate representation to the concerns of "Third World" women. In a postmodern critique of feminist scholarship and colonial discourses, Chandra Talpade Mohanty demonstrates how much Western feminist writing about Third World women produces Third World women as a singular category defined by their victim status. "Colonialism," she argues, "almost invariably implies a relation of structural domination, and a suppression – often violent – of the heterogeneity of the subject(s) in question" (Mohanty et al. 1991, p. 51). In Western feminist writing, this effect is achieved by the implicit assumption that Western feminism is "the yardstick by which to encode and represent cultural others" (p. 55). The production of the Third World woman as a subject, who is a victim by virtue of her sex, suppresses differences, denies historical specificity, and renders the operations of power, both negative and positive, and the potential for resistance invisible. Mohanty argues against starting with a pre-given category, "Third World women." Third World women are constituted by the social relations in which they engage and these are constituted by class and ethnic interest as well as gender.

As Mohanty's critique suggests, it is crucial to be aware of the specific discursive power relations in play when one uses theory. In practice different and competing theories do not have equal social or institutional status, nor can their material effectivity be divorced from the actual existing context of power relations within which they are articulated and which they seek to affirm or transform.

Postmodern feminism stresses the need for such awareness. As Nancy Fraser and Linda Nicholson argue:

> In general, postmodern-feminist theory would be pragmatic and fallibilistic. It would tailor its methods and categories to the specific task at hand, using multiple categories when appropriate and forswearing the metaphysical comfort of a single feminist method or feminist epistemology.   (1990, p. 35).

PART II

AFRICA, ASIA, LATIN AMERICA, AND EASTERN EUROPE

9

Latin America

OFELIA SCHUTTE

In Latin America, institutionalized feminist philosophy is a recent phenomenon, dating for the most part since the 1980s. Historically, the gifted writer/philosopher/poet Sor Juana Inés de la Cruz (1651–95, Mexico, Colonial Period) and the utopian socialist activist Flora Tristán (1803–44, France and Peru) are especially recognized for their original feminist contributions. The Uruguayan philosopher Carlos Vaz Ferreira (1872–1958) wrote the moderately pro-feminist treatise *Sobre feminismo* (On Feminism) in 1918, during the suffragist phase of the movement. Contemporary feminist philosophy has followed the general theoretical trends established since the 1970s in Western European and Anglo-American feminist philosophy and theory. Feminist philosophers have challenged traditional androcentric readings of the canon (Hierro 1985) and have pursued alliances with colleagues in Women's Studies programs. As of the mid-1990s, a firm tradition of feminist studies has been established in several countries. Important feminist journals and publications include *Debate feminista* (Mexico), *Estudos feministas* (Brazil), *Isis Internacional* (Chile), and *Feminaria* (Argentina); *Hiparquía* (Argentina) currently publishes feminist and non-feminist articles by women philosophers.

This article focuses on recent trends and issues in *feminismo filosófico* (philosophical feminism) as developed particularly in Mexico and Argentina since the 1980s. Given the limitations of space, three general questions will be addressed: (1) how are the terms *género* (gender), *mujer* (woman), and *mujeres* (women) understood in feminist theory written in the Spanish language?; (2) should feminists adopt a feminism of equality or a feminism of difference?; (3) what are some of the directions taken by feminisms of difference?

Género as a category of analysis in the Spanish language

Feminist theory is affected by the different meanings attributed to *género*. Traditionally, *género* has a formal classificatory connotation (as in *genus*, a class containing several species), or it can refer to a *kind* (in the sense of *group*, or *kin*) as in *el género humano* (humankind). It can also refer to *kind* in the sense of the manner or mode of doing something. Another of its meanings is *sex* or *gender* (as in the masculine or feminine gender). In grammar, it refers to the gender of nouns, pronouns, articles, adjectives, and other gendered particles in language.

With the advent of the category *gender* in Western feminist theory, new senses of *género* have been introduced. Because the terms *género* (gender), *mujer* (woman), and *mujeres* (women) can be used ambiguously, it is important to keep their senses clear.

Senses of *género* currently found in feminist writings include: (1) *género* as a strictly logical category marking the distinction between women and men as conventionally accepted by various societies, a category useful for establishing criteria of formal equality between women and men; (2) *género* as a collective term useful for speaking about women or about issues concerning women (*género* being understood here as short for *el género femenino*, the feminine gender); (3) as a ramification of (2), *género* as a designator of elements of group identity or kindred relations among women, useful for speaking about women or women's issues from an involved standpoint (*our* gender rather than *the* feminine gender); (4) *género* as a power-laden concept used to regulate the sexual identities of women and men, therefore, both a tool of analysis, insofar as it is an indicator of differences, and a target of deconstruction, insofar as the differences so marked are judged to be politically or ethically unacceptable.

The second sense of *género* is based on a loose association between *gender* (short for *the feminine gender*) as a classification that groups all women, and *women* (mujeres) as the group so designated by the classification. This sense of gender appears to function as the successor to *La mujer* (woman), a term used in Spanish to speak about a woman or women in an abstract manner. *La mujer* is used to refer to *women*, as a class, in a collective or group sense, but also (often ambiguously) to the eternal form or essence of Woman which essentialists believe inheres in every woman. Women's Studies programs are designated by the general categories *género* or *la mujer*, as in PIEM (Programa Interdisciplinario de Estudios de la Mujer, El Colegio de México); AIEM (Area Interdisciplinaria de Estudios de la Mujer, Universidad de Buenos Aires); Cátedra de la Mujer, Universidad de La Habana, Cuba; PUEG (Programa Universitario de Estudios de Género, Universidad Nacional Autónoma de México, Mexico City).

For many speakers *la mujer* (woman) can evoke an explicit essentialism; changing the reference to *género* does not necessarily eliminate this problem. The use of *género* as a designator of women in a collective sense lends itself to a closet essentialism unless the distinction between empirical and normative constructs of *women* and *the feminine* is made very clear. For example, one thing is to note, in an empirical sense, that most women are mothers; another is to suggest that in order to really be a woman one must be a mother or a special kind of mother (patient, self-sacrificing, and so on), thus locking women's identity to certain ways of being or kinds of activity in an essentialist–normative sense. Despite the danger of essentialist connotations of *la mujer* and of some uses of *género*, if interpreted critically both terms may be appropriated by non-essentialist feminist theorists. The plural term *mujeres* (women) is also used in feminist discourse. Its limitation is that, unlike *la mujer* and *género*, *mujeres* lacks a collective sense, offering only a plural connotation. In many important contexts, however, a focus on the plural meaning of *mujeres* is central to feminism. A feminist use of *mujeres* is found in discussions dealing with the category of agency, which presupposes the notion of women (subjects) as agents empowered to act or make choices regarding their own lives. The category of *sexual difference* is often used by feminist psychoanalysis to criticize the binary oppositions according to which cultural constructs of men and women evolve. In this case, the plural *mujeres* is used as a privileged term in feminist discourse to emphasize the differences among and within women – differences that go against the grain of the gender stereotypes prevalent in a particular culture.

The gendered construction of knowledge and women's experience

While feminists agree that the existing organization of knowledge has served men's ends and that the experiences of women have remained marginalized or invisible, there are different approaches as to how to best represent the interests of women in academia and in society.

In Argentina a moderate wing of women philosophers prefers to speak of "gender theory" than of philosophical feminism or feminist philosophy (Santa Cruz 1994, p. 48). This position argues that as long as there are many different perspectives within feminism (not all of which any particular feminist might endorse), it is more appropriate to use the more encompassing, more neutral term *gender theory* than *feminism*. It also holds that "gender theory" is a preferable category for feminist work than "women's studies," charging that *women's studies* is too restrictive a designation since it suggests women are either the exclusive subjects or objects of such studies. The point that the object of study should be defined by gender-related rather than women's issues as such may be of strategic importance for women philosophers who, as a rule, work with the traditional canon.

Santa Cruz subscribes only to the formal, classificatory sense of *gender* mentioned above. Gender is defined as "the form of the possible kinds of assignation [given] to human beings in dual, familial, or social relations, concerning properties and functions imaginarily tied to sex" (Santa Cruz 1994, p. 51). This position accepts a social constructionist view of gender, holding that gender distinctions are conventional because they are based on social relations, not biological characteristics, and because conceptions of gender vary according to historical conditions, time, and place. A feminine or masculine gender-assignation is a product of historical factors, not an ontological essence. Moreover, since individuals' social identities involve a number of other factors besides gender, such as race, social class, occupation, sexual orientation, religion, and so on, gender should not be considered an independent category in the systems of social assignation (Santa Cruz 1994, pp. 50–1). This formal egalitarian position rejects perspectives on gender associated with feminisms of difference. The sociopolitical model proposed is a "complex" kind of egalitarian society (not a utopia), whose logical structure can be contemplated as a possible object prior to its actualization (Santa Cruz 1994, p. 53). In such a society, gender would not be regarded as

89

foundational to human identity. Still, it would not be unfair to continue assigning the conventional gender identities (M/F) to individuals as long as gender was not thought to interfere positively or negatively with the use of reason, on the basis of which the principle of the equality of persons is established.

At least two lines of objections confront this formalist gender position. One line would question the possibility of a value-neutral or merely formal concept of gender difference as a regulative ideal detached from the gender models and stereotypes prevalent in a particular society. Is not the formal classification (M/F) itself a product of culture and history, thereby tinged with values regarding the dual and/or complementary status of the sexes and of masculine/feminine attributes? This line of objection would argue for the deconstruction, not the ahistoricized abstraction, of the regulative sense of gender (cf. Lamas 1994). A second and different line of objection would question, strategically, why feminists should opt for a regulative ideal that minimizes the connection between gender and personal identity, appealing to the abstract concepts of human equality and a complexly egalitarian society. How can women's interests be represented and negotiated in a male-dominant society – how can there even be a women's movement? – if the ideal is to bypass the mark of gender, given its contingency and historicity?

The second line of objection is implicit in the methodology adopted by feminists who work with the second concept of gender outlined above, the collective sense of women's experiences as women. These theorists focus on women's issues and then adopt an explicitly feminist perspective to reconsider the norms that should govern an understanding of women's rights and responsibilities in society. A case in point is the analysis of women's rights as human rights, an important issue that has arisen in some Latin American countries out of a national political context. One strategy for denouncing human rights abuses against women is to establish the legitimacy of "group" or "collective" rights, taking into account the collective entity or the group "women" as a legitimate subject for the assignment and exercise of such rights (Maffía 1994, p. 67). Once some of the gender-specific sexual abuses against women are identified (such as the beating and the rape of women's bodies), the dichotomy between the public and the private spheres breaks down. Feminists argue that if female oppression were seen as political oppression whether it occurs in the domestic or public realms, then, regardless of where the violence against women occurs, such acts could more easily be recognized as violations of women's human rights in a gender-specific sense (Maffía 1994, pp. 71–2). Criticizing the practical implications of androcentrism, they point out that women's advances cannot simply be monitored by using the male as the standard for the whole human species; a reconceptualization of the human must be made to include the experiences and needs of both women and men.

In Latin America, the gender-specific approach to human rights and other civil and political freedoms typically involves: a critique of traditional male models for understanding political culture; an insistence on the link between private and public; a consideration of specific activities of women which have failed to achieve recognition in the public view or mind; a consideration of women's needs when establishing priorities for social policy and social action; and (possibly the most difficult of all) the establishment of new conceptual paradigms that will effectively place women's heretofore invisible needs high on the social and political agenda (Jelin 1990, Schutte 1993). This approach takes the concept of women's gender specificity as foundational for a feminist analysis, even though the ultimate goal is equality. In so doing it exemplifies a moderate feminism of "difference," moderate in that its ultimate goal is to reach an inclusive representation of women and men in the universal concept of the "human." The main limitation of this approach is that it does not confront directly the question of essentialism, possibly incorporating a closet or, at the least, a stategic essentialism. What mostly concerns this theory is not the source of women's beliefs about their gender identity but, once having this identity, the action they take in society on behalf of women's perceived interests and needs.

Feminisms of equality and difference

The differences in approach regarding what senses of gender to adopt are linked to the debate over whether feminism should follow a paradigm of equality or difference. Debates on the European continent among French, Italian, and Spanish feminists have influenced the direction of feminist theory in Latin America, particularly in Mexico, Argentina, and Chile. In the 1990s, with the rapid ascent of postmodern critiques of the universal subject of modernity, feminisms of difference are on the rise. The Spanish feminist philosopher Celia Amorós, whose work has been widely read in Mexico and Argentina, has argued extensively, however, on behalf of an Enlightenment-based feminism of equality and against a postmodern feminism of difference. According to Amorós the essential difference between the two positions lies in whether the principle of the universalizability of moral laws (códigos) is accepted (Amorós 1994, p. 55). If universalizability is granted as an intrinsic value in moral reasoning, everyone (as a rational agent) is held in principle to be equally subject before the law. The political result of this principle is favorable for women, she insists, because universalizability makes possible the legitimation of a larger number of new political subjects. If taken to its ultimate consequences, universalizability will also abolish the double standards that place women in a differential relation to the law. To the standard objection, why universalize when the model is male?, Amorós has one basic reply: there is no other choice, since men (whose codes are currently in power) will not reverse the process of universalization toward women's standards. (Amorós 1994, pp. 56–7).

Amorós defends a feminism of equality over feminisms of difference based on the continuing validity of the European Enlightenment project, arguing that when political rights are subject to the principle of equality, as they are in the modern state, such rights are capable of subverting patriarchal authority. This is because patriarchal authority is characterized by a pact among some men which excludes women, making women objects rather than subjects of the agreement;

91

the modern state, in contrast, establishes laws before which all rational agents are equal, in principle making women subjects, not objects of, or outsiders to, the social contract. Insofar as some versions of the feminism of difference posit the notion of women as differently positioned collective subjects not only to denounce but to overturn their inferior status in society, Amorós concedes that this has been helpful for feminism (Amorós 1994, p. 66). The relevance of difference is accepted on the conditions that the end goal is to uphold the principle of universality and that the depiction of women's differences is not reduced to a gender essentialism (Amorós 1994, 79–82).

Against this position, perhaps the most interesting defense of an anti-egalitarian radical feminism of difference to reach Hispanic American feminists has come through a reading of the Italian school of radical feminists known as *Rivolta Femminile*. One important objection raised by Italian radical feminists against using the male subject as the model for women under a paradigm of equality is that women do not find themselves reflected in this model, not because they belong to an oppressed social group (as reformist and socialist feminists have held), but because they perceive themselves as differently sexed individuals (Rubio Castro 1990, p. 188). The Italian feminist movement of the 1970s and 1980s held that adherence to an ethical imperative of equality is not sufficient to change a woman's self-concept of gender difference or the cultural images representing her as "other" (negatively construed) of the man. If feminism is to change the relations of power in society so that women are enabled to transform the spaces of inequality into spaces of equality – a goal advanced by Amorós – then a self–critical understanding of sexual difference is needed, if only as a prior psychological requirement for the empowerment of women. The social goal of a "complex equality" advocated by Amorós and other egalitarian feminists cannot be reached except by a radical break with the logic of equality found in the politics of modernity (Rubio Castro 1990, p. 193).

But how is *sexual difference* to be understood? Is this position trapped in essentialism? On the contrary, a nonessentialistic reading of *sexual difference* holds that these terms need not refer to a feminine essence. Rather, they can question the distance between a woman's sense of self and the ideological conceptions of the feminine prevalent in her cultural and social environment (Rubio Castro 1990, p. 194). The principal difference referred to in *sexual difference*, then, is not difference between that which is masculine and that which is feminine, in which case one would remain trapped in an essentialism of the feminine (as of the masculine), but the difference, or distance, one would like to establish between one's sexual/gender identity and the entire representational ideology of the masculine and the feminine. This critique of gender ideology often works in conjunction with a feminist psychoanalysis. For example, the idealization of heterosexual romantic love and the double standard of sexual morality affecting women are shown to be among the more powerful symbolic constructs of masculinity and femininity contributing to psychological conflicts affecting women in traditional sectors of Latin American societies (Fernández 1992).

In this discussion, the debate over the constituency of the feminist subject hinges on whether feminists should take the short cut to equality through the appropriation of the male model or whether they should reject equality, resisting assimilation to the paradigm of the male citizen-subject not to remain trapped in the feminine difference, but to deconstruct both it and its masculine counterpart. This crucial aspect of the feminist project is being developed by some radical feminist projects outside academia but also by cross-disciplinary work in cultural studies and feminist theory.

The feminist movement and feminist cultural studies

The Mexican anthropologist Marta Lamas, editor of the leading journal *Debate feminista*, uses a poststructuralist analysis on gender effectively to obtain what she defines as the ethical and political goal of feminism: to offer a new symbolic and political definition of "what it is to be a *person* – a human being and a subject – , whether it be in the body of a *woman* or of a *man*" (Lamas 1994, p. 29). She defines gender as a cultural construct whose function is to give meaning to the sexual difference through the binary opposition man/woman, and whose logic is one of "sexism and homophobia" (Lamas 1994, p. 18). The logic of gender also establishes a differentiated regulation of sexuality and a double morality for men and women. To reach a feminist account of sexuality it is not enough to deconstruct an essentialistic view of gender, as Foucault has done in his analysis of the history of sexuality. There must also be an analysis of the counterposition of the sexes created by the gender binary and a deconstruction of the latter, which forms the framework of the symbolic structures regulating the meaning given to male and female sexuality (Lamas 1994, p. 26). Interestingly, Lamas does not oppose her view to Amorós's feminism of equality. on the grounds that Amorós does not reduce equality to sameness, accepting differences attributed to gender as long as the latter are not essentialized (Lamas 1994, p. 21). Here the agreement between one poststructuralist and one Enlightenment feminist over the critique of essentialism takes precedence (for Lamas) over their disagreement over the relevance of postmodern perspectives to feminist theory.

While a poststructuralist feminist psychoanalysis has argued against essentializing the gender and sexual difference (Lamas 1994, Fernández 1992) so as to free women from the ideological constraints of the masculine/feminine gender difference, feminist literary criticism at times privileges essentialism. Building on positions offered by Julia Kristeva and Luce Irigaray, some critics, including the Chilean Lucía Guerra, have commented on the maternal body, a theme of extraordinary appeal to the Hispanic gender-normative culture where *mujer* is often simply taken as a synonym of *madre* (mother). In essentialist poststructuralist readings, the maternal body is symbolized as the site of plurality and heterogeneity but also as the body of *la mujer* (woman/women) (Guerra 1994, pp. 170–2). For this type of feminist criticism the danger in feminist theory is not the essentialist projection of symbolic maternity on woman, the female body, or the authentic feminine (now represented as maternal-erotic instead of virginal).

Rather, the danger is abstract thinking (Guerra 1994, pp. 165, 182–3), which is interpreted as the phallogocentric denial of the mother's body.

In contrast to poststructuralist essentialism, an influential nonessentialist position in literary and cultural studies is offered by the poststructuralist critic Nelly Richard, editor of the Chilean journal *Revista de Crítica Cultural*. Richard takes a deconstructionist position on identity. She argues that the signs *masculine* and *feminine* should be displaced from the reference to the bodies of men and women (Richard 1994, p. 133). She offers a strong reminder that "just as 'being a woman' ('ser mujer') does not guarantee by nature the critical exercise of a femininity that necessarily questions hegemonic masculinity" neither does " 'being a man' ('ser hombre')... condemn the subject-author fatally to be in favor of the power codifications of the official culture or of automatically reproducing its mechanisms" (Richard 1994, p. 134). More vital to feminist criticism, she argues, is to separate, regardless of the sex of the author, texts that rebel (particularly stylistically) against the official culture, as happened in Chile during the resistance to the dictatorship of Augusto Pinochet, whether such texts are authored by men or by women (Richard 1994, p. 135). Richard opposes the "ghettoizing" of women's texts on the basis of gender-difference characteristics.

Outside the academy and its spin-off cultural productions (cultural criticism), feminist militancy is linked to what is widely known as the women's movement. For some, self-consciousness groups ("grupos de autoconciencia") are the process that leads and sustains women in their struggles. Others have entered the movement through joint involvement in women's rights issues and popular education, ethnic struggles, the labor movement, political work and organizing, legal work, lesbian rights, and so on. At present, many NGOs (non-governmental organizations, often funded by foreign donors) are promoting women's groups in various Latin American countries. These groups generally promote women's greater participation in democratic processes and in the basic institutions of civil society (economic production, popular education, the media). Differences arise between the radical and the establishment-oriented sectors of the women's movement. Radical feminist activists insist on the primacy of linking the personal and the political and on criticizing bureaucratic-style leadership. Some are critical of the present (post-Cold War) global economic order, particularly its impoverishing and displacing effects on the populations of the periphery, an important issue for the political Left in Latin America. A central criticism is how the male model of power is used to legislate not only over world politics but over ethical systems dictating the meaning of life and death. Some feminists propose the notion of a time-off from the economic-political masculine system. The time to create alternatives and to enjoy individuals' most intimate desires is referred to as "women's time." "The time to make another reality, women's time, neither is nor can be the system's time" (Bedregal Sáez 1995, p. 15).

Despite the effort of many academic feminists to link their work or their activities outside of work with the women's movement, the relation between feminist philosophy and feminist practice, or militancy, sustains a tension. A

94

juxtaposed kind of "theory" (born of activism) sometimes emerges in language that combines aspects of philosophical feminism with strong critiques of academia as a site where knowledge is reserved for the elite. Taking all currents – established and marginal – into consideration, then, feminist theory can be said to exist inside a discipline, such as philosophy, in a space that traverses several disciplines (cross-and interdisciplinary programs), and outside of the disciplines (though not necessarily uninfluenced by them), in that space known as "the women's movement." In the latter space, consciousness-raising workshops and groups, together with community and political organizing activities on behalf of women's rights continue to comprise a vanguard. *See also* Article 47, COMMUNITY.

10

Africa

SOPHIE OLUWELE

Origins

Most of the existing works that can be classified as African feminist literature today are mainly the result of pioneering researches into the conditions of African women both in the past and in contemporary times. Many scholars and writers working within sociohistorical disciplines have engaged in feminist criticism of a rigorous type. But when it comes to philosophy proper, it appears that the main figures in the discipline have almost, in a conspiratorial way, avoided feminist discussion.

Feminism in the West today refers to a wide range of approaches and theories, all of which address different aspects of social discrimination against women. We have seen functional, structural, Marxist, socialist, psychoanalytic, and, more recently, postmodernist feminism. These sociopolitical movements and theories sometimes raise and discuss philosophical issues. However, their common goal is to identify policies and programs that will be useful in promoting the social, economic, and political emancipation of women.

Feminist philosophy, however, is an involvement in direct critical examination and analysis of different worldviews and philosophical stands on the nature of reality, of man and woman, as these serve as justifications for the type of relationship that exists between the two sexes. The primary goal is to expose different scientifically false theories, rationally unjustifiable principles of human existence and inconsistent moral norms which have hitherto served as reasons for the different arrangements of men and women in most human societies. Often, feminist philosophers propose alternative principles of understanding male–female differences and adequate relationships that can justifiably exist between them.

The development of African feminist philosophy therefore presupposes the existence of some clearly identifiable worldviews and philosophical positions in which claims about women and of principles that ought to guide their relationships with men have been made. However, it is not an understatement to say that the main area of African philosophy today remains basically unsettled. This is because there is no general agreement about the nature of African philosophy or about a specific worldview which is (generally) accepted as representative of African intellectual ideology. This article therefore starts with a short survey of the major trends in contemporary African philosophy. This is then followed by a critical analysis of the main trends likely to determine the future development of African feminist philosophy.

Major trends in contemporary African philosophy

Negritude and ethno-philosophy

The first group of Western writers who characterized African thought and worldview was made up of travellers, missionaries, and colonialists. The group was later joined by ethnologists and anthropologists whose major claim to competence in African thought was the knowledge of casual references to black men made by Greek and Roman writers, many of whom never stepped on the soil of Africa. The other weapons with which these social scientists were equipped were their intense interest in the study of primitive peoples of the world and Western education. Most of these earliest writers described Africans as people with little or no rational thought, people given to mythical and magical beliefs about nature and reality. Some even doubted African people's capacity to think in abstract and rational terms.

The first black Africans who defended African culture and worldview against what they regarded as racial intimidation by Western intelligentsia were poets, essayists, and nationalists. They include Edward Wilmot Blyden (1832–1912), Aimé Césaire (1912–) and Léopold Sédar Senghor (1906–). Their aggressive reactions marked the beginning of the intellectual opposition between Western and African thought. These pioneering efforts were enviable, even though the analyses and conclusions they provided were mostly not referred to textual fact, and hence remain both theoretically and factually questionable.

The term "negritude" was coined by Césaire to identify an African personality which Blyden had dealt with in great detail. Later on Senghor characterized an African consciousness, a peculiar African way of knowing and understanding. These scholars were eager to articulate an authentic African intellectual culture (i.e. one put in place by African indigenes) in which Western Logos and nous are replaced by ratio and vital force. The basic argument is that the cold, distant comprehension of nature which results from the separation of the object from the subject by Western thinkers gives way in an African gnosis which entails participatory relationship between the knower and the known.

Neither Blyden, nor Césaire, nor even Senghor claimed to have identified negritude as African philosophy. In fact none of them was a professional philosopher. What they all tried to characterize was an African worldview, a uniquely African *Weltanschauung* whose features do not necessarily coincide with the Western worldview, nor with any particular school of thought within the discipline of philosophy. However, the conventional identification of British and German philosophies, for example, as empiricism and idealism respectively, easily led many scholars to misunderstand the phrase "African philosophy" as a

97

demand for the proof of one metaphysical and/or epistemological position commonly shared by every African. Yet the initial problem was one of positing a Western worldview against a cogent African alternative. And this, by its very nature, cannot be a matter of identifying and characterizing one school of philosophy to which every African, dead or alive, belongs.

The real philosophical confusion that triggered off the debate about the existence of African philosophy was initiated by Rev. Father Placide Tempels who used the term "philosophy" to characterize an African body of thought. In his book *Bantu Philosophy* (1959), Tempels proposed that an implicit intuitive philosophy lurks behind the thought, language, religion, and social principles of behavior of the Luba people of the former Belgian Congo (now Democratic Republic of Congo). Holding the view that the people are incapable of an eloquent presentation of that philosophy, he regarded his own rational systematization of the people's worldview as adequately representative of their beliefs, views, and moral values.

Tempels identified *ntu* as the ontological axiom that replaces Western nous. From it, every other Luba principle of existence follows. Tempels, we are told, lost his job for making Africans too rational and philosophical. The argument was that, if they truly were rational and philosophical, then there would be no need to civilize them. If they are not, his work constitutes a religious heresy. On each count he could not possibly have remained as a missionary in Africa.

Tempels was not a professional philosopher but a Catholic priest versed in the Aristotelian tradition. He used the terms "African Bantu," "nature," and "savages" interchangeably and actually titled his book *Bantu Philosophy*. He can thus justifiably be identified as the father of ethno-philosophy, having postulated the existence of a single and primitive philosophy shared by at least every member of an African society.

Several Western and African scholars hailed Tempels's work, seeing it as a breakthrough in the annals of the search for an indigenous African philosophy. However, one of the earliest reactions came from another Catholic priest, this time a Luba. Rev. Father Alexis Kagame was a knowledgeable historian, anthropologist, linguist, theologian, and philosopher (Mudimbe 1988). Kagame did not disagree with Tempels's discovery. His primary objection is that a people's philosophy is best discovered in their linguistic structure rather than in their social and moral beliefs, as well as behaviors. Tempels's failure to understand Bantu thought was, for Kagame, due to the fact that he (Tempels) was not a scholar.

Using the same Aristotelian system, Kagame exposed Bantu philosophy through the application of formal logic, ontology, theodicy, cosmology, and ethics. For him, the collective, deep, implicit philosophy of the Bantu is a profound system of lived thought which is superior to the "solitary labor of a licensed thinker amid a literate civilisation" (Mudimbe 1988). He too identified *ntu* as the Bantu term for being and reality and as their basic principle of understanding nature and human experience.

Critique of ethno-philosophy

The first vigorous attack on ethno-philosophy came from F. Crahay, a professional philosopher who taught logic and modern European philosophy at Lovanium University, Kinshasa, in 1965. He made basic distinctions between the narrow intellectual discipline known as philosophy and the "broad" and "vulgar" use of the same term to refer to a people's worldview. Crahay insisted that there is nothing like intuitive or implicit philosophy, and that a lived philosophy like the one identified by Tempels and Kagame is a *Weltanschauung* which should never be confused with "explicit, analytical, radically critical and auto-critical, systematic, at least in principle and nevertheless open, bearing on experience, its human conditions, significance as well as the values that it reveals" (Crahay 1965). The *Weltanschauung* presented by Tempels, he said, contains prescientific beliefs, views and doctrines in which religious claims replace abstract, objective and scientific principles. Crahay, therefore, condemned *Bantu Philosophy* as, at best, a work of ethnology. Following a similar line of argument, Robin Horton saw African thought as coterminous with philosophy as an art. The fundamental difference for him is that while Africans use religiously coated terms to obtain religious and emotional satisfaction, Westerners use objectively specific terms to explain reality for the purpose of attaining scientific knowledge. But even then both systems employ similar rational procedures in their efforts to make sense out of conflicting human experiences. The other difference he saw was that while the African system of thought is closed because it does not recognize possible alternatives, the Western system is open because it is built on the notion that a theory today may change beyond recognition tomorrow. Some African scholars have argued that because African thought was accommodative of conflicting views, it did not develop into the adversarial style of science. For these scholars, ancient African thinkers never developed "strict" philosophy because of the non-literate and non-industrialized social conditions that prevailed in most pre-colonial African societies.

Professional philosophy

Meanwhile, around the 1950s, a number of Western-trained Africans, some of whom later dabbled in studying and teaching philosophy, had come on the scene. None of them studied African languages and culture in the way they studied Western classics and history. Neither did they see the need for doing so even when they entered into the debate about African philosophy.

But, like the professional scholar Crahay, they all felt that their discipline was being cheapened, even insulted, by ethno-philosophers. While not denying the existence of coherent rational systems of thought in some ancient African societies, these scholars defended Western paradigms of thought as universal, valid canons of ideal methodologies and procedures of formulating scientific and "strict" philosophy in contradistinction to formulating "broad," "debased," and

99

"vulgar" philosophies or worldviews. They therefore advocated the adoption of Western intellectual style as the only way of moving Africans from the level of mental primitivity to that of development and civilization. This option is sometimes seen as a choice between good and evil, even between life and death (Masolo 1992).

The point, however, is that there is, today, no unanimity about what makes some literary works African philosophy (that is, African in origin and conception) and others not. While Hountondji, for instance, insists on the authors being African in origin apart from writing for the interest and benefit of Africans (1977), Wiredu opts for a conscious African search for solutions to African problems of existence, even though one may adopt Western scientific methodology to analyze African concepts (1980). According to him, this must be done within an African understanding. It is not yet clear under what conditions a literary piece originated and developed in a language foreign to Africa can be adequately regarded as an expression within African understanding. As to what makes such a work qualify as philosophy, every professional African philosopher in this school of thought agrees that every discourse that passes muster as strict philosophy must pay necessary homage to human experience and reason, in just the way this is done in the West.

Sage philosophy

The late Professor Henry Odera Oruka dropped out of the professional school very early, even though he still distinguished between "popular" and "strict" philosophy (1972, 1976). His major concern has since been to demonstrate that some indigenous African sages who are untouched by Western education do produce philosophies that can pass both of these tests. The work of Barry Hallen and J.O. Sodipo also belong here, even though Oruka believes otherwise. For him the Yoruba *Babalawo* interviewed by Hallen and Sodipo (1986) are sages only in the sense of being uncritical custodians of traditional wisdom, as Ogotemmelli is among the Dogon.

Part of the objection to this approach is that contemporary African sages cannot but be affected by Western civilization. This, coupled with the fact that Western-trained interviewers are coproducers of the sages' thoughts, show that the African authenticity of "sage philosophy" is open to serious doubt (that is, their authenticity in the sense of being a product of African thinkers who initiated the ideas without copying foreign ideas or style of reasoning in the first instance). The other problem touches on the difficulties of drawing a clear distinction between the sage as a critical thinker and the sage as a nonreflexive custodian of folk wisdom. However, a noncritical thinker is hardly ever called a sage in most traditional African societies.

Contemporary developments

This chequered history of the major trends in answering questions about African philosophy reveals that several problems remain unresolved. What exactly does the phrase "Western philosophy" mean if it is to be posited against "African philosophy"? If the former label can accommodate German, French, and American philosophies, for instance, what is wrong in condoning the existence of Yoruba, Igbo, Bantu, or Akan philosophies in the latter?

Some have, for instance, argued that since it was possible for the Austrian-born Ludwig Wittgenstein to write British philosophy, it should be possible for non-Africans to write African philosophy. This argument misses out on a strong point. It fails to recognize the fact that Wittgenstein studied under the most influential British philosopher of his time – Bertrand Russell. It is therefore very doubtful whether Wittgenstein could have successfully done what he did if his tutelage had *not* been in the British tradition of philosophy. What this shows is that one can hardly talk of British philosophy, for instance, if there is no specific tradition so identifiable. This may not necessarily mean that cultural philosophies are adequately characterized as the common sharing of one metaphysical and/or epistemological position, as is done in the cases of British, German, or French philosophies. At least Africa is not just a country, but an entire continent. However, there is the need to identify and be trained within a universe which can accommodate various forms of philosophical position. Discussion about the existence of African philosophy is a rational requirement which cannot be easily wished away. This perhaps explains why a number of different groups still continue to address one or another of these crucial issues.

The historical group

According to Oruka, members of this group record African oral passages without characterizing them. D.M. Masolo, Claude Sumner, Henry Olela, Y. V. Mudimbe, and Lucius Outlaw are all classified here. The last two have, however, been charged with accommodating almost every African text, without showing particular interest in arguing for or against their being classifiable as African philosophy.

Critical traditionalists

Members of this school try to critically examine, analyze, and identify some basic concepts like witchcraft, reincarnation, destiny, truth, God, etc., as perennial problems of philosophy. The trend is to demonstrate that although the precepts of both experience and reason are adhered to in African thought and understanding, no permanent solutions to these issues exist either in the West or in Africa. Gyekye, Sodipo, Makinde, and Oluwole can in a sense be classified here.

This approach has been challenged as carrying out analyses which can be adequately done by language experts. This is similar to Noam Chomsky's argument, which involves a confusion of the semantic and linguistic analysis of language with the philosophical endeavor to critically examine the metaphysico-epistemological underpinnings of language. However, Mudimbe's charge that many works here contain orthodox and purely speculative undertakings must be given some merit. But his claim that many of the subjects discussed are scandalous is mainly directed against "Africans who wrote in Europe when there was no Germany" (Mudimbe 1988).

The universalists

There are some professional philosophers who still insist that logos and nous are inviolable elements of every "strict" philosophy anywhere in the world. Their recognition of the possibility of culturally defined and relative truths does not debar them from seeing philosophy as the search for absolute certainty. Hence, although most of them believe in the possibility of local creations, they refuse to give up the idea that some logical and scientific strictures are universally valid canons of assessing every local philosophy. The dilemma here is obvious. To preach the grafting of African ideas onto a Western conceptual structure defeats the very purpose of mental decolonization in philosophy which many of them now call for. The point is that there are no rational procedures of demonstrating the absolute certainty of the basic assumptions of any one particular conceptual system. Every cultural and/or rational variation necessarily becomes relative to a particular ideology, or set of axioms, etc.

The Egyptologists

These philosophers are engaged in an effort to revive the belief in the existence of a traditional African intellectual culture. They claim the existence of an existing African intellectual tradition of philosophy on which a modern African philosophy can be built. Innocent Onyewuenyi and Lansana Keita are prominent names here.

Future prospects and difficulties

Some scholars now claim that all cultural identities are imaginary and consequently tantamount to a creation of myths (Appiah 1985); others continue to warn against a wholesale adoption of Western theories and methodologies – most especially Western gnosis. The contemporary concern of many African scholars, however, is the deconstruction of the myth of African mental inferiority and the reconstruction of a rationally viable African intellectual culture. And this, it is assumed, can be done either by taking a cue from an existing African tradition of philosophy or by starting a completely new tradition in the belief that no viable one existed before the colonial era.

Over and above these are others whose major interest lies in formulating social theories which will move Africans forward from their present state of underdevelopment. This group is made up mainly of young scholars who maintain the socialist perspective that philosophy is meant to change the world. Regarding the Western style of philosophizing as adequate, they want to fill into its grids elements of African experience, during colonial and postcolonial times.

Condemning all forms of negritude and ethno-philosophy as mythological, they argue that African unity and identity can only evolve from the common recognition of the problems of colonialization and contemporary economic exploitation of Africans by neocolonialists.

Two major objections can be raised against the last view. Africa had existed long before colonialism. Its identity cannot therefore solely be derived from that "short parenthesis." The claim that different peoples of the continent had nothing in common before colonialism has been shown as false by many historians. Secondly, if liberation means accepting entirely foreign paradigms and parameters, then we may need a new understanding of the relevance of African mental liberation.

Hermeneutic orientation

The hermeneutic approach stresses the importance of studying African oral texts in their original forms and within the social conditions of their production: myths, legends, fables, proverbs, aphorisms, etc., most especially those that relate to political, economic, and religious principles that guide human existence. The goal is neither to celebrate nor to condemn every element of ancient African thought. African philosophy, when situated within the intellectual heritage of Africans, should present a true picture of an African tradition of thought – a distinctive, rational endeavour which can yield theories whose execution will promote the socioeconomic conditions of the peoples of Africa.

This trend, as promoted by scholars like Lucius Outlaw (1987) and S. B. Oluwele (1996), coincides with some basic tenets of postmodernism which recognize that philosophical theories are as much universal as they are contextual and culturally determined. The attitude is to respect local creativity and examine each text within its own axioms and framework. An African approach to philosophy may, therefore, be judged as distinct yet not overshadowed by the so-called universal precepts.

African philosophy, for this group, will emerge within a discipline which can demonstrate the adequacy of its peculiar features and style of reasoning. Like Western philosophy, African thought-process may not necessarily meet all the demands of Crahay and Hountondji, but it would have enough evidence of its being critical and strict if and when it pays due homage to the essence of its own logic, as well as develop cogent justifications for its own way of understanding reality.

Many practical and theoretical problems bedevil this view. Since there is little or no written record of various developments in African thought, the intellectual yardstick for treating some African narratives as philosophy is sometimes not easily available. This means that any text of oral literature may be treated as communal or anonymous. The lack of an adequate means of establishing the possible existence of different schools of thought and subcultural variations in ancient African thought is a serious problem, yet the viable alternative is to relapse back into ethno-philosophy.

It is important, however, to note that no phenomenal rupture in the form of a true revolution has actually occurred in African philosophy since Levy-Bruhl's statement about an African prelogical and prescientific mentality (1978). The proposed theoretical cogency of African religico-mythological systems by some anthropologists and philosophers links up very well with Levy-Bruhl's claim of African weakness in logical and scientific thought. And this, when combined with the new claim of the necessity of written texts, leaves African (intellectual) culture in the original inferior position as assigned it by some Western thinkers.

African feminist philosophy

Feminist philosophy, some will argue, "has existed for centuries" in the West (Nagl-Docekal 1990). The same claim cannot, however, be made for African feminist philosophy. Feminist discussions among most African scholars belong mainly to African women's studies: attempts to document various forms of female oppression both in modern and traditional African societies.

Many generations of Western writers have characterized the African woman as timid, passive, and family-oriented. African women in the traditional setting have been depicted as victims of the worst type of male chauvinism, while Western women are said to have become dynamic and knowledgeable beings who have fought against similar oppressions in their traditional societies and have won for themselves social, economic, and political liberation. This group of foreign scholars was later joined by some internationally based, Western-educated Africans whose expertise and knowledge of African cultures did not go far beyond their being Africans by origin.

Again, the urge to present a homogeneous image of the "African woman" prevented the recognition of the heterogeneity of precolonial African societies. Authentic African views about the male–female relationship in their societies became blurred by Western ideology and the unquestioned assumption that sexism occurred under similar parochial conditions of male chauvinists in all human societies.

The predominant Western views about human nature and reality that determine male–female relationships are to be found in the entire spectrum of their intellectual culture – in Western religion, history, literature, their sciences and philosophy, and, more recently, in the social sciences. The ideal human being in Western thought is man. In religion, the woman is an appendage, an afterthought whose evil deed brought woe to the entire race of mankind and their generations. In science, the woman is regarded as the weaker sex; as a more feeble, less intelligent, less objective species of human beings more given to moral and religious piety.

One of the fundamental problems of the development of African feminist philosophy today is the lack of actual texts in which the existence of specific African views on women can be identified, apart from merely drawing inferences from anthropological studies of the socioeconomic and political roles of women in different traditional African societies.

Quite fortunately, however, this lack of sizeable written documentation of ancient African thought does not totally rob us of several traditional views on men, women, and human relationships. There are many African societies today where several verbal arts are still practiced and where great collections of songs, liturgies, proverbs, stories, and aphorisms which express specific beliefs and worldviews can still be found. Some predominant views about women and socially accepted principles of their relationships to men can be directly located in several of such texts. It is these traditional views that some African feminist philosophers, as well as female writers, have started to identify and expose to critical analysis and synthesis for possible future development.

The oral traditions of many societies on the continent of Africa characterize many women as initiators and practitioners of verbal arts, as successful professionals and inventors of food technology. It has now been established through oral history, archaeology, and other forms of research that women dominated the economic, social, and political spheres of life in many traditional African societies. A number of researchers believe that African women were able to do all this because they were traditionally accorded extensive opportunities for self-realization and development. Some historians, like Professor Bolanle Awe (1977), argue that African women were economically disempowered and politically disenfranchised during the colonial era, even though they did not enjoy equality with men in many traditional societies.

Some African writers and researchers believe that many African women, most especially at grassroots level, are still strongly committed to the survival of their family, even of their immediate society, mainly because they continue to employ these basic traditional principles of the male–female relationship.

There is, however, another school of thought which cautions against the dangers of eulogizing the success of a few women in traditional African societies. The need to understudy the exploitative structures that made the achievements of such women possible is being stressed. The argument is that the reality of a few successful women in traditional Africa must not be allowed to overshadow the oppression of millions of other women, even by these aristocratic females. The conclusion is that African women still need liberation and empowerment programs if they are to keep pace with women's development in other parts of the world.

Future prospects: tradition and continuity

African feminist philosophers can make legitimate contributions in the main area of African philosophy only if clear distinctions are drawn within the discipline itself. Mere sociological and/or anthropological characterizations of African women and their different roles in society do not constitute African feminist philosophy. Interested scholars have to go beyond identifying and discussing social issues as they affect African women. Feminist philosophy must challenge

105

basic African assumptions about the nature of reality, man, woman, and knowledge such that they can critically examine the intellectual edifice on which African types of sexism are or were based. This is what will provide the basis for a better understanding of the African brand of sexism and the validity or otherwise of different justifications for recommending positive changes within existing principles of male–female relationships in African societies. The expected radical revolution in societal values and ideals will never occur if this fundamental step is not taken. The recognition of the dignity of all human beings depends largely on the development of an adequate African worldview that justifies male–female equality.

For philosophers to discover, understand, and appreciate African traditional views about womanhood, about male–female relationships, it is not necessary to create a black ghetto as an antithesis to Western paradigms or to completely step out of the demand for rationality as some have hitherto tried to do in African philosophy per se. The point is that unless the basic ideas, beliefs, and principles of human existence upon which African principles of organizing society are founded are identified and adequately analyzed, it may be difficult to change the present social attitudes of men towards women's rights in politics, economics, and other social spheres of human life.

A number of African writers and scholars have made some proposals about what they regard as African traditional worldview. For example, the late Professor Zulu Sofola explained:

> According to African world-view, existence is perceived as a positive expression of the creative energy whose reality can only be sustained through a harmonious balance within its essence and through a peaceful co-existence of all its parts... .
> From this type of world-view. the African (sees) society as an organic reality. as inclusive rather than exclusive; xenophilic rather than xenophobic; communal rather than an individualistic entity. (Sofola, in Hudson-Weems 1996)

Sofola was of course mindful that this lofty worldview did not make African thinkers blind to the negative side of existence. She noted that while African men never treated their women as equals, they never regarded them as possessors of only negative qualities. The philosophical implication of this worldview is that it provides a basis for the better understanding of the unequal treatment of men and women in many traditional African societies.

One fundamental question must still be raised and, if possible, adequately answered: Are there actual oral texts which bear testimony to the existence of this identified African view about women and the male–female relationship? Do we have these principles directly expressed in words or are they mere machinations of some contemporary African philosophers who want to chart an enviable course for African traditional thought?

The unsettled situation of African philosophy itself is likely to hold back cogent answers to these and other relevant questions within African feminist philosophy. Yet as long as we continue to neglect serious investigations into both contemporary and traditional expressions of ideas and beliefs, so shall the development of professional African philosophy and along with it that of African feminist philosophy be retarded. Philosophy is a concern with human thought rather than a concern with the direct analysis of social actions. African feminist philosophy is not likely to take off until serious attention is paid to the study of African oral texts as the source of all African thought. It is African-expressed ideas that feminist philosophers have to investigate, critically analyze and examine, and interpret, after full understanding.

This conclusion points to the inescapability of the adoption of the hermeneutic orientation, first in African philosophy and by implication in African feminist philosophy. Philosophy itself cannot continue to neglect the study of African thought both in the past and in the present. A people's body of beliefs and ideas constitute the basic materials philosophers work with. If African feminist philosophy is ever to develop as a serious area of philosophical studies in Africa then African views and ideology, their specific style of thinking and formulating principles of existence must be directly analyzed and cogently criticized. Otherwise all talk of African feminist philosophy may be nothing more than an involvement in another version of African women's studies and hence an exercise subject to suspect as a cogent philosophical endeavor.

11

China

LIN CHUN, LIU BOHONG, AND JIN YIHONG

What is feminist philosophy? A difficult question for feminist scholars in China. Women's studies in the Chinese mainland are characteristically policy-oriented, geared to practical concerns and moral urgency. Empirical research projects engage many pressing social issues related to the changing situation of women in a rapid marketification of society and commercialization of culture since the post-1978 reform movement. Here are some examples: migrant female workers and their working conditions in the urban centers; the impact of rural industrialization on women in the countryside: discrimination against women in employment as well as in other aspects of social life; marriage and sexual relations. What follows in this article however, represents an effort to identify and categorize trends in emerging feminist theories. The main questions that might be seen as in one way or another philosophical are located in the historical context of the transformation of Chinese socialism. As we have only very limited access to publications in Hong Kong and Taiwan, to avoid mispresentation we regret that we cannot discuss the feminist work developed in these areas.

The emergence of women's studies

Since the late 1970s, China has entered an era of economic and political reforms and an opening-up to the outside world, aiming at a "socialist market economy" with "Chinese characteristics." The new problems with regard to women's rights and interests brought about by wide-ranging social changes generate challenges to the established Communist ideology of gender equality and its public consensus. It is against this background – retreat of the state and advance of the market – that women's studies and other autonomous activities are beginning to flourish. These movements have involved active participation from both official institutions, in particular the All-China Women's Federation (ACWF) and its local as well as research branches (which now all claim to be nongovernment organizations (NGOs)), and the newly formed NGOs and concerned individuals of both sexes.

This development can be roughly divided into an initial stage, from the early 1980s to 1989, and a consolidation and expansion stage, from 1990 onwards. The campaign for "liberating the mind" (1978–9) indicated a fundamental reorientation of the party line. But it also paved the way for the creation of autonomous spheres more or less independent of the state authority, first and

108

best constituted and represented by the women's movements. Despite all the subsequent setbacks, the flow of information and traveling of ideas, free thinking, communicating, and even organizing became feasible. Many scholars also began to become aware of "Western feminism," still taken as largely homogeneous with regard to either the "West" or "feminism." They also put on the agenda the legitimization of women's studies as an interdisciplinary field of scholarly invest-igation.

The second stage featured growing feminist discussions and impact after the Tiananmen Square incident (1989) and the collapse of the Soviet Union. These internal and external crises helped some Party ideologues to resist "bourgeois liberalization" by resuming some political control. It was remarkable, however, that the "Woman Question" soon broke the silence within intellectual circles. This might be due partly to the uncontroversial legitimacy in the Communist tradition of discussing women's liberation; and partly to the ironic marginality of the question which was never politically threatening for the authorities. More-over, there was also a common recognition of the actual need for a feminist answer to the mounting social problems in the 1990s. More recently, attention to gender issues showed an even stronger presence in national affairs, high-lighted by the fourth UN Conference held in Beijing (1995) and works under-taken around it. Other intellectually significant events include, to mention just a few, the 1993 Tianjin feminist seminar in which the concept of "gender" was introduced into Chinese ("shehuixingbie" or "social sex"), waves of translation and publication of feminist readings, and the 1995 Beijing international sympo-sium on feminist thought (Philosophy Summer School), which facilitated lively exchanges between Chinese and foreign participants.

The Marxist tradition

But the awareness of the gap between experience and needs of the women of China and those in the West remains overwhelming. The dominant tradition within women's studies in China continues to be, by and large, Marxist in political terms. Quite often it is difficult to clearly distinguish government policy statements from the actual convictions of concerned women. In other words, the long standing consensus on a feminism conceived in universalist and socialist terms persists in spite of doubts, contentions, and outside influence. In an attempt to reaffirm the official commitment to women while countering "bour-geois feminism," the Party General Secretary (Jiang Zemin 1990) found an occasion to restate the standard Marxist views such as the historical nature of women's oppression, their participation in social production as a precondition for gender equality, and the liberation of women as a natural measure of the degree of social emancipation.

Beyond these familiar principles, feminist scholars working within the Marxist tradition have tried to update the issue by asking new questions. Paying no attention to the poststructuralist dismissal of "origin," these scholars wish to explore the origins of women's subordination in human civilization in general and also in a socialist society in particular. Since it has always been an established argument within the historical materialist framework that private ownership and class exploitation are the root causes of gender inequality (summarized in Luo Qiong 1986), then what is the explanation for the unfulfilled liberation of women after a thoroughgoing socialist revolution in China, in which private property was eliminated and the exploiting classes overthrown? To what extent might this be explained by economic backwardness? By what was believed to be the imperative necessity of "internal accumulation"? By political and cultural "vestiges of the old society"? By the persistence of traditional gender division of labor under socialism, despite women's massive participation in public productive and other activities (the "double-burden," job restriction, social expectation on gender roles, etc.)? By the claim that universal liberation was incomplete because of the absence of a fully democratic citizenry (involving not so much gender relations as the power relationship between women – and men as well – and the state)? These questions become all the more pressing when reform has seriously revalidated private property rights and exploitation (to a limited degree), and has hence further complicated the case for a Marxist interpretation to be upheld in a "socialist market" environment.

Marxist scholars commonly take the development of productive forces as the primary material basis of women's liberation. The assumption that there is a positive correlation between economic growth and the advance of women is, however, largely accepted without critical examination (e.g. Li Jingzhi et al. 1992). The "central task" of the women's movement, as some leading theorists (Tao Chunfang et al. 1991, p. 223) argue, "is to develop social production and meanwhile, seek liberation by pushing forward social development." Very often "social production" and "social development" are used more or less interchangeably. Even those who acknowledge that material and technological progress cannot automatically liberate women do not doubt that the ultimate eradication of women's subordination lies in economic modernization (cf. Guan Tao 1993). It is thus a commonplace in women's studies that the gender issue must be brought into the overall project of socioeconomic construction. As the ACWF Vice-President (Huang Qizao 1992) put it, serving the Party's central line of economic development "is to safeguard the rights and interests of women in the most fundamental way." Such a conviction, apparently with a ring of economic determinism, nonetheless has less to do with any doctrine than with the popular desire for breaking away from poverty. More recently, however, this confidence in the productive forces has been increasingly questioned. Scholars in women's studies begin to see the distinction between economic growth and social development as a matter of creative and normative contestation, and have introduced the UN notion of (socially and ecologically) "sustainable development" into public awareness.

The theme of productivity as the "driving force of history" coincides well with the traditional Marxist assertion that women's liberation is an integral (though not thereby automatic) part of the universal cause of proletarian class struggle, social revolution, and human emancipation. The Chinese revolution served as a

110

vindication of this assertion. It is so in the sense that the female population was seen and duly articulated in the Party program as among the foremost victims of the old powers – imperialism and its local agents, in particular the indigenous "feudal" rule and tradition mingled with patriarchal clanship – which the revolution had defeated. The post-revolutionary regime's pro-women legislation and policies demonstrated deliberate continuation of the Party's commitment to women, which made a tremendous positive difference in women's fate and lives in China. However, many flaws in this Communist feminism might be identified. For example, the epistemological foundation of state protection is preoccupied not only with women's social victimization but also, prejudicially, with their "natural" disadvantages, defects, or disabilities as a physiologically "weaker" and otherwise variously troubled sex. The much concerned problem of "dependency" – a mentality of women that features their relationship with the government – is also attributable to state-sponsored feminism and its paternalistic discourse. But these, and other possibly valid criticisms, cannot lead to an overall dismissal. For, to say the very least, to comprehend Chinese women's appreciation for the revolution in which they themselves voluntarily participated is to locate their ideas and actions today in their proper historical context.

In fact, it becomes more difficult than ever before to insist on any absolute unity between women's and "social" needs being represented by a socialist state (an immediate but complicated case is the government's one-child policy, which simultaneously corresponds and conflicts with "women's interests" – we may assume that women have some basic common interests, including multiple reproductive rights, and yet the policy has a rather broad support, especially among urban women). Likewise, the leadership role of the Communist Party in women's liberation is losing priority and, for some, even relevance. It is not enough to recognize the "specific interests" of women in a reciprocal relationship between them and the general public interests of the people as a whole, partly because these diverse and sometimes conflicting interests depend to a large extent on political struggle, manipulation, and articulation. Not to get into the open question about the nature of the transformation of Maoist socialism, one simply cannot overlook all kinds of contradictions of the reform process. Market preference or "economic rationality," for example, can be at odds with women's employment with the maternity and other benefits hitherto protected by the law. Should women support a reform, then, whose market logic and commercial values begin to dictate social attitudes against equality but, on the other hand, whose political liberalization makes room for individual freedom, self-realization, and voluntary organization? Although generally speaking women have been themselves conscious reformers (while class, regional, professional, age, and other divisions, including political difference among them, must not be ignored), it is by no means self-evident that the path to their liberation runs parallel to a single-minded national economic development. Being conscious of this, feminism in China inevitably becomes a representative moral voice of social conscience.

It is clear that the mainstream of women's studies as recounted above is recognized as Marxist mostly in a practical political and strategic sense. What

111

Marxist feminism has gone through in the West – in various ways deconstructing and reconstructing Marxism – has not happened in China. However, scholars have increasingly appreciated the openness of Marxism as a scientific inquiry rather than a state ideology, which should lead to serious intellectual engagement. Major breakthroughs in theory would in turn be likely to assist the confrontation of politically sensitive questions, such as democracy, political reform, and independent union movements which would involve women workers. The existence of a state agenda for women, institutionalized with a nationwide women's organizational network, has been of genuine lasting effect. But when a top-down pattern of mobilization is no longer viable, it becomes practically urgent to clarify such issues as who should and can represent women, why women's political independence is so important, where to forge battles against discrimination and abuse, and what should constitute a feminist program for China's social reform.

Feminism

From within the Chinese Marxist tradition, for the first time a revisionist trend has emerged, advocating a gendered identity of women, which amounts to a conscious resistance against a gender-blind Marxism centered only on class analysis. Historically, women in Communist China used to believe that the degree of their liberation was rather high, surely incomparably higher than all the previous generations in an ancient civilization and probably also higher than women in most other contemporary countries. (Why does the apparent contradiction here, between the judgment of women's advance in the conditions of economic backwardness and the tendency toward economic determinism noted earlier not appear to be a problem?) To be sure, the actual achievements of Chinese socialism for women sustained such a belief. But the misleading social experiment of equality through sameness also left a powerful imprint. It is misleading because, as is now widely realized, the traditional image/knowledge of fixed gender roles and male supremacy can be rejected without challenging the false universality of male desires and abilities. Economic reform has been a catalyst, especially for the educated, to reevaluate the situation: women are still way behind in many aspects of life in China, and there is no such thing as automatic or inevitable simultaneity between progress in the conditions of existence of the two sexes, between class and women's liberation, and between women's advancement and national modernization. Moreover, as a revolt against that artificial sameness, with all its political and ideological implications, there has also emerged a sidelight fetishism, aided by commercial forces, of an equally artifical "femininity" and even of the traditional gender norm.

This new consciousness of identity, self-described as an awakening, has undergone an intellectual operation of a series of "separations." That is, theoretically, separate women's liberation from the "proletarian emancipation" or the "socialist revolution;" academically, separate women's studies from traditional knowledge production of the humanities and social sciences; and strategically, separate the women's movements from state molding and control. Central to the project is to make "women" a distinct category vis-à-vis the concept of "class," and hence considering women's liberation to possess some meanings and goals which are different from or beyond those of class liberation and elimination. (This of course does not necessarily diverge from the view of classical Marxist thinkers, who sometimes see women as making up a special underclass, or even as the very first exploited socioeconomic class. While on a par with other exploited, oppressed, and marginalized people, the question of women is for them not identical with that of others.) A pioneer theorist (Li Xiao Jiang 1989, p. 34) asserts that

> women and class are two different categories: the former is human ontological and the latter, social historical. The making and evolution of the female sex was prior to the formation of classes and intrinsically transcends class relations. Under certain historical circumstances, women acquire class identities through [their relationships with] men and are indirectly dictated by the commands of class struggle. However, the issues of class antagonism and its resolution by no means embrace the issues of women....

This passage, from our point of view, is in a sense transitional, representing only an initial thought exercise. Given the specific Chinese background, that women normally did not own property and a female individual's class status was determined by the Communist authorities on the basis of the economic status of the male head of her family, it is an understandable observation that the class identities of women are imposed from outside their "original" places. However, this is not a tenable theoretical proposition: if women are by themselves "classless," then they are essentially excluded from the social web which also absorbs and transforms gender relations along with other specific relations, and which is the very context where their subordination and liberation would make sense. Moreover, isn't regarding class emancipation as a male or male-dominated process exactly what feminism intends to resist?

But what is striking is perhaps the essentialist inclination of this statement by a splendid scholar and organizer who soon came to proclaim that the (intellectual) task of separation was basically fulfilled and women must now, apparently in the sense of reconciling particularities with something more universal, "rejoin society." The problems which confront us today, she (Li Xiao Jiang 1993, pp. 31–2) points out, "are not merely, even not mainly, women's problems." A narrowminded and narrowly defined feminism no longer fits China's great social transformation. Later on she has implicitly abandoned the view that the identity of women is somehow pregiven and "ontologically" fixed rather than historically and socially produced. However, many in women's studies disagree with her assessment of the completion of "separating." The new slogan of "connecting with the international track" of the women's movements worldwide, inspired by the UN Conference and by such notions as "empowerment", has also reinforced the desire to defend a "room of one's own" for women. Meanwhile, it is puzzling

113

that women's studies in China in general remain preoccupied by versions of reductionism, especially by a biological deterministic perception. The biology of reproduction, for example, is rarely recognized at the conceptual level as itself construed and institutionalized variously in particular historical settings. This is indeed surprising, given the all too familiar Chinese practice of human intervention in the supposedly natural process of procreation: the forceful cultural preference for giving birth to boys, or direct state control in family planning.

The separation project is from the outset also a project of seeking an independent female subject and subjectivity in both social being and thinking. From the "gendered personality" to a "gender-woman angle of view" (Du Fangqin 1993b), from "making up the missed lesson" of (re)constructing a collective consciousness of women to liberation beyond participation and equality (Li Xiao Jiang 1995), the new terms and ideas are all directed toward a repositioning of women in "history" and "society." Speaking of epistemology, a noted historian (Du Fangqin 1993b, p. 7) advocates "a female viewpoint" that will enrich human understanding of the world and of themselves. It can fill the gaps in our cognitive past created by male bias and social prejudice, she says, hence contributing to a more complete system of knowledge. The job intended here, as we see it, is no more than to supplement and adjust a distorted picture that we were taught to conceive. Should we, however, expect something fundamentally reordered or redrawn? Also, compared to male eyes, do women see things differently and acquire different knowledge? Do they even occupy an epistemologically privileged standpoint? But why and how should it be so, and who is this female knowing subject in the first place? Is she already and always there, homogeneous, coherently recognizable, and without ambiguity and contingency? After all, any "subject" would have to possess some (situated) knowledge about itself, then how is that knowledge actually produced? These questions are not addressed in China, nor any substantial elaboration of what is exactly wrong with what we know. The urge to "deconstruct" a universalist outlook, however, is clearly expressed.

At the political level, it is also obscure to us as to whether there is such a thing as a given but lost identity which is only to be rediscovered. Whether and in what way the subject and subjectivity of women existed before (one could argue, for example, that there was, even in a typically male-dominated Confucian culture, a persistent literary tradition that cherished the humanity and independence of women) and vanished at some points on the tortuous paths toward Chinese modernity? In particular, was the female as subject really suppressed by national and social emancipatory struggles from the mid-nineteenth century? In that case, were men also subordinated, and what about their subjectivities? Or, were the revolution and modernization, as critically elaborated mostly outside China, themselves masculine and even patriarchal in nature? Indeed, if a conscious female subject was actually absent in tradition, had these modern-day, historically transformative movements actually started the process of building it, while perhaps falling short of its eventual formation? The debate among feminist scholars over the timing of "completing" this process and hence "returning" to the social whole also revealed that they in the end agree with each other upon the resumption of the ultimately supreme value of the "universality," as soon as its connotation undergoes a feminist scrutiny and reinterpretation.

It is clear that the "separation" movement differs considerably from conceptualization of "difference" and identity politics in Western feminism, especially in terms of power relations. Much due to the public character of patriarchy under state socialism and the effects of public education and intervention in domestic lives against what the Chinese learned to call "feudal" attitudes, one is tempted to say that the female population are by and large more liberated at home than in the public sphere as citizens. The market reform has begun to reset the scene, but the feminist concern in China is still not mainly with "private" relations around the family and sexuality (although scholarly works have begun to appear, e.g. Min Jiayin 1995), also because the physiological difference between the two sexes is often seen as decisive among other (consequential) differences, fixed or even fatal. Rather, the Chinese concern is fundamentally with the relationship between women and the supposed universal totality. It is this relationship – which is changing and viewed from concrete historical experience – between women on the one hand, and the state, the nation, the society, the commonality on the other, that primarily dictates and situates the language, the strategy, the future program and direction of Chinese feminism. Somewhere connecting these two divergent concerns should be the role of the political authority in the processes of gender differentiation and identification; but this is not discussed. Also missing in the separation discourse are such topics central to feminism in the West as "ethnicity," "cultural identity/difference," religious and sexual orientations, etc. ("race" is irrelevant when the discussions are confined to a racially homogeneous society).

Could there be exclusions, therefore, in the universalizing identity of "Chinese women"? Scholars in women's studies in China are always conscious of diversities among women, especially big gaps between urban and rural conditions, and different experiences between the Hans and the national minorities. This recognition, however, does not prevent them from seeking a common ground and a unified category of identity for women. This particular universalism is articulated in a simplified manner without touching deeper philosophical questions of "human nature" or female (human) nature. Feminist reason is also made instrumental when, in a dialectical twist, it is viewed as best representing the universal interests of the country, when what constitutes (gender) equality is distinguished from that of liberation (if only because of the familiar reality of the equal share among men and women of social inequalities), when feminism is taken as a project of creating free individuality and democratic citizenship. There is no such division of labour in China, for example, as the male discourse of rights and justice and the female ethics of care. Indeed, somehow distant from "theory," Chinese feminism speaks first and foremost for basic social justice in a "socialist market" situation: against poverty, abuses of women and children including child labor, economic polarization, social disparities, corruption, money fetishism and

115

commercialization of cultural values; for government accountability and open policy discussions, education especially of neglected rural girls, equal employment, public medical service and women's health care, environmental protection, and so on. Its rhetoric is feminine and its concern, also in the form of social criticism, is universal.

Against gender politics

There is a smaller trend in women's studies, involving both female and male scholars, which seems to claim an a priori universalist humanism while rejecting any "gendered judgement." An influential sociologist of sexuality (Pan Suiming 1989, pp. 176–7) insists that since "gender problems are generated by (intellectual) genderism," or the assertion of gender itself creates problems, the unbound development of human beings would require an elimination of gender consciousness in every aspect of life. Making judgment least on the ground of gender difference, he writes, is "the only way out for women to resolve their own problems and problems in sexual relations." If the tone of this appeal carries some Marxist inspiration, its astonishingly ahistorical perspective does not. However, if we consider the question of (re)constructing democracy, it is worth debating whether gender differences should become nonpertinent to the concept of social citizenship.

Different from such deliberate gender blindness, there is also a tendency similarly against politicized gender identity but celebrating female particularities and sexual difference. A young scholar (Zhou Yi 1996) has proposed to (re)build a theory of "natural balance": male and female interactions "jointly demonstrate both their internal and external social values." Rejecting construing gender inequality as being rooted in the gender division of labor, she believes that "the more sophisticated the division of labor is, the more the mutual dependence and integration of the two sexes become. The result, as a human voluntary choice, is inevitably equilibrating." Here we have these preexisting and biologically determined categories of men and women, who (should) live in harmony and whose differences are mutually beneficial. The concept of "equality" thus becomes almost irrelevant, so does the false dilemma of equality versus difference that trapped so many feminists in the West. It is also an ironic contrast to note that the introduction of antiessentialist feminism, including postmodernist and postcolonial polemics, into China, has turned to help various attempts in not so much "deconstructing" as destroying feminist consciousness and promises from a premodern position of Chinese traditionalism.

It might indeed be worthwhile for women's studies in China to look closely at our traditional culture which is, after all, not one single tradition. Although much of that culture may be fundamentally conservative and repressive, especially with regard to the place of women, we will be able to emancipate ourselves from it only through careful and critical evaluations. The core of essential humanism in Chinese philosophy, for example, is to see Yin and Yang, the two opposing principles in nature respectively represented by feminine and masculine, as in a harmonious unity. Is there anything valuable in this proposition? Is there even some affinity in its recent revival, in effect, for the socialist aspiration for cooperation and solidarity? It is also interesting to notice that the scholars exploring possible feminist implications of Confucianism and neoConfucianism, notably in ethics of care, are mostly Chinese living overseas (cf. Tao 1995).

Conclusion

It is a delicate position to be on one front confronting current Western ideas with suspicion ("orientalism"? cultural imperialism? imposed representation or misrepresentation of the "other?" foreign fetishism? dogmatism?) while on the other front facing the Chinese heritage of political culture with ambivalence (national dignity and socialist pride versus "Asiatic mode" of cultural production? "Oriental despotism"? "feudal" patriarchy? manipulation? backwardness?). This of course is not new, and the conflict between modernism and nationalism is a permanent puzzle that modern Chinese intellectuals must solve in our country's prolonged struggle for prosperity and recognition. There is something illuminating here in the trajectory of Chinese women: Women's liberation has taken a unique route which selectively explored foreign influences, while women's studies are taking shape by reading their similarities and differences from Western feminism. Yet feminist theorizing in China is only in its initial stages. It has just begun to look deep inside many aspects, personal as well as social, of the historical "woman." It will flourish, however, if only because women's studies are indispensable in orienting and reorienting the transformation of Chinese society.

Note

The authors wish to express their gratitude to the following friends and colleagues for their stimulating discussions and suggestions: Cai Yiping, Du Fangqin, Feng Yuan, Li Dun, Liu Dongxiao, Pu Wei, Tan Shen, Wang Zheng, and Yan Haiping. Alison Jaggar's encouragement and help, as well as Robert S. Cohen's critical comments, were indispensable and most appreciated. The English text was prepared by Lin Chun who is responsible for any errors.

12

The Indian subcontinent

VRINDA DALMIYA

Meta-theoretical comments

> Feminism, as appropriated and defined by the West, has too often become a
> tool of cultural imperialism. The definitions, the terminology, the assump-
> tions, even the issues, the forms of struggles and institutions are exported
> from west to east. (Kishwar 1990)
> When the dominant strand in Western feminism articulated its own solutions
> to (those) problems, it did so in a way that only addressed the contra-
> dictions principally as women from such social formations experienced
> them. Other contradictions, which had their source, say, in patriarchy as it
> was historically constituted by class, by colonialism, or by caste, which would
> have shaped the subordination of a working-class woman in India ... and
> determined her selfhood or subjectivity, were simply not addressed. (Tharu
> and Lalita 1991)

The politics of the us/them or West/East divide forms the backdrop to philosophizing about, for and by women in India. Starting with an awareness that
"Western woman" cannot mean the same as "Indian woman," the philosopher
here is easily led to an antiessentialism and explosion of a monolithic idea of
woman. With such diffusion comes also a variegation in a monochrome "feminism"; for if subjects are multiple, so also are the blueprints for their emancipation.
Resting content with a plurality of feminisms might seem an obvious solution
here; but then, it is also natural to wonder whether a simple grammatical
pluralization can create space for genuine conceptual diversity, given the
entrenched (and Western) associations of the term.

The decision to reject the label "feminism" or to retain it as a family resemb-
lance term does not exhaust the battle against cultural imperialism. The attempt
to grow something uniquely *ours* demands an aggressively fresh start –
beginning with the material conditions and lives of women in India (to identify
issues) and dipping into the indigenous cultural and philosophical tradition (to
articulate alternatives). But even this is problematic. Firstly, there is no *one*
tradition in India. Pasts are made and traditions invented by ideologically guided
principles of selection. Secondly, given its hopelessly patriarchal structures, any

configuration of traditional material can hardly be seen as yielding a *women's* philosophy. And finally, even if a feminist reinterpretation of the tradition were possible, the difference in paradigms of traditional rationality can easily generate skepticism about obtaining a feminist *philosophy*. Feminist philosophy in India is thus doubly subaltern. The struggle to show that "feminism" appended to "philosophy" does not generate an oxymoron is well known. In the context of India, the imputed incoherence is also between "Indian" and "feminism" and, more insidiously, between "Indian" and "philosophy." It is not surprising, then, that some have chosen to go beyond tradition in their assertion of "Indianness," or have not cared whether their prescriptions for the emancipation of women in India were "Indian."

What emerges is a metaphilosophical terrain where the basic patriarchal split between outer(public)/inner(private) is interwoven with two other dichotomies – West/East(India) and modern/traditional. A plethora of "feminist" positions can be plotted vis-à-vis these polarities. What follows below is a collage of only some ideas thrown up by this dialectic.

Some voices from the mainstream

Mention of women philosophers is found even in sources as classical as the *Upaniṣads*. Maitreyi and Gargi are the oft-cited examples. Lesser known, but more interesting, is Ubhayabharati, the wife of Mandana Misra. In a historic debate between Sankaracarya (the founder of Advaita Vedānta) and Mandana (a follower of the rival school, Mīmāmsā), Ubhayabharati was made the umpire. Seeing her husband lose ground, she is supposed to have taken over the questioning and stumped the celibate Sankara by asking questions pertaining to sexuality and intercourse! Such examples of a "golden age of Indian womanhood" – though important in the colonial/nationalist discourse (Chakravarti, 1989) – tend to cloud the fact that the female figures dominating popular imagination, like Sitā (who followed her husband Rāma into exile, was abducted and recovered by Rāma, only to be abandoned on the grounds of no longer being "pure") and Draupadi (who was married to five husbands and was wagered and "lost" to the enemy in a game of dice) – are women embodying the virtue of "pativratā" (loyalty to one's husband). However, a close study of the texts shows that even they decry their husbands at crucial junctures of the relevant narratives. Picking up on this, contemporary literature and theater often (re)casts them as voices of protest.

Women and environment

A connection between nature and women is neither uncommon nor unproblematic in feminist discourse. In India, we see it when the "world" is spoken of as a "menstruating body" or when various geographical locations are identified as different organs of a Female Body (*Śākta Pīṭhas*) or when creation is said to be a manifestation of the feminine principle of *Prakṛti*. The last of these indigenous

119

links is retrieved by theorists like Vandana Shiva (Shiva 1988) into a powerful ecofeminism that envisages freedom not as an emancipation from the "realm of necessity" (nature) but as rediscovering our submersion in it. This materialism, she claims, is neither a "commodified capitalist" nor a "mechanical Marxist" one (Mies and Shiva 1993).

The notion of Prakṛti occurs in the orthodox "systems" of high philosophy. But Shiva's Prakṛti-idea can be recovered from oral traditions and rural practices and underlies grassroots environmental movements. In this form, Prakṛti is a metaphysical principle – a living, conscious, and creative energy. Everything that there is – animate and inanimate – is a manifestation of this power which pervades and yet transcends the plurality of the manifest world. It is represented as feminine and is revered as a Goddess (The Mother).

A creative use of this ontology first leads to radical changes in *ethics* and *epistemology*. If Nature is as conscious and self-willed as humanity – and sacred to boot – we lose the ethical rationale for treating her as an inert "resource" to be exploited. The relation between human and natural realms is reconceptualized along idioms of "participation" or "reconnection" rather than "mastery." The epistemological consequence of the stress on interrelations *within* the manifestations of nature is an abandoning of the "methodological atomism" of reductionist science, while interrelations *between* nature and us explode the myth of an objective "knowing from the outside." These two paradigm shifts in turn develop into a powerful political critique. The postcolonial ideology of "development," "modernization," and even "poverty" in the Third World is based on the sanctity of a market economy with its twin pillars of manipulation of nature for profit and technological piecemeal fixes of the consequent environmental degradation. The ethico-epistemological attitude-changes implicit in the Prakṛti-idea thus debunk development as "maldevelopment" and replace it by what is called the "subsistence perspective," which emphasizes satisfaction of common human needs of life rather than maximization of commodity production and crass consumerism.

In the final stages of the argument, it is concluded that in subsistence economies "women's work" is typically not rendered invisible, thus reinstating women as "producers." Verification by controlled experimental situations in laboratories is deprioritized to validation through experience and participation in the production of subsistence. And since the latter is, *ex hypothesi*, the domain of marginalized rural groups and women, they become reinstated as cognitive "experts." While it would be interesting to explore whether this constitutes an epistemological "feminist standpoint," the anti-imperialist implications of such epistemic empowerment is important in the present climate. For example, multinational corporations claim patents and intellectual property rights over genetically engineered seeds, produced from germ plasm preserved by sustainable indigenous farming practices over the ages in the Third World, simply because such practices (unlike biotechnological approach) are not regarded as "knowledge" or as exercising the "intellect" (Shiva 1992; Mies and Shiva 1993).

Such ecofeminism has been vigorously criticized for "essentializing" rural women and ignoring their differences of class and caste, for ignoring the material and political structures within which ideological constructs alone manifest themselves (Agarwal 1992, Dietrich 1992). Instead of rehearsing these objections, I want to explore the feminization of Nature implicit in saying that, though leading to "categories of liberation for all, for men as well as for women," Prakṛti is a *"feminine principle."*

Etymologically Prakṛti, like individual women, *gives birth* (to the world) and "makes things grow": The maternal metaphor is clear. But Nature conceptualized as Prakṛti is more than the simple assertion of an Earth *Mother* in an ordinary sense. Two points should be carefully noted: first, generation by Prakṛti is not biological but due to her *creative impulse* (will). It is a conception that does not need a male – in fact, there is nothing other than Prakṛti ("I alone exist in this world," says the Goddess in *Durga Saptasati)*. Second, procreation itself is conceptualized as a kind of *activity:* the texts are unambiguous in asserting the *active principle* to be feminine. The full import of a "femininity" along these lines is thus understood only by stepping outside the usual associations of motherhood and into a construct that is a negation of passivity and may be even androgynous. Prakṛti is also divine, whereas simple maternality need not include godhood. Before turning to the ramifications of this last qualification, it should be noted that Shiva stresses not only reproduction but also "connectedness" as feminine. Buried in the tradition is yet another notion of the feminine that might be relevant here. As far back as the *Rig-Veda* and the *Bhagavad-Gita*, "speech" (*Vāk*) is spoken of as a (glorified) woman. Interestingly, the word "prakṛti" also means "grammatical root" (of a word). What emerges as the "feminine principle" is thus a generativeness/connectedness that is not biological procreation. Feminization via *generativeness of language/grammar* is different from adoption of the maternal model and remains a rich and unexplored terrain for feminist scholars.

Goddesses and spirituality

In India, high Hinduism and folklore present us with many female deities. The feminist impact of female divinity is bound to be complex in a culture overpopulated by goddesses and is totally different from the use of "goddess" in monotheistic religions.

As "consorts" of gods, it might seem that goddesses are basically appendages. But iconographically, divine sexual union is often depicted with the female in the dominant position. Conceptually, women are the embodiment of power (*Śakti*), the absence of which renders male deities "unable to move even a blade of grass." However, power is not necessarily autonomy, and the cult of the *Mahādevi* abandons the image of consortship altogether for that of the Cosmic Queen who creates even the gods. In Tantric literature, the Goddess (Devi) assumes ten forms – the *Mahāvidyās* – (which are, to mention a few) *Kālī* dancing naked with a garland of skulls; pot-bellied (pregnant?) *Tārā*; *Chhinnamastā*, who, having decapitated herself, holds in her hand, her dismembered head into whose mouth flows one of the three jets of blood spouting from the severed neck; a

121

buxom *Bhuvaneśwarī* giving nourishment to the world; *Ṣoḍaśī*, a sixteen-year-old astride the body of Shiva; *Dhumāvatī*, old, disheveled, and widowed. In the smaller traditions, we find mention of a group of goddesses who are inimical to children but are, fascinatingly. called *Mātṛkās* (meaning "mothers" and also. "phonemes") and *village goddesses* with demanding, ambivalent natures.

Such postulation of female goddesses, of course, is not in itself a feminism; in fact, the transcendental–empirical dichotomy may be a compensatory device that gives to women in the other-worldly realm what they are denied in the empirical world. (Actually the tradition seems to be aware of this strategy, for in many myths mortal women often *become* goddesses in a rage over some societal insult.) But still, the sheer visibility of female power in the pantheon opens up possibilities of creative forms of revolt. A striking example is the manipulation of the phenomenon of "possession," where a woman uses belief in a goddess "taking over an individual as her vehicle" to wrest advantages for herself in hostile situations. In a short story, *Sanjh Sakaler Ma* (Mother at Dawn and Dusk), the contemporary Bengali novelist, Mahesweta Devi (1993), writes of how a widow "becomes" possessed during the day and, with the offerings she receives, becomes an ordinary mother feeding her son after sundown. She thus manages to survive by a temporal splitting of divine and biological motherhood!

Furthermore, even if the creation of divine mothers is a motivated patriarchal move, to *succeed* as "compensation," what is imputed to women in their glorified forms – autonomy, power, sexuality – must be deemed important for ordinary women. Hence, analyzing the nature of female goddesses remains an important tool for unearthing the concept of "womanliness" in a community. The juxtaposition of what in the West are deemed opposites – the maternal and the erotic, the terrible and benign, the hungry and nourishing, represents a metaphysic of synthesis and interrelation. Life and death are cyclically related. The Divine Mother must sometimes kill to protect and must herself eat to feed. The image of "maternal care" that follows (even though the "mothers" here are divine) is far from a self-sacrificing and self-effacing sentimentalism and could serve as a base for a robust "feminine ethic." Furthermore, our sample of embodied divinities invites rethinking of the female subject itself as embodied. And the deification of sexuality, menstruation, birth, aging – all the *biological* aspects of a woman's life-cycle – indicates an acceptance of the female body in all its stages. Of course, the concern of contemporary Indian feminists with issues of women's health, and sexual and domestic violence suggests an awareness of the fact that female embodiment can easily slip into bondage. The importance of the category of the "lived body" grounded in such embodiment is differently *experienced* by differently located gendered subjects.

Moving away from the "canon" to lived religious experience, we encounter women saints of the *Bhakti* movement. (For an overview see *Manushi* 1989 50–2;). The regional and sectarian differences between, for example, *Mira* (Rajasthan), *Akka Mahadevi* (Karnataka), *Lal Ded* (Kashmir), and *Muktabai*

(Maharashtra), should caution us against generalizations, but certain central themes do emerge. *Bhakti* is a direct apprehension of God through love. The devotion of a *bhakta* is expressed in passionate love poetry directed to a chosen, intimate and reciprocating God, as in the following:

> ... O Siva
> when shall I
> crush you on my pitcher breasts
> O lord white as jasmine
> when do I join you
> stripped of body's shame
> and heart's modesty.   *(Akka Devi; see Ramanujan 1985)*

To enact such single-minded love or a monogamous marriage to God, woman had to forsake the security of domesticity and earthly wedlock. But even so, the expression of *Bhakti*-love was often in the idiom of the very patriarchal structures it initially subverted, as in "Mira is the servant of her beloved Giridhar." Kumkum Sangari's exemplary work on Mira (Sangari 1990) indicates the complexities of cooption and/or willful appropriation to legitimize revolt and form dissident communities through *Bhakti*.

Part of the revolt of the *Bhakti* movement was against knowing God through theoretical scriptural learning and austerities. So it too could well be a resource for alternative epistemological paradigms. Exploring *Bhakti*-love can join hands with Shiva and the trend in Western philosophy that is trying to establish alternative, value-laden and emotional "women's ways of knowing."

Another interesting dimension of *Bhakti* emerges from its use by *men*. *Bhakti* is in a sense an "immersion in powerlessness" (Sangari 1990) and thereby, its conduciveness to the female voice. Manhood, associated as it is with privilege and power, becomes an *obstacle* in this context. So just as women *Bhaktas* cast off forms of domestic security, the man had to ultimately cast off his maleness and *become* female to be a true *Bhakta*. It is well known how the modern saint Sri Ramakrishna Paramhansa, when approaching Krishna in the "mood of a female lover," not only dressed as a woman but tried to emulate the female gait, speech, and gestures down to the minutest detail. This curious juxtaposition and the resulting androgynous state of male sainthood implies an understanding of gender as a social–functional construction. Some women saints (Akka Devi and Lal Ded) went around naked. This might be an attempt at androgynous gender-construction or asexuality: nakedness, wandering in the search for like-minded souls, etc., is typically *male behavior* associated with male ascetics or a mark of childlike innocence.

A fascinatingly new area within women's spirituality that could be called "feminist theodicy" is implicit in Veena Das's work on violence (Das 1995). Das shows how apparently "benevolent" processes – the medical, legal, and bureaucratic discourses – initiated by the state in the aftermath of the Bhopal gas leak and the Partition riots, inadvertently ended up *legitimizing* the very systems responsible for the violence. Even though intending to articulate their misery, these processes resulted in a "professional transformation of suffering" that actually rendered the victims voiceless. A "theory of suffering" *from the point of view of the victim*, says Das, eschews explanations. The healing process is one where victims come to terms with undeserved suffering through a realization that "certainties" and abstractions of science, religion, and law are unable to make their pain comprehensible. In such a "cosmology of the powerless" the world is contingent and chaotic – in diametrical opposition to, say, the neat system of Shiva's Prakṛti-vision. An acceptance of basic ontological *incoherence* becomes the only coherent alternative and paradoxically, the rejection of theodicy (as *intellectual systematization*) becomes the only acceptable "theodicy" now understood as an existential response attempting to make unbearable suffering bearable.

Mortal mothers, domesticity and the third gender

The "mother" tends to engulf the "woman." In India, a "good" woman is not only one who gives birth but birth to *sons*; and with this definitional stricture, individual women lose control over their bodies and sexuality. Women are the "field" in which man sows seed. He "owns" her as well as the "fruits" which she passively bears. The biological mother is simply a "passive factor of reproduction." Even mother goddesses give the ideology of motherhood a normative status that pressurizes individual women to thrust motherhood on themselves.

However, motherhood became a political symbol in the context of the colonial experience. At the turn of the century, the Nationalist movement introduced the powerful image of "Mother India" to evoke the concern of the (colonized) emasculated male child for a mother in distress. This was tremendously successful in mobilizing the masses because "the sense of personalised well-being generated by the mother is beyond the reach of an impersonal concept of a 'nation'" (Bagchi 1990). The feminist import of this is ambiguous. On one level, the role of individual women remained, like that of Mother India, the production and nourishment of heroic sons. However, the fact that the mother-myth *could* be so effective in electrifying the masses probably points to sentiments like "the mother is equivalent to a thousand fathers," which is just one of the "discrepancies" in the general patriarchal backgrounding of mothers in traditional Indian society (Bhattacharya 1990). Second, even if the value of mothers in political slogans is "instrumental" – a plea to fill her colonial sons with Śakti – we are back to the idea of males having to be energized by the female principle.

The confinement of women to the private–domestic sphere implicit in their roles as mothers was further politicized by an identification of the truly "Indian" with the private/spiritual/home as opposed to the "Western" realm of public/material/"worldly" excellence. Women thus became the repositories of cultural essence and identity. Gandhi – often called by feminists "the benevolent patriarch" at best – introduced an interesting twist here. His slogan of *Swadeshi*, of spinning *khadi* as symbols of self-reliance was a brilliant move to infuse this private/domestic realm – the decision of what to wear, for example – with *political* significance. Women, in this way, were made active agents in the free-dom struggle *without questioning of their traditional role.* But in the absence of an agenda for economic empowerment, this "emancipation" was limited. The over-all Gandhian strategy was to recast the classic symptoms of women's oppression – their capacity for suffering and their leanings to non-violence – as the paradigms of strength and heroism for all humankind. Sara Ruddick has encashed the potential of this by linking it to a feminist peace politics. But consequences of emphasizing "maternal thinking" in the Indian context is both bound to be ambiguous (given the mother-obsession) and bound to signify more than the simple assertion of a "feminine virtue" (given the nationalist appropriation of the feminine). Ashish Nandy argues that the exaltation of maternal qualities and practices as examples of strength implies the following threefold subversion: (i) the Brahminical tradition prioritizing intellection; (ii) the *kshatriya* or the Indian martial tradition prioritizing militancy; and (iii) the colonial equation of masculin-ity with aggression and femininity with passivity. Seen in this light, the Gandhian revolution consists in the "legitimacy" given to femininity, not via a spiritual deification but as "a valued aspect of Indian self-definition" (Nandy 1980).

The reason this worked – to the extent it did, if at all – lay in the deep-rooted symbol of the *ardhanarisvara* (literally, "Lord who is half a woman") – the androgynous form of Lord Siva, where his/her body is split down the middle, with one half being male and the other female. Wendy O'Flaherty (O'Flaherty 1980) has documented the subtleties and differences that occur within this principal representation of bisexuality, but the general idea suggests the incorp-oration of femininity in any individual identity. Note that this basic androgynous symbol can be variously conceived – as being *both* male and female (in Prakrti?) or as transcending the dichotomy altogether and being *neither* male nor female (in *Bhakti*-saints?). Roop Rekha Verma (Verma 1995) is concerned with the second interpretation in her theory of a "personhood" transcending male and female essences. Nandy uses what looks like the first interpretation to argue that women here "do not start with as great a handicap as they do in many other societies ... . The Indian woman can more easily integrate within her feminine identity the participation in what by Western standards are manly activities" (Nandy 1980).

The *hijra* community in India of "men in a sari," visible at the fringes of society but participating in the mainstream through their traditional role of dancers to celebrate births and marriages, is living testament to a gender-identity con-structed beyond the neat dichotomy of male–female. Not all *hijras* are born intersexed (hermaphrodites), but include men who are forced/choose to join this highly structured community because of their "effeminacy," cross-dressing and, sometimes, homosexuality (Nanda 1986).

The "real" Indian woman?

The fracturing of the category "Indian woman" began almost simultaneously with its construction in the pre-Independence era. The low-caste, peasant, and

125

adivasi movements presented counter-narratives to the nationalist discourse. The construction of "the" Indian woman by contemporary activists, on the other hand, is determined by the specific contexts of their struggles – which vary notoriously (see Akerkar 1995), while the urban elite emerges as the "new Indian woman" in contemporary media and commercial advertisements (Sunder Rajan 1993). Thus, we began with a counterposing of "Indian woman" against "Western woman" but find the former disappearing, as quickly as the latter.

The recent Shah Bano case (in 1985, Shah Bano, a divorced Muslim woman, sought maintenance under Prevention of Vagrancy clauses of the Criminal Procedure Code – in a series of subsequent events, this came to be perceived as a threat to the identity of the entire Muslim community by posing a challenge to the Muslim personal law that did not give women this right) and Roop Kanwar case (Roop Kanwar, a young widow from a small town in Rajasthan, committed/was forced to commit *suttee* amidst celebrating crowds in 1987 – this led to a confrontation between women's groups and some Hindu organizations that raised the issue of minority rights and religious self-determination of a community) frame the question: Who is the *Indian woman?* rather dramatically. They indicate contexts where many individual women abandon the secular "feminist" platform of fighting patriarchy across religious and caste lines to align themselves with communities with frankly communal agendas (Sarkar 1993). The voluminous literature on this intertwining of feminist and fundamentalist agendas throws up some distinct philosophical issues concerning the construction of self-identity.

First, selfhood as requiring fixed and definite criteria is replaced by a "fluid identity." The subject is not lost when the nexus of exclusions and assimilations surrounding it is changed. It is possible for an individual to assume an identity that cuts across caste and creed and excludes men; but then, in certain situations, to affiliate herself with a larger communal identity that excludes other women. This suggests a "positional definition of the subject" (Alcoff 1988). The appeal of a communal or religious identity for an individual also needs to be rethought. It might lie in a promise of pluralism – of the assertion of cultural rights in the face of homogenizing influences of the state. Paradoxically, however, the self-definition of the *community* is based on leveling out *individual* voices in the re-creation of a common past – the very same authoritarian device used in the self-definition of the state. An internal tension thus erupts between the individual and community.

Is there an alternative and non-authoritarian basis for community? The juxtaposition of the theme of embodiment mentioned earlier, with the ideas of Sunder Rajan and Das on *pain*, might prove suggestive here. Sunder Rajan (1993) suggests emphasizing "sati-as-burning" instead of the usual "sati-as-death" (murder or suicide) to underscore the (historicized) "subject of/in pain" in the constitution of female subjectivity. Such a subject is necessarily a dynamic *agent* (rather than a passive victim) because the subject-in-pain by definition is struggling toward a state of non-pain. Das (1995) speaks of how the infliction of bodily pain can be a medium through which a society "marks" an individual as belonging to it (the classic example, of course, being initiation rituals). The *body* and (given the prevalent gender ideologies) *women* bear the stamp of such initiation and become the mediating signs between the individual and society. But a daring use of Wittgenstein's private-language argument leads Das to conclude that an *expression* of pain by the victim is an invitation to enter into a language-game with her. Taking up this invitation is a (non-sentimental) "sharing pain" and even experiencing it in my body. This "forming of one body" through "public" rituals of mourning and listening is the alternative ground of a collective identity that does not erase individual specificities. Could "Indian womanhood" or perhaps even "womanhood" reemerge as identity-in-difference in this manner? After its exuberant contributions to ethics, epistemology, ontology, economics, and religion, feminist philosophy in India, as elsewhere, must finally confront this question if it is not to annihilate itself. Without subjects and their collectivities, positive emancipatory agendas make little sense and without some such agenda, neither does "feminism."

13

Eastern Europe

DAŠA DUHAČEK

My first attempt to gather material for East European feminist philosophy through systematic library research was discouraging: the computer had no matching titles for my search. However, the concept of East European feminist philosophy is not totally nonexistent. Any statement about Eastern European feminist philosophy, therefore, should be preceded by a definition of the terminology in question. For example, even feminism and philosophy construct a phrase: feminist philosophy. This phrase, this neologism, can even be regarded as self-contradictory. On the one hand it seems to adhere to the traditional classification of knowledge, which maintains a privileged position of philosophy and, on the other hand, feminism stands for the disruption of traditional, especially hierarchical, paradigms and classifications.

But the overriding problem is defining Eastern Europe. The concept refers to a placement, a geographical position, but requires a wider definition (or a narrower one, having been called "a non-region" in a press release at the 1995 Beijing conference), a common denominator that stands for the former socialist countries, or, to be more specific, for those European countries which share a history of "truly existing socialism" (including. therefore. the countries which historically and geographically belong to Central Europe). What these countries share is a geographical situation of heavy political consequence: they were either a part of the former USSR (for seventy-five years), or shared a border (for forty-five years) with it.

The historical diversity of the region cannot be overemphasized, even within the shared part of its history. This diversity is twofold. Firstly, the history before World War II, which reveals on the one hand, industrialized countries, with a developed civil society (e.g. Czech lands) or, on the other hand, rural, patriarchal cultures (e.g. some parts of the Balkans). Secondly, the context of World War II itself, which presented some parts of the region as either centers, or at least, independent movements of resistance to fascism (e.g. the former USSR, the former Yugoslavia). This may have been one of the factors which led to the different levels of the implementation of the dogmatic system, and laid uneven cultural practices, uneven access to communication, different flows of books and translations, autonomy of the universities or lack of it, and so on.

Understanding this diversity includes a recognition that some parts of the region are relatively ethnically homogeneous, and have homogeneous religious traditions (e.g. Poland), or are, in those respects, mixed (e.g. the former

Yugoslavia). Finally, today, some of these countries have the benefit of peace, whereas some are at war.

Turning to feminism in Eastern and Central Europe, one issue presents itself as almost a point of departure. Namely, do we consider the Western world as the one that defines feminism? How do we speak of feminism which is other *than* Western feminism, if not as a feminism which is the other *to* it, which would presuppose Western feminism as the parameter? Could we even begin to consider any official ideology, as a whole, for whatever it is worth, as "feminist"? If society was obliged to adhere to the principle of equality between women and men, does that make its ideology feminist? Can an equality within a lack of freedom be a guarantee of equality? Or does this line of reasoning question the position of who is defining what feminism is?

In summarizing the important contributions of Eastern European feminist philosophy, I must admit to several limitations. First, the issues presented here will take into account only those raised in the texts written *by* Eastern European feminists; and not issues raised in numerous, and, for the most part, excellent texts *about* them. (For example, the work of Cynthia Cockburn, Barbara Einhorn, Zillah Eisenstein, Nanette Funk, Susan Gal, Celia Hawkesworth, Gail Kligman, Ann Snitow, and many others.) Also, every effort will be made to rely on the texts written by philosophers but, where important issues have been raised, by theorists from other fields (which poses the question of where is the dividing line between feminist theory and feminist philosophy). Literary theory, since it is a vast and a distinct field, is not included, and is cited only exceptionally.

Finally, the linguistic diversity of the region severely limits research in this area. The texts taken into account are either in one of the East European languages (spoken by the author of this article) or, for the most part, texts translated into English, which in itself raises many questions. Which audience are they addressing? (A complete survey of this aspect of Eastern European feminist theory should also present data on translations of Western texts.) Owing to the constraint of language barriers, there is little evidence of theoretical exchange between Eastern European feminist philosophers. The internal theoretical debates concerning feminist issues, which engage philosophers within a single-language intellectual scene, and include nonfeminists, are also absent. In the light of all this, my article is merely a proposal for further comprehensive research of Eastern European feminist philosophy, which is itself very much in the making.

Philosophical traditions and feminism

In exploring the diversity, rather than assuming that the philosophical tradition is uniform, the first question should be, what are the respective national philosophical traditions of Eastern Europe (if philosophy, like economy, borders, taxes, and the like, is to be primarily locally determined)? In posing this question the presupposition is that the current philosophical moment is a continuation of its past, regardless of whether it is in agreement, or, much more often, in disagreement with it. There exists no present philosophy that has lost its relationship to its own past. Therefore, feminist philosophy is the il/legitimate heiress of its mediated and immediate past.

The philosophical tradition of Eastern Europe, diversified as it is, does share one common denominator, the philosophy of Marxism. Nonetheless, within the Marxist tradition there are significant differences. There was, in all probability, a whole army of anonymous philosophers doing theoretically barren research in a scholastic manner, while taking care to strictly adhere to dogmatic Marxism–Leninism. Conversely, we can just remind ourselves of some who not only stood out, when Marxism was the official ideology – and, for the most part, paid a price for it – but who are still today surpassing the scope of the "national," like Lukács and the Budapest circle, Kolakowski, Kosik, Schaff, Patochka, Gajo Petrovic and members of the Yugoslav Praxis group, the Lvov–Warsaw school, Tarski, Tatarkiewicz, and so on. A great deal could be said about their work, and could be expanded on, but, suffice it to say that at least two avenues need to be explored further: one, stemming from the fact that some of these philosophers were very much a part of the Marxist, albeit nondogmatic, tradition, and another, arising from the immediate fact of the, so to speak, philosophical diaspora – which was a consequence of dissidence from the official ideology – and, beside other questions, including the following: can philosophers be viewed as national and locally framed (Kolakowski, Agnes Heller, and many more come to mind)?

Going further back into the philosophical tradition, the question of this classification, among others, reveals itself as inherently more complex. Some authors (B. Smith 1993, p. 167) insist on a sharp distinction between a Latin- and a Byzantine-rooted culture in a way which makes this distinction function as hierarchical binary. The dividing line cutting across the Balkans would place Bosnia, Croatia, Hungary, and anything west of them as Latin-rooted culture; and conversely, everything east of them would be designated as Byzantine-rooted culture. However, beside being Eurocentric, this distinction denies the permeability of ideas which has always been the ultimate value of the spaces in question. In the older philosophical tradition, the prominent figures of Bernard Bolzano, Franz Brentano, and Nikolai Berdyaev, in different ways, shaped the tradition of Central and Eastern Europe.

Contemporary philosophy in this region is only a brief snapshot of processing, brewing, and crystallization. In this unpredictable flow and reshaping, not only is there a presence of women philosophers, but it is a presence recognized as that of the feminist philosophers, for example, Dmitrina Petrova (McBride and Raynova 1993, p. 127) and Tatyana Klimenkova (Swiderski 1993, p. 154). In some parts of Eastern Europe some feminist research was carried out prior to the events of 1989. Blazenka Despot has done extensive research within the Hegelian–Marxist framework. Rada Ivekovic has engaged in an exchange with postmodernism. Although promising and commendable as far as it goes, she maintains, postmodernism has been noted for its absence of the Other (given the possibility in language, the form is gendered as feminine), meaning not only the feminine, but also the non-Western. The absence of the feminine in Lyotard's and Deleuze's texts is characterized as insufficient awareness of the specificity, the materiality of the feminine (Ivekovic 1988, pp. 111, 118).

Political presence and economic independence

Most of the texts of Eastern European feminist philosophers discuss issues within their "historical-philosophical consciousness," their shared past. The theoretical basis for the analysis of the position of women was class analysis, which seldom allowed for an independent posing of the problem of women: it was subsumed under the priority of class (Voronina 1993, p. 109).

For the most part these texts remind us that the system which they shared was egalitarian in its ideology, which meant that women were nominally and officially declared equal to men (Havelkova 1993a, 1993b, Petrova 1993, Voronina 1993, 1994). It further meant that women were economically independent, which was one of the least disputed advantages of the shared "real socialism." The immediate consequence was what was commonly called a double- (Miroiu 1994) or even a triple-burden day (Petrova 1993), meaning that women, beside wage-earning, also had the tasks of housework and child care. Their third daily burden was society's expectation that they engage politically.

However, as is also well known, it was not a matter of individual choice (Havelkova 1993), but women were liberated from men in order to be enslaved by the state (the reality of the state never exceeded the concept of the patriarchal mutant of the modern state), because it was precisely women's labor "that held up [the] extensive economy for many long years at a low cost" (Voronina 1993, p. 101). As for the expectations that they should take their rightful place within public space, "women were only marginally represented in planning, decision and leadership positions" (Kiczkova and Farkasova 1993, p. 85), or some feminist philosophers state that, simply, even to this day, "women want to work, but they still do not want to govern" (Petrova 1993, p. 26).

Z. Kiczkova and E. Farkasova use an enlightening metaphor of a "building" to designate the public space which women were, in "real socialism," free to enter. What Kiczkova and Farkasova emphasize is that within that building women never felt at home, so to speak. Although their conclusion is that women don't want to leave the "building" en masse and require the revision of its structure, revolving around that metaphor is more of a nostalgia for the safe space of the private, the family. "It meant the loss of women's identity, because women had to adapt themselves to the architecture of the "building" and had no chance to become aware of and determine themselves what it meant to be a woman .... . The cost of entering the building was too high" (Kiczkova and Farkasova 1993, p. 87). M. Miriou, H. Havelkova and others point out that precisely owing to the fact of major disillusionment with the public and the political women not only made the decision of retreating to their family and privacy during the period of "real socialism," but seem to have adhered to this latent inclination well after 1989. The family is almost seen as the site of the public, or at least its

131

compensation, its supplement, which is a reversal of the Western feminist theoretical designation. "Because the family remained the last bastion of freedom, it took over many of the former functions of the public sphere" (Havelkova 1993b, p. 92). However, there is little awareness of the trap this line of argument would support. When discussing the fact that women chose their work for the sake of conveniently fulfilling their "family duties," Havelkova also concludes about men's choices: "they sought jobs, *offering as much creativity* as possible and wanted to avoid direct state control" (Havelkova 1993b, p. 93, emphasis added). It would appear that feminist philosophers complied with the fact that within this divide women are assigned duties, and creativity is left to men.

The economic attire of the public/private split in Eastern Europe engaged in political crossdressing. For example, in Hungary, concessions to private property, albeit limited, did nevertheless pave the way for "an erosion that gradually permeated all institutions ... [W]omen had a major role in this erosion, even if [their] influence did not manifest itself in the classically political forms" (Szalai 1991, p. 153). What is probably on the agenda for Eastern European feminist theory is a redefinition of the public and the political, with an emphasis on the local.

The system of "real socialism" is, on the one hand, defined by some feminist philosophers as "precapitalist," "feudal" (Havelkova 1993b, p. 90); and, on the other, as the system where industrialization was taking place in a communitarian framework (Klimenkova 1994). These two viewpoints are at odds inasmuch as the former designates "real socialism" as a premodern society and the latter as the society that reached modernity in the process of its own self-construction. The line of argument T. Klimenkova follows juxtaposes not only East and West, the future and the past, but also the individual and the communitarian theoretical frameworks, which is all of consequence for feminist theory. She views the historically existing "real socialism" as communitarian in comparison to what exists today, which is oriented toward the individual; and, while there is a lack of critique of what she euphemistically calls "communitarian," she rejects what, in the texts of other feminist philosophers, albeit questioned, functions as the desired, namely, the political model of liberalism.

The main theoretical question addressed in all these, and some other texts, is whether women should continue to demand equality granted in the period of "real socialism."

The experience of "real socialism" has somewhat blurred the fact that the demand for equality is not a *differentia specifica* of "real socialism" but is the demand of modernity, and, therefore, of both liberal and socialist thought. Liberal philosophy placed this demand having in mind the rights and the freedom of the individual. Here equality is the *assumption*. The socialist project, stemming from the (communitarian) motive of social justice, uncritically applied the principle of equality as the awaited and the expected *conclusion*, annihilating the fruitful concept of differences. Needless to say, this allowed for the space of its horrifying alienation in Stalinism. However, what is relevant for feminist theory is to keep in mind that whatever the advantages of the dissemination of differences, the denial of equality many East European feminists are prone to "may have a boomerang effect and lead to the reinforcement of the patriarchal presumption of the inequality between women and men" (Duhacek 1993, p. 135). Also for feminist theory, East or West, the theoretical models of both liberalism and socialism, and any other, should be critically assessed and none dispensed with automatically. Surely no serious theory can allow itself to conflate the "real socialism" with the socialist project and, consequently, dispense with one articulation of leftist politics. What should the process of critical sifting and feminist assessment be based on? Perhaps, on how much space for disrupting hierarchies any theoretical position leaves?

Controlling the body

Beside the issues of political participation and economic independence, the equality principle would have to confirm and enact the right to decide about one's own body, which relates, among other questions, to the question of abortion. Most countries of the Eastern bloc had, while they were a part of it, relatively liberal abortion laws (with some exceptions, e.g. Romania). However, what Eastern European theorists fully realize is that this legislation was not based on woman's right to choose, but, at best, on the concern of the state to protect women. "The aim of the law is stated clearly in its preamble: to protect women's health from abortion in unsuitable conditions by nonphysicians" (Fuszara 1991, p. 242; see also Zielinska 1993, p. 53). More often the legal status of abortion was based on what the state saw as its own interest at a given moment, e.g. demographic concerns, or pressure on women to join the workforce (Zielinska 1993, pp. 49–50). What has also, necessarily, been reflected on is the fact that in most of the former socialist countries the right to choose abortion has either been threatened (for example, Serbia, Croatia, etc.) or suspended (Poland). The discourse in use stemmed from the opposition to real socialism; undoubtedly, respective churches played a part. "The Catholic church played an important political role, in part because over the past forty years, the church was the only voice independent of the state" (Fuszara 1991, p. 249).

Issues of the body have not been under much scrutiny concerning sexuality or pornography, but, necessarily and sadly, have emerged and exploded in the war in the former Yugoslavia, amidst inconceivable violence and the mass rape of women. With some exceptions (Meznaric 1994), and perhaps understandably, these issues have been less addressed theoretically. Meznaric has based her analysis and conclusions on extensive research. One of the pivotal questions arising from her text is the ethnic appropriation of the identity of women for political purposes.

However, great efforts have been made to document and draw public attention to the atrocities against women. "It is therefore important that we constantly break the silence of male violence against women, that we encourage one another to speak and speak aloud" (Mladjenovic 1995, p. 74). Most of the feminist activity has also focused on the demand that rape be declared a war crime.

Nationalism and war

The reality of war in more than one part of Eastern Europe and, according to some, the possibility of it spreading has made it something painful but inescapable to speak and write about. Feminist philosophy claims that "the war in the former Yugoslavia is in significant ways an affair of 'brotherhood' and not of 'sisterhood'" (Ivekovic 1993a, 1993b, p. 115). In creating the conflictual, the flammable, warring, symbolical system is highly gendered. Consequently, so are nationalism and war. Rejecting a priori any essentializing of the category "woman" (and women have been complicit), Rada Ivekovic claims that women's boundaries are more relational, their incorporation of the "other" is evidenced by their bodies and they represent a meeting, a mixture. As such women are, as the mixed urban culture of the cities is, a target for destruction. Women, though not absolved from partaking of nationalist ramblings, have much less investment to do so. "The suicidal drive in nationalism ... is the result of the insane attempt to *be born by oneself, from oneself*, not to owe anything to the other" (Ivekovic 1993b, p. 123, original emphasis).

In most of the writing of former Yugoslavia's feminist theory the reality of war and the discourse of nationalism is gender identified. "Because of the absolute domination of the Nation's interest, *any other, civilian, politically democratic*, peace making, and alternative strategy against the War itself is, at the very first step seen as "cowardly', *unmanly*" (Papic 1992, p. 12, original emphasis).

What also runs like a thread through these writings is the need for these feminist authors to ground themselves in the sanity of peace, absolute rejection of any nationalism, and a reminder of multicultural frameworks of the former Yugoslavia. "[A]ll my intellectual framework was and is Yugoslavia and, of course, also cosmopolitan. ... A journalist told me recently that Yugoslavia was a fiction. But then I must be a fiction too" (Ivekovic 1993a, p. 65; see also Lukic 1996, Papic 1992, Slapsak 1994).

There are approaches within which feminist philosophy is, while also using as a point of departure the sanity of peace, treating the issues of war and nationalism without the nostalgia for the former Yugoslavia, multicultural or otherwise. Along that vein runs Renata Salecl's book, *The Spoils of Freedom, Psychoanalysis and Feminism after the Fall of Socialism*. This is a pathbreaking text inasmuch as it is, by every parameter, feminist philosophy originating from this region. Her analysis of the fall of socialism, beside being feminist, is embedded in the psychoanalytic approach of Lacanian orientation; consequently, the main thesis of the text stems from her presupposition that any analysis of the political has to include psychoanalytical insights. She maintains that the law – and women are a symptom of rights – in socialism has been constructed so as to be systematically transgressed, because the priority was the content – defined as an ever-elusive "interest" of the people – and not the form. "The sad conclusion one can draw from this is that some kind of a master is always in place, regardless of how much we deny its existence" (Salecl 1994, p. 140). The master opted for here is the dead father, who represents the law, the empty form of authority. However, what a text such as this needs to distinguish more sharply is the socialist project from "real socialism."

In conclusion

An array of issues is being fully discussed within Eastern European feminist philosophy. For example, in a work on ecofeminism Mihaela Miroiu has "developed the radical feminist idea that being a woman is a strong ground for self-respect and the ecological idea that being a member of a community including non-human beings is fundamental for understanding ourselves" (Miroiu 1996, p. 7). However, some still present a blind spot and are still waiting to be addressed, such as issues of race and lesbianism.

Feminist philosophy is emerging through the work of the young generation. This generation has the knowledge of East and West, contemporary French and Anglo-Saxon philosophy, the experience of the old and the new world and, so far, cannot be bought; they possess the rigor of traditional European systematic approach to philosophy, but have no problems in deconstructing it. In that vein, following a thesis on feminist interpretations of Descartes and a number of articles on Spinoza, Kristeva, and Irigaray, a book was published, a *Dictionary*, soaked in the best contemporary feminist theory (Arsic 1995). Rearticulated in it are the concepts of city, library, heart, mirror, gaze:

> Library is the scene of history. Library is, like the female body, a stage on which wars, victories and losses, loves, betrayals and deaths simultaneously take place. Library is like a female body, a stage on which all the languages are spoken and all the writing are written at the same time. Library is, like the female body, a stage of eternally unsatisfied desires and irretrievably lost chances. (Arsic 1995, p. 20)

Branka Arsic draws not only on the European modern philosophical tradition but also on its literary tradition (Proust, Mallarmé, Beckett, Tzvetayeva). Her play with words makes her a master and mistress of words at the same time. Although her text is woman-centered, it does not readily yield to the pressing issues of feminism, but, rather, will reveal itself to have a long-term contract with it. Although writing such as this deserves detailed attention, suffice it to say that it is a very fine weaving, and it is up to the interpreter, feminist or otherwise, to read it as a fragile cobweb, which will fall apart when touched, or a firm pillar that one can hold on to.

If this overview is more inclined to open up problems and pose questions rather than give answers, it is because it portrays the picture, or an incomplete mosaic, of Eastern European feminist philosophy. Every aspect of the very existence of this philosophy and its definition is a process, an unfolding which is central not only to itself, but to feminist philosophy as a whole. Given that philosophy is at its best where it provokes and disturbs, rather than settles, I consider the questions to be more important than the answers.

PART III
LANGUAGE

14

Language and power

LYNNE TIRRELL

Language casts sheaves of reality upon the social body, stamping it and violently shaping it.   (Wittig 1992, p. 78)

Most of us – those of us who are women; to those who are men this will not apply – probably check the F box rather than the M box when filling out an application form. It would hardly occur to us to mark M. That would be like cheating or worse, not existing, like erasing ourselves from the world ... For since the very first time we put a check mark on the little square next to the F on the form, we have officially entered the sex-gender system, the social relations of gender and have become engendered as women; that is to say, not only do other people consider us as females, but from that moment on we have been representing ourselves as women. Now I ask, isn't that the same as saying that ... while we thought that we were marking the F on the form, in fact the F was marking us?   (de Lauretis 1987b, pp. 11–12)

Language matters to feminism because language is a structure of significances that governs our lives. It contains and conveys the categories through which we understand ourselves and others, and through which we become who and what we are. Our linguistic practices are constituted largely by inferences which in turn constitute or contribute to our understanding of the connections (causal and otherwise) between things. These inferential roles and patterns, which are normatively inscribed, give order and significance to the categories. Once we realize that our linguistic categories reflect and are reflected by our social categories, and once we see that our discursive practices are normative, it is a short step to see language as an arena of political struggle. Feminism is, at the very least, a struggle to end sexist oppression by eradicating both the means by which oppression is carried out and the ideology that seeks that it be carried out. As our most powerful and yet nuanced symbol system, language is perhaps the primary means by which the ideology of sexism is developed and reinforced; it is not news that language is an instrument of oppression. A narrow focus on sexist semantics is of limited use to feminist philosophers, for at best such studies yield lists of past and present harms, with little more to add than "stop it, *now*." The real promise of philosophy of language for feminists is an understanding of articulated normativity; by understanding how language really works, we

139

might just understand how the rabbit of normativity gets pulled from the hat of articulation. Language is normative in its production and reproduction of social norms by way of its content, by way of its forms, and most especially by way of its constitutive discursive practices. Once we understand how women are paradoxically constituted by and yet erased from discourse, we may use what we know of these processes of articulation and legitimation to effect and explain our reconstitution as whole.

Feminism is characterized by a dual consciousness which is aware of injustices in past and present social practices, and yet is marked by an apprehension of possible futures in which women can flourish. As Sandra Bartky argues, "the very *meaning* of what the feminist apprehends is illuminated by the light of what ought to be" (Bartky 1990a, p.14). This general pattern is equally true of feminist attention to language. Early work on language focused on diagnosing harmful practices, such as the use of the so-called generic "man," naming practices, titles declaring marital status such as "Mrs" and "Miss", category terms, and so on (Spender 1980, Frank and Anshen 1983, Miller and Swift 1991). Such diagnostic work may seem strictly descriptive, or to some it may seem thoroughly political, but it is both normative and descriptive. Some feminists, like Mary Daly, have worked to recover lost meanings of words, revealing common words which harm women as well as recovering those which might give us power, such as "spinster," "crone," "a-mazing"; with Jane Caputi, Daly has created an entire dictionary of such terms (Daly and Caputi 1987; see also Graham 1973, Kramarae and Treichter 1985). Many feminists have coined new terms, given us new concepts, and worked to create liberatory discursive practices. As attention to *practices* has become more explicit, feminist philosophers have increasingly addressed the politics of discourse, specifically asking who gets to speak, when, where, and why. More recent feminist work on language is less frequently seen as philosophy of language because it juggles its linguistic investigations with investigations of politics and metaphysics.

The interweaving of philosophy with linguistics and literary theory makes feminist philosophy of language significantly different from traditional philosophy of language, although they share some methods and concerns. Feminist concern with finding "the woman's voice" led to understanding the importance of hearing the many voices of our diversities, and to exploring the tensions between the relatively powerless position of being a woman and the relatively more powerful position of being a speaker or author. Feminist revisionings of women's testimonies about our lives show that linguistic change is of primary importance, but not all by itself (Rich 1979a, pp. 33–50). For example, a domestic worker paid (under the table) less than a minimum wage with no health benefits should fight for better compensation as a worker, but she should also care that her employer calls her a "girl," because the employer's conceiving of the worker *as a girl* is connected to her not being treated as an adult with real financial responsibilities (Merriam 1974). Language matters because it at least reinforces and may even create forms of

140

behavior. As feminist work on discursive practices shows, those who seek to change that social order must not ignore the language that embodies it.

Feminists have found that we are simultaneously marked and erased by discourse, for we are marked as objects, while we are erased as speaking subjects. This article begins with a preliminary sketch of an approach to language that should be of general use to feminists. The next section addresses feminist philosophical/linguistic work on marking and erasure, and suggests that concern about specific harms, such as belittling labels and semantic erasure, has always had a broad normative significance for gender identities. The following section addresses feminist philosophical/literary discussions of the speaking subject with an emphasis on this paradox of marked inclusion and forced exclusion. Finally, I briefly address recent work on pornography that illustrates a trend in contemporary feminist philosophy of language toward understanding the metaphysical power of discursive practices in their particular social and political contexts.

Language: some preliminaries

Language is a dynamic complex of processes and practices; it is not a static, enduring thing, although it has some thing-like features. The linguistic practices that constitute and reinforce our social and material reality fall along a continuum of normativity, with explicitly normative practices at one end and deeply embedded, barely discernibly normative practices at the other. "Mary is a good mother" wears its normativity on its sleeve, as do other "good mother" claims, used to reinforce certain behaviors as well as to counter behaviors deemed undesirable. "Mary is a woman" does not seem to be explicitly normative, nor does the practice of identifying the sex or the gender of human beings. Many feminists have sought to show that although such claims seem merely descriptive, in fact they only appear so if one has already accepted a rather large set of norms (Beauvoir 1952, Hoagland 1988, Penelope 1992, Wittig 1992, Butler 1993). The norms concerning sex and gender are so deeply embedded in our culture that they have become *naturalized*. We speak and write at least in part in order to establish, reinforce, or undermine social, political, epistemological, metaphysical, and moral norms. These norms are not confined to our discourses; working in tandem with other practices, our discursive practices create complex social structures within which we construct our lives. This view of language as thoroughly normative is at odds with the more commonly accepted views that language is primarily descriptive or expressive – that its purpose is to capture or convey what we think, what we feel, how things are. A normative approach to language recognizes that language serves expressive and descriptive functions, but emphasizes that the structures of our discourses establish norms that govern what can and cannot be said, and with that what can and cannot *be* (Brandom 1994, also Butler 1990, 1993).

A descriptive/expressive approach to discourses would take sex to be a set of given facts about bodies that exist prior to their being described, and which do not alter under their description or in the face of attitudes expressed about them.

141

The most blatant descriptivist amongst philosophers was the early Wittgenstein, who in his *Tractatus* argued that words are the names of things and sentences are pictures of states of affairs. Most twentieth-century philosophers of language have taken language to be descriptive or expressive rather than constitutive of reality. On such a view, women are women and men are men, and while there may be a few unfortunate individuals who are biologically indeterminate or in transition, they are simply the exception that proves the rule. The rule, of course, is sexual dualism, a linchpin of heterosexism. Descriptivism is also a form of realism and physicalism, and it eschews linguistic constructivism.

Linguistic constructivism need not deny that there is an antecedently existing physical reality prior to language, but it holds that in order to apprehend this reality we must use our discursive practices, which then govern the attention we give to what we apprehend. This differential attention then creates a practical emphasis that can in fact transform the object to the point that it no longer much resembles what it was to begin with (Nietzsche 1974, 58). Linguistic constructivists do not generally hold that it is simply because people believe in the stories they tell that these appearances become facts; rather, the belief generates practices which ultimately provide grounds for the belief. A cycle of creation and discovery is formed, one which mystifies the creation and glorifies the "discovery."

In his *History of Sexuality* (1978), Foucault argues that sex itself is the *product* of discursive practices. saying "the notion of 'sex' made it possible to group together, in an artificial unity, anatomical elements, biological functions, conducts, sensations, and pleasures, and it enables one to make use of this fictitious unity as a causal principle, an omnipresent meaning; sex was thus able to function as a unique signifier and a universal signified" (p. 154). Notice that Foucault does not argue that there are no bodies or behaviors prior to the creation of the artificial unity we now call "sex." Neither does Wittig when she says "there is no sex. There is but sex that is oppressed and sex that oppresses. It is oppression that creates sex and not the contrary" (Wittig 1992, p. 2). According to Wittig, the conceptualization of the body *as sexed* was a power play which benefited men by conceiving them as superior in socially significant ways. The many differences amongst human bodies are *literally insignificant* as long as these differences are *unmarked*. Without a social context, they do not signify. Only within and against a structure of norms can these mere differences become something more: an organizing principle establishing who has greater access to what the society deems valuable.

The descriptivist would say that we see human bodies and simply describe what we see – heads, eyes, hands, arms, legs, feet, etc. The constructivist would urge that we see hands because hands matter to us, and that hands matter to us because we have projects to which they are useful (see E. Martin 1987). We think we simply see a body before us, but as Wittig argues, "what we believe to be a physical and direct perception is only a sophisticated and mythic construction, an 'imaginary formation', which reinterprets physical features (in themselves as neutral as any others but marked by the social system) through the

142

network of relationships in which they are perceived" (Wittig 1992, p. 12). This network of relationships is embodied in our discursive practices as well as in our more generally understood social practices. Linguistic constructivism has less initial intuitive appeal than descriptivism or expressivism, because we are all raised to be realists. What constructivism offers, however, is an analysis of discursive power as effected through discursive practice.

Marilyn Frye's classic "In and out of harm's way: arrogance and love" (in Frye 1983) offers an insightful analysis of the process of construction-by-interpretation enacted by discursive and other practices. Frye's "To be and be seen" (1986) explains the erasure of the lesbian by way of rendering her existence unintelligible. "Lesbian 'sex'" (1988) provides a similar treatment of the way the very concept of sex is heterosexistly blind to what lesbians do; this blindness puts lesbians outside the discourse and outside the conceptual space of mainstream (heterosexual and heterosexist) society. Sex is shown to be a regulatory norm which, as Judith Butler argues, "qualifies a body for life within the domain of cultural intelligibility" (Butler 1993, p. 2). At issue is how language serves to shape us *as women* and to keep us from being lesbians, hags, spinsters, crones, and other forms of life deemed undesirable to the reality defined by what Julia Penelope calls the Patriarchal Universe of Discourse. These essays show how our discursive practices and the practices to which we are subject shape our gender identity. These and other works by Frye, Penelope, Daly, Wittig, and Butler show us that the language is not neutral and the language is not ours. They reveal the power of discursive practice to shape and reshape our lives.

The language is not neutral and the language is not ours

Early feminist discussions of sexist language emphasized the ways that the content of what is said tends to trivialize women, to label us as exceptions when we succeed, or to erase us from the discourse entirely by using so-called generic terms that are not in fact generic (Moulton 1981, also Straumanis 1978). Such discussions are important for understanding the details of the practices that constitute our "socialization to powerlessness" (Penelope 1990, p. xxxi). Feminist philosophers and linguists have shown that women are oppressed by discursive practices in two primary ways. First, women are *marked*. Marking draws attention to the woman's femaleness and carries implications of inferiority. The woman is present, but only as lesser. Marking is achieved by pronouns, prefixes, and by sex-specific words and naming practices. Practices of marking women as diminutive, secondary, or amateur serve to diminish us, particularly when such marking fits into a systematic cultural pattern of women's trivialization (Frye 1983, also Vetterling-Braggin 1981). Secondly, women are *erased* as subjects. Discursive practices set women up as outsiders, as objects in texts, but not straightforwardly as speaking subjects. The speaker or writer of a text claims an authority that women are generally presumed to lack (Wittig 1992). There is a paradoxical tension between the way traditional

143

discursive practices both mark us and exclude us, making us present and absent, like the sign itself.

Mary Vetterling-Braggin's collection, *Sexist Language* (1981), includes many of the key articles written by philosophers on sexist language during the 1970s; it remains the central collection on the subject. Vetterling-Braggin points out that there are at least six different construals of "sexist" operating in the anthology, each yielding different accounts of sexist language (Vetterling-Braggin 1981, pp. 3–5). Different conceptions of sexism do in fact yield different accounts of sexist language, as do more or less robust theories of language and its powers. A linguistic remark is sometimes said to be sexist because it reveals certain sexist attitudes and beliefs about the speaker, or because it perpetuates the oppression of women, or because it does both. When we look closely at a remark, we can see that three different kinds of cases arise. Sometimes what is deemed sexist is (a) *what* is said, in the sense of the content of the remark; or (b) the *saying* of it, that is, the speech act of saying it; or (c) the *sayer*, the agent. As philosophers, feminists have not paid much attention to (c); we have instead focussed on words and sentences and their meanings in speech acts.

Cases with explicit sexist content, fitting (a), are relatively easy to see. The two cases that are hardest to see are (1) when what is said is not sexist but the saying of it is (this would be a pure case of (b), a sexist speech *act*); and (2) when the content may be sexist but the saying of it is not. Let's look more closely at these cases.

> *Case 1: what is said is not sexist but the saying of it is.* Ms Smith is a beautiful woman; everyone agrees. Generally, there isn't sexist content in merely saying that someone is beautiful. But when Ms Smith applies for a job at the university philosophy department and the men doing the hiring say "she is beautiful" in the context of discussing the qualifications of candidates for the job, that is sexist.

Some would say that this is sexist because her beauty is not relevant to her qualifications, while others would say that the problem is that her beauty is *made* relevant and that's the sexism of it. Either way, the content is inappropriate in this context. Feminist philosophy of language takes seriously the interplay between context and content.

> *Case 2: what is said is sexist but the saying of it is not sexist.* In a class on feminist approaches to language, students offer examples of sexist comments they have heard. They generate a collective list, and discuss a math professor's recent utterance of "Women are lousy at math." This sentence, first uttered in the math class, is said many times during the discussion. In every instance, a logician would say it is *mentioned* and not *used*. It was not asserted, it was simply displayed.

Sometimes even displaying or mentioning something is a problem, because even mere display can reinforce a norm. The mere utterance of a sexist bit of discourse does not ensure that charges of sexism against the speaker or against the utterance should stick; the question is whether the speaker has *endorsed* the sexism or eschewed it. The fact that the utterances in Case 2 were all merely mentioned suggests that no one endorsed the content of the claim. Notice also that the broader context matters here. Because this was a feminist classroom, there were prior anti-sexist statements which created a context of interpretation for the current claim. Alternatively, if a linguistics professor who has often made explicitly anti-feminist comments gives students this sentence to parse, its being mentioned rather than used does not save it from promoting sexism. The professor's past comments create an interpretive context for the current merely mentioned sentence. Listeners presume a speaker endorsement, again depending upon the interplay between context and content.

The practices that mark us as women are problematic both on the microscopic level of the specific traits they attribute but also on the macroscopic level of practices of attribution. Even very early discussions were attuned to this duality. Elizabeth Lane Beardsley's "Referential genderization" (1976) argues that the very practice of requiring speakers to specify a gender whenever speaking about human beings is the "foundation stone for building these other forms of genderization" such as gendered self-image, psychological gender identity, status differences between the sexes, etc. Beardsley notes that although sex-neutral terms exist, such as "person", or "someone," nevertheless colloquial usage usually requires us to avoid these terms in favor of sex-determinate terms. So, rather than "There's someone here to see you," colloquial usage requires "There's a man [or: woman] here to see you." This practice may have changed due to feminist efforts in the last twenty years, for a receptionist today is more likely to say "There's a client [or 'patient,' or 'student'] here to see you" than to explicitly identify the person by gender. The problem reemerges, however, if the speaker says "Miss Jones is here." Beardsley also points out that required referential genderization feeds our tendency to "make a differential appraisal wherever [we] have made a distinction" (see also Beardsley 1977, 1981). Being required to make the distinction in order to be grammatical creates conceptual frameworks that foster widespread sexist discrimination. To couch Beardsley's point in terms later introduced by Frye, sex-marking and sex-announcing in language are cornerstones of sexism (Frye 1983). We are included in the discourse, markedly.

The theme of false inclusion was present in early feminist work on the allegedly generic uses of "man" and its cognates to refer to all people. In an influential article which argues that the neutral "man" is a myth, Janice Moulton introduced the concept of *parasitic reference* into the philosophical discussion of linguistic sexism. Moulton argues that such uses of "man" to refer to all people are like using "Clorox" to refer to all bleach, yielding to men the same sort of increased name-recognition (and economic advantage) garnered by the brands that get such treatment (Clorox, Kleenex, etc.). Moulton's breakthrough was to introduce a way to explain the normative slant of such brand-names posing as generics. Even if they have become generic (which she denies in the case of "man"), the brand-name advantage still sticks – that brand sets the norm. Similarly, men set the norm for the generic class – humanity – with which they share their name (see also Kittay 1988).

The normative slant of the terms of our language is not just a matter of brand-names. Words about women have always had strong normative import, and so feminist approaches to the politics of discourse have always focussed on words. Eleanor Kuykendall explains that, "Like Wittgensteinian analysis the application of feminist linguistics to philosophy is a kind of therapy, and like Austinian analysis it attempts to lay bare the realities speakers use words to talk about, by examining the words themselves. Feminist linguistics proposes that uses of words help constitute the world in which speakers act" (Kuykendall 1981, p. 133). Feminists tend to believe in the potency of words; words have the power to make what they describe, denote, or depict seem real. The investigation of this power to create social ontology through normative categories disguised as descriptions is *normative metaphysics*. When someone calls you "queer," you feel the potency of the category whether you own it or not. This is not to say that feminists have gone mystical, thinking that saying simply makes it so. Calling me "queer" does not change my sexual orientation any more than calling me "black" changes my race. The potency of words is multidimensional; saying I was a vegetarian motivated me to make it so, but saying I drive a Ferrari would provide no such motivation. The first is a *self-prescriptive performative*, while the second would simply be a lie. Here, the self-prescriptive performative is part of the process of making myself vegetarian, putting others on notice of my change in lifestyle, and bringing on the ramifications of such a change. Feminists have been discovering and creating vocabularies that enable us to undertake these self-prescriptive performatives, to describe and prescribe ways of being.

The power of words shows most clearly in the case of humankind terms; this vocabulary, together with the practices in which these terms play, serves to reflect, reinforce, and even establish a social order. Julia Penelope makes the normativity of words explicit when she says,

> Words exist and are created because they serve the values and attitudes central to a culture. Dictionaries record cultural meanings. Definitions of *womanly, mannish,* and *manly, feminine,* and *masculine* ... reveal the cultural values modifiers denote and perpetuate. As long as women use these words as though they describe something real or explain observable phenomena, we lend credence to the idea that people can and should be characterized by the dichotomy they represent. (Penelope 1990, p. 52)

Penelope's position is emphatically constructivist, for she argues that withdrawing support from the practices that constitute the Patriarchal Universe of Discourse will change the reality of our lives and experiences. Ceasing to use terms that seem like ontological primitives within that discourse is a major step. Similarly emphasizing the connection between words and power, Andrea Dworkin argues that "words matter because words significantly determine what we know and what we do. Words change us or keep us the same. Women, deprived of a forum for words, are deprived of the power necessary to ensure both survival and well-being" (Dworkin 1988a, p. 30; see also Penelope 1992, pp. 39–49). Words preserve or transform us.

If indeed words do have such metaphysical and epistemological significance, we need urgently to address why words for women tend to be so derogatory. Even apparently neutral words that mark us are problematic; "female" ranks among the more neutral words one could use, and yet Beauvoir claims that "the term 'female' is derogatory not because it emphasizes woman's animality but because it imprisons her in her sex" (Beauvoir 1952, p. 3). Carolyn Korsmeyer extends Beauvoir's insight by exploring the metaphysical presuppositions of common terms for women, which, she argues, "promote a notion of female nature that is quite out of balance with that of the male, for [they continue] to identify a woman primarily in terms of her sex" (Korsmeyer 1977, p. 150). In her study of semantic derogation, Muriel Shultz found "roughly a thousand words and phrases describing women in sexually derogatory ways" and "nothing approaching this multitude" for men (Shulz 1975, p. 72). Korsmeyer offers the hope (but no assurance) that changing to more neutral language should "have more than a cosmetic effect." But what effect would ending semantic derogation have? To paraphrase Dworkin, perhaps by creating "a forum for words," women would garner "the power necessary to ensure both survival and well-being."

Mary Daly's concern with "the power of naming" captures two aspects of feminist philosophical concern: (a) finding the words we wish to use; and (b) effectively baptizing, which requires that others give our words uptake. Daly's work on language began with *Beyond God the Father* (1973) and so far has culminated in *The Wickedary* (1987) – in which she and Jane Caputi attempt to unravel the meanings of phallocratic language and reclaim archaic and more feminist meanings of words. Daly and Caputi say that "*The Wickedary* is a book of Crone-created New Words"; it is fundamentally a meaning-making work, for it offers a philosophical picture of language that has the potential to reshape our understanding of the politics of discourse and the significances of its histories (Daly 1987, p. 240). Daly encourages women to discover the words of women's past and to reanimate them as a means to empowerment. What is less emphatic in the presentation of the work, but clearly woven throughout it, is the importance of the forum for our words, of creating contexts in which we count as speakers, in which we "hear each other into speech," and so hear each other into a new kind of being (Rich 1979, p. 185).

There is a strongly normative vision at work here; it is work illuminated by the light of how things ought to be for women. Julia Penelope's explorations of the Patriarchal Universe of Discourse are a more linguistically explicit version of Marilyn Frye's courageous dance with meaninglessness in *The Politics of Reality* (1983) and both complement Mary Daly's work on creating and discovering meaning. These works show us that the language is not neutral, that its presuppositions do not serve our interests, that (to mix Wittgenstein's metaphors) it is a toolbox we must approach with caution, that its games are not played on a level field. As Dale Spender argues,

> For generations women have been silenced in patriarchal order, unable to have their meanings encoded and accepted in the social repositories of knowledge. The

process has been a cumulative one with silence built upon silence. When women's voices do penetrate, that same cumulative process can apply in reverse. Woman-centred meanings will multiply as the pattern of women's existence begins to emerge in both formal and informal contexts.   (Spender 1980, p. 74)

To imagine our own games, to create our own practices and our own meanings is a generations-long challenge. To meet this challenge, we must learn well what other women have already said, discovering their lost meanings. To meet this challenge, we must also gain semantic authority, and become speakers in our own right.

Neutral isn't neutral: credibility and situated subjectivity

As we have already noted, the power of naming is not just about finding or inventing the words for what we want to say; it is also about having contexts and communities within which such saying matters. Speaking subjects need interlocutors to whom they have credibility (Tirrell 1993). Seeking the authority of an author, a woman claims an authority that she, *qua* woman, is generally presumed to lack. Insofar as a woman seeks to write or speak authentically of her own experience as a woman, she runs into the problem of either losing credibility because her work is seen as not yet quite universal or of losing the experience because she has tried to universalize it. Wittig explains that

> Language as a whole gives everyone the same power of becoming an absolute subject through its exercise. But gender, an element of language, works upon this ontological fact to annul it as far as women are concerned.... The result of the imposition of gender, acting as a denial at the very moment when one speaks, is to deprive women of the authority of speech, and to force them to make their entrance in a crablike way, particularizing themselves and apologizing profusely.   (Wittig 1992, p. 81)

Similarly, Simone de Beauvoir argues that female subjectivity is often a liability, for she finds "In the midst of an abstract discussion it is vexing to hear a man say: 'You think thus and so because you are a woman'; but I know that my only defense is to reply 'I think thus and so because it is true,' thereby removing my subjective self from the argument" (Beauvoir 1952, p. xviii). Beauvoir and Wittig highlight a problem that still plagues women – the problem of needing to assume a false neutrality and objectivity in order to gain credibility. The importance of finding a voice and having an arena in which it is credible is especially important for women of color, for whom "coming to voice is an act of resistance," which, bell hooks explains, serves as "both a way to engage in active self-transformation and a rite of passage where one moves from being object to being subject" (hooks 1989, p. 12).

Feminists have sought to show that the supposedly unsituated credible voice is really a voice from a different situation; thus Beauvoir continues by observing that "it is understood that the fact of being a man is no peculiarity." Truth and the appeals to truth, the forms of logical argument and analysis, the "objective" discourses taught in philosophy and science, promise to provide a kind of haven for those whose subjectivity is suspect – people of color. white women *qua* women, the very old and the very young. Such haven is provided by treating all speakers as if they were "the normal speaker" – generally a white middle- to upper-class male. Like television news anchors, speakers are not supposed to have accents or attitudes. The credibility that much early work in feminist philosophy of language sought was bought by adopting a white male subjectivity. Early efforts at analyzing sexist language focused on institutional contexts and public speech, "official discourses," even as these apply in personal contexts. These analyses were part of the project of proving that a woman (usually a white woman) can make it in a man's world (i.e. a white man's world). They set out the ways women's speech deviates from men's speech, challenged the assumptions that men's speech should dominate, and also provided an unwitting roadmap to the practices of discursive power. To adopt these practices is to adopt a voice that has become embedded as a norm of objectivity.

These "neutral" discursive practices have their price: not everything can be said in every voice. Concerning her own writing about the law, Patricia J. Williams asks "What is 'impersonal' writing but denial of self? If withholding is an ideology worth teaching, we should be clearer about that as the bottom line of the enterprise." Williams warns us that we "should also acknowledge the extent to which denial of one's authority in authorship is not the same as elimination of oneself; it is ruse, not reality" (Williams 1991a, p. 92). An even more serious danger is that the ruse may *become* reality, that a temporary denial of self, a series of short-term self-stiflings may in fact lead the woman, the thinker, the person to lose track of her long-term interests. Adopting an impersonal style requires us to enter the conversation scuttling "crablike."

For many women, it is a major achievement to gain credibility from adopting "the neutral voice" of a recognized style, discipline, or school. It is an achievement, however, that transforms the *subject* without transforming the *practice*. The credibility that feminists seek for situated subjects has the potential to transform *practices*. Carol Gilligan tells a story of two children arguing about whether to play Pirates (his idea) or Neighborhood (her idea). Gilligan argues that a "fairness" approach (equal time for each game) leaves the games intact, whereas the girl's ultimate suggestion, that they play Pirates-in-the-Neighborhood, changes everything. The pirate is different for living in a neighborhood and the neighborhood is changed for including a pirate (Gilligan 1988). Similarly, giving situated subjectivities credibility transforms the practices that generate semantic authority; authority now takes on new meaning when it does not require the particular individual to absent herself from the text to speak.

Philosophy, with its mission of finding objective truth and universal theories, generally demands impersonal prose. In her "Ethics of Method," Joyce Trebilcot urges women to stop trying to develop general (or worse: universal) theories; she wants stories from situated women who let their readers or listeners know who

149

they are and why they tell these stories. Trebilcot's own "ethics of method ... includes the idea that it is good when feminists and lesbians write about aspects of reality by telling stories, that is by saying what they have to say in terms of their lives and the lives of women they care about" (Trebilcot 1991, p. 50). But why *should* women tell the stories of our lives, how should we tell of our experiences, and to whom should we speak? As Maria Lugones and Vickie Spelman argued, "It matters to us what is said about us, who says it, and to whom it is said: having the opportunity to talk about one's life, to give an account of it, is integral to leading that life rather than being led through it; hence our distrust of the male monopoly over accounts of women's lives" (Lugones and Spelman 1986). The issue is the power of articulation, the power to put our lives together inside and outside discourse (Tirrell 1990). Giving an account of something involves categorizing that thing, identifying its features; we must choose our words and find or create a genre within which our stories may emerge. The categories we choose and the structure of articulation imposed by adopting a genre may be more or less accurate. Lugones and Spelman make the moral and metaphysical claim that women should not have to live their lives within the confines of categories which do not fit, or which do fit, but at a significant cost. This cost is what Wittig identifies when she argues that she must "insist on the material oppression of individuals by discourses" (Wittig 1992, p. 25). The process of self-articulation promises empowerment.

Pornography: discursive practice writ large

Finding empowerment through self-articulation requires fighting the dominant practices that lead to women's simultaneous presence-and-absence in discourse. The paradox of female presence-and-absence is particularly overwhelming in pornography, which is one reason feminists who think about language are also thinking about pornography. Another reason is that pornography is an arena in which the male monopoly over articulation has been very explicit. Yet another is that pornography, like language more generally, is a symbolic system in which the line between semantics and pragmatics is hard to draw. So, Catherine MacKinnon expresses her rage that anyone could think of pornography as "only words" and argues that in pornography "to say it is to do it" (MacKinnon 1993b, p. 25). And so, Carlin Romano thinks the best way to argue against MacKinnon is to begin his critique with a description of his imagining raping her – he thinks this makes his point that saying it isn't doing it (Romano 1993). The anger and pain of the many women who feel that they too have been violated by his ugly little "thought experiment" show that saying it is often some kind of doing it. In the context of these arguments, ordinary language philosophy comes to life – issues of the relation between semantics and pragmatics, questions of the intricacies of illocutionary and perlocutionary force, and other philosophical matters now have clear relevance.

Susan Griffin's *Pornography and Silence* (1981) painfully portrays the way pornography includes women as objects with limited subjectivity (just enough

150

to be capable of humiliation). She makes a powerful case that women are silenced by way of our false inclusion in pornography, that is, by way of our presence-but-absence in those texts and images. Describing "the metaphysics of pornography," Griffin says that "woman will either be excluded, and her presence made an absence, a kind of death of the mind, or she shall be humiliated, so that the images we come to know of woman will be degraded images" (Griffin 1981, p. 14.) Like other forms of discourse, pornography does not get its power all by itself; Griffin emphasizes that "all the structures of power in [a woman's] life, and all the voices of authority – the church, the state, society, and most likely even her own mother and father – reflect pornography's fantasy." To become what she is supposed to be, the girl must repress what contradicts the image, and so "that part of her which contradicts this pornographic image of womanhood is cast back into silence" (Griffin 1981, pp. 201–2).

Griffin's thesis is echoed in MacKinnon's *Only Words* (1991), where MacKinnon also makes the claim that pornography silences women, and also charges that pornography is a totalizing context – it is ubiquitous and largely inescapable. MacKinnon argues that pornography is the agent of the social construction of the sexes, saying, "Pornography makes the world a pornographic place through its making and use, establishing what women are said to exist as, are seen as, are treated as, constructing the social reality of what a woman is and can be in terms of what can be done to her, and what a man is in terms of doing it" (MacKinnon 1991b, p. 25). Thus, the sexes are defined by what they are said to be, and by what can and cannot be done to them. Recent work in feminist philosophy of language, focussing on speech acts, on what we do by saying what we say is especially vivid in feminist philosophical discussions of pornography. Some, like Jennifer Hornsby and Rae Langton, have gone back to Austin, providing a corrective to rather freewheeling analyses of the way speech acts. Hornsby, for instance, argues that Ronald Dworkin's critique of MacKinnon's silencing claim goes wrong because "he helps himself to some erroneous views about the workings of language" (Hornsby 1995, p. 220). Langton also uses a careful analysis of Austin's work to defend and refine MacKinnon's claim that "pornography subordinates," and in the process she offers an insightful general account of subordinating speech acts (Langton 1993b).

As this recent work shows, feminist philosophy of language is integrated into our work on metaphysical, epistemological, moral, and social issues. There is not much current work on defining and describing what makes sexist language sexist, the project of the 1970s. Today, speech act theory applied to pornography, for example, yields important insights about each. We see how speech acts, and come closer to understanding how language shapes the social reality that renders us women. Feminists working on philosophical and political issues arising in pornography are working against an oppressive construction of "woman." Philosophy of language looms large in this crucial work. On the flip side, Marilyn Frye's latest work argues that "it is a vital political function of feminist community and politics to construct a positive category of woman" which, unlike earlier conceptions of "woman," must be

151

conceived within an explicit logic and practice of pluralism (Frye 1996). Examination of these practices of interpretation and category construction is crucial work for feminist philosophers of language. We must understand, master, and create new norms of articulation.

Where to now?

Feminist linguists and sociolinguists have catalogued many ways in which our linguistic practices suppress women's full participation in "the conversations of humanity." What work is there for feminist philosophers to do? We need to develop more sophisticated accounts of how our discursive practices construct and reinforce the norms that govern our social ontology. Put baldly, there is much work to do to explain how the practices that govern what can be said to and about women serve to make women out of us and keep us present as women and absent as spinsters, or crones, or hags, or dykes, or tortilleras, or . . . . We use these words as means to self-empowerment. Sometimes we use them as self-prescriptions, sometimes as descriptions, always as ways of claiming categories as viable for self-respecting animation. In claiming them, we say these are categories to be lived. To be who and what we want to be, we must explore strategies of resistance to discursive practices as well as to other sorts of social practices. As feminist philosophers of language, we must learn more about the dynamics of meaning change, within linguistic communities, and also across linguistic communities. We must discover the resources that have grown out of languages of resistance in the past, and we must create new strategies and new languages to foster creative growth in the future. We must learn how to become the many selves we are by describing and prescribing ourselves into being.

152

15

Semantics

ANDREA NYE

Early in the resurgence of feminist philosophy that accompanied the "second wave" of the feminist movement in the 1960s and 1970s, language was recognized as a key issue. Because personal relations, politics, economics, religions, and academic disciplines are defined and carried on in language, practical reform or transformation in these areas is often blocked by insistence on logics, rules of grammar, systems of meaning, and uses of words that carry sexist implications. The question immediately presented itself as to whether these barriers are changeable uses of words and reformable conventions of grammar, or constitutive of rationality and so not removable without risking unintelligibility. Is language a variable and flexible tool that can be used to describe independently existing differences between men and women, or are those differences projected in language? Even more important for feminists is the question of the relation between language and thought. Is language constitutive of thought so that any intelligible communicable thought is framed within established perimeters of possibly sexist meaning? Or can feminist beliefs and aspirations achieve independence from established meanings and lay groundwork for radical changes in human relations? Even more important: is the self constituted in language, or can freely thinking feminist selves hope to create more adequate means of communication and more truthful ways of naming reality?

Feminist reflection on these issues, whether dealing with pragmatic aspects of language use, or grammatical structures, or theories of meaning, has several distinctive characteristics. First, feminist philosophers of language have tended to use resources from a variety of disciplines, drawing on psychoanalysis, linguistics, sociology, law, psychology, and literary theory to illustrate, explain, and proscribe for sexist language. Second, feminist linguistics is both descriptive and prescriptive, concerned with not only identifying language that degrades or misrepresents women, but also with projecting new ways of speaking, writing, thinking, and describing reality. Third, such a linguistics understands questions about the nature of language to be unanswerable without attention to uses of language that maintain forms of dominance. Fourth, feminist philosophy of language is strongly objective in the sense developed by Sandra Harding. It is critical not only of the empirical adequacy of specific results but also of its own stance and methods.

Pragmatics

In the 1970s feminist linguists studied differences between men's and women's use of language. Using descriptive and statistical data, they showed that women listened more, interrupted less, used more correct forms of grammar, added more hesitant questions onto the end of statements, used less slang, and made more disclaimers. Sociolinguists studied women's and men's talk as the speech styles of different social groups, exposing the way language can be used to create solidarity, exclude opposing groups, ridicule subordinates, and create exclusive identities (see Kramarae 1981 for a detailed description of these studies, and also Lakoff 1975, Spender 1980). Linguistic differences between men and women were explained by saying that the sexes employ different verbal "strategies," or by identifying women as a "muted group" forced to use language to propitiate or manipulate men with power.

Already in this descriptive work, disputes arose between male and female linguists. Did diagnosing for woman's speech patterns go beyond the proper scientific task of neutrally describing reality? Were feminists tainting objective scientific judgment with politicking? A call for a more rigorous "feminist empiricism" was one answer to these doubts, but already at this early stage of feminist reflection on language, there were deeper issues at stake. Even if it could be proven that women as a social group use language differently than men, it was not clear what conclusion should be drawn from that fact. Is this one instance of inevitable social inequality in which oppressed groups depend on other dominant groups, as some sociologists argued? Or are normative questions involved? And if normative questions are involved, what judgment should be made? If women use language differently from men, should women change, take debating and assertiveness training, learn to talk liké men? Or alternatively should men learn to talk like women, seeking consensus and alternative accommodating viewpoints? When questions like these are asked, core philosophical issues surface. What is language? Is language a cognitive tool for mastering reality? A device cast up by evolution? A means of individual self-expression? A way to weave an interpersonal view of reality? The decision as to what, if any, feminist practice follows from recognition of the fact of different male and female speech styles depends on the answers to these questions about the nature of language.

Another line of more narrowly philosophical work raised similar issues. Analytic philosophy, the dominant school of philosophy in English-speaking countries in the latter part of the twentieth century, focussed on language as the means to philosophical understanding. Understanding of reality, including psychic reality, now seemed to be the province of science. With the logical positivist project of prescribing an ideal logical language for that science abandoned, English-speaking philosophers turned to conceptual studies that mapped "ordinary" uses of words and dispelled metaphysical confusions. In the 1970s, feminist philosophers trained in the methods of analytic philosophy began to use those techniques to show how it is possible, in the words of the speech-act philosopher John Austin, "to do things with words," things that are sexist.

Typical were papers included in the "Sexism in ordinary language" section of an early collection of feminist philosophy edited by Mary Vetterling-Braggin and others (1981). In her introduction to the language section, Vetterling-Braggin cited Wittgenstein as authority for the view that the way we talk reflects the way we think. In addition, she pointed out, the way we think determines the way we act. Therefore, study of sexist language use can elucidate and diagnose sexism. The papers that followed explored the proper definition of sexist language, the ways in which different character traits are evaluated depending on sex, generic uses of masculine words, and differential joking about men and women. Another prototype for feminist analytic work was Marilyn Frye's classic dissection of the term "male chauvinism" (Frye 1975).

Again, feminist aims – understanding ways in which language maintains male dominance – required attention to deeper issues. Are sexist uses of language constitutive of intelligibility or are linguistic conventions human choices that can be evaluated and revised? A nuanced answer to that question was given by Judith Butler in a second generation feminist appropriation of speech act theory (Butler 1993). Gender identity, Butler argued, is a performance and not determined by fixed biological nature, but it is not a performance at will. The conventions by which we are "named" "girl," "boy," "queer," or "gay" are constituted in language. Butler went on to use the resources of analytic speech act theory and reference theory to understand how the linguistic mechanisms that produce normal and abnormal bodies, normal and queer subjects, might be cooptable or interruptable to produce new sexual/social identities.

Grammatical studies

Until the twentieth century, philosophers drew on Aristotle's projection of Greek grammar as reflective of primal metaphysical reality. Grammatical categories like subject, object, verb, or gender were thought to mark extralinguistic realities. In the twentieth century, the replacement of Aristotelian logic by modern mathematical logic as well as the ascendence of structural rather than descriptive studies of grammar led to a revised conception of grammar as a formal system onto which are "mapped" meanings which provide reference to reality.

Neither view of grammar proved adequate to increasing feminist awareness that it is not only voluntary "uses" of words but more permanent aspects of grammar that carry sexist implications. Virtually all feminist writers noted the pernicious effects of grammatical conventions that mandate the generic use of masculine terms (Lakoff 1975, Spender 1980, Moulton 1981). Feminists argued that terms like "mankind" or the grammatical rule that the pronoun "he" agree with any sexually nonspecific subject suggest that women are less human than men and that men are the only ones who do things. Nor does grammatical gender as a basic organizing feature of Indo-European languages spoken by Western academics seem to be easily eliminated. In many of these languages, nouns as a matter of grammatical convention are categorized male, female, or neutral, making dichotomous sexual difference a primary and seemingly unescapable division of reality. Even languages like English which do not have formal grammatical gender have a system of covert gender, which matches up masculine pronouns with words like "lawyer" or "doctor," pairs weaker feminine adjectives with female subjects, and reserves adjectives denoting mastery and control for masculine subjects. The result is that female powerlessness seems to be coded into the conventions of proper grammatical usage.

But feminists were unwilling to see such grammatical forms as either reflective of unchanging reality, or as an aspect of neutral or "wired-in" cognitive structure. Language that forces dichotomous gender identity, or that suggests that women are not fully human, or that all agents are male reflects and legitimatizes social behavior which harms women. As such, grammar is subject not only to description that exposes prejudice but also to feminist reform. Feminist response to studies of grammatical gender, therefore, typically involved prescriptions for change. A considerable movement ensued to devise and enforce guidelines for nonsexist language which eventually became standard in publishing and writing, including philosophical writing (Miller and Swift, 1991).

Feminist reform of grammar was not without its critics, as attested by considerable debate as to whether forced linguistic change accomplished any material gain for women. Again, the question of the relationship between language and reality and language and self was involved. Is it possible to change language at will? Even if people can be made to change their external verbal behavior, will the effects be determinable? Does language determine thought, so that it might be hoped that forced linguistic change might eventually make people think and act differently, or is any such change superficial, throwing up illusions of neutrality behind which old patterns of discrimination continue to operate eventually to taint any politically correct usage? Might the forced use of "she" rather than "he" by male writers only cover up the fact that it is men's and not women's thoughts that are being expressed? Some feminists argued that "humankind" is a euphemism that only hides the fact that culture is a male creation (Daly 1978). Others called attention to deep logical structures, less obviously linked to sex and less mutable at will, that install and maintain masculine styles of thought no matter what choices are made as to surface grammatical forms (Nye 1990).

Even as some feminist philosophers applied logical techniques to sexist arguments and concepts, others expressed suspicion of logic as contributing to adversarial masculine speech styles (Moulton 1983a). Even more controversial was the claim that the embedding of prescriptive logic in descriptive studies of grammar imposes on language forms designed by men to automate inference and close off debate. In a series of studies, I, for example, argued that the logical form which supposedly constitutes the deep structure of any intelligible language makes language into a truth machine barricaded from egalitarian speech and interpersonal conceptual revision. Seemingly technical issues such as the difference between subject and object in simple predication (Nye 1992), the translation of indexicals and personal pronouns into logical notation (Nye, forthcoming), the attempt to make of grammar a unified "structure" (Nye 1987), have implications for relations between speakers, their logicist resolution often ratifying forms of authoritarian speech.

Constantly critical of aims, goals, and the presuppositions of disciplinal methods and conceptual frames, these studies, like much of feminist philosophy, have the distinctive characteristic of "strong objectivity" defined by epistemologists such as Sandra Harding. Nowhere is that feature more evident than in philosophy of language, which by definition requires critical reflection on the terms of thought. It was not only formal systems of grammar or conventional uses of words that feminists called into question, but the ways in which the grammatical forms and individual words which are the vehicles of thought acquire meaning.

Theories of meaning

To develop a theory of meaning that makes strong objectivity possible might be taken as the goal of a feminist semantics. Again, early linguistic studies of lexical organization which encoded female inferiority pointed the way to deeper questions about the nature of language and the ability of words to refer to reality. Linguists noted in vocabularies the disproportionate number of derogatory words for women (Stanley 1977), the frequent use of euphemisms for women (Lakoff 1975), asymmetrical opposing pairs such as "master" and "mistress" (Lakoff 1975, Kramarae 1981). Remedial guidelines for correcting these inequities were included in publishing and writer's guidelines (Miller and Swift 1991) with further debate as to the superficiality of the changes mandated. Ms might be required as symmetrical with Mr to replace the traditional Miss\Mrs, but did sexist thinking and action change? Or might Ms, pulled back into asymmetrical usage, become, for many speakers, a derogatory term for pushy feminists? Reformist movements for language change continued to be criticized by some radical feminists. Mary Daly, for example, emphasized the aggressive wilfulness of male speakers and actors and proclaimed a more violent and subversive transformation of language in life-affirming separatist communities of women (Daly 1978).

Meanwhile, a different line of feminist reflection on language was developing in France. Is the sexual discrimination written into lexicons simply expungeable, or is it symptomatic of deeper generative structures of meaning? Although structural linguistics in the United States tended to be limited to studies of grammaticality, on the Continent the work of the French linguist Saussure inspired a far-ranging structural approach to meaning of all kinds. A key influence for French feminist philosophy of language was the structuralist psychoanalytic thought of Jacques Lacan. Language was the key, according to Lacan, to understanding that the self is not a primal consciousness that uses neutral and malleable language to express private and individual thoughts. Instead the self is a "subject" that acquires a stable identity only in language. In that language, gender plays a primary role. According to Lacan, opposition between masculine phallic presence and feminine lack is the very organizing motif of language

157

which, as a matter of course, is reflected in asymmetrical lexical features noted by feminists. Inequalities of semantic structure, therefore, are not repealable, but are corollaries of an immutable "law of the father" that makes meaning and identity possible. Lacan argued that women will always be at a disadvantage in language. Coded as inferior object rather than as masterful subject, they will never, as women, use words with the same authority as men.

This line of structuralist thought, along with the equally provocative post-structuralist deconstruction theory of Jacques Derrida, provided the matrix for an alternate line of continental reflection on language and its implication in sexism. Julia Kristeva, a noted linguist, contrasted the logical structure of rational language theorized by Lacan with a sub-rational maternal semiotics which provides expressive underpinnings for linguistic forms (Kristeva 1974). Kristeva's heroes were not specifically women, whose writing Kristeva sometimes deprecated as self-indulgent and sentimental, but rather male modernist poets who, in tune with the maternal, tap semiotic expressiveness but still manage to return to forms of rational structure that reconstruct social relationships. In contrast, Hélène Cixous theorized and tried to instantiate in her own work a writing that escaped logical structure altogether to speak a woman's body with all its passionate drives and impulses (Cixous 1979). Luce Irigaray followed Lacan's lead in relating rational structures to philosophical tradition. She psychoanalyzed the writing of canonical figures such as Descartes and Plato to find in the rigid concepts and linear logic of philosophical argumentation a defensive logocentrism in rejection of the maternal body. Again in contrast to Kristeva, Irigary evoked an alternative female idiom, generated in repressed female experience, formless, fluid, nonrestricted by the law of noncontradiction (Irigaray 1985).

Inherent in these approaches was the characteristic assumption of structuralism: meaning is systematic, dependent on relations between elements rather than on any element's singular reference to predetermined reality. There can be no one-to-one relation between a word and a thought, or between a word and an object. Instead, words have meaning by way of contrast with other words. Female means not male. Father means not mother. Meaning is built up in patterns of such oppositions. However, Cixous and Irigaray went beyond both Lacan's acceptance of patriarchy and Derrida's disruptive deconstruction of logocentric oppositions to project the possibility of another visionary mother language that escapes the oppositions on which logical forms depend and that is shaped by a woman's and not a man's imagination. Irigaray envisioned a fluid, associative, ambiguous, feminine play with words that did not allow itself to be defined or restricted by logic's law of noncontradiction. Cixous imagined a woman writer free from masculine forms of academic thought and discourse, expressing her own sensations and feelings.

Other feminists resisted this literary approach to linguistic liberation, charging elitism and failure of reference to material reality. One critic of poststructuralist feminisms was the legal philosopher Catherine MacKinnon. The purpose of language, she argued, is not to express either a masculine or a feminine imaginary, but to refer to material experiential realities like sexual harassment and rape, many of which go unnoticed when it is only men who do the naming (Mac-Kinnon 1987b). Power, she said, is in the naming of reality on one's own terms in a way that is adequate to one's experience. Nowhere is this more evident than in the law, where official and supposedly consensual language shapes thought and behavior. If naming is private, understood only by oneself or by a special enclave of writers or associates, its power is limited. Alternately, if naming is necessarily caught up in alienated symbolic structures, it has no reference to reality. But, said MacKinnon, words can be made to *respond*, both to women and to men, and in that process a legal system and a legal language might evolve that is both referential and nonsexist.

MacKinnon understood the logic that structures linguistic meaning in the context not of philosophical systems or theories, but of legal reasoning that structures actual behavior. In a fresh feminist approach to logic, Carroll Guen Hart described such a logic as "part of our attempt to regulate our inferences, to check our system of assumed meanings, to test our judgements." Such a process involves complex systems of meanings and principles that fundamentally provide general "ways of acting" that in turn delineate sets of traits defining various "kinds" (Hart 1993, p. 205). In the legal context, which Hart takes as a place where a feminist logic might flourish, this involves working out rules of evidence, degrees of guilt, assignment of punishments that reflect a true social consensus as to sexual behavior, and, ultimately, as to what sex is.

Again the status of logic is in question. Is logic the inherent form of any language that is communicable and has reference to objective reality? Or is logic a masculine imposition on an expressive mother tongue to contain and repress? The form in which these questions are posed often implies that one monolithic logic is inherent in masculine speech or in masculine theorizing about language, a logic that might have variants or be represented in differing idioms, but that always has a common core, the law of noncontradiction. Hart and MacKinnon suggest that there are various logics for various purposes, including the purpose of creating a social consensus adequate to both women's and men's experience, as well as the purpose of enforcing consistency of ideas. In support of that view, in historical studies, feminists found that the forms and the uses for which logics are designed are specific to different periods and different socio-cultural settings (Nye 1990).

Even in contemporary Western analytic philosophy, feminists noticed competing versions of logical semantics, as pointed out in a groundbreaking article by Merrill and Jaako Hintikka (Hintikka and Hintikka 1983). The Hintikkas argued that currently popular truth-theoretic semantics deals with the "structural system" of language and takes the "referential system" for granted. The result is that relations between language and the world which are the input for the structural system go unexamined, along with "tacit evaluations or interests" on which those inputs or meanings are dependent. The Hintikkas' claim that reference to reality is elided in truth-theoretic semantics had implications beyond the announced aim of their paper: to prove that Jaakko Hintikka's game-theoretic semantics is preferable to truth-theoretic semantics, implications that converge with recent work in feminist epistemology. How are the objects of science or of any truth-telling language determined? How are thoughtful nonscientists concerned about the state of the world to understand a science which constructs its own objects – atoms, neutrinos, quarks, neural brain-links – if those objects are identifiable only in terms of scientific theory? Must we accept a "division of linguistic labor," trusting to science to tell us the truth about the world? If science defines "IQ" and then, using that definition, proves that IQ is linked to race or that women are less intelligent than men, must that be taken as truth?

The suggestion that the logic that informs various semantic systems is not a given to be discovered but rather a criticizable theory of language proved one of the most controversial of feminist philosophical claims. For many philosophers, logic is at the heart of philosophy, the source of its independence and vitality. In an age of science, the mapping, legislating, translating of logical order can seem to be the only tasks left for philosophy. Recently efforts in this area have found an important application in computer programming which depends on translation of linguistic elements into binary machine language, and on constructing automatic inferences and rigid definitions. Philosophers' exploration of artificial intelligence – the construction of computer models of human cognition – justifies and implements the increasing computerization of decision making and operational strategies. Feminist suspicion of logic, of semantic theories rooted in logic, and of the automated inferences that result calls into question the assumptions behind this professional success.

More important for feminist semanticists than professional credibility, however, has been the recovery of reference. Feminism requires the linguistic means to refer to and prescribe for the reality of sexist action and thought. Feminism as an egalitarian movement also requires the linguistic means to provide reference to reality, seen not from the perspective of any elite group privileged by class, education, or culture, but as experienced by many diverse women. Much twentieth-century semantics, whether generated in competitive attempts to ingeniously solve long-standing philosophical puzzles and win professional acclaim, or dedicated to defending the sovereignty of science against superstition, does not answer to these feminist needs. As the Hintikkas argued, truth-theoretic semantics elides questions of reference by adopting Tarsky's definition of truth within a formal system. Similarly, cognitive psychologists posit a mysterious wired-in "language of thought" from which linguistic elements get their meaning. Functionalists argue that relations between sensory input and behavior output that provide the reference for words are markers not for reality, but for biological patterns that insure "survival." Some philosophers, like Quine, give up on the idea of providing a semantic theory of reference to a common object, arguing that understanding is a matter of interpreting or translating verbal behavior into one's own conceptual scheme. Others, like Donald Davidson, go even further to argue that no sense can be made of the notion that others could have a conceptual scheme different from one's own. Although these positions make sense within the context of a professional philosophy concerned with problems generated in a line of intellectual history increasingly closed off to social, political, and existential concerns, they cannot provide an adequate response to feminist concerns about language.

Feminist political and social concerns required a critical perspective on the inherent aims, effects, and institutional commitments of semantic theory. The insistence on forms of language that describe reality accurately and the attempt to theorize thought that is not only self-consistent but that accommodates differing points of view have initiated studies of language in which theoretical and technical issues merge with existential concerns which give those issues substance and meaning.

PART IV

KNOWLEDGE AND NATURE

16

Rationality

GENEVIEVE LLOYD

Feminist critique of reason

The feminist critique of reason has formed a large part of the dramatic expansion in the literature of feminist philosophy since the early 1980s. (See Rooney 1994 for a useful overview.) The critique has been controversial. It has often been seen – both by its practitioners and by its outraged opponents – as a critique of prevailing ideals and practices of philosophy. Some have seen it as the legitimate expression of the concerns of women alienated from, and marginalized within, the prevailing structures of professional philosophy. Others have seen in it nothing but a perversely reasoned commitment to irrationalism. Here the close connections between ideals of reason and the self-definition of philosophy can make it difficult to get the issues clear.

In the Western philosophical tradition the history of ideas of reason is as complex and shifting as that of philosophy itself, which has defined itself in relation to reason. The connotations of "rationality" are of objectivity, abstraction, detachment. Yet the term itself evokes strong emotions. "Rationality" acts as a symbol of all that the Western philosophical tradition holds dear; philosophy has appropriated to itself the aspirations and intellectual virtues associated with the rational. The claims and pretensions of philosophy are thus at stake in the debate over the claims and pretensions of reason. It is not surprising, then, that many feminists, disaffected with the prevailing practices of philosophy, should have attempted to develop sustained criticism of reason; or that their efforts should have met with bemusement and frequently hostility. But to engage in the critique of reason and of prevailing philosophical practice is not necessarily to reject either reason or philosophy. The history of philosophy, after all, is full of such critiques and challenges. Properly understood, feminist critique of reason can be seen as an enrichment and revitalizing of philosophical practice – to the benefit of all philosophers.

Yet it must be acknowledged that there can be something puzzling and even disconcerting about contemporary feminist criticism of reason. Is it rationality itself that feminist philosophers challenge? Or is it rather the accompanying rhetorical trimmings and trappings of the received ideal? Ideals of rationality are so integral, both to the philosophical tradition and to the broader intellectual tradition with which it interacts, that there can seem something paradoxical about the attempt to criticize reason. The procedures of argumentation on which the critique depends are themselves part of the object under attack. The perplexities and exasperations of debate on these issues have been compounded by the difficulty of getting the claims properly articulated within the restraints of the dominant modes of philosophizing. The expression of feminist dissatisfaction with prevailing practices of philosophy frequently itself falls victim to those very practices. The polemic between feminist critics of reason and their opponents can quickly become sterile unless the terms of the debate are broadened to include the practices of philosophy in which the claims of the "maleness" of reason are addressed.

Much feminist work in this area is concerned with the symbolic aspects of constructions of reason and of philosophy. But modern English-speaking philosophy has given little attention to rhetorical and symbolic dimensions of philosophical discourse. By the time the alleged maleness of reason is articulated in a form in which philosophers can hear it, the imaginative and affective dimensions of discourse are often filtered out. What is left is a pale abstraction, easily reduced to absurdity. Feminist claims that reason is male are taken as a reaffirmation of female irrationality or as a misleadingly literal claim of exclusion from the practices of professional philosophy.

The following sections will survey some of the ways in which feminists have attempted to bring gender to bear on ideals of rationality – their concern with metaphor and imagery; their skepticism about the claims of a universal, gender-neutral reason; their attempts to dismantle dichotomies which traditionally opposed reason to imagination and emotion; and their exposure of the interconnections between philosophical ideals of reason and the norms of philosophical practice.

Metaphor and the "philosophical imaginary"

In a philosophical culture which sees metaphors and imagery as incidental to philosophical content, the alleged maleness of reason is readily seen as an incidental accretion, wrongly exaggerated by feminists into a problem about rationality itself. (See Rooney 1991 and the Introduction to Lloyd 1994.) Feminist critics of the maleness of reason have often focussed on the tensions between the explicit philosophical content of texts and the covert privileging of maleness carried by philosophical metaphors and imagery. But if metaphor is seen as external to philosophical meaning, the alleged "maleness" is inevitably trivialized. Here the work of Michèle Le Doeuff has helped to uncover some of the obstructions to constructive debate on issues of rationality and gender. (See especially Le Doeuff 1990a, 1990b.) Much of what is problematic in the idea of rationality, and in the practices of philosophy, she suggests, is located in the "imaginary" of philosophy – in its symbolism, its metaphors. For Le Doeuff, much of the imagery discernible in philosophical texts is not incidental, external decoration to philosophical thought. It functions to mask aspects of the philosophy which cannot be readily articulated at the level of abstract concepts, and to organize the values implicit in philosophical texts. Often the meanings conveyed by images in a text, she points out, sustain things the system cannot itself justify, which are nevertheless needed for the text's proper working. It is at this nexus of philosophical meaning and the symbolic dimensions of texts that much feminist work on the maleness of reason is most fruitfully located.

Feminist criticism of rationalism and the Enlightenment tradition

Much of the feminist philosophy devoted to critique of the universalist pretensions of reason, and of the supposed gender neutrality of the knowing subject, has centered on critical discussion of specific figures in the history of philosophy. Feminist critique of rationality has gone on within the broader exercise of rereading key texts of the Western philosophical tradition from feminist perspectives. Here seventeenth-century philosophers – especially those associated with rationalism, and their influences on the subsequent Enlightenment tradition – have been particularly important (see Article 2, MODERN RATIONALISM).

Feminist readings of Descartes, for example, have challenged the supposed universality of his ideals of reason, sometimes from the perspective of modern psychoanalytic theory. Susan Bordo has offered a reading of Cartesian ideals of clarity and detachment in the light of ideas of separation drawn from modern developmental psychology. Cartesian reason, rather than expressing the universal essence of human minds, involves a masculinization of thought, posing as a neutral objectivity (Bordo 1987). And Naomi Scheman has suggested that psychological repression and projection may have a role in the constitution of Descartes's version of the disembodied knowing subject (Scheman 1993a).

The figure of Rousseau has also been central in feminist critiques of reason in the history of philosophy. (See Gatens 1991, Green 1993, Le Doeuff 1990a, 1990b, Lloyd 1983.) Here, as in other feminist work in the history of philosophy, attention has been given not only to the more notorious sections of the texts where women are discussed disparagingly or dismissively, but also – and more importantly – to the ways in which the male–female distinction has been caught up in other, apparently gender-neutral, parts of the text. Rousseau's articulation of distinctions between reason and nature, and his treatment of the passions, have been seen as interacting with his views on women in ways that reinforce conceptual connections between reason and maleness, and between emotion and femininity. Some feminist discussion of the writings of Mary Wollstonecraft has also highlighted her dissatisfaction with aspects of Rousseau's treatment of reason, of nature and of virtue, which intersect with his disparagement of women (see Green 1993, Mackenzie 1993).

Not all feminist work in the history of philosophy is directed to uncovering a latent gender bias or to deconstructing alleged gender neutrality. The feminist critique of reason incorporates attempts to reclaim neglected moments in the tradition where the supremacy of an affectless reason have been challenged. Some feminist discussions of Spinoza, for example, have looked to his philosophy as a source of positive insight into how issues of sexual difference and equality might be better articulated; and for inspiration on how ideals of reason might be brought into closer relationship with imagination and emotion (see Gatens 1995c). And David Hume's emphasis on sociability and reflection on passion has prompted Annette Baier to suggest that there are affinities between his treatment of knowledge and some of the concerns of recent feminist epistemology (see Baier 1993b).

Reason and emotion

Against this background of concern with the interaction between the male–female distinction and parts of the philosophical tradition which polarize reason from other, supposedly lesser, aspects of being human, it is not surprising that feminist philosophy has also been concerned with the description and revaluation of the emotions. Many feminist discussions of the relations between reason and emotion have emerged from attempts to rethink prevailing assumptions of ethical theory. Feminists have highlighted the role of emotion – both in the complex moral contexts within which moral theory must be applied, and in the processes of moral reasoning. Other work has been oriented toward the understanding of specific emotions caught up in the social construction of sexual difference, and in the politics of sex and gender. Elisabeth Spelman has explored philosophical aspects of anger in relations to the politics of subordination (Spelman 1989), and the ways in which emotions such as regret, embarrassment, guilt, and shame can be revelatory of moral attitudes operating within the politics of feminism (Spelman 1991). Sandra Bartky has also explored pervasive patterns of gendered emotion, especially in relation to shame (Bartky 1990a, pp. 84–98). The point here, as Bartky stresses, is not that particular emotions are gender-specific but rather that they have a different meaning in their "total psychic situation and general social location." Out of the consideration of the differences, Bartky develops a philosophical account of shame, which treats it as not so much a particular feeling or emotion as a "pervasive affective attunement to the social environment." The way emotions are experienced and expressed reflects different power relations between groups; and the different assumptions and expectations which operate in attitudes toward men and women make for sexual differentiation within emotions (Bartky 1990a, p. 85).

Unity and diversity

What Le Doeuff calls the "philosophical imaginary" has helped constitute the unitariness of rationality and of philosophy. But feminist philosophy itself, as Le Doeuff suggests, has been in some ways complicit in these symbolic operations. The unity of "woman" or "the feminine" is just as much a construction of the philosophical imaginary as is "rationality" or "philosophy." Ironically, in challenging the unitariness of rationality and philosophy in the name of "woman" or the "feminine," feminist philosophy can itself generate unities which mask difference. Whether feminist philosophy should be conducted in the name of a unitary "feminine," or whether it should rather resist the construction of such unities, is one of the theoretical issues around which feminist discussions of reason divide. Rather than seeking new distinctively female versions of – or alternatives to – rationality, some feminist philosophers have instead attempted to focus on the particularities of female experience, highlighting the ways in which socially constructed gender differences provide a context in which to situate the purportedly neutral and universal subject of reason. Insistence on particularity and context, and a rejection of the privileged position of the individual knowing subject, has been a prominent feature of feminist epistemology. (See Article 17, EPISTEMOLOGY).

Issues of the implied unitariness of philosophy, of "male" and "female," have been central to debates about the feminist critique of reason. Contemporary feminists have come to see the unitariness of "woman" or "the feminine" as requiring demystification no less than the unitary "reason" which has in the Western tradition so often been defined in opposition to the feminine. In its resistance to the claims of a unitary and universalist reason, some feminist philosophy here converges with some aspects of "postmodernism." It is this convergence which has prompted some critics to see in feminist critique a repudiation of philosophy in favor of irrationalism. The unity of philosophy, Brenda Almond has argued, depends on a commitment to the unity of reason which is under challenge in contemporary thought, both from postmodernism and from feminism. With the rejection of the ideal of a common reason, philosophy has "nowhere to go" (Almond 1992, p. 215).

The similarities between feminist and postmodernist critiques of reason have been constructively explored by Seyla Benhabib. There are affinities, she has pointed out in *Situating the Self*, between feminist attempts to demystify the "Male Subject of Reason" and postmodern critiques of Enlightenment ideals (Benhabib 1992, pp. 1–19). However, feminist critique of reason is not committed to a wholesale rejection of Enlightenment ideals of reason, any more than all versions of postmodernism are. It is possible, as Benhabib argues, to reconstruct Enlightenment ideals of reason in ways that take account of postmodern and feminist critiques of the supposed universalism and unitariness of the "knowing subject" idealized in that tradition.

A great deal of debate within feminist philosophy centers on this issue of how gender bears on the supposed unity, neutrality, and universality of reason. The alleged sexlessness of reason – its transcendence of all bodily difference – has been seen by many feminist critics as masking differences under an idealized sameness, to the disadvantage of women. It has been argued that what passes as an egalitarian ideal is, in fact, a covert privileging of maleness. The issue then becomes: what can be salvaged and restated of the traditional ideals? How might "rational thought" change if gender differences – whatever their origin – are taken seriously, rather than masked in an idealized sameness of soul?

169

Feminist critique of philosophical practice

The issue of how exactly sexual differentiation applies to moral and intellectual character has been the focus, too, of some feminist-inspired critical discussion of philosophical methodology. Here, feminist challenge to the supposed gender neutrality of reason has extended into critical debate on prevailing modes of philosophical practice. Janice Moulton, in an influential paper critically discussing the "adversarial paradigm" of philosophical debate (1983), has argued that an apparently neutral philosophical technique, on closer examination, carries a different social meaning for men and women. The adversarial approach – identifying positions which can be readily subjected to refutation – operates, she suggests, to the advantage of those whose socialized gender identity best fits a combative practice. Behavior seen as appropriately assertive in men is readily construed as "aggressive" in women. As well as subtly reinforcing the privileging of maleness, the dominance of the adversarial paradigm impoverishes philosophical practice, excluding other, more exploratory approaches which may in some contexts be more fruitful.

Moulton's paper illustrates how a reflective awareness of the interaction of gender and philosophical practice can transform philosophical methodology in ways that enrich the discipline for both women and men. There is no endorsement here of an alternative, distinctively feminine way of philosophizing. Rather, a subtle analysis of the real differences in the application of a supposedly gender-neutral practice opens space for a revision of philosophical practice in ways that make it genuinely accessible to both women and men.

Feminist philosophy interweaves with trends in contemporary philosophy which are not primarily motivated by a concern with issues of gender. Some feminist philosophy has had a confrontational tone of resistance to a discipline seen as hostile or oppressive toward women. But much of it can be seen rather as drawing on – and in turn reinforcing and expanding – shifts in the agenda and in the practice of contemporary philosophy which are differently motivated. Feminist philosophy converges with other attempts to transform philosophical practice. It complements, enriches, and is itself enriched by some of those developments. Questions of the relations between reason and emotion, and of the rationality of emotion itself, for example, have been on the contemporary philosophical agenda. And interest in the operations of metaphor and imagery in philosophical writing has been stimulated by more general concern with the relations between philosophy and literature.

Feminist critique has played an important part in articulating and addressing the restraints and the exclusions of inherited ideals of rationality, and in challenging the philosophical practices which have both formed and been formed by them. But feminist critics of reason are not always readily distinguishable as a distinct group within the diverse practices of contemporary philosophy; and many of them welcome this lack of fixity. Questions of identity, of self-identification and of self-constitution are themselves under debate in contemporary social

170

philosophy; and the identity of the "feminist philosopher" is itself an interesting issue. Feminist philosophers are often more readily identifiable by their motivations and by the recurring patterns of salience in their philosophical interests than by any allegiance to philosophical positions or commitment to any distinctively feminine forms of thought. The core of the feminist critique of reason resides in the exploration of what happens when received ideals and practices are confronted with the complex realities of gender difference, and forced to adapt to those realities. But there is no one legitimate feminist outcome to such explorations. And often the thinking-through of the assumptions and procedures that mask the differences that hang on gender will take the feminist philosopher into unexpected territories, forming at least temporary alliances with developments in other, differently motivated, challenges to intellectual traditions.

Future directions

The work of contemporary French philosophers has had a strong influence on feminists working within English-speaking philosophy. Le Doeuff, as we saw earlier, has focused on neglected imaginative dimensions of philosophical writing. The work of Luce Irigaray has also been a powerful influence in the exploration of operations of both imagination and affect in philosophical texts (see especially Irigaray 1985, Whitford 1983, 1991). But the literature of feminist philosophy displays a wide range of philosophical styles and orientations. Although much of the feminist discussion of reason has drawn on contemporary European philosophy and social theory, there is a growing interest in using the techniques of analytical styles of philosophy to explore gender-related aspects of norms of rationality and objectivity; and to clarify claims of a sexual differentiation of reason (see especially Haslanger 1993, Langton 1993a).

Feminist philosophy has contributed to significant transformations of philosophical practice. It has played an important role in the emergence of modes of intellectual enquiry which aim for engagement with social context, sensitivity to difference, and attunement to developments in other areas of thought. Is it also committed to developing a new feminine rationality or new alternatives to reason? There is, as we have seen, no unity among feminists about this issue. Some articulate their vision of the future in terms that suggest new feminine thought-styles. Others dismiss such visions as a perpetuation of stereotypes which would be better left behind; and, as always, there is a range of positions in between.

Attempts to sketch what might be new, preferred thought-styles are perhaps themselves best seen as exercises in what Le Doeuff has called "the philosophical imaginary." Dissatisfied with intellectual practices epitomized in professional philosophy, feminist philosophers try to imagine alternative thought-styles – intellectual spaces in which we glimpse possibilities excluded through past polarization of reason, imagination and emotion. We might imagine, for example, conceptions of objectivity which allow for detachment from our own standpoint – without commitment to the possibility of a way of knowing that transcends all standpoints. And we might find in neglected parts of the philosophical tradition itself resources for constructing unities of affect, imagination, and intellect which resist the polarizations of the past without sacrificing ideals of rigor or disinterestedness.

Women and men, differently situated in relation to the past exclusions and privileges of their shared intellectual tradition, may well have different perspectives on rationality; and different attitudes to what can be hoped for from its transformation. But whatever differences there may be here are in principle accessible to an informed philosophical imagination, regardless of gender. The most important upshot of the feminist critique of rationality has perhaps not been the emergence of – or even the aspiration to – a thought-style that is distinctively "female." Perhaps it has been rather a sharper articulation of the different strands – intellectual, imaginative and affective – involved in human ways of thinking; a resistance to their polarization; and a greater appreciation of the strengths and limitations of different ways of bringing them together. Different kinds of unity between intellect, imagination, and emotion are appropriate or inappropriate in different contexts. Feminist efforts to think through the strengths and the weaknesses of different ways of bringing together those elements of knowledge have yielded a heightened awareness of the ways in which philosophers can constructively engage with, and intervene in, the social practices through which our humanity – in all its diverseness and all its commonalities – is expressed.

17

Epistemology

LORRAINE CODE

Introduction

A relatively late arrival on the philosophical scene, feminist epistemology has evolved and undergone multiple refinements since, in 1981, I posed the then still outrageous question: "is the sex of the knower epistemologically significant?" At the time, that question was beginning to receive affirmative answers, within philosophy, from the essays in Sandra Harding and Merrill Hintikka's *Discovering Reality: Feminist Perspectives on Epistemology, Metaphysics, Methodology, and Philosophy of Science*, from Nancy Hartsock's *Money, Sex, and Power: Toward a Feminist Historical Materialism*, and from Alison Jaggar's *Feminist Politics and Human Nature*, with its chapter on feminist epistemology, all published in 1983. These writings were mapping a new epistemic terrain within professional philosophy that was also being opened out in the work of such non-philosophers as Dorothy Smith (1987), Carol Gilligan (1982a), and Nancy Chodorow (1978). Nonetheless, in the philosophical projects of the late 1960s and throughout the 1970s, even as feminist moral and political philosophy were growing to constitute an impressive body of critical-constructive literature, the suggestion that analogous interventions were not merely indicated, but urgently required, in epistemology, philosophy of science, and even logic still sounded like a preposterous manifestation of ideological excess. Knowledge, science, and logic seemed, virtually by definition, to stand secure as the repositories and guardians of truth and objectivity, occupants of a space isolated and protected from the vagaries of politics and of gendered specificities.

Mainstream Anglo-American epistemology had defined itself around a conviction that its principal task was to determine the necessary and sufficient conditions for objective, uniformly valid "knowledge in general," thereby refuting the skeptic: a conviction that explicitly precluded its having any but a universal, abstract, and a priori pertinence. The very title – *feminist epistemology* – sounded, within these discursive assumptions, like a crass oxymoron, for epistemology properly conceived eschewed taking subjectivity, with its manifold specificities, into account. The point was to preserve the alignment of knowledge with an objective, impartial detachment that could justify its apolitical self-presentation. Feminists, by contrast, in seeking explicitly to address issues of gendered epistemic subjectivity and agency, and to expose the politics of knowledge, cast doubt upon their claims to be "doing" epistemology worthy of the title.

173

Yet the period since 1983 has witnessed a proliferation of feminist epistemological projects so meticulous, so searching, and so varied as to contest most of the fundamental presuppositions of traditional inquiry into questions of knowledge. and to expand the range of epistemological investigation well beyond the confines within which it was hitherto practiced. Feminists have moved on from demonstrating the epistemological significance of the sex of the knower as he appears, at best, as a shadow figure in the pages of mainstream analytic epistemology, to exposing the androcentricity of "the epistemological project" in most of its Anglo-American mainstream forms. They have shown further that even attributions of androcentricity are far too crude, for they fail to capture the extent to which philosophical theories of knowledge are drawn from, bear the marks of, and perpetuate structures of power and privilege that are sustained as much by racial, class. religious. ethnic. age. and physical ability differentials as they are by a sex/gender system that could be discretely and univocally characterized. In the late 1990s it is clear that a revisioned epistemology has to concern itself as minutely with matters of subjectivity as with questions about knowledge; and that epistemological issues not only pervade most areas of philosophical inquiry, but are tacitly operative in most other academic disciplines and in the practices that inform and are informed by them. Disciplines and practices commonly work from embedded assumptions about what counts as knowledge worthy of the name, and whose knowledge merits acknowledgment. Frequently these assumptions confirm the presuppositions around which the epistemologies of the analytic mainstream are constructed, to produce uneven, and often unjust, multiple standards of credibility, authority, responsibility, and trust: standards that perpetuate white affluent male epistemic privilege while discrediting and discounting the knowledge and wisdom made in places and by knowers other than those legitimated by the current, authoritative knowledge-makers.

Demonstrations of the epistemological significance of the sex of the knower owe a large debt to three theorists whose work, in the early and mid-1980s, exposed the historical and cultural specificity of even such putatively "perennial" philosophical ideals as reason and rationality, objectivity, and knowledge itself. Genevieve Lloyd's *The Man of Reason* (1984, 2nd edition 1993), Evelyn Fox Keller's *Reflections on Gender and Science* (1985), and Susan Bordo's *The Flight to Objectivity* (1987) opened up conceptual spaces that had literally not been available in Anglo-American philosophy before these thinkers began circulating the material published in these books.

In a careful rereading of the canonical texts of Western philosophy, Lloyd shows that even throughout marked historical variations, there is a striking coincidence among the definitions, symbolisms, and associations of masculinity and those of Reason. Reason is not an independent item one simply comes across in the world. It is symbolically, metaphorically constituted all the way down: its constitution in association with ideal masculinity stakes out a rational domain that is inaccessible, or accessible only uneasily and with difficulty, to people whose traits and attributes do not coincide with those by which ideal white masculinity has defined itself. The conceptual-symbolic dichotomies that such

174

alignments generate – of which reason/emotion, mind/body, abstract/concrete, objective/subjective are typical samples – align also with a male/female dichotomy, both descriptively and evaluatively. And those dichotomies work to establish the features of ideal. universally valid knowledge as a product of rational endeavor, and to separate it from opinion, hearsay, particularity, which come to be associated with (stereotypical) femininity (see Article 16, RATIONALITY).

Keller's and Bordo's analyses are more psychosocial than symbolic. For Bordo, Cartesian objectivism is of a piece with a seventeenth-century "flight from the feminine," consequent upon a prevailing conviction that the primary epistemic task, both practical and theoretical, was to tame the chaos of "the female universe." Only by adopting a *masculine* epistemic stance, best manifested in detached and self-controlled objectivity, could a knower hope to complete this project successfully. And that stance was, of necessity. removed from the particularities of embodiment, time, place, idiosyncrasy, and *a fortiori*, from the object itself. In an account that is indebted to object-relations theory (see Chodorow 1978), Bordo reads all of these requirements as strategies to dispel a pervasive anxiety produced by a (distinctively masculine) separation from the mother and, derivatively, from "reality."

In a similar vein, Keller argues that conceptions of rationality, objectivity, and the will to dominate nature at once inform a particular vision of masculinity, and work to institutionalize a "normal" science that is uniquely adapted to the traits of such (male) practitioners. Keller's respect for scientific method and the achievements of empirical science is palpable throughout her writings. Yet she too demonstrates, in readings of historical texts and of twentieth-century scientific experimentation, that the alignments Lloyd and Bordo (variously) discern among dominant conceptions of reason, masculinity, knowledge, and scientific practice are as plain in the thought of Plato and Bacon as they are in the exclusions that twentieth-century science effects. The refusal or inability of the scientific establishment to accord timely recognition to the eminent geneticist Barbara McClintock has some bearing – Keller persuasively argues – upon McClintock's divergent (from the masculine norm) scientific style (Keller 1983).

Although the claims that Lloyd, Bordo, and Keller advance are often contentious, their works count among the texts – and function as producers of the contexts – which, explicitly or implicitly, have made feminist epistemology possible.

Feminist epistemological projects are located both within and in opposition to the received epistemologies of Anglo-American philosophy: they often move in and out of these theories, drawing on those of their resources that can withstand critical scrutiny, even as they work to eradicate their exclusionary, oppressive effects. As will be apparent in this article, many of these projects draw inspiration and substantive content from critical interrogations of philosophy of science and social science. Few of them believe that feminist political ends could be achieved simply by counting women among the knowers, and knowledge about "women's issues" as part of the knowledge that revisioned epistemologies will study; and most of them resist positing unified and essentialized "women's ways of

175

knowing" that might run parallel to, but would not disturb, established mainstream knowing. Yet the scope of feminist epistemology is broader than and different from that of feminist philosophy of science, even though commitments to a set of common causes allow for cross-fertilizations that are both fruitful and innovative. Thus feminists start from a realization that epistemologies, in their trickle-down effects in the everyday world, play a part in sustaining patriarchal and other hierarchical social structures, both in the academy and throughout Western societies. They achieve such effects in consequence of the kinds of knowledge that they tacitly legitimate, the kinds of knowers to whom they – again often tacitly – accord epistemic authority, and the exclusions and credibility differentials that they consequently produce. Abandoning any goal of constructing idealized accounts of what abstract knowers should do, most feminists attempt to ground their normative conclusions in the epistemic demands that real, embodied, specifically located knowers face in endeavoring to construct responsible and reliable knowledge that can serve them well in real-world (and/ or in real scientific/social scientific) circumstances (see Code 1987).

Mapping how feminist interventions were reshaping epistemological inquiry in the early 1980s, Sandra Harding, in *The Science Question in Feminism* (1986), set out a taxonomy that served in that initial period to distinguish feminist approaches from one another and from other successor epistemology projects, starting from within philosophy of science, yet claiming wider pertinence. Harding discerned three principal strands of inquiry: feminist empiricism, standpoint theory, and postmodernism. This ordering attests to descending levels of radicality, with empiricism retaining the closest allegiance to principles that govern traditional theories of knowledge, postmodernism departing most sharply from them, to challenge them at their roots. This taxonomy has been superseded as it has become clearer that feminist projects cannot be summed up so discretely and neatly as the first two categories imply, and as the postmodern import of the whole endeavor has been differently conceived. Nonetheless, I begin with a sketch of some versions of empiricism and standpoint theory as a way of mapping these changes.

Empiricism and standpoint theories

Feminist empiricism takes as its starting-point the contention that feminists – like other would-be knowers – have to base their knowledge on empirical evidence if they are to move capably about the physical world and engage effectively with the social, political, and "natural" realities that constitute their environments and inform their experiences. Such claims hold both for everyday and for academic/scientific knowledge. Yet classical empiricism grants exclusive pride of place to items known in ideal observation conditions by separate and interchangeable knowers whose specificities of embodiment and subjective location disappear in its processes of evaluating abstract and allegedly generic knowledge claims. Starting from a modern-day analogue of a (Lockean) tabula rasa, many orthodox empiricists work with the fiction of knowers as detached and neutral information-processors, whose natural and/or locational particularities should have no bearing on the cognitive products they derive from observational evidence, and whose access to that evidence is assured by their simply encountering it. The model of evidence as self-announcing, and knowers as uniformly ready to receive it (of knowledge as found, not made), dominate empiricism in its analyses of everyday knowledge and in its elaborations within natural and social scientific practice.

Yet far from yielding neutral, universally valid conceptions of knowledge and epistemology, empiricism is indelibly shaped by its creators and attests to the specificities of their epistemic locations. For orthodox empiricists, historical, gendered, locational differences between and among knowers reduce to bias or aberration: errors to be eradicated and thence discounted in formal justification procedures. Thus for all its alleged experiential grounding, the experience with which empiricism works is an abstraction in which cognitive specificities are homogenized under one dominant conception of what counts as knowledge and of who qualifies as a knower. In practice, those conceptions mirror and replicate the experiences that their (usually white, male, prosperous, and educated) creators are positioned to regard as exemplary.

For feminists in the late 1990s, the goal of inquiry is to yield knowledge, both secular and scientific, that is neither androcentric nor marked by racist, classist, sexist, or other biases. While reaffirming the impressive successes of empirical investigation in enabling people to live knowledgeably, both in their everyday lives and in the laboratory (see Article 3, EMPIRICISM), feminists contend that an unabashedly value-laden yet rigorous empiricism can produce more adequate knowledge than an empiricism whose practitioners are ignorant of the effects of their own specificity and of their complicity in sustaining systems of asymmetrical epistemic power and privilege. In this revisioned empiricism, inquirers are answerable as much to the epistemic community as to the evidence; details of a knower's epistemic location and interests count among the conditions that make knowledge possible, and are likewise open to critical scrutiny. The idea is that politically informed inquiry fosters a better empiricism, and generates a stronger, more rigorous objectivity than an objectivity that defines itself by bypassing the circumstances of its own possibility. Feminist-informed cognizance (and racial, class, and other "difference"-sensitive awareness) of the effects of subjective positioning on the very possibility of achieving good observations and deriving sound conclusions enhance objectivity, increasing the stringency of its demands. They do not thwart it. Components of the knowers' epistemic locations require empirical analysis as rigorous as the analyses that evaluate the knowledge claims he/she/they advance(s).

This reconfigured notion of objectivity contests the principal tenets of a positivist–empiricist tradition for which sensory observation in ideal conditions is the privileged source of objective knowledge, knowers are detached, neutral spectators, and the objects of knowledge are separate from them, inert items in knowledge-gathering processes. According to this orthodoxy, knowledge claims are formulable in *propositions*, uniformly verifiable by appeals to observational

177

data. Each individual knowledge-seeker is singly and separately accountable to the evidence, though *his* cognitive efforts are replicable by any other knower in the same circumstances. Yet feminists contend that the idealized view from nowhere – the "god trick" (Haraway 1991d) – on which such a conception of objectivity relies is as politically implicated as it is impossible to achieve: it sustains and is sustained by the hegemonic epistemic values and ideals of autonomous, self-sufficient subjectivity that its promulgators are positioned to regard as neutral and natural. The illusion of this stark objectivity, escalated into an objectivism that knows no bounds, can be deflated only by showing, as objectively as possible and despite the self-referentiality that such a requirement invokes, just how it bears the indelible mark of the situations and circumstances of its articulators. Thus the conclusion emerges that a realistic, responsible objectivity *requires* taking subjectivity into account (Code 1993).

Departures from an enclosed, unilinear conception of epistemic accountability (from observer to evidence) that move toward community-located theories of knowledge characterize the leading neo-empiricist feminist epistemologies of the 1990s, which have developed primarily from within philosophy of science.

Helen Longino's contextual empiricism centers around the claims that science is social knowledge and background assumptions play a constitutive part in knowledge acquisition and evaluation (Longino 1990). Scientific inquiry cannot be value-free, as traditional empiricists required, for cultural and social values make knowledge possible. Although such assumptions are embedded in the communal wisdom from which inquiry is generated, they are nonetheless open to rigorous critique. Such critique cannot restrict itself to the "context of justification," for value-laden assumptions go much deeper, shaping the conceptualization of projects, the hypotheses that guide and regulate inquiry, and the taken-for-granted beliefs about what counts as evidence and what amounts merely to an aberration. Indeed, Longino shows that diverse background assumptions can produce radically different readings of "the same" natural phenomena. Yet "scientific knowledge is constructed not by individuals applying a method to the material to be known but by inquirers in interaction with one another in ways that modify their observations, theories and hypotheses" (Longino 1990, p. 111). Within a research community, those interactions may not of themselves succeed in exposing background assumptions, which tend to be invisible to the very people whose thinking they shape. Hence Longino urges the need for "outsider" critical voices as participants in a dialogic community hospitable to "transformative criticism" (p. 112). Hers is a pluralistic conception of inquiry in which multiple, diverse voices will claim a hearing and contribute to sustaining community standards of respect for the evidence, accountable cognitive agency, and reliably collaborative knowledge-seeking. Objectivity, on her reading, is an explicitly communicative, communal achievement.

Lynn Nelson's empiricism draws its initial inspiration from the work of W. V. Quine who, she argues, has more to offer to successor epistemologies than orthodox empiricists (Nelson 1990). Nelson rethinks the whole idea of evidence within a conception of knowers as collaborative agents, whose epistemic projects are shaped by, and require evaluation within, the communities where their knowledge-producing practices occur. She argues that "the collaborators, the consensus achievers, and, in more general terms, the agents who generate knowledge are communities and subcommunities, not individuals" (1990, p. 124). In affirming the radical potential of Quinean epistemology, she finds the resources for a robust version of empiricism that is respectful of the evidence and of the impressive achievements of the natural sciences, yet resistant to representing items of knowledge as discrete or autonomous, isolated from the "webs of belief" that contain them and make them possible. Quine, in her reading, eschews classical, passively receptive, "one man, one knowledge claim" assumptions to work with a conception of science as a "bridge of our own making," and of beliefs, embedded in theories, as evolving holistically as those theories are tested against new evidence, put to work in diverse contexts. She elaborates the promise of "naturalistic epistemology" in her critical rereadings of sociobiology and of hunter-gatherer theories in anthropology. Her point is at once to applaud Quine's turn toward real knowledge-making (at least as scientific psychology investigates it) as the place from which epistemologies are generated, and to expose the gender, race, and class insensitivities carried within the going theories of social science, including the very scientific psychology which, for Quine, becomes the place where epistemology is made (see also Code 1996).

Jane Duran's proposed merger between naturalized and feminist epistemology also treats knowledge as communally acquired, corroborated, and elaborated (Duran 1991). Whereas the feminist import of Longino's and Nelson's theories attaches to their critical sociocultural rereadings of the background assumptions (Longino) and webs of belief (Nelson) that perpetuate the androcentricity of received scientific ideology, Duran maintains that feminists can preserve the spirit of analytic philosophy even in "creating a model of epistemic justification that is simultaneously naturalized and gynocentric" (p. 124). The model will make the most of what Duran regards as essentially feminine principles and modes of reasoning. It will draw on object-relations theory, psychoanalysis, and cognitive science to examine how male and female knowers are psychologically produced and reproduced. Duran believes that the model's empirical–analytic rigor will counteract an elusiveness she finds in standpoint theory on issues of truth; its postmodernism, drawn from psychoanalysis read through French feminist theory, will allow it to address female specificity.

According to standpoint theorists, not even the most rigorously feminist empiricism can offer a sufficiently radical analysis of the historical-material circumstances that produce both subjectivities and knowledge. Standpoint theorists construct an analogy between the epistemic position of women under patriarchy and the economic position of the proletariat under capitalism. Just as capitalist ideology represents proletarian subordination to the bourgeoisie as natural, so patriarchal ideology represents women's subordination to men as natural. And just as Marxist analyses take the material-historical circumstances of proletarian lives as their starting-point, so feminist analyses start from the material-historical circumstances of female lives. Patricia Hill Collins, Nancy Hartsock, Hilary Rose, and Dorothy Smith were the principal articulators of standpoint epistemologies in the 1980s, and in the late 1990s are still among its most eminent spokeswomen.

A feminist standpoint is not to be confused with a "women's standpoint," which would be theirs just by virtue of their femaleness; nor is it merely an interchangeable perspective which anyone could occupy just by deciding to do so. On the contrary, it is a hard-won product of consciousness-raising and social-political engagement that exposes the false presuppositions upon which patterns of domination and subordination are built and sustained. Standpoint theorists contend that the minute, detailed, strategic knowledge that the oppressed have had to acquire of the workings of the social order just so as to be able to function within it can be brought to serve as a resource for undermining that very order. Taking refined and elaborated, local and global practices of consciousness-raising as their principal interrogative strategies, standpoint theorists expose the unnaturalness of a patriarchal social order that has successfully represented itself as "natural," to oppressed and oppressors alike. Yet their project is not to aggregate women within a single, unified, or putatively representative standpoint. It is, rather, to honor the material, domestic, emotional, intellectual, and professional labor that women engage in as knowledgeable practices, radically constitutive of knowledge and subjectivity. These theorists aim to revise the social structures that have devalued women's labor (see Ruddick 1989, Rose 1994, Harding 1991), according its practitioners minimal social-political authority even within the professions; and, empowered by those new understandings, they aim to generate radical transformations of the social order.

Both empiricist and standpoint theorists focus not just on knowledge, but also, to varying degrees, on "the knower(s)"; for on this new epistemic agenda, epistemologists can no longer rest content with examining impersonally presented knowledge claims to ascertain their warrant. Questions about who the knower is enter the discussion at every turn. Yet empiricists pose these questions differently from those in whose work Marxist and/or postmodern influences are more explicitly operative. Most feminist empiricists eschew the starker abstract individualism that characterizes classical empiricism and underwrites the methodological solipsism on which it often relies. Yet – to different degrees – the new empiricist knower, even when he or she is represented as embedded in an epistemic community, still comes across as a separate individual, capable of formulating his or her knowledge claims monologically and independently, even in presenting them for community corroboration and critique. The community emphasis redistributes burdens of evidence-gathering and proof and reconfigures patterns of accountability in ways that should drastically alter epistemic practice. Yet even such innovative empiricists as Longino and Nelson, for whom knowledge-production is an explicitly, ineluctably communal activity, offer little analysis of how selves and communities are themselves socially/communally produced within powersaturated structures of domination and subordination. And despite Duran's appeal to psychoanalytic theories of ego development, she fails to consider how the characteristics she reads as quintessentially feminine are products of networks of class, race, and sex/gender privilege that normalize and naturalize the very traits she judges "typically" feminine. Those same structures of power and privilege legitimize psychoanalysis as the producer of truth about male and female adult self-realization, glossing over its complicity with patriarchal power in so doing.

One of the major differences between empiricists and standpoint theorists, then, is in their analyses of subjectivity. Nancy Hartsock (1983) shows how affluent Western societies, whose ethos is governed by economic and political exchange, inevitably produce "rational economic man" as a regulative figure whose competitive, exploitative practices in the public world generate dominant ideals of knowing and being. In such societies, possibilities of common interest and concern give way to self-interested, autonomous. mutually independent knowledge and action. And Hilary Rose (1983) argues that societies that privilege an illusory ideal of detached, intellectual knowing rely on a truncated conception of scientific-epistemic practitioners which bypasses the extent to which hands and hearts are integral knowledge-and-subjectivity-productive aspects of common and communal human *praxes*. As Sonia Kruks (1995) convincingly shows, their conceptions of the mutually constitutive effects of *praxes* and subjectivities differentiate standpoint theorists most strikingly from feminist empiricists.

Beyond empiricism and standpoints

In a landmark article that draws critically on empiricist and standpoint insights, while aligning itself explicitly with neither, Donna Haraway argues for "situated knowledges" which maintain a strong commitment to objectivity – to learning to see well – while denying that everyone will see in precisely the same way, as epistemologies that rely on "the god-trick of seeing everything from nowhere," or on a picture of the knower as neutral and perfectly replicable, take for granted (1991d, p. 189). For Haraway, "seeing well" is not just a matter of having good eyesight: it is a located activity, cognizant of its particularity and of the accountability requirements that are specific to its location. It refuses to posit any subject/object split in the production of knowledge, insisting on "the critical and interpretive core of all knowledge" (p. 191). In situated knowledge-making projects, embodied knowers engage with active objects of knowledge, whose agency and unpredictability unsettle any hopes for perfect knowledge and control. Haraway's primate studies offer exemplary instances of the politics of such knowledge at work; and she finds in ecofeminist engagements with the world as active subject a notable place where feminists have been able to recognize that "we are not in charge of the world" (p.199). Haraway's commitment to "seeing well" preserves an empiricist-realist belief in a world that is independent of the knower, about whose deliverances she or he can be right or wrong. Her emphasis on situatedness and materiality attest to commonalities both with standpoint theorists, and with postmodern critics of the unified and perfectly knowable subject and object of the Enlightenment legacy.

181

My own approach to questions of knowledge is residually empiricist in acknowledging the resistance of the physical, material, and social world to casual restructurings or interventions. Yet my emphasis on the specificity of epistemic agents and the particularity of diverse cognitive circumstances attests to the influence, also, of standpoint and postmodern thinking (Code 1987, 1991, 1995, 1996). My work is as much about subjectivity as about knowledge. Following Annette Baier, I contend that persons are essentially "second persons" whose achieved subjectivity is interactive, dialogic (Baier 1985) and socioculturally embedded. Knowing other people acquires an exemplary status equivalent to the status traditional epistemologists accord to knowledge of middle-sized material objects, for appropriately responsive knowledge of/about people can be less reductive, and more adequate to the heterogeneous constructive-interpretive features of real, everyday knowledge-gathering than standard versions of empirical knowledge have been. The methodological pluralism that emerges from my inquiries owes a debt to Foucault's thinking about "local knowledges." It resists homogenizing under one unified model the people, artifacts, material objects, or events that become the "objects" of knowledge, to work by analogy (and disanalogy) from one knowledge-making situation to another. Knowers face choices in knowledge-making that evoke responsibilities as much to epistemic communities as to the evidence. Hence, where traditional theories of knowledge focus almost exclusively on perception and memory as sources of knowledge, I argue that testimony is at least as salient a source of knowledge, within a politically sensitive epistemology. The multiple patterns of incredulity that acknowledge or dismiss testimony, according to whose it is, who is speaking, within power-infused structures of authority and expertise map, with remarkable accuracy, the rhetorical spaces where the politics of knowledge are enacted. I locate those patterns within an ecologically modeled knowledge and subjectivity, to work toward a (naturalized) understanding of cognitive interdependence, and of the radical interdependence between human lives and the natural–social world (Code 1991, ch. 7, 1996).

Postmodernism?

The very existence of feminist epistemological projects attests, to varying degrees, to the effects of postmodern contestations of "the Enlightenment project." Such contestations are evident, for example, in Linda Alcoff and Elizabeth Potter's introduction to *Feminist Epistemologies* (1993), with its representative samples of state-of-art inquiry, written by many of the leading practitioners in the field in the early 1990s. The language of emancipation, embodiment, power, materiality, and oppression that runs through the introduction culminates in the authors' reference to "the contradictory relationship of feminism to philosophy": in their bold contention that "feminist work in philosophy is scandalous primarily because it is unashamedly a political intervention" (p. 13). Such a claim succinctly attests to the extent to which feminist epistemology has departed from the aims and claims of modernism, with its explicit commitments to apolitical inquiry.

182

Postmodern thinkers resist aggregation under one theoretical rubric. Yet they concur in refusing to believe that the multiplicity of knowledge-making practices can result in a universally valid meta-narrative. Nor are they prepared to conceive of epistemic agents on the model of the unified, coherent, disembodied, perfectly transparent, self-aware Enlightenment self. In the theoretical strands I have traced here, the empiricists tend, in general, to concentrate more on the knowledge question than on questions of subjectivity, and thus to retain closer allegiance to the projects of modernity. Standpoint theorists devote more theoretical attention to questions of subjectivity. Their disruptions of the unified-subjectivity assumptions of the tradition mark these inquiries, also, as postmodern, as they move epistemology away from the abstractions of modernity into real-world, historical-material practice (*praxis*), performed by embodied subjects whose specific experiences have to be taken seriously.

Yet postmodern thinkers who explicitly own the label are usually more radical in their thinking than either empiricists or standpoint theorists. With an indebtedness to "continental" philosophy and to psychoanalytic thought that is at least as great as standpoint theorists' debt to Marxism, postmodernists insist on the opaque and often contradictory, incoherent features of subjectivity. The tone of their discursive assumptions is strikingly audible in Kathleen Lennon and Margaret Whitford's collection *Knowing the Difference: Feminist Perspectives in Epistemology* (1994). Lennon and Whitford observe in their introduction that the postmodern element that becomes visible in most of the essays in the volume is apparent in a "recognition that all of our interactions with reality are mediated by conceptual frameworks or discourses, which themselves are historically and socially situated ... [and that] fragmentation and contradictions are inevitable and we will not necessarily be able to overcome them" (p.5). Postmodern thinkers find themselves, then, caught in a set of tensions that may be unresolvable. Yet it is these very tensions, at this critical-revisionary moment, that can generate the energies feminist epistemologists need if they are to negotiate the complexities of a situation in which it is as important to be objective in order to contest oppression with well-established facts as it is to be strategically skeptical in order not to allow closure that could erase experiences and differences under an assimilationist rubric. It is as important to affirm identities and allegiances as politically informed, active thinkers as to acknowledge the falsely essentializing, solidifying tendencies of identity politics and political categories to impose premature structures on events and circumstances that need to be open to transformative intervention.

Feminists are adopting creative and innovative techniques to work within these tensions. No longer content to try to develop theories of knowledge that could serve philosophical ends alone, epistemologists have turned to interdisciplinary, cross-disciplinary projects where the knowledge at issue has to be worked at, unearthed, and analyzed not just in standard epistemologists' rarefied "S-knows-that-p" propositions, but in its workings at the heart of local, specific inquiry and action in such domains as law, moral deliberation, social science, and policy-making. To cite just one such example, Patricia William's mappings of

183

the effects of systemic racism produce knowledge specific to the (regional) experiences of a professional black woman in the United States, yet translatable by analogy to racism and accountability issues in much wider spheres of relevance. Similarly, feminists are turning to literary texts and cultural production as sites of knowledge-making that interrogate the complacency of mainstream assumptions about power and privilege, sexuality, race and gender, age and disability. These multi-layered, multi-directional projects are naturalizing epistemological inquiry in a new way: producing natural histories of human beings in the myriad activities, both professional and "private" that comprise their lives, and in which they have to be able to know well. Such projects challenge the boundaries of philosophy in general and epistemology in particular, as they reveal that questions about knowledge run through people's lives in ways that no mono-logic, disinterested theory of knowledge could hope to address.

18

Natural sciences

KATHLEEN LENNON

The scope of this article is feminist philosophical engagement with the natural sciences. As a starting point we can view science as having the objective of "producing general propositions about nature, the physical 'out there,' that can be tested empirically where appropriate, and that are rational in character" (Jordanova 1989, p. 17) but we also need to recognize the fluidity of the term "science"; for to term something "scientific" is honorific. It is signaled as something to be trusted and relied on, and there are political as well as intellectual debates concerning what is to be dignified with this title.

Intellectual and political background to feminist philosophies of science

Several intellectual and political movements form the background to feminist critical engagement with the natural sciences. One important movement manifested itself within postpositivist philosophy of science with the work, for example, of Thomas Kuhn and Paul Feyerabend (Kuhn 1962, Feyerabend 1975), who argued against the position that scientific theories were produced and accepted purely on the grounds of empirical adequacy. Following Quine (1963), who pointed out both the underdetermination of theory by data and the lack of brute empirical facts, such writers argued that our classifications do not simply reflect an already categorized reality but rather mediate our observations of the world. Moreover, our choice of theory and accompanying classificatory system is dictated not only by predictive and technological success, which fails to favor a single scheme, but also by social, historical, cultural, and aesthetic factors.

A second contextualizing movement yielded the radical science critiques, especially of the late 1960s and early 1970s. The movement originated from the Left, but challenged a strict Marxist division of science from ideology, recognizing that science, under capitalism, was structured to reflect bourgeois and imperialist interests. Here, with a concentration on the global political economy of science, the distinction between pure science, as knowledge pursued independently of its applications, and technology as good or bad uses of this knowledge, was being undermined. It became clear that the direction of scientific research, including the high proportion devoted to military- or defence-related projects (Rose 1994), was dictated by the profit-making or imperialist objectives of its private and public funders. These radical science movements were, however, noticeably silent on the interrelations between gender and science (Rose 1994, Introduction).

The third important contextualizing movement came from sociologists of knowledge, insisting that there are sociological factors structuring the kinds of knowledge which we produce (Mannheim 1960). Such accounts could take the form of pure social constructionism, in which the idea that knowledge is constrained by an independent reality got lost; but, at their most modest, insisted that the social and historical position of the producers of knowledge was implicated in the knowledge produced. Again, little attention was paid to gender as a significant determinant.

As second-wave feminism emerged, an important area of activity was the formation of women's health groups. Through a network of such self-help groups women shared experience of, and information about, their bodies and their treatment by health-care professionals. Campaigns in the West were paralleled by campaigns of women in developing countries over, for example, the uses of the contraceptives Depro Novera and Norplant as part of Western aid packages and their effects on women's bodies. Certain characteristics of the women's health movement were influential in the more wide-ranging feminist science critiques that followed. The movement used collective methods of knowledge sharing, disseminating information without reference to, or the creation of, authoritative scientific experts. The movement prioritized the voices and experience of those the knowledge concerned. It insisted that anchorage in and answerability to such experience were central criteria of the legitimacy of the knowledge created.

Another important political movement in the West was the women's peace movement. Developing from decades of anti-nuclear protests, a network of women-only peace groups were organized, participating in direct-action strategies opposing, in particular, nuclear weapons. Here a direct association was made between military technology and forms of masculinity articulated as power-hungry, violent and technological (Griffin 1978, Shiva 1989). In the "developing" world women were involved in opposing the Green Revolution and saw the movement to cash crops as a rationalistic technology destroying the ways of life and patterns of ecological balance of generations. This "scientific" agriculture was seen as ignoring the know-how of those who for generations had tended the forests or evolved resistant but ecologically balanced crops. These political movements involved feminist activists in challenging the authority of science, responding to its perceived masculinity, and insisting on attention to evidence and experience which it had failed to accommodate. These movements then fed into the way feminist intellectuals engaged with scientific thinking.

Science as "male"

It was against this background that the feminist critiques of science and technology as "male" emerged. This claim came in many different forms which require careful unpacking. The easy and uncontroversial point is that the science which is dignified as such and passed on in academic and industrial circles is primarily done and taught by men. Certain men also hold the purse-strings via state or industrial funding for research, and their interests and preoccupations serve to determine the direction of the research. Here military-directed research is taken as a prime example. Women become involved in research objectives only as potential consumers (for example, of contraceptives or microwave ovens).

It has also been suggested that the gendered life experiences and subjectivities of the men who practice science have conditioned not only the direction and objectives of the research but also the theoretical narratives which provide the explanations. Such a claim is particularly associated with an appeal to object-relations theory to provide an anatomy of male and female gender character-istics, generated by the position of women as primary carers (Chodorow 1978, Keller 1985, Harding and Hintikka 1983). The predominant motifs are of detached, unemotional, and individualistic men and relational and integrated women. These male gender characteristics are then read into the character of the scientific theories which were produced. So, for example, theorizing the living world as one vast arms race, or images of the immune system as a battlefield or the "master molecule" approach in genetics (Haraway 1991b) can be viewed as reflections of masculinity. These approaches, when first introduced, were seen as the gendered subjectivity of the producers of science being reflected in the product which they produced. What was suggested was the partiality and situatedness of theories which made claims to impartiality and universality. The implication was that with different producers, situated in different locations, different objectives would be pursued and different explanatory narratives pro-duced. Evelyn Fox Keller, in her famous study of the biologist Barbara McClintock (1983), suggests that McClintock's approach showed the possibility of altern-atives. In studying maize, "McClintock shortens the distance between the obser-ver and the object studied and considers the complex inter-action between the organism and its environment" (Tuana 1989, p. 9). Such an approach, for Keller, reflects a sense of relatedness to others and connectivity with the world (Keller 1985, p. 117). One way of reading this early work sees fixed gendered identities as having a formative influence on the construction of scientific the-ories and science's conception of its own enterprise. There are, however, other ways in which the scientific enterprise can be seen as "male."

There are examples from Francis Bacon through to Richard Feynman (in his 1965 Nobel Prize speech) (Rose 1994, p. 18), in which the nature that scientists investigate is conceptualized both as female and an object of invasion, domina-tion, and control (Jordanova 1989, p. 25). Pervasively, the imagery of nature "unveiling before science" is used; with the analogy of revealing the mysteries of the female body (Jordanova 1989). "Science as heroic quest and as erotic technique applied to the body of nature are utterly conventional figures" (Har-away 1991c, p. 205). Even without such revealing metaphors, however, the most commonly articulated account of the scientific process is a gendered one. Here the key terms are those of objectivity and rationality. The validity of scientific knowledge, it is claimed, is achieved via a process of objective testing which ensures that the subjectivity of the knowledge producers is removed by the application of universal and rational procedures. The conceptualizations of objectivity and rationality employed here are placed inside a symbolic order which constructs these notions alongside its constructions of conceptions of masculinity and femininity. The way in which the notions of objectivity and rationality are understood echo our gender norms. It is woven into our hegemonic conceptions of (white, professional European) masculinity that men are capable of detaching themselves from the objects of their study and reaching judgments untinged with emotion, by the application of universal rational principles (Irigaray 1989). It is woven into our hegemonic conceptions of femininity that women are anchored in the sensuous, the emotional and the particular and have difficulty in making detached judgments. (A key study spelling out these interdependencies is Lloyd 1984.) Parallel remarks can be made about the culture of technology. What gets to count as technological is conceptualized with an articulation of masculinity as requiring technological expertise. It is because of these interdependencies that girls can be seen as "doing femininity" in rejecting science and technology. A recognition of this leads us to sophisticate our account of the relationship between gender and science and technology. It is not simply the case that already fixed gendered identities are having a formative influence on the nature of the scientific process. Rather what gets to count as scientific or technological is being constructed interdependently with what is recognized as normatively male and female.

The complexity of the way in which science is gendered is increased when we recognize that science itself yields some of the major texts informing our conceptions of masculinity and femininity. The principal source of these texts have been the biomedical sciences, which have served to naturalize oppositional difference between men and women. These are viewed as being a consequence of nature or biology, given with hormones or brain size and not opposable without damaging cost. There are clear parallels here with scientific work concerned to provide a biological anchoring for the concept of distinct races. Sex-difference research at both the physiological and psychological level is still an ongoing preoccupation, alongside preoccupations to find a gene for homosexuality or to find differences in the brains of transsexuals (*Guardian*, March 12, 1996). Parts of sociobiology locate the different social behavior of men and women in the patterns required to maximize the survival of their respective genes (Lewontin, Rose, and Kamin 1984). A whole range of animal studies interrogate the animal world through the lens of our own social order and read back functions which legitimate that social order as "natural" (Bleier 1988, Haraway 1989). The female body is frequently seen as being at the mercy of hormones which require medical intervention to keep in balance (Oudshoorn 1994).

Feminist critical engagement with this range of theories has been twofold. First, and unproblematically, there has been very careful empirical research which sought to expose the *empirical inadequacies* of much of this work (Bleier 1984, Hubbard and Lowe 1979, Hubbard et al. 1982, Fausto-Sterling 1985).

Second, attention was focused on the *ideological* structuring of these scientific narratives. That is they were shown to be structured in such a way as to support the hierarchical differences between men and women in society. Seeing scientific theories as ideologically masculine in this way was engaging in a more damaging critique than that of incompleteness or limitation of research objectives. The resultant theories are discredited in a more thoroughgoing way. It is important to notice the distinction between these two lines of criticism. The recognition of the ideological function of these naturalizing stories allowed attention to be paid to scientific theories as *texts*, susceptible to the kinds of deconstructive techniques initially at home in the arts and humanities. Attention to the language, metaphors, and symbols employed both in science's conception of itself and in its theoretical narratives about the world reveal that the process of legitimating and naturalizing the position of male dominance is embodied in the imagery and conceptual forms employed. They are made evident by a careful unpicking of the oppositional categories, absences, and marginalities of the scientific text (Keller 1993). Donna Haraway's work on primatology has been exemplary here (1989 and 1991a). She explores the connections between the theoretical accounts of the scientific primatologists and the images and associations of primates in the surrounding culture. These core narratives both direct scientific observation and structure interpretation. She also explores the way in which they legitimate positions of power, of both men and the European races. Haraway's work signals changes in such narrative structures over time. It also highlights the way that feminist primatologists have produced new stories, of female activity and power and cooperative societies. These accounts, however, are nevertheless stories, although answerable to different kinds of agendas.

Appreciating the *textuality* of the scientific enterprise enables us to see that "scientific texts are woven from the materials of the social imagination" (Duden 1991). Consequently the way in which science is gendered is not simply in reflecting the interests and experiences and subjectivities of those who mainly produce it. The conceptual frameworks which scientists employ can be gendered in ways that are not necessarily modified by the entry of women into the profession. In the words of Evelyn Fox Keller, whose recent work adopts such a deconstructionist approach to scientific texts, "Gender norms come to be seen as silent organisers of the mental and discursive maps of the natural worlds we simultaneously inhabit and construct – even of those worlds that women never enter" (Keller 1993: 13) and, we might add, those that do not explicitly talk about men or women.

Accompanying this deconstructive turn in feminist philosophy of science, feminist theorists began to engage in systematic archaeologies of the emergence of scientific theories. Here, by means of careful historical excavations of the emergence of particular theories, attention is paid not only to the patterns of conceptualization employed in particular scientific texts but also to the concrete material practices employed in scientific laboratories and the negotiations

189

between different sites of power out of which scientific "facts" emerge. Donna Haraway's work incorporates such archaeologies. Another exemplary text is Nelly Oudshoorn's *Beyond the Natural Body*, which explores the emergence of theories of sex hormones, out of which came classification of hormones as male and female, and a conception of the female body as being at the mercy of its hormonal balance. "Science is not just words .... . The development of scientific knowledge depends not only on ideas, ideologies or theories, but also on complex instruments, research materials, testing practices" (Oudshoorn 1994: 13). The emergence of theories of sex hormones rested not only on gendered cultural assumptions but also on contingencies such as the availability of urine from gynaecological clinics or mares' urine from stables, enabling the production and investigation of the so-called female sex hormone. Crucial to this process was the shifting power-balances between clinicians and laboratory scientists and the links to a pharmaceutical industry which transformed a concept into a chemical substance that could be manufactured.

What becomes most philosophically salient from both the deconstructionist and the archaeological work is the recognition of the *contingency* of the scientific narratives, and the possibility of alternative ways of dealing with the data which might better suit our epistemological objectives.

Feminist philosophies of science

The impact of the feminist critiques of science as male led to feminist philosophers of science sharing moments of thought with other postpositivist philosophers of science. There was a rejection of the givenness of observation, an acceptance of the underdetermination of theory by data, and a recognition that science is "story-laden." The deconstructionist and archaeological turn in feminist philosophy of science, however, provided tools for exploring the social and political dimensions of scientific storytelling in ways that could not be addressed within analytic postpositivism. For feminist philosophers of science the stories which science tells reflect: the conceptual resources available in the culture, the practices accepted as constituting proof and disproof, the power relations between those involved in the construction of theory, and the power relations in society at large which established who could take part in the construction of the scientific stories in the first place. It is from this complex set of factors that "facts" emerge, and what is to count as "nature" becomes established.

Most feminist philosophers of science accepted that this was a reflection of science as usual, not of "bad" science, and rejected as unrealizable a project of producing knowledge which did not bear the marks of its material and cultural conditions of production. However, once we recognize that it is not just in the production of ideologically distorted theories that the account of nature is mediated by culture, we are confronted by epistemological dilemmas. Theories cannot be assessed simply as being more or less adequate reflections of reality, nor by reference to universal norms of rationality. These are themselves situated, textual and variable. For some writers, often identified as postmodernist feminists

(Nicholson 1990), such a recognition forces the abandonment of traditional epistemological questions concerning justification. Instead, our defence of preferred narratives becomes strategic and small scale, and possible only amongst those who already share agreement in judgments. For many feminists engaging with science, however, such a "postmodern" moment is especially problematic. Many feminists have wished to discredit and displace certain scientific theories, for example, those employing naturalizing discourses around sex differences. Moreover, feminists need narratives about the world which will facilitate effective interventions, or enable certain practical forms of life (for example, we want to know whether the quality of vaginal mucus is a reliable predictor of fertility, or how the Internet functions).

Recognition of the textuality and locatedness of scientific knowledge has not therefore led to the abandonment of epistemological questions, but has simply highlighted their complexity. As Haraway points out,

> the practices of the sciences force one to accept two simultaneous, apparently incompatible truths. One is the historical contingency of what counts as nature for us; the thoroughgoing artifactuality of a scientific object of knowledge that makes it inescapably and radically contingent ... . And simultaneously scientific discourses make claims ... physically ... they have a sort of reality to them which is inescapable. No scientific account escapes being story laden, but it is equally true that stories are not all equal here. Radical relativism just won't do. (Haraway 1991b)

Despite their differences, therefore, most feminist philosophers of science have worked within a framework of critical realism, recognizing that our narratives are answerable to something independent of them which plays an active role in their construction and can resist certain modes of articulation. Naomi Scheman talks of a realism that recognizes the world as "not dead or mechanistic" but as "Trickster, as protean, ... always slipping out from under our best attempts to pin it down. The real world is not the world of our best physics but the world that defeats any physics that would be final. that would desire to be the last word" (Scheman 1993b, p. 100).

A respect for such critical realism requires that we retain criteria of empirical adequacy insisting our theories make sense of what we simultaneously encounter and produce. However, along with other postpositivist philosophers, feminist philosophers of science are aware that there will be more than one account which can satisfy these demands. Moreover, what seems empirically adequate rests on a whole background of assumptions. All of the standardly referenced studies on the causes of heart disease have been done using only male subjects. This research appeared empirically adequate because there was an assumption that the male body was the norm, and that differences between male and female subjects were insignificant outside the area of reproduction. What this makes clear is that the notion of empirical adequacy is not "innocent." What gets to count as such is conditioned by sets of beliefs which cannot be neatly disentangled into "factual" and "evaluative" categories. These points have been highlighted in an article by Lynn Hankinson Nelson (1993b), in a discussion of the nature of evidence. Once we recognize that an uninterrogated conception of empirical adequacy is not sufficient to act as a criterion of theory choice, we need to pay attention to what epistemological virtues we want our theories to additionally display. It is here that it is possible for our philosophy of science to be explicitly politicized, and cognitive and social aims brought into play to ensure that our scientific narratives are answerable to the evaluations and commitments of the communities they serve. We are anxious to develop explanatory narratives which allow empowering interventions. We want to reject those which serve explicitly ideological purposes; and we can build such criteria explicitly into the objectives we wish our theories to display. When feminist primatologists produced new narratives, of female activity and power and cooperative societies, their accounts were constrained by requirements of empirical adequacy, but they were not politically neutral. They were looking for empowering accounts. Nelly Oudshoorn (1994) discusses a period when despite previous classification into male and female hormones it became clear that neither set was found in bodies without the other. What had been regarded as male sex organs did not develop without so-called female hormones. It was also the case that attention to hormone presence, increasingly seen as a marker of sex difference, didn't dictate a division into just two sexes. There was rather a continuum and patchwork of similarities and differences. Gender divisions within culture told against the creation of a theoretical narrative here which did away with the division into just two sexes. Recontemplating this moment now with altered political sensibilities might, however, open up the possibility of alternative accounts.

Widening the range of epistemological virtues in this way, however, requires that we learn to pay attention to the textuality of science, to its language, metaphors, and narrative structures in addition to and interdependently with assessing its empirical adequacy. This opens the door for linking together more traditional epistemological concerns in philosophy of science with deconstructive ones. The deconstructive readings of scientific texts and archaeological accounts of theory production, including crucially the power relations which feed into the emergence of scientific texts, can then provide evidence relevant for their assessment. Recognition, for example, of the ideological role of the naturalizing narratives concerning gender and race can count as evidence against them. Within this framework the notion of the answerability of theory to evidence remains a central concern, but what counts as evidence widens.

The range of epistemological virtues our science should promote in addition to empirical adequacy is, however, a highly contested matter. It forces attention to the constitution of scientific communities by whose practices these virtues become established. For Nelson, our assessment of evidence is a communal enterprise, and "my claims to know are subject to the knowledge and standards constructed by the various communities of which I am a member" (Nelson 1993b, p. 186). For Helen Longino (1990, 1993b), such a community must contain diversity to enable the background assumptions, against which an assessment of relevant evidence is made, to become visible. For Sandra Harding (1991, 1993a), attention to the perspectives of those who have been marginal in the production of knowledge brings into relief sources of evidence invisible to dominant groups, makes explicit background assumptions which are otherwise taken for granted, and exposes ideological structuring of narratives. (For further discussion of Harding and Longino and associated issues of objectivity see Article 17, EPISTEMOLOGY).

Despite internal differences, feminist philosophy of science has been marked by what Hilary Rose terms "responsible rationality." The responsibility here is both to a world which is not of our creation, and to the diverse communities of which we are a part, and which our science is intended to empower. Such a responsibility requires that our research objectives are linked to the diverse needs of these communities and that their experiences are incorporated into our empirical data. It requires that scientists develop a reflexive sensitivity to the way in which science reflects the social imagination, and interrogate their language, metaphors, and narrative structures to ensure that they reflect and empower the communities they wish to serve. It also crucially requires that, for interconnected, political and epistemological purposes, we diversify the community of those who bear the mark of "scientific professional."

19

Biological sciences

LYNDA BIRKE

What is the "biological body"?

Our bodies are ourselves: yet we are also more than our bodies. In the early years of "second-wave" feminism in the West, embodiment was acknowledged implicitly in the action of women's health groups, and campaigns for reproductive rights. But simultaneously, bodies failed to enter our theorizing. Central to theorizing then was a distinction between "sex," (which anatomically distinguishes males and females) from "gender" (the processes of becoming "woman" or "man"). Although recent feminist writing tends to decry that simple opposition (see Article 29, GENDER), the ghost of biology still haunts us: biological sex, the biological body, remain problematic concepts for feminist theorizing.

But what does the term "biology" connote? It can mean a particular discipline, part of the natural sciences. "Biology" implies the study of living organisms and their processes. But the word can also be synonymous with those processes, as in "human biology." In this sense, the term "biology" all too often invokes dualism, as it is taken to include bodily processes, and nature "out there." This sense of biology, and of "biological," tends to be troublesome for feminism.

Biological arguments have all too often been made in ways that buttress gender divisions. Such biological determinism has, for example, been adduced to argue that women are, say, genetically predisposed toward nurturing behavior while men are inclined toward adventures and fights. Politically, then, feminists have tended to oppose biological determinism and to insist on some form of social constructionism of gender, or of other social categories (such as sexuality).

In this article, I will examine some of the ways in which we have analyzed arguments rooted in biological claims. In particular, I draw on the work of feminists challenging the philosophical and theoretical underpinnings of biological ideas. Mainstream philosophy of biology covers many areas: it shares with other studies in philosophy of science a concern with issues such as empiricism and positivism, with objectivism and realism, for example. But it also has its own concerns, with, for instance, theories of evolution or genetics. Here, what is at issue includes the nature of explanation and evidence when, say, biologists speak of phenomena such as natural selection or adaptation (e.g. Hull 1988, Sober 1993).

Feminist engagement with philosophical issues in biological thinking has covered several quite disparate areas. These include: ecology (Gross and Averill

194

1983, Plumwood 1993); immunology (Haraway 1991b, E. Martin 1994); evolutionary theory and molecular biology (Keller 1993, Masters 1995); bioethics, including new reproductive technologies and genetic engineering (Hubbard 1990); the relation between concepts of humans and other animals (Birke 1994); and the body and its developmental processes (Bleier 1984, Birke 1986, Fausto-Sterling 1992).

Yet, while apparently very diverse, these approaches share certain themes which I will draw out here, using one or two areas as illustrative. As other articles in this volume point out, feminist scholars are critical of the logical positivism that characterizes scientific thinking; rather, they have insisted on the social situatedness of the knower and on the theory-laden nature of scientific inquiry (see Article 20, SOCIAL SCIENCES).

Another strand of critiques of positivist biology, however, is opposition to epistemological reductionism. General critiques of reductionism (e.g. Koestler and Smythies 1968, Dialectics of Biology Group 1982a, 1982b, Lewontin, Rose, and Kamin 1984) are joined by feminist versions, which analyze ways in which epistemological reductionism contributes to biological determinism, and thence to particular ways of conceptualizing gender.

Helen Longino, for example (1990), examines the prevalent linear-causal model of explanation in the biology of behavior. She focuses particularly on assumptions of linear causality implicit in hormonal explanations of human or non-human behavior. Hormones, that is, are assumed to lead to particular kinds of behavior through their action on the adult or prenatal brain (similar analyses of the linear-causal model can be found in Birke 1986 and Oudshoorn 1994).

Longino thus examines theory-laden assumptions operating in research into behavioral sex differences. Implicit stereotypes (rumbustious boys, and passive girls, for instance) run through much of this research, inevitably influencing the processes of hypothesis construction and interpretation of data. The linear model, she notes, assumes the brain to be a black box, positioned between hormones and behavior, and assumes that the organism lacks agency; behavior results from hormones acting on the box's hard wiring.

As an alternative approach, she advocates selectionist views of brain function, which insist on brain complexity and agency (this draws on recent work in cognition, emphasizing, for example, how the brain uses parallel processing and complex sorting of information). Whatever the merits of this particular theory, it does, she insists, return agency to the organism.

Longino argues for "contextual empiricism." By this she means that she does not want to lose some aspects of empiricism: "what we see is what we experience," she insists (1990, p. 215). Like Sandra Harding's (1991) advocacy of "strong objectivity" which takes account of the social positioning of knowers, Longino seeks a social account of objectivity which acknowledges background assumptions in evidential reasoning, yet at the same time avoids the pitfall of extreme relativism of truth claims. This role of background assumptions, she argues,

is grounds for unbridled relativism only in the context of an individualist conception of scientific method and scientific knowledge. If our conception of the methods
of knowledge construction in science is broadened to embrace the social activities of
evidential and particularly conceptual criticism, we see how individual subjective
preferences are minimized in the final products.   (p. 216)

Feminist analyses of biological thought typically start from such premises:
evidential reasoning in biology, as elsewhere in science, is very much a social
activity, and includes social values. It is therefore, an activity with which
feminist and other critics can engage. Moreover, feminists usually advocate
more complex, and context-dependent, approaches to the "biological" world.
These are seen to be less overdetermined than the prevailing linear models,
and hence more likely to have explanatory power. While feminist theorists are
often wary of arguing for any absolute truth, the insistence on more complex,
context dependent views of biology implies a belief that such views are more
"true" – at least in the sense that they better explain how nature works than the
simpler, linear models.

It is not only the validity of truth claims at issue here, however. One important
reason why feminists have insisted on context-dependency has to do with the
political effects of simple reductionist models. Not only does reductionism imply
violence toward nature in its assumption that nature is best understood by
analyzing component parts, but reductionism and linear-causal models can
lead to "magic bullet" answers. So, rather than try to understand the complexity
of a problem, scientists sometimes turn to surgery, drugs, or genetic solutions.
Claiming a "gene for learning disability" conveniently lets educational systems
off the hook (Hubbard and Wald 1993).

Challenging reductionism in biology

There are, then, many ways in which critics have challenged epistemological
reductionism in biology (methodological reductionism, the methods by which
science proceeds analytically and experimentally, is less often criticized: see
Longino 1990). There are two main, though overlapping, threads to these
challenges; first, critics insist on viewing nature/biology as more complex and
less fixed than many reductionist accounts allow, and second, they insist on
interactive models of causality.

One example of the first thread comes from work analyzing scientific accounts
of animal behavior (Haraway 1989, Birke 1994). Those who argue biological
determinism typically use stories about "what animals do" in order to argue for
biological determination of human behavior. But those stories are written in
language implying inferiority and fixity in non-humans in the first place, which
is then read back onto human behavior. Animals become, for example, little
more than bundles of instincts in (human) social theory (see Birke 1994,
pp. 105–9). Yet, there is plenty of evidence that the behavior of non-human
animals is more complex than we tend to assume; moreover, the ways in which

scientists have reported animal skills and capabilities is itself rooted in all kinds of concepts of hierarchy and domination (Haraway 1989, Birke 1994). If we construct images of non-humans as stupid, then seeing such species as mirrors of human behavior is certainly problematic for humans. Notions of stupidity, moreover, fuel the Enlightenment belief in the superiority of (human, male) rationality.

What is at issue here is the social situatedness of scientific knowledge (and its dependence on Western cultural assumptions about animality and humanity), and a concern to "rewrite the stories" to produce different kinds of knowledge claims. These draw on available evidence, but might use that to generate different hypotheses or conclusions.

Examples of the second thread, using more complex and interactive models, come from ecological and evolutionary theorizing. Critical theorists concerned with evolutionary ideas, for example, often deplore the growth of neo-Darwinism, with its insistence on competition in nature, and concepts of "selfish genes." Among other things, critics point out, such discourse is both rooted in, and makes justificatory claims for, a particular form of late capitalist society (e.g. Bleier 1984).

Such conceptions of nature assume a dead, static view of an organism's environment. In her critique of modern evolutionary theory Judith Masters (1995) notes how ecological and evolutionary theory speaks of "niches" which have to be "filled" by species – surely a passive notion. We should, she believes, insist on viewing environments as themselves composed of interacting organisms which change all the time, thus changing "niches." Organisms and their surroundings co-adapt, she insists, rather than one adapting to the other as conventional neo-Darwinism would have it.

Opposition to reductionism, then, forms an important part of feminist theorizing. This work maps onto some mainstream philosophy of biology (in relation to evolution, say). But its focus differs, being concerned also with developing other ways of thinking biology. Such themes – opposition to reductionism, and a concomitant concern to infer different accounts from available evidence (in less reductionistic frameworks) – run through most feminist work on biology. I want now to turn to theorizing about the body and to analyze in some detail feminist approaches in philosophy and in biology to the body.

The body is good to think with? Living the body in 1980s feminism

"The body" is a focus of growing intellectual interest, both within and without feminism. Some writers, such as Moira Gatens, employ earlier frameworks to transcend dualisms such as sex/gender. She suggests returning to Spinoza's metaphysics, in which the "body is not part of passive nature ruled over by an active mind but rather the body is the ground of human action" (1988, p. 68). This, she claims, would allow us to acknowledge cultural and historical specificities while moving beyond the traditional political assumption of bodies as given.

197

Although forms of social constructionism still prevail, some theorists attempt to transcend the mind/body dichotomy through phenomenological approaches emphasizing the *lived body* (e.g. Young 1990b). This is a body that is not given but is both signifying and signified, historically contingent and social (see Grosz 1994c). "The body" in this theorizing becomes central to understanding women's experiences but is not fixed or presocial. It becomes instead, "a body as social and discursive object, a body bound up in the order of desire, signification, and power" (Grosz 1994c, p. 19, and Butler 1993).

Insisting on the "lived body" is important, and understanding how it is signified – and lived – is critical for feminist theorizing which no longer ignores the body. Yet gaps remain. First, it fails to pay much heed to the body's *interior* and its processes; and secondly, it does not sufficiently address bodily development. Both of these fall within the remit of "biology": as such, it has fallen largely to feminist biologists to begin the task of retheorizing.

Feminist theorists continue to deconstruct texts and visual images; yet the abstractions called "diagrams of the body" rarely merit much attention, except as historical artifacts. Thomas Laqueur (1990) notes how representations of the reproductive organs have changed during recent centuries. From carefully executed drawings, shaded to show fine details, anatomical illustration has moved to highly abstract, stylized images. These, which most of us would take for granted in biology textbooks, need more detailed feminist analyses.

Picturing the body's interior is, nevertheless, evident in two important feminist works, both dealing with immunology. Donna Haraway (1991c) and Emily Martin (1994) work with changing images of the immune system and how these are culturally mediated. Here, at least, the interior of the body enters the realms of cultural production and feminist theory. I want to emphasize two aspects of these texts. The first is the stress on cultural understandings, so that "the immune system" can be understood principally (perhaps only) in terms of the language and images with which it is described. Thus, Emily Martin notes the ways in which narratives of immune bodies have changed dramatically from one of bodily defences, under siege from external pathogens, to bodies responding flexibly to external demands.

The permeability of the body's exterior is the second theme. The postmodern immune system, suggests Haraway, is part of a "network-body"; it is "everywhere and nowhere" all at once (1991d, p. 218). The body – as bounded, as the quintessential individual – is threatened even by the discourses of science itself. Its boundaries become permeable, opening it up to networks of influence inside and out.

We can see in these accounts feminist insistence on the situatedness of scientific knowledge, and on biological complexity. Nevertheless, apart from these studies of the discourses of immunology, there is rather little consideration of bodies *as* biological. Indeed, it seems to me that much feminist thinking still harbours an underlying belief in the biological body as fixed – even when that belief is apparently denied by statements that we cannot understand our biological selves *except* through culture. Where does that leave (say) the action of nerves, the functioning of immune systems, or the development of embryos from

198

fertilized eggs? That *level* of bodily working seems to remain forever outside culture, fixed into "biology." In important ways, that underlying assumption that some aspects of "biology" are fixed becomes itself the grand narrative (albeit implicit) from which feminist and other social theorists are seeking to escape.

While the new focus on the body is welcome, it perpetuates an additive model. There is always a level of "biology" that seems beyond the cultural analysis – usually, the body's interior. Interestingly, it is also the workings of the interior that largely escape the attentions of mainstream philosophers of biology, who tend to focus on areas such as evolution or genetics. Physiology seems doomed to narratives of mechanism and reductionism, unsullied by philosophical attention.

Most of the time, our physiology seems constant; it is a part of our bodily "nature." Now there is an important reason for assuming such constancy, which comes from the study of physiology itself. For those of us trained in the biological sciences, the body's functions – physiology – can be roughly categorized into systems: nervous system, endocrine system, immune system, and so on. A central principle of how these systems work is homeostasis, the body's ability to maintain a constant state. So, for example, body temperature is normally around 37 degrees Celsius, and levels of sugar in the blood usually (except in some disease states) remain within certain limits.

Scientific language of separate systems maintaining constancy becomes part of a wider cultural language, assumed even within accounts of the "socially constructed body." Thus, health is a matter of maintenance, or keeping things constant, while disease represents perturbation. This way of thinking is paralleled by the abstraction and reductionism of the language of genetics as fixity, a language increasingly moving from laboratories and into the street. Biological bodies, within these narratives, become fixed by the parallel languages of genes (determining who we are) and homeostasis (which ensures we stay that way). Yet isn't such language itself a social and cultural construction?

Bodily interiors need to emerge from the confines of physiological discourse into wider cultural criticism. We need to insist on thinking about the biological body as changing and changeable, as *transformable* (Birke 1986. 1994. Fausto-Sterling 1992, Hubbard 1990). All our cells constantly renew themselves, even bone (which is always remodeling, especially when we put loads on it in exercise). There are, nevertheless, constraints, imposed by one part of the body on another; as a result, our overall bodily appearance changes relatively little in adulthood.

Living the body means experiencing it *as* transformable, not only as cultural meanings/readings, but also within itself. Whatever physiology may say, I do not know whether we would experience the interior workings of our bodies in similar ways if the culture in which we live were to change dramatically. People with diseases, or some forms of physical disability, may well experience their bodily interiors differently from persons who are well or able-bodied: but part of that experience depends upon the cultural experience of living out medical definitions of pathological functioning. In that sense at least, culture shapes our internal experiencing.

199

Moreover, "homeostasis" can be turned around, decentering the "constancy" theme and focusing instead on fine changes involved in keeping within gross limits. How might we understand potential changes in these, and how they are culturally contingent? Over time, too, bodies are transformable; the type of muscle fiber predominating in any one muscle mass is at least partly a product of the kind of stress put on the muscle in exercise. Judith Butler's concept of performativity (1993) is useful here: She focuses on gendered performance, analyzing in detail the cultural production of gender transgression. But might performativity (in the sense of iterated performance, whether or not to do with gender) itself also influence the "way the body works," its interiority? We perform many roles, any or all of which could influence bodily workings.

Meanwhile, our internal organs and tissues also perform. Physiological language is deeply mechanistic – it speaks of control systems, and feedback loops serving to stabilize them. Yet implicit in these systems is *active* response to change and contingency, bodily interiors that constantly react to change inside or out, and act upon the world.

The body becoming

Even fetuses enter culture, through the use of techniques of prenatal visualization and screening. Yet, human development – the processes of becoming human as we enter the world, or of becoming adult as we grow – seems to be missing from feminist insistence on "lived bodies" or social constructionism.

We can emphasize human development in terms of transformability, in opposition to the fixity implied by some concepts of "the gene." The discourse of "the" gene is gaining ground; Dorothy Nelkin and Susan Lindee argue that: "The findings of scientific genetics – about human behavior, disease, personality and intelligence – have become a popular resource precisely because they conform to and complement existing beliefs about identity, family, gender and race" (1995, p. 197). So, while feminist and postmodern theorists increasingly question notions of identity, such ideas are reinforced in the wider culture within a (dangerous) discourse of "genes."

Within this discourse of identity and determinism, "we" unfold from the genes laid down when sperm meets egg. It is a modern version of preformationism – the eighteenth-century idea that we unfold from a tinier version of ourselves housed comfortably in sperm (or egg). Genes as blueprints is a similar and persistent idea, as Susan Oyama (1985) pointed out.

Yet there are other ways of thinking about our becoming. Even within science, there are other positions, such as emphasizing active engagement of the embryo in its own development (see, for example, Fausto-Sterling 1989). The embryo actively makes over its environment, engaging with its own development; it is thus a self-organizing entity, rather than a passive victim of genetic inheritance (see Goodwin 1994). Its essence, if there is one, is not fixity, but transformability. The embryo/fetus in this story is like the physiological organism as I conceive it above; it is constantly changing and having agency in that change.

Reinventing the organism

In thinking about organisms or development as transformative, I recognize that the organism itself becomes a more fluid and permeable concept (with implications for selfhood and subjectivity). Elizabeth Grosz (1994c) suggests an association with gender in notions of fluidity: "women's corporeality is inscribed as a mode of seepage," she argues (1994c, p. 203). Female bodies thus culturally echo themes of seeping liquids and formless flow, of uncontrollability.

Donna Haraway's vision of the cyborg (1991d) also implies fluidity. She speaks of "polymorphous, information" systems, emphasizing rates of flow across boundaries rather than bodily integrity. While both Haraway's vision and Grosz's description of female fluidity are compatible with my insistence on transformation, I want also to retain some sense of organisms as entities. Haraway opposes holistic/organismic views (and related stories of development as progress), as fostering a kind of solipsism. In her utopia, organisms seem to disappear into webs of complexity, with entities dispersing into information; they become "strategic assemblages ... ontologically contingent constructs" (1991b, p. 220).

But organisms are more than just strategic assemblages of cells/information: they are self-actualizing agents. Insisting on organisms as entities/agents returns them conceptually to the study of biology – from which whole organisms have almost disappeared in the world of genes as prime movers. If, as Haraway insists, it's problematic to think of organisms in terms of a path of (genetic) progress (a narrative deeply embedded in Western culture), then we should certainly use other metaphors. One approach retaining organismic entities is provided by Brian Goodwin (1994). Drawing on the sciences of chaos, he describes ways in which emergent order can arise from apparent chaos in nature. Organisms (bodies), in this view, are *self*-organizing; they *are* processes. And they have value, he suggests, as entities – a position arguing against the extreme reductionism that takes organisms apart to reconstitute them (as, for example, in genetic engineering or the use of animals as organ "donors" for transplant surgery).

Ascribing agency and transformativity to organisms/bodies works against the social devaluation of the body and its interior that contributes to women's (and others') oppressions. Moreover, it works against simple dichotomous classifications of mind/self versus body, for both exemplify the same or overlapping agencies. Elizabeth Grosz (1994c) similarly emphasizes the need for feminist philosophy to seek an "embodied subjectivity" (p. 22).

To see organisms/bodies as having agency and the ability to be self-organizing also implies that social constructions and experiences of gender can themselves be part of a process. "Sex" cannot thus be prior to gender, but itself shaped by, and contingent to, gender. Put another way, processes involved in creating and continually recreating (sexed) bodies are partly material and partly social/experiential. Out of those are created the marked bodies, the bodies of difference, that feminist writers such as Grosz insist upon.

Remaining uncertainties

In examining feminist work on embodiment in relation to scientific explanations, I recognize two tensions. First, I draw on both postmodernist insistence on science as narratives *and* on belief in some form of realism. These are not necessarily incompatible, and tension between them seems inevitable – indeed, desirable, if we are to escape from such binaries as narrative versus realism itself.

Secondly, "transformation" may not always serve feminist political ends. My insistence on transformability is for thinking about organisms. Genetic reductionism, however, also (somewhat paradoxically) permits discourses of transformation, by moving genes around, *within* the rhetoric of reductionism. Surgical transformation may not serve progressive interests, either; cosmetic or transsexual surgeries, for example, involve literally making the body over to achieve desired goals. But in neither is the material body thought of as having internal agency; rather, it is a fixed entity which is at odds with what is desired. (I am not saying here that thinking of agency will necessarily make the desired changes, simply that seeing bodies as reducible to interchangeable bits is part of the discourse of fixity.)

Yet the fact that bodies are alterable within reductionist logic is not itself an argument against transformation and complexity. We need urgently to find ways of thinking about bodily processes (or about "biology" more generally) that move away from simple reductionism, and that simultaneously allow us to theorize bodies lived *in* culture.

The search for alternative models, for different stories to tell, lies at the heart of feminist theorizing about biology. Feminists insist on more complex, nuanced, ways of interpreting biological processes. Partly, we do so because even empiricism allows different ways of interpreting evidence. Complex models better describe how things work: they also provide alternative narratives, in the postmodern sense, which challenge Enlightenment concepts of one truth (see Hekman 1992).

A second, more clearly political, reason for feminist struggles to rename nature through complexity and transformation is that we can thus challenge persistent dualisms. Seeing gender opposed to the bedrock of sex is one example. Others include the dualisms of organism/environment, human/animal, bodily fixity/cultural lability, nature/nurture, and so on. As feminist critics often note, dualistic thought is deeply problematic – not least because it feeds dualisms of gender.

In opposing reductionism, and ensuing dualisms, feminists must insist on the uncertainty and indeterminacy of bodies. Yet we must also recognize that indeterminacy and transformability are not without limit. Bodies may constantly undergo interior change, but within apparent sameness. Perhaps nowhere is this more apparent than in the bodies of those with physical disabilities. Transformation may be the modus operandi of the body's interior, but it is unlikely to lead to sudden able-bodiedness. And nor will thinking of bodies in terms of transformation alter the present cultural reproduction of disability.

While recent feminist work insists on cultural contingencies in describing bodies as marked, as signifiers of culture, it rarely goes beyond bodily surfaces. Culture is inscribed *on* those surfaces. In doing so, we run the risk, as Elizabeth Grosz rightly recognizes, of leaving the body's interior in the realm of biological fixity. Yet that risk rests on how we conceptualize biology itself. Bodies are good to think with only when we think of indeterminacy or transformation. "Biology" is not always the ultimate limitation.

20

Social sciences

MARY HAWKESWORTH

Social sciences seek to understand and explain human existence in all its complexity. Thus they encompass the study of individual consciousness and behavior, social relations and cultural practices, social systems, and structural forces. Investigations of these diverse phenomena proceed in accordance with modes of inquiry sanctioned by the academic disciplines of anthropology, archaeology, cultural studies, economics, geography, history, political science, psychology, sociology, and women's studies.

Philosophers of the social sciences investigate the nature of social science inquiry and the epistemological warrants for the methodological practices within these diverse disciplines. In the twentieth century, debates within the philosophy of social sciences have engaged the problem of "demarcation" (how to distinguish science from non-science), the problem of validity (how to distinguish truth from error), and problems pertaining to the theoretical constitution of facticity (the recognition that what is perceived as reality is mediated by presuppositions that are culturally freighted). Over the past thirty years, the field has undergone systematic transformation as positivist and critical rationalist approaches have been supplanted as a result of challenges raised by historians of science, sociologists of science, postmodernists, and feminist scholars.

The central tenets of logical positivism included the verification criterion of meaning (the view that a proposition is meaningful if and only if it can be empirically verified), the fact/value dichotomy (the belief that value-neutral observation, description, and explanation are possible and are constitutive of the unique domain of science), the unity of science (the belief that the logic of scientific inquiry is the same for all fields), the inductive method (observation of particulars as the basis for empirical generalizations), and the covering law model of explanation (events are explained when it is demonstrated that they could have been expected, given the presence of certain initial conditions and the general laws of the field). These tenets shaped the behavioral approach to the social sciences which gained ascendancy in the United States in the 1960s and which conceived the social sciences in terms of "value-free," quantitative studies designed to discover the "laws" of social behavior.

Although positivism still structures the practices of many of the social science disciplines, philosophers of science have demonstrated serious defects in its major tenets. The verification criterion of meaning is self-refuting. The fact/value dichotomy misconstrues the psychology of perception, the role of language in description, the role of theory in hypothesis formation, and the disciplinary practices of scientists. Both the reflexivity of human beings and the cultural specificity of social practices suggest that methods devised for the study of the natural world will fail to explicate social reality adequately. Induction cannot guarantee the validity of scientific knowledge, for no amount of confirmations can conclusively prove a universal generalization or negate the possibility that the future may be different from the past. The covering law model conflates explanation and prediction, taking correct prediction as an indicator of truth while failing to recognize that an incorrect theory can generate correct predictions.

Postpositivist approaches to the philosophy of science emphasize that the practices of social scientists are inherently theory-laden. Theoretical presuppositions shape perception and determine what will be taken as fact; they confer meaning on experience and control the demarcation of significant from trivial events; they afford criteria of relevance according to which facts can be organized, tests envisioned, and the acceptability of scientific conclusions assessed; they accredit particular models of explanation and strategies of understanding; and they sustain specific methodological techniques for gathering, classifying, and analyzing data. Theoretical presuppositions set the terms of scientific debate and organize the elements of scientific activity. The implications of the postpositivist conception of science are the subject of ongoing debate among proponents of various versions of empiricism (scientific/critical realists, contextualists, naturalists, historical/dialectical materialists, critical theorists, and postmodernists) who are attempting to resolve questions concerning truth, theory choice, and cognitive practices in relation to a social reality that is theoretically constituted and in which all theories are underdetermined (Bernstein 1976, 1983, Hacking 1983, Harre 1986, Hesse 1980).

Feminist philosophers of the social sciences have made important contributions to the postpositivist critique of positivism. Taking feminist social scientists' demonstration of the persistence of androcentrism in the social sciences as their point of departure, feminist philosophers of the social sciences have sought to explain how assumptions about and experiences of gender are factors in social scientific theorizing (Harding 1986, 1991, Longino 1990, Marshall 1994, Nelson 1990, Wylie 1991a, 1991b, 1991c, 1992). They have demonstrated that gender symbolism and analogies drawn from contemporary gender relations structure allegedly "neutral" scientific claims to such an extent that gender must be understood not only as a constitutive force in social relations, but also as constitutive of perception and reasoning in scientific endeavors (Harding 1986, Kessler and McKenna 1978, Scott 1986, Wylie 1992). Feminist use of gender as an analytic category has generated a range of critiques of traditional conceptions of scientific objectivity, scientific methodology, and of experience. Exploring the practices of feminist social sciences, feminist philosophers of the social sciences also have raised complex questions about the relation between the political project of emancipation and disciplinary norms of truth (Alcoff 1989, Longino 1989, 1993b, Wylie 1992).

Critiques of objectivity, methodology and experience

In the context of traditional scientific investigations, an objective account implies a grasp of the actual qualities and relations of objects as they exist independent of the inquirer's thoughts and desires regarding them (Cunningham 1973, p. 4). Objectivity, then, promises freedom from distortion, bias, and error in intellectual inquiry. Feminist critiques of objectivity have been triggered by breach of promise. Feminist scholarship across the social science disciplines has revealed that androcentrism routinely surfaces in scientific investigations. Observations, beliefs, theories, methods of inquiry, and institutional practices routinely labeled "objective" fall far short of the norm. A significant proportion of feminist scholarship involves detailed refutations of erroneous claims about women produced in conformity with prevailing disciplinary standards of objectivity. Feminist scholars have documented extensive androcentrism in diverse scientific methods manifested in the selection of scientific problems deemed worthy of investigation, research design, definition of key terms and concepts, decisions concerning relevant evidence and counterexamples, data collection and analysis, interpretations of results, and assessments of practical falsifications (Farnham 1987, Fausto-Sterling 1992, Duerst-Lahti and Kelly 1995, Spender 1981, Westkott 1979, Wylie 1992). Feminist scholars have also demonstrated that when investigating women, social scientists often ignore or violate the methodological constraints of their fields, generate contradictory claims about women that undermine the internal consistency of their arguments about human beings, and fail to notice that the hypotheses they advance about women are inadequately warranted (Bleier 1984, Eichler 1980, Fausto-Sterling 1992, Fee 1983, Haraway 1989, Hubbard et al. 1982, Longino 1990, Westkott 1979). The frequency with which such problems arise in the context of "objective" modes of inquiry implies both that existing strictures of objectivity are insufficient to attain truth and that there are serious deficiencies in the dominant conceptions of objectivity (Bleier 1979, 1984, Eichler 1980, Fausto-Sterling 1992, Fee 1983, Hubbard et al. 1982, Westkott 1979).

Feminist philosophers have suggested that the core assumptions concerning objectivity within science are seriously flawed. Behavioral social scientists often conflate objectivity with adherence to method, adoption of a dispassionate attitude, and reliance upon a naive conception of "brute" facts. Yet none of these assumptions can withstand scrutiny.

In contrast to broad construals of the scientific method in terms of formulating, testing, and falsifying hypotheses, feminist scholars have pointed out that "science has many methods," all of which are discipline-specific and most of which are closely linked to the phenomenon under study (Harding 1986, p. 36). Moreover, whether the specific method of investigation involves induction, deduction, or controlled experimentation, no method can guarantee the validity of its results. The attainment of truth cannot be assured by adherence to a simple procedural formula (Berman 1989). Thus conceptions of objectivity that turn on adherence to an appropriate disciplinary method are seriously defective. Nor can an appeal to replicability save the belief that scientific method guarantees the objectivity of results. Intersubjective testing and confirmation cannot be taken as reliable tokens of truthfulness. For, as the history of scientific and philosophical claims about women so clearly demonstrates, conventional misogyny sustains verifications of erroneous views (Ruth 1981). Multiple investigators deploying identical techniques may produce the same conclusions, but such intersubjective consensus cannot attest to the veracity of the claims. Consider, for example, male political scientists' continuing "verification" of the claim that women are uninterested and uninvolved in politics, a claim that has been systematically refuted by feminist scholars who abandon their male counterparts' exclusive focus on national elections as the sole venue of politics, and who investigate structural barriers to women's full political participation rather than attributing women's underrepresentation in elective office to lack of interest (Lovenduski 1986, Guy 1992, Vianello et al. 1990).

In contrast to the systematic skepticism that critical rationalists ascribe to scientists, feminist scholars have demonstrated that many scientists not only never question popular gender stereotypes, but incorporate culturally-specific gender roles in their hypotheses about various animal species, cellular organisms, and social systems (Bleier 1979, 1984, Haraway 1989, Longino 1990, E. Martin 1991). Claims of detachment, disinterest, distance, and universality may merely serve as mechanisms for male hegemony, substituting certain men's perspectives for the view from nowhere (Keller 1985, Jaggar 1989, MacKinnon 1987b, Young 1986).

Like many postpositivist critics, feminist scholars have pointed out that notions of "brute facts" or "unmediated experience," like myths of value-neutrality in methods of inquiry or attitudes of inquirers, seriously misconstrue the nature of cognition, overlooking the theoretical presuppositions that shape perception and interpretation, masking the processes of selection and omission that inform description, and concealing the disciplinary practices that frame research problems and accredit evidence (Fee 1983, Hawkesworth 1989, Jaggar 1989, Longino 1990, Wylie 1992). Scientifically accredited "facts" are not the hard, incontrovertible, immutable givens they are purported to be, but rather, theoretically constituted propositions, supported by theoretically mediated evidence, and put forward as part of a theoretical formulation of reality (Hawkesworth 1988a). Many feminist philosophers are currently involved in efforts to develop more sophisticated accounts of facticity and its relation to non-discursive reality, in order to explain how feminist investigations provide non-arbitrary accounts of social relations that correct the defective views of androcentric social science, while acknowledging the fallibility and situatedness of human knowers and giving full credit to unique dimensions of social life such as reflexivity, agency, innovation, self-fulfilling prophecies, unintended consequences, emergent properties, and systemic effects (Grant 1993, Grimshaw 1986, Hartsock 1983, Harding

207

1986, 1991, Hawkesworth 1989, 1991, Jaggar 1983, Kaufman-Osborn 1993, Longino 1989, 1990, 1993b, Wylie 1992).

Several feminist scholars have also argued that the persistence of androcentrism in science illuminates problems of knowledge overlooked by traditional philosophers of science (Longino 1990, Hawkesworth 1991, Wylie 1992). Conceptions of scientific objectivity premised upon self-purging of bias, value, or emotion, as well as those dependent upon intersubjective correction of the same sources of error, imply that the fundamental threat to scientific knowledge is idiosyncrasy. Both share the Baconian view of subjectivity as an obscuring, "enchanted glass, full of superstition and imposture, if it be not delivered and reduced" (Bacon 1968, VI, p. 276). Both locate the chief obstacle to the acquisition of truth within the individual. Thus the techniques of scientific inquiry, whether conceived in terms of acts of pure intellect or intersubjective emendation, are designed to protect against "the capacity of the knower to bestow false inner projections on the outer world of things". (Bordo 1987).

The feminist discovery of persistent patterns of sexist error in "objective" inquiry suggests that the target of the various corrective strategies has been mislocated. The conviction that the central problem of objective knowledge lies with the emotional and perceptual quirks of the subjective self that distort, confuse, and interfere with objective apprehension of phenomena neglects the social dimensions of inner consciousness. Situating the issue of objectivity in a contest between the inner self and external reality masks the social constitution of subjectivity. The recurrence of a profound degree of sexism that filters perceptions, mediates arguments, structures research hypotheses, and "stabilizes inquiry by providing assumptions that highlight certain kinds of observations and experiments in light of which data are taken as evidence for hypotheses" (Longino 1990, p. 99) indicates a remarkable uniformity in the kinds of distortion that impede the acquisition of truth. Such uniformity challenges the myth of radical idiosyncrasy. Social values incorporated within individual consciousness present an important obstacle to objective knowledge. Norms of scientific inquiry that blind the individual to their role or assure the individual that intersubjective consensus is a sufficient remedy therefore fail to produce objective accounts of the world. For if certain social values structure conceptions of self and perceptions of the social and natural worlds, then neither isolated acts of pure intellect nor intersubjective testing will suffice to identify them. On the contrary, the belief that subjectivity is the fundamental obstacle to objectivity will preclude detailed investigations of shared observations and intersubjectively verified theories. Rather than being perceived as a potential source of error, values such as sexism and racism that are widely held will escape critical reflection. Their very popularity will be taken to certify their validity, thereby truncating further inquiry into their merits.

As an alternative to binary constructions of objectivity/subjectivity and objectivism/relativism, feminist attention to the social constitution of consciousness has generated discussions of cognition as a human practice – a conception that recognizes the complex interaction among traditional assumptions, social norms, theoretical conceptions, disciplinary strictures, linguistic possibilities, emotional dispositions, and creative impositions in every act of cognition (Hawkesworth 1989). Within the context of cognition as complex social practice, social science investigations entail both cultivating critical reflexivity on the part of individual investigators and intersubjectivity in the form of transformative criticism within the scientific community (Longino 1990). The point of intersubjectivity within this framework is not to confirm shared assumptions about what is normal, natural, or real, but rather to subject precisely what seems least problematic to critical scrutiny. Critical intersubjectivity constitutes one means to probe tacit assumptions and foundational beliefs of various cultures and disciplines.

If the social sciences require systematic probing of precisely that which appears unproblematic, then feminist philosophers have suggested that who does the probing may be a matter of central concern to those committed to social science inquiry. For what is taken as given, what appears to be natural, what seems to fall outside the legitimate field of investigation may be related to the gender, race, class, and historical situatedness of the investigator. Feminist scholars have argued that understanding the role of sophisticated intersubjective critique within the social sciences has implications that transcend the quest for an appropriate intellectual procedure. Convinced that "methodological constraints are inadequate to the task of ruling values out of scientific inquiry" (Longino 1990, p. 15), some feminists have argued that the social sciences must become an inclusive practice (Hawkesworth 1988b, 1991, Longino 1990, Wylie 1992). Sophisticated intersubjective criticism is unlikely to be attained within the exclusive preserve of privilege – whether it be the privilege of Whites, the middle class, heterosexuals, or men. To the extent that social values mediate perception and explanation, exclusionary practices can only help insulate questionable assumptions from scrutiny. A commitment to sophisticated intersubjective critique within the social sciences embraces diversity as a means. More and different guides to the labyrinths of reality may help us to confront the contentious assumptions most deeply entrenched in our conceptual apparatus. The inclusion of people from different social backgrounds, different cultures, different linguistic communities, different genders, and different sexualities within science and philosophy cannot guarantee, but it might foster, sustained critique of problematic assumptions long entrenched in the academic disciplines.

Feminist social sciences

Feminist philosophers of the social sciences have also investigated the practices of feminist social scientists to glean insights into the nature of feminist research methodologies. Although feminists use a multiplicity of methods developed within the social science disciplines, feminist social science, like feminist theory and critical theory more generally, is "explicitly directed by liberatory political goals" (Harding 1991, p. 98). Feminist researchers place women's experiences at the center of their analysis and use gender as an analytic category in order to develop a comprehensive analysis of women's oppression and to identify strategies for egalitarian social transformation (Jaggar 1983). Giving voice to "others," celebrating differences, "making the invisible visible, bringing the margin to center, rendering the trivial important, putting the spotlight on women as competent actors, understanding women as subjects in their own right rather than objects for men" (Reinharz 1992, p. 248, Stanley and Wise 1983) and developing an "egalitarian research process characterized by authenticity, reciprocity, and intersubjectivity between the researcher and her subjects" (Mascia-Lees et al. 1989, p. 21) are the hallmarks of feminist research.

Beyond characterizing the dimensions of feminist social science, feminist philosophers of science have engaged the complex issues pertaining to the emancipatory project of feminism and questions of truth. There is significant disagreement among feminist philosophers concerning the possibilities for truth and the criteria for theory choice within a postpositivist framework, which recognizes that reality is always richer than our theories about it and which accepts that all theories are necessarily underdetermined by evidence.

Some feminist scholars have endorsed a conception of truth that recognizes the situatedness and fallibility of all knowers yet eschews judgmental relativism, insisting that cognitive practices afford a range of standards that enable us to distinguish between knowledge and opinion, between partial views (the inescapable condition of human cognition) and false beliefs, superstitions, erroneous assumptions, and willful distortions (Harding 1986, 1991, Hawkesworth 1989, Longino 1990, Marshall 1994, Nelson 1990, Wylie 1992). Alison Jaggar (1983) has described such standards in terms of the systematicity and comprehensiveness of the explanatory account, the consistency and coherence of theoretical presuppositions, and evidentiary confirmation in relation to available data. Sandra Harding (1987b) and Lorraine Code (1994) suggest criteria related to successful transformative strategies. According to Harding, "the questions an oppressed group wants answered are rarely requests for so-called pure truth. Instead they are queries about how to change its conditions, how its world is shaped by forces beyond it; how to win over, defeat, or neutralize those forces arrayed against its emancipation, growth, or development" (Harding 1987, p. 8). On this view, "it is precisely their commitment to a developing, changing feminist practice that will provide the self-regulating guidelines that can keep feminist inquirers from having to equate 'pluralism' with the 'anything goes' spectre of relativism that has haunted philosophy since Plato" (Code 1994, p. 189).

Some postmodern feminists, on the other hand, have called for abandonment of conceptions of truth as fundamentally incompatible with the partiality of individual perspectives. "We may yearn for a world in which truth claims can be justified by reference to a metanarrative, but we no longer live in such a world, if we ever did. The metanarrative that held sway for so long rests on a false claim to universality; any metanarrative that might replace it will be similarly partial" (Hekman 1995, p. 16, 1990, Scott 1991). Kirstie McClure has argued that abandonment of notions of truth are crucial if feminists are to achieve their transformative goals. According to McClure, feminist efforts to identify criteria for theory choice drawn from disciplinary standards such as systematicity and comprehensiveness are themselves implicated in modernist practices that politicize science without disrupting the general privilege accorded scientific explanations in the broader world of scientized politics. They confirm the "quite modern political sensibility that casts the "political" as coextensive with the organization and management of a system of social relations and that consequently renders political action importantly dependent upon the production of properly scientific knowledge of that system." In so doing, feminist quests for theoretical adequacy operate to the detriment of the political character and possibilities of feminist critical practice by constituting feminism as unitary and univocal, thereby masking divisions within feminism, eliding differences among feminist visions, and foreclosing the possibility that new knowledges, agencies, and practices might reconfigure the political world (McClure 1992, p. 351).

Linda Alcoff has suggested that the central differences in this debate can be understood in terms of divergent ontologies. She notes that all participants to the debate explicitly embrace a coherence criterion for theory choice, yet this apparent agreement masks significant distinctions between proponents of a *"holistic model"* of theory choice and proponents of a *"constructivist model"* of theory choice. The holistic model endorses a paradigm-dependent conception of truth that avoids radical relativism by suggesting that the underdetermination of theories does not imply the absence of all constraints upon belief. Within this framework, non-discursive reality sets limits upon what can reasonably be believed. Thus Alcoff suggests that the holistic model operates with a correspondence *theory* of truth even while it explicitly adopts coherence as a *criterion* of truth.

> With this conception of truth we have a schism drawn between reality and the knower, wherein knowledge claims are expressed by a knower and are about reality. Although our given criterion of truth, coherence, can involve the particularities of the knower or the scientist, the ultimate arbiter of truth value for any statement is reality. What makes a statement true is not its coherence or its experimental verification but its correspondence to reality. The resulting conception of reality is as an autonomous entity, certainly changing spatiotemporally but not necessarily changing between coherent frameworks or fields of belief. (Alcoff 1989, p. 93)

The constructivist model, on the other hand, suggests that all knowledge is discursively constituted: one can never get outside the text. Particular discourses that are historically specific and contingent provide the background conditions that give meaning to scientific claims. Within this framework, relativism cannot be escaped because truth is an "emergent property" of historical and contingent discourses and practices.

> The schism between the knower and the known has been eliminated .... Truth is the product of a process which involves observation, practices, and theories, rather than a correspondence relation between a proposition and ... reality. The process

211

of knowing constitutes what is true, which makes truth something constructed rather than discovered ... . Truth is about reality, but reality itself is in historical development, an emergent property of discourses and practices. (Alcoff 1989, pp. 94–5).

Alcoff's analysis helps to illuminate what is at stake in the current debate among feminist philosophers of the social sciences. At issue are competing accounts of reality and competing conceptions of truth. The challenge of feminist philosophy of the social sciences remains the explication of a conception of knowledge that situates the emancipatory interests of feminist cognitive practices in relation to the contingencies of and innovations in, as well as the structural regularities and the modicum of permanence in, social relations.

21

The environment

VAL PLUMWOOD

The diversity of feminist ecology

Feminists working in the area of environmental thought argue that ecology is a feminist issue. They have drawn widely on the conceptual and critical resources of feminist philosophy both to develop a more complete feminist account of the world, and to expose masculinism where it appears in both traditional Western ecological thought and in modern environmental philosophy, producing a rich variety of feminist approaches to environmental philosophies. Their efforts have contributed to extending the critical resources and scope of both feminist thought and environmental thought, bringing to each a further major set of concerns, perspectives, and theoretical constraints.

There are several different but overlapping projects and characteristic issues in the broad area of feminist ecology. The main projects are:

(1) To explore the issue of connection between women and nature.
(2) To apply the methods, scholarship, and characteristic insights of feminist philosophy to the problems of environmental philosophy, and to critique masculinist forms of environmental philosophy.
(3) To connect feminist and ecological perspectives and critiques by developing "a feminism that is ecological and an ecology that is feminist" (King 1989). Not only must feminist thought temper environmentalism, ecological thought must modify feminism. Thus Warren (1987) critiques the neglect by many branches of feminism of ecological embeddedness.

Stereotyping and essentialism

"Just as there is not one feminism, there is not one ecofeminism," writes philosopher Karen Warren (1991, p. 111). Nevertheless, all forms of feminist ecology face serious problems of stereotyping, especially in relation to essentialism. Since feminist ecology began over twenty years ago (D'Eaubonne 1974, Ruether 1975), its period of development has coincided with a period of major change and controversy in feminist theory, associated with the displacement of radical or cultural feminisms by antiessentialist postmodern feminisms emphasizing marginalized perspectives and women's diversity. These changes have been reflected within feminist ecology, where maturity is similarly marked by more careful critical scrutiny of assumptions (Slicer 1994).

213

It is incorrect to treat feminist ecology generally as "essentialist." At one stage a number of feminist writers saw women's nurturance (whether biologically or socially based), or some aspect of "the authentic female mind" (Spretnak 1989), as giving them special qualities of connection to nonhuman life which positions them socially as defenders of nonhuman nature (D'Eaubonne 1974, Dodson 1979, Griffin 1978, Salleh 1984, Shiva 1988). Recent ecofeminism tends to reject generalizations about women's nature, uncritical approaches to nurturance, and representations of women on the model of "the angel in the ecosystem," as examples of the ecofeminine rather than the ecofeminist (Cuomo 1992, Mellor 1992, Plumwood 1986, 1988, 1993, Davion 1994, Slicer 1994, Merchant 1994). It views such connections, where they exist, as variable, local, and contingent, and developed in the context of women's subordination. (Whether this trend represents an oscillation from an overfeminization of women to an underfeminization remains to be seen, but in my view it is important to note that affirmation need not be uncritical). Critics who indiscriminately stereotype ecofeminist work as essentialist (Biehl 1991, Johnson 1994) neglect major critical discussions, are themselves "essentialist" in falsely universalizing, fail to note development within the area, and abandon an important critical resource for environmental thought.

Exploring the woman–nature association

An important thesis of feminist historical philosophers such as Genevieve Lloyd (1991, 1994) and Carolyn Merchant (1980, 1994, 1996) has been that women in Western culture have been historically associated with the "lower" order of nature and materiality, and men with the contrasting "higher" order of mind, reason, and culture. Much feminist ecology problematizes the Western tradition's naturalization of women and feminization of nature, as constructed in the context of intertwined and mutually reinforcing forms of domination (King 1989). "The idea that one group of persons is or is not closer to nature than another group assumes the very nature–culture split that ecofeminism denies," writes Karen Warren (1987, p. 15, Griscom 1981). The association between women and nature is not a universal one, as Ortner (1974) claimed, but is inflected historically and culturally (McCormack and Strathern 1980); it is problematic for women because it has so often been used to oppress us (King 1989, Plumwood 1988).

Feminist ecologies also differ according to how the idea of mutual reinforcement between oppressions is understood and elaborated. Some accounts associated with gynocentric forms of radical feminism tend to reduce both forms of oppression to matters of male dominance, treating gender, which they see as underlying the degradation of nature just as it does other forms of oppression, as the primary axis of oppression, having explanatory or strategic priority (Collard et al. 1988, Spretnak 1989, Doubiago 1989, Birkeland 1993, 1995). In contrast, accounts rejecting gender reduction and aiming for greater harmony with contemporary feminisms of race and class resist ceding this privileged explanatory and strategic status to gender (Warren 1989, Plumwood 1993, forthcoming, a, Mies and Shiva 1993, Mellor 1992, Slicer 1994).

There is an important division within feminist ecology, between those who understand women's historical connection with nature in positive terms as a special connection to be affirmed and elaborated, on the one hand, and, on the other, those for whom it is simply a source of oppression which must be discarded. Gynocentric forms of radical feminism tend to the affirmatory side of this divide, while androcentric forms of liberal feminism tend toward the negative side of striving for equality in terms which do not query the dominant masculinist constructions. Several philosophers have argued that this is a false choice (Plumwood 1988, 1993, King 1989), between a feminism of uncritical reversal which distances women from culture, and a feminism of uncritical equality which absorbs women into a masculinist model of the human as distant from and opposed to nature. Feminism can only escape the dilemma between uncritical equality and uncritical reversal by developing a more complex response of critical solidarity, which rejects women's exclusion from culture, but also contests the dualistic and masculinist construction of human identity developed in the context of the Western tradition, as well as the negative and oppositional role ascribed in the rationalist framework to the subordinated sphere of alterity cast as "nature."

Feminist environmental philosophy

Problematizing masculinist models of the human and of nature

Feminist ecophilosophers draw on feminist resources of critical thought about the male/female boundary and concepts of masculinism in philosophy to interrogate the dualistic construction of the human/nature boundary. They query both the construction of the human as a hyperseparated category outside nature (Midgley 1980, Plumwood 1991, 1993), and conceptions of humanity, animality, and nature as naturalized categories beyond politics (Haraway 1989, 1991). The work of Donna Haraway exposes and destabilizes the political construction of concepts of nature, animal, human, and machine in modern science, problematizing the assumption of a complete and apolitical human knowledge and mastery of a passive and unresisting category of "nature." In her rich, groundbreaking work, *Primate Visions* (1989), Haraway shows how the "neutral" discipline of primatology, as well as associated disciplines of anthropology and biology, have been informed by the perspectives of an imperial, white patriarchy, defining scientific manhood severally against women, against "natives" and against the animals themselves, all modelled as minors. The discipline of primatology located its chimpanzees and gorillas in a scientific origin narrative which represented them as "pure" and objective natural objects, the plastic but elusive raw material of nature which underlies human culture. So conceived, they present a free playground for the forces of rational engineering still forbidden unconstrained access to humans themselves.

215

My own work discusses the concept of nature as defined historically in contrast not only to the human but also in contrast to what has been taken to be the chief characteristic of humans and ground of human culture – reason (Plumwood 1991, 1993). The conceptual and historical framework which has shaped the dominant Western concept of reason as a sphere of mastery and nature as a sphere of diverse subordinated others is therefore that of rationalist philosophy. Reason has been constructed in this context as the privileged domain of a master subject who conceives nature as an instrumentalized and inferiorized other, representing the sphere of materiality, subsistence. and the feminine split off and constructed as a lower sphere identified instrumentally as providing raw material for his needs. Reason and nature are constructed in terms of a dualism of contrasting oppositional spheres which are arranged as radically distanced, as higher and lower, as center to periphery, as active to passive, as mind to mindlessness, as unmarked all-knowing subject to marked object of knowledge. The guiding project of progress with which these conceptions have been variously associated at different stages of the history of the West is that of the colonization of nature (both within and without the human sphere) through appropriation and rational engineering.

Dualism and the logic of oppression

The logic of colonization or oppression is linked to the concept of dualism or binary opposition. a key concept in feminist thought which constructs identity and boundaries in terms of exclusionary contrasts, as in the case of male/female and human/nature boundaries. But the concept of dualism has many unclarities, and some interpretations would collapse it back into difference or distinction. In Plumwood 1993 I develop a detailed critical account which draws on the work of a number of feminist thinkers to clarify the concept of dualism for use in feminist ecology. From feminist psychology comes a concept which can be used to explain the gulf between dualised categories – that of hyperseparation, as a form of identity constructed by an emphatic or maximal separation from or exclusion of the other's qualities, conceived as inferior. As Frye (1983) points out, the members of dualized classes are both hyperseparated and homogenized, that is, assumed to be both very like one another and very unlike the members of the opposed group (Frye 1983, Collard et al. 1988).

In the case of women, the effects of dualism are polarized, complementary, or complicit forms of identity which ascribe to women a nature, role, and fate subsidiary to that of men. In the case of human/nature dualism, the result is a polarized construction of both gender identity and human identity which conceives humans as above and discontinuous from the lower order of nature, which has the homogenized status of "the Other." These distortions of identity, which locate the best, most authentically human type as maximally distant from and outside of nature (taken to include both the animal and "primitive"), are implicated in both mechanism and contemporary failures of ecological rationality. But although countering them requires us to reclaim continuity. it does not warrant a denial of difference or oblige us to reconceive dualized items as merged or indistinguishable in the fashion often suggested by deep ecologists.

Differences over the interpretation of concepts of dualism and of nature result in stronger and weaker forms of social constructionism in feminist accounts. One possible direction for developing a human/nature parallel with gender dualism would treat nature as strongly socially constructed, as in some versions of postmodernism, and envisage boundary breakdown and blurring as the main strategy for overcoming oppressive constructions of oppositional categories. The antidualist analysis suggests, however, that a generalized fostering of boundary breakdown is a shallow and imprecise strategy for gender liberation, since breakdown is an ambiguous feature which can occur in oppressive as well as liberatory ways; although reclaiming the denied elements of continuity is crucial, certain kinds of boundary breakdown imply failure to respect another's boundaries, and are implicated in projects of colonizing and erasing the other.

The methodological principle that social distinctions posed as natural and inevitable should be treated as permanently open to contestation as political and constructed, and therefore to relegitimation and reshaping (Bennett and Chaloupka 1993) has high appeal to feminists and to others oriented to social change. But this principle does not require or legitimate strong forms of social constructionism for nonhuman nature which screen out its difference and independence and are insensitive to the colonizing politics involved in treating nature as only a human or cultural construction. Thus while showing how extensively animal societies have been used in the rationalization and naturalization of the oppressive orders of domination in human society (1989, 1991b), Haraway clearly rejects the reduction of nature to the status of "a blank page for social inscription" (Haraway 1991b). Haraway (1989) recognizes the independence and agency of nature as well as that of human society, insisting that knowledge is a co-construction between human knowers and nonhuman known.

A strong social constructionist approach which reductively dissolves nature into little more than the noumenal "raw material" of culture is thus not supported by an antidualist analysis of the nature/culture contrast, and fosters the anthrocentric illusion that as humans we are in complete charge of the world. In contrast, the critical account of the human/nature relationship in terms of dualism suggests strategies of retaining but reconceiving this distinction in nondualistic and nonanthrocentric ways. Differences over this set of methodological issues have implications over wide areas of feminism, and in feminist ecology itself lead to different approaches to the body and to the key ecological concepts of nature and wilderness (Plumwood, forthcoming, a).

Anthrocentrism and androcentrism in ecofeminist epistemology

The concept of anthrocentrism has been central to environmental philosophy, connecting the nature and animal branches of ecological thought and action, and linking ecology to other social movements and forms of radical thought. But the concept is now under a cloud, ecophilosophers having failed to develop

217

accounts of anthrocentrism which have wide acceptance, explain why it is problematic, or connect clearly with practical environmental activism. Both critics of the central ecophilosophical project who treat anthrocentrism as inevitable and benign. and ecophilosophers associated with deep ecology who regard anthrocentrism as dispensable and malign, assume problematic readings of this key concept. A poorly theorized concept of geocentrism has provided the most popular model for anthrocentrism, and the extensive theoretical attention feminists and other oppressed groups have given to such parallel "centric" concepts as androcentrism, phallocentrism, ethnocentrism, heterocentrism, and eurocentrism has been neglected. The dominant readings follow a masculinist dynamic in locating the problem with geocentrism in "parochialism," conflated with particularity, and in prescribing a dose of universality and impartiality as the cure. Correspondingly, avoidance of anthrocentrism is thought to require the achievement of a view-from-nowhere, perfect detachment from all human "bearings," perspectives, values, and preferences. The difficulty of realising these masculinist understandings is held to demonstrate that alternatives to anthrocentrism can be neglected, and that challenges to anthrocentrism must fail.

A standpoint feminist epistemology of "studying up" suggests an alternative focus on models such as eurocentrism and androcentrism, and attention to their origins in multiple projects of colonization (Plumwood, forthcoming, a). The relationship of colonizer to colonized begins by assuming a dualistic "us" and "them," a context of polarity which treats the other as a stereotypical member of a sharply separated and inferior group. But it adds to this dualistic relationship of colonizer and colonized a further set of logical features which define the colonizer as the conceptual, ethical, and epistemological center. For example, the colonizer locates the colonized on the value periphery and places himself at the center of importance and value. Simone de Beauvoir's classic analysis of women's positioning as Other shows how, in androcentric culture the identity of the male, as the conceptual center, is defined as "absolute," while that of the woman is defined in relation to this "colonizer" center as a lack, an absence of valued qualities; the colonizer assimilates the Other, treats them as deserving respect just to the extent that they can be reconstructed as a version of self, as copies or inferior versions. The colonizer *backgrounds* the colonized, conceiving them as *inessential* in relation to self, and *denies dependency* on their labour or contribution, as the basis of exploitation. And the colonizer defines the colonized in *instrumental* terms, denying the existence or importance of their agency and self-definition and conceiving them in passive or in purely functional terms as mere means to the colonizer's ends, as resources. The gaze of the colonizer, as unmarked epistemological center, can completely unveil the marked, objectified Other, recognizing no resistance, limitation, or excess. If dualism characteristically enforces exclusion and polarization as a philosophical expression of privilege, this gaze from the center characteristically builds on this exclusion by taking the right to define the difference of the Other.

If the dominant human culture has given its relationship to nature a form in which its gaze and goals toward the naturalized other have issued from the position of the colonizer, feminist analysis opens up space for reformulating many of the characteristic insights of environmental ethics in terms of a politics, an epistemology, and an ethics of decolonization. The kind of (re)consideration the dominant human technoculture must now give to nature acknowledges the need for a redistribution of value, space, and resources in favour of the other, for a negotiated relationship which acknowledges that the interests and needs of nonhuman nature present a limit to human ambitions, designs and demands. It must acknowledge the human continuity and interdependence with nature it has denied in its dualized conception of human identity: but it must also acknowledge the independence of nature it has denied in constituting itself as the center and treating nature as no more than a set of replaceable and inter-changeable units answering to its needs.

This is not just a matter of justice or altruism. but also one of longer-term survival: anthrocentrism, like androcentrism and eurocentrism, results in pervas-ive and dangerous distortions of selfhood, perception, and distribution (politics). Some of the most dangerous symptoms of this are the denial of human depend-ency on nature and the failure to acknowledge its limits. A program of action for countering anthrocentrism would aim to disrupt dualistic and mechanistic understandings of nature and animals which have denied their capacity for subjecthood, mindfulness, and communication, while still acknowledging their independence, difference, and specific, complex order. Feminist analysis opens the way for a conception of nature and animals as active agents in a practical and knowledge relationship reconstrued as involving dialogue and active exchange (Haraway 1989). In contrast to masculinist accounts stressing detachment, feminist methodology stresses relationship and communication as goals for prac-tical ecological interaction.

Feminism, animal ethics, and critical vegetarianism

Feminist animal ethics and critical vegetarianism is a vigorous and exciting area of ecofeminist thought represented in recent collections (Warren 1994. Gaard and Gruen 1995, Slicer 1991) and in work by Carol Adams. The neglect of animals in contemporary ecophilosophy is critiqued by Kheel (1985), while Slicer (1991) and Donovan (1993) criticize rationalism in animal rights theory. Although some feminists treat violence toward women and violence toward animals in terms of a critique of multiple, related oppressions, others analyze masculinity as the primary source of meat-eating and focus on the role of males in the violent abuse of women and domestic animals and in hunting. A strong radical feminist influence is apparent in some of the issue focus and explanatory orientation. Leading texts invoke the figure of "man-the-hunter" (Collard et al. 1988) as explanation, rather than focusing on the contribution of masculinism and anthrocentrism to the broader systems of knowledge and accumulation which enable the appropriation of both domestic and wild animals, as well as their ecological contexts. The explanation of male proclivity for violence to women and animals, which assumes the centrality of supposed traditions of

219

male hunting for masculine identity (Collard et al. 1988), overlooks feminist criticism of this assumption (see Haraway 1989, 1991). It also involves a false cultural universalism, since in some indigenous cultures hunting by women is a common practice. Some feminist vegetarians treat animal oppression mainly in terms of violence and abuse, pursuing a parallel between animal dismemberment and pornography (Adams 1990). Feminist vegetarianism raises some of the same issues of feminist pluralism as in the case of pornography, as feminist vegetarians criticize the involvement of other feminists in meat-eating.

Carol Adams (1990) aims to denaturalize the eating of meat, establishing first, its general social construction, second, its specific formation in terms of the dynamics of sexual politics, and third, its universally oppressive and ethically insupportable character. The first goal of denaturalization is well argued and convincing, but the second is more problematic, to the extent that sexual politics is explicated mainly in terms of the role of males and articulated from a Western, urbanized consumer perspective which assumes that alternatives to meat are always available. Adams's account of the ethics of contemporary farming and diet discourse and practices is on firmer ground, pointing to many of the features of the logic of oppression we have noted in the case of human/nature dualism and anthrocentrism. "Meat" animals and humanized non-meat animals (for example, pet dogs) are treated as belonging to *radically separate* and polarized categories of privilege (Adams 1990, Collard et al. 1988). The "meat" animal is *backgrounded* or conceived as inessential as a living animal through "absent referent," a form of denial which enables us to disconnect "meat" from the animal and erase it as a conscious, independent being. The animal is *incorporated* or assimilated through its definition in relation to human needs, as "meat," and in factory farming especially is reduced to an extreme condition of *instrumentalization* ("cows turned to milk machines") in which its entire life and development is subordinated to its function as a human food commodity. Critical disruption of this logic of oppression opens the way for feminist solidarity with all animals, but especially with female animals, oppressed as females by exploitation of their capacity for motherhood.

Although ecofeminist vegetarianism argues for the reconceptualization of animals as fellow subjects and active agents, it has not yet sufficiently reconciled its thinking with broader ecophilosophies locating animal and human identity in the ecological community. Any ethics of nonviolent eating which appeals to universalism or to some version of the Golden Rule faces a problem about violence in the larger food chain of which human eating is a part. It must address this problem with special care if it hopes to place its ethic in the context of an antidualist ecophilosophy which stresses humans and animals as both embedded in nature (Adams 1991), and sees humans themselves in ecological as well as ethical terms. Ecofeminist vegetarianism has not consistently met this challenge, nor has it fully confronted the problems inherent in its cultural universalism (Gaard and Gruen 1995, Adams 1991, 1993a, 1993b, 1995): thus if Adams's argument above establishes the oppressive character for animals of dominant Western food commodity practices, it does little to show that carnivorous practices which do not satisfy these conditions (for example those of some indigenous peoples) are unethical. A more carefully contextualized and nuanced version of vegetarianism will be necessary to resolve these problems.

Feminist approaches to environmental ethics

Many ecological feminist philosophers have been inspired by feminist critiques of masculinism in ethics. These critiques have shown how the dominant streams of ethical thought have made ethics turn on androcentric concepts of universality and reason associated with masculine lives and with the public sphere, and neglected or devalued ethical concepts and practices drawn from the areas it has associated with women's lives, with the body and with nature.

The impetus to extend new feminist approaches derived from the critique of reason/nature dualism in ethics to environmental ethics gains added momentum from the difficulties and limitations the dominant accounts of ethics encounter when extended to the new area of ecological ethics. *Kantian*-style ethical theories encounter difficulty in trying to extend to all living things the respect in their own right Kantians accord humans, because Kantian ethics is extremely dualistic and reason-centered. The other major traditional approaches to environmental ethics, the *ethics of rights* and the *ethics of utilitarianism*, can be applied relatively unproblematically to domestic animals in human care, but encounter severe problems in application to wild nature and animals, and have been critiqued by feminists (Kheel 1985, Warren 1990, Plumwood 1991). These three approaches are applied with great difficulty to non-animal parts of nature such as ecosystems, and also suffer from the problem of moral extensionism, of extending ethical concern to the other just to the extent that they exhibit human-like features.

The fourth approach of *deep ecology*, in its dominant form, hopes to circumvent these difficulties through reducing ethics to phenomenology, generating ethical concern for nature by incorporating it into the moral sphere of self. Among its problematic features are an inability to recognize the independence of nature, and reproduction of the familiar masculinist themes of rationalist ethics which emphasize detachment and distrust of the sphere of personal attachment, mistakenly equated with the selfish. Thus both rights theory and deep ecology have built ethical theories of respect for nature on the idea of moral progress as distanced from the personal, the emotional, and the local (Cheney 1987, 1987a, 1989b, Plumwood 1991), while Kantian-inspired ethical theories explicitly treat the "lower self" of inclination and the body as the enemy zone, opposing particular attachments to abstract ethical universalization. These masculinist conceptions of ethics not only continue to place an oppositionally-conceived reason at the centre of ethical life, but construct their proposed alternative on inferiorization of the very sphere they aim to revalue, that involving local, concrete, bodily relations associated with the emotions, with women, and with nature.

221

In this situation feminist care ethics has appeared to many ecological philo-sophers as a potential savior. Extensions of a feminist ethics of care to ecology have brought a new set of ethical concepts and issues to the fore, have stressed the importance of modest and localized ethical concepts drawn from the sphere of personal life, such as care, gratitude, friendship, trust, generosity, and attentive-ness and openness to the other, seeing a potential for wide application to the practice of ecological concern and to respect for animals and nature, both wild and domestic. Advocates of a feminist ecological ethics of care have seen it as grounded in identity and the concept of the self as expressed in relationship to others (Plumwood 1991). Theorists who criticize the abstraction of conventional ethics celebrate the new ethical approach as contextual and narrative, emerging from relationships and identity (Cheney 1987, 1989a, 1989b). Thus Karen Warren (1990) constructs the narrative of a rock-climber who relates to the rock in terms of care, loving attention, and gratitude, as an example of the way such local ethical concepts can be employed in particular contexts of relationship to nature. The account shows how these concepts can overcome the limitations of the ethical extensionism implicit in the conventional ethical positions, and apply to moral subjects in no way assimilated to the human.

However, extensions of care ethics into ecology partake of the same ambigu-ities and differences which appear in the case of care ethics more generally, and there are considerable differences in the way they are understood by theorists in the area of ecological ethics. As in the original position of Gilligan, there is both an ambiguity between the feminine and the feminist ethic, and an unclarity about whether the "ethic of care" is seen as capable of replacing conventional ethics accounts in terms of rights and value or whether it is seen as supplement-ing and enriching them. If replacement is intended, there is a problem about how ethical concepts thus based on narrative and identity can stand alone. We have still, as one critic of care ethics insists (King 1991), to ask the question: which narratives should we listen to and respect? And answering these questions seems to require a larger ethical framework than that of the narrative provided, or indeed of care ethics itself, as explicated so far in the work of care theorists. Other approaches under development to complement or supplant care ethics include communicative and virtue ethics (Plumwood 1993), and ecofeminist moral epistemologies of nature (Gruen 1994).

PART V

RELIGION

22

Christianity

CATHERINE KELLER

Unlike the nontheological articles, this one must, for the sake of its coherence in this volume, define its basic discipline before its specific feminism can be articulated. Theology, "god-word," a term coined by the pagan Plato, became the language game of Christian intellectuals within a century of the death of Jesus of Nazareth. This Jewish life, its premature termination, and the virtually unprecedented spread of the spiritual movement he had initiated managed to attract philosophical minds such as Clement of Alexandria and later, Augustine of Hippo, in the meantime converting the emperor as well. So the philosophical logos of the cultural elite established itself as the discourse of the Christian movement – hence theo-logos. Indeed, the author of the fourth gospel had already identified Jesus himself as the incarnation of the cosmic logos, the principle of meaningful order for Stoicism, the Word of God for the Jews. This translation of Hebrew metaphor into Hellenistic philosophy prefigured the institutionalization of a set of rationalized symbols as the creeds (in Greek, *symboloi*) of Christendom. That institutionalization sought at once to organize Christian spirituality around belief, that is, around discursive propositions to which one assents or not; and to homogenize a tumultuous, subversive, and multifarious movement around the political expediency of unifying both Church and Empire.

That organization of faith required aggressively patriarchal practices of discourse and leadership. A relative gender egalitarianism had prevailed in some early Christian communities, and a certain fluidity of gender imagery for the divine was discernible in such tropes as that of the Holy Spirit as Mother, or, in the language of Clement's *Pedagogos*, of that of Christ as the breast milk by which God the Father nurtures those adults reborn in baptism (Clement of Alexandria 1983, Book I, Chapter 6, p. 221). Such discursive spaces were virtually eliminated by the fourth century. Feminist theology in the twentieth century therefore arose as a protest against the exclusively masculine imagination of the divine – in all three of its "Persons" – and the corresponding exclusion of women from positions of ordained leadership in the churches. Yet it has been an "inside outsider's" protest, to transpose Audre Lorde's phrase. We have known of the early potentiality of the Jesus Movement for egalitarianism since Elisabeth Schüssler Fiorenza's *In Memory of Her* (1983) revolutionized the field of biblical studies with its demonstration of the systematic overlay already within the canonical gospels of androcentric interpretation. Releasing the emancipatory energies of the earliest tradition has thus become a motivating force of all

225

liberation and progressive theologies. Moreover, we have gleaned the stories of women creating openings for themselves. And especially within the ecumenical protestant denominations, we have seen significant institutional progress as to the ordination and placement of women, as well as attention to issues of gender symbolism.

So those feminists who work within Christianity have been unwilling to damn the Church to its own sexism. And this tenacity is not just for the sake of the Church itself, but for our own interest in combining the work of the intellect with ethical spiritual practices. For it is perhaps by now apparent that in the history of Christian theology, quite unlike that of philosophy, no clear separation can be drawn between issues of institutional power and the thought which justifies or resists it. Claims to orthodoxy do not hide behind appeals to pure reason. Foucault has shown all disciplines to be subject to this messy inseparability of knowledge/power. Then we might claim that theology, especially as engaged from the forthrightly political perspective of feminist critique, has the advantage of displaying the terms of its power struggles with relative transparency. Moreover, to play its language game, one never speaks merely as a scholar of God-language – that would be a form of religious history or philosophy of religion rather than theology or philosophical theology. One speaks as a participant in the tradition, however one chooses to criticize and reinterpret its practices and beliefs. One circulates with its signs through the vortices of its struggles for both power and meaning.

Feminist theology thus comes entangled in the question of God – a matter of the relationship of language and power within our ancient branch of what we might call the signocracy. In the sign-language of the first creation story of Genesis: human beings are "made in the image of God; male and female God made them" (1:26). Women would seem therefore to be as entitled as men to make God-signs in our image – to mirror as men have always done our sense of our own cosmic significance. So why cannot we correct the systematic oversight of two thousand years or so and invest a few female metaphors with their overdue holiness? Cardinal O'Connor of New York made headlines by simply declaring "God is a man." More subtle representatives of the tradition argue: "You can't make God a woman. The biblical images are just metaphors for God. He has no gender." Very smart folk seem taken in by the innocence of that little pronoun.

Let me reemphasize that the matter of God-language and thus of its gender is no trivial or supernatural pursuit, but a way of encoding the gender of ultimate values. Theology signifies much more than logos or theos – for both language and God themselves always signify more than themselves. Let me suggest somewhat metatheologically that in its feminist deconstructions, "God" produces a version of what Gayatri Spivak calls "catachresis" (not to be confused with catachesis!) – it is "brought to crisis." When we reconstruct God as a woman, we produce a valuable sense of contradiction: of ourselves as female flesh, mimicking but not imitating the personhood of a flesh-transcendent masculinity, claiming discursive authority within the patriarchy of theological authorship.

226

To function as field of discourse at all, feminist theology has no recourse but to move into an uncertain space beyond both premodern patriarchy and late modern reductionism. The postmodern – if it distinguishes itself from the ultra-modern – evokes this opening. If we direct the emancipatory energies of a tradition against its own hegemony, we do so for the sake of vision and action on behalf of "the creation" and all its creatures today. For as Amos put it at another apocalyptic moment, "without a vision the people perish." But the visions of feminist theology have no meaning outside of what Sharon Welch, reading Foucault through Mary Daly for the sake of a social–theological ethic, called "communities of solidarity and resistance" (1990). The proposals which follow demonstrate and presuppose participation in the significatory practices, at once liturgical, conceptual and political, which characterize such communities. So there will be no separate section on the ethical practices implied by feminist theology, as its ethical implications remain at every stage inseparable from its theory, and indeed do not vary significantly from that of progressive academic feminism in general, except in the particulars pertaining to such socioreligiously charged issues as abortion and the religious right. What differs most prominently is perhaps, as I have argued, the overtness with which normative moral positions are espoused within theological institutions.

Christian God-language had early resisted its own monism by breaking into three: known as the Father, the Son, and the Holy Ghost, the three "persons" of the Godhead. In what remains a trinitarian rhythm will therefore guide us schematically through key themes of feminist constructive theologies. This pro-cedure will make possible an epitome of US Christian feminist theologies. But I will add an anthropological spin to each of the three divine "personae" – the Latin for "masks." In other words, what appears as a way of divine being will unmask itself (temporarily, at least) as a mode of human self-construction. In order to clarify the operative method, more space will necessarily be allotted to the "First Person," "God the Father." This does not indicate "his" relative importance, however. The subversive potential of the second and especially the third persons will, I hope, become clear in the contrast. It should also be under-stood that the trinity itself is a postbiblical abstraction from multiple metaphors, much criticized by liberal theologians, and invoked in the present context partly for the sake of its neat organizing capacity, partly in the spirit of what Judith Butler calls "performative parody" (1990, ch. 3). So in the following exercise, I will be not just surveying but performing feminist theology.

"God the Father"

1

As Person: Nothing in the iconography of our tradition communicates more persistently and more paradoxically as to the nature of the First Person of the trinity than "his" sex: his fierce and authoritative manhood, not attested by a pagan genital display but rather by those attributes marking the ideal patriarch in Jewish and then Christian culture. His authority, his penetrating, unsmiling gaze, commanding, judging, and occasionally touched with compassion, perhaps even touching – another man, as in the familiar Michelangelo. To be a "personal God," God needs a sex, since we reportedly cannot imagine a sexless person. But therein lies the perplexity: that same God must above all be sexless. Indeed, his very above-all-ness depends upon his transcendent asexuality. Both the biblical Yahwist-prophetic tradition and modern biblical scholars construct divine transcendence against the foil of pagan "fertility idols," who voluptuously admit of either feminine or multiple genders and tempt us to conceive of the divine as immanent in the material world. Given the paradox of God's nonsexual sex, the divine masculinity was virtually never discussed but always silently presupposed, left to the visual imagination, a metaphor congealed into the orthodoxy of the unchanging and performed in its institutions of authority. Note that such construction of transcendence just happens to correspond to the masculinity constructed in the image of this God: a patriarchy both indelibly marked by its sex and defined as a rational essence, that is, as sex transcendent. One might infer that atheist or agnostic feminists ignore the God-word at their own peril.

So the originary task of theological feminism – as book titles like *Beyond God the Father* by Mary Daly (1973), *Sexism and God-Talk* by Rosemary Radford Ruether (1983), *Sex, Race and God* by Susan Brooks Thistlethwaite (1989), and *The Body of God* by Sallie McFague (1993) suggest – lay in the mytho-institutional confrontation with the First Person. As Mary Daly put it in the classic formula in the above text: "if God is a male, then the male is God" (p. 19). (Written at the point of her "exodus from the patriarchal church," she performed her theology: as the first woman invited to preach at Harvard's Memorial Church, she concluded her sermon with an invitation for all who would separate from Christian patriarchy to process with her down the aisle. A couple hundred women and several men did.) So feminist theology has pursued a double strategy. First, to blow God's cover: either "he" is male or the fatherhood of God is truly a metaphor and hence negotiable. Then, to propose alternatives: either choosing an iconoclastic gynomorphism (just call the Holy "Goddess" for a while: this will test the notion that "he" has no sex, counseled Nelle Morton, a grandmother of feminist theology), or calling for "inclusive language" ("God" as God's own pronoun, or words like God/ess or the divine which take "it," thus leaving the biblical masculine imagery intact as historical text while picturing female and neutral images of ultimacy today).

Let me suggest that in order to tease out the implicit anthropology of such apparently metaphysical moves, we treat the personal divine attributes (person, father, creator, author, for example) as adverbs of human self-understanding rather than as substantives of divine substance. Feuerbach invented such an anthropological inversion for atheism. In an age in which much more reflection on the self-referential character of language has proceeded, in other words, in which we tell the difference between metaphors and their literal referents, I replicate it for theism. It only makes explicit what is implied already in the "imago dei": that with God-words we have to do with the construction of our self-image in its widest context, of our ego-ideal mirrored by its lack: its abyss of unknowing, to use the old mystical language. Such metaphors cannot decide the existence of the "transcendental signified" of the symbol "God," which will always remain an open question. The problem is not "God" per se but the fact that one group of one species has claimed a monopoly on the divine mirror. Moreover, that group defined that ego and its self-knowledge in terms of the Cartesian divide between subject and object. So we might say that the theological episteme refracted through a feminist lens is less object-knowledge (knowledge of self or other) than a way of knowing; therefore less knowledge of God than, in ancient parlance, godly knowing. This has always been true but often repressed: therefore to confess belief in the First Person as Father means to know the world from a fatherly perspective. What "fatherhood" means, like its corollary constructions of "motherhood," comes of course encoded in the sociolinguistic fabrications which structure personal existence. So one might argue for first of all coming clean as to the profoundly constructed character of personhood and thus all the more so of divine personhood.

One might then be able to reconstruct the personhood of the first person from a feminist perspective. Disputing that sex or any particular sex provides the essence of humanness or holiness, we might under the sign of the First Person affirm that we know ourselves as personal: that is, that knowledge of self and world registers in our own experience as persons, as specific, interpersonally wired bodies of experience. We do not then so much gaze at the divine personae, the "masks of God"; we look through them. The personal is that which embodies its knowledge interpersonally; accordingly, it issues in an epistemology of attention to the complex integration of self with the multiple dimensions of its experience, intimate and political but always personalized, with others.

2

Feminist reflection on the First Person, traditionally the Creator, has led to our own version of what feminist theologian Rosemary Radford Ruether called the "urgent task ... to convert human consciousness to the earth" (1992, p. 250). This embrace of the ecological was not an easy move, given on the one hand the antinaturalism of Protestant theology and the natural law orthodoxy of Catholicism, and on the other the anthropocentrism of progressive social theory. Feminist theologians tended in the first round to react against the earth-centered "goddess feminists," who joined in the insistence that Jewish or Christian feminism was a contradiction in terms, that "God" in the biblical tradition is as irreversibly male as the conservatives claim "He" is. But the differences ran deeper than divine gender. Theological feminists, among them the earlier Ruether, who first tended to assume the biblical bias for history over nature as the site of divine revelation, readily joined the historicism of socialist feminists and other social justice movements in dismissing the "naturalism" of the goddess movement, with its tendency to romanticize female biology. But the dialogue ripened, its maturation marked by the moment Radford Ruether defined God as the divine matrix of life (which she renamed "God/ess") (1983, pp. 70–1). This name marked the deconstruction of the binary opposition of culture and nature; it took up the cross of the planetary ecosocial justice crisis.

Epistemologically, then, this line of development suggests that the attribute of Creator of Heaven and Earth, already redirected within the late Jewish context of apocalypticism to "New Creation" – renewal of creation – converts the character of human creativity. Our works of creation no longer claim either the security of a Creator in control of the Creation nor the pride of an enlightenment epistemology of the Knower who transcends "his" objects and thus the knowable world. So how do we, at the apocalyptically charged turn of a millennium, know in the light of a reconstructed, feminist version of the First Person of Heaven and Earth? We would know earthily. That is, our processes of perception are recognized as thoroughly ecological: there is no epistemic process to which we have access which is not through and through the matter of embodiment.

Feminist theology presumes psychoanalytic accounts of the patriarchal dread of matter, the matrix, as matter, but need not therefore fixate itself on a Divine Mother. Of course the emergence of maternal metaphors for the deity can be criticized as "essentialist"; but inasmuch as they encode the difficult possibility of a biocentric understanding, they need not evoke feminine earth-mother stereotypes. Rather, they can be read as marking the intersection of the corollary degradations of maternal and earth bodies (Williams 1993). Ecological knowing attends to the ways we come as cultural–linguistic creatures always inseparable from the ecological vitalities to which our spirituality might discipline our attention. Faith in a creator and re-creator of heaven and earth means a praxis of re-creation of land, the ocean and the atmosphere which are being apocalyptically devastated by the Western "dominion over the earth" (Genesis 1:26). Ecotheology strategically reclaims the ancient biblical obligation to "stewardship" – *oikonomia* – "householding," the root of both "ecology" and "economy" – to counter the decontextualized modern exploitation of the biblical dominion rhetoric. Indeed, ecofeminist theologians must beware playing the housewives of creation.

3

Such theological moves stimulate another attribute of the First Person, and thus another aspect of our own personhood: that of authority. "God the Father" preeminently inscribes claims of universal power, mirroring millennia of what Schüssler Fiorenza calls the "kyriarchy" – the system of patriarchal domination by which male elites, largely white and Christian, exercise dominion over everyone and everything else (1994). Feminist debate about whether to claim power for ourselves, to reject the idea of power, or to reconstrue power as empowerment, seems not accidentally to parallel debates about God-language: shall we claim it for ourselves, reject it, or reconstruct it? Let me merely suggest in the present context that the Foucaultian reading of Power as not that of an authoritative Subject of Power at the top, but as exercised, flowing through our flesh and in the capillaries of our total network of social relations, is proving most suggestive for feminist theological ethics (Welch 1990, Chopp 1989). Feminists may work the attribute of divine power as the epistemology of ethical attention to human power. Understanding empoweringly means first of all attending to the power which we already embody, for good and for ill. Such self-scrutiny, as it turns up not only our capacity to change self and world but also the gaze of the patriarchy internalized as inner god, requires something very like a spiritual discipline.

To claim authority as women leads, then, to the ethics of mutuality which Christian social ethicist Beverly Harrison began to articulate in the 1970s in relation to poverty, racism, and abortion. In *Making the Connections* the empowerment of "right relations" redefined the work of justice (1985). For it is as a response to the wrongful relations of injustice that power becomes an issue: both in the biblical tradition of exodus and the prophets and in its postpatriarchal transformation. To know through the First Person becomes a matter of knowing empoweringly, to register the interpersonal and the political currents of power as cut through by force-fields of dissent and possibility; to practice a knowledge never value-neutral and always ethically accountable. In this mutual knowingness, we begin to embody a new authority; indeed, to exercise the epistemic privilege of the new creation as authors even of theology.

So then: personally, creatively, earthily, empoweringly, and authoringly, the First Person, denuded of its transcendent Fatherhood, may open up alternate spiritual spaces for self-understanding and its worldly practices.

"God the Son"

1

At the point of the Second Person – the Christ, the Logos, the Son of God – the trinity really gets personal. Only as Father of an equally divine Son is the erstwhile One God said to reveal "himself" as father – and vice versa. And only as Son, that is, the mythological title of Jesus of Nazareth, does the Word of God become human flesh. For Christian feminism, that "Incarnation" for which Miriam/Mary was the "vessel" bears at once promise and disappointment. It could seem to restore the holiness of our materiality within a classical context, increasingly defining body as that entrapment, marking humans as "born of a woman." For women the incarnation has invited intimacy with this exceptionally "sensitive male." But inasmuch as Jesus was early figured as the ultimate exception to the human condition, he merely proves the rule – the rule of the immaterial Father. Orthodoxy permitted Christians only this single point of divine immanence, concentrating in itself all the signals of transcendence. At the same time the elevation of a Son to a status which by definition can never be attained by a Daughter still functions to exclude Catholic women from ordination and Protestant women from a full exercise of vocation. Feminist theology has therefore understood christology to be our "thorn in the flesh" – in the designation of the unique, once-for-all embodiment of the divine the Word of patriarchy becomes final. Mary Daly declared a "Second Coming of Women" – but only after exodus from our captivity to the Christian Word. That logos nonetheless subsequently inspired a wave of feminist christologies, renarrating the historical Jesus as a finite, charismatic Jewish male who gathered around him an egalitarian sociospiritual movement.

Out of the icon of the cross the church fathers had developed an orthodoxy of atonement understood as redemption by the Son of God's innocent suffering. Precisely here have irrupted women's protests against the use of christology to enforce an obediently suffering daughterhood: feminist christology understands the crucifixion as an effect not of divine will but of human sin. In the light of the revelation of the pervasion of US family life by the physical abuse of children, including prominently the sexual abuse of girls, feminist theologian Rita Nakashima Brock, in her influential *Journeys By Heart: A Christology of Erotic Power* (1988), has recognized in substitutionary and surrogacy constructions of atonement "cosmic child abuse" (Nakashima Brock 1988): the imputation to God the Father of the need for the physical torture, humiliation and sacrifice of the child. Delores Williams, in *Sisters in the Wilderness* (1993), has developed a womanist analysis of the parallel between the surrogacy of slave women and the surrogacy of the atonement doctrine. She challenges black women to question beliefs which encourage them to accept suffering. We are also outgrowing the (especially white) feminist tendency to construct ourselves as the innocent victim of patriarchy. Instead Nakashima Brock has proposed an "erotic power." Eros, not in the genital but in a politico-cosmological sense, cashes Christ into a cipher of mutual relation. Thus the point is not the heroism of a particular individual, but the healing and enlivening quality of the relationships he generated around and beyond himself.

Through the mask of the Second Person we glimpse the thoroughly vulnerable finitude which defines human life: the incarnation of our significance as radically specific, ethnic, mortal. Our indelibly carnal knowing is born of the fleshly desire for mutuality with the others out of whose lives we come and whose futures we affect just by being "members one of another" (1 Corinthians). Hence Paul's metaphor of the "Body of Christ." Our bodily knowing is the knowing of communal bodies: bodies which are themselves organic communities, enmeshed in endless networks of sociality and ecology beyond themselves. These relations become christological – indeed, "atoning" – only as they become the subject of mutual attention. The Second Person, after all, masks and unmasks love. Not that this mutualism cannot surrender to the exclusivism which the Pauline metaphor of communal body has supported. Iris Marion Young's warnings against idealizing community are valuable for feminist christologies of eros (1990a). Also, theologian Kathleen Sands has offered a challenge to any feminist theological overbelief in our eros-driven mutualism, evoking literary analysis in favor of the radically plural and ambiguous (1994). Feminist mutualism under the sign of the Second Person, in whom the First Person of empowerment achieves limitation, incarnation and crucifixion, inscribes the God-word in all that has suffered the harsh truths of love.

2

Epistemologically as well as mythologically, the logos echoes the Jewish *Hochma/ Sophia* – "Wisdom," a feminine personification of the canniness of cosmic order. She is at once divine and human. Thus Schüssler Fiorenza has developed a biblical theology of the historical Jesus as child of Miriam, prophet of Sophia (1994). Christology was originally inseparable from Sophialogy. But the convenience of the masculine logos for the Gospel of John's figuration of the cosmic Christ and the subsequent privilege of the trope of Sonship over even the logos neatly eclipsed this lingering Sophia. At the level of Schüssler Fiorenza's historicist rhetorical criticism, she develops an exegetical basis for a christology of wisdom as the prophetic praxis of "the Jewish emancipatory movement of wo/men" around Jesus (p. 88). She disallows, however, any theological construction, and therefore any cosmological, let alone theological, content for Wisdom. Here I need to expose a deep tension in present feminist theology. She would "abandon and replace" (1994, p. 57) the relationalist christologies of lesbian theologian Carter Heyward and Asian-American theologian Rita Nakashima Brock. While she raises incisive questions about the implication of feminist mutualism in the sex/gender system, she deploys an antiessentialist polemic of the supercessionist sort more philo- sophical feminists have begun to rout. (See, for example, the work of contributors to *The Essential Difference* [1994], edited by Naomi Schor and Elizabeth Weed.) Indeed, its combination, with an appeal for an "uncompromising liberationist practice" and "a critical feminist theology of liberation," seems more character- istic of other forms of uncritical identity politics (1994, p. 189).

Nonetheless, despite our conflicting attempts to incarnate the wisdom of justice with love, this *Hochma/Sophia* seems to be returning by way of the feminist version of that Christian Second Person under whom she was repressed. Accord- ing to Proverbs, she "cries aloud in the streets" (p. 12). Christologically I recommend then theologian Rebecca Chopp's poststructuralist inscription of "proclamation" – from the New Testament Greek *kerygma* – as a trope of women coming to voice, to word to authority and authorship (1989). The theological understanding which might have atoning power for women, too, will not keep silence: it knows proclaimingly. Only so does the spirit which was in Christ, the spirit of prophetic resistance to the religious and political orders, the spirit as one always interprets it today, work. And without its works, its prac- tices, it bears no fruit and is worthy, like the barren fig tree in the hard word of Jesus, only to be cut down.

"God the Spirit"

It is "in the Spirit" that an epistemology suited to a feminist theological anthropology comes into its own. The charismas of the spirit (otherwise known

233

as the Holy Spirit; or by those preferring the King James version, "the Holy Ghost") are precisely modes of knowing already in the first century deemed strange and disruptive: the ecstatic and prophetic gifts as well as those of teaching and interpretation, even of healing, are spirit-practices which cut against not only modern modes of cognition but ancient sophistication as well. *Pneuma*, or *ruach*, the words in Greek and Hebrew respectively for either wind, breath, or spirit, was said to "blow where it will." It "in-spired" practices resistant to the cognitive disciplines of the culture. Hence Paul's highly charged ambivalence about the Holy Spirit: "Never try to suppress the Spirit," he wisely warns (I Thessalonians 5:19); but, worried by the direction experiences of the Spirit were taking in Corinth, he orders the gifts according to his sense of communal hierarchy (2 Corinthians 11: 12 ...). New Testament scholar Antoinette Wire has argued persuasively that Paul's disciplinary stance toward the Corinthians was provoked by their female prophets – to whom the Spirit had granted far too much proclamatory public power for that patriarch to tolerate in women (1990).

If therefore we take into account the intriguing gender-ambiguity of the Spirit – its feminine *ruach*-form, its elemental, nonanthropomorphic manifestations in fire, water, and wind, its appearances in early Christianity, as nursing mother and power of rebirth – its personhood invites feminist pneumatological speculation. Yet so far, the heavy masculinity of the First and Second Persons has defined not only ecclesial orthodoxy but feminist response. This andromorphic circumscription of spirit is not surprising, given its inspiration of nonscholastic epistemologies and occasional social revolutions (Bloch 1986). The spirit was thus left to flap around within the private pietisms of antirationalist traditions, often deeply associated with feeling and femininity, but unable therefore to reshape the operative epistemologies of mainline faith and culture. While Mary Daly dedicated *Pure Lust* (1984) – a decisively post-Christian prophetic work – to "the spirit," most feminist theologians have simply avoided the disembodied, ahistorical pietism of "spirituality." But they have thereby colluded in the rationalist dismissal of the spirit as a spook for kooks.

Roman Catholic theologian Elizabeth Johnson, a nun and a feminist who has survived heavy surveillance from Rome, broke the pneumatic barrier within feminism. Indeed, in her magisterial *She Who Is* (1992), the Third Person becomes the First. Her moves are radically sophialogical, working the metaphor of Sophia for both its active gynomorphism and its relational potential: thus "Spirit–Sophia" initiates her systematic theology, which then moves (in reverse trinitarian fashion) through Jesus–Sophia and Mother–Sophia.

The breezier openings of the spirit into postpatriarchal discourse have only begun to be explored. If, in the meantime, to know the Third Person is to know spiritually, then the personification of spirit does not comprise some ghostly reification but a sense of the spirit of all of life in one's own personhood. But then that personhood constructs our personalities as always already interpersonal and indeed transpersonal – perhaps therefore theomorphic. Nothing spooky there: the personhood of the Third Person invokes something like our relation to the dynamism of relation itself, as it figures a universe in which nothing is what it is in abstraction from its circumambient matrix of interdependencies. This may count after all as a version of Augustine's pneumatology of "love itself." But differently from Augustine, the predicate of "love" is not here subordinated to the substantives of "Lover" (Father) and "Beloved" (Son). Rather, we may recognize such personifications as themselves discursive abstractions from the field of relations constituting the creation: invalid only as absolutes, meaningful as metaphors relativized to the entire matrix of relations.

"God" as spirit then does not merely perform but is love [cf. 1 John]. What matters, that is what materializes, this love, to the extent that it does materialize, is the total complex of our life practices at any given moment. Spiritual practice is in any religion a reflective and intentional participation in the multidimensionality of that complex. Through "gifts of the spirit" we may cherish, enhance, and expand the boundaries of our "body." But such a body, personal and transpersonal, will no longer serve the militant imperialism of the missionary movement after Constantine. It appears instead, from this feminist perspective, as the potential for a collective Body committed to metanoia (change of mind; repentance) for the devastating effects of the pathologized Body of Christ upon the body of creation: upon the bodies of Jews, of women, of slaves, of the colored and the colonized, upon the nonhuman systems of life itself. The task is so overwhelming as we approach the millennium, so fraught with apocalyptic resonance, that I am convinced that only revitalized and ecumenical spiritual practices – as opposed to the mere progressive verbiage of Word abstracted from Spirit – will sustain the needed commitment. Only so can we "ground the spirit" (Sharon Betcher, unpublished dissertation) as a force of renewal rather than escape. Grounding is a matter of ecosocial justice and its animating sensibility, not of foundations.

So if the First Person deconstructs and reconstructs Author-ity, and the second, the Word ... then the Third, which is "blowing in the wind," might provide us with a draft feminist theology. But while spirit traces possibilities of new relation and new creation, it inscribes itself always and only in the drafty circulation of the present: in it we know what we know presently, and therefore not quite. Such a project is meaningful, and is worthy of the evolving potential of feminist theology, only as a strategy to materialize loving, vital bodies of greater justice and mutuality.

23

Islam

BASHARAT TAYYAB

Introduction

This article aims to introduce nonIslamic readers to Islamic feminism. The central text mainly draws upon the Qur'an and the sayings of the Prophet Muhammad. However, because the Indo-Pakistan subcontinent is the author's natural background, a few of the traditions and points of view mentioned may not conform with the traditions and points of view regarding the role and status of women in other parts of the Islamic world. However, they form an essential part of the author's personal views, based on her direct experience of the Indo-Pakistan culture and society.

Muhammad and the Qur'an

Islam claims to be the culmination of Judeo-Christian tradition, in the sense of establishing a middle-path religion avoiding the extremes of Judaic transcendence and Christian immanence. It began in seventh-century Arabia, a vast, arid peninsula. Socially, the Arabs were organized into tribes and lived mostly in widely scattered groups. There existed no central government. A few cities like Mecca and Medina thrived, mainly as centers for trade and religious rites.

Revealed to Muhammad by God between 610 and 632 was the Qur'an, the basic Islamic text, and the pivot around which the whole of Muslim life runs. Muhammad lived a private life until the age of forty, during which time he worked as a shepherd and later became the agent of a wealthy businesswoman of Mecca, Khadija. After he had worked for five years, Khadija proposed marriage to Muhammad when she was forty and Muhammad was only twenty-five years old; they married and the marriage lasted for twenty-five years, until Khadija died.

At the age of forty, Muhammad received the first revelation from God. He now gradually achieved the status of religious leader and moralizer, and later he also gained the status of law-giver, after establishing the first Islamic state at Medina in 623.

Muhammad remarried; unrestricted polygamy was the custom among Arabs of that time. Female infanticide was largely practiced, as women were looked down upon and they possessed little or no social or religious status.

The Qur'an, the revealed word of God to Muhammad, contains the general reforms of Islam. The most important legal enactments of the Qur'an are on the

236

subject of women, improving the status of women in various spheres. It gave women a fully-fledged personality. Spouses are declared to be each other's "garments" (2:187). Women have been granted the same rights over men as men over women, except that men, as breadwinners, are protectors and supporters of womenfolk. Unlimited polygamy was strictly regularized as the number of wives was restricted to four, with a rider that all four would be treated justly. To this was added a general principle that "you shall never be able to do justice among them, no matter how desirous you are (to do so)" (3:128), the overall logical consequences amounting to the banning of polygamy under usual circumstances. The Qur'an gives women the right to inherit a share of property, a right to divorce, and gives widows the right to remarry. Islam attributes to women equality of creation and spiritual worth: "Oh mankind, be careful of your duty to your Lord, who created you from a single soul and from it created its mate and from them have spread abroad a multitude of men and women" (4:1).

Woman's spiritual equality with man is established, as she has received divine revelation as in the case of Mary, mother of Jesus. Similarly, the Qur'an is a guide both for men and women and both would be rewarded or punished equally. In many places the Qur'an addresses its readers as "Muslim men and women, believing men and women, devout men and women" (33:35).

The pursuit of knowledge is incumbent on every male and female in Islam. Some very well-known sayings of the Prophet Muhammad hold; "Seek knowledge even if it takes you to China." "Seek knowledge from your cradle to your grave." "Every Muslim man and woman is obliged to seek knowledge" (Bukhari 1938).

Even though Islam recognizes the male as the main economic head of the family, it does not forbid women from taking part in professional activity and rising to the pinnacle of their profession; they are entitled to the same pay as their male counterparts. Nursing mothers are allowed to leave their children with other nurses: "Mothers shall suckle their children ... and if you wish to give your child out to a nurse" (2:233).

Islam bestows on women the right to own and inherit property: "From what is left by parents and from the nearest related there is a share for men, and a share for women, whether the property be small or large, a determined share" (4:7).

Islam also recognizes the equality of men and women as regards moral and legal issues. A woman is regarded as an independent legal personality and not an adjunct of her guardian. She is also entitled to the same punishment, neither less nor more, for any crime she commits, and is also entitled to the same reward as a man for her achievements. "Whoever doeth right, whether male or female and is a believer, Him verily we shall quicken with good life, and we shall pay them a recompense in proportion to the best of what they used to do" (18:97). They can vote, be members of the Shoora (Islamic Parliament), be a minister, a head of state (though there is a difference of opinion about this), or a judge (see Musheerul Haq 1989).

Interpretations of the role of women in Islam: traditional, eclectic and modern

Even though many Islamic countries in modern times constitutionally recognize the equality of men and women as perceived by the Islamic ideal, as in Pakistan, where Muslim women are recognized as legal individuals possessing the right to vote, to have an education, to be elected to Parliament, and to become head of state, women still suffer from extreme social oppression, except in the case of the higher and upper middle classes, where women enjoy all the privileges of free individuals. In fact, Muslim women are not perceived to have enviable roles. For much too long, Muslim women have been living under a shadow; voluntarily, out of habit, or because, traditionally, their menfolk have put them there.

However, the contemporary gender perception can be broadly classified as: (a) traditional (orthodox); (b) eclectic; and (c) modern.

Traditional

The traditionalists constitute the backbone of the Islamic intellectuals who represent the feudal–tribal rather than the Islamic way of thinking. They seek to place women under the control of men. They are powerful and effective in their influence as they form the backbone of both social and political leadership in Muslim societies because of their religious influence. The conservatives regard womenfolk as inferior to men in their intellectual capacities; woman is taken to be the cause of most of the evils of society in general, she cannot appear in public, she must be completely veiled when appearing in public, her domain of activity is restricted within the four walls of her home, she can marry only with the consent of her father or male guardian, she has no right to divorce, and polygamy is seen as justified.

Maryam Jameelah, a spokesman of orthodoxy writing in the 1970s, maintained, "In Islam the role of the women is not the ballot box but maintenance of home and family. Her success as a person is judged according to her fidelity to her husband and the rearing of worthy children. A Muslim woman is expected to live in privacy; Pardah is an indispensable means to this end" (Jameelah 1988, p. 9).

A contemporary Muslim scholar, Dr Asrar Ahmad, in his *Islam Main Aurat Ka Maqaam* (1984), maintains that women must take the wives of Muhammad as their model, since only they could guide Muslim women in their vocation of childbearing and childrearing. He further argues that the Prophet Muhammad is a model for men only (Ahmad 1984, p. 48). Dr Ahmad's position, in fact, limits the scope of the teachings of Muhammad as being guidance for men only, and in this way he is also able to limit the scope of the activities of women, to the tasks of childbearing and childrearing.

Religious scholars (*ulema*) used pseudo-traditional and historical norms to resolve woman problems. Patriarchy and male chauvinism of the feudal and capitalist systems converted women into the private property of men (Hussain

238

1984, p. 29). Using all forms of social control, the *ulema* try to prevent any deviation from the roles prescribed by them. Maryam Jameelah writes, "The movement for female emancipation should be recognized by all Muslims for what is – a malignant conspiracy to destroy the home and family and eventually wreck our entire society" (Jameelah 1988, p. 29), implying that women's emancipation is the cause of all evil in society. In order to retain the superiority of men over women, many sayings of the Prophet were fabricated to construct the one which mentions three causes of interruption of prayer, that is, dogs, asses, and women (Farid 1994, p. 75). The Qur'anic verses were often misinterpreted to the advantage of men. Regarding the notion of male superiority, verse 34 of chapter Nisa (Qur'an) is often quoted, according to which men are in charge of women as God has made them to excel over women. The misinterpretation consists in ignoring the next verse of the same chapter, which makes men in charge of women only because they provide for them. The difference between men and women is not because of any fundamental difference between the two, only because of certain functions.

Eclectic

The eclectic school of thought, originating from Muhammad Abduh of Egypt and Maulana Maududi of Pakistan, has a slightly better perception of the gender roles in Muslim society. Elaborating his stance on Muslim women in his book *Purdah and the Status of Women In Islam*, Maududi maintains that Islam has in fact introduced the concept of giving rights to women and a place of honour in society. The slogan of women's emancipation and education was first raised by Islam. However, after having accepted all the parameters of the equality of man and woman in society and religion, Maududi refers to the order of the social system of Islam, which he regards as natural. Talking now of the natural social order rather than the Islamic order, Maududi claims that Islam wants to keep the social environment clean of all sexual stimulation, to enable man to develop his physical and mental abilities in a pure atmosphere and to prepare him to play his role effectively in the building-up of civilization, with conserved energies. Restricting sexual relations to marriage only, Maududi now segregates women's sphere of activity from that of men's. They should shoulder different responsibilities according to their respective natures and must not transgress by entering the domain of the opposite sex. Man should have the status of a governor in the family and the other members should obey him (Maududi 1981, p. 159). On the basis of this philosophy Maududi enjoins purdah – complete segregation of the sexes in social life – he denies women the right of becoming a political head in society except in exceptional circumstances, and he allows women to appear in public only when completely veiled apart from her face and hands (ibid. 1981, p. 23). This is how Maududi sees a glimpse of naturalism in Islam, by recognizing the natural superiority of one partner over the other. Working on the foundation that biological and psychological differences between men and women do exist, he employs these differences for determining their place and responsibilities in the social system.

Modern

The modernist approach to Islam and to gender perception in particular is that of reconstruction. The modernists lay greater emphasis on understanding human situations and feel that the substantive teachings of the Qur'an are for action in this world. Important from the feminist perspective are the modernists of the late nineteenth century: Syed Ahmad Khan in British India, Ali Shariati in Iran, Fazlur Rehman in Pakistan, and Qasim Amin in Egypt.

The title of Shariati's book, *Fatima is Fatima*, symbolizes the identity of Muslim women as against other women. It exhorts every woman to "make" herself, to "create" herself, that is, it emphasizes the necessity of being responsible for herself as well as for the society in which she lives (Shariati, n.d., pp. 6–7).

Shariati insists that a Muslim woman needs to develop her own form of Islamic values. She must aspire to be "a woman of a society who wishes to make decisions on the basis of reason and choice and relate them to a history, culture, religion, and society which received its spirit and origins from Islam .... A woman who in this society wants to be herself, 'herself' to build herself, 'herself' She wants to be reborn, in this rebirth, she should be her own midwife, she neither wants to be a product of her heritage nor a superficial facade" (ibid, pp. 23–4).

For Shariati the Islamic role model was the best solution to the woman problem, and a weapon for creating a conscious struggle within the new generation of Islamic societies. The model selected for this purpose was Fatima, the daughter of Muhammad, who symbolizes the woman which Islam wants. Various dimensions of being a woman are symbolized in her personality – a daughter, a wife, a mother, a responsible fighting woman when she needs to be, an Imam (prayer leader), a guide. Thus, Muslim women are those who play an active role in the historical development of their society: they possess social, political, and economic freedom and are independent human beings, respected as women.

Muslim women in the Indo-Pakistan subcontinent

In spite of progressive views like those of Shariati on women, the real situation of women remains inferior and oppressed in various Islamic cultures and societies throughout the world – South and South-east Asia, of course, being no exception to the above rule. In fact, from the ideal position originally established as early as 1400 years ago, the gradual downgrading of women in society started soon after the death of the Prophet Muhammad. The Indian subcontinent, from the tenth century up to 1857, remained under the rule of Muslim conquerors, who brought with them the Arab and Central Asian tribal cultures, after which it remained under British colonial rule for about a hundred years thereafter, declaring the independence of India in 1947 with the formation of Pakistan as an independent Islamic state. However, in 1970, Pakistan disintegrated to form Bangladesh, a secular state with a predominantly Muslim population. Prior to this, the Indian subcontinent ran along Hindu sociopolitical lines. In Hindu India, social life was stratified by the caste system. The lawgivers, like Manu, prescribed cruel penalties for women who deviated from Hindu norms, where they were the victims of their own religion, the institution of suttee (the practice of women to be burnt to death on their husband's funeral pyre) and "deva dasies" (slaves of gods – young, Hindu girls who served Hindu priests). Islam provided salvation to many Hindu women who sought conversion to Islam to avoid suttee and temple prostitution. Soon the Muslim rulers were corrupted and their palaces maintained harems entertained by dancing girls. The professions were closed to women as morality decayed, the only course open to them being that of prostitution. The women of wealthier classes were kept strictly segregated. Power and wealth corroded Muslim rule and the British set in for 100 years. The corrupt pseudo-Islamic scholars who condemned the acts of Muslim rulers proved to be a retrogressive force for the Muslims of the subcontinent, who now took to protecting tradition in the name of Islam. Islam was compromised to suit the needs of feudal elites, the bureaucracy, and military power.

The religious political parties in Pakistan and Bangladesh are hence extensions of feudalism, expressing traditional, customary morality regarding women. Women are basically. in the feudal order, instruments for producing male progeny – heirs to their fathers' wealth. Hence, the religious ideology of the retrogressive forces was to institute a male-dominated system where women were strictly guarded, either at home, or in the harem. Hence the Islamic institution of purdah (segregation of sexes) was introduced. The religious scholars justify polygamy and servile behavior and regard birth control as anti-Islamic.

It is because of all this that successive governments have failed to secure and recognize the role and rights of women in Pakistan, though numerous social, cultural, religious, and professional women's organizations have emerged. One of the most important of these is APWA (All-Pakistan Women Association). The efforts of APWA resulted in the enactment of the Family Law Ordinance of 1961 which dealt with the injustices of marriage, divorce, and polygamy. This ordinance has, ever since, remained a subject of controversy. Orthodoxy believes that it has deprived a Muslim husband of his eternal Islamic right to divorce his wife, and has constrained his right to have four wives simultaneously. The provisions in the ordinance for the registration of marriages and the use of a standard form of marriage contract (*nikah nama*) are unacceptable to them (Patel p. 91).

In spite of giving some protection to Muslim women, the Family Law Ordinance still does not treat women the same as men in matters of divorce. According to the law, a man who wishes to divorce his wife has to pronounce *talaq* (divorce) and submit a notice to the chairman of the local council. If no reconciliation takes place within a period of ninety days the divorce becomes final. The woman, however, does not have such a right. If she wants to dissolve her marriage (*khula*) she may do so after foregoing her benefits through marriage (ibid. p. 93).

In 1979, under the process of "Islamicization" of laws in Pakistan, the Hudud Ordinance was introduced. This consists of a collection of five criminal laws promulgated in 1980. One of them relates to the crime of rape, abduction, and adultery. Criminals under the Hudud Ordinance are sentenced to whippings or

241

any other mode of punishment prescribed in the Qur'an, e.g. stoning to death for *zina* (adultery and fornication), amputation of a hand for theft, etc. These laws, again, are controversial even to this day. Yet few want them to be repealed, as it may endanger the process of Islamicization. The promulgation of the zina ordinance has not only been widely criticized by women but also by the International Commission for Jurists as a gross violation of women's rights. The ordinance contains provisions for its misuse, to the disadvantage of women. Jawed Iqbal, Chief Justice of the Lahore High Court, cites certain examples of its misuse in a lecture given at a workshop on "Women and Law" on 5 November 1994, held in Karachi. He quotes from the journal, *All Pakistan Legal Decision*, Vol. XL.

The obsession with the virginity of females will illustrate to some extent how women are treated as private property in most Islamic societies. The preference for a virgin wife has caused numerous oppressive practices. Parents get their daughters married off as soon as possible, to get them off their hands. Further, the segregation of women imposes exclusion from the reach of males. In the Indian subcontinent, if proof of the bride's virginity is not evidenced on the wedding night, it is taken as sufficient grounds for abandoning the bride for the rest of her life.

Feminist movements in the Muslim world

Various women's organizations exist in the Muslim world to safeguard the interests of women against unjust practices. These organizations, besides fighting against woman's oppression, also join hands with nationalist struggles aimed at achieving political independence, asserting national identity, and modernizing society. This has been the nature of indigenous feminist movements of the Islamic world. The feminist movements of the late nineteenth and early twentieth centuries have arisen in societies fighting against imperialist domination of foreign and local landowners and capitalists. Women in these societies were the cheap source of labor for plantations and factories. For the colonial rulers, local women had to be educated, in order to be able to handle the modern industrial work. Whereas the local male reformers needed women to be adequately Westernized in order to enhance the modern image of their country. Women of all classes went out into the streets to demonstrate on issues of national concern, for example, in India, in the nationalist struggles of 1903 and 1947, in Iran in 1906, 1911, and 1979 (the Iranian Revolution), and during democratic revolutions in Egypt. Many eminent women activists gained popularity, among them Kartini (Indonesia), Sadiqa Daulatabadi and Khanum Azamodeh (Iran), and Huda Sharawi (Egypt).

In Egypt, the crossroads to Asia and Europe, feminist stirrings are linked with modernizing the country's educational, cultural, and administrative structures and also in the growth of nationalism and the anti-imperialist order of the British. The Egyptian reformers started a debate on the rights of women in Islam, one of its pioneers being Sheikh Muhammad Abduh. He was outspoken on the status of women, denouncing polygamy as unIslamic and condemning the practices of concubinage and women's slavery – citing the Qur'an on women's education, he regarded backwardness of Arab women as detrimental to the future of the Arab world. It was Abduh's disciple Kasim Amin, with his book *Women Emancipation* (n.d.), who argues, on the basis of religious texts, that female seclusion, the veil, arranged marriages, and the prevalent divorce practices are unIslamic. He advocated women's rights to work and legal reforms to improve their status. Many influential women writers wrote extensively on feminist issues in the first decade of the twentieth century. Malik Hiba wrote on marriage, divorce, veiled seclusion, and women's education. Another area for women was philanthropy. Hidiya Afifi formed a network of women's clinics in 1906, and in 1919 she formed another network of girls' schools, orphanages, and child-care centers. Open political agitation by women began with their participation in the nationalist movement against the British after World War I. Huda Sharawi organized women's demonstrations.

Attempts at women's emancipation in Afghanistan were influenced by similar attempts in Turkey and Egypt. Claiming the emancipation of women as the keystone of the future of Afghanistan, Amanullah Khan, the ruler of Afghanistan from 1919 to 1929, introduced a family code in 1921. The code forbade child marriage, encouraged girls' schools, banned polygamy for government employees, and ordered women to wear Western dress. In 1929, his wife Suraya appeared unveiled in public. However, after his succession in 1929, Nadir Shah annulled those measures which were beneficial to women in order to appease orthodox opinion.

While in India, agitation for social reform for women was led by both Hindu and Muslim women, yet many issues which agitated Hindu women did not apply to Muslim women as Muslim law allowed for the remarriage of widows, divorce, and a share from parental property. Yet concern was expressed by Muslim male reformers in the fields of education, polygamy, and purdah. Muslim feminist pioneers included Begum Nawab Mirza, who founded an orphanage, and Shareefa Hamid Ali, who began a nursing center. Local women's associations were also formed at various urban centers. In 1906, the Begum of Bhopal formed the All-India Muslim Women's Conference. The Khilafat Movement (agitation against the dismemberment of the Turkish Empire in India) brought women into the public sphere. Muhammed Ali's mother, Bi Aman, his wife, and Hasrat Mohani's wife addressed women's meetings, and later a separate women's wing was added to the Muslim League which struggled for the establishment of Pakistan. Miss Fatima Jinnah and Begum Rana Liaquat Ali Khan are but a few examples of women who took part in nationalist struggles. Since the establishment of Pakistan, women have been active participants in national politics. Benazir Bhutto, former Prime Minister of the country, headed a leading political party.

In Indonesia, Islam being the dominant ideology, many Indian cultural patterns persist. This is due to Hindu and Buddhist beliefs, which have caused the absence of purdah and other similar practices. However, one of the first Indonesian women to work for women's emancipation was Kartini, whose writings show the desire for emancipation through education, rejection of polygamy, access to the professions, and personal freedom. In 1928, the first Indonesian

243

Women's Congress was held, bringing together about thirty women's associations, and in 1929, the Federation of Indonesian Women's Associations was formed, which worked for women's interests.

In the last analysis, it would not be too wrong to conclude from the above that many practices acquired religious status in many Islamic societies, the nature of such practices being primarily cultural and social rather than religious. Purdah (segregation of the sexes), an institution now identified exclusively with Islam, is primarily a pre-Islamic institution practiced in ancient Persia, the Jewish nation and some parts of ancient India. Similarly, polygamy, an Arab tribal tradition, has been identified as an Islamic practice (for the history of the feminist movement in the Muslim world see Jaywardena 1986).

Conclusion

Many feminist writers (e.g. Farid 1994) believe that Islamic texts need to be reinterpreted in view of the changed social conditions of the postmodern age. Islamic law, commonly known as *Shar'ia*, was first developed during the eighth, ninth and tenth centuries, and since then it has hardly grown. It is generally believed by the Muslims that the Qur'an is a book primarily of religious and moral principles rather than a legal document, though it may embody certain legal enunciations issued during the final state-building process of Medina (the first Islamic state). Qur'anic legislations primarily address themselves to the society in existence at the time. However, ignoring the historical, legislative aspect of the Qur'an, Muslim *ulema* dogmatically took to apply the legal structures developed during early Islam to any society, no matter what its inherent dynamics. This has led to the stagnation of Islamic sociocultural structures.

It is believed that as far as feminist issues are concerned, Muslim women will have to struggle against both the internal forces (religious orthodoxy) and external forces (feudal tribal social structures). This struggle will have to be carried out by interpreting the true Islam for themselves. This interpretation of Islam by women is yet to emerge. Against misinterpreted and misconceived views of the orthodoxy, there is an urgent need for an academic approach to study the primary Islamic texts at first hand, without attempting to fill in the blanks with preconceived notions. We must interpret the Qur'an against women's background, skills, procedures, practices, and so forth prevalent in existing society. The built-in mechanism providing room in Islam for such interpretation is the long forgotten institution of *ijtehad*. To employ *ijtehad* is to "exert." The Qur'anic verse regarding *ijtehad* is "And to those who exert we show our path" (29: 69).

Finally, a word of caution for the Islamic feminist movements: they need to guard against the dangers of confusing the real feminist issues with those of Westernization. It is the element of Westernization, when confused with feminism, which causes reaction amongst the more conservative elements of Muslim society. The real feminist perspective, however, needs to be highlighted so as to lend vitality and meaning to Muslim feminism.

24

Judaism

RACHEL ADLER

The problem of philosophical theology as a Jewish form

The initial problem for feminist Jewish theology has been its very definition as theology. Whereas, from its beginning, Christian feminism has defined the transformation of theology as a major goal, the nature and boundaries of the Jewish feminist project have been more amorphous. In part, this is because the theological tradition to which Christian feminists react is highly systematized. The nature and methodology of theology are more open questions in Judaism. Biblical and rabbinic Judaisms embody a variety of theologies in narrative, prayer, law, and textual exegesis. While in every period of postbiblical Judaism there have been influential theologies utilizing philosophical forms and categories, there is no standard way of systematizing their Jewish content. That is because Jewish philosophical theologies serve dual purposes.

Whereas Christian theologies are principally conversations within the faith community constructing and clarifying the content of accepted rubrics, Jewish philosophical theologies are both intracommunal and intercommunal conversations. As internal conversation, philosophical theologies extend, defend, and negotiate the boundaries of normative Jewish discourse. As intercommunal and interfaith conversations, they respond to challenges from the larger social environment and its impact upon Jewish thinking and practice by examining Jewish concepts and categories in the light of this larger discussion. At worst, the result is polemics and apologetics. At best, constructive, not merely reactive, theology emerges.

Jewish feminist theology, then, shares some patterns and motifs with other Jewish philosophical theologies. It responds to transformative events in the larger social environment which present a challenge to the thought and practice of Judaism. It is addressed to both internal and external audiences: feminist Jews seeking to critique and to reconstruct Judaism, non-feminist Jews whose concerns must be addressed, and non-Jewish feminists with whom both common language and crucial differences must be clarified. It too, in the absence of standardized rubrics to reformulate or react against, has had to carve out its theological categories afresh. In consequence, the opponents of Jewish feminism in the 1970s and 1980s classified its writings as sociopolitical polemic rather than theology. Even today, few feminist Jewish scholars identify themselves as theologians, although their work may be covertly or even overtly theological. Yet

245

Jewish feminist thought has had an immense impact on every variety of modern Judaism. Like the theological upheaval that produced Reform Judaism in response to the Enlightenment and Emancipation, it has produced major changes in Jewish thought and praxis.

Historical context of Jewish feminist theology

The feminist critique of society and culture initiated in the 1960s and 1970s posed profound challenges to every branch of Judaism. Before this time, in no form of Judaism did women have equal access to communal participation, leadership, or religious education. Liberal Judaisms influenced by Enlightenment universalism made women invisible by regarding them as "honorary men" (Prell 1983) but did not, in fact, give them the religious opportunities afforded men. Discrimination on halakhic (Jewish legal) grounds was common, not only in Orthodoxy but in all the other branches of Judaism. Halakhic discrimination is considerable. Women may not be included in the minyan and hence, may not lead worship. They may not called to the Torah. Their credibility as witnesses is severely limited. Moreover, they are powerless to effect changes in their own marital status. Orthodoxy, which affects not only its own practitioners but all Jewish Israeli citizens, does not permit women to initiate divorce. Women whose husbands are untraceable, insane, or simply unwilling may not free themselves to remarry. If they remarry civilly and bear children from the second relationship, those children bear the status of bastardy and are barred by halakha from marrying other Jews.

At the core of Judaism is the devotion to sacred text and to the interpretive process which continually recreates the text. Yet these texts often ignored or marginalized women, and women were excluded from the interpretive process.

Traditionally, the main duty of women was to enable the Jewish observance of men. Modern Judaisms, reeling from postenlightenment assimilation and from the loss of one-third of the world Jewish population in the Holocaust, augmented women's responsibilities for enabling Jewish survival. They were to repopulate the Jewish people, maintain a warm and inviting Jewish domestic environment, and be the volunteer labor force for communal projects and institutions. The earliest feminist critiques of Judaism, then, were depicted by their opponents not only as unfeminine and unnatural, but as selfish, syncretistic, and threatening to Jewish survival.

Despite opposition, Jewish feminist thought and practice succeeded in changing modern Judaism profoundly. Between 1973 and 1983, the Reform, Reconstructionist, and Conservative movements began to ordain women as rabbis. In all branches of Judaism, access to religious participation, communal leadership, and higher Jewish education took a quantum leap. New rituals were advanced to address previously ignored events in women's life cycles. The prayerbooks of the Reconstructionist and Reform movements have begun to address problems of inclusive language in liturgy. New academic research on the construction of gender and new evidence regarding women's activities in different periods have affected Jewish historical and textual scholarship.

The impact of feminist theory

Two crucial controversies regarding feminist theory affect the nature and extent of feminist impact on Judaism. The first of these controversies asks whether the central feminist goal is *equal access* for women to existing structures, categories of knowledge, and practices or the *transformation* of structures, knowledge, and praxis. A fierce battle has been fought for women's equal access in Judaism. Traditionally women's religious behavior was home-centered and involved enabling rather than leadership roles. Since Torah study was the preeminent obligation/privilege of men, women's religious educations were rudimentary. Without access to education, women could not speak authoritatively in a religion defined by its devotion to texts. Even had they been permitted, they would have been incompetent to assume liturgical leadership roles, since this required Hebrew scholarship and other specialized knowledge. Without equal access, women could not be other than peripherally Jewish (Adler 1973). However, equal access integrates women into structures created by men. If equality means only the erasure of women's difference, it makes women invisible by making them honorary men (Prell 1983). If, however, transformation is the goal, the very content of prayer, study, and praxis must be reconsidered. Judaism itself must be studied and practiced differently. Identifying these problematic issues, and creating and institutionalizing feminist alternatives, is the core task of a feminist Judaism.

A second and related feminist controversy concerns the nature of gender difference, for problems and solutions imply underlying definitions of what it means to be a woman or a man. Are there *essential feminine and masculine natures* that remain constant through different historical periods and cultural locations? Or is gender a *social construction* in which the desires, characterological features, and social functions that typify femininity and masculinity are contingent upon socio-historical context and hence vary widely? Orthodox Judaisms which affirm an historical divine revelation tend to embrace ahistorical, essentialist understandings of femininity. However, essentialism tempts even non-Orthodox Judaisms because it offers religious roles and rituals for women that can be accommodated with little disruption of existing institutions and without the participation of men. New Moon celebrations, women's Passover seders, prayer groups, special classes concerning women in the Bible or Talmud which originate as creative responses to women's invisibility in liturgy and learning (Adelman 1986, Broner 1993, Levine 1991, Umansky and Ashton 1992, Orenstein 1994) can be coopted as additional programming to strengthen women's traditional roles. Essentialist rereadings of Levitical purity laws, for instance, destigmatize menstruation and childbirth but enable continued observance (Adler 1973, 1993).

In contrast, acknowledging gender as a social construction opens the door to theological questions that challenge traditional assumptions and render some

247

practices problematic. Non-Orthodox Judaisms do not believe in an unvarying, timeless revelation. Since their inception, they have accepted the premises of modern historiography that societies are human constructions that cannot be adequately understood without reference to context. It is hardly tenable to claim that gender is the single exception to this rule. However, non-Orthodox Judaisms have been slow to pursue the implications of the constructedness of gender. If gender is a social construction, then the impact of gender on Judaism cannot be pigeonholed as a women's problem. Masculinity is no less constructed than femininity and no less context-dependent. Rather than postulating a pure form of Judaism unaffected by gender considerations, onto which historical or literary information about women can optionally be appended, one must assume that *all* representations of gender in text and tradition require critical scrutiny. This would profoundly affect the methods and processes of textual interpretation and the adjudication of Jewish law.

In addition, critical examinations of gender expose Judaism's incomplete adjustment to modernity (Heschel 1983). They spotlight instances where sacred texts and hermeneutics, religious laws and praxis, conflict with Enlightenment principles that the majority of American religious groups claim to revere: equal respect for all persons, and tolerance for difference. Thus, contextualizing gender creates ethical challenges for Judaism. Both gender and the boundaries of sexual expression are deeply implicated in social structures of domination and hierarchy. To claim that gender is contingent upon social context is to acknowledge that gender injustices can be rectified by reconstructing society (Plaskow 1990). If gender discriminatory practices or sexual ethics are found to rest upon archaic or oppressive structures or discredited assumptions, there is an ethical duty to reevaluate them. For example, how should men's and women's bodies be perceived and valued? If sexual orientations are influenced both by biology and by social possibilities, what are responsible ways to live them out? How should choices and responsibilities regarding childbearing and childrearing be reconfigured, and how will this affect decision making about birth control, abortion, fertility technology, definitions and organizations of family? Must organizational structures and processes be hierarchical? What are the effects in models where information and authority are more broadly distributed? What is the place of human beings in a populous and interdependent universe, and how are its claims and desires to be balanced against those of other entities? Questions such as these clamor to be addressed as soon as the values of past Judaisms are acknowledged to be context-dependent.

A brief taxonomy of major theological problems

If a tradition is an entity whose rules are ahistorical and unchangeable, then women cannot be invited into it in the first place. But if a tradition is a conversation, a number of questions follow: What does it mean to invite women into a conversation from which they have been excluded for centuries, an interchange whose past topics, language, and categories were framed by interests and experiences other than their own? How does the conversation itself change when women bring their experiences, needs, and desires to it, and how are conversations from before their inclusion reviewed in retrospect? Once in conversation with religious traditions, women bring new perspectives on old questions as well as new questions altogether. These questions have far-reaching implications for redistributions of social power and religious authority and leadership. They require reevaluations of canon, hermeneutic, and praxis. The following are a few of the areas affected.

The critique of Jewish law

One of the earliest and most persistent theological questions identified by feminist Jews concerns the authority of Jewish law (halakha) (Adler 1971, 1993, Greenberg 1981, Plaskow 1983, Ozick 1983, Orenstein 1997). Because the theological implications of halakha are realized in praxis, its subordination of women is no mere theoretical issue. Orthodox feminists maintain that discrimination against women is historically conditioned rather than a manifestation of divine will, and that it can and should be amended through existing legal mechanisms. Others argue that halakha is merely a structure for maximizing male power and authority in Jewish communal life and can serve no useful purpose in a feminist Judaism. Yet others claim that lawmaking in partnership with God is a defining feature of Judaism, but merely amending discriminatory laws is insufficient. Halakha must be radically reenvisioned, the narratives that ground it must be reinterpreted, and the power to create and maintain law must be distributed equitably throughout the community of those who commit themselves to it.

A further question is whether feminist issues are necessarily legal problems. Jewish feminist theologians originally formulated some issues in halakhic terms simply because there was a halakhic literature on the topics of gender, the female body, and sexuality, whereas these topics had no precedent in Jewish or non-Jewish philosophical theologies of the past. Access questions such as whether women could count in a minyan, be called to the Torah, or be ordained as rabbis, were phrased in legal language because the male-dominated institutions that controlled access insisted on phrasing them in these terms. However, the tendency to articulate all feminist issues as halakhic questions permits halakhic language and categories to hold hostage what are essentially theological questions and to refrain from addressing equally crucial non-halakhic questions concerning exclusively masculine God-language and androcentric sacred narratives (Plaskow 1983).

The feminist debate over halakha also reawakens the familiar theological challenges of modernity: If beliefs and behaviors are shaped within social contexts that vary from place to place and change over time, how can any revelation be eternally true and binding? What sanctity should be accorded to tradition? Has the past any claims upon us? By what processes is revelation reshaped within historical time, and who has the authority to do this reshaping?

249

Representations of God and Israel: language and imagery

Another approach to feminist theology gives precedence to issues concerning the representation of God and Israel in language and imagery. Gross (1983) and Plaskow (1983) charge that depicting God as male both constructs and justifies a world in which power and authority are allocated to men. The primary responsibility for making women "the Other" rests not with halakha but with theological conceptions of God as male embedded in stories and prayers. An exclusively masculine God-language is ethically objectionable because it fosters injustice, but it is also theologically inadequate. This discussion has produced both new theology and new liturgy.

Many feminist thinkers have revived interest in feminine God-imagery and in nongendered images drawn from nature, some of them traditional in origin, for instance God as rock, lion, or tree (Gross 1983, Falk 1989, Plaskow 1990). Marcia Falk has produced a prayerbook which not only incorporates such imagery but replaces the masculine language of time-honored canonical formulas (Falk 1996).

A related innovation are feminist spiritualities that reconstruct the metaphoric language of Jewish mysticism. These spiritualities are in dialogue with a form of unitive mysticism promulgated by Reconstructionist postmodernist theologians. Both feminists and Reconstructionists fear the reifying power of the traditional language of transcendence, feminists, because, invariably, what is reified is God's masculinity, and Reconstructionists, because they regard the very attribution of personality to God as a reification. The quintessential spiritual experience in this reconstructed mysticism is a fusion that dissolves boundaries between self, world, and God. While its most common anthropomorphic metaphor is sexual intercourse, images connected with water, light, and fire also abound. Unitive spirituality is appealing because metaphors of hierarchical relations are inapplicable and gender differentiation irrelevant. It is unnecessary to prove that anthropomorphism is inadequate because that has already been acknowledged, and alternatives are welcome.

Some major theological problems, however, are raised by relinquishing the notion of God as an Other (Adler 1997). First, covenant requires the existence of a divine Other; if God is not distinct from self and community, the theological language of partnership is not usable. Second, given how bitterly feminists have fought for integrity of selfhood, for not being subsumed or swallowed up by others, the experience of fusion makes an odd foundation for a feminist spirituality. Finally, if the boundaries between God, self, and world are collapsed, there can be no stories; the foundational narratives of Judaism must be regarded as archaic and vestigial.

Hermeneutics: dealing with androcentric or misogynistic texts

Like legal texts, Biblical narratives, rabbinic exegesis and stories (*midrash* and *aggadah*), and commentary can marginalize, demonize, or efface women's presence altogether. Until feminist interpreters problematized these representations or invisibilities, they were simply accepted as givens. But claiming a share in the Torah and utilizing it as holy text are fundamental to Judaism. How can women imaginatively enter the world of a text that misrepresents or marginalizes their difference? Yet if feminist interpreters problematize sacred texts, how can they then claim them? One solution lies in a feminist hermeneutics which makes wrestling with the text a holy activity.

Another solution is to claim that a canon designated by a male elite is not the only possible source of holy texts. Texts written by women can be rediscovered through historical research (Umansky and Ashton 1992). Contemporary texts by Jewish women and men can be incorporated. It has been proposed that women did contribute to canonical texts (Goitein 1988, R.E. Friedman 1987), but a further question is whether the polytheistic texts that formed part of Jewish women's traditions in ancient times should be acknowledged canonically (Plaskow 1990), or whether there should be a canon at all.

Another solution is to create feminist *midrash* that, like classical *midrash*, tells new stories about biblical stories (Plaskow 1976, Gottlieb 1995). These new *midrashim* flesh out women's actions and motivations and bring them to center-stage in stories in which they were peripheral. They are both commentaries on traditional texts and new creations.

New rituals and ceremonies

Orthodox Judaism knows of only two life-cycle rituals for women: weddings and funerals. The woman is equally silent at both. Traditionally, women are not counted as participants in communal prayer, nor do they lead home rituals such as the Passover seder. Consequently, feminist Jews have both demanded equal access to life-cycle ceremonies and communal prayer and invented religious ceremonies and religious language to address previously unacknowledged experiences in women's lives (Orenstein 1994). *Bat mitzvah*, the first ceremony to which women attained equal access in non-Orthodox American Judaisms, exactly parallels the boy's *bar mitzvah*. However, the demand for *bat mitzvahs* among women who were not given Jewish educations as children has given rise to adult *bar* and *bat mitzvah* ceremonies in which grown women and men celebrate, not their religious coming of age, but their attainment of religious competence.

One important ceremony to which women cannot have access is circumcision. Baby boys are traditionally initiated into the covenant through circumcision. At this event they are named and take their places in the historical community of Israel. There is no comparable ceremony to affirm the entrance of baby girls into the covenant. This issue had to be addressed both ritually and theologically. What is the nature of the covenant to which the child is being pledged? If women lack the covenant of circumcision, are they included in the convenantal people or are they an addendum to it? Feminists who argued that Judaism has an equal access covenant innovated *b'rit bat* ceremonies to

251

welcome baby girls into the covenantal community. The ritual act by which this is to be accomplished has been the subject of much debate, the most extreme (theoretical) proposal being hymenotomy. There is as yet no standard form of the ceremony, though predominant rituals involve light or water. An emerging feminist critique suggests that the association of circumcision with the covenant inherently glorifies the penis and grounds masculine privilege in Judaism. The proponents of this critique propose an alternative covenant ceremony for boys as well as girls.

A variety of innovations articulate the possibility for holiness in women's experiences and concerns. New blessings and rituals celebrate menstruation, childbirth, weaning, women's entrance into elderhood and wisdom, and offer healing for traumas such as miscarriage, rape, and hysterectomy, A variety of liturgical events draw upon rabbinic references to women's celebration of *Rosh Hodesh*, the New Moon. Many women's groups also celebrate an additional Passover seder, with *haggadot* focusing upon redemption from the bondage of sexism.

Many of these rituals are as permissible to Orthodox as to non-Orthodox women. If they fill a liturgical vacuum rather than replacing some preexisting liturgical form, and if they are separate events for women only, classical Jewish law has no precedent for forbidding them. At the same time, because such rituals inhabit an intermediate space between private and public, where attendance is optional and restricted to invited guests, they do not require the larger community to integrate women's experiences and concerns into the genres of institutionalized liturgy and the ritual events of public synagogue worship.

PART VI

SUBJECTIVITY AND EMBODIMENT

25

Self/other

MICHELLE M. MOODY-ADAMS

Feminist reflection on the nature of the self

Belief in the existence of individual selves who are both knowers and agents in the world is for many philosophers an indispensable component of a reasonable view of experience. To be sure, some feminist and nonfeminist philosophers alike have challenged the ontological and epistemological commitments of conventional conceptions of the self. These philosophers have questioned, for instance, whether the self is some kind of unity which persists as a unity over time, and whether self-knowledge is (at least in some degree) possible. Those who challenge these commitments appear to deny the plausibility of the very idea of the self – though many would insist otherwise, or at least argue that the implausibility of that idea would pose no great difficulty for the project of making sense of human subjectivity. Yet many feminist philosophers presuppose both the reasonableness of the idea of the self and the importance of that idea to understanding human subjectivity and identity. In fact, some of the most important developments in feminist philosophy have involved efforts to understand the nature of the self.

Recent feminist reflection on these matters has by and large taken one question as central: whether the nature and identity of the self can be separated from contingent facts about concrete social, historical, and physical circumstances, or whether such facts are fundamentally constitutive of the self. Following in the tradition of such thinkers as Wollstonecraft and Mill, some contemporary feminists embrace the classical liberal conception of the self as an autonomous, selfsufficient individual essentially independent of all contingencies (Wollstonecraft 1975, Mill 1983). But for many feminists, facts about the social, historical, and physical circumstances of human existence are inseparable from the nature and identity of particular selves. Some feminists have suggested that biological differences between men and women may create fundamental differences between masculine and feminine selves. But many feminist philosophers have come to take a different category of social, historical, and physical facts as most important to the constitution of the self: facts about the self's relationships to other selves. Those who defend this view usually maintain, further, the fundamental interrelatedness, or interconnection, between the self and various others. They thus defend what may be called relational theories of the self – theories which, as a whole, constitute one of the most influential components of recent feminist thought.

The relational theories defended by feminist thinkers take different forms, depending upon the particular kind of relationship posited as fundamental to the constitution of the self. Two kinds of relationships have been appealed to most often. By far the largest group of relational theories takes the close personal relationships most typical in families, such as relationships between parents and their children, to be fundamental to the nature and identity of the self. On most of these views, however, the central identity-constituting relationship is that between parents who serve as primary caregivers for children – who are, historically, principally mothers – and the children for whom they are responsible (Held 1993, Noddings 1984, Ruddick 1989). The second main group of relational theories contends that friendships are at least as important in the constitution of the self as are familial ties between caregivers and children. Indeed in some of these theories, the ties of friendship are held to be more fully constitutive of the mature self than the ties of family – principally in virtue of the voluntariness (or quasi-voluntariness) of the bonds that exist between friends (Friedman 1993, Code 1987b).

There are important tensions between some of the fundamental assumptions underlying the two principal variants of relational theories. This is no doubt why some of the most influential relational theories emphasize either the ties of friendship, or the bonds between mother and child – but not both – as fundamental in constituting the mature self. Relational theorists who appeal primarily to the bonds created by childbirth and mothering have often argued that these appeals constitute the only way to give women's experience its due in philosophical discussion. On these views, feminist theory makes a distinctively feminist contribution to philosophical thinking only when it illuminates some aspect of women's experience that has been neglected or altogether ignored by the philosophical tradition – especially some experience not shared by men (Held 1993). Other theorists are concerned that theoretical appeals to bonds between mothers and their children are limited in scope. These theorists question, first, whether insights linked with mothering could ever be fully accessible to women who never become mothers (Moody-Adams 1996). They suggest, further, that appeals to the ties of friendship are more likely to yield insights into the constitution of the mature self (and relations between that self and others) that will be genuinely accessible and instructive to human beings (female and male) generally (Friedman 1993).

Such tension between the two principal variants of relational theories has meant that debates between their respective proponents often end in argumentative impasse. There may be a way beyond this impasse in feminist reflection on the self, though it will most likely require a more eclectic approach than most currently available theories offer. Such an approach might appeal to the identity-constituting properties of a variety of personal and associational relationships – including those in families, friendships, and even the associational ties of communities and groups organized around various professional and personal interests. Increasing numbers of feminist philosophers have begun to question whether it makes sense to privilege any one kind of relationship

256

between persons as most fundamental to the nature and identity of mature selves (Code 1987b). More eclectic approaches to the relational theories so often associated with feminist thought may come to seem more plausible as this question takes on even greater importance.

Feminist presuppositions of relational theories of the self

It might be wondered precisely how relational theories offer distinctively feminist insights, or rest on distinctively feminist methodological presuppositions. After all, a variety of nonfeminist philosophical conceptions (those appealing to the thought of Aristotle or Hegel, for instance) are to some degree committed to some variant of a relational theory of the self. Many such conceptions – including the communitarianism recently defended by some political philosophers seeking to reject the seeming atomism of liberal social and political theory – defend the idea of the "encumbered" or "situated" self, whose nature and identity are defined (at least in part) by social roles (Sandel 1982, MacIntyre 1981). Like the relational theories defended by feminists, such conceptions claim to provide important alternatives to the individualist theories which presume that persons are essentially separate from the contingencies of social roles and personal relationships.

Yet the relational theories defended by feminist philosophers typically rest on two assumptions not shared by nonfeminist philosophers. First, virtually all feminist philosophers agree that nonfeminist philosophy has largely ignored the perspectives of women, and that it has done so to the detriment of philosophy itself. Feminist theories of the self claim that analyses of central features of women's experience (and of women's allegedly distinctive modes of knowing and thinking) will yield richer understandings of the nature of the self than any nonfeminist accounts. Among the most important subjects for analysis, relational theorists contend, are the social roles that women have typically occupied to the general exclusion of men (especially their roles as the primary caregivers for children), the developmental processes that have long determined the character of female childhood and adolescence, and even the sui generis relationship between a pregnant woman and a developing fetus. But many feminist philosophers of the self also accept a second assumption: an adequate account of the self will necessarily be in some degree critical of the ways in which conventional social relationships have sometimes contributed to the oppression of women (Ferguson 1987). This assumption has generated some particularly vehement feminist resistance to communitarian accounts of the situated self. Appealing to sociological and historical investigations, as well as to psychological theories of gender construction, many feminist philosophers insist on the theoretical relevance of the ways in which women have often been stifled by – and sometimes sacrificed to – conventionally accepted social and cultural roles and relationships. These theorists then argue further that, as a rule, communitarian accounts are inattentive to the ways in which conventional social and cultural roles often not only define but confine the development of female selves

257

(Friedman 1993, Code 1987b, Benhabib 1987, 1992b). Concerns about the potentially oppressive components of some communities' traditions thus create important areas of divergence between many relational theories defended by feminist philosophers and accounts of the situated self defended by communitarian thinkers.

But the very concerns which lead to this divergence between feminism and communitarianism have also generated serious theoretical conflict within feminist thought itself. In particular, feminists who defend relational theories by appeal to women's roles as primary caregivers for children have been criticized by feminists for whom such appeals seem to reaffirm historically developed social conventions that are potentially oppressive to women. The ensuing debate has raised a pressing question: can feminism find a genuinely transformative vision of social and political life by appeal to those conventions which have historically defined the social and personal roles and relationships primarily occupied by women? This question has special importance for feminist thinkers because feminist philosophy attempts more fully than most philosophy to bridge the familiar divide between "theory" and "practice." Indeed most feminist philosophers view their theoretical investigations as, at least in part, contributions to a broader effort to transform the social, economic, and political circumstances of women. This suggests that future feminist reflection on the nature and constitution of the self will be inextricably linked with efforts to determine which kind of relational theory – if any – will best harmonize the theoretical and practical aims of feminist philosophers. Many feminist philosophers are optimistic that it is possible to harmonize feminist theory and practice and still appeal to the centrality of motherhood and care to many women's lives (Held 1993, Ruddick 1989). Others remain skeptical, however, about the possibility of reconciling such optimism with familiar facts of social life (Moody-Adams 1996). To consider just one source of relevant concern, even as ever larger numbers of women take on increased responsibilities outside the homes in which most childcare takes place, women remain more subject than men to stringent normative demands associated with the care of children – and, in general, with the stewardship of the domestic household. Some feminist philosophers believe that such developments should challenge faith in the transformative potential of insights drawn from social roles conventionally occupied primarily by women.

Moral and epistemological implications of relational theories

In addition to their obvious importance for shaping moral reflection on the social, political, and economic status of women, feminist theories of the self (like all philosophical theories of the self) have crucial implications for understanding the nature of morality and the moral foundations of social and political life. To begin with, the notion that there is fundamental interdependence between the self and (at least) some particular others casts doubt on familiar assumptions of a fundamental opposition between self and other (Whitbeck 1983). Relational theories of the self thus fundamentally challenge moral and political theories which posit a self for whom most interactions with others must be fraught with competition and conflict. The conception of a self for whom community and cooperation are in some interesting sense not "natural" – or are potentially threatening to its integrity – is incompatible with the central claims of relational theories. But relational theories also undermine familiar conceptions of the "other." Many influential moral theories contend that impartiality towards others is the only stance genuinely compatible with a mature moral point of view. But we often encounter situations, feminist thinkers argue, in which it is morally necessary to attend to the concrete identity, history, and needs of the other – situations in which a stance of impartiality would, in fact, be incompatible with what morality requires. As Seyla Benhabib puts it, relational theories remind us of the moral importance of the "concrete other" (Benhabib 1987, 1992b). On relational theories, situations demanding attention to the concrete other are not contingent exceptions to the requirements of moral maturity, nor can they be consigned to a realm of purely "personal" and essentially non-moral concerns. Such theories thus constitute a fundamental challenge to central assumptions implicit in much non-feminist moral theory. Still further, feminist theorists claim that in focusing moral attention on the interconnectedness of persons (and ultimately on some of their common needs and desires), relational theories are more likely to yield useful insight into the moral importance of norms of friendship, love, and care – norms which demands for impartiality generally ignore.

Central components of relational theories also challenge influential versions of the view that the ideal moral agent is an autonomous being. The fullest (and most contested) development of this view is contained in the moral philosophy of Immanuel Kant. For Kant, the ideal moral agent is autonomous in at least two senses. First, the identity of the ideal moral agent is essentially separable from the social and historical contingencies of particular human relationships and roles. But, second, the autonomous moral agent gives the moral law only to itself, by means of legislation in accordance with universally applicable demands of reason. Autonomy, so understood, is for Kant the ultimate source of all morality. The moral implications of relational theories are antithetical to central features of this Kantian conception. Some relational theorists take the Kantian emphasis on the demands of reason to be insufficiently attentive to the moral importance of emotions in affirming the fundamental interconnectedness of self and others (Baier 1987a, 1994b, Code 1987b). Other relational theorists have sought to develop an alternative to the Kantian conception of moral autonomy – a conception more compatible with a morality that could be adopted by agents who affirm the interdependence of selves, and who give moral priority to caring in human relationships (Meyers 1987). On such views, it is possible to capture what is important in the idea of the self-governing moral agent without ignoring the moral importance of the interrelatedness of self and others. Indeed, some feminist philosophers suggest that feminist concerns about discrimination and oppression may require feminist discussion of the importance of respect for the moral – as well as the personal – autonomy of agents.

259

Relational theories of the self may also have important epistemological implications that are analogous to their implications for moral reflection and action. Just as the ideal of the autonomous moral agent who is essentially separate from particular social and historical circumstances has been deemed inattentive to the essential interrelatedness of self and other, the ideal of the autonomous human knower – who must attempt to free her reflection from all prior beliefs, physical encumbrances, and external testimony of other human beings – has been challenged as incompatible with insights provided by relational theories (Code 1987b, Baier 1985). Indeed, even the conception of knowledge typically associated with the idealization of the autonomous human knower – on which genuine knowledge is the autonomous, self-sufficient product of "objective" theoretical investigation – has come under attack (Code 1987b). Most of these claims await further development, but it has been suggested that the epistemological implications of relational theories will be importantly similar to contemporary pragmatist challenges to traditional defenses of cognitive autonomy – especially to that pragmatism inspired by the work of Peirce and Dewey (Code 1987b, Rorty 1991). There is much of value in this suggestion. Thus, for instance, pragmatist reminders of the interdependence of human inquirers as members of knowledge-seeking communities are certainly echoed in many feminist treatments of central epistemological concerns. Yet while there are important points of convergence between feminist and pragmatist views about human knowledge, there may ultimately be far more important areas of divergence – analogous, perhaps, to the divergences in moral theory between feminism and communitarianism. Even contemporary pragmatists who have emphasized the convergence between feminism and pragmatism acknowledge the potential for divergence. Richard Rorty, for instance, has noted that – considered as a body of philosophical claims about objectivity, truth, and knowledge – pragmatism is essentially neutral between feminism and a "masculinism" that is unsympathetic to the socially transformative aims of feminist philosophy (Rorty 1993). (See Article 5, PRAGMATISM.)

Problems and prospects of relational theories

Many of these implications of feminist philosophical reflection on the self – especially its implications for moral thinking – are a function of concerns which first generated extensive feminist discussion of the nature and identity of the self. That discussion has been powerfully influenced by a long-standing debate in developmental psychology concerning the nature of moral maturity, and of the moral domain and the nature of the self which properly underwrite mature moral reasoning. This debate began when the psychologist Lawrence Kohlberg claimed to have discovered, through empirical psychological research, that mature moral reasoning always involves appeals to moral notions of justice, fairness, and rights (Kohlberg 1981). After attempting, unsuccessfully, to apply Kohlberg's claims in her own empirical research, the psychologist Carol Gilligan became convinced that there are serious difficulties with Kohlberg's view of moral maturity (Gilligan 1982a). Gilligan claimed that attention to the ways in which women think about morality and the moral domain would reveal a different, but equally mature and plausible, moral voice: one that relies primarily on the language of care, and on the notion of responsibility in caring relationships, rather than on notions such as justice and rights. The moral language of care and responsibility, she maintained, is rooted in a conception of the self not accessible on the perspective described and defended by Kohlberg – a conception on which self and others are fundamentally interdependent. Indeed, on the most mature versions of this moral perspective considerations about justice and rights will often prove inappropriate and morally insufficient. The morality of rights, she concluded, too often gives priority to non-interference as a fundamental moral demand just where a morality of care would demand far different responses. Many feminist philosophers trace their conviction of the theoretical importance of relational theories of the self to the influence of Gilligan's claims. For these thinkers, Gilligan's empirical research has shown that mature moral reasoning can presuppose a relation of interdependence between the self and other – not interminable competition and conflict that must be regulated by the notion of moral rights (Noddings 1984, Baier 1985, 1987a, 1994b, Ruddick 1989). Once again, the link between feminist theory and practice turns out to be crucial to understanding important developments in feminist philosophy.

Gilligan's work also offers many feminist philosophers grounds for believing that in order to appreciate fully the theoretical possibilities of relational conceptions of the self, it is necessary to attend to central features of women's experience – even where that experience might be different from the experience of men (Held 1993, Whitbeck 1983). Developing this view, feminist theorists have supplemented appeals to Gilligan's work by reference to theories of gender construction developed by psychoanalytic feminists exploring the problems of female social and psychological development (Chodorow 1978, Dinnerstein 1976). But this turn to the experience of women may open the door to some important criticisms. Defenders of nonfeminist approaches, for instance, may charge that theories of the self have always sought to abstract from the particularities of experience (whether male or female), and that feminist appeals to empirical claims about the experience of women are insufficiently general in scope. To be sure, feminist theorists have responded to such criticisms. Most often they contend that theorizing offered as non-gendered reflection on universal facts about humankind is often little more than generalization of the experience of men (Code 1987b, Held 1993, Benhabib 1987, Whitbeck 1983). But such responses fail to address the fundamental concern about generality of scope. Some feminists have even suggested that certain kinds of generalizations about the experience of women – for instance, about the experience of pregnant embodiment and birth, and the activity of mothering a child from birth to maturity – may be incapable of yielding sufficiently general reflection on the nature of the self. In fact, these thinkers have wondered whether appeals to the experience of motherhood can even provide genuinely useful insights for all women – let alone all human beings. After all, some women either cannot, or do not, become mothers. The outcome of debate about such issues is likely to have a profound effect on the future of feminist thinking about the self.

Yet most relational theorists, even those whose theories appeal to the relation between mother and child, do want to claim that their theories illuminate the nature and identity of both male and female selves. That is, even theorists who focus on relationships between mothers and children contend that their theories need not ignore questions of the nature and constitution of the mature self of the non-mothering woman, or the typical man. A principal aim of many relational theories – whether they appeal to the bonds of friendship or the ties of mothering – is to show that certain relationships conventionally deemed "personal" or "private" might provide rich new insights about how to reconfigure the "impersonal" or "public" relationships of political, legal, and economic life (Young 1986). Thus relational theories of the self are often defended as part of substantive efforts to transform "public" life by appealing to moral insights drawn from the "private" realm. The importance of such efforts to the development and defense of relational theories provides more evidence of how fully feminist philosophy seeks to bridge the gap between theory and practice. But in so doing, they also raise the difficult question of whether insights drawn from the "personal" and "private" realms to which women have often been confined may remain too embroiled in oppressive social and cultural conventions to possess genuinely transformative potential. Some of the most powerful challenges to relational theories, especially from within feminist thought itself, are profoundly pessimistic about the transformative potential of the relationships (even friendships) to which such theories most often appeal. Future feminist reflection on these matters – and, more generally, on the plausible outlines of a philosophical theory about the nature and constitution of the self – cannot afford to ignore the theoretical and practical import of these concerns.

26

Postmodern subjectivity

TINA CHANTER

Let me forego all the usual caveats about the vagueness of the term postmodern, our inability to determine what postmodern might mean without first undertaking an exhaustive review of modernism, and the synchrony and dissonance of postmodernity with the equally problematic term poststructuralist. I'll just assume that Derrida, Foucault, and Lacan are among the important thinkers to have influenced the feminist demand to rethink subjectivity, and that Luce Irigaray and Julia Kristeva are two of the most significant and interesting thinkers to have inflected this demand in feminist directions in the French context (see Article 8, POSTMODERNISM).

At the heart of feminist rejections of traditional models of subjectivity – as defined by the Western philosophical canon – is the impasse that is reached when Cartesian assumptions about subjectivity remain unquestioned. If Descartes's mind/body dichotomy is allowed to dictate the opposition between subjectivity and objectivity, along with a series of related distinctions, including reason versus emotions or feelings, feminism inherits a tendency to posit the subject as essentially rational, as unified, and as capable of becoming more or less fully transparent to itself through reflective awareness of its own acts and judgments – of which it is assumed to be more or less in control. While the post-Cartesian subject overcomes mind/body dualism in some way, it remains bound to its inheritance in other ways. Filtered through the lenses of transcendental philosophy and phenomenological reduction, the existential subject takes on the capacity to explore the bodily and emotional aspects of experience that were previously disqualified as legitimate topics of philosophical enquiry. Although the existential subject is no longer confined to a rigidly rationalist conception of what it means to be human, the lived body remains ensconced in the foundational ontological framework that prevents a full articulation of the social, historical, and cultural dimensions of subjectivity (see Article 7, EXISTEN TIALISM AND PHENOMENOLOGY).

Universalist pretensions pervade even the most radical phenomenological analyses, and it is here perhaps that postmodernism might be said to offer something new. By providing ways in which difference, multiplicity, and fragmentation might be not only thought but mobilized, postmodernism distances itself from the assumed rationality, unity, coherence, and mastery of the Cartesian subject, in favor of multiple subjects rather than one ideal subject. This plurality of actors are not assumed to act rationally all the time, or in unison

263

with one another. They experience conflicting and contradictory demands that are sometimes incapable of neat resolution either within a subject or between a community of subjects. Subjects are not always able to make sense of, or gain control of their situations. and may be prey to political forces that elude attempts to harness them.

To admit that subjects are exposed to influences that neither can nor should necessarily be completely negated, contained, or controlled is to see that we are constituted in part by social dimensions that exceed our rational control, as moral and epistemological agents. It is to accept that there are limitations on independent agency, and to acknowledge that part of who we are is dependent on our political location in given institutional, local, national, and international networks of power. Moving away from the idea of atomistic, isolated, solitary thinking selves, postmodernism is more willing to admit than rationalists that individuals are formed through a complex interaction that is played out between the ego and others, between consciousness and unconsciousness, between an always already socially situated self and the society which helps to shape us, forming the background against which we act out our responses, subversions, and transformations of the social norms it offers us.

A conscious subject, potentially capable of indubitable knowledge of the world, able to freely and independently manipulate the world, is no longer assumed as a starting point. The subject is no longer seen as essentially a consciousness capable of knowing the world, or as productive and creative origin, defined as an autonomous agent and by its capacity to produce rational decisions. We are no longer assumed to be the only authors of our social scripts. Institutional and political power is not assumed to emanate purely and simply, like a ray of consciousness from a central subject that is in all significant respects identical to other subjects. Rather, inequities between subjects, imbalances of power are admitted. Forces that bear energies that are irreducible to individual actors are acknowledged, impersonal flows of energies are posited as more fluid and mobile than the picture of subjects with essentially Cartesian consciousness allows.

The well-worn arguments that pose as the mutually exclusive alternatives freedom or determinism, social constructionism or biological reductionism, relativism or universalism, become susceptible to a nuanced, contoured revision that is not content to reduce the subject to one of two extremes, both equally undesirable. On the one hand there is the ideal disembodied, transcendental subject who enjoys a "view from nowhere" – with its pretensions to objectivity, neutrality, and universality. On the other hand the subject is seen as a passive puppet whose strings are pulled by any number of forces outside its control – biology, society, and the state become interchangeable placeholders for some form of determinism. Jettisoning these two unhealthy visions, a more believable picture emerges.

Individuals may be at the mercy of social and biological forces – and part of the interest here lies in the impossibility of ever definitively separating out the strands of that veritable Scylla and Charybdis, nature or culture – but we are not completely passive or without resources in the face of such culturally and

264

historically specific determinants. Although the available resources at the disposal of individuals will themselves be implicated in political agendas, never innocent and neutral, always liable to exploitation, and to subversion by the social forces that produce and maintain the systems against which and in terms of which individuals define themselves, these resources are not completely negligible. Subjects are capable of adopting strategies that can harness power with varying degrees of success, that can produce new power relations, negotiate new communities, and overturn or transform well-established lines of power.

Rethinking sex and gender

One of the axes around which it is useful to rethink subjectivity is that of sex and gender. Gatens argues convincingly for the need for feminists to revise typical conceptions of sex and gender, which adhere to fundamentally Cartesian assumptions about the ease with which gender can be thought independently of sex. Just as it no longer seems viable to many feminists to separate out thinking from bodies and passions, as if thought either is or should be disembodied and purely rational, so it no longer seems credible for feminists to focus exclusively on the category of gender at the expense of sex. Rather than ignoring sex – which had become for some feminists symbolic of all that was wrong with the patriarchal world, the site of women's difference from men, the sign of their apparent inferiority, an index of their inability to become like men – Gatens (1996a) points out in the opening chapter of *Imaginary Bodies* that we cannot adequately think gender unless and until we think it in relation to, and not in abstraction from, sex.

Gatens's insistence on the need to raise the question of sexual difference by thinking through the relation between sex and gender can be read as a useful corrective to the view that sex can be seen as an entirely normative domain, that there is no real distinction between gender and sex – both are part of a discursive realm that comes to be constituted by a divergent network of often inconsistent claims that are made on what we used to call our "identity." Drawing on Foucault (1978), Butler suggests in *Gender Trouble* that there is a parallel to be drawn between the way we think of sex, and the tendency to naturalize, or posit as a foundational and unchanging ground the fictional or discursive category of women (Butler 1990). Much as the category of women is posited as the subject of feminism not merely by feminism itself, but by the very system of representational politics that feminism takes itself to be combating in its struggle for emancipation, sex is taken to be natural, biological and bodily in ways that are not politically or culturally circumscribed. Butler points out, however, that sex is constituted by way of exclusionary claims that may be more or less invisible to those of us who are caught up in the socially variegated discourse of feminism, a discourse which itself is not immune to the heterosexual, racial, and class prejudices that help to structure and maintain the status quo against which feminism positions itself – but to which it is still related in ways that may exceed the critical purchase feminism seeks to develop.

265

Bodies

A number of diverse factors converge on present bodies – resistant as they undoubtedly are to analyses – as urgent topics of enquiry to feminist theorists. Among these factors is the truculent absence of bodies from the feminist rhetoric of the gendered 1970s and 1980s, which disposed feminists to debate at length the acquiescence of female bodies to masculine paradigms, effectively obliterating not only the specificity of bodies, but almost incidentally rendering invisible bodies themselves. It is not accidental that the invisibility of feminist bodies rendered not only sex and sexuality invisible, but also race (Spelman 1988). If the extent to which feminism found it necessary to ignore female bodies was bound to issue in a reaction that tried to rehabilitate the spurned bodies of feminist theory (see Butler 1993, Braidotti 1994, Grosz 1994c, and Gatens 1996a) – other circumstances conspire to render visible the blind spot that marked the absent place of the body in feminist theory.

Developments in medical technology have helped to put bodies on the feminist agenda, confronting feminism with the challenge to accommodate itself to dramatic shifts in reproductive possibilities – transformations that challenge the boundaries we used to take for granted between the body and culture, nature and history. Now that reproductive technologies enable women to reproduce in ways that vastly attenuate the role of men, not only is pregnancy no longer the more or less exclusive province of heterosexually coupled women, but what used to count as culture, and what used to count as nature is up for grabs. The female body is no longer a stable ground defined by clear-cut reproductive capacities. What we used to regard as anatomy is itself shifting, settling into different grooves that are continually being redefined by medical sciences and technologies.

The boundaries between technology and bodies are shifting not only through processes of artificial insemination and in-vitro fertilization, but also through the increasing proliferation of gender identity clinics (the very name of which betrays an oversimplification that betokens perhaps a naive attempt to legislate culturally what bodies are allowed to be). As trans-gender identities are more easily accommodated through sex-change operations, so bodies assume the status of symbols that come to represent a subject's idea of what gender they are, rather than contradicting that idea. The symbolic value that bodies acquire is a further testimony to the need to depart from any simple equation of sex with an unchanging and unchallengeable natural domain hitherto presumed to be beyond human and technological control. A woman who previously felt trapped in a man's body is freed from the material signs of masculinity, and granted the right to be a woman at the physical, empirical – and also, we now see, symbolic – level.

If Butler's work reminds us that gender is not only an unavoidable and pervasive imperative but that it is one that also functions in a binary and polarized way. she takes this insight beyond its probably Derridean source

(1978). Why are there only two sexes? Because there are only two genders – and it is not only femininity or masculinity that are prescribed, but also heterosexuality. Why do we not have a third sex to designate feminine men, or a fourth sex to designate masculine women? What does society do with hermaphrodites, androgyny, or any other challenge to our received and mutually exclusive categories of who is allowed to be feminine and who masculine? Medical technology provides ways of clarifying the issue at a bodily level, and psychiatrists provide counselling to help people find out who they "really are." Of course, increasing the number of sexes would not really address the issue, since it still assumes that there is a biological base onto which gender is constructed. The point is to disrupt the binarism of thought – both at the level of the bifurcation into sex and gender, and at the level of masculine and feminine.

Essentialism

In so far as the classical notion of the subject assumes that there is an essence of humanity, a real core underlying the superficial bodily covering of materiality, the question of essentialism must be investigated by feminists who want to rethink subjectivity from a postmodern perspective. Humanism is under attack from many sides, but the idea that there is an ideal or innate human essence is hard to eradicate – it recurs under different guises. In feminist discourse, the accusation of essentialism has been mobilized in a variety of ways, and has come to mean anything from biological reductionism to social universalism (see Grosz 1995). Sometimes it serves a useful purpose, as when it is used to ward off metaphysical beliefs underlying appeals to specifically feminine experiences – beliefs which implicitly or explicitly turn on the essential similarity of all women in virtue of a shared commonality. To appeal to a female nature that all women share is to repudiate the ultimate importance of race, class, sexual preference, and the like, a gesture that ostensibly endorses the supposedly neutral and ideal subject, which often ends up being white, middle-class, heterosexual, and whatever else marks privilege in a given society.

To take differences seriously need not be a reactive celebration of women as fundamentally feminine, caring, or nurturing. Taking differences seriously can be a way of taking into account the specific social circumstances women face in a given society. The differences between women's and men's experiences need not be timeless or universal – they can be temporary, and socially defined, and as such subject to change. Still, we should bear in mind that a society in which there are no differences at all between the sexes is not an ideal that we necessarily want to uphold as desirable.

The sameness/difference dilemma

Equality has often been taken by feminists to indicate the basic sameness of sexed subjects, so that any differences between men and women are treated as incidental and unimportant. At best women's differences from men are dismissed as

267

trivial, at worst they are seen as embarrassing and to be denied at all costs. For example, arguments to establish equal pay for equal work appeal to the equal competence of men and women, and dismiss as insignificant physical and reproductive differences between women and men, once again playing down the salience of the body, while emphasizing the potential similarity of the sexes. By focusing on the fact that women can measure up to men, feminists concede inadvertently that men's traditional roles are more valuable than women's traditional roles. Work by Gilligan, even if it was in its first formulations rather theoretically naive, and based on an empirical group that reflected classist, racist, and heterosexist privilege, had the merit of overturning the assumption that men's practices, and the values that are celebrated in a masculine world, are inherently superior to women's (Gilligan 1982a). Women may see things differently, but their values are not inherently inferior to men's.

Feminists working in the area of legal studies (see Rhode 1990a, Minow 1991b, P.J. Williams 1991b, Cornell 1991) and social and political philosophy (Jaggar 1980a) have recognized the need to acknowledge that there are important respects in which women's needs are different from men's, and that women consequently require different treatment. As long as women remain the primary caretakers of children, they should be treated differentially with regard to child care, maternity leave, or responsibility of whether to carry an embryo to term. Arguments such as these, that are contingent on relevant aspects of the situation remaining stable, avoid the charge of essentialism or universalism. In a particular situation, a particular party's interests differ significantly from those of others, and these differences should be taken into account in deciding how to treat people equally. Nothing need be claimed about human essence, feminine essence, or universal judgments.

Beyond equality

While it seems possible to make significant claims that are informed by feminist insights without appealing to eternal or metaphysical grounds in order to legitimate them, it remains true that there is a tendency for any knowledge that is produced to be co-opted by those that are privileged in a given society. Thus corporations can claim feminist motivations when they make day care available, but in fact increase of profits remains the major motivation for the retention or attraction of female employees. Feminism cannot – and perhaps should not want to – maintain its immunity from the inevitable coercion of its aspirations, but it can be more or less wary of its effects, more or less vigilant about observing what is claimed in the name of feminism.

Luce Irigaray, for example, is wary of identifying with the quest for equality because she is suspicious of the extent to which striving for equality with men allows feminism to gloss over not only the differences both between men and women, and among women, but also the question of what grants subjectivity. Women have been systematically defined in relation to men, and as such have been denied a specific identity of their own. Such coherence. unity, and significance as women have been granted accrues to them in virtue of their opposition to, or difference from, the masculine norm. Usually this being in virtue of what-men-are-not, this non-being, signifies the inferiority of women to men, of feminine to masculine.

To insist upon viewing women as subjects in their own right may provide a partial and corrective solution to the historical disenfranchisement of women, but to operate only on this reactive level carries with it the danger of simply reinscribing the problematic claims of universal ontology. Postmodernism avoids ontologically grounding the subject, or granting it universality by appealing to the purity and transparency of core identities implicit in traditional Western metaphysics. Rather, theorists such as Foucault and Derrida view the subject as operating in a multiplicity of ways, some of which challenge both the assumed unity of its identity, and any assumptions about the homogeneity and fixity of sources of authority that constitute subjects. Feminists influenced by Derrida and Lacan emphasize the extent to which the apparent solidity and coherence of subjects often amounts to a fiction bought at the price of repressing or denying whatever aspects of ourselves do not fit neatly into the stories we tell ourselves about our capacity to master or control our lives. Foucault has emphasized that the repressive forces which subjects often experience as representing some form of prohibition are neither merely negative, nor the only mechanisms of power. To imagine that subjects are simply the passive repositories of higher authorities is to ignore both the productive effects of power, and the fact that subjects themselves can make power a resource. The powers that facilitate subjects need not be envisioned as capacities over which the subject maintains total or constant control. Rather, subjects are a nexus of various lines of force which converge and overlap at particular concentrations or nodes. Subjects can tap into these flows and eddies, thereby mobilizing energy in particular ways and creating new local and temporary centers of power, which are not orchestrated in any direct way by a centralizing, autonomous higher agency. Networks and alliances are therefore irreducible to one single and overriding mechanism of power, whether this is identified with patriarchal, racist, or heterosexist ideology.

Thus postmodern feminism does not merely authenticate the female subject by providing it with the same legitimation as male subjects – extending political privileges and rights to women, for example, it also questions the adequacy of construing subjects only as repositories of equal rights. Exploring female morphology is one way in which Luce Irigaray has challenged the predominant product-oriented, phallogocentric imagery, which values distinctions between subjects and objects, in the service of rational teleological projects (see Irigaray 1993a).

If the work of Foucault and Derrida has contributed to feminist projects in positive ways, it has not been received uncritically. As Jana Sawicki (1994) points out, Foucault's writings often display a masculinist bias, and his skepticism about the discourse of emancipation can be read as pessimistic, but this does not prevent feminists taking up his work and applying his insights fruitfully, with an appropriate wariness of the dangers inherent in the strategies available to us for liberation. Feminists are also skeptical of Lacan because he tends to write in a way that obfuscates rather than clarifies, he tends to be overtly sexist, and because of the view that psychoanalysis rehabilitates the individual to the world, rather than seeing what's wrong with the world, and working politically to change it. Despite this, I contend that feminists can learn from psychoanalysis – and psychoanalysts can learn from feminism. Tensions remain to be explored within what might be called the unhappy marriage of feminism and psychoanalysis (see Brennan 1989).

Psychoanalysis and subjectivity

In an interview that was first published in 1974, and has become a notorious site of tension between sympathizers and critics of postmodern feminism – all the more so because it appeared in a collection that represented the first exposure of many English readers to "French feminism" – Kristeva famously declared "a woman cannot 'be' ... feminist practice can only be negative ... . In 'woman' I see something that cannot be represented, something that is not said" (Kristeva 1981, p. 137). In the background of this statement is Lacan's even more notorious claim that "There is no such thing as *The* woman" (Lacan 1983, p. 144). Read quickly and out of context, these statements seem to amount to the same pejorative views of women and of feminism – women do not exist, and feminism is a waste of time. Read more carefully and slowly, and taken in their respective contexts, this particular statement by Lacan is not offensive to feminists, and Kristeva's claim indicates something much more helpful to feminism than the derisive dismissal for which it is often mistaken. The completed statement by Lacan runs as follows: "There is no such thing as *The* woman, where the definite article stands for the universal." With this qualification, it can easily be seen that Lacan's point, far from representing mere invective or polemics, coincides with the belief of many feminists that there is no one, ideal, universal, woman – no essence, no eternal feminine, no natural and unchanging stamp that marks all women. To assume that there is would be to fail to take seriously not only cultural, religious, ethnic, racial, and class differences, but also sexual preference. There is not one ideal woman, there are many different women. Women may be encouraged to live up to some ideal – and nonexistent – image of female beauty, virtue and chastity, but no single individual embodies such an ideal, which is precisely a fictional, symbolic, mythical construct of a particular society.

When Kristeva says "a woman cannot 'be'" she adds, in a series of statements that clarifies the claim,

> it is something which does not even belong in the order of *being*. It follows that a feminist practice can only be negative, at odds with what already exists so that we may say "that's not it" and "that's still not it." In "woman" I see something that cannot be represented, something that is not said, something above and beyond nomenclatures and ideologies   (Kristeva, 1981, p. 137).

To say that a woman cannot be is to deny the adequacy of positing an ontology of woman, as if the construct "woman" could be universally determined across time and space, irrespective of cultural and political coordinates. By denying that women can be pinned down, defined – "that's not it ... that's still not it" – Kristeva reminds us that women are not just one thing – they are not only nurturing, they are not only gendered. Women are not all the same, not always unified and coherent in the choices and judgments they make. To construe feminism simply as a struggle for equal rights concedes the point that men are better than women, and that women should strive for what men have and the values they have traditionally represented. While some feminists may take umbrage when Kristeva denies that women can be represented – a denial which appears to just repeat the masculine invocation of women as indefinable and ineffable, as mysterious other – her point can be read more sympathetically. She is calling for a resignification of the subject of sexual difference that does not merely adopt models that are already available.

To think through subjectivity at the level of sexual difference is not to assume that the goal of feminism is the degendering or the desexualization of society. It is to try to think differences without suppressing multiple sexualities, without demanding the conformity of gender to a binary opposition, and without subordinating all other differences to gendered differences.

27

Psychoanalytic feminism

TERESA BRENNAN

Psychoanalytic feminism is that body of writing which uses psychoanalysis to further feminist theory and, in principle, feminist practice.

Origins

The myth of the origin of psychoanalysis for feminism goes like this. A long time ago in the early 1970s, our feminist mothers were bewildered. They found that despite their intellectual and political commitment to feminism, they still indulged in bad old masculinist practices, like loving (men) too much and being relational rather than thinking consequentially. Could it be that patriarchy was after all biological? Or was there some other explanation for the tedious stereotypical pattern-repeats of the bad old days?

Enter the unconscious. According to the first book on the subject, Juliet Mitchell's *Psychoanalysis and Feminism* (1974), the unconscious, rather than biology, explained the repetition of roles. It explained why stereotypical masculinity and femininity persisted, even when one wanted to change. This was the beginning of the way in which much of the subsequent debate in and on psychoanalysis and feminism has been organized around the bifurcation between the biological and the social. The debate gives birth to a third category, the psychical, as we shall see.

Mitchell's polemical target was the condemnation of Freud that held sway in early feminist circles, in the works of Kate Millet, Shulamith Firestone, Germaine Greer, Eva Figes, and of course Simone de Beauvoir. But despite the generally negative attitude to Freud that permeated the work of the feminist founders, and despite the apparent novelty of psychoanalysis-for-feminism, a case can be made for seeing early feminist interest in psychoanalysis as an extension of the formative practice of the women's movement: consciousness-raising.

Consciousness-raising was based on the assumption that one had a false consciousness, which buttressed oppression through its identification with the "feminine stereotype." There was also a feminist consciousness, an awareness of the manifold ways in which one bought the false stereotype, ways ranging from the recently rediscovered "beauty myth" to the conviction that a woman's appropriate destiny was that of wife and mother. The rejection of the stereotype was simultaneously the opening-up of myriad possibilities for how one could be in the world. It was a rejection that was sudden, and that had qualities associated with a conversion experience. The world and woman's place within it was seen in a new light; the old ways were rejected. A new truth, experienced with absolute and energizing conviction, came into being.

Because of its emphasis on changing consciousness, the second feminist movement was anchored in the psyche from its inception. But the ties between that interest and the potential of psychoanalysis for furthering it were obscured by the biological aspects of Freud's theory. Millet, Firestone, Greer, Figes, and Beauvoir, to various degrees, emphasized the salience of biology in Freud's writing on femininity, and the fact that in the last analysis he referred the deficiencies of femininity (of which he thought there were many) to penis envy. These writers assume that the penis is biological. Well, you may say, but it is, isn't it? Not exactly, said Mitchell. There is a distinction to be drawn between the penis and the phallus, she continued, introducing Lacan's version of psychoanalysis into feminist theory for the first time. Moreover, she seemed to add, penis-envy is a small price to pay for the illumination Freud's account of "the making of a lady" shed on feminism's concern with stereotypic femininity.

Freud's biological residues, as Mitchell termed them, mattered far less than his discovery that sexuality was constructed rather than given. One is not born, but becomes sexual. The libido is not predetermined, but draws on various contributory currents: oral, anal, scopic, phallic, even a drive for mastery. These drives have obvious reference points in biological experience, but there is no necessary teleology in how that experience shapes each tributary current, let alone in how the overall stream of libido intertwined (Freud 1905). Freud's idea of a constructed sexuality was revolutionary in its time. It was also a condition of furthering the cardinal interest of the second women's movement, namely, there is no natural or *essential* sexuality. The contrary view, embodied in claims such as "women are by nature more nurturing (and therefore should stay at home)" or "men are essentially more aggressive" was labeled essentialist.

In retrospect, Mitchell's was a two-sided move. On the one hand, feminist concerns with change received a tremendous boost via the concept of the unconscious, and the idea that sexuality is a construction. On the other, there was a simultaneous deflection into Freudian and Lacanian theory, a deflection whose yield has not always been self-evident. The subsequent history of psychoanalysis for feminism has maintained this initial tension between the desire to explain ourselves to ourselves, in terms of everyday oppression and the wish to change it, and the desire to comprehend fascinating and often ineluctable theory that may or may not further that explanation. This will become plainer as we go along, beginning with Lacan.

Lacanian views

As noted thus far, in Mitchell's reading of Lacan, a reading developed in a subsequent book with Jacqueline Rose, *Feminine Sexuality: Jacques Lacan and the Ecole Freudienne* (1982), biology is less salient because of the difference between phallus and penis. The penis is the biological organ (everyone agrees on this); the phallus is the Master Signifier. The phallus is a representation of the penis, but it is also the only way we have of signifying that the basic purpose of language is to plug up the hole at the center of all being. Language fills this gap because it communicates, and by enabling us to communicate with one another overcomes the emptiness at the core of each of us. But it only overcomes it temporarily and to a very limited extent. Not only that, words never get it quite right. There is a difference for Lacan between what we want to say (the need), and what we actually say (the demand). That difference he calls desire.

For our purposes, the most salient thing about desire is that it refers specifically to a psychical reality. Desire is not only about biological need, nor is it solely a matter of social response and social interaction. It exists in a territory between the biological and the social. This new territory is the psychical reality of what Freud had earlier labeled "the other scene," the *andere Schauplatz* (literally "the other showplace") of mental life (Freud 1900). In that scene, the psychical governs.

Psychical reality complicates the initial bifurcation along biological and social lines. The nature of the complication becomes more evident once we turn to the next major contribution to psychoanalytic feminism: that of object-relations theory in general and Nancy Chodorow in particular.

Object-relations perspectives

Chodorow's is the best-known intervention using object-relations theory for feminism but, two years before its publication, Dorothy Dinnerstein published a marvellous and underused book drawing on Kleinian object-relations theory (*The Mermaid and the Minotaur*, 1976). At some point, this book deserves a revival. But keeping for now to Chodorow, her *The Reproduction of Mothering* (1978) is described by its author as a sociology of gender. Its focus is entirely on how social relations are internalized by the psyche, via a kind of direct mapping: the psyche is meant to be an accurate reflection, a transposition, of the social. It is this direct mapping that was challenged by Lacanians and Kleinians alike: both schools emphasize the significance of psychical reality, in which social interactions, events, and relationships are always mediated by fantasy or desire.

A Kleinian baby might have the "best mother" in the world, a mother who loves it, feeds it whenever it is hungry, and so on. But in the minute between when that baby first feels its hunger and vocalizes its need, a paranoid fantasy of deliberate deprivation can enter the psyche (and frequently does). Women can henceforward be blamed for deliberately keeping one in a situation of pain. A Lacanian theory baby might be well on its way to internalizing the apparent social relations in its family constellation when it is zapped by the *unconscious* desire of the other: that baby's father may be a very model of virtuous equal parenting, while unconsciously desiring that his baby daughter provide him with a feminine mirror to flatter his narcissism.

But for the student of psychoanalysis and feminism, "psychical reality" is complicated precisely because Lacan and Klein speak from different traditions;

274

moreover Klein is properly regarded as an object-relations theorist, as indeed, are the theorists drawn on by Chodorow. We have already seen some of the parameters of Lacan's thought. We need to see more about the object-relations tradition, stressing that it gives rise to one school which emphasizes psychical life (the Kleinians) and another which dwells on social factors (the object-relations school).

Chodorow herself gives a first-class introduction to the social object-relations theories; amongst others, she uses the work of the Balints and Winnicott (A. Balint 1965, M. Balint 1968, Winnicott 1965). She lays particular stress on the assumption (common to these thinkers) that mother and child form a primary undifferentiated unit, from which the child has to emerge with a distinct sense of its separate existence. This social baby has to go through a phase of individuation–separation from the mother. In this phase, its psyche is shaped by the social relations it internalizes.

The prototype for all object-relations theory is Freud's description of the ego in Freud's "Mourning and Melancholia" (1917b), a description that is amplified in *The Ego and the Id* (1927). Freud argues that "the ego is a precipitate of abandoned object-cathexes." Where we love, but are forced to give up what we love, either because it is socially or ethically inappropriate, or because it gives us up, or whatever, then we cope with the loss by identifying with the object we loved. To identify is to take on the object's characteristics: the nuance of voice, the hidden ambition, the appalling politics, and so on. Freud calls on this theory in *The Ego and the Id* when he discusses how it is that the boy is heir to the world of the father, whose characteristics he takes on when he has to give up his desire for his mother.

The identification with the lost object became the cornerstone of the object-relations approach, insofar as this identification explains how the object becomes internalised. A focus on identification is common to both object-relations schools. The difference is that for the Kleinians, as I have indicated, the identification is mediated by fantasy. For the object-relations theorists Chodorow favors, the actual social relation is internalised.

And so back to *The Reproduction of Mothering*. As it belongs to the social object-relations school, it emphasizes how the existing social relations to the mother and the father are internalized. It assumes, as did Freud, that the parent with whom one identifies is the parent of the same sex. Girls identify with the mother, boys with the father. Because Chodorow assumes a family in which mothers are the primary caregivers, this means that girls identify with the "caring" parent, the relational mother, while boys identify with the distant parent, the father. They identify with the father, and in doing so turn out to the world. Girls are more predisposed toward an inward turning, if not to the family circle, then at least to "the relationship." The result is that boys grow up to be distant, objective, and detached; girls are more focused on relationships, intersubjective interaction, and in permanent peril of merging with those they love.

This theory has great strength and great weakness. Its strength is that it touches strong chords of recognition in the experience of many women who

275

find themselves cursed with connectedness. At this experiential level Chodorow's work found numerous followers. Chodorow's theory contributed a continued and more subtle interrogation of the relation to the object and feminine masochism in Jessica Benjamin's work *The Bonds of Love* (1988); it influenced Carol Gilligan's new feminine ethics based on connection, and the salience of the concrete rather than the abstract value in ethical decision making (*In a Different Voice* 1982a); it helped form a feminist philosophy of science, in terms of its substantial influence on the work of Evelyn Fox Keller, and her investigation of the psychical origin of the scientific categories: "subjective" and "objective" (*Reflections on Gender and Science*, 1985).

Chodorow's weakness is that the theory is too successful. It cannot explain why any girl would ever escape the relational net, or the confines of heterosexuality. Chodorow freely admits that her theory cannot handle lesbianism. More generally, it cannot explain masculinity in women or femininity in men. It loses the explanatory force of Freud's own theory, which at least did explain why a woman or a man could depart from the social norm.

Queering the norm

The Freudian subject is always split. He or she goes through a negative as well as a positive Oedipus complex. In the former, a girl desires her mother, a boy his father. The triumph of the positive Oedipus complex is precisely a matter of social norms. These cement libidinal pathways in one direction whilst repressing, without eliminating, the other pathways and possibilities that live on in the unconscious, from time to time disrupting or overpowering the prescribed heterosexual outcome.

There is another problem with the social object-relations perspective. This problem in fact is endemic to Freud's account of loss and identification. Boys actually do not identify with the object they have lost: the mother. They identify with the father, an identification based on the promissory note that they too can have the mother, or a woman like her one day, provided they repress and defer the desire to have her now. Girls do identify with the mother, but how they lost her is not explicated in Freud's account. This loss, however, is central in Irigaray's theory. We will come back to this.

For now, it should be noted that the theme of "Mourning and Melancholia" has been pursued in the queer theory literature. "I never loved him, I never lost him," is how Judith Butler (*Gender Trouble*, 1990) describes the psychical response of the straight man to the negative Oedipus complex, in which he loved and desired his father, or a man like him.

The potential of the theory of the split subject for explaining deviations from the heterosexual norm begins with Freud's account of the negative Oedipus complex, but it does not end there. There is a more general interest in the instability of identity, or the notion that a given identity is a fragile construction. Just as "the ego is a precipitate of abandoned object-cathexes," so too is identity. Jacqueline Rose was the first to stress how "the stability of identity is always threatened by disruption" (Rose 1982), but the theme has since become popular, not only in queer theory but in "constructionism" overall.

But with the significant exception of queer theory, there is little in much of the contemporary literature on deconstruction and Lacanian psychoanalysis that seems to bear on felt experience. In fact writings on the instability of identity have prompted many critiques of their putative esoterica, and their apparent general inadequacy in terms of politics and political programs, and especially their neglect of race (see hooks 1992a). Such critiques are often intertwined with an affirmation of "identity politics," which eschews constructionism and "high theory" on these grounds. It is necessary to espouse some form of essentialism in order to claim the identity necessary for political action: as a "woman," African-American, or person of color. Partly because of these arguments, the opposition to essentialism has abated somewhat. But it remains an issue, which we will refer to again in a discussion of the work of Luce Irigaray and "French feminism."

Irigaray and others

Irigaray has made many contributions, but two of them are especially significant here. As I have indicated, the first contribution concerns loss in the girl's relation to the mother; this loss is figured, for Irigaray, within the broader context of how the cultural symbolic does not provide models and images, myths and stories of the relation between mother and daughter (Irigaray 1985a). The relation between mother and son is symbolized, as of course is that between father and son. But, since the myth of Demeter and Persephone, there has been no symbolization of the mother/daughter relation. For Irigaray, this failure to symbolize is at the root of much of a girl's (and a woman's) experience of deep melancholy. The melancholy is worse because she does not know what it is she is mourning; there is no familiar code in which the loss can be recognized.

Moreover, it is a grounding in the culture's symbolic order that gives the psyche leverage. We are able to move forward when we recognize ourselves as part of a tradition in which we have a place. To be without a place is to be without boundaries, and hence to never be sure of who one is. This offers a different perspective altogether on the phenomena Chodorow observed, namely, woman's greater tendency toward merging and the concomitant importance of relationships in her life. It is an explanation ultimately founded in Lacan's theory, in which "finding one's place" through the symbolic order of language is the condition of becoming a relatively sane subject.

For many Lacanians, the assumption has been that girls will be less able to find their place, and ultimately their sanity: they do not have a privileged relation to the phallus, and hence to a symbolic governed by the law of the father. Irigaray insisted (and for this insistence was expelled from Lacan's *Ecole*) on conceiving of the place afforded by language, and of the relation to the phallus, in broader cultural terms. Language after all is grounded in culture, and Irigaray broadened the definition of the symbolic to encompass culture directly.

This takes us to the second of Irigaray's contributions which I will discuss here. It was not only the relation to the mother that should be symbolized. It was the female body as such which had to be written in all its specificity. Irigaray first gained attention in English-speaking countries. and notoriety as an ostensible essentialist, for her focus on the "two lips" of the woman's genitalia (Irigaray 1985b). Her appeal to the imagery of the woman's body was read as an essentialist claim about woman's nature: a claim that women thought in plural rather than singular terms because of their genital morphology. In fact, as Margaret Whitford (1991) has shown definitively, Irigaray was actually concerned with the *symbolization* of the female body, with speaking what had no name in patriarchal culture. However, like the other two main French feminists in the psychoanalytic camp, Hélène Cixous and Julia Kristeva, Irigaray was read as writing in ignorance or defiance of the Anglo-American strictures on essentialism. Despite this, Irigaray's work went on to achieve considerable acclaim, especially in the decade 1985–95.

Cixous's work on writing and difference has also had some impact, especially in literature. One thinks immediately of "The laugh of the Medusa" (1979) and of course *The Newly Born Woman* (1986). Julia Kristeva has had a broader impact, in philosophy as well as literature. Like Irigaray, she has been interested in melancholy, amongst other things (*Black Sun*, 1989). But she was first known for her great work, *Revolution in Poetic Language* (1984), in which she stressed the importance of the pre-Oedipal phase of psychical life in the formation of the feminine. For Kristeva, there is a "before" of language; it consists of the biorhythmical cooing and babbling that language will later formalize, and repress, at the expense of the music and poetry which seep out the sides of subject–predicate structures. In this seepage lies one source of opposition to the rigidity of patriarchy, and the linguistic law of the father.

As with Irigaray's, Kristeva's *oeuvre* is much richer than I have indicated here. As with Irigaray, she was initially influenced by, but subsequently distanced herself from, Lacan. To my mind the similarity ends there. Kristeva is an original thinker whose explanatory yield is only beginning to make itself felt, while Irigaray's has been relatively mined. Kristeva has a coherence which is often absent in Irigaray, and she also has the humility of a mind given to ongoing inquiry. Indeed it is her curiosity about felt experience, on issues ranging from motherhood to the powers of horror (*Powers of Horror*, 1982), and to the varieties of love, that lends her deployment of theory its compelling effect. In this, she differs from some of the English-speaking theorists, also influenced by Lacan as well as Freud, who have led the debate on psychoanalysis for feminism since 1985. That debate has concentrated increasingly on questions of theoretical exactitude concerning the works of Freud and Lacan.

Politics now

I think it fair to say that whatever their theoretical merits, the applications of Freudian and Lacanian theory in English-speaking countries have not had the same widespread intuitive appeal of the earlier branches of psychoanalytic feminism, especially Mitchell's and Chodorow's. However, the more subtle theoretical explications of Lacanian theory especially have produced a very rich body of theory bearing on English and comparative literature. As my focus in these brief notes is primarily social and philosophical, I will not attempt to explore that literature here. The point rather is that psychoanalysis-for-feminism now flourishes best in literary theory, and this reflects the distance that currently exists between the initial concerns that prompted the psychoanalytic turn and the theoretical state of the art. By this, I do not wish to imply that literary theorists have taken psychoanalysis-for-feminism away from practice, any more than philosophers or social theorists (practice is the issue for Alice Jardine in "Notes for an Analysis" (1989) amongst other literary theorists). The question rather is whether the theoretical elaborations of more recent psychoanalytic feminism can bring forth more touchstones in analyzing how we change women and men. Queer theory has shown that this can be done. But the experience of heterosexuality remains underanalyzed *in this respect*, which leaves us with the conclusion that it is an experience that is peculiarly resistant to change, or adroit at avoiding prolonged interrogation. After twenty years of psychoanalysis for feminism, it may be time to turn elsewhere.

279

28

Human nature

NANCY HOLMSTROM

Are women human? A puzzling, even bizarre, question, yet one raised by many philosophical theories regarding human nature and women. Human beings are a species, and species are defined, albeit in a very complicated way, by their biological attributes. Women, of all groups that have ever been oppressed, are most clearly and undeniably differentiated by their bodies. Since men have always been taken as the norm, the question was posed as to the implications of *women's differences* from this norm. Although few philosophers seriously questioned whether women were a distinct species from men, many explicitly denied that women had the properties they defined as human, or else they designated traits historically more true of men as characteristically human. Aristotle referred to the female character as "a sort of natural deficiency."

I will not review this sorry history except to note that philosophical theories of human nature are always a mix of the descriptive and the normative. As Alison Jaggar (1983) explains, "the core of any theory of human nature must be a conception of human abilities, needs, wants and purposes; but there is no value-free method for identifying these" (p. 20). And they have always been put to political purposes – either to defend existing societies, as best suited to human nature, or to criticize them, for failing to fit, and as a basis for alternative positive visions. Such theories always have some presuppositions about the nature of women and men as well (just who is presumed to fall within the scope of "human nature?"), which are also both explanatory and normative.

The traditional sexist question – do *women* have a distinct nature? – can, however, be put in unbiased terms: does human nature take sex-differentiated forms? In one sense, it clearly does. There are many variations among humans, from trivial to profoundly important, and sex is obviously one of them. Leaving aside the question of where on this spectrum sex would lie, it is important to see that sex-differentiated natures cannot be identified with the defining biological differences between the sexes. For then it would be tautological to claim that men and women have distinct natures, and this claim was never supposed to be a trivial truth. On the contrary, it was supposed to be an especially deep, profound truth. Whether the basis was metaphysical, religious or scientific, whether it was alleged to be universally or statistically true, the claim was that women had distinct intellectual, emotional, and moral capacities which lead to distinct behavioral tendencies and both did *and should* lead to distinct social roles with attendant duties and virtues. And this was believed to be impossible or difficult to

280

change. Given the explanatory and normative role that these allegedly sex-differentiated cognitive, emotional, moral capacities and tendencies play, it is they that should be understood as the alleged distinctive nature of the biologically defined groups, women and men. *By themselves* the biological attributes could not play the explanatory role natures are supposed to play, much less the justificatory one. The debate over "women's nature," then, is, first of all, over the existence of such psychological traits, and second, if they exist, their source and mutability. In contemporary language, such traits are part of the meaning of "gender," the other aspects of gender being the norms and the social structures they both reflect and reinforce. So let us call the claim that there are such natures "gender essentialism."

While all feminists deny that differences in nature between women and men justify sexual hierarchy, their reasons vary. Some avoid the question of natures, arguing that how we should organize society, including whether there should be sex roles, is fundamentally a moral question, and whether men and women differ "in nature" is irrelevant or secondary; male domination is unjust, regardless (Midgley 1988). Most, however, are committed to some position on the "natures" question. While some accept differences in nature and others are agnostic on the question, probably most reject the idea that women have a distinct nature; in fact the idea of a common human nature has often served as a key premise in arguments for equality. After looking at some influential historical antecedents we will examine contemporary debates related to human nature and women. What we will see is how many positions oppose the idea of human nature, though for different, even contradictory, reasons. We will also see a revival of a feminist humanism.

Feminist foremothers and fathers

Plato is an ambiguous father-figure. In *The Republic*, Plato argued that everyone should do the work for which nature had fitted them. He granted that in one sense, of course, women and men differ "in nature" but argued that there are *all kinds of differences* "in nature," but the question was their *relevance*: "natural gifts are to be found here and there ... one woman will be fitted by nature to be a Guardian, another will not ... . So for the purpose of keeping watch over the Commonwealth, woman has the same nature as man" (p. 449). Plato proposed, therefore, that women be included among the Guardians, the ruling class of the elitist utopia he outlined in *The Republic*, and be educated equally with men. Nevertheless, Plato believed that fewer women than men had these natural gifts and "woman is for all purposes the weaker."

An unambiguous foremother was Mary Wollstonecraft who, inspired by the French Revolution, wrote "A Vindication of the Rights of Woman" (1790), undoubtedly influencing John Stuart Mill's better-known classic of liberal feminism, *The Subjection of Women* (1869). Their arguments regarding women and human nature are very similar, including the ambiguities. Physical qualities, sex-differentiated or not, are not important to them, morally, but rather what

281

distinguishes human beings from other animals – "the simple power ... of discerning truth ..." (Wollstonecraft 1975, p. 303). Thus reason is the essential quality of human nature, all others accidental, a normative dualist conception typical of liberal feminism (Jaggar 1983).

However, both Wollstonecraft and Mill are somewhat ambiguous as to whether, beyond this common rational foundation, human nature is sex-differentiated. Both frankly acknowledge that women and men display different attributes; describing women as "almost sunk below the standard of rational creatures" (Wollstonecraft 1975, p. 287). But was this the result of nature or society? Despite occasional comments suggesting a natural complementarity, most of both Wollstonecraft's *Vindication* and Mill's *Subjection* are devoted to refuting the idea that male domination is natural, their arguments applying to the claim that *nonhierarchical* sex roles are natural as well. Acute observers of their societies, they detail the vastly different ways in which girls and boys are raised, the "hothouse" manner in which certain capacities are cultivated, others left to wither. Mill contends that what is called the nature of women is "an eminently artificial thing." Are men and women essentially the same, then? Though Mill and Wollstonecraft often seem to take an agnostic position, which is sufficient to argue for equal opportunity, they often take a stronger position. Wollstonecraft's deepest conviction seems to be that sexual differences are the result of the greater freedom boys have. "A wild wish has just flown from my heart to my head ... I do earnestly wish to see the distinction of sex confounded in society" (Wollstonecraft 1975, p. 397). Wollstonecraft's wild wish can be defended, I believe, not with certainty, but with reasonable probability. Her acute observations of the different social environments surrounding the two sexes, strengthened by later social scientific research, are quite adequate to explain any significant psychological differences that might exist between the sexes. While there could conceivably be biological factors pushing in the same direction, this is a hypothesis that fills no explanatory need. Thus, in my opinion, the principle of methodological simplicity bids us reject it. Some of Mill's and Wollstonecraft's statements suggest this methodological stance. For example, Mill says, "however great and ineradicable the moral and intellectual differences between men and women might be ... . Those only could be inferred to be natural which could not possibly be artificial – the residuum, after deducting every characteristic of either sex which can admit of being explained from education or external circumstances" (1983, p. 24). Wollstonecraft answers those who claim that women have inherently inferior reasoning capacities by saying "Let men prove this" (1975, p. 305).

On the liberal view, then, all normal human beings share the essential capacity to reason and the desire to be free, if these have not been extinguished by repression. For Wollstonecraft, these facts are the basis of natural rights which are inconsistent with rigid sex roles. For Mill, sexual restrictions are wrong on Utilitarian grounds because "After ... food and raiment, freedom is the first and strongest want of human nature" (1983, p. 95).

Marxists, particularly Friedrich Engels (1972), deepened the critique of essentialist justifications of hierarchical sexual relations. Rejecting normative dualism, they say that these start with real material beings, who, in all modes of production, must eat and have shelter and must labor to satisfy these needs. Humans are also the only animals who engage in free, conscious activity and can satisfy animal needs in distinctly human ways. Thus the idea of transhistorical needs and capacities – human nature – is important for Marxists. However, this human nature is always exemplified in specific social historic forms. By interacting with the world through labor, Marx says in *Capital* (1967) that man changes his own nature. Engels calls absurd the idea that women have always been slaves to men, contending instead, that male domination came into existence at a certain stage in the history of property forms ("the world-historic defeat of the female sex") and would go out of existence with socialism. Though Marx and Engels do not seem to have applied their insight regarding the interpenetration of the biological and social to the reproductive roles of the sexes, treating these simply as "natural" without qualification, they did not believe these biological facts would, or should, lead to invariable gender roles. The family, they stressed, is not only a biological, but a social relationship, hence historically variable. The first premise for women's emancipation was that women be integrated into the public workforce and that domestic labor be socialized. In socialism, when labor is under conscious collective control, both sexes would engage in free, conscious activity, and there is no suggestion that this labor would take sex-differentiated forms. Thus women and men are understood as sharing the same fundamental human nature, although I have argued (Holmstrom 1994) that Marxist theory allows for the possibility that particular social-historical forms of human nature are differentiated by sex. Whether Marxism has been appropriated, rejected, or transformed, it has greatly influenced feminism.

Simone de Beauvoir's groundbreaking *The Second Sex* [1952] (1973) opens with one of the most famous statements in feminist literature, "One is not born, but rather becomes, a woman" (p. 301). However, Beauvoir saw women's reproductive function as an obstacle to their realizing the radical freedom existentialists believe humans have to determine their own essence. Relying on Hegel's master-slave narrative, she contended that men were able to define women as the Other because men were often required to put their lives into danger, which raised them above the animal. To the idea that giving birth is the most fundamentally creative act, Beauvoir replied that giving birth and suckling are not *activities* at all, but "natural functions; no project is involved" (p. 71). Raising a child *could* be a valid project, but only if it were freely chosen, next to impossible in a maledominated world. Women's increasing freedom consisted primarily, she maintained, in the fact that women were increasingly able to escape the "slavery" assigned to them by their reproductive role. Though existentialists say they reject human nature, what they reject is static predetermined conceptions, holding instead a normative and dualist view of human nature whose most important aspect is radical freedom. In order both to gain equality

283

and to realize their human potential, women must transcend their distinctive femaleness to lead the kind of life men do.

Contemporary discussions: essentialisms and anti-essentialisms

Within the enormous and ever-evolving variety of opinion among second-wave feminists (from the 1960s onward), several strands challenged notions of human nature.

Many critics pointed out how biased most conceptions were. Both Wollstone-craft's and Mill's liberal conception and Beauvoir's existentialist one extolled activities associated with men and devalued activities associated with women and bodies. The negative portrayal of childbirth and motherhood typified by Beauvoir and carried to more radical conclusions by radical feminist Shulamith Firestone (1970) elicited a particularly strong reaction. Some critiqued it as reflecting a dualist bias against the body common throughout the history of Western thought; others saw a more specific distaste for *women's* bodies (Jaggar 1983, Spelman 1988). These critics challenged the content of the concept of human nature as well as its scope of application. Iris Marion Young (1985) characterized these critiques as a distinct perspective, "gynocentric feminism," as opposed to the earlier humanist feminism. In contrast to earlier feminists, many in this period emphasized biological differences between the sexes. Poet Adrienne Rich (1976) argued that what women needed was not liberation *from mother-hood*, but liberation *from male domination of motherhood*. For Rich, rather than women's bodies being an obstacle to realizing their most human potentialities, on the contrary, women's reproductive functions make them *better* able than men to realize a uniquely human potential of rationality and physicality, referring to women's bodies as "the corporeal ground of our intelligence" (p. 31).

Some gynocentric writers went beyond critiquing male bias in ideas of a common human nature and put forward theories of essential differences between women's and men's cognitive and emotional attributes sufficiently important to be called sex-differentiated natures. Gender on this view is essential. Particularly influential were Mary Daly (1978) and Susan Griffin (1981), radical feminists whose views had evolved into a distinct perspective called cultural feminism. To Daly and Griffin, women's bodies and sexuality made them closer to nature, and therefore more intuitive and creative. A familiar theme in anti-feminist thinking, what defines these thinkers as feminist is their reversal of the usual (male) evaluation of these (alleged) male–female differences. Women's bodies are cel-ebrated rather than deprecated, and seen as the source of superiority, intellectual and moral, rather than inferiority. In order to become whole persons women must free themselves not of their femaleness, but of the artificial femininity imposed by men and must each get in touch with her wild natural self. It is not clear why Daly supposes there is this true self beneath women's socialized one, why she does not allow the same possibility for men, and why the "true self" must be a distinctively female one. More generally, one can ask how gender essentialists think their theories can avoid biological determinism, or if not, why biological determinism is any more defensible when they propound it than when conservatives do. While gender essentialists offer a thoroughgoing critique of a male-dominated world, they have no basis for opposing "separate-but-equal" sex roles, a less radical position than Wollstonecraft's "wild wish" to deny any social importance to the sex distinction.

Most contemporary feminists have opposed the idea of sex-differentiated natures and the biological determinism on which it rests. While the empirical heart of the critique has come from scientists like Ruth Bleier, Ruth Hubbard, and Anne Fausto-Sterling, who have subjected the allegedly scientific claims to detailed critique, both on specific and methodological grounds, philosophers have also made contributions to these debates. Alison Jaggar (1983) has shown the extent to which political theories rest on theories of human nature, and, in turn, how much theories of human nature (and women's nature) are influenced by political and other normative theories. Radical scientists have shown this is true of scientific theories as well. Jaggar and others, including myself (Holmstrom 1982, 1984), have argued against identification of the natural with the biological and a too simple contrast of the biological and the social. In fact the two interpenetrate. While human biological needs and capacities certainly have influenced the societies humans have constructed, so also have social conditions influenced human biology, for example, our size, shape, and even our reproductive capacities. Thus sex is not a pure biological substratum beneath a socially constructed gender, as is sometimes assumed.

Gender essentialism was not the only tendency in this period to make talk of human nature suspect. At the other end are extreme social constructionists who extend the anti-essentialist arguments to sex as well as gender (Dworkin 1974, Wittig 1981, 1992, Butler 1990). Recognizing that there is no pure biological sex uncontaminated by society these thinkers go further, contending that "Gender created anatomical sex" (Wittig 1992). Since human nature is understood as partly a biological concept, this entails its rejection. Dworkin, ironically, rests her case for androgyny at the social level only because she believes in it at a biological level. Given that the several aspects of sex identity do not always fit together, but nevertheless everyone is neatly divided into two and only two sexes, she concurs with Wittig that this shows the basis is political, namely, usefulness for heterosexism. More recently, influenced by Foucault and deconstructionists, Judith Butler (1990) has argued that there is no body prior to its construction by phallocentric significations.

Extreme social constructionism is problematic since nothing is "a given fact of nature" in the sense presupposed. Social elements enter into decision making in all sciences and classifications are not so neat in natural science either. Classifications, in natural as well as social science, are not on the basis of similarity and difference of properties alone, but how important the common properties are. Why else would German Shepherds belong to the same species as Chihuahuas, and not wolves? The actual distribution of properties among organisms is such that, contrary to the Aristotelian view, most taxa names can only be defined

285

disjunctively. Any of the disjuncts is sufficient and the few properties that are necessary are far from sufficient, making most concepts of so-called natural kinds what are called "cluster concepts." Thus whether women (and men) have distinct natures depends first, on their properties and second, on the importance of these properties. But "importance" can only be evaluated within a specific theoretical context (Holmstrom 1982). Given that the sex difference is what allows for reproduction of humans and most other kinds of things, and that the difference between creatures that produce sexually and those that produce asexually has great importance for biological theory, the division into two sexes also has great importance for biological theory. Why then should it not be considered a natural or biological division, taking these terms to mean something like "the object of biological theory"? (Their argument does apply, however, to the roughly 4 percent of humans who do not fit neatly into one or the other sex; Fausto-Sterling 1992.) Extreme social constructionism is also deficient politically. The political importance of the revelation that supposedly natural categories like race and gender are actually social in origin is greatly reduced if *everything* turns out to be social. Moreover, how does one support the demand for reproductive rights as especially critical for women, except in virtue of their distinctive bodies?

Another factor leading away from discussions of human nature was an increased attention to differences among women. Just as gender essentialists rejected the idea of a common human nature as being overly abstract and biased, theories regarding "women" were criticized for ignoring important differences among women, and being implicitly biased toward the speaker/writer, who was usually white and middle-class (Zinn 1986, Collins 1990, Spelman 1988). Marxists had long made this point with respect to class, and lesbians had objected to heterosexual presumptions, but it was primarily women of color who pushed this issue to the foreground, particularly in the United States. While logically speaking there is no inconsistency between the concept of human nature and a recognition of the importance of all its many variations, the emphasis on "difference" meant a turn away from such a universal concept. It was held to be impossible, in practice, to achieve a bias-free perspective. Moreover, certain theoretical tendencies became influential that held this to be impossible even in principle, for example, postmodernism that precluded "totalizing" theories like liberalism or Marxism. The stress was on "particularity" and "location." The popularity in this period of relativism, of all kinds, also precluded such theorizing.

Recently, however, a number of voices have been heard defending the validity and importance of general concepts like sex, gender, and human nature. One could even speak of a new feminist humanism. In response to criticisms of universalistic projects like her theory of "humanist justice" (1989a), Susan Moller Okin (1995) has argued forcefully for the political importance of the category gender, by which she means that "it is possible to generalize about many aspects of inequality between the sexes. From place to place, from class to class, from race to race, and from culture to culture, we find similarities in the specifics of these inequalities, in their causes and effects, although not in their extent or their severity" (1995, p. 294). Calling this a "qualified defence of essentialism" may be misleading, however, since Jane Flax (1995) has criticized her for assuming that gender and race are separable and that gender is internally undifferentiated and conflict-free. Neither of these assumptions is necessary to Okin's conclusion. General terms, even species names (as we saw), can be usefully employed even if there are only family resemblances among their instantiations. Attention to differences and generalizing about commonalities should not be counterposed.

On the international level recently, activists and attorneys have had some success arguing that violations of women's rights are violations of human rights (Peters and Wolper 1995). *The Human Rights Watch Global Report on Women's Human Rights* (1995) documents some abuses unique to women because of their bodies, e.g. forced pregnancy and virginity examination, and others that primarily affect women, e.g. rape and sexual servitude. Many kinds of violence against women that have been ignored because they are allegedly "private" (domestic violence) or "cultural practices" (female genital mutilation) are argued to be violations of the human right not to be tortured. Other less sex-specific abuses like denial of the right to employment also serve to maintain women's subordination. Without the ideas of sexual difference on the one hand, and of a human nature common to women and men on the other, it is not clear how such arguments could be made. For reasons like this, some philosophers have defended the explanatory and political importance for feminism of the concept of human nature (Assiter 1996, Holmstrom 1994, Midgley 1980, Nussbaum 1995).

Alison Assiter is an interesting voice in this debate whose positions accord with much of what I have argued above. Challenging postmodernism, she defends realism, human nature, and a sex/gender distinction, but in ways that reflect criticisms of these concepts by postmodernists and others. For example, defending the concept of a "minimally necessary set of biological features ... which enables us to identify the person as female" (p. 25), she stresses that the properties need not be present in the same quantities in all women, nor need they be fixed exclusively by nature. Nevertheless these bodily features are important to women's lives (humans are, after all, embodied beings) and therefore important politically. However, Assiter's identification of this as a female nature is problematic. "Women's nature" has never been *identified* simply with their distinctive biology, because then it would be tautological. The concept is supposed to support generalizations about ways in which women think, feel, and act that men do not that are relevant to gender roles. Assiter does not advance proof that this is the case. The only relevant evidence she offers is that anatomy is important in determining gender *identity*, which she allows is only one aspect of our identity – and this is not the same thing.

In a series of papers over the past decade, Martha Nussbaum has developed in an explicitly Aristotelian direction the capabilities approach to evaluating quality of life associated with economist and philosopher Amartya Sen (1985). Calling her position a defense of essentialism of a very particular kind, she argues that a conception of the human being and human functioning is the best basis for evaluating women's position around the world. Though Aristotle himself did not believe women shared this human nature, Nussbaum calls this a problem of scope of application, rather than the concept itself, claiming that the Aristotelian ideal is sufficiently "thick" and "vague" to accommodate historical and cultural variations in its exemplification. Starting from the intuitive idea that "human capabilities exert a moral claim that they should be developed" (1995, p. 88), she proposes two thresholds of capabilities: the first, below which a life would not count as human at all, and a higher threshold beneath which it would not count as a good human life. The capabilities in the latter conception (which is strikingly similar to Marx's ideal of fully human flourishing) are all individually necessary, and include such items as: (1) "Being able to have good health ... adequate nourish(ment) ... shelter, ... opportunities for sexual satisfaction and choice in matters of reproduction" and (2) "Being able to use the senses; being able to imagine, to think and to reason – and to do these things in a way informed and cultivated by an adequate education" (pp. 83–4). Arguing that there is no basis for the position that women and men should have different norms of human functioning or that they should exercise the same norms in different spheres, Nussbaum recommends specific policies and legal rights to secure equal capabilities for women. Her approach has both influenced and been influenced by debates about development policy through conferences sponsored by the World Institute for Development Economics Research (WIDER) of the United Nations University. Whether or not Nussbaum is right that her approach is the best basis for an ethics of development, I believe that any adequate feminist theory and practice will presuppose something like this conception of human nature common to women and men.

However, it does not follow that this human nature is always more important than its many variations, particularly when they are hierarchically related. Which aspect is most salient – causally or morally – depends on the context and will remain an issue of theoretical and practical contestation. There was never just one humanist tradition any more than there is just one variety of feminism. Hopefully, the new feminist humanism combines the respect for differences characteristic of progressive movements since the 1960s with the universalistic aspirations of earlier liberatory traditions.

29

Gender

LINDA NICHOLSON

The term "gender" has played a key role in feminist theory and politics since the late 1960s. Debates over its meaning reflect major turning points within the women's movement of the past thirty years.

Prior to the late 1960s, English language-speakers used the word "gender" to refer to the understanding of certain words as masculine or feminine. For example, the word "ship" has often been thought of as feminine. During the 1960s, English-speaking feminists extended the meaning of "gender" so that it came to describe the understanding of not only words but also types of behavior as female or male. Feminists wanted to make the point that the association of specific types of behavior with females or males was as much a social convention as was the association of specific words. Prior to this time, the dominant understanding was that such phenomena were "naturally" linked with males or females. It was thought that the biological distinction between women and men, often referred to as the difference between "the sexes," caused women to behave one way and men the other. Feminists wished to emphasize that such differences in behavior were not a consequence of biology but of social convention. By including these under the category of "gender" rather than "sex," they hoped people would come to see such differences as socially rather than biologically caused.

Within feminist discourse, a distinction soon developed between "sex" and "gender." It became widely accepted that while "sex" referred to those differences between women and men that were biologically given, that is, grounded in the differences in women's and men's bodies, "gender" referred to the differences between women and men that were a product of society. In short, feminists came to view differences between women and men as having two dimensions: (1) the biological and (2) the social, with "sex" referring to the former, and "gender" to the latter. Because biological phenomena are often viewed as immutable, feminists frequently thought of the biological aspects of male/female differences as those that were unchanging across history and culture. Differences of "gender," however, or in how societies elaborated these biological differences in terms of expectations regarding behavior, were thought of as variable across cultures. In other words, for many feminists, some differences between women and men – most notably their bodies – were unchanging, while other differences – such as expectations regarding their respective behaviors – were variable. Feminists regarded this way of viewing the differences between women and men as representing an important advance over older perspectives, which understood the social conventions regarding male and female behavior as "natural" and thus impervious to change.

The questioning of sex versus gender

In the early 1980s, some feminists began to find problems with this framework. For one, they began to ask whether even the biological differences between women and men were as unchangeable as many thought. Contrary to the received feminist wisdom that unchanging bodily differences underpinned changing social differences, Alison Jaggar pointed out that changing social practices have led to changes in the body. Thus, she noted that women are becoming physically stronger as strength in women has become more socially acceptable. Moreover, changing social practices can affect not only women's external physical structure but also their internal biology, and include changes in their genetic endowments. Thus, a cultural preference for smaller women in certain societies may have resulted in the greater selection of such women for reproductive purposes. Jaggar claimed that the interactive causal relation between biology and social practice made theoretically problematic the idea of a sharp line between nature and culture (Jaggar 1983, pp. 106–13).

Moreover, some feminist theorists began to question the distinction between "sex" and "gender" for other reasons. One problem with the distinction as formulated by feminists in the 1960s was that it assumed that the biological distinction between women and men, or "sex," was a given, unaffected not only by social practice but also by social interpretation. But many feminists were coming to recognize that all distinctions, even those dubbed "biological" or "natural," were formulated from within a particular theoretical perspective. This meant that even the biological distinction between women and men was socially constructed, and thus as potentially variable as the social conventions which were thought of by feminists as part of "gender." Joan Scott expressed this point in the following way: "It follows then that gender is the social organization of sexual difference. But this does not mean that gender reflects or implements fixed and natural physical differences between women and men; rather gender is the knowledge that establishes meanings for bodily differences" (Scott 1988, p. 2).

This realization that even the biological differences between women and men are socially constructed from within a given theoretical framework was receiving further support from work being done by historians. Both Linda Schiebinger and Thomas Laqueur argued that the contemporary Western construction of the biological differences between women and men as polar opposites emerged only around the eighteenth century (Schiebinger 1987, Laqueur 1987, 1990). Prior to this time, the hegemonic perspective within Europe was to view women as less developed versions of men along a continuum. This meant, for example, that men's sexual organs were not seen as completely different from women's, but rather as more developed versions of them. Pictures of women's and men's sexual organs in medical texts of the time tended to emphasize the similarities between these organs, rather than their differences as became the case later on. But, around the middle of the eighteenth century, this older view began to give rise to a newer perspective which placed great emphasis on the differences. The result was not only the inclination to view the sexual organs of women and men as completely different but also the inclination to emphasize the differences in all aspects of women's and men's bodies, including their respective skeletons and nervous systems.

In sum, by the late 1980s and early 1990s, a growing body of literature was beginning to challenge the idea that the old distinction between "sex" and "gender" was useful. Many came to believe that this distinction obscured the crucial point that "sex" itself was a social construction and thus was a part of and not separate from "gender." Moreover, as some were coming to see, the failure to see "sex" as a social construction had important political consequences. For example, I argued that the feminist tendency to separate "sex" and "gender" and to view the former as the unchanging constant upon which variable social constructions of the latter are built – a position I labelled "biological foundation-alism" – encouraged feminist tendencies to minimize differences among women (Nicholson 1994). I claimed that the idea that the body provided certain constants in women's experiences led to theories depicting women's situation as fundamentally similar across history and culture. Inevitably, however, such theories tended to assume the meanings given to the body and the types of experiences associated with those meanings which were most familiar to those creating the theories. For example, some feminists have taken women's smaller size relative to men, a physical difference highly emphasized in postindustrial societies, to possess the same meaning and importance in all societies. In sum, the tendency to view "sex" as separate from "gender" contributed to feminist tendencies to homogenize the experiences and situations of women.

The essentialist debate

Within feminist discussions, the issue of the relationship between "sex" and "gender" soon came to be superseded by the question whether the concept of "woman" possessed any "essential" meaning, that is, any meaning common to all understandings of the term. Certainly the idea that "sex" is naturally given – and consequently distinguishable from the social constructions that constitute "gender" – strongly contributed to the idea that there exist some commonalities in the meaning of "woman" across cultures. However, the idea of a unitary or "essential" meaning of woman could survive even in the face of the breakdown of the distinction between "sex" and "gender." It might be argued, for example, that while the body is always viewed from within a particular theoretical framework, and thus is a part of and not separate from "gender," across all or most of human history one interpretation of the body has contributed to some commonality in what it means to be a "man" or "woman." Consequently, what became central to feminist debate was less the question of the relationship between "sex" and "gender" and more the question: does "gender" – or the social construction of what it means to be a "woman" or "man" – possess any unitary or "essential" elements across cultures? Certainly, by the late 1980s, most feminists had come to acknowledge that differences among women were much more extensive than had been recognized in the past. However, many still wished to claim that despite important differences there were also some common features in women's experiences which gave unity to the concept of "woman" and made possible the united political struggle that was feminism. However, others argued that the idea of "woman" possessing an "essential" meaning led to political outcomes antithetical to feminism. In short, was "gender," or the social construction of what it meant to be a "woman" or "man," to be understood as containing both homogeneous and heterogeneous elements or as being heterogeneous through and through?

Arguing for the latter perspective, Elizabeth Spelman elaborated some of the ways in which essentialist understandings of "woman" have been present in second-wave feminist theory (Spelman 1988). Spelman noted that such understandings have often been associated with the idea that feminists can isolate the "woman" part of who we are from other parts, such as those which describe our racial, ethnic, class, etc., identities. This has resulted in tendencies to think about identity in additive ways, or as Spelman describes it, in terms of a type of pop-bead or "tootsie roll" metaphysics. In accord with such a metaphysics, who we are is a composite result of our gender, race, ethnic, class, etc., identity, with each element being separately describable. From within this perspective, while African-American women are recognized as possessing a different racialized identity from European-American women, this different racialized identity is perceived as something external and additional to the common gender identity which women from both groups are assumed to share.

Spelman points to the many problems with this type of perspective. Most seriously, the so-called "common" woman part of identity tends to be described in terms of the characteristics of dominant groups. The racial, ethnic, class, etc., identities of these groups tend not to be seen as distinctive, that is, white women often do not see themselves as possessing a distinctive racial identity. Consequently, members of dominant racial, ethnic, class, etc., groups often fail to see how their own gender identities are affected by their racial, ethnic, class, etc., identities. As a result, they tend to see their own gender identities as "universal" and gender identity in general as separable from other aspects of self-identity. Moreover, in seeing the racial, ethnic, class, etc., identities of people as separable from their gender identities, members of dominant groups tend also to see the racial, ethnic, class, etc., identities of others only in negative terms. Thus, from within the perspective of a "pop-bead" view of identity, African-American women are perceived by European-American women as being "just like us" except for the fact of also suffering from racial oppression. This perspective overlooks those positive aspects of being a woman which are distinctively African-American.

Other feminist theorists have argued against essentialist understandings of "woman" for different reasons. Chandra Talpade Mohanty has claimed that

292

such understandings, being based upon imputed commonalities in experience, tend to rest upon a conception of experience as given and individual, that is, as personal rather than social. Since experience is abstracted out of its social context, differences among women, which include differences in power, are ignored.

> The *experience* of struggle is thus defined as both personal and ahistorical. In other words, the political is *limited* to the personal and all conflicts among and within women are flattened. If sisterhood itself is defined on the basis of personal intentions, attitudes or desires, conflict is also automatically constructed on only the psychological level. Experience is thus written in as simultaneously individual (that is, located in the individual body/psyche of wom*a*n) and general (located in wom*e*n as a preconstituted collective).   (Mohanty 1992, p. 82)

Thus, a purely psychological understanding of experience leads to a view of women's collective experience as merely the composite and shared result of what each woman experiences at the individual level. This understanding eliminates from analysis those experiences women have as members of particular social groups, experiences which differentiate women from each other. Such differences include those of power, necessitating, as Mohanty argues, that the politics of feminism become that of internal as well as external struggle.

Judith Butler's work on "gender" also entails a critique of "woman" as possessing any "essential" or unitary meaning (Butler 1990). As Butler has argued, the idea of woman as unitary is a fiction in the service of the very oppressive regime that feminism seeks to overthrow. The belief that "woman" does have some common meaning serves to coerce individuals into behavior aimed to exhibit such meaning. In other words, the idea of "woman" as unitary operates as a policing force which generates and legitimizes certain practices, experiences, etc., and curtails and delegitimizes others. Moreover, the idea of "woman" as unitary and situated in opposition to "man" works to sustain the status quo by supporting the norm of heterosexuality. The idea of "woman" and "man" as possessing a unitary meaning in opposition to each other supports the idea of sexual desire as "the attraction of opposites." The feminist project which assumes such a unitary meaning therefore ends up reproducing both the very sexist and heterosexist social order it aims to eliminate.

Other feminists, however, have taken very different types of positions in the essentialist debates. Some have raised concerns that the "anti-essentialist" position has led to a "chilly climate" in feminist scholarship for anyone attempting generalizing moves. Jane Martin has claimed that the epithet "essentialist" has functioned as a type of scare word, warning off feminist scholars from searching for any commonalities among women that may in fact exist. It has worked to privilege differences in advance of investigation (J. Martin 1994b). Susan Bordo makes a similar argument when she claims that the effect of feminist arguments against essentialism is "to delegitimate *a priori* the exploration of experiential continuity and structural common ground among women" (Bordo 1990, p. 142).

Moreover, as both Martin and Bordo argue, the problem is not only that the warnings against essentialism have created a climate where commonality among women is excluded from consideration *a priori*. In addition, the very recommendations scholars have made about avoiding generalizations are inconsistent. As both of these theorists point out, all theorizing is generalizing. To avoid generalizations altogether is to limit scholarship to descriptions of particular events at particular points in time. Because it is impossible to carry out such recommendations and still do theory, Bordo and Martin claim that the recommendations against generalizing tend, in fact, to be inconsistently applied. While many feminists have been arguing against generalizations based upon gender, few have been arguing against generalizations based upon other categories, such as those of race or class (Bordo 1990, pp. 145–6). But consistency here would mean condemning talk about "black women" as much as it would mean condemning talk about "women" as such.

> Just as the category of women masks everything that the category black women does and more, the category black women masks everything black Caribbean women does and more. The same is true of the category black Caribbean women in relation to black Jamaican women, of the category black Jamaican women vis-à-vis twentieth-century black Jamaican women, and so on. (J. Martin 1994b, p. 637)

Finally, as many feminist theorists have argued, anti-essentialist arguments have conservative political implications. Such arguments leave feminism without a political subject. How is it possible for feminism to exist as a political movement without making claims about the needs or situation of women, claims which involve generalizations about "women"? Anti-essentialist arguments appear to ally feminism with liberal assumptions that "we are all just individuals." Feminism emerged as a challenge to the idea that many of the problems individual women faced could be explained by reference to idiosyncratic features of their lives. Rather, feminism claimed that such problems were rooted in the situation of women *as women*. Because of the importance of generalizations to feminist politics, some theorists, such as Nancy Hartsock, have linked the emergence of anti-essentialist arguments with a backlash against feminism.

> Somehow it seems highly suspicious that it is at the precise moment when so many groups have been engaged in "nationalisms" which involve redefinitions of the marginalized Others that suspicions emerge about the nature of the "subject," about the possibilities for a general theory which can describe the world, about historical "progress." (Hartsock 1990, p. 163)

Resolving the debate

The debate between "essentialism" and "anti-essentialism" seems one in which neither side can be completely right. On the one hand, talk about woman's "nature" or "essence" has worked to minimize understandings of differences among women. It has also provided the means where women from privileged groups have falsely generalized their own situations and problems. On the other hand, feminism relies on generalizations in both its theory and its politics. How can feminists both sufficiently emphasize differences among women while also creating effective theory and politics?

One possible resolution to this dilemma is to adopt what has been called "strategic essentialism." The idea here, often associated with a suggestion first made by Gayatri Spivak, is that feminists explicitly recognize claims about women as political interventions (Grosz 1984/5, pp. 175–87). In other words, claims about "women's situation" would be viewed as generalizations geared to the attainment of specific outcomes rather than as apolitical depictions of reality. A related suggestion made by Diana Fuss is that "woman" should not be understood as indicating "a natural class" but as the construction of a coalition politics (Fuss 1989, p. 36).

This attempted resolution has generated some critical reactions. In a later interview, Spivak herself stated that she wished to reconsider her original suggestion. As she argued, the use of the phrase "strategic essentialism" within a particular academic culture "gives a certain alibi to essentialism" (Spivak and Rooney 1989, p. 128). Iris Marion Young has articulated two arguments against the kind of proposal suggested by Fuss. For one, it fails to avoid one of the problems of essentialism raised by Judith Butler. All generalizing claims about women, even those understood as the outcome of politics and not of nature, are normalizing. Young also claims that this type of proposal seems to make the generation of feminist politics arbitrary.

> Some women choose to come together in a political movement, to form themselves as a group of mutually identifying agents. But on the basis of what do they come together? What are the social conditions that have motivated the politics? Perhaps even more important, do feminist politics leave out women who do not identify as feminists? (Young 1994a, p. 722)

Are there ways in which the insights of both the essentialist and anti-essentialist positions can be maintained? Let me propose a resolution to some of the issues involved.

For one, as Nancy Fraser and I have argued, the issue should not be understood as whether feminists should employ generalizations or not (Fraser and Nicholson 1990). Feminists need to make generalizations. The anti-essentialists are correct in noting that what made feminism a political movement was that it began describing the situation of women in *general* terms. However, what they have stressed less strongly is the problematic nature of many of the generalizations that feminists made from the 1960s through the 1980s. These were generalizations whose boundaries were so vaguely formulated that they functioned either explicitly or de facto as universalizations. For example, while individual scholars might have claimed that the generalizations they were putting forth were only true for women "in patriarchal societies," typically the boundaries of what constituted "patriarchal societies" were left so poorly articulated that such claims were taken as applying to most, if not all, women. Indeed one could claim that it was the vagueness of the boundaries of the claims made rather than their status as generalizations which generated outcries from African-American women, lesbians, working-class women, etc., protesting that such claims did not adequately tell their stories.

Of course, it is always an open question how precisely any generalization needs to be framed. As Martin and Bordo correctly note, claims about "black women" are just as potentially subject to charges of vague boundaries as are claims about "women." But the conclusion of this point is not that charges of vague boundaries must be inconsistent. It is rather that since boundary issues can always arise, whether they do or not is a political – not a logical – issue. Again, it was because many African-American women saw the need to differentiate their situation from that of European-American women that the charges of problematic boundaries were invoked when European-American women began making claims about "women." If class conflicts within the African-American community should surface more than they have to date, one would expect to see poor African-Americans demanding that generalizations about the plight of African-Americans be qualified in relation to class. Again, the argument that African-American women among others were making was not that generalizations per se were being made but rather that the generalizations which were being made did not have the kind of qualifications they thought it politically important to make.

The above argument reinforces a claim made by Judith Butler, that we need to understand the term "woman" as the site of permanent openness and resignifiability (Butler 1995, p. 50). During the 1960s and 1970s, generalizations about "women" were a first crude, though perhaps necessary, way of articulating gender as a social rather than a personal issue. As feminism grew, and the voices of those it claimed to speak for obtained greater representation in public debate, so also did the political call for qualifying its claims become stronger. But who those voices were and how they articulated the need for qualification were dependent upon the ways in which political issues and identities were framed at the time. There is no reason to assume that such issues and identities will remain stable. As new political demands are raised and new social identities are forged, so should we expect new claims made about needed qualifications to the category of "women."

When I say that the meaning and boundaries of "women" are political, I do not mean that claims about the commonalities or differences in women's situations represent mere "strategic" moves in a political game plan. One of the problems with the idea of "strategic essentialism" was that it assumed one could or should distinguish between commonly understood meanings of "women" and those meanings political agents advanced for the sake of specific ends. Rather, my point is that what can or cannot be understood in the name of "women" is political in a deeper sense of the term; how we understand the term and what kinds of claims we believe can be made on its behalf are tied to our diverse situations and needs.

This means that the social distinction between "woman" and "man" becomes a distinction without a necessarily common content. But the lack of a common content does not mean no connection among the diverse meanings of "woman" and "man" which do exist. Instead of thinking that either there must be a common meaning to "woman" across contexts or that there merely exists a disparate assortment of such meanings with no connection, we can instead understand the meaning of the male/female distinction across cultures in another way. We can see it as encompassing a complex web of distinctions evidencing threads of overlap within a field of discontinuities (Fraser and Nicholson 1990, p. 35). It is this kind of understanding of "gender" that I believe we need today to support a viable feminist politics. Having given up on the idea of a common meaning to "woman" or "man," we can begin the task of figuring out where and where not shared understandings exist.

30

Sexual difference theory

ROSI BRAIDOTTI

Sexual difference theory can best be explained with reference to French post-structuralism, more specifically its critique of the humanist vision of subjectivity. The "post" in poststructuralism does not denote only a chronological break from the structuralists' generation of the 1940s and 1950s, but also an epistemological and theoretical revision of the emancipatory programme of structuralism itself, especially of Marxist feminist political theory. The focus of poststructuralism is the complex and manifold structure of power and the diverse, fragmented, but highly effective ways in which power, knowledge, and the constitution of subjectivity combine. Poststructuralism questions the usefulness of the notion of "ideology," especially in the sense developed by Louis Althusser, as the imaginary relation of the Subject to his/her real conditions of existence. In a feminist version, ideology refers to the patriarchal system of representation of gender and, more specifically, to the myths and images that construct femininity. Subjectivity is conceptualized therefore as a process (*assujettissement*) which encompasses simultaneously the material ("reality") and the symbolic ("language") instances which structure it. Psychoanalytic notions of identity, language, and sexuality – especially in the work of Jacques Lacan – play a central role in the redefinition of the subject as a process, rather than in the more traditional sense of a rational agent. The notion of difference emerges as a central concept in the poststructuralists' critique of both classical humanism and of the humanist legacy of Marxist-inspired structuralist social theory. It includes both differences within each subject (between conscious and unconscious processes), as well as differences between the Subject and his/her Others.

The American reception of poststructuralist theories of difference, which Domna Stanton (1980) described in terms of a transatlantic "disconnection," resulted in a series of polemical debates about the interrelation between the material and the symbolic reality and language, which tended to focus on the structure of power and the possibility of resistance to it. As Elizabeth Wright argues (1992), a stalemate debate around "essentialism" opposed French-oriented sexual difference theories to American-based "gender" theories throughout the 1980s. Whereas "gender" theorists understand the construction of masculinity and femininity as more determined by cultural and social processes, sexual difference theorists also understand it as determined by unconscious processes such as identification and internalization. A critical reevaluation of the whole debate was undertaken in the 1990s, under the joint impact of postcolonial theories, the work of black women, women of color and of lesbian and queer theorists, as well as by an increasing diversification of positions within the European philosophies of sexual difference.

In order to avoid the polemic, while attempting to do justice to the complexity of the issues raised by sexual difference, I will concentrate on the work of Luce Irigaray because, as Whitford argued (1991), she is the most prominent figure. I will distinguish between three different aspects of this theory: its analytic or diagnostic effect; its function as a political cartography; and the utopian aspect.

Sexual difference as diagnostic map

Sexual difference theory states the obvious but in so doing also radicalizes it. The main philosopher of sexual difference, Luce Irigaray, following on from Simone de Beauvoir's analysis of the dialectics of the sexes, focuses at first on the difference between masculine and feminine subject positions [1974] (1985a). Irigaray relies on the theoretical toolbox of poststructuralism, however, especially on Lacanian psychoanalysis, linguistics, and literary theory, to bring into focus the dissymetrical power relations that underlie the construction of woman as the Other of the dominant view of subjectivity. This dominant view is defined in terms of phallogocentrism. This term refers simultaneously to the fact that, in the West, thinking and being coincide in such a way as to make consciousness coextensive with subjectivity: this is the logocentric trend. It also refers, however, to the persistent habit that consists in referring to subjectivity as to all other key attributes of the thinking subject in terms of masculinity or abstract virility (phallocentrism). The sum of the two results is the unpronounceable but highly effective phallogocentrism.

This notion involves for Irigaray both the description and the denunciation of the false universalism which is inherent in the phallogocentric posture: one which posits the masculine as a self-regulating rational agency and the feminine "Other" as a site of devaluation. Going beyond the Hegelian scheme, so prevalent in Beauvoir, Irigaray focuses on the perverse logic of this dualism. It assumes that the phallogocentric system functions by constituting sets of pejorative "Others," or negative instances of difference. In such a system, "difference" has historically been colonized by power relations that reduce it to inferiority. Furthermore, it has resulted in passing off such differences as "natural," which then made entire categories of beings into devalued and therefore disposable entities. Power, in this framework, is the name given to a strategic set of close interrelations between multilocated positions: textual, social, economic, symbolic, and other sorts of positions. Power, in other words, is another name for the political and social currency that is attributed to certain notions, concepts, or sets of meanings, in such a way as to invest them with either "truth value" or with scientific legitimacy. To take the example of misogyny and racism: the belief in the inferiority of women and people of color – be it mental, intellectual, spiritual, or moral – has no serious scientific foundation. This does not prevent it from having great currency in political practice and in the organization of society. The corollary of this is that the woman or the person of color as "Other" is "different from" the expected norm: as such s/he is both the empirical referent for and the symbolic sign of pejoration. Because of this specific position, however, the devalued Other functions as a critical shaper of meaning. Devalued or pejorative Otherness organizes differences in a hierarchical scale that allows for the management and the governability of all gradations of social differences. By extension, therefore, the pejorative use of difference is no accident, but rather it is structurally necessary to the phallogocentric system of meaning and the social order that sustains it. It just so happens that the empirical subjects which are the referents for this symbolic pejoration experience in their embodied existence the effects of the disqualification. At this level, sexual difference is a powerful critique of philosophical dualism and of binary habits of thought. In the same vein, it also challenges the categorical binary opposition of the symbolic to the empirical within psychoanalytic theory.

The sexual difference approach, in other words, dislodges the belief in the "natural" foundations of socially coded and enforced differences and of the system of values and representation which they support. Moreover, this approach emphasizes the need to historicize the very notions and concepts it analyzes, first and foremost among them the notion of difference. This emphasis on the historical embeddedness of concepts, however, also means that the thinker needs some humility before the multilayered and complex structure of language.

The implications of this analysis are far-reaching: phallogocentric logic is embedded in language, which is the fundamental political myth in our society. In the poststructuralist framework, language is not to be understood as a tool of communication, following the humanistic tradition. It is rather defined as the site or location where subject positions are constructed. In order to get access to language at all, however, one has to take up a position on either side of the great masculine/feminine divide. The subject is sexed, or s/he is not at all.

Against the tendency of Freudian psychoanalysis to fix psychic structures through biological references, Irigaray and other sexual difference theorists problematize the question of the connection of morphological men and women to culturally coded roles of masculinity and femininity. Morphology replaces biological deterministic readings of the body with a psychosexual version of social constructivism. Morphologies refer to enfleshed, experiential understandings of the bodily self. As Elizabeth Grosz points out (1989), these experiences are mediated through discursive practices (biological, psychological, psychoanalytic discourses) which construct social representations. Embodied subjects are expected to adhere to these representations by internalizing them. Thus, although language is posited as a structure that is prior to and constitutive of subjectivity, the sexed subject positions that structure identity (M/F) are neither stable nor essentialistic. A fundamental instability in the subject's attachment to either masculine or feminine positions is proposed instead as the site of resistance to fixed or stable identities of any kind. The subject is both sexed and split, both resting on one of the poles of the sexual dichotomy and unfastened to it. The "linguistic turn" thus defined therefore provides sexual difference philosophy with a materially grounded historicized and yet ubiquitous structure on which to base its vision of subjectivity.

It is important to stress the political implications of this definition of language: the phallogocentric code being inscribed in language, it is operational no matter who happens to be speaking it. This emphasis on the in-depth structures or syntax of language implies that there is no readily accessible, uncontaminated, or "authentic" voice of otherness, albeit among the oppressed. This turns into an attack on the essentialism of any radical epistemological claim to authenticity. Claims to epistemological or political purity are suspect because they assume subjectpositions that would be unmediated by language and representation.

Irigaray radicalizes the psychoanalytic insight by showing, especially in her psycholinguistic studies, how morphology interacts with linguistic definitions in a very dynamic manner. Moreover, she focuses on female morphology as a privileged site of production of forms of resistance to the phallogocentric code. To conclude the diagnostic map, I would say that sexual difference provides a political anatomy of the in-depth structures of phallogocentrism, which is defined as intrinsically masculine, universalistically white, and compulsorily heterosexual. Moreover, it locks the feminine in a double bind: on the one hand it glorifies maternal powers to the detriment of the empowerment of female subjectivity, but on the other hand it stresses the fact that matricide is the foundation of the male psychosocial contract as well as femininity. Phallogocentrism is, in fact, the Law of the Father and it confines the mother to symbolic insignificance. Feminist resistance to phallogocentrism consequently takes the form of a reappraisal of the maternal as a site of empowerment of woman-centered genealogies. Irigaray claims these counter-genealogies as the start of an alternative female symbolic system.

Sexual difference as political cartography

The philosophy of sexual difference suggests that, because the specular relation between Subject and Other is dissymetrical, especially in terms of power relations between the sexes, there is no possible reversibility between their respective positions. Moreover, this dissymetry is proposed as the foundation for a new phase of feminist politics, especially in the Italian feminist reception of Irigaray's work (Milan Women's Bookstore Collective 1990). The argument runs as follows: the fact that the two poles exist in a dissymetrical power relation toward each other also affects their respective relationship to otherness. In the phallogocentric system, argues Irigaray, women's "otherness" in relation to each other remains unrepresentable because the peripheral "other" is conceptualized in function of and in relation to a masculine center. Irigaray refers to the former as "the other of the Other" and to the latter as "the Other of the Same." Under the heading of "the double syntax" Irigaray defends this irreducible and irreversible difference not only of Woman from Man, but also of real-life women from the reified image of Woman-as-Other.

Hence the feminist poststructuralist critique of Beauvoir's "emancipationism," or "equality-minded thought," which is perceived as naive insofar as it assumes that women can simply "grab" transcendence as a point of exit from the paradox of femininity as a systematically devalued site of otherness. Irigaray argues instead that the terms of the dialectical opposition are not reversible, either conceptually or politically. The theory of sexual difference rather banks on the politically subversive potential of the margins of excentricity that women enjoy from the phallogocentric system: it is women's relative "non-belonging" to the system that can provide margins of negotiation for alternative subject positions. Whereas Jacques Derrida's deconstructive philosophy is quite contented with confining the feminine to such margins of noncoincidence with the phallic signifier, sexual difference feminists aim to use these margins to experiment with alternative forms of female empowerment. These margins, however, must be negotiated through careful processes of undoing hegemonic discourses at work not only in dominant culture, but also within feminist theory itself.

Sexual difference as a strategy of empowerment thus is the means of achieving possible margins of affirmation by subjects who are conscious of and accountable for the paradox of being both caught inside a symbolic code and deeply opposed to it. This is why the feminist philosophy of difference is careful in speaking of margins of nonbelonging to the phallic system. In reverse, one could also speak of areas of belonging by women to the same system they are trying to defeat. The point worth stressing is that, willingly or not, women are complicitous with that which they are trying to deconstruct. Being aware of one's implication or complicity lays the foundations for a radical politics of resistance which will be free of claims to purity but also of the luxury of guilt.

Sexual difference theory thus stresses the positivity of difference, while opposing the automatic counter-affirmation of oppositional identities. Feminists need to revalue discourses and practices of difference, thus rescuing this notion from the hegemonic connotations it acquired in classical philosophical thinking. This reappraisal of difference is proposed as a political practice, which coincides with the critique of a humanistic understanding of subjectivity in terms of nationality, self-representation, homogeneity, and stability. This view of the subject is questioned in the light of its dualistic relation to otherness. More specifically, sexual difference theorists politicize habits of metaphorization of the feminine as a figure of devalued difference. Thus, Irigaray pleads for a feminist reappropriation of the imaginary – that is to say of the images and representations that structure one's relation to subjectivity. Language thus becomes a site of political resistance.

I argued earlier that psychoanalytic theory plays an important role in theorizing the fractured vision of the subject. One of the lasting lessons of psychoanalysis is the insight that the notion of "Woman" refers to a female sex being morphologically constituted and socialized so as to conform to the institution of femininity. In keeping with Foucault's understanding of embodied subjectivity, femininity is understood as both a monument and a document. It is both a set of social conventions and a set of social, legal, medical, and other discourses about a normal, standardized female type. In opposition to essentialistic and biologically or psychically deterministic accounts of femininity, psychoanalysis suggests that one is constituted as a woman through a series of mostly unconscious identifications with feminine subject positions (see Article 27, PSYCHOANALYTIC FEMIN-ISM). In a more political reading of this idea, Irigaray suggests Beauvoir was not systematic enough when she asserted that "one is not born, one becomes a woman": this assertion must be extended to cover unconscious structures and forms of identifications which resist willful and conscious processes of political transformation. Irigaray's emphasis on the in-depth structure aims at radicalizing Beauvoir's formula by extending it to unconscious identity formations. The vision of the subject that emerges from this is firmly anti-Cartesian in that it challenges the classical coincidence of subjectivity with consciousness. Feminist politics challenges the structure of representation and the social and political values attributed to Woman as the Other of the patriarchal system, but also extends this challenge to the deep structures of each woman's identity.

The corollary of the above is crucial: it implies that the women who undertake the feminist position – as part of the process aimed at empowering alternative forms of female subjectivity – are split subjects and not rational entities. Each woman is a multiplicity in herself: she is marked by a set of differences within the self, which turns her into a split, fractured, knotted entity, constructed over intersecting levels of experience. Irigaray, as most psychoanalytic feminists, focuses especially on the discrepancy between unconscious desires and willful choices. This deeply anti-Cartesian vision of the subject is not gratuitous, but it rather aims at providing a more adequate and consequently politically more effective mapping of the complexities that surround female agency. It complexi-fies and updates an important question: why do not all women desire or long for freedom and autonomy? Why do they not desire to be free?

The feminist subject, in other words, is not a purely volitional or self-representational unit: she is also the subject of her unconscious and, as such, she entertains a set of mediated relationships to the very structures that condition her life-situations. There is no unmediated relation to gender, race, class, age, or sexual choice. Identity is the name given to this set of potentially contra-dictory variables: it is multiple and fractured; it is relational in that it requires a bond to the "others"; it is retrospective in that it functions through recollections and memories. Last but not least, identity is made of successive identifications, that is to say of unconscious internalized images which escape rational control.

Sexual difference as utopia

The question then becomes: how to unfasten one's attachment to and identification with certain images, forms of behavior and expectations that are constitutive of femininity? In answering this question, sexual difference becomes a theory of female empowerment, based on a strategic use of repetition. It is utopian as in a-topos, that is, it has no foundations as yet, it is "nowhere" – but it does point to a process of significations that has already started. Irigaray calls "mimesis" the strategy that consists in revisiting, reappraising and repossessing the female subject-position by women who have taken their distance from Woman as a phallogocentric support-point.

The starting point for the project of sexual difference is the political will to assert the specificity of the lived, female embodied experience. This amounts to the refusal to disembody sexual difference into an allegedly "postmodern" subjectivity; while it reasserts the will to reconnect the poststructuralist project of deconstruction of fixed subjectivity to the social and political experience of embodied females. The philosophy of sexual difference argues that it is historic-ally and politically urgent to bring about empowered notions of female subjec-tivity. Feminism is the strategy of working through the sedimented layers of meanings and significations surrounding the notion of Woman, at the precise moment in its historicity when, because of the decline of classical humanism, this notion has lost its substantial unity. Thus, as a political and theoretical practice, feminism unveils and consumes the different representations of Woman in such a way as to open up spaces for alternative representations of women within this previously fixed essence which has been challenged by postmodernity. Postmod-ernity has made femininity available to feminists as that which needs to be deconstructed and worked upon.

Mimesis as the politics of "as if" is a careful use of repetitions which confirms women in a paradoxical relation to femininity, but also enhances the subversive value of the paradoxical distance that women entertain from the same feminin-ity. The political gamble is clear and the stakes are high: for sexual difference theorists, the new is created by revisiting and burning up the old. The quest for alternative representations of female subjectivity requires the mimetic repetition and the reabsorption of the established forms of representation for the post-Woman women. The signifier woman cannot be relinquished by sheer volition: it must be consumed and reappraised from within.

As I suggested briefly before, an important element of the mimetic repetition is, for Irigaray, the sense of women's genealogies, which I read as a politically activated counter-memory. A feminist is someone who thinks through her experience as a woman and through shared experience with other women. A feminist is someone who forgot to forget her bond to other women: a bond that is made not only of a shared oppression, but also of commonly experienced joys and ways of knowing. I refer to this subject-position as "the female feminist." Genea-logies constitute a symbolic legacy of female embodied and embedded experience, the starting point for which is the enfleshed location of the body. Remembering that the enfleshed or embodied self is, for Irigaray, a de-essentialized entity, which she reads with psychoanalytic insight, the bodily self can best be described as the intersection of many fields of experience and of social forces. In a phallogocentric system, women are socialized into thinking through a masculine symbolic structure which is sustained by an imaginary that reduces them to "the Other of the Same." Female feminist genealogies as counter-memories are a way of breaking through the mighty power of the phallic signifier and opening up spaces for women to redefine collectively their singular experiences as "Other of the others."

Sexual difference is not to be understood, therefore, as an unproblematic category, nor is it to be radically separated from the workings of other categories, such as class, race, ethnicity, and other coded social differences. It does continue to privilege, however, sexed identity – the fact of being embodied female – as the primary site of resistance. This site is defined as a process of constitution of multiple, complex, and potentially contradictory facets or subject-position, as Teresa de Lauretis suggests (1987b).

One of the most interesting new perspectives is offered by the intersection of sexual difference theory with other differences. The French school of sexual difference has come under criticism for its color-blindness and its disregard of race and ethnicity issues. Following Butler and Scott (1992) the question can be reformulated in terms of the points of convergence between poststructuralist critiques of identity, and recent theories by women of color and of black feminists to expose the whiteness of feminist theory. In postmodernity, what is needed are new transversal or intersectional alliances between postcolonialism, poststructuralism and post-gender theories (Trinh T. Minh-ha 1989, Spivak 1987b). This would correspond to new interdisciplinary dialogues between philosophy and fields such as legal studies, critical studies and film theory, social and political thought, and economics and linguistics. The common running thread could be: which accountability is available to feminists working outside the reference to a universal, coherent, and stable self and yet still committed to agency, the empowerment of women and to theoretical and methodological accuracy?

Another important new area of study is the relation between philosophical style and political agency. Sexual difference as a highly distinctive mode of philosophical thought has brought a new style into feminist philosophy: in a radical redefinition of interdisciplinarity, sexual difference thinkers open the discipline of philosophy up to dialogical exchanges with all sorts of other (non-philosophical) discourses. Moreover, the utopian dimension of sexual difference inaugurates a visionary mode of thinking where the poetic and the political intersect powerfully.

Moreover, the anti-Cartesian vision of subjectivity which is implicit in sexual difference philosophy has the advantage of allowing for a political reading of affectivity. Thus, feminism gets redefined as the passion of sexual difference, that is to say as an object of desire for women who no longer recognize themselves in the phallogocentric "Other of the Same," that is, Woman. A female feminist could thus be seen as someone who longs for and tends toward the empowerment of other representations of being-a-woman. The feminist project is no longer described only in terms of willful choice, but also in terms of desire, that is to say un-willful drives. Consequently political passions, and the political analysis of affectivity that accompanies them, emerge as a central issue. This

305

also requires a critical reappraisal of the notion of desire itself. Irigaray, not unlike Deleuze, challenges the equation between desire and negativity or lack, which also constitutes a Hegelian legacy in Lacanian psychoanalysis, and proposes instead desire as the positive affirmation of one's longing for plenitude and well-being – a form of felicity, or happiness. What the feminism of sexual difference wants to free in women is thus also their desire for freedom, justice, self-accomplishment, and well-being: the subversive laughter of Dionysus as opposed to the seriousness of the Apollonian spirit. This political process is forward-looking, not nostalgic: it does not aim at the glorification of the feminine, but rather at its actualization or empowerment as a political project aimed at alternative female subjectivities. It aims to bring into representation that which phallogocentrism had declared unrepresentable and thus to do justice to the sort of women feminists, in their great diversity, have already become.

31

Sexuality

JACQUELINE ZITA

Finally, in order to talk about sex we find that we must overcome both internal and external resistance, for we live in a culture that is, in general, inhospitable to critical analysis of sex, and one in which female sexuality, in particular, has been simultaneously manipulated by taboo, glorification, and degradation. To speak at all, and then to speak in opposition to those manipulative traditions, is to invite strong reaction.   (Freeman and Thorne 1984)

Feminist philosophical writing on sexuality is both concentrated in specific areas and dispersed throughout feminist philosophy. This is because feminist philosophers usually incorporate in their writing some notion of what sexuality is and its relevance to women's social oppression and liberatory projects. Feminist thinking on sexuality can also be found in many writings on sexual violence, reproductive and erotic rights, sexual ethics, sexual politics, sexual law, sexual harassment, sexual deviance, sexual practices, sexual commerce, sexual identity, and sexual pleasure. Additionally, feminist thinking on sexuality appears in the critical rethinking of biological and social sciences and in a variety of new discourses seeking their interdisciplinary homes in women's studies, gender studies, queer theory, and cultural studies. To carve out from all of this a domain of feminist philosophical work on sexuality seems difficult if not perilous.

This discursive ubiquity of feminist thought on sexuality is counterbalanced by academic philosophy's professional reticence to write directly about sexuality, perhaps a vestige of philosophy's traditional disdain for the body and its salacious sexual functions. Consequently, major feminist reconceptualizations of sexuality have mostly occurred outside of academic philosophy. These new ideas have emerged in feminist movement literatures, in creative writing and art, in philosophy's neighboring disciplines (such as political science, history of consciousness, anthropology, literary criticism, history, political science, etc.) and in new interdisciplinary fields. Feminist academic philosophy has been responsive to these other sources and steady in its attempt to rethink and clarify the contemporary passages of sex in feminist thinking and the relevance of sexuality to more traditional philosophical problems. This results in a curious epistemic hybridity that marks an important difference between feminist philosophical work and what little there is of other philosophical work on sexuality. In feminist philosophy, there has been a steadily consistent interdependency on writings and sources outside of academic philosophy which have in common a commitment to rethink sexuality and to make intelligible its relation to women's experiences and to the social institutions and practices that cause women's oppression. In this overview of the last quarter-century, I will attempt to trace these emerging complexities in the work of feminist philosophers, as they join a larger reflective project to rethink sexuality in feminist terms.

Before beginning this brief chronological overview of what feminist philosophers have written about sexuality, I would like to ennumerate several themes which seem recurrent in this body of thought. These are theoretical projects or questions that have been pursued, sometimes with success and sometimes with frustration, but always with a commitment to the disciplinarity of philosophical inquiry and its practices of critique and dialogue. These projects include attempts:

(a)   to explore more authentic forms of female sexuality or languages of sexuality more fitting to the physicalities and desires of female bodies;
(b)   to understand some forms of female sexuality as sites of resistance to male dominance or as radical transgressions against heterosexual hegemony;
(c)   to comprehend some forms and contexts of female sexuality as significant areas of women's social oppression and potential and systemic sites of violence against women;
(d)   to expand the notion of sexuality as an erotic that is inclusive of, but not limited to, genitally-focused acts;
(e)   to comprehend sexuality as socially constructed and as implicated in various social hierarchies of gender, race, class, and reproductive practices, that raise important questions about agency, resistance, and power;
(f)   to articulate sexuality as a quasi-autonomous social domain to be explored by alternative interpretations, norms, and values;
(g)   to clarify the notion of sexuality identities and related gender formations.

The personal is political – beginning in the 1970s

Thrown by the historical jolt of 1970s feminism and the theoretical gambit that *the personal is political*, a few courageous women philosophers found a moment of intellectual discovery in women's hitherto unexamined sexuality. In feminist movement literatures, sexuality was becoming a place where much of *the personal* seemed political, as a primary location where many women experienced oppression, personal harm, and identity crisis. Consciousness-raising groups focusing on such experiences were later lauded by feminist philosophers, such as Sandra Lee Bartky, Catharine MacKinnon, and Naomi Scheman, as exemplary sites for the articulation of women's subjugated and experiential-based knowledge. However, the emerging feminist philosophy of the 1970s, though often influenced by earlier work of Simone de Beauvoir's *The Second Sex* (1952), was in varying degrees reticent to fling open the door of philosophy to sexuality, an apparent hazard arising from philosophy's bodiless commitment to thought and the plebeian nature of sex talk.

An essay by Ann Garry, "The philosopher as teacher: why are love and sex philosophically interesting?", written as late as 1980, was one of the first to ask directly why sex and love might be of intellectual interest to feminist philosophers. In that essay, Garry describes three different paradigms of consciousness-raising, psychotherapy, and feminist philosophy, noting that the latter differs from the other two in the lack of a direct commitment to social change or to personal emotional growth. For Garry, feminist philosophy on love and sex, while related to women's experiences and to a feminist theoretical foundation for socially bettering the conditions of women, stays committed to conceptual work:

> Philosophy about love and sex leads to the same things that any philosophy leads to: the goal might be truth, plausible theories, clearer concepts, or uncovering nonsense – as one finds appropriate.... Conceptual clarity is especially important for concepts such as love, dependency, sex, need, autonomy, and trust, which come in clusters and are overlayed with emotion. Not only do the concepts form a complex cluster, but different people's input on their meaning is important. For we look at trust and need in importantly different ways. Also of philosophical interest are the moral problems that arise when analyzing concepts in this area. (Garry 1980, p. 29)

While Garry provides a traditional philosophical justification for studying love and sex, even though they are concepts that "happen to be ones that have bearing on our emotional lives" (Garry 1980, p. 30), she supports a professional innovation to merge philosophical craft with an understanding of how sex and love are institutionally constructed. Two points are worth noting here. Garry claims that such feminist philosophy may release emotions important to the topic and that a diversity of perspectives are equally called for. This begins to erode the rigidly Cartesianized boundary separating the interiority and apositionality of reason from the emotions and from the philosopher's personal experience, a boundary that has often separated philosophical from other kinds of writing. Second, in recognizing the feminist notion that sex and love may be institutionally constructed and implicated in social relations of power, the subject matter of such feminist philosophy already rests on a social hypothesis that could be used to interpret male-dominated traditional philosophy as a possible bastion of sexist rhetoric and biased arrogance. Both the challenge to reason's pure interiority (its absence of emotional disturbance) and to its possible conflation with hidden rhetorical bias reveal the deeper subversion that feminist philosophy brings to its professional discipline. The efforts of feminist philosophers to write about sexuality, using familiar and unfamiliar tools of philosophical analysis, could thus be construed as an oppositional practice of philosophy, cast by the hegemonic eye as undisciplined and too close to smell of women's bodies.

309

In contrast to philosophy's caution, by the late 1970s and early 1980s, discussions on sexuality among feminists had reached a high pitch, especially under the signs of *victim* and *survivor*. An historical corridor had been opened in which women began to discuss and "speak out" on their experiences of rape, incest, child abuse, sexual battery, sexual harassment, and sexual displeasures with men. In feminist writing, the sexual repression hypothesis was becoming gendered and political, a paradigm that would be consolidated in Catharine MacKinnon's (1982, 1987b) and Andrea Dworkin's (1974, 1981, 1988b) analysis of pornography as a fundamental site of women's sexual oppression. The repression hypothesis was also articulated in the notions of rape culture (Russell 1975) and sexual slavery (Barry 1979), conceived as transhistorical oppressions shared by all women. Under the wing of this new paradigm, feminist philosophers found gainful foundations for the next decade in rethinking traditional philosophical concepts, such as agency and autonomy (Hoagland 1988), respect (Tong 1982, Morgan 1986), consent (MacKinnon 1982, Frye 1978, 1986, 1988, 1992a), responsibility (Trebilcot 1982), personhood (Kappeler 1986, Green 1989), dependency (Hoagland 1988), and sexual objectification (Hill 1987, Bartky 1984, 1990a, Kittay 1983a, McCormack 1993). Feminist philosophers could at least bring *the personal* to discourse by disciplining feminist thinking to these more familiar philosophical concerns.

These were, however, treacherous ventures as female minds and bodies in philosophy were becoming visible. The principle of articulation – *the personal is political* – encouraged feminist philosophers to think more widely and daringly about sexual experience and the body. As Linda Nicholson analyzes this, failure in the realm of *the personal* was seeking a larger social interpretation as a failure in relations between the sexes.

> If failures of the private sphere were not necessarily a function of the personalities of individuals, then the process of eliminating them might require something other than individual adjustments. If social norms and practices were what lay behind problems in the personal sphere, then removing such problems might require a social or political movement. This conclusion was also expressed in the slogan "The personal is political." (Nicholson 1981)

With this new paradigm, radical feminists began to inspect the norms of heterosexuality with a new lens that encouraged feminist philosophers to explore heterosexuality more directly. Lesbian separatism and heterosexual surveillance were discursive practices that began to emerge in the work of lesbian feminist philosophers, such as Allen, Card, Daly, Frye, Hoagland, Raymond, Trebilcot, and Wittig. The meaning given to "lesbian" varied in these philosophical writings, but they shared in overlapping ways an effort to challenge the meaning and norms of womanhood (Wittig 1981, Frye 1978, Hoagland 1988), heterosexual femininity (Daly 1978, Dworkin 1974), female emotional and sexual dependency on men (Frye 1978, Allen 1986) and to expand the meaning of "lesbian" beyond genital sexuality (Rich 1980) to include a wide range of woman-centered experiences and a more diffuse eroticism (Lorde 1984, Frye 1988, Rich 1980). There were attempts to expand the term "heterosexualism" to include other forms of nonconsenting relations of domination (Hoagland 1988) or to map the contours of less obviously apparent heterosexualized activities, as for example in Naomi Goldenberg's (1990) work on baseball or Cynthia Enloe's (1990a, 1990b) work on military practices.

In a fashion consistent with the profession of philosophy, many feminist philosophers writing on sexuality promoted the work of conceptual clarification and normative analysis, while also exploring discursive transformation as a way of resisting male dominance. By changing paradigms, language, values, perspectives, and definitions, these conceptual moves would hopefully have their real effects on social and political reality (Wittig 1992, Frye 1978). Later critics of the radical feminism (such as Danmer 1992, Duggan 1992, Echols 1989, Feinberg 1993, Stein 1992, Rust 1995, King 1986, Rubin 1984) have represented this discursive faith as a utopian gap and as the intellectual arm of "cultural feminism," which these critics have characterized as a further repression of sexual diversity in the name of sameness and gender essentialism. I venture, however, that a careful reading of radical feminist philosophical writings reveals a commitment to a strategic essentialism (Fuss 1989) that was effectively deployed to organize female oppositional practices and communities. In these writings, this was differently nuanced as resistance to heterosexual reality (Raymond, Frye), heterosexual ethics (Hoagland, Card), heterosexual semantics (Frye, Penelope) and heterosexual culture (Card, Frye, Ferguson, Hoagland, Trebilcot). It is worth noting that this earlier work brought the body and sexuality into philosophy in a way that grounded theory on women's experiences and produced philosophy for a wider women's readership, as well as academic feminist philosophers.

One upshot of the early lesbian feminist critique of heterosexuality is that it prompted some women to abandon feminist philosophy. Only gradually was this critique taken up philosophically by heterosexual and later by bisexual feminist philosophers. Over the years, several heterosexual feminist philosophers have developed analyses of the cultural construction of heterosexual female bodies (Bartky 1990a, Bordo 1993, Heise 1984, Young 1990a), sometimes siding rather pessimistically with the hope for less oppressive heterosexual practices (Hamblin 1983, Krasner 1993). However, in whatever ways women's heterosexuality is thought to be socially constructed or oppressive, this does not necessarily negate the possibilities of heterosexual resistance and resiliance. Some of the most optimistic writing on this has been done by lesbian philosophers (Ferguson 1991a, Frye 1992a, Zita 1997) and in the new writings by bisexual or omnisexual philosophers (Clausen 1990, Bedecarre 1997, Burchard 1996a, Danmer 1992, Heldke 1997, Rust 1995, Udis-Kessler 1990, Wilkerson 1997).

Writing as a heterosexual feminist philosopher, Barbara Krasner has explored in her essay "Impossible virgin or why I choose not to be a heterosexual" (1993) a possible strategy for heterosexual resistance:

311

> If feminism is about identifying the sources of and ending oppression, and if heterosexuality is based on a construction of gender that is oppressive to any people involved in a heterosexual relationship, and if whom you are sexually attracted to is an issue separate from the political institution you subscribe to, then it is quite possible to be a feminist and be sexually attracted to and involved with men, so long as it is not done on the heterosexual model... women cannot be feminists and heterosexual where heterosexuality is understood as a political institution that is based upon our operating construction of gender that lends itself to the oppression of women. (Krasner 1993, p. 2)

Courageously entering into the fray of sexual responsibility, sexual choice, and sexual resistance, Krasner calls for heterosexual resistance to an institution of heterosexuality based on gender polarization, limited sexual scripts, and reproduction of oppressive power relations and prescriptive categories of behavior between the sexes. Relying on earlier radical feminist norms, that promoted a more equalitarian distribution of power between the sexes and the values of intimacy and love, Krasner does not deny her physical attraction to men, but evokes a new kind of relation between the sexes that challenges "the social construction of what you are biologically" (Krasner 1993). Heterosexuals have a choice on how to express and deploy their sexual practices, and for Krasner how "to choose to be with a man without compromising my personhood" (Krasner 1993, p. 33).

In summary, the first generation of contemporary feminist philosophers developed a paradigm for rethinking female sexuality with a focus on the objectification and dehumanization of women through sexuality. There was philosophical objection to this objectification, whether embodied in Hugh Hefner's sex kittens of the 1960s, the norms of standard heterosexual practice, or violent sexual abuse of women that had become a new common knowledge – an *open secret* – in the 1970s. Feminist thinking about sexuality was linked to an attempt to understand women's experience of male sexual violence and the many facets of female socialization and sexual agency under sexual oppression. However, while feminist philosophers continued to explore ideas within this paradigm over the next two decades, the dominant shape of feminist philosophical discourse on sexuality would be profoundly changed in the coming years, a discursive shift occasioned by the so-called sex wars, the AIDS crisis, a generation of women coming to philosophy through the conduits of queer identity and politics, and a return to a more isolatory and esoteric form of philosophical writing.

1980s: sex kittens meet the war machine, the AIDS epidemic, and the question of difference

In earlier lesbian feminist philosophy, the idea of lesbianism was often depicted as the most radical personal and political solution to women's sexual oppression, creating a discursive space in which lesbian feminism was given the positive political significance of prima facie resistance to male dominance, but with very little further reflection on lesbian sex itself. Marilyn Frye's (1988) remarkable essay "Lesbian 'sex'" accounts for this as a lack of language, a silencing of marginal articulation. Others saw in the reiterative definition of "lesbian" as everything *not* heterosexual an attempt to homogenize the category of lesbian without revealing its own specific content (Fuss 1989, Butler 1990, Roof 1993). "Lesbian" had become its own unmarked sign, a magical sign of liberation and creativity (King 1986, Farwell 1988, Wittig 1992), leaving many of its closeted secrets for later analysis. Claudia Card (1995c) was one of the first feminist philosophers to write about the less positive aspects of lesbian battering, lesbian stalking, and lesbian incest, matters that had been previously and exclusively deferred to the meaness of men.

Similarly, critics have challenged the category of woman supporting 1970s feminism as not sufficiently responsive to race, ethnic, class, disability, and other differences (Feinberg 1993, Hollibaugh and Moraga 1983, Lugones 1987, Nestle 1987, 1992; Pérez 1991; Spelman 1991, Trujillo 1991, Wendell 1996). Women of color and women writing from non-middle class and disabled perspectives have written most effectively and provocatively on these issues, revealing the contours of whiteness, middle-class assumptions, and able-bodied privilege that have often determined the limits of feminist philosophical thinking on sexuality. This confrontation with *the question of difference* has been commonly character-ized as an attack on an identity politics, especially whenever feminist identity politics ignored the diversity of women and homogenized those differences under the sign of *woman*. In emphasizing the heterogeneity of women's experiences in sex and love, including the nuances of class, race, gender, disability, age, and other social factors, as well as sexual orientation, the category of "female sexu-ality" appeared not only as a social construction (to be deconstructed) but also a category of multiplicity, inconsistencies, and conflicting political inferences. The *question of difference* seemed to challenge the epistemic foundations of a feminism that required a homogeneous and monolithic rhetoric of women's liberation.

In a similar exploration of difference, the feminist category of sex was con-fronted by its own critics. This is reflected in Gayle Rubin's foundational piece, "Thinking Sex: Notes for a Radical Theory on the Politics of Sexuality" (1984), in which she argues that feminist theory should reconsider sexuality as encompassing its own dynamics of sexual oppression, not reducible to the oppression of women. In contrast to Rubin's 1975 essay, "The traffic in women," where she developed a structuralist social analysis of Oedipalized con-structions of female sexuality, her rethinking on sexuality in the 1984 essay created a new problematic:

> In contrast to my perspective in "The Traffic in Women," I am now arguing that it is essential to separate gender and sexuality analytically to more accurately reflect their separate social existence ... . For instance, lesbian feminist ideology has mostly analyzed the oppression of lesbians in terms of the oppression of women. However, lesbians are also oppressed as queers and perverts, by the operation of sexual, not gender, stratification. (Rubin 1984, p. 308)

313

This intellectual maneuver casts serious philosophical suspicions on feminist theories of sexuality based on an understanding of women's oppression. Under this new paradigm, sexuality is still perceived as socially constructed, but the agency of oppression is now heterosexual hegemony. rather than male dominance. With a swift inversion, the repression hypothesis was turned against radical feminists and especially lesbian feminists for their alleged philosophical hijacking of sex in the name of an insulatory feminist politic. This sentiment, typified by Amber Hollibaugh, was echoed as a sexual grievance that was to become the mantra of the new pro-sex advocates in the 1980s: "while lesbianism is certainly accepted in feminism, it's more as a political or intellectual concept. It seems feminism is the last rock of conservativism. It will not be sexualised. It's prudish in that way ... . Sometimes, I don't know how to handle how angry I feel about feminism" (Hollibaugh and Moraga 1983, p. 403). In this mood, multiple voices in support of pornography, prostitution, sex workers, s/m practitioners, pedophiles, fetishists, transsexuals, bisexuals, and others came forward in part to challenge the ideas of 1970s feminism and to proclaim their own marginal identities. This confrontation could have opened a wider discussion on sexuality – instead it was scripted as a "sex war" – a war machine in which positions became highly polarized and verbally incommensurable.

Feminist philosophers responded to the "sex wars" in a reflective and ethnographic mode, clarifying what the debates were about and what issues required deeper philosophical attention (Bar-On 1992, Cohen 1986, Creet 1991, Rich 1986, Ferguson, et al. 1984, Valverde 1989, Willis 1982, Zita 1992a). In "Sex war: the debate between radical and libertarian feminists," Ann Ferguson (1984b) described the mental and emotional geography of the "sex wars" as two opposing paradigms, reflecting different ways of comprehending sexuality:

Radical feminists' views of sexuality include the following:
1. Heterosexual sexual relations generally are characterized by an ideology of sexual objectification (men as subjects/masters; women as objects/slaves) that supports male sexual violence against women.
2. Feminists should repudiate any sexual practice that supports or "normalizes" male sexual violence.
3. As feminists we should reclaim control over female sexuality by developing a concern with our own sexual priorities, which differ from men's – that is, more concern with intimacy and less with performance.
4. The ideal sexual relationship is between fully consenting, equal partners who are emotionally involved and do not participate in polarized roles. (Ferguson 1984, p. 108)

This radical feminist paradigm Ferguson contrasts with the second paradigm, the libertarian–feminist paradigm, which she summarizes as follows:

1. Heterosexual as well as other sexual practices are characterized by repression. The norms of patriarchal bourgeois sexuality repress the sexual desires and pleasures of everyone by stigmatizing sexual minorities, thereby keeping the

majority "pure" and under control.

2. Feminists should repudiate any theoretical analyses, legal restrictions, or moral judgments that stigmatize sexual minorities and thus restrict the freedom of all.
3. As feminists we should reclaim control over female sexuality by demanding the right to practice whatever gives us pleasure and satisfaction.
4. The ideal sexual relationship is between fully consenting, equal partners who negotiate to maximize one another's sexual pleasure and satisfaction by any means they choose. (Ferguson 1984, p. 109)

Ferguson reviews the difference in these two paradigms as a difference in primacy placed on an intimacy established by a balance of power in relationships or on the pleasure produced by any means necessary between two consenting adults. While the concept of consenting adults is common to both paradigms, maintaining a feminist rejection of "forbidden sexual practices," such as rape, incest, and sexual violence, women's consent to sex is more suspect in the radical feminist paradigm where sexuality is viewed as a tool of male domination and as socially constructed through gender, family, and social relations of male power (Wagner 1982). Consent in the libertarian–feminist paradigm is an individual matter, negotiated between individuals and often championed when transgressing socially condoned sexual norms. The radical feminist paradigm puts sex into a politic that unites women against the excesses of male violence and the "normalization" of sadomasochism of many heterosexual practices. The libertarian–feminist paradigm puts sex into politics as a site of transgression and release from sexual repression, creating alliances between sexually transgressive women and other sexual minorities.

Ferguson resolves some of the tension between the two camps by calling for more reflection on what she calls "risky" sexual practices. A "risky" practice differs from a forbidden sexual act such as rape, insofar as a "risky" practice is suspected of leading to a dominant/subordinate relationship, although there is not conclusive proof of this as there is with rape and incest victimization. Ferguson calls for more feminist tolerance of the middle zone of "risky" sexual practices while holding firm on a commitment to end social subordination of women, reinforced by "forbidden" sexual violence and domestic abuse of women. "Sadomasochism, capitalist-produced pornography, prostitution, and nuclear family relations between male breadwinners and female housewives are all risky practices from a feminist point of view. This does not mean that feminists do not have a right to engage in these practices" (Ferguson 1984, p. 111). Feminists should be free to choose between casual and more committed sexual love, co-parenting, and communal relationships and "risky" practices "without fear of moral condemnation from other feminists" (Ferguson 1984b, p. 112).

Once the smoke screens of "political correctness" and "sex policing" were lifted, the "feminist sex wars" actually raised some interesting new questions about sexual risk and power (Califia 1981, Ferguson 1984, Rubin 1984), sexual essentialism (Butler 1990, Fuss 1989, Grosz 1994c, de Lauretis 1987a, 1988; Roof 1993), sexual ethics (Card 1995c, Hoagland 1988, Singer 1993), the rights and wrongs of pornography (Bensinger 1992, Cameron 1992, DeCew 1984,

J. Hill 1987, Teachout 1987, Tong 1991, Turley 1986, Vadas 1987), and prostitution (Green 1989, Jaggar 1991, Schrage 1989, Pateman 1983), violence and the body (Burchard 1996a), the use and abuse of the phallus in sexual acts (Butler 1992a. 1992b. Findlay 1992. Reich 1992). In various quarters. feminist philosophers took up positions on these debates. These differences, according to Freeman, raised basic questions about sexuality and political discourse:

> The debates draw, quite dramatically, on the plasticity of sexual meanings. What, it has been debated, is sexuality basically "about"? Power and violence? Pleasure? Intimacy? If sexuality is, at least in part, about fantasy, how does it relate to the "real," which is tied to the political? If sexuality is socially constructed (a belief most feminists affirm), are sexual practices and experiences not shaped by social structure, and should they not be subjected to political scrutiny? But do we want a movement where such scrutiny results in the labeling of some sexual practices as "politically correct" and other as "incorrect"?   (Freeman and Thorne 1984, p. 104)

By the end of the 1980s, feminist philosophy had made the issues of sexuality and the body not only more acceptable in some alcoves of professional philosophy, but its own intertextual cottage industry. The writing practices of feminist philosophy continued to hybridize with other areas of discourse engaging a wider reflection on a new diversity of political practices. Above all the AIDS crisis of the 1980s made a strong impact on feminist sex theory, calling for a response to the plight of persons living with AIDS. cultural representation of AIDS. increased visibility of gay men and other sexual minorities as victims of social suffering, as well as the continued silence on women's, and in particular woman-to-woman, HIV transmission risk. In a new age caught up in a moral AIDS panic, the logics of radical feminism and the grip of lesbian separatist practices never fully recovered from the discursive explosions affecting fundamental feminist categories – such as "woman," "gender," "sexuality," and "power" – and from the increasing pressures to make alliances with sexual minorities (Zita 1994). Sexual theory began to embrace a more widely cast repression hypothesis in which contemporary sexual tyranny affected more than the oppression of women in the struggle against male dominance.

1990s: sexual (f)right and the (dis)solution of difference

With the emergence of postmodern sex theory, the categories of sexuality were stretched by deconstructive maneuvers that further destabilized the meaning of sexual identities and practices. In *Tendencies*, Eve Sedgwick (1993) aptly characterized this new sexual theorizing as "the mesh of possibilities, gaps, overlaps, dissonances and resonances, lapses and excesses of meaning where the constituent elements of anyone's gender, of anyone's sexuality aren't made (or can't be made) to signify monolithically." For feminist philosophy, the impact of postmodern theory has resulted in a renewed interest in questions of sex and gender ontology and foundationalism (Butler 1990, 1993, Scheman 1996) and in a scattering of new writings that challenge the stability of sex and gender categories from a transgender-identified perspective (Dolan 1993, Hale 1996, Nash 1992, Zita 1992a). In this work, sex and gender categories were becoming more fluid and less able to sustain a discursive difference based on an unexamined essentialism, creating new philosophical questions about the matter of bodies and the materialization of sexualities (Butler 1993, Grosz 1994b, Bordo 1993).

These philosophical writings on sexuality emerged in a time overwhelmed by an epidemic that had encouraged more direct sex talk about sexual behaviors rather than sexual kinds. Concurrent with this as a new academic interest in postmodern theory (perhaps best rendered as a new liberalism of anti-identity politics) is a new and virulent white supremist and queer-hating conservative politic that is also catalyzing the disappearance of identity politics. Consistent with this scene, conservative attacks on women's studies and feminist philosophy (Patai and Koertge 1994, Sommers 1994) have called for a depoliticization and reprivatization of *the personal* and the silencing of personal voice in the feminist classroom. In all of these discursive maneuvers, what Bar-On (1994) has called "the feminist connection of experiential marginality, difference, sexuality, and consciousness as foundational for a political stance" is under siege.

The newly emerging paradigm of postmodern feminist philosophical writing on sexuality contrasts with earlier work of the 1970s in the following ways:

(a) the libidinal excitement of sexual writing has shifted to postmodernism's *romantics of transgression* as the privileged form of sexual radicality rather than resistance to male sexual domination (Rubin 1984);

(b) a new Butlerian (1990) construction of gender as performative and citational makes less readily apparent the discursive delineation of gender assymetries in male power, misogyny, and violence against women;

(c) power inequalities in sexual practices are given a new erotic reading in prosex agency (Vance 1984, 1990, Califia 1981), diffusing a dogmatic reading of gendered dominance, abuse, and danger to women and children;

(d) the body has become a transcendental pivot of quasi-indeterminacy in the play of gender and sexuality categories (Butler 1993, Grosz 1994a), diffusing the use of the body as a primary site of women's sexual oppression, sexual violation, and the "breaking silence" narrations of the self;

(e) sexuality is rendered more isomorphic with capital economies (Griggers 1993, Ebert 1996) and also privileging of male practices of sexual pursuit and pleasure over more typically identified feminine needs for emotional intimacy, community, and sexual equality;

(f) heterosexuality as a category of material and historical practice has become a performative category that can be reproduced in lesbian and gay relationships, and vice versa, diffusing a clear sense of social privilege and material hierarchy by introducing a panoply of sexually transferable acts, pleasures, and fantasies (Sedgwick 1993, Butler 1992) and a new erotic language of amorphic surface linkage (Grosz 1994a).

317

My penchant for characterizing this generational transition from the paradigm of radical to postmodern feminism as a "diffusion" or "dissolution" is meant to emphasize the loss of clear and "boundaried" categories supporting the radical feminist theories that mobilized many women to the barricades of the 1970s. The "dissolve" created a multitude of new identities and modes of resistance, the need for a politics of alliance and coalition, and a retreat to the individual and a politics of radical specificity (Phelan 1991, Mann 1994). Secondly, I have purposefully overdrawn a polarized tension between postmodern and radical feminism to create a rich and inviting terrain for future feminist philosophical work. The questions which emerge in this tension remain profoundly philosophical: what is the ontology of sex, what is its relationship to power, agency, desire, and oppression, what kind of political or ethical analyses are best suited for sexual identities, practices, and struggles, and to what extent is sexuality a discursive fiction with or without ontological or experiential reference? During this most recent period, the feminist "sex wars" continued, but now as a debate often influenced by the rhetorical strategies of postmodernism (Dolan 1993, Hart 1994a, Williams 1989) and by a fierce resurgence of radical feminism (Jeffreys 1993, Reti 1992). The female body and its sexual desire are central to this fertile tension between radical and postmodern feminisms and to further developments in feminist philosophy.

For postmodern feminism, the influence of Michel Foucault cannot go unremarked upon. Although Foucault's importance rests in his intellectual allegiance to the margins of sexual hegemony and in his commitment to the discursive construction of sex categories, the incorporation of Foucault's ideas into feminist philosophical work on sexuality has not been without its feminist critics (more recently V. Bell 1993, B. Martin 1994). Foucault's conceptualization of sexuality has added fuel to the postmodern attempt to understand sexuality as an epistemic category, discursively constructed by power, authority, and institutional practices. Not only does this approach minimize the impact of male dominance on women's sexuality, but uncharacteristically, new Foucauldian theorists of sex often ignore Foucault's cautionary note that the trajectory of sexual liberation, in and of itself, may not be the best path of liberation. At the end of his first volume on the *History of Sexuality*, Foucault ventures this claim: "the rallying point for the counterattack against the deployment of sexuality ought not to be sex-desire, but bodies and pleasures" (Foucault 1978, p. 157). Given the way sex is now inflected in postmodern theory, its bursting but narrow trajectory may in the end secure more for the domination of sex than for a strong oppositional movement capable of resisting a relapse into ultra-conservative sexual politics, a renewed means of male domination and other capital atrocities. Teresa Ebert (1996) echoes this concern even more critically, although somewhat dogmatically, in her call for feminist theory and philosophy to return to the materialism of history rather than the *matterism* of postmodernist theory.

Poststructuralism removes one kind of subject (the Cartesian subject of consciousness), which has become historically irrelevant to late capitalism, and invents another kind of subject (the subject of the body). Consequently, it also puts in question one kind of consciousness (consciousness of the divine), which has become dysfunctional, and in its place institutes another form of consciousness (consciousness of sensuality and pleasure).   (Ebert 1996, p. 160)

Conclusion: remarks on the discursive revolutions of sex

This brief overview of what feminist philosophers have written about sexuality is by no means finished as philosophers will continue to create new questions, debates, and analyses. Philosophical predilection for questions of ethics, epistemology, and ontology will always inform this discussion, as well as the historical and personal struggles that a feminist philosopher brings to the inquiry of her life work. The effort to put the female body and sexuality into philosophy as a legitimate area of scholarship is an achievement largely carved out by feminist philosophy, and more recently queer theory. However, there is, in any philosophy which aims toward *the real*, a hazard of discursive seduction, a belief that the power of words can change the world. The discursive turns of feminist sexual theory – the first in the 1970s and the second in more recent postmodern feminisms of the 1990s – reflect at times a commitment to what Wittig has coined a plasticity of the real to language (Wittig 1989, p. 44). This way of putting sex into discourse has perhaps put too much discourse into sexuality, but I will leave this as a cautionary note for a future revolution in feminist philosophy.

Finally, I would like to comment on the quantity of non-heterosexual philosophy I have reviewed in this article. This reflects a scarcity of writing on heterosexuality by heterosexual feminist philosophers willing to reexamine heterosexual practices and pleasures. Philosophical reflections on monogamy or adultery are, of course, of philosophical worth but are often treated as universal problems that take for granted heterosexual practices. For me, the more interesting contemporary work on sexuality has been written by philosophers who aimed to expose sexualities as social constructions of scattered hegemonies and power relations. Philosophers writing as lesbians, bisexuals, and sexual minorities, while also becoming increasingly cognizant of the interpolation of race, class, and other social differences in sexuality, have had a lot to say about sexuality that was out of the ordinary and philosophically courageous. Additionally, the void created by commercialized overpromotion of heterosexuality and the twin signs of *victim* and *survivor* of heterosexual atrocity in feminist writing have created a troubled space for more positive feminist writing on heterosexual bodies and desires. Perhaps this trouble can become productive, rather than silencing.

Although there are some outstanding exceptions (Bedecarre 1997, Krasner 1993, Young 1990a), a deeply self-reflective pro-heterosexual presence has been missing from feminist philosophical writing on sexuality, a silence that registers a privilege of power as well as an interesting epistemic difficulty. The two are related as I see it. For example, in my own attempts to understand the content of my own whiteness, I often draw a blank. As Ruth Frankenberg (1993) suggests, the epistemic privilege of whiteness is its apparent formlessness. I suspect that there is a similar experience for heterosexual feminist philosophers, if they take seriously some of the lesbian, bisexual, and sexual minority critiques of heterosexuality. Analogous to the meaning of whiteness, heterosexuality remains unmarked and diffused, *the way things are*, a norm that has the privilege of not naming itself, while serving to measure all that is different, and in this case "sexually deviant" from itself. Postmodern sexual theory, as a new philosophical paradigm which accommodates everything in its repertoire of ludic transgressions and shifting categories, is beginning to reopen this important dialogue of difference under the sign of *sexual pluralism*. Unfortunately, the category of lesbian as we have known her has become antiquated and historically irrelevant in this new dialogue on sexual aesthetics and the materialization of performative sexualities. I leave this as my second, and perhaps generational, cautionary note for a future revolution in feminist philosophy.

32

Body politics

SANDRA LEE BARTKY

1. "One is not born a woman, but, rather becomes one"

Webster's Dictionary defines "femininity" as "the quality or nature of the female sex" (p. 803); the *Oxford English Dictionary* as "the quality or assemblage of qualities pertaining to the female sex" (p. 982). Both are wrong. One can be a member of the female sex and yet fail or refuse to be feminine; conversely, one may be biologically male and a drag queen. Femininity is a certain set of sensibilities, behavioral dispositions, and qualities of mind and character. It is also a compelling aesthetic of embodiment, "a mode of enacting and re-enacting received gender norms which surface as so many styles of the flesh" (Butler 1985, p. 11). What follows will focus on the ways in which some feminist thinkers have theorized the norms that govern the production and behavior of an ideally feminine body.

Simone de Beauvoir's *The Second Sex* (1952), perhaps the most influential work of feminist theory in the twentieth century, makes use of Sartrian categories to support the striking claim that "one is not born a woman, but, rather becomes one" (Beauvoir 1973, p. 301). Being-in-itself, non-human being, is that which simply is what it is, whatever that happens to be. Being-for-itself or consciousness, is not what it is, which is to say that it can always choose to be *other* than what it is now and what it has been in the past; it is human freedom. Finally, there is Being-for others, whereby the absolute freedom of the subject is threatened by the freedom of every other subject. Sovereign in my own world, I am an object for the Other whose gaze bestows on me an outside, a nature; since he can define my existence, he is a potential enemy whose very subjectivity "alienates" me from myself. But the Other is an object in my world as well; my gaze can steal his being, just as his can steal mine. Hence, the relationship between selves is fundamentally agonistic, a circle of conflict in which are attempted various recuperative strategies – domination, seduction, indifference.

For Beauvoir, woman has always already been bested in this primordial conflict. This situation of woman is that she – a free and autonomous being – nevertheless finds herself living in a world where men compel her to assume the status of Other, an Other typically inferior to whatever man imagines himself to be. Social definitions of womanhood have most often condemned her to immanence, to the brutishness of the in-itself, that is, to the mind-numbing repetitions of household maintenance and to bodily functions such as childbearing and lactation which, while necessary for the survival of the species, do not raise woman's existence above an animal level.

Whence man's ability to compel? Women are bound to their oppressors, says Beauvoir, by male control of the dominant institutions and the dominant ideology, by women's lack of solidarity with one another, by the biological necessity that requires coupling, by the very antiquity of oppressive arrangements that makes them appear natural, hence unalterable – and sometimes by women's complicity. "A woman may be well-pleased with her role as the Other" (p. xxi). The temptation to allow oneself to be defined by another is an effort to escape the heavy burden of freedom that is, inescapably, the mark of humanity.

Shulamith Firestone's *The Dialectic of Sex* (1970), one of the first and most influential works of US second-wave feminist theory, takes up Beauvoir's call for an escape from the immanence of the reproductive female body. Firestone argues that the disabilities and dependency of pregnancy made women vulnerable to the domination of men in the past. What was past is also present: the disabilities of pregnancy are still a factor in our oppression. But progress in reproductive technology is preparing the way for women's liberation. While Firestone's extensive and visionary program for the liberation of women captures something of the political imagination that was characteristic of the period in which it was written, it was her call for extrauterine reproduction that provoked the most controversy. Unaddressed in Firestone's text is the question under whose auspices the new technology will be developed and who will control its use.

2. "Feminine writing" and female pleasure

Many feminist theorists have taken issue with what they believe to be Beauvoir's repugnance toward the female body, her idealization of male pursuits and denigration of the domestic sphere. Many women find positive value, even joy, in pregnancy, childbirth, and nursing. Beauvoir's rejection of the ordinary pleasures of womanhood, some have contended, skews her account of woman's condition and thus limits the usefulness of *The Second Sex* as an organizing text for a mass-based movement. Moreover, one of woman's characteristic functions in the domestic sphere – maternal caregiving – is said by some to be an occasion for the exercise of virtues and of value-laden activity undreamt-of in Beauvoir's philosophy; indeed, care should become a model for the feminist transformation of the traditionally masculine spheres of government and the economy (Noddings 1986, Ruddick 1989).

A younger, psychoanalytically oriented generation of French feminists has argued against thinkers such as Beauvoir that a liberatory feminine writing (*écriture féminine*) can arise directly from aspects of women's bodily experience that have remained uncolonized by male culture. Luce Irigaray maintains that the specificity of woman's sexual desire has never been recognized; the sexuality of both male and female has been understood by reference to a phallocratic model that is centered on the penis, imperious, and driven by the pursuit of orgasm. Female sexuality, on the contrary, is multiple, decentered, and diffuse.

Unlike men, women have multiple sex organs (e.g. breasts), hence multiple possibilities of satisfaction, not all of which are orgasmic. This is captured in Irigaray's image of the two labia – The Two Lips that Speak Together, always touching (Irigaray, 1985b). As Irigaray associates phallocratic constructions of sexuality with the linearity and rationality of male discourse, proper attention paid to the specificity of the female body will prepare the way for an authentic articulation of female experience – nonlinear, and not necessarily rational, at least as "rational" has traditionally been understood.

In "Breasted experience" (in 1990b), Iris Marion Young follows Irigaray in claiming that women's sexuality is importantly different from men's and that it offers pleasures unique to women. Male culture fetishizes women's breasts: the "'best' breasts are like the phallus: high, hard and pointy" (p. 190). Enormous importance is attached to the look of women's bodies and since so few breasts measure up to patriarchal standards, many women experience their breasts as a source of shame. "Phallocentric culture alienates us from our bodies" (p. 192). Young challenges us to imagine breasts as they are, or might be, not for men or suckling babies, but for women themselves. The recovery by a woman of, e.g., a nonspecular erotic pleasure that may accompany the nursing of a child, threatens the separation of motherhood and sexuality on which, Young claims, much of patriarchy is founded. Hence a decolonized, potentially empowering sexual pleasure in motherhood is possible. An ethic of care and nurturance would indeed change the public sphere for the better. "But we must also insist that nurturers need, that love is partly selfish, and that a woman deserves her own irreducible pleasures" (p. 200).

3. Alienation and the fashion/beauty complex

Here is one way to periodize second-wave philosophical writing about the female body: from the late 1960s to about the mid-1980s, work that dealt particularly with the internalization of patriarchal norms of feminine bodily acceptability drew heavily upon the concept of "alienation." After 1980, ideas and methods associated with postmodern thinkers such as Foucault, Lacan, and Derrida slowly assumed a new prominence. Young's "Breasted experience" is a piece in transition. Phallocentric culture is charged explicitly with the alienation of women from their bodies, but at the same time, Young's critique of the privileging of sight over touch is a poststructuralist inheritance from Heidegger, while the deconstruction of the pair sexuality/motherhood owes much to Derrida.

"Alienation" may be defined as a *fragmentation* of the human person and a *prohibition* on the full exercise of capacities, the exercise of which is thought necessary to a fully human existence. So for Marx, in whose early work the concept of "alienation" is very prominent, workers are alienated under capitalism both from the products of their labor and from their own laboring activity – activity thought necessary to fully human existence. The concept of alienation appealed to feminist theorists of the 1970s and 1980s for a number of reasons. The first was the continuing influence of Simone de Beauvoir. The Other, she maintains, "alienates" me from my being. Man has defined woman as "Other" and in so doing, he has stolen from her the opportunity for self-definition, substituting myths and stereotypes, that, in the absence of any opportunity for self-definition, she is irresistibly led to internalize. The idea of alienation was also compelling due to the continuing influence on this generation of theorists, many veterans of the New Left, of various Marxist and neo-Marxist ideas. Some thinkers speculated about the possibility of a new theory of alienation that could bring together feminism and a radically altered Marxism (Bartky 1990a, Jaggar 1983).

The medicalization of childbirth that robs women of agency in the birthing process could be construed as a form of alienation, as could the historic exclusion of women from most forms of cultural expression (Jaggar 1983). It seemed obvious that women had been alienated from their own sexuality, both by their ignorant or indifferent male partners and by the medico-psychiatric establishment (Koedt 1973, Weisstein 1970, Young 1990b). The fragmentation of women's bodies – actual, as in violence, linguistic ("I'm a tits (or ass) man"), and pictorial, both in pornography and advertising, seemed to be a form of alienation of women as well. Soble argued that these forms of alienation are due to the specific sexual alienation of men under capitalism (Soble 1986).

A "fashion–beauty complex," as much an articulation of patriarchal capitalism as the "military–industrial complex," presides over the forms in which the sexual objectification and self-objectification of women manifest themselves (Bartky 1990a). Overtly, the fashion–beauty complex glorifies the female body; more important is its covert aim, which is to depreciate this body. The media images of perfect female beauty that bombard us daily leave no doubt that we fail to measure up: we live inside our bodies with a pervasive sense of bodily deficiency, even of shame. Women in Western societies live out an estrangement from the body; on the one hand, we *are* the body and are scarcely allowed to be anything else; on the other hand, we must exist perpetually at a distance from our physical selves, fixed in a permanent posture of disapproval. The fashion–beauty complex has not produced. but it refines and deepens feminine anxieties that would accompany the status of sex-object in any case (Bartky 1990).

In an early and now classic paper, "Throwing like a girl: a phenomenology of feminine body comportment, motility and spatiality," Iris Marion Young argues that the norms of feminine bodily comportment forbid women the fullest realization of their bodies' potentialities. A space seems to surround women in imagination; this manifests itself both in a reluctance to reach, stretch, and extend the body to meet resistances of matter in motion and in a typically constricted posture and general style of movement. A woman's space is not a field in which her unalienated bodily intentionality can be freely realized but an enclosure in which she feels herself positioned and by which she is confined (Young 1990b).

Not all feminist work on the body done in this period drew explicitly or implicitly on the alienation paradigm. Linda LeMoncheck, for example, treated sexual objectification not as a species of alienation but as a denial of rights

(LeMoncheck 1985). The idea of normative femininity as alienation, though still compelling, has given way to other approaches, for a variety of reasons. A younger generation of feminist theorists appeared who had not been part of the New Left or the student movements of the 1960s, hence had little exposure to Marxist theory but were much influenced by theoretical approaches that had, particularly in France, superseded Marxist–Lacanian psychoanalysis, Foucault's neo-Nietzscheanism, and Derridean deconstruction. Postmodernism became the order of the day; as in all such transitions, something of value was lost, something gained.

4. Postmodern feminism and the postmodern body

The alienation paradigm fared badly in postmodernism. "Totalizing theory" was now forbidden, for it was assumed (somewhat a prioristically) that any very general theory *must* marginalize someone's experience. Anyhow, the wedding of Marxism and feminism had not come off, though the courtship produced some very fine work. Alienated labor is ordinarily resisted by workers, while femininity is sought eagerly by many, if not most women. Moreover, the precise characterizations of alienation tended to rely upon a phenomenological method: phenomenology can and to some extent did take as exemplary the consciousness of the theorist and her circle; even a very large circle could not disguise the fact that most theorists were white, middle-class, and heterosexual, hence that the theory produced was partial at best, racist or class-biased at worst. It should be said in defense of phenomenological feminism that it tries to present not only the contents of actual consciousness, but also the social norms that define ideal femininity, whatever a woman's race or class. Perhaps the most serious objection to the notion of alienation is its purported essentialism; the very idea of alienation, it was charged, presumes a true self or core self, pure and uncontaminated, that will manifest itself when the causes of alienation are removed. Such a self is regarded as mythic, also coercive, for the very idea of a "true" or "core" self is said to act as a norm with which to bludgeon selves that fail to measure up. But does the idea of an *un*alienated self entail the claim that there is an *actual*, if buried core self? Can the idea of an unalienated self be understood politically, as a vision of what human beings might be like in a world without domination? So understood, the "unalienated" self would belong not to ontology but to a political program, where it can become, quite properly, an occasion for political contestation. At any rate, the eclectic and experimental character of much feminist theory has meant that many thinkers have moved, with no great sense of incoherence, between various conceptual paradigms, using Foucault, alienation theory, or Derridean deconstruction as it suited them.

Of all French postmodern thinkers, Foucault and Derrida have most influenced feminist philosophers. Brevity forbids anything like a general characterization of postmodern philosophy, hence, given his pervasive influence, Foucault can be taken as an exemplar of this philosophical tendency. Radical feminists have understood the domination of women to rest on physical and psychological

325

terror, as well as financial entrapment (Frye 1983); Foucault, however, has a more complex conception of the operation of power than the model of victim and victimizer. Power, for Foucault, is not a possession, nor is it centralized or exercised from above. Disguised, it circulates throughout the body politic, where it regulates "the most intimate and minute elements of the construction of space, time, desire and embodiment" (Bordo 1993, p. 27). Subjectivities, including, of course, gendered subjectivities, are constituted through individual self-surveillance and obedience to norms that arise with "regimes" of knowledge/power–"discourses." On this view, gross violence is not necessary to subjugate women, just a gaze. The theme of the gaze recalls Sartre and Beauvoir; Foucault historicizes the gaze and adds to its workings a very minute analysis of the specific ways in which power gains control of both bodies and minds (Foucault 1973).

It has been suggested that the imposition of normative femininity upon the female body requires modes of training that are properly described as "disciplinary practices" in Foucault's sense – systems of micropower that are fundamentally inegalitarian and asymmetrical – and that are ultimately disempowering to the woman so disciplined (Bartky 1990a). The norms of feminine body comportment, dieting, some forms of exercise, hair care, skin care, etc., all satisfy Foucault's criteria for disciplinary practices. Within a sexist society, the mastery of these disciplines can give a woman more power than she might have otherwise; this is part of their widespread appeal. A thorough examination of the disciplines of normative femininity would have to explain not just why and how they are oppressive, but why they are, for women themselves, seductive. A full account would have to describe the barriers to renouncing them, both objective and subjective. It would have to explore the following circumstance: in order to *be* at all, in this society, one must be a body that is masculine or feminine: the prospect, then, of abandoning the practices that perpetuate femininity must induce in many women a kind of ontological vertigo (Bartky 1990a).

No discussion of the norms of feminine self-presentation in modern industrial societies can ignore the growing preoccupation of women with body shape and body weight. Susan Bordo (1993) puts forth the idea that extremes of behavior – here anorexia and bulimia – can reveal much about "normal" cultural preoccupations. By examining the psychic states of anorexic girls, Bordo probes the immense attraction of the slender body of fashion – a body that resembles more a prepubescent girl than a mature woman. While anorexia and bulimia are complex disorders having multiple causes, certain themes are sounded over and over, themes that have been prominent in Western philosophy: the dualism of body and spirit with its concomitant hatred and distrust of the body and the issue of control of the body, source of error and sin. "Thinness represents a triumph of the will over the body, and the thin body (that is to say, the non-body) is associated with purity and spirituality" (Bordo 1993, p. 148). Issues of control have special resonance for women. "Normal" women who want a svelte appearance must learn not only to control hunger but, if they are to conform to the norms of femininity, to control anger and aggression, and not only their own sexuality but that of males as well. The normal emotional needs of women are routinely regarded by many men as excessive (p. 199).

In "Hunger as ideology," Bordo examines the discourse of mass media in regard to women's hunger. There is a taboo on women's capitulation to "rich, exciting food," this in spite of ever more seductive "sinfully delicious" images of food in magazines and on television. Women in ads take small mincing bites if they eat at all; men are often shown eating lustily. Transgression in regard to food is sexualized: the overweight are the new sinners, their flesh an outward sign of an inner weakness of will. Hunger is by no means a new metaphor for female desire: "Anxiety over women's uncontrollable hungers, sexual and other-wise, appears to peak during periods when women are becoming independent and are asserting themselves politically and socially" (p. 161). The promise of a technological fix for the unwanted results of both aging and eating are producing the image of a plastic, "postmodern" body, a body whose materiality is disap-pearing into a space increasingly occupied by cosmetic surgery and the idea of a designer body. Moreover, the ads that trumpet choice and self-determination are in fact legislating conformity to highly oppressive and clearly racist standards of white, Anglo-Saxon beauty.

Judith Butler's *Gender Trouble* (1990) is perhaps the most thoroughly post-modern treatment of the body in the feminist philosophical literature. Ever since Beauvoir, many feminists have argued that gender is a cultural configuration of male and female bodies understood as "natural kinds": while it might be imposs-ible to characterize human biology except in language, no one doubted that there was a biological substrate independent of culture. But Butler pulls the rug from under biology, "natural kinds," the "natural" body. True to the linguistic turn in French poststructuralism ("There is nothing outside of the text" – Derrida 1974, p. 158), Butler argues that sex as well as gender belongs to the realm of discourse. Moreover, just as earlier feminists had attempted what would now be called a "deconstruction" of gender, Butler's aim is the deconstruction of sex. She argues that much biological "science" as well as our very experience of the body is filtered through metaphors (E. Martin 1987) and organized within rigid and hierarchical dualisms: everyone is either the one sex or its "opposite." Any conception of the "natural" is a "dangerous illusion" of which we must be "cured else we will capitulate to the ultimate weapon in the armamentarium of sexist ideology – the 'naturalness' of male and female" (p. 93). Biological sex is not the bedrock on which gender is erected; rather, it is part of the Gestalt that is performed as "gender." Gender itself is understood as a performance in which an important role has been scripted for the body.

In a more recent work, *Bodies That Matter* (1993). Butler addresses critics who claim that the earlier work ignored the "materiality" of the body. She does not claim "that the materiality of bodies is simply and only a linguistic effect which is reducible to a set of signifiers" and she grants that "to think through the indissolubility of materiality and signification is no easy matter" (p. 30). The embodying of norms of gender is compulsory, but they are, nonetheless, "never

327

quite carried out according to expectation" (pp. 231–2). Further, "gender norms are almost always related to the idealization of the heterosexual bond" (p. 232). Hence, the compulsory gendering whereby one becomes a self is an articulation of compulsory heterosexuality. Butler interrogates at length the complex links between gendered identities, gender norms, sexual practices, and sexual orientation; feminist theory in this instance is incorporated into "queer theory." Drawing sustenance where it can, queer theory must nevertheless keep its theoretical and political independence (p. 240).

5. Subversion and resistance

The case against the fashion/beauty system is strong. The "disciplines" of femininity are an enormous drain on women's time and, in a miserable world that could use it more wisely, their money. The standards of feminine body-display are racist and exclusionary. The expense of time and money required for the project of conformity are out of reach for poor women: so to the shame attached in our society to poverty is added the additional shame of overweight, or of a lifetime of "bad hair days." The project of ideal embodied femininity is a "set-up" for most women, for its standards are largely unattainable. The taboo on aging may poison a woman's maturity. Her infantilized body must take up as little space in the world as possible, this when women are demanding more entry into and control of public space; her infantilized face must not betray the marks of strong emotion or deep thought. The extraordinary importance given to women's appearance produces in many a narcissistic preoccupation with the body that alternates between infatuation and self-disgust. Women are now experiencing shifts in the kinds of power that are ranged against them, shifts that, according to Foucault, Western society as a whole underwent in the transition from the classical to the modern age: power is no longer vested in *individuals* – husband, father, priest; instead, it is pervasive, anonymous, and disguised. The tying of social acceptability, perhaps even identity, to the repressive norms of ideal embodied femininity requires constant surveillance and self-surveillance and constant surveillance, as even the British royal family has discovered, can be disempowering (Bartky 1990a).

Finally, the vexed question of resistance – vexed not only because of quarrels among theorists about strategies of resistance, but because of the high cost of ignoring the codes of the dominant culture. Butler's "performative" theory of gender holds out some hope: the idea that compulsory gendering is never fully determining is cause for optimism. However we are not told why, when or by whom such major or minor mistakes occur. Butler also calls for "gender-bending" – drag, parody, transvestism. But Honi Haber has warned us of the ease with which patriarchal ideology is able to coopt subversive imagery (Haber, forthcoming); moreover, it is not at all obvious that drag, an impersonation, destabilizes or in fact requires the conventional gender imagery on which it depends.

There are those who call for women to defy the disciplines. Radical lesbian theory and practice, for a time, called for the adoption of what was essentially the garb of working-class men: the rejection of femininity led to a taboo on fantasy, self-ornamentation and self-display, perhaps a needless asceticism. On the other hand, aging in radical lesbian communities is often seen to enhance a woman's sexual allure, not to signal its disappearance. As has been shown in Section 2, feminist writers have called attention to capacities of the female body for pleasure other than the reflected pleasure she may take in the satisfaction of patriarchal norms. Many women have taken up bodybuilding and martial arts: this is clearly resistance. Many of the millions of readers of *The Beauty Myth* are resisters or potential resisters (Wolf 1991).

Feminist theorists have not always agreed as to the effect and propriety of calls to resist. Kathryn Morgan's critique of plastic surgery is clearly a call to resist. Such surgery, she claims, is dangerous and expensive: the decision for face-lifting, tummy-tucking or breast augmentation must be evaluated in the light of the cultural colonization of women's bodies. Such choices cannot be truly free, as they are made within a context of coercion (Morgan 1991). Kathy Davis, in a most interesting study of women's decisions to undergo plastic surgery, takes issue with Morgan's claim: the women in her study, she argues, were competent agents for whom plastic surgery was a way of gaining more control of their lives. Morgan's summary dismissal, says Davis, misses the ambiguity and complexity that mark such decisions (Davis 1995).

The positions of Davis and Morgan are not irreconcilable. Davis is by no means a defender of plastic surgery. Given things as they are, she says, the decision to go under the knife might well be the best decision for a woman to make, within the constraints of her situation. Both Morgan and Davis – and many of the women Davis interviews – deplore "things as they are." The question then is how to alter these circumstances radically, that is, how to develop a truly liberatory feminist aesthetic of the body.

When the women's movement is in a position to go once more on the offensive, it must develop, as part of its cultural politics, a new politics of the body, an invention of new "styles of the flesh." This new aesthetic will require a new sensibility, altered modes of sexual desire, the disappearance of mandatory gender markers, the overthrow of a racial hegemony of the image. This revisioning will extend our ideas of physical beauty far beyond the narrow limits within which they are now confined.

33

Disability

ANITA SILVERS

How can women with disabilities be feminists?

As both the promise and the influence of feminism have grown, women with disabilities have, with increasing intensity, pronounced themselves to be disregarded within the women's movement to an extent little different from how patriarchal society devalues them. Deborah Kent (1977), blind since birth, comments:

> When I joined a women's consciousness-raising group a few years ago ... I listened in amazement and awe as the others delivered outraged accounts of their exploitation at the hands of bosses, boyfriends, and passersby ... it was impossible for me to confess my own reaction to their tales of horror, which was a very real sense of envy .... Society had provided a place for them as women, however restricting that place might be .... For myself and for other disabled women, sex discrimination is a secondary issue.

Writing close to two decades later, Carol Gill, Kristi Kirschner, and Judith Panko Reis (1994) observe: "Of great frustration to women with disabilities has been the reluctance of many women's right groups to include them and recognize their issues as women's issues. Women with disabilities are one of the most isolated and invisible minority groups in this country" (see also Klein 1992).

Jenny Morris (1991) speaks directly to the question of theory. At age thirty-three, Morris – a mother, a victorious politician, an activist buoyed on the rising tide of a flourishing feminist movement – tumbled off a wall at the bottom of her garden, injured her spine so that she lost the ability to walk, but retained her political knowledge and skills, her relation with her child, her disposition to fight for social justice. Very little about her that had been of social value changed after the fall. Yet, in the eyes of others, hers was a social as well as a physical fall. She comments:

> The fact that disability has not been integrated into feminist theory arises from one of the most significant problems with feminism's premise that "the personal is political" ... . Disabled people – men and women – have little opportunity to portray our own experiences within the general culture, or within radical political movements. Our experience is isolated, individualized .... This lack of a voice, of

the representation of our subjective reality, means that it is difficult for non-disabled feminists to incorporate our reality into their research and their theories, unless it is in terms of the way the non-disabled world sees us.

Because their difference from other women is inescapable and in most cases can be concealed – if at all – only at formidable cost to their energy and self-esteem, the existence of women with disabilities tests the inclusiveness of feminist theory and its capacity to embrace "difference" in a way that escapes being platitudinous. Initially, feminism does speak to the isolation of the 16 percent of women who have disabilities (Asch and Fine 1988a, 1988b). It repudiates the exclusion that controls their social lives by associating them with many other oppressed women who all are to be enfolded in a freshly empowered group. But having promised group inclusion to women with disabilities, feminism in some of its central manifestations then dismisses them by magnifying themes that deny them standing as women.

By definition, disability is any physical, emotional, or cognitive impairment sufficiently serious to impede performance of one or more major life activities and so to limit function significantly. Either their actual impairments, or the social construction of their disability, result in severe limitations to their lives, restrictions which bar women with disabilities from performing life functions considered customary for women. Elevating what is typical of women into an ideal evokes the "tyranny of the normal" which oppresses people with disabilities (Silvers 1994), thus distancing women with disabilities. Thus, feminist theory that identifies what it is to be a woman with the personal or social roles in which women normally function risks marginalizing those with disabilities so as hardly to acknowledge them as women at all.

For example, women with disabilities fare very poorly on two themes of increasing importance to feminist discussion: grounding womanhood in a distinctive kind of embodiment, and identifying women with a distinctive kind of interpersonal relating. To remedy the general culture's suppression of women, these theories celebrate and elevate personal functions and social roles customarily assigned to or associated with women. They privilege images of how the "normal" woman functions, magnifying these until they become standards of womanhood against which disabled women shrink into invisibility.

Embodiment, dysfunction, and suffering

Embodiment – understood as rooting one's identity in the reality of one's body – is a principle of many feminist philosophies. As a feminist motif, embodiment represents the fact that in patriarchal Western culture women's bodies have functioned as objects that are possessed and controlled by men. Elizabeth Grosz (1994c) comments that "patriarchal oppression ... justifies itself ... by connecting women much more closely than men to the body, and through this identification, restricting women's social and economic roles." Initially, this analysis speaks affectingly to women with disabilities, who disproportionately

331

experience themselves as being the physical objects of other people's abuse and control. According to Gill, Kirschner, and Reis (1994), "abuse is the rule rather than the exception in the lives of disabled girls and women, much of it perpetrated by family members, personal assistants, and employees of institutions who knowing their victims 'need' them, count on the power differential to keep their crimes unreported." As Sandra Lambert (1989) writes: "I pretend to forget how deeply disabled people are hated. I pretend to forget how this is true even within my chosen home, the lesbian and feminist communities. My survival at every level depends on maintaining good relationships with able-bodied people."

More than others, women with disabilities must endure health-care and social-service systems that coerce them into compliant behavior and exploit them as a source of livelihood for the systems' providers. In the "poor law" system from which our social-service institutions evolved, physical or cognitive impairment give the presumption of incompetence, regarding impaired individuals as meriting assistance because socially defective. Despite the lesser expense and greater productivity of developing accessible living venues and workplaces where people with disabilities can function competently. this system prefers segregated arrangements where people with disabilities are physically controlled by and for the advantage of the able-bodied. Categorized both by gender and by impairment as incapable of self-direction, women with disabilities thus are immensely vulnerable to ensnarement by custodial systems which possess and control their bodies.

Like other women, women with disabilities find their knowledge of their bodies distorted and dismissed by the oppressive cognitive authority (Addelson 1983, Hanna and Rogovsky 1991) assumed by medical professionals. Moreover, the anguish of women whose bodies fall away from cultural ideals is as intense for those with disabilities as for others, so liberating feminist analyses such as Susan Bordo's (1993) on the coerciveness of our culture's somatic idealizations are broadly and helpfully applicable. But retaining control over one's own body may not cure one's alienation from it. So some theories exhort women to regain authority over the reality of their corporeal being through heightened awareness of their bodily functions, experienced as embodied sites of distinctively female energy or performance.

However, for many women with disabilities, the principle of elevating the female body as the primary locus of womanhood threatens to make them less than women. For treatments of embodiment rarely confront experiences of bodily suffering, choosing instead to focus on the pleasures occasioned by well-functioning bodies, as Susan Wendell (1989, 1996) points out, detecting here the unabated influence of the masculinist obsession with the perfect body. Extolling embodiment misleads us, she says, by making us think that self-mastery of our bodies and endorsing our bodies by getting our social, political, and cultural positions right make us feel right about our bodies and equally make our bodies feel right. But both physical and emotional impairments can prevent bodies from feeling right.

As a class, women with disabilities fall away from both the patriarchal standard of having control over their sensual bodily functions and the feminist ideal of achieving gratification through the natural responses of their fleshly functions. Some try to disregard their bodily functions to dispel their consciousness of inhibiting limitation, debilitating pain, or frustrating lack of physical mastery. For the physically disabled, Wendell explains, distancing themselves from their dysfunctional bodies is at the same time a necessity and a luxury. Disregarding their bodies is necessary when it is pointless to wait for respite or healing to occur. But ignoring their bodies constitutes a luxury because performing major life functions if one is severely impaired demands constant attentiveness to the states of one's body.

Quality of life and right to life

Reproduction is another area where the sensibilities of disabled women may depart from the norms of feminist perception. The right to determine not only whether to bear a child, but what sort of child to bear, is often thought of as a corollary of the proposition that women have the right to control their bodies. But from a disability perspective, a prejudicial disparity is evident in how and why this right is exercised.

Because the lives of physically and cognitively impaired people typically are seen by the general culture as burdensome not only to themselves but to family, friends, and society as well, it is to avoid their birth that the freedom to abort a pregnancy most often is invoked and least often challenged. Adrienne Asch and Michelle Fine (1988b) believe that feminist activists "exploit the disabled fetus as the good or compelling reason to keep abortion safe, legal and funded." Deborah Kaplan argues (1989) that much of society's thinking about prenatal screening expresses our cultural aversion to disability. This antipathy impels rejection of possibly damaged fetuses, regardless of whether they are likely to be seriously, moderately, or only mildly impaired. After all, aren't normal or perfect persons self-evidently preferable to defective ones?

Morris (1991) writes:

> Arguments about the potential quality of life for a disabled child take place in the context of a society which is generally hostile towards disabled people ... Nondisabled feminists have generally failed to confront the judgments which are an integral part of this debate .... Feminism has let disabled people down by failing to confront these "quality of life" arguments .... Feminism itself is the poorer for this."

Women with disabilities fear that feminism cannot be expected to press for reform of conditions that constrain behaviors in which "normal" women desire to engage. Some (Kaplan 1989, Gill, Kirschner, and Reis 1994, Hershey 1994) suspect that a perceived disconnection from or, even worse, a projected conflict between feminist concerns and issues raised by disability deter the women's movement from addressing the latter. Even more disturbing is the suggestion of outright inequitable inconsistency in the way the women's movement values the lives of women with and without disabilities.

For fear of jeopardizing women's right to self-determine their reproductive activities, the women's movement shrinks from criticizing the practice of nonselecting impaired offspring. But – this time with no concern for compromising reproductive self-determination – it vigorously criticizes the practice of nonselecting female offspring. Yet both practices serve women who cannot bear to bear culturally devalued offspring, and curbing either is, equally, a constraint on reproductive self-determination.

Nor does the women's movement defend the reproductive self-determination of women with disabilities, whom the general culture discourages from bearing and rearing children. They are the most frequent sufferers of surgical sterilization, and the women most frequently challenged for custody of their children. To be a woman with a disability thus is to be distanced from full sisterhood by the alienating recognition that till now feminism has been especially vigorous in defending the right to prevent people like one's self from being born, but exceptionally passive when it comes to defending the right of people like one's self to embody reproductive functions.

Socialization

Census data from 1984 show that women with disabilities have a much lower sociocultural participation rate than their nondisabled and male counterparts. More than half of nondisabled men and women, and disabled men, are employed, but less than half of women with disabilities have employment. They are the group most likely to remain unmarried. Among persons who have married and are not widowed, 12 percent of male nondisabled, 15 percent of female nondisabled, 11 percent of male disabled, but 25 percent of female disabled are divorced or separated (Bureau of the Census 1984). These data show the sociocultural participation rate of women with disabilities descending below the combined straight-line projections of the participation rates of nondisabled women and men with disabilities, thereby suggesting that, combined, the two stigmas have a more than additive negative effect (Deegan and Brooks 1985, Hanna and Rogovsky 1991).

Why is this? Disability impedes women both from performing one or more major life activities and from assuming a woman's social roles. While the former consequence is definitive of disability, the latter is culturally contingent. In antiquity, disability decreased a woman's intrinsic value, but did not necessarily affect her functional value. Herodotus cites with approval a practice he attributes to the Babylonians: namely, that to ensure that the disabled girls also would be married, marriage to the most beautiful girls was auctioned off at high prices as a means of dowering the disabled girls (Garland 1995).

Yet today, as Roberta Galler (1984) points out, disabled women are assumed to be asexual as a consequence of the degree to which they fail to embody the

334

standard of the normal body. Hanna and Rogovsky (1991) found that disability was equated with both unattractiveness and incompetence. From a cultural perspective, modernity has naturalized the magnification of deficit so that physical dysfunction now both signifies and is blamed for social dysfunction. Iris Marion Young (1990b) cites this trope in tracing deficits in women's physical activity to the coercion of a patriarchal social structure which cannot abide to have women manifest full proficiency: "Women in sexist society are physically handicapped. Insofar as we learn to live out our existence in accordance with the definition that patriarchal culture assigns to us, we are physically inhibited, confined, positioned and objectified." As with Bordo's work, this analysis elucidates the condition of women both with and without disabilities.

Attesting to the effects of an analogous trope, the aforementioned Hanna/ Rogovsky (1991) study reveals that even their relatives and friends could not envision disabled women as functional wives and mothers. Addressing the disparity between disabled men and women in respect to marital status, one of their subject's comments: "There is a big difference between a disabled husband and a disabled wife. A disabled husband needs a wife to nurture him, but a disabled wife is not seen by society as capable of nurturing a husband who is not disabled." The researchers conclude: "Women in general, in contrast with men, are typically seen as having nurturing roles in our society. Our interviews suggest that women with physical disabilities are viewed differently .... Rather, they are often seen as incapable of nurturing, indeed, as dependent people who must themselves be nurtured." In a similar vein, Wendell (1996) reports being struck by how women disabled as adults "struggle with shame and loss of self-esteem at being transformed from people who took physical care of others (husbands and children) to people who were physically dependent."

Caregiving

These observations bring us to another feminist theme that magnifies the "normal" woman's role. This is the proposal to make the caregiving traditionally associated with female family members the central model for ethics. One of the most sophisticated proponents of this view is Annette Baier, who charges liberal morality with being unrealistic in its attempt to portray those bound together by moral relationships neutrally. In contrast to the justice ethic, which glorifies the free acceptance of moral duty, Baier (1987b) explains, "the emphasis on care goes with a recognition of the often unchosen nature of responsibilities of those who give care."

Not all feminists venerate caregiving. For example, Janet Finch (1984) writes, it depends "on the substantial and consistent input of women's unpaid labor in the home, whilst at the same time excluding them from the labor market." But for Baier (1987b), caregiving is an inescapable reality, one which women more than men accept. So she urges that "the best moral theory has to harmonize justice and care."

Justice, Baier thinks, presumes an environment in which individuals are similarly powerful or similarly weak. But in most real-world relations there is an asymmetry, rather than an equality or neutrality, of positions. People are always unequal, Baier asserts. because some are vulnerable to others, a permanent or temporary asymmetry of position which morality not only need acknowledge but embrace. Some people are less capable than, and therefore are dependent upon, others who are more capable. And all of us sometimes become vulnerable to others, often at times and in ways we do not choose.

Because women customarily have the social responsibility of caring for the very young, the very old, the ill, and the disabled, theories which render caring as central to social virtue elevate conduct which customarily is theirs. However, women with disabilities belong also to a class whose social role is to receive care rather than give it, and their access to social roles which offer scope for caregiving is diminished. Reviewing *Feminism and Disability* (Hillyer 1993), Karen Hirsch (1994) writes, "In Barbara Hillyer's world all caregivers are women, and a woman is either a caregiver or she is disabled and needs care to be provided for her. Thus, there is no place for the experiences of disabled women."

But morality focused on protecting those seen as deficient too readily lends itself to harming the putatively dependent by requiring them to accept lesser-quality care than they could administer to themselves. For a dependent stance is advantageous only if genuine – that is, if the putative dependent is truly incompetent. So in a system in which caring is the primary way the able-bodied relate to the disabled, it becomes socially incumbent upon the latter to profess incompetence even where they are more competent than the former (Scott 1969). It was not too long ago, remember, when all women were expected to dissemble in this way. to make men more secure in their masculine roles.

Feminists should be mindful that welfarism – the belief that virtue is determined above all by how much one contributes to the well-being of (other) people – is inherently paternalistic because it authorizes distribution of benefits whether or not in conflict with the recipients' wills. Joan Tronto (1993) is among a minority of advocates of ethics of care who acknowledge the power imbalance inherent whenever caregiving thus becomes institutionalized:

> caregivers may well come to see themselves as more capable of assessing the needs of care-receivers than are the care-receivers themselves .... The only solution I see is to insist that care needs to be connected to a theory of justice and to be relentlessly democratic .... What would make care democratic is its focus on needs, and on the balance between care-givers and care-receivers.

But how such a balance could be maintained remains obscure. Tronto sometimes thinks that the solution lies in reconfiguring the relative valuation of dependency and autonomy, so as to elevate the value of dependency and to replace interests with needs as the central consideration in political deliberation. Political rearrangements meant to make dependence more desirable cannot resolve the inherent power imbalance and potential for oppression between caregiver and care receiver. In some personal relations, the reality of this imbalance may be benign. But when depersonalized, abstracted from, and theorized into a vehicle for feminist reform, caring cannot help but be a perilous foundation on which to build an inclusive feminist philosophy.

Martha Minow (1990) suggests that persons with serious disabilities are among the most stubbornly limiting cases in respect to the homogenization of moral personhood. They would then seem to be among the best candidates to be treated adequately by an ethics of care which places deviation rather than homogenization at the core of moral associations. But modeling morality on caring and being cared for renders compliant behavior *obligatory* for persons with disabilities. For them, submissiveness becomes the price of good treatment. We can grasp this consequence by noting that helping relationships are voluntary, but asymmetrically so. Helpgivers choose how they will help, but helptakers cannot choose how they will be helped, for if one's connection to others is as the recipient of help, rejecting others' choice of proffered help leaves one solitary (Silvers 1995).

In a framework of moral relations in which some must make themselves vulnerable so that others can be worthy of their trust – namely, in paternalistic systems where those viewed as incompetent are coerced into compliance "for their own good" – women with disabilities are typecast as subordinate. According to Asch and Fine (1988a), it is for this reason that nondisabled feminists are reluctant to engage with disabled women, namely because they perceive them not as powerful, competent, and appealing females but instead as dependent, passive, and needy (see also Reinelt and Fried 1991).

Morris (1991) writes:

> it is the loss of reciprocity which brings about inequality within a relationship – and disabled and older people are very vulnerable within the unequal relationships which they commonly experience with the non-disabled world .... Very little attention has been paid to disabled and older people's experience of physical and emotional abuse within caring relationships.... Research needs to examine what makes "caring for" in a "caring about" relationship possible in a way which meets the interests of both parties. Many disabled people have clearly identified that "caring for" in a "caring about" relationship cannot work unless there is real choice based on real alternatives.

This is not to say that no disabled people need nor should be given help from others. There are many who do and, as Wendell (1989) reminds us, they are condemned to be devalued in any society which values self-reliance over interdependence. Moreover, nothing argued so far suggests that caring and being cared for must be repressive, for bonds of affection encourage mutual helping, and bonds of respect support reciprocal helping. But as Tronto (1987) notes: "In focusing on the preservation of existing relationships, the perspective of care has a conservative quality." If this is so, substituting the ethics of caring for the ethics of equality entrenches the subordination now suffered upon women with disabilities in virtue of their enduring stigmatization. In sum, as Alison Jaggar (1995a) reminds us,

> Despite the virtue of care thinking, its emphasis on the quality of individual relations seems to preclude its addressing the structural oppositions between the interest of social groups that make caring difficult ... between members of these groups. Similarly, care's reliance on individual efforts to meet individual needs disregards the social structures that make this virtually impossible in many cases.

The tyranny of normalizing female roles

The conviction that women are better served by revaluing, rather than by revising, their customary social roles magnifies the importance of their traditional functions of pleasuring and nurturing. This strategy may be advantageous to women generally because it avoids making them compete with men for roles from which they traditionally have been excluded. Elevating functions that are "normal" for women thus negotiates the difficulties of positing an undifferentiated equality between men and women. But it debars women with disabilities from a womanhood narrowly defined by roles from which they are excluded in virtue of their own limitations or the social construction of their impairments. Thus the strategy of revaluing constituents of paternalistic social systems appears to prolong rather than transcend inequity (cf. Butler 1990).

Not unexpectedly, in their new context these functions, validated by the tyrannical concept of the "normal," simply reimpose the old pattern of subordination on women with disabilities. To itself escape imposing the repression it so often deplores, feminism should cease to conserve and magnify the existing social norms for gendered roles. Instead, feminism should innovatively relocate women to a place where their distinctive social functions and interactions are equally accessible to all who wish to take their place as women.

Is a project with this goal executable by any women, or does pursuing it require the special perspectives that differentiate women with disabilities? This depends on whether the reasons which inform disabled women's choices can be appreciated by any and all other women, for even here there may be no escape from the tyranny of "the normal."

To begin, we should notice that while race, class, and sexuality frequently are acknowledged by feminist theory as causing theoretically significant differences among women, issues of disability and age are not uncommonly dismissed as being inconsequential or so transparent as to need no consideration. That is because age and disability are seen as deformations and therefore as distractions from "universal woman's" essential or central concerns. Caroline Ramazanoglu (1989) typifies this response when she argues that these differences are neither stable nor stubborn enough to warrant much attention. Explaining why her analysis of women's oppression omits disabled and older women, she explains that "while these are crucial areas of oppression for many women, they take different forms in different cultures and so are difficult to generalize about. They are also forms of difference which could be transformed by changes of consciousness."

Let us turn, then, to the question of whether feminism itself can be a source of such a transformation of consciousness. Ordinarily we bond with those who are different from us by imagining what other persons' ambitions in view of their interests and needs *normally* would be were they in my place or I in theirs. But performing major life functions such as moving one's body, seeing, and hearing, is so intimate an element of the fabric of our experience that one cannot accurately imagine how it would be if to live normally were to live otherwise.

What we view as within our reach in the world around us – and thereby what we take as the objects of our ambition – is directly a product of the scope of our functioning. Thus, the very prospect of being seriously impaired may paralyze most women's normalizing imagination so severely as to prohibit their confronting how life is experienced and satisfaction is craved by women with disabilities. And whether or not any and all nondisabled women can learn to understand disabled women well enough to speak for them also is not clear. Wendell (1989) believes that, because fear of suffering and of losing bodily control are so deeply embedded in our culture, as much for women as for men, the disabled usually are debarred from communicating their experiences effectively.

How women with disabilities can be feminists

These considerations indicate that it requires the presence of women with disabilities in women's activities and their voices in theorizing, not merely well-meaning acknowledgement of their existence, to "encourage the satisfaction of personal need and desires through inclusive positive interaction of individuals or groups," the objective that leads Young (1990a) to urge feminists to value disabled women's differences. Analyses of difference like those by Addelson, Bordo, and Young, cited earlier, guide us to common ground. But inclusive positive interaction is difficult to achieve if, as Wendell (1989) suspects, the able-bodied "resist the assimilation of ... disabled people" because "they may *need* someone to carry the burden of the negative body as long as they continue to idealize ... the body." And relatively few disabled women's voices are heard elucidating feminism. As Young might say, the dilemma faced by women with disabilities who wish to be feminists is that the parts of their identity – their identification of themselves as women and also as disabled – are in categorical opposition to each other because nondisabled women – bound by the denials which still permeate our culture – fear making permeable the categorical border between themselves and the disabled.

By extending Wendell's point, we see that whether the disabled remain distanced when feminist values replace paternalistic ideals benchmarks the completeness of the movement's reform. This is because being a woman who has a disability makes one more vulnerable, and therefore more sensitive, to the presence of paternalism. This observation marks an interest common to both the minority and the larger group. For feminists generally as well as for women with

339

disabilities, increasing visibility of the latter within the theoretical framework created by feminists is an important test of whether the movement has sufficiently disentangled itself from paternalism. And so whether women with disabilities can comfortably be feminists turns on their inclusion in the company of feminists, which in turn turns on whether feminist theory reforms our construction of women's personal and social identity as earnestly, as positively, and with as much independence from prevailing social and cultural norms, as it has revolutionized our approach to women's political power.

One reason women want to be feminists is our conviction that feminist theory is powerful enough to liberate us from the negative effects induced by the general culture's gender tyranny. And in their desire to partake in this release, some women with disabilities trace their marginalization within the women's movement to its psychosocial periphery rather than to its conceptual core. They take as regrettable but incidental that feminists operate within, and thereby are subject to the failings of, the general culture. They assume that feminism itself cannot be faulted for failing to overcome base emotions induced by the general culture (Asch and Fine 1988a, 1988b, Hershey 1994). But this defense is puzzling, for it portrays the very same feminism that is forceful enough to liberate its adherents from gender oppression as helpless against similarly repressive reactions to disability.

To the movement's credit, recognition of the significance of overcoming this challenge recently has expanded interest in the possibility of assimilating women with disabilities. In this regard, the strategy of personalizing disability by increasing interaction between women with and without disabilities may seem attractive because feminists stress so often that the personal is the political. But if personal experience is to energize political action and, as well, political organization to shape personal experience, not mere shared acquaintance, however assiduously pursued and nurtured, but a theoretically compelling commonality of experience must be identified. This will be an experiential core approached through discourse liberated from the general culture's assignments of functional female roles and accepting of nontraditional expressions of women's ambitions. If successful, this effort will strengthen feminism's conceptual frame to better support inclusiveness and embrace difference. And it will clarify how women with disabilities can be feminists.

PART VII
ART

34

Aesthetics

CORNELIA KLINGER

"The sins of omission"

The first and most important impetus motivating a feminist engagement with the complex of art and aesthetics is – as has been the case in many other realms of social life – the exclusion of women from participation in the respective sphere of activity: the denial of women's entry into formal and institutional education, training, active practice in the profession, and the continuous discrimination and marginalization that women have had to endure even after the end of their formal exclusion. A second stage in the feminist engagement with art and aesthetics is reached when the considerable accomplishments are made visible that women have attained despite all obstacles, although these achievements have so often been overlooked, forgotten, denied, or overtly suppressed. The discovery of the resistance women have always mounted to all hindrances placed in their way, the (re)discovery of "women worthies," takes place in the fields of art, literary, and music history much in the same way as feminism has begun to dig up the lost memory of women's efforts in the fields of history, science, and so on.

Given the demands for justice and equal participation that the egalitarian-minded women's liberation movement had voiced since the end of the 1960s, it was only logical that women would also demand equality of the sexes in artistic expression, as well as in access to training and securing a job in the artistic and cultural sectors. Women claimed, and, through the discovery of their forgotten and suppressed accomplishments, proved to deserve, full citizenship in the realm of art. Yet, the fact that these just and self-explanatory demands met with so much resistance drew attention to deeper layers of the problem, and thus led to the emergence of the third stage of the feminist engagement with art and aesthetics.

The structural and symbolic background of women's exclusion: the masculinity of aesthetic ideology

A closer investigation into the "sins of omission" leads feminist analysis very soon to the discovery of the *symbolic* mechanisms underlying the exclusion of women: "Arguing that women's marginality manifests itself not simply by the sociological fact of their exclusion from art institutions, but in the very criteria and vocabulary of aesthetic evaluation, feminists have shown that a purportedly universal and transcendent canon is dramatically skewed toward masculine norms" (Felski 1995, p. 433). The subject matter of art and the concept of a philosophical aesthetics are closely bound to the same metaphysical, universalist, and essentialist assumptions of the Western philosophical tradition that appear highly suspect from a feminist perspective in relation to other fields of male-dominated theory formation.

Consider an aesthetic theory which, like Hegel's, affirms the following principle: "The purpose of all art is the identity, brought forth by the spirit, in which eternity, divinity and truth is revealed to our perception, to our mind and imagination, in material appearance and form" (Hegel 1970, p. 572). Such a principle presupposes a concept of man, of human essence, that is endowed with transhistorically and transculturally valid criteria of perception, representation, and taste, as well as with universal judgment, that is, a type of aesthetic reason. In the same vein as the capacity for reason has been denied to women in the Western tradition, thus rendering their participation in the status of being human peripheral and precarious, women have also been considered incapable of this specific aesthetic rationality, unable to exercise aesthetic judgment. That the supposedly gender-neutral "human" carries specifically masculine traits is true not only of the "man of reason" in general, but also of the subject of aesthetic judgment in particular.

Even more emphatically masculine than the traits of the viewer of art are the qualities of the producer of art. The idea of the artist as genius contains a marked intensification of the belief in the subject's sovereignty, autonomy, and creativity. As a consequence, this implies that the masculine characteristics bound to this traditional conception of the subject are heightened and the opposition to the feminine is sharpened: "the pervasively androcentric metaphors and myths of creativity ... have defined 'women' and 'artist' as mutually exclusive terms. ... From Romanticism to modernism and postmodernism, the figure of the artist has become closely identified with an ideal of transgressive masculinity, while women have been seen as at best capable of reproduction and imitation" (Felski 1995, p. 432). Taken together, these three components – the philosophical expectation that art is or reveals eternal truth, and the concepts of a universal aesthetic judgment in the recipient and genius in the producer of art – form the core of what can be called "aesthetic ideology." Numerous feminist critiques that examine how its masculinist characteristics devalue femininity and discriminate against women have emerged over the last two decades.

But indeed, the questioning of this "aesthetic ideology" began long before and outside the practice of feminist criticism. Above all, the revolution that the arts experienced in the first quarter of the twentieth century and that led to a specifically modern idiom in the arts, a specifically aesthetic modernism, contributed greatly to the decline of the traditional concept of aesthetics:

– A new, revolutionary art and literature take shape, which not only originate new ways of perceiving, feeling, and imagining, but which also endeavor to pave the way for a new social order. Art and literature begin to retreat from a

344

universal and transhistorical ideal of truth and beauty, and develop a new and different relation to time and reality. In the term "avant-garde," the concepts of an art that engages with reality and of an art that plays the role of the vanguard of the future are united;

– Along with this orientation toward the future, and the social and political situating of the artist and of the work of art, the position of the viewer and of the perception of art change as well. The concept of disinterested pleasure loses significance, and the normative elements of the category of taste are subjected to a critique which detects its ideological aspects;

– Many artists in the course of the twentieth century have dealt ironically, critically, parodically with the myth of genius and have derided the idea of the godlike creativity of the artist. The deconstruction of the cult of genius has taken many forms. and is a major issue in the artists' grappling with their professional identity.

Not only the practice of art but also aesthetic theory has, despite all the differences among its various approaches, worked toward the dismantling of aesthetic ideology. In particular, the development of analytic aesthetics around the middle of the century contributed heavily to its demise as this approach brought to the fore a nonessentialist concept of knowledge that was oriented toward the empirical sciences, thus leaving behind the idealist philosophical tradition. Still more radically, a postmodern aesthetic theory began to distance itself from the classical assumptions:

> In refusing to assign representations to an author or a controlling producer, they [postmodern tendencies in aesthetic theory, C.K.] explain texts by means of an intertextual series of traces, echoes of echoes, which preclude any idea of a singular or decidable origin. ... This not only dissolves the notion of a creative or originary source, but also problematizes the presumption of a pregiven unity attributed to the text or artwork, which is now seen more as a fragment within a history and context of other fragments.   (Grosz, 1994a, p. 140)

What holds true for the production side of art is also valid for the reception of art:

> The open-endedness or indeterminacy of texts means that not only are they prised free of their (authorial/artistic) origins and the intentions of the singular creator, but perhaps even more radically, that they are also freed from any determinate reception: any fixed body of receivers, any audience constitutes simply an inter- prétative moment in the "life" or survival of any text or artwork; reception is a provisional arrival of a text, always potentially divertable, ... always potentially reversible by the next interpretation or use.   (Grosz 1994a: 144)

However, in spite of all the challenges, deconstructions, and ironizations, it cannot be overlooked that substantial elements of the traditional aesthetic ideo- logy still persist in artistic practice and aesthetic theory throughout the twentieth century: "First of all, it is rarely questioned that art's value transcends cultural

345

differences and is a source of timeless and everlasting value" (Brand and Korsmeyer 1995, p. 6). Second, with regard to the reception of art, the idea of aesthetic judgment, as well as all other traditional characteristics of competent art criticism, prevail. Third, little has changed in the image of the artist as an exception to the norm of the bourgeois way of life. Even if he is not perceived as a genius, he appears at least as a revered and privileged outsider, a visionary of an "other" reality. And even those aesthetic theories that have distanced themselves sharply from the tradition of idealistic aesthetic ideology, like analytical theory, remain more closely bound to it than one may have at first expected: "if analytic aesthetics developed by challenging romantic essentialism and expressionism, it did not altogether rid itself of romantic tenets, such as the uniqueness, gratuitousness and autonomy of works of art" (Shusterman 1989, p. 5).

Insofar as twentieth-century aesthetic theory and practice have by no means completed the process of overthrowing the classical idealist aesthetics, it comes as no surprise that the masculinist traits of aesthetic ideology are still in place. The masculinism that continues to pervade artistic and literary activities today can be read as an index for the incomplete victory of modern art and aesthetics over the remnants of the obsolete aesthetic ideology. And although a feminist critique of aesthetic ideology shows many similarities with other critical perspectives, none of the post-classical art forms or theories have contributed to the dismantling of the masculinist assumptions of the aesthetic tradition, nor have they acknowledged the contribution of feminist approaches to the critique of aesthetic ideology.

On the contrary, the aesthetic avant-garde of the early twentieth century was notorious for an extreme masculinism, despite its declared opposition to the aesthetic ideology. It broke with neither the privileging of the masculine inherent in aesthetic ideology, nor with the exclusion of the feminine. In fact, it intensified both significantly. This tendency can, for example, be traced in the core categories of aesthetics, namely the beautiful and the sublime. The category of the beautiful, which traditionally was perceived as the first and foremost principle of art and aesthetics, was always closely associated with femininity. But for a long time the category of the beautiful has been on the wane as a founding principle of aesthetics; it is increasingly shut out from the realm of serious art and art theory, and relegated to the fields of advertising and design. Whereas the beautiful has been completely eclipsed, the once marginal category of the sublime has come to the fore of aesthetic theory and practice in the course of the twentieth century. And well into the twentieth century the category of the sublime carries with it clearly masculine overtones. In the works of, for example, the abstract expressionist Barnett Newman, one can see that the explicitly masculine characteristic of the sublime has not diminished in the least.

It is precisely at this point – the privileging of the category of the sublime along with its specific masculinism – that a red thread can be traced from the avant-garde to the postmodern theory of the immediate present. It is not without irony that, of all people, Jean-François Lyotard, who has won a reputation in initiating and establishing the concept of postmodernism, remains bound to an explicitly modernist aesthetic, or more specifically, an avant-garde aesthetic, because of his particular interest in the sublime (Lyotard, 1989). Although the concept of the avant-garde has been dismantled from many sides, a postmodern theorist like Lyotard firmly professes his faith to the avant-garde, especially to its masculine aspects.

Even more vigorous than Lyotard's postmodern pledge of faith to the avant-garde is that of German philosopher Wolfgang Welsch: "The congruence of postmodernism and 'hard' modernism may still seem surprising today; tomorrow this will be self-evident" (Welsch 1987, p. 201). The affinity between the postmodern and the avant-garde, and the pronounced, "hard" masculinism that acts as a connecting link between them have not, however, remained unnoticed and uncriticized (Tagg 1989, p. 3).

The refined and intensified analysis of the symbolic dimension of gender hierarchy in general and of the masculinist elements at work in aesthetic theory and practice in particular, have shown that earlier hopes of a straightforward integration of women into the fields of art and literature were naive. The more radically the aesthetic ideology is subjected to a feminist critique, the further away the possibility of an easy dismantling of the exclusion of and discrimination against women in art seems. And the more aware women become of the fact that "the articulation of my sex is impossible in discourse, and for structural, eidetic reasons" (Irigaray 1985, p. 149) the more a search for an exclusively female form of expression that is completely independent of the male symbolic order suggests itself.

From the feminist insight into the masculine character and male bias of the aesthetic tradition inevitably arises the reverse question of and quest for a "feminine aesthetic."

The unavoidable conclusion: is there a "feminine aesthetic"?

This next step that ensues from the feminist critique of art and its institutions is in keeping with the development that the feminist approach takes in other disciplines. The question of a feminine aesthetic, a feminine art, an *écriture féminine*, corresponds with the question of a feminine ethic, a feminine epistemology, a feminine science, etc. These questions arise in the process of transition from an egalitarian or "humanist" feminism to a gynocentric direction that occurred during the 1970s. In this latter perspective the idea of an ontologically founded duality of the sexes overrules the vision of a genderneutral, universal humanity beyond sex and its differences.

The positive answers to the question of whether there is a "feminine aesthetic" in art and literature differ significantly from each other. Rita Felski differentiates two directions the gynocentric, or feminine, aesthetic may take:

– first, the counter-proposition of a feminine concept of genius and canon, as, for example, developed by Christine Battersby (Battersby 1989);

347

– second, a type of feminist populism according to which "any appeal to artistic value is read as symptomatic of an elitist and patriarchal world view" (Felski 1995, p. 434).

While the former approach attempts to reconstruct the tenets of aesthetic ideology from a feminine/feminist perspective in order to apply them to theorize women's artistic and literary activity, the latter seeks to reject aesthetic ideology radically:

> The list of abandoned problems includes the characterization of aesthetic "disinterest," the distinction between various art forms, as well as differences between craft and art, high art and popular art, useful and decorative arts, the sublime and the beautiful, originality, and many puzzles that have to do with the cognitive versus the affective character of aesthetic experience.   (Hein 1995, p. 455)

Actually, all the critical arguments against aesthetic ideology brought forth earlier by the avant-garde and aesthetic modernism are reformulated in a feminist perspective. The argument is directed at the universalist expectation that art is or reveals truth, at the cult of genius, at the position of the disinterested (sublimating) spectator, at the concept of good taste, at the separation of art from "life" and nature, at maintaining a hierarchy of aesthetic categories according to the criteria of their distance from the sphere of sensuousness and use, etc. In addition to these critical trends, the attempt is made to derive positive, alternative aesthetic categories from woman's nature and essence, and/or from specific historical, cultural, and social experiences of women: "Enthusiasm ran high that something like a woman's art or a feminine sensibility could be discerned" (Brand and Korsmeyer 1995, p. 11). It goes without saying that the aesthetic categories derived from femininity in all aspects appeared to be the reverse of the traditional male-oriented aesthetic ideology.

Critiques of the concept of the "feminine aesthetic"

Just as feminist essentialism has come under critical scrutiny from postcolonial and deconstructive perspectives since the late 1980s, the idea of a "feminine aesthetic" has also been subjected to a variety of criticisms. Most arguments center on the universalist, ontologically founded and therefore normative term, "feminine." Many critics protest that the characteristics ascribed to the feminine by gynocentric feminists only reproduce traditional – masculine – clichés. The attempt to provide the feminine aesthetic with an historical foundation, an origin that is often searched for in a prehistoric matriarchy, is shown to be directed more toward a fictitious past than toward radical transformation. And a definition of woman based on the body identifies woman with nature and hence reduces her to nature. The archetypal attributes of feminine identity deduced from this perspective base the feminine aesthetic on a few bodily, body-like elements ("cunt art," in the intentionally provocative words of Judy Chicago and Miriam Schapiro (1973)). Many critics object to "the image of a woman's art that relies on the worn out myth of woman's natural potential, resulting in a uterus-art of gurgling amniotic fluid, of guttural lullabies and fundamentally benevolent knitting patterns" (Sichtermann 1987, p. 68). Such disapproval has issued not only from feminists and feminist critics, but also – and especially – from women artists, writers, and composers. Many, if not most, of them have refused to be identified with or restricted to a "feminine aesthetic. "

In fact, the aesthetic productions of women are highly various, and they follow the traditions, schools, directions, and conventions in which the artists are socialized and with which they identify, rather than a common understanding of femininity that is imposed upon them. The objection that has often been articulated over the past years – that the feminist essentialism which underlies the concept of a "feminine" worldview and thinking cannot do justice to the entire range of women's experiences – has also made its mark in the realm of aesthetics.

Both versions of a "feminine aesthetic" have come under attack. On the one hand, those efforts to reformulate specific concepts, categories, and values of the traditional aesthetic ideology from a feminist perspective are rejected. Its critics argue that such attempts simply repeat the old positions and their problems under a new rubric. In substituting the idea of feminine creativity or a female genius for masculine creativity and a male genius, the dualism of the One and the Other is reproduced. Thus, we fall victim precisely to the structure that we should criticize and leave behind: "The suggestion that women embrace the notion of a separate women's discourse, women's art, feminist aesthetics, is ... untenable. It simply inverts and thereby valorizes the oppositional dichotomy that has denied women and their projects as other" (Waugh 1995, p. 412). On the other hand, the radical, "populist" version of a "feminine aesthetic" with its complete rejection of all elements of the aesthetic ideology runs counter to many conventions of institutionalized art and literature which explicitly or implicitly still draw upon this heritage. A radical departure from this legacy on the part of women therefore entails the problem of women's self-marginalization in the enterprise of art. Insofar as the residues of the aesthetic ideology continue to govern the institutions, market and business of art and culture, the gesture of radical refusal simply strengthens the existent tendencies that exclude and isolate women.

For these and other reasons, the majority of women artists and critics have arrived at the conclusion: "There is no single, totalizing feminist aesthetic theory and none is sought" (Hein 1995, p. 455).

The "feminine aesthetic" in historical perspective

Despite a few dispersed oppositional voices, in the 1990s, we find ourselves "*beyond feminist aesthetics*" (Felski 1989) or rather, "*beyond feminine aesthetics.*" In other words, we have reached a point when an essentialist way of thinking in feminism is definitely passé. But, at the same time, we are at this point far enough *beyond the critique* of "feminine aesthetic," and given the distance that

349

separates us from the essentialist gynocentric position, we can find the freedom to take a fresh look at this whole complex.

First, every thesis about women's writing, thought, and creativity voiced by gynocentric theorists, artists, and writers does not have to be taken up as a statement of truth about all real women, at all times in history and in every culture on earth. In some respects, the essentialist position was actually more provocative and polemical, more rhetorically intended, than it may appear at first glance. Second, we must remember that such provocation produced real effects:

> While the idea of a categoric women's art may be philosophically dubious, it was a valuable creative principle for the historical Feminist Art movement, which drew in its early stages upon a form of female essentialism – a belief in the unitary reality of the category female – as its source of artistic inspiration ... right or wrong it was an enabling myth.   (Broude and Garrard 1994, p. 28)

What was, or would have been, undoubtedly misguided as an authentic expression of a universal feminine essence, did, in fact, possess a certain sense and significance as an aesthetic and theoretical expression of a social and political movement during a specific period. Its historical and conceptual limitations should not make us blind to the value and effect that it had within these confines. Finally, we must not forget that the essentialist emphasis on sexual/ gender difference undoubtedly meant a certain progress compared to the naive egalitarianism of the preceding phase in the development of feminism, as it was grounded on a deeper understanding of the symbolic mechanisms of asymmetry between the sexes. While the representatives of the egalitarian position of the 1970s were convinced that "the only aesthetic freedom worth fighting for is the freedom to do the same" (Mainardi in Broude and Garrard 1994, p. 23), the proponents of the difference position recognized that not only legal, social, political, and economic obstacles bar the way to justice in gender relations. It was from the gynocentric perspective of difference that the philosophical and symbolic dimensions of the problem were brought into the debate. When we look at essentialism in this way, we can regard it as a vital intermediate step on the way toward the discovery of the gender axis in the coordinates of the social and symbolic order.

Feminist aesthetics after the departure from the concept of the feminine

How can a feminist aesthetic be defined, what are the topics, tasks, aims, and perspectives of the feminist encounter with art and aesthetics? These questions win new meaning and importance after we have come to see that it is neither enough to reconceive aesthetic categories like genius, creativity, and the sublime from a feminine point of view nor to radically challenge and renounce the aesthetic ideology in the name of absolute feminine otherness.

From the 1980s, the emphasis shifted from the search for a specifically feminine in aesthetics to the analysis of the manifold aesthetic aspects of the existing gender system. This project takes shape within the context of the post-structuralist theories of the era. The core assumption here is the notion that reality in all its aspects is an effect produced by complex historical and cultural processes. From this perspective, all social relationships are denaturalized. There is a growing awareness that even the most apparently "natural" forms of life, like the family, or the ways in which the relations between the sexes and generations are organized, and in the last instance even the human body, sexuality, and sex, are constructs created by society. As a result of this new awareness, critical attention turns to the specific rules and mechanisms according to which these constructs function. From semiotics comes the important insight that "meanings are not innate or given in the nature of things. Meaning is an effect, produced by signs" (Pollock 1992, p. 27). In the first place this statement refers to the production of meaning by *linguistic* signs. But it can be and, in fact, must be extended to the realm of aesthetic sign production in general. Only when the entire spectrum of symbolic production is subjected to a feminist consideration will we reach a thorough understanding of the constructedness of gender and sex.

These reflections correspond to a change in the concepts of art and literature: they not only depict a given existing world, but they also play an active part in the construction of that world. In other words, they help create reality in all its aspects by providing schemes and patterns of perception. This is the underlying cause of the recent and noticeably growing interest in the notion and theory of representation, with its dual position between aesthetics and politics: "This enquiry into the relations between representation, ideology and the subject has proved extremely productive for feminists and for feminist artists" (Iversen 1991, p. 86).

The mechanisms of representation, the production of linguistic and aesthetic signs, play a significant role in the constitution of social systems in general, but they exert a particularly important influence on the social ordering of gender and sex. It is precisely in the constitution of gender identity, gender difference, and gender hierarchy that aesthetic categories play a central role. The sex/gender difference finds its expression in dualisms like visible–invisible, or in the categories of the look, the "droit du regard," or the "male gaze." Sex and gender difference is even translated into the language of aesthetics, as for example in the identification of sublimity/dignity with masculinity on the one side, and beauty/charm with femininity on the other. While the identification of masculinity with the sublime and with dignity remains relatively loose, the aesthetic categorization of feminine identity is firmly set. The feminine connotations of beauty make the "fair sex" the aesthetic sex in general, thereby subjecting woman to a certain male control.

The analysis and critique of the aesthetic aspects of the sex/gender system can be seen as the genuine and most important object of study by feminist aesthetics today. But the analysis of the aesthetic components of the sex/gender system

351

does not only take place in and through theory; it also occurs in the artistic production of women. The work of Cindy Sherman and Barbara Kruger serve as frequently cited examples of this form of critique: "The production of such art is at once a theoretical and a confrontational act, literally an intervention in the socially produced gender system. It calls attention to that system, displays it in detail and renders it intelligible" (Hein 1995, p. 452).

In this sense, feminist aesthetics and the art it inspires are political. This is already apparent in the fact that its historical development correlates closely with the various stages of development in the women's movement and in feminism. The political character of the feminist aesthetic and art differs substantially from the concept of engaged art and literature formulated by the avant-garde during the first quarter of the century. Feminist critics and artists for the most part do not subscribe to the avant-garde belief in a future utopia of universal emancipation, or in the belief that art is the forerunner of and pathbreaker to a liberated society. It is likely that representatives of a feminist aesthetic would tend to stand closer to Roland Barthes's post-avant-garde position: "The forces of freedom which are in literature depend not on the writer's civil person, nor on his political commitment ... nor do they even depend on the doctrinal content of his work, but rather on the labor of displacement he brings to bear upon the language" (Barthes 1982, p. 462). At the end of the 1990s, however, also the potential of such aesthetic displacement to change consciousness is regarded more skeptically. The formal aesthetic advances of art are today no longer equated with progress in the social or political sense. Permanent transgression has been incorporated too fully into the business of aesthetics for such a belief anymore. The role that art and aesthetics can play as the foundation for individual and social change of consciousness now appears more questionable than ever before.

In other words, the political character of feminist aesthetics develops less on the level of a vision for a better future than in accordance with the analysis and critique of a sex/gender system that comes from a long tradition and still prevails today. It would, however, be a misunderstanding to believe that feminist aesthetics obliges its adherents to a particular aesthetic or political program. It is not expected that every producer or receiver of art makes it her task to critique and analyze the sex/gender system. Instead, the available achievements of feminist aesthetics allow women the possibility to begin their own new artistic projects on the basis of a critical reflection on their historical, cultural, and social conditions.

35

Film theory

CYNTHIA FREELAND

Feminist philosophy of film is a young field that is rapidly growing but that has as yet no distinct disciplinary presence within philosophy. Articles by feminist philosophers on film began appearing in aesthetics journals and anthologies in English only in the late 1980s and 1990s. In film studies, as in aesthetics more generally, disciplinary boundaries are fluid. Writers from many fields – literature, art, communications, cultural studies – make critical contributions on film, addressing philosophical issues and drawing upon philosophical theories. Many questions discussed in the general field of film theory are philosophical ones, and among these are topics important for feminist philosophy and aesthetics: Is film an art, and if so why? What is the essence of film? How does film depict subjectivity? What is the nature of our emotional reactions to and interest in film? How is the photographic nature of film used in constructing realistic or other forms of representations of the world? How is ideology at work in the Hollywood production system and in the circulation of filmic images in the popular culture industry? It would be not only difficult, but arbitrary and misleading, to restrict the label or practice of "feminist philosophy of film" to professional philosophers. It is best to approach this subject, then, by situating it in relation to other fields, including feminist film theory, film theory in general, philosophical work on film, and feminist aesthetics. Feminist philosophy of film is rapidly expanding as philosophers with diverse interests turn their attention to film. The inclusion of feminist essays by philosophers in two anthologies on film in the mid-1990s (Freeland and Wartenberg 1995, Bordwell and Carroll 1996), together with the appearance of the first issue of the journal *Film and Philosophy*, suggest that this field is on the brink of a period of rapid growth and change. I will discuss possible new directions of growth, and connections with feminist philosophy broadly considered in the conclusion.

Feminist film theory

Feminist film theory is recent, dating from the 1970s, but it has become a large and complex field (for an overview, see Erens 1990). In the early days of the women's movement, critics focused on filmic "images of women" in studies that examined how women were depicted in films – as, for example, either mothers or whores (Haskell 1974). This approach waned, however, following publication of

Laura Mulvey's essay "Visual pleasure and narrative cinema" (Mulvey 1975). In this essay Mulvey utilized Lacanian psychoanalysis and semiotics to construct an account of the gendered nature of visual pleasure in traditional Hollywood narrative cinema. Briefly, she argued that traditional cinema presupposes a male viewer to whom it offers visual pleasure that can be explained in terms of unconscious processes of voyeurism and fetishism. The female body is displayed as a "bearer not maker of meaning" before the intense gaze of the male watcher. In a movie like Hitchcock's *Vertigo*, the female body is fetishized and displayed before the camera and viewer's eyes as beautiful and perfect. However, this fetishized image continually threatens to open up and reveal what it is hiding, the female's castrated body. To overcome this threat of castration the viewer must shift from visual pleasure to intellectual identification with the male protagonist who carries forward the narrative to some resolution. Thus in surrogate he "owns" the woman, and the links are reinforced between maleness and activity and femaleness and passivity.

Mulvey's work has been enormously influential. Often reprinted, it is also frequently cited, not just within feminist film theory but more generally in discussions of television, painting, photography, and advertising. Mulvey's essay both suggested avenues for further research and also raised some obvious questions, and so it immediately prompted a wide variety of further articles and books. This work ranged from studies of particular filmmakers (Sirk, Hitchcock, Fassbinder) and genres (horror, pornography, melodrama), to criticisms of the basic framework and its problems, such as her apparent inability to account for male masochism, female visual pleasures, or differences of race, class, or sexual preference among women viewers (see Erens 1990). Despite the fact that it has been much criticized and she has herself revised it (Mulvey 1990), in some ways Mulvey's framing of basic categories for discussion and analysis remains dominant in the field, since many film theorists still share a common view that the main task of feminist film theory is to account for aspects of gender in relation to visual pleasure. Major recent books continue to assume a psychoanalytic framework. For example, Kaja Silverman's *Male Subjectivity at the Margins* begins with the claim, "The starting point for virtually every formulation this book will propose is the assumption that lack of being is the irreducible condition of subjectivity" (Silverman 1992, p. 4). As recently as 1990 the feminist film journal *Camera Obscura* devoted a double issue to considerations of the "spectatrix."

The philosophical basis for Mulvey's essay and the tradition it launched is a distinctively continental blend combining elements of Althusserian Marxism, semiotics, and Lacanian psychoanalytic theory (which can be called philosophical due to its theses about the self, symbolic representation, desire, etc.). Film theory in general, and feminist film theory in particular, have been constructed to a great extent in France, and so this type of theoretical influence from continental philosophical theories should not be surprising. Recently, however, this dominant emphasis within film theory has come under attack from analytic philosophers. These attacks have clear relevance for mainstream approaches to feminist film theory. At stake are such questions as whether film studies needs theory and how theory should be construed in this realm. Attacks by philosophers trained in traditional aesthetics reflect a split or "schism" between Anglo-American philosophical aesthetics and the academic field of film theory (Plantinga 1993). From the standpoint of philosophers, film theorists are overly tempted by universalizing Theory with a capital "T" ; they lack rigorous analysis from well-argued foundations; and they are more interested in reaching viable political conclusions than in logic or empirical evidence. On the other hand, film theorists reply by noting that philosophical aestheticians are relatively uninterested in film as an evolving historical force or social technology that interacts with culture in general; and they are inattentive to film's political role and impact. As philosophers of film follow up on implications of these philosophical critiques for feminist film theory, they may find themselves torn. On the one hand, the criticisms do apply to aspects of feminist film theory; but on the other hand, philosophers are likely to share film theorists' general interest in connecting film to history, politics, and culture. Feminist philosophers share film theory's desire for a more historically positioned account of film, one that is in tune with feminism's broad political goals.

Philosopher's attacks on film theory and their proposed alternatives have clear relevance for feminist film theory, and so it is important to look at some key points raised in these recent disputes, and in particular at work by philosopher Noel Carroll, who concludes that film theory "has been nothing short of an intellectual disaster and should be discarded" (Carroll 1988, p. 26). Film theory is problematic, Carroll argues, because it relies excessively on complex theoretical jargon, and it exploits puns or metaphors that purport to uncover real, but actually magical or unempirically validated links between essence and outcome. Further, film theorists regularly invoke, without defending or considering alternatives to, other theories – psychoanalysis, Althusserian Marxism, and structuralist semiotics – that themselves lack evidence; and they cite as explanations entities that are themselves nebulous and vague such as "desire," "absence," "the imaginary," "subject positioning," etc. A central target of Carroll's criticisms is that "Theory" as used in film theory is "top-down," or totalizing. Carroll recommends instead a more piecemeal or particularist approach that will aim to construct smaller theories of particular genres or aspects of film production and ontology. In his essay "The image of women in film: a defense of a paradigm" (Carroll 1990), Carroll applies these same criticisms to Mulvey's reliance upon psychoanalytic theory. Mulvey's approach was problematic because she did not consider alternative accounts of the emotions and pleasure, relying simply on an available, but heavily contested, "science" – psychoanalysis. Carroll points out obvious counter-examples to Mulvey's general claims, such as the fact that male movie stars from Valentino to Stallone have been presented as visual objects to be ogled in films, and that women like Katharine Hepburn and Rosalind Russell were often "doers" in Hollywood movies. Carroll defends the older "images of women approach," and he suggests it can gain a requisite amount of theoretical unity from an alternative, more cognitivist, philosophical account of the

355

emotions. On this account, emotional behavior is learned from "paradigm scenarios" that may reinforce sexist standards for behavior and appraisal, and films may provide one source of such scenarios – and a corresponding target for feminist critiques.

Other philosophers agree with Carroll's general line of thought and seem to accept his proposal for a more "piecemeal" approach to theorizing about film. Accordingly they have also pursued alternative, more cognitive, strategies of feminist theorizing on film. For example, Laurie Shrage (1990a) argues that a concentration on film texts leads to unfortunate universalizing of psychological subjects who view films and an overemphasis on reader/viewers' passivity. Shrage proposes a "contextual" approach that recognizes considerable variation among an audience's "cinematic habits." As a modification of Mulvey-type feminist film theory, Shrage argues that we ought to "regard the absence, passivity, or treacherousness of the female gaze, not as the inevitable product of global patriarchy, but as a local variant inscribed in the viewing habits of Euro-American audiences and in certain films themselves" (Shrage 1990a, p. 142). In keeping with this proposal Shrage offers her own reading of a potential "liberatory cultural politics" in the 1933 film *Christopher Strong*.

Others also explore a "piecemeal" approach by examining particular film genres. For example, another approach to films in the general category of melodrama, traditionally regarded as a "woman's genre," is offered by Flo Leibowitz (1996). She utilizes a rhetorical and cognitive approach, rather than a psychodynamic approach founded in the scientifically problematic kind of psychoanalytic theory that is typically unquestioned in feminist film studies. Leibowitz's recommended alternative emphasizes that emotions are cognitive and "not intrinsically irrational." She applies this kind of cognitive model to an analysis of processes of audience identification with certain forms of melodrama, including, for example, *The Piano*. Focusing on a rather different genre, horror, which has itself been much studied, and much criticized, by feminists who regard it as quintessentially misogynistic, I have also criticized psychoanalytic and psychodynamic assumptions that are dominant in feminist film theorizing (Freeland 1996). I suggest an alternative approach that focuses on horror films' gender ideologies, and that finds surprising possibilities for disruptive and subversive readings of this especially experimental and participatory genre.

It should be mentioned, however, that some philosophers and other scholars do make interesting use of alternative versions of French feminist/psychoanalytic theorizing in constructing readings of individual genres or films. For example, Nickolas Pappas (1995) draws upon Luce Irigaray's theories about the exchange of women in patriarchy to construct critical readings of the "new film noir" movies such as *Fatal Attraction* and *Sea of Love*. Kelly Oliver (1995) uses Irigaray's account of motherhood to construct a critique of what she calls the Hegelian ideology of women and "natural" relations among them in Ingmar Bergman's *Persona*.

Another important contribution made by philosophers writing about film is to question the philosophical and theoretical goals of feminist film theory as theory (and with them, of film theory more generally). This is in accord with recommendations of recent writers in feminist aesthetics, such as Hilde Hein, who argues that feminist theory in general can learn from aesthetic theory:

> Feminist aesthetic theory serves both as a model and a point of departure for feminist theory more broadly understood. Clearly addressed to the works of art and phenomena that are its data, there is no question that feminist aesthetic theory is experientially grounded. And open to the new data that are constantly proposed to it, feminist aesthetic theory has no alternative but to be a "musing on the circumference." (Hein 1990, p. 286)

Karen Hanson (1995) offers another general attack on film theory. She recommends an alternative approach that does not construct totalizing theory or regard criticism as itself atheoretical. Hanson asks bluntly, "Serious film study often takes the form of theory. Is there any reason why this should be so?" (Hanson 1995, p. 33). She criticizes film theorists who argue that their discipline should aim at the status of *science*. Film *theory* sets itself up as superior or foundational to film *criticism*; supposedly, as a *science* film theory offers greater objectivity, truth, systematicity, and explanatory power. But, Hanson points out, film theorists naively invoke many concepts that philosophers of science regard as quite contested – concepts such as explanation, justification, and systematicity. And there does not even seem to be any operational agreement within the discipline for what will count as evidence, testing, or confirmation of a theory. Instead of trying to make the study of film rational through a sort of reductive unifying drive for artificial systematicity, Hanson suggests that understanding may result from looking at the particularity of film, from the inside. She cites as philosophical support passages about rational inquiry from the pragmatist philosophers, for example William James's discussion in his essay "The sentiment of rationality" of a "sister passion" that accompanies broad theoretic goals: this is the passion for "specificity, detail, distinctions, a clarity of cognition unrelated to theoryconstruction" (Hanson 1995, p. 45). Hanson refers to Stanley Cavell as an example of someone who offers deeply theoretical and philosophical readings by exploring films individually and attentively.

Cavell's writings must be mentioned in any discussion of philosophical writing about film. While they certainly do attend to gender issues in complex ways, whether they should be labeled feminist is a matter for debate. In *Pursuits of Happiness* Cavell (1981) describes the active women, and the spectacle of the passive male body, in the 1930s and 1940s film genre he calls "the comedy of remarriage". These kinds of observations count against some of the universalizing claims made in Mulvey's essay; Cavell points out how male actors are often portrayed as objects to be desired by female stars and presumably by the viewing audience as well. However, on the other hand Cavell appears to endorse what he reads as these films' assertions that male characters must become passive in order to "free" or "teach" women how to acknowledge and express their own desires. Again, in writing about the "melodrama of the unknown woman,"

Cavell (1987) seems concerned to valorize both an often-criticized genre and to emphasize the significance of women's roles in these films. He writes, "[F]ilm ... is from first to last more interested in the study of individual women than of individual men ... . Men are, one could say, of interest to it in crowds and in mutual conflict, but it is women that bequeath psychic depth to film's interests" (Cavell 1987, p. 29).

Cavell's work is not without problems for feminists, who have disagreed about its usefulness for philosophical reflection about gender roles, sexual relations, or the social values reflected in marriage. Clearly his work does offer a springboard for philosophical critiques of the specific kinds of assumptions about subjectivity and pleasure that are still dominant in the Mulvey tradition of feminist film theorizing. This has been done, for example, by Naomi Scheman (1988). Nevertheless, Scheman also is critical of Cavell, questioning, for example, his inattention to the absence of links in the remarriage comedies between mothers and daughters. Scheman contends that both the genres Cavell has focused on, remarriage comedies and melodramas of the unknown woman reflect a feminine but not feminist gaze. The gaze in each case is problematic because it can be "conscripted" by a masculinist world. This occurs in remarriage comedies through a positive identification of women (heroines) with men (their fathers), allowing only "a dubious legacy of female self-realization" (Scheman 1988, p. 75). It occurs in melodramas through setting up unresolvable tensions between the mother–daughter bond and heterosexual love. Scheman proceeds to locate a search for more promising forms of female subjectivity in film, to recent broader critiques within feminist epistemology of the "specular economy of patriarchy" (Scheman 1988, p. 88).

Feminist aesthetics and feminist approaches to film

The past twenty or thirty years have seen important recent developments in feminist aesthetics, tied in complex ways to developments of feminist art and feminist art history [see Article 34, AESTHETICS]. Certain kinds of practices in say, painting of the 1970s, and consequent discussions about the relevance and problematics of essentialist imagery in women's art, have not been so prominent in the field of film studies, although there have been interesting debates about whether avant-garde feminist film practices are progressive, or elitist and problematic (see Erens 1990). Just as feminist musicologists and art historians have examined construction of a canon of great artists, so also some of this same work has been done in film studies. This involves reconsidering the work of women in film as directors, writers, etc., or by valorizing women's films that depict women and their everyday lives, such as Chantal Akerman's *Jeanne Dielman* (1975), "a film about the routine daily activities of a Belgian middle-class and middle-aged housewife, and a film where the pre-aesthetic is already fully aesthetic" (de Lauretis 1987b, p. 131). Writers in film theory, as in aesthetics, also often raise questions about distinctions between "high" and "low" art forms along gendered lines. It is likely that film studies has included more attention to reception theory, through empirical extensions of a Mulvey-type concern with the viewing audience and its experiences and motivations in watching traditional Hollywood films (see Erens 1990).

As a filmmaker herself, Mulvey also had the goal in her criticism of opening up paths to construct an alternative kind of approach to filmmaking. In other writings on film theory, similar connections are drawn between feminist aesthetics and feminist counter-cinema. Teresa de Lauretis's (in 1987b) essay, "Rethinking women's cinema: aesthetics and feminist theory," draws a more explicitly political picture of the aims and nature of feminist film theory, characterizing it as working, together with feminist cinema itself, to create a transformative social technology of gender, or a new feminist aesthetic. The creation of a feminist counter-cinema is tied to broad political aims of social transformation: "Our task as theorists is to articulate the conditions and forms of vision for another social subject, and so to venture into the highly risky business of redefining aesthetic and formal knowledge" (de Lauretis 1987b, p. 134). De Lauretis draws heavily upon Foucault's discussion of technologies of sex in *The History of Sexuality*, in her account of how cinema functions as a "technology of gender": "[G]ender, too, both as representation and as self-representation, is the product of various social technologies, such as cinema, and of institutionalized discourses, epistemologies, and critical practices, as well as practices of daily life" (de Lauretis 1987b, p. 2).

Much recent work in film theory is in accord with these recommendations, and uses more subtle and complex accounts of "difference," not just the category of gender alone, to study filmic representation. For example, in a number of recent studies film theorists make use of philosophical ideas about "gender trouble" in constructing analyses of queer representation or such phenomena as women in camp, or of femininity in male homosexuality (Silverman 1992). Also, much work has been done within the broad field of cultural studies to examine links between race and gender in film and to explore how these factors interweave with others such as social class in affecting the politics of filmmaking and film viewing (hooks 1992b, Wartenberg 1995). This work follows up on more traditional forms of Marxist ideology critique, including attention to gender among other topics.

Prognosis

Feminist philosophy of film is new, especially in relation to feminist film theory. There is no doubt much of value in film theory for feminist philosophers to use and build upon. Work on the gaze, for example, can be the basis for feminist philosophical accounts of subjectivity and body image, or for examination of the epistemological biases of traditional philosophers like Descartes (Scheman 1988). Feminist film theory includes significant, subtle, and detailed work on genres like horror or pornography. This work on dominant forms of representation of important social issues may be usefully considered by philosophers who want to criticize and move beyond current positions on topics such as domestic violence, the eroticization of rape, and the current feminist pornography debates (for example, see Williams 1989). Recent work by film theorists concerning the construction of masculinity or of gender transgressive behavior, of "camp" and the self-conscious performance of gender in certain films, will also prove of much interest to philosophers who consider representations of gender to be significant in formations of conceptions of the self and identity. This is true even when the philosophical assumptions used within film theoretic discussions could be considered problematic by philosophers (e.g. the use in Silverman 1992 of Foucauldian theory to analyze films of Fassbinder).

However, clearly feminist philosophy also has much to offer feminist film theory. There are approaches within contemporary feminist philosophy that could well prove useful for discussing films but that have not yet had any impact. For example, discussions in the field of feminist ethics (maternal ethics, the ethics of care, or lesbian ethics) might provide a theoretical framework for constructing detailed readings and/or critical analyses of numerous kinds of films, such as ones depicting female friendships, love affairs, or mother–child relations. Philosophers may choose various approaches to these films. They could use ethical theories to provide critical readings of films, or alternatively could turn to films as sorts of empirical data to test their theories. Again, there are many current threads within philosophy of science that offer good bases for constructing critiques of filmic depictions of "natural" behavior reflecting supposed biological bases of sex or gender. Feminist analyses of documentary films in particular would certainly benefit from recent work in feminist philosophy of science critiquing stereotypical associations of race with gender or gender with illness, etc.

Although de Lauretis (1987b) has drawn attention of feminist film theory to "technologies of gender," surprisingly little feminist work has been done on the changing role and impact of film technology itself. Philosophers might go on to construct alternative, more positive and liberatory feminist readings of science fiction or even horror films that are often seen as misogynistic (as for example, de Lauretis does in her reading of Lizzie Borden's science fiction film *Born in Flames*). The assessment of film technology should not be restricted to considerations of women's relations to productive technology of filmmaking, but also should explore the role of technological change in women's access to or experience of film. For example, Linda Williams's *Hard Core* (1989, p. 231) cites statistics indicating that, with the advent of the home video market, women's participation as consumers of X-rated film pornography has dramatically increased (up to 40 percent in 1987).

It is difficult to forecast the nature of feminist philosophizing about film, because the philosophic study and use of film is itself relatively new and varied. At the very least however, film is starting to be seen as itself a source of philosophical reflection, in the same way that works of drama and literature are. This offers a final important avenue for further exploration by feminist philosophers, who can find ways of reading the creative and potentially transformative social visions in films themselves.

PART VIII

ETHICS

36

Moral epistemology

MARGARET URBAN WALKER

Moral epistemology investigates sources and patterns of moral understanding. Its questions include: To what extent does morality consist in or depend on knowledge, and of what kind(s)? What makes possible moral knowledge, and how is such knowledge grounded or justified? What is the relation between philosophical claims about morality and the moral understanding any of us has, that is, what has ethics – the philosophical representation of morality – to do with morality itself? Feminist moral epistemology asks how social divisions of labor, opportunity, power, and recognition which reproduce gender and other hierarchies affect both the ways these questions have in fact been answered, and the ways they might be.

One might expect to find feminist moral epistemology at the point of intersection of feminist ethics and feminist epistemology. But these two well-developed areas of feminist philosophy have formed largely in parallel, in response to different problems. Feminist epistemology examines dominant paradigms and practices of knowledge in Western philosophy and science. It seeks practices of justification that expose and correct (rather than abet and conceal) biases rooted in the structures of gender and other forms of social domination. Feminist ethics reveals gender bias in established traditions of morality and moral philosophy, and constructs alternatives which draw on women's gendered experiences, feminist activism, and practices of solidarity among women and with men who suffer oppression (Jaggar 1991).

Feminist ethics has been heavily weighted with epistemological themes. I begin by reviewing ways this work challenges existing pictures of moral understanding and proposes others. The challenges pose fundamental questions about the adequacy and the authority of representations of "our" moral lives, including, it turns out, the representations of feminist ethics. I will argue that it is by connecting the epistemological themes of feminist ethics with recent developments in feminist epistemology that this ethics can best go forward.

Questionable positions

Feminist ethics finds gender bias in dominant theories of Anglo-American ethics. Certain modern moral theories, such as Kantian, utilitarian, contractarian, and rights-based ones, command most attention, set problems for discussion, and

363

influence standards of evaluation in journals, conferences, classrooms, and text-books of twentieth-century Anglophone ethics. Academically institutionalized views mirror and reinforce publicly authoritative discourses of rights, obligations, and welfare in industrialized Western countries.

Feminists find a kindred set of preoccupations, assumptions, and points of view in these discourses and theories. They mirror spheres of activity, social roles, and character ideals associated with socially advantaged men; they reflect norms of masculinity that apply at least to men so privileged, if not to men generally (Baier 1994a, Benhabib 1987, Friedman 1993, Held 1987a, Whitbeck 1983). Dominant views idealize relations of nonintimate, mutually independent peers seeking to preserve autonomy or enhance self-interest in rule- (or role-)bound voluntary interactions. The normative subject thus conjured up is, in a now (revealingly) unmentionable phrase, "free, white, and twenty-one" – and male. That is, "the" moral agent so envisioned is not (typically) a woman, a child, a person of disadvantaged or despised economic, educational, racial, caste, ethnic, sexual, or religious identity or position, or a person with temporary, chronic, or progressive disabilities of body, mind, or spirit.

This moral agent is none of us at all times, and many of us at no times. More specifically, this image of normal moral agents and their contexts of choice ignores or distorts a great deal that *women* in Western societies, even across class and racial groups, have historically been expected and required to do. Women are typically assigned variable and discretionary responsibilities to care (in physically and often emotionally intimate ways) for others, either as paid or unpaid labor. Often, the others to be cared for are dependent and vulnerable, and women are expected to care for them with dedication and restraint. Women are expected to perform in subordinate or dependent economic, social, and political roles obediently and loyally, if not selflessly. Women are pressed or forced to accept domestic, reproductive, and sexual arrangements set and enforced by male authorities; many such arrangements offer limited possibilities for individual expression or negotiation of terms (Okin 1989a, Mann 1994). Dominant moral theories thus seem to see a moral world from typical situations and familiar positions of some men, but (even now) few women; this shows something about what theory makers have been able or likely to know about "our" moral world (Frye 1983).

The canonical form of moral judgment in dominant theories tracks gendered social positions and prerogatives as well. Moral judgment or justification is rendered as the uniform application of law-like, impersonally action-guiding principles to cases relevantly similar from an impartial point of view. In this "theoretical–juridical" picture "the" moral agent in action resembles a judge, manager, bureaucrat, or gamesman, exercising patterns of judgment appropriate to legal, institutional, or administrative contexts, or games (Walker 1992). The picture suggests either the reciprocal social positions of participants or competitors in a rule-structured practice, or the positions of those with authority to apply law or policy impartially to cases. Since positions and operations like this characterize roles, offices, and activities that are historically reserved to men in

Western societies, again it seems that theory makers know what some men (are supposed to) know.

The imagery – a fraternity of robustly independent peers invoking the authority of laws to deliver verdicts – is so pervasive in academic moral theory that some philosophers think the project of Western ethics itself is hopelessly discredited. Is ethics not only gendered but "race, class, and history specific" (Frye 1990), the canonization of views from positions of governance in hierarchical social orders (Hoagland 1988)? Or do we need better ethics? Better ethics would mean conceptions of morality *descriptively* adequate to diverse social positions and the moral understandings they require, and *normatively* equipped to support social and political critique. Many feminists have thought adequate moral theories must at least articulate the moral knowledge resident in women's characteristic gendered locations and roles. But these are parts of a social order that is unjust or oppressive to women and many men, and they are coercively assigned, and coercively and manipulatively maintained, within gender and other hierarchies. So what is the status of the knowledges they include for an understanding of how to live?

Problems of representation

Feminist critiques of ethics do not show that moral philosophy is simply mistaken in its claims to represent moral life. Rather, feminist critiques show how moral philosophers have in fact represented, in abstract and idealized theoretical forms, aspects of the *actual* positions and relations of *some* people in a certain kind of social order. This social order is the kind where the availability or typicality of these positions depends on gender, age, economic status, race, and other factors that distribute powers and forms of recognition differentially and hierarchically.

So dominant moral theories depict the self-images, prerogatives of choice, required patterns of moral reasoning, and anticipated forms of accountability of people placed in societies like ours in certain ways, not just in any or every way. It is the moral agency of people "like that" that is dignified and "normalized" by its portrayal in culturally authoritative philosophical accounts. The portrayal puts forward a certain position as representative of real, or full, or unproblematic moral agents. Anyone who isn't or can't be "like that" is either left unrepresented in such accounts, or is effectively represented as different, problematic, less than fully fledged from a moral point of view. Yet such moral theories are invariably put forward as accounts of "the" moral agent exhibiting the intuitions, sense of justice, practical wisdom, or patterns of rational choice characterizing "our" moral life (Calhoun 1988).

In pressing on these theories to find where and if women's lives, labors, and responsibilities figure, feminist critics lean on a faultline in modern moral theories. If these theories derive authority from their supposed representation of a moral life common to all (or even most, adult ones) of us, they are in trouble; they depict some aspects of the lives of the few, rather than most of the lives of the many. If the credibility of claims to represent is saved by admitting that what

365

is depicted is representative of rather little of the moral lives of most of us, then these views lose their authority as representative of "our" (much less "human") moral life.

In this way feminist criticism puts the authority and credibility of representative claims about moral life under harsh light. Since so much of philosophical theorizing about morality takes the form of such claims, or relies upon them, the practice of moral theorizing is itself on the spot. Who in fact is the "we" that does this representing? How adequate are the representers' *positions to know* and *means of knowing* to the matters they undertake to represent? The answers to both these questions bear on whether claims *about* morality and moral knowledge are justified. They also test the credibility of claims *within* morality: how are judgments of good, obligation, responsibility, and entitlement affected by the concrete social positions from which they are made? Are all positions available in a given social order coherently expressible in the moral terms that order provides? And what terms apply to the moral acceptability of a social order itself?

One strategy to remedy the exclusion or distortion of women's lives in moral theory is to represent fully and sympathetically women's moral perceptions, senses of value, and understandings of agency and responsibility. The aim is to give expression to moral understandings embedded in practices that have been and still are "women's work." The result has been a rich lode of creative work on ethics of care, maternal and friendship paradigms of moral relations, and moral responsibilities in situations of interdependency, vulnerability, and trust (Baier 1994a, Cole and Coultrap-McQuin 1992, Held 1993, 1995b, Manning 1992, Noddings 1984, Ruddick 1989, Tronto 1993, Whitbeck 1983).

This literature confronts the monologic, universalist, and deductivist picture of moral judgment in dominant theory with the following epistemological themes. Adequate moral understanding is best achieved in particular, finely responsive attention to actual others. Close attention to particular people includes awareness of specific histories of these people and their relationships. Analogies to familiar paradigms probe the moral significance, and narrative constructions articulate the specificity, of actual personal and interpersonal histories. Pasts are mapped on to possible futures, exposing meanings and costs of different choices. Many narratives are continuing stories of connection; they are all continuing stories of moral identity and integrity, or the lack or loss of them (Meyers 1994, Walker 1996b). Moral relations are not just sites for unilateral choice based on fixed principles, but are places where we negotiate and acknowledge each other's identities, the relationships that construct them, and the values they express. Communication and collaboration at points of moral decision are seen as central, best-case features of responsible moral deliberation. Moral competence draws on propositional knowledge – "knowing that" – but also on perceptive, imaginative, and expressive capacities supported by habits of emotional response.

All these capacities and understandings are shaped in particular cultural settings that present us with certain practices and relations, and with the moral and other discourses that make sense of them. The terms and trainings supplied, however, may not be uniform, or uniformly understood. In societies stratified and segmented by the interactions of gender, race, class, and other factors, "we" may not all come to know the same; "we" may not be intended to occupy interchangeable moral positions, to be equally or similarly responsible. In fact, differentiated moral–social orders with different relative moral positions seem to be the rule with humankind, rather than the exception. Whether this, where true, is a moral problem is one issue. That it presents an epistemological challenge, however, may now be clear.

Feminist moral epistemology confronts dominant moral theory's representative pose of reflecting or rationally reconstructing what we – indifferently or interchangeably – know morally. Although some views in feminist ethics overlap with nonfeminist views (e.g. Aristotelian, pragmatist, or communitarian ones) in their criticisms of the theoretical–juridical formation of modern ethics, the distinctive achievement of feminist ethics is its challenge to epistemic and moral authority that is politically engineered and self-reinforcing. Yet here feminist criticism turns back upon itself. Claims to represent "women's" moral experience have been contested in much the same way that feminists have contested a tradition and practice of representing "our" moral life that has been dominated by some men. Not all and not only women find the voice or view to be theirs (Lugones and Spelman 1986). Has feminist ethics represented "the" moral experience of "women"? Is there such an experience, and which women's experience would count as it? And if there are women's experiences in a social order that is morally blemished by gender hierarchies, why should experiences under or of oppression be paradigms of moral understanding? Might they not be symptoms of accommodation or survival scenarios in a morally distorted and deforming environment (Card 1990a)?

The reception of psychologist Carol Gilligan's work exemplifies the pitfalls of attempting to render "women's" moral understandings visible, coherent, and authoritative. Gilligan (1982a) argued that her moral development research revealed two distinct but comparably integrated and mature moral orientations, "justice" and "care," and that care reasoning was significantly more likely to be used, especially as a predominant moral approach, by female subjects in her (socially advantaged) samples (Friedman 1993, Walker 1989b, see Article 38, CARE). While Gilligan's claims sparked care ethics, they also ignited controversy over whether care thinking is really linked to "women," and whether it is a resource for politically liberatory ethics for women (Grimshaw 1986, Hanen and Nielsen 1987, Kittay and Meyers 1987, Larrabee 1993, Moody-Adams 1991, see also Article 37, AGENCY).

Ironically, alongside the claims about care and women, a little-remarked theme announced at the outset of Gilligan's book foreshadows precisely the problem of whose moral views carry authority and have representative status. Gilligan said her point was not to generalize about either sex, but to "highlight a distinction between two modes of thought and to focus a problem of interpretation" (Gilligan 1982a, p. 2). The problem is "a problem in the representation, a limitation in the conception of human condition, an omission of certain truths

367

about life" (p. 2). While Gilligan was out to reveal "a consistent observational and evaluative bias" (p. 6) in the use of men's and boys' views to establish norms of moral development, the problem she mentions is completely general.

In a segmented and stratified society it would be surprising if there were not some significant differences in views about the nature, salience, structure, and rational resolution of moral problems among people very differently placed and experienced. Differently situated people will tend to have different moral problems or experience similar ones differently. They will have reasonably different understandings of costs, risks, and relevance. They will see different responses realistically open to them, and find different strategies of resolution sane. It would be surprising if this were not true unless morality were modular relative to other social practices and understandings in ways it is very unlikely to be.

If a segmented or stratified social order is apt to produce different, potentially competing styles of moral understanding (and perhaps different conceptions of agency and responsibility as well), there is going to be a "problem in the representation." These styles may compete not only for relative status, but may compete to be considered "moral" ones at all. Are all of them, some of them, or none of them the ones that set the standard for the *kind* of thing a normative moral theory (or a moral psychology) is supposed to represent? The problem here is to define the field of inquiry itself: whose moral understandings, vocabularies, senses of relevance, strategies of resolution, conceptions of agency, and notions of responsibility are authoritative, even relevant? These questions *will* be answered in academic disciplines, and in large and small arenas of social life, but the answers, and the authority and credibility of what is built on them, beg review and remain open to contest. Still, projects of amplifying muffled moral voices – of many women and many men – are vital. They yield objects of comparison which help us track dominant and recessed voices to real social locations. They reveal the multilingual moral–social world which inheres in a differentiated social one. Moral philosophy and its epistemology must address this.

Where, then, to begin? Some philosophers remain convinced that well-established traditions of moral thought and their allied epistemologies, in particular those of Kant and Aristotle, can be effectively recruited to feminist criticism (Herman 1993a, Homiak 1993, O'Neill 1993, Nussbaum 1995). I argue instead that feminist ethics needs recent feminist epistemology. This tells us, in the manner of naturalized epistemology, to begin where we are, but to pay close attention to how we got there. It shows how we can help ourselves to critical strategies that start from places we no longer wish to be, but that show us where we need to go.

Epistemology socialized

Feminist epistemology critiques the philosophy and practice of science and the normative knowing subject of modern philosophies of knowledge. Some feminist epistemologists maintain that knowledge is necessarily an *intersubjective* achievement. They also claim that it is *communities* rather than individuals in them who are the subjects of knowledge; communities sustain the discursive and other material resources, and the social and cognitive practices, for producing and legitimating knowledge (Alcoff and Potter 1993, Longino 1993a, Nelson 1990, Scheman 1993b). These feminist epistemologies reject foundationalism that posits given, self-evident, or incorrigible bases of justification (Antony 1993). They urge us instead to examine actual practices of forming and fixing beliefs or generating and confirming hypotheses. This requires a look at the structures of communities that underwrite these processes.

Practices and relations of cognitive authority are embodied in real people and institutions, as well as in methodologies and instruments, discourses and background assumptions. By checking the effects and reliability of these, using everything at any time that we have good reasons to think we know, we qualify and disqualify as we go both claims to knowledge and ways of arriving at them. One thing we now have very good reasons to believe is that de facto cognitive authority may follow distributions of social power. Feminists, for example, have hard-won knowledge of histories and politics of unreliable theorizing driven by privileged men's dominance of culturally authoritative knowledge-making and women's socially enforced incredibility and credulity (Code 1991).

Rebuilding the ship while at sea is not a new idea about knowledge. Using analyses of the social worlds of knowledge makers, informed by what is (fallibly) known about social powers and oppression from diverse critical perspectives, is still a novelty viewed with suspicion. Yet to do so is not to shift theory of knowledge away from evidence and justification but toward a more demanding and critical view of them. Epistemic communities are epistemically responsible for examining the discourses, instruments, practices, and relations of authority by which knowledge is made (Addelson 1991). Feminist epistemologies argue for standards of objectivity that recognize the social placement of knowers and its meaning for what is known (Haraway 1991b, Harding 1993b). These are politically critical epistemologies of knowledges produced by and for communities.

Feminist ethics profits from viewing moral knowledge as a communal product and process constructed and sustained in interactions among people, rather than an individually action-guiding theory within people. I call this conception of morality an "expressive–collaborative" model (Walker 1996a). Moral discourses furnish shared terms and patterns through which people express and account for their identities, relationships, and values in mutually recognizable (but also revisable, negotiable) ways. Socially embedded practices of moral accounting enable people to allot, assume, or deflect responsibilities; shared moral understandings allow them to grasp the interpersonal implications of doing so. Moral practices are not and cannot be modular; they are shaped around and shape specific folkways, relations, institutions, and environments.

Moral–social worlds are held fast or changed by many pressures and powers, including the power of representations of moral life from places of authority and the pressures of people's understanding how they actually live. We sustain mutual intelligibility to the extent that practice, understandings, and the

369

demands people's lives put on them remain in rough equilibrium. This equilibrium is reflective when we can make its conditions and consequences explicit among us. Sometimes in doing this equilibrium is disturbed or shattered. Although disequilibrium occasions disorientation or conflict, it can also open opportunities for criticism and change. Feminist ethics both creates and exploits these opportunities.

Feminist critiques push moral arrangements and understandings of them toward greater *transparency*, toward that condition in which we can see more clearly who is doing (or is in a position to do) what, and what terms are available to recognize, evaluate, and apportion responsibility for these doings (or derelictions). This allows us to see what our terms and arrangements really are, what it takes to sustain them, how their costs are distributed, and how habitable is the common life to which they lead, for people variously placed within it.

Even where the life of collectivities in which people invoke shared moral terms is in some ways common, the sense of its habitability may not be. People differently placed may view differently, and value differently, what these arrangements have been and might be. These differences may prompt or force new shared understandings, in which applications of familiar moral terms shift, or novel moral discourses emerge around new or newly visible practices. Neither the opportunity for change nor the success of it are guaranteed; they depend on powers and pressures available to actual (or would-be) participants.

Feminists expose, for example, a moral shadow economy of caring and affective labors (not only gendered, but raced and classed (Tronto 1993)). The official moral fraternity relies on these activities without being able to recognize in official terms either the indispensability of this support system, or the coercive measures required for its replication (Baier 1994a). This exercise in transparency was made possible by social and economic changes, including unprecedented participation by women in the paid labor force. It was also enabled by many women's novel access to the cognitive authority of academic and professional discourses, by the moral–political compass and sense of authority provided by women's movements of the 1970s and 1980s, and by the concepts and theories that grew out of these new positions and practices. Caring labor is still overwhelmingly gendered, raced, classed (and often undocumented), and stark sexual divisions of paid and unpaid labor remain a fact of contemporary life. Even so, feminist moral discourses now provide some of the tools for exhibiting and criticizing these arrangements in ways that spur change.

Shorn of universalist claims to represent "the" experience of "women," feminist ethics continues its pursuits of transparency. It finds resources and invents techniques to expose the rhetoric and politics of public, professional, and folk discourses of ethics. Moral practices of communities of feminist activism and practical dialogue (Jaggar 1995b), and moral understandings among women and men of nondominant cultural identifications, display actual alternatives and provide revealing comparative models (Anzaldúa 1990, Collins 1990, hooks 1984, Lugones 1991). Collectivist moral theory teaches how moral knowledge is enacted and hidden in social interactions structured by differentials of cognitive

370

authority and political access (Addelson 1994a). Interpretive moral ethnography illuminates cultural presuppositions of moral understandings, creating conditions for intercultural understanding, and political compromise within and between societies (Shrage 1994). It also helps us to denaturalize those largely invisible views that reveal what it means to be "us." Critical analysis of our actual flawed and differentiated social–moral orders allows us to see how being "us" is no one thing in actual communities (Card 1996, Moody-Adams, forthcoming, Walker, forthcoming). Cracking codes that propagate culturally normative prejudice in communities and multiplying practices of refiguration are both exercises in transparency and political actions (hooks 1994, Meyers 1994, Nelson 1995, Young 1990a).

The epistemological part of feminist ethics searches for practices of thought and justification that lead to better moral understandings between people and to better understanding of morality as a social institution. Better understandings of both kinds are those that resist hierarchies of social domination, including gender, and the allocations of responsibility and definitions of agency that maintain them. To achieve these better moral and political understandings, we need to have more accurate and sophisticated accounts of what moral knowledge is like. We need to know what it is, where it comes from, what human capacities (not only for knowledge) it requires, and how it is lodged in, and is reproduced by, the practices of communities whose knowledge it is.

An old self-understanding of moral philosophy stands in the way of both kinds of better understanding. This is the view of ethics as "pure," disinterested inquiry into timeless moral truths about individuals, available to individuals, by reflection and reasoning within individuals. I believe desertion of this old view is necessary for a fully critical and politically responsible feminist ethics. At the same time, it sets a good example and different tasks for philosophical ethics at the close of the twentieth century.

37

Agency

DIANA TIETJENS MEYERS

The problem of moral agency

A moral agent is an individual who is capable of choosing and acting in accordance with judgments about what is right, wrong, good, bad, worthy, or unworthy. Such individuals are thought to be free and hence responsible for what they do. The obstacles to freedom and responsibility raise philosophical problems in regard to moral agency.

The first obstacle to moral agency can be framed in terms of the contrast between activity and passivity. Since people are profoundly influenced by their social experience, no choice is insulated from cultural norms and pressures. Thus, social conformity is the rule. Moreover, it may seem that conduct that defies socially prescribed norms stems from drives or psychological disorders that no more express individual freedom than conduct stemming from internalized norms does. On this view, if people's choices and actions are not determined by their social environment, they are determined by their internal compulsions. Thus, people are passive conduits for forces they cannot control, and active agency is an illusion. A second obstacle to moral agency can be framed in terms of the contrast between morality and amorality. A moral agent is not motivated solely by egoistic concerns. Self-interest may be among a moral agent's concerns, but it cannot altogether eclipse consideration for other people. Yet, it may seem that people have no end in view except pursuing their own selfish interests and that helping others or refraining from harming others is merely incidental to securing their own interests. Thus, people are essentially amoral, and morality is an illusion. To overcome the dual threat of passivity and amorality, many philosophers seek to explain how individuals can use reason to choose and act freely and responsibly.

Feminist philosophers have politicized the concept of moral agency, for they have detected the taint of gender bias throughout the canonical treatments of this topic. Whereas classic accounts of moral agency take the moral experience of privileged men as paradigmatic, feminists insist that diverse women's moral experience be taken equally seriously, though not endorsed uncritically. This attention to women's experience brings to light heretofore neglected contexts of moral choice and action that are conventionally associated with femininity, notably, intimate interpersonal relationships. Feminists insist that an account of moral agency must be adequate to these contexts, as well as to contexts

372

involving relations between strangers or nonintimate associates. Likewise, the heterogeneity of women's experience highlights novel issues. Feminists see male dominance as multiformed, multifaceted, and pervasive, and they demand that an account of moral agency make sense of both the capacity to recognize this injustice in whatever guise it may assume and the capacity to oppose it effectively.

Major philosophical traditions have ignored or denigrated forms of agency that are symbolized as feminine, and gender-based domination and subordination restrict and distort women's agency. Yet, since women's agency is necessary for women's emancipation, feminist philosophers have made this issue a priority.

Feminist critique of traditional philosophical accounts of moral agency

Critique of the major philosophical accounts of moral agency has generally been incapable of assuming an objective and impartial viewpoint. This conception of people as free and equal atomic individuals has been a prime target of feminist criticism.

Many feminists express astonishment and dismay that atomic individualism has gained such a powerful hold on the philosophical imagination. Acceptance of this view denies or, at least, philosophically occludes the reality of physical dependency during infancy and childhood and during periods of frailty or infirmity later in life, and also the reality of lifelong psychic dependency on others for emotional sustenance and fulfillment and for intellectual stimulation and enrichment. Many feminists interpret this denial of human interconnectedness as a misogynistic repudiation of maternal caregiving and of the emotional labor conventionally expected of women (Baier 1987b, Benhabib 1987, Code 1987b, Flax 1983, Held 1987a, 1987b, 1993). The role that is culturally coded feminine and the concerns and contributions of many women are deemed irrelevant to moral and political philosophy.

Still, it is doubtful that the independent individual's social contract theory posits are really as self-sufficient as they are supposed to be. Susan Moller Okin traces a subtext of reliance on women's traditional work running through major works of Western moral and political theory (Okin 1979). Philosophers who extol the citizen – the free and equal man who takes part in debating social issues and governing society – assume that women (in some theories, slaves too) are working in the background providing indispensable, though inferiorized, domestic support services. Even philosophers who proclaim the political equality of women (and denounce slavery) fail to explain how this work is going to get done once women (and all men) are participating as political equals. Taking into account the social inertia that generally favors the status quo, failing to propose and vigorously champion a program of redistributing domestic labor means that few women will ever be more than nominal political equals. Despite the obligatory lip service contemporary philosophers pay to gender equality, pernicious assumptions about women's subordinate status and their correlative lack of agency continue to infect prevailing conceptions of the moral subject.

Obstacles to women's moral agency

For feminists, diagnosing obstacles to women's agency is an important project – a project that illuminates complex relations between culture, social structures, developmental experience, interpersonal relationships, and individual identity. Some feminist theorists appropriate the notion of false or colonized consciousness from the Marxist and anticolonialist traditions (Bartky 1990a, Hartsock 1983). Cultural ideals of feminine beauty and demeanor, together with norms of feminine duty and conduct, function to subordinate women, yet women often embrace these very ideals and norms. Moreover, when women fail, as they frequently do, to measure up to these ideals or to conform to these norms, they blame themselves and feel inadequate instead of contesting such conceptions of femininity and opposing the subordination they reinforce. Once oppressive standards have been internalized, women's frustration and anger are turned inward and transformed into shame and self-hatred. Overt force is not needed to secure women's compliance, for their potential for critiquing these standards and demanding change is effectively neutralized.

A number of feminist scholars contend that the ethic of care is one form that these seductive, yet self-defeating feminine norms assume and that women's acceptance of this ethic helps to perpetuate male dominance (Bartky 1990a, Card 1990a, Houston 1987, Morgan 1987; for an account of care ethics, see Article 38, CARE). The attention to others and the altruistic responsibilities that are integral to the ethic of care can stifle the needs and aspirations of the caregiver. Moreover, capitulating to the widespread social presumption that women should give care unstintingly and that men and children should receive copious care traps women in an unreciprocated care syndrome that ensures their continued subordination. Thus, the perils of self-effacement and servility incurred by exponents of a care ethic are undeniable.

In a related vein, some theorists analyze the moral double binds that snare women. "Womanly" virtues are despised as vices, but acquiring "manly" virtues stigmatizes women as unfeminine (Morgan 1987). Women are powerless; so they protect themselves in various ways. They may succumb to the temptation to pervert "womanly" virtues – ostentatiously delivered, overweening care can be used to manipulate and coerce beneficiaries. Or they may shirk responsibility – taking responsibility for events over which they have no control while disavowing responsibility for their own decisions (Gilligan 1982a). Since there is no way to be truly good and a woman, women's moral agency is confounded.

374

Feminist approaches to reconstructing women's moral agency

Plainly, the prime tasks of a feminist theory of moral agency include explaining how women can overcome colonized consciousness, how women can enact the value of care without collaborating in their own subordination, and how women can break out of the double binds of femininity that distort their self-perception and hence their life choices. Feminist scholars have used two interestingly divergent strategies to pursue these aims. One is to see the experience associated with women's traditional role of mother and caregiver as a repository of socially disdained, but genuine values and thus as affording an opportunity to reconfigure our conception of what it is to think insightfully about moral questions and what it is to act morally. This strategy asks what we can learn from reinterpreting and revaluing so-called feminine experience. The second strategy focuses more on women's economic and political marginalization and on various forms of abuse to which they are vulnerable at work, in the home, and when socializing. This strategy asks how it is possible for women to gain a critical perspective on and resist their mistreatment.

Though distinct, these approaches share some assumptions. Both strategies regard the self as social. Socialization shapes one's beliefs, values, goals, and so forth, and one's social context dictates one's social identity. Still, feminists treat women's experience as a resource that must be respected, and they see consciousness-raising coupled with feminist practice as a method that respects and builds on this experience. Both strategies seek to establish an alternative discursive community – either one in which traditional feminine activities are revalued and their feminist potential is mined, or one in which the subordination and victimization of women is decried and subversive initiatives are undertaken. As these different foci suggest, these strategies frame the problem of feminist moral agency in significantly different ways. One yields a care-based account of moral agency; the other yields an oppositional account of moral agency. I shall now turn to these two accounts.

Care-based moral agency

Although feminist accounts of care vary in many respects, they share a relational conception of the self. Feminist proponents of care see the moral subject as a self-in-relation – an individual who values and enjoys intimacy, whose identity is in significant measure defined through her interpersonal ties, and whose concerns are interdependent with those of other people. Embedded in a web of relationships – some voluntary, others nonvoluntary; some between equals, others with dependents – a self-in-relation construes moral choice in terms of the question of how to respond to others in a way that avoids harm and maintains relationships (Gilligan 1987).

375

In developing a care-based account of moral agency, some feminists hearken to experiences of pregnancy and giving birth and to the nurturance that mothers are expected to give and that many mothers do give children (e.g. Baier 1986, Held 1989, Ruddick 1989). However, other feminists have explored a broader spectrum of interpersonal relationships, including relations between lovers, adult family members, and friends (Walker 1987, Friedman 1993). When inquiry into moral agency is situated in these intimate contexts, a different set of moral capacities and skills becomes salient from that which is salient when relations between strangers are taken to be paradigmatic of moral relations.

Firstly, care-based moral agency is particularistic. A caregiver must pay attention to and meet the needs of a distinctive individual. Secondly, care-based moral agency cannot mechanically derive decisions from general theories and must proceed improvisationally. A caregiver must be alert to fluid, sometimes peculiar, circumstances that give rise to special needs or necessitate a reordering of priorities. Thirdly, care-based moral agency is interactive. One cannot presume to understand the needs of another person; one must open lines of communication and listen attentively. Fourthly, care-based moral agency does not exclude emotion. Affective ties to others can enhance moral sensitivity, and emotional receptivity can sharpen moral perception.

All of the capacities I have mentioned so far are other-directed. Consequently, they bring to mind the objections to self-sacrificial altruism that have prompted some feminists to doubt that care furnishes a tenable feminist ethic. Feminists who would reclaim women's experience in intimate social contexts must show that a care ethic can be extricated from its historic role in women's subordination and cooptation.

Feminist scholars repudiate the stereotype of feminine care that attributes to women an unflagging disposition to serve the interests of others. Because caregivers are equally deserving of care, caregivers must include themselves in the orbit of care. Since caring for oneself presupposes knowledge of one's own needs, desires, values, aspirations, and the like, introspective skills together with the imaginative, calculative, and volitional skills that enable one to realize one's plans are indispensable to care. However, because self-knowledge and self-affirmation may lead to interpersonal tensions and conflicts, feminist care theorists construe care as a form of moral thought that calls on characteristic cognitive and expressive capacities and that eventuates in discerning judgment. Care-based agency requires balancing skills that enable individuals to weigh the moral concerns that are at issue and to find a course of action that keeps these concerns in equilibrium. Also, it requires expressive skills that enable individuals to assert their needs and represent their choices without rupturing relationships. In sum, care mobilizes a repertory of skills – a moral competency – that enables an individual to define her own moral identity and to improvise enactments of her moral identity that take into account both her empathic understanding of others and her introspective understanding of herself (Walker 1987, Meyers 1987, 1994). Care mandates responsiveness both to others and to oneself.

376

Although the feminist account of care-based moral agency originates in a commitment to reclaiming and revaluing activities and experiences that are culturally coded feminine, the capacities this account calls upon have far wider application than their derivation from maternal practices and other intimate relationships might suggest (Benhabib 1987, Ruddick 1989, Tronto 1993). Moreover, feminist care rediviva does not submerge women's identity in the identities of other people, does not divert women's lives into vicarious satisfactions, and does not block women's self-fulfillment. Indeed, care may mandate breaking off harmful relationships, and opposition to harmful social practices may be mounted in the name of care. Thus, there is growing consensus that an ethic of care or, perhaps better, an ethic that incorporates certain care themes is an important component of a feminist ethic (Ruddick 1989, Manning 1992, Held 1993, Tronto 1993, Baier 1987b, Kittay 1995). Still, there is reason for skepticism, for it is arguable that care's presumption in favor of accommodating others, reconciling competing interests, and sustaining existing relationships deflects and dilutes social critique and blunts oppositional politics. In light of these misgivings, many feminists advocate an alternative model of the self and moral agency.

Oppositional moral agency

Whereas the self-in-relation grounds feminist accounts of care-based moral agency, feminists have premised accounts of oppositional moral agency on two principal conceptions of the self – a materialist conception stemming from Marxism and a discursive conception stemming from postmodernism. The materialist view stresses the role of social institutions and practices in shaping the individual. Gender difference is a function of the sexual division of labor – unlike men, women are responsible for child care and for household maintenance and production (Hartsock 1983, Jaggar 1983, Ferguson 1984a). Unpaid and privatized, "women's" work is scorned, and women are held in contempt. In contrast, the discursive view stresses the role of symbolic systems in defining the individual. Gender difference is codified in systems of hierarchical binary oppositions that associate women with otherness, that is, with subordinated difference (Scott 1990). Discourses furnish gendered subject positions with which individuals identify and which individuals perpetuate by reproducing norms of behavior that express the social meaning of gender (Butler 1990, 1993, Mouffe 1992).

A common theme in discussions of oppositional moral agency is that the impact of social forces, whether material, discursive, or both, is profound and inescapable. On this view, then, the question of how women can critique and resist the social forces that construct them is vital. Proponents of different views of oppositional moral agency adopt essentially the same strategy for addressing this question. They deny that social forces are monolithic, and they appeal to the salutary interplay of a multiplicity of social forces.

Ideologies contain inconsistencies, and these discursive faultlines can be exposed and interpreted (MacKinnon 1982). Likewise, since people are expected to act differently in different social spheres, and since everyone enters into different social spheres, no one has a unitary identity, and everyone is obliged to juggle incongruous internalized values and norms (Ferguson 1984a, Mann 1994). In culturally pluralistic societies, people encounter diverse values and practices (Friedman 1993). Even in comparatively homogeneous societies, historical change begets diachronic conflicts in gender norms, while the proliferation of faulty replications of gender norms synchronically exposes the arbitrariness and mutability of these norms (Bartky 1990a, Butler 1990). Moreover, emotions are not amenable to lockstep regimentation, and spontaneous emotional responses that convention deems misdirected or disproportionate can kindle suspicions about the legitimacy of the social order (Jaggar 1989). Finally, to be a competent speaker of a language is to be endowed with the capacity to generate new sentences and thus the capacity to articulate novel social forms and to entertain novel ways to live (Meyers 1989, Hekman 1991). Though hegemonic, social practices and discourses that embody gender regimes are not totalizing.

An important corollary of this view of the self is its sensitivity to the role of race, class, ethnicity, age, sexual orientation, and the like in constituting identity. Since gender is not isolable from these other dimensions of identity, a feminist theory of oppositional agency must accommodate the complex consciousness and crosscutting allegiances of, say, a Latina lesbian or an African-American grandmother (King 1988, Spelman 1988, Lugones 1990, Crenshaw 1993). Likewise, it is important to recognize that repressed racism, class snobbery, xenophobia, homophobia, and misogyny split the self. As a result, a person's avowed egalitarian beliefs are contravened by unconscious bigoted beliefs. Though the latter are denied, they are operative and find expression in exclusionary and subordinating conduct (Piper 1990, Young, 1990a, Kristeva 1991, Meyers 1994). On the one hand, people who repress bigotry are dangerous, for they refuse to admit they are prejudiced, and they adamantly defend the fairness of unjust conduct and policies. Yet, on the other hand, the indecipherable feelings and perplexing conduct that result from such fragmentation can spark self-scrutiny and critical moral reflection.

Evidently, neither the material nor the discursive construction of the self bars innovation. Still, the socially constructed self has a sinister side. It is disquieting that influential thinkers are trumpeting the dissolution of the self and agency just when women are claiming agentic powers and gaining recognition as moral agents (Flax 1987). Also, feminists must resist an account of subjectivity that entails dismissing moral agency as an anachronistic illusion, for they must make sense of the distinction between progressive, feminist policies and retrograde, antifeminist policies. A feminist account of oppositional moral agency must inventory the emotional, intellectual, discursive, and organizational capabilities that enable women to chart a feminist politics of critique and empowerment.

Oppositional moral agency must counteract the dismissive treatment that women's emotions commonly receive, for these emotions can be symptomatic of socially unacknowledged injustice or oppression. "She's bitter," "She's hysterical," and "She's hypersensitive" are potent rhetorical ploys that often succeed in reducing feminist protest to emotional pathology and distract attention from compelling demands for change. Women who can neither name nor claim their anger cannot identify and resist the wrongs they suffer (Frye 1983, Lorde 1984, Spelman 1989, Scheman 1993b). Likewise, to renounce bitterness and cheer up may be to lose one's emotional comprehension of wrongs one has suffered and thus to betray the truth about one's life (McFall 1991). Negative emotions sometimes provide clues to concealed social realities.

Emotions can be revelatory, but they are not transparent. They require interpretation, as do other aspects of women's experience. Consciousness-raising groups function as enclaves in which women's heterodox perceptions are given their due and in which these perceptions are consolidated into feminist theory.

Unfortunately, the will to credit other women's experience cannot be summoned by fiat. Thus, consciousness-raising enlists emotions for two more purposes, namely, to build feminist unity and to catalyze feminist interpretation. Some theorists maintain that the personal emotions of love or friendship are needed to bridge the experiential gulfs that separate women of different races, classes, ethnicities, ages, and sexual orientations, while others make a case for the political emotion of solidarity (Lugones 1987, Lugones and Spelman 1986, hooks 1984, Meyers 1994). All see emotional ties as enabling women to tap into and profit from one another's experience – that is, to analyze the commonalities and differences between diverse women's social positions and to shed light on their meaning.

Still, it is necessary to ask what validates feminist theories and the political demands that flow from them. Most feminist thinkers describe a dialectical process of mutual adjustment between experience, theory, and practice. Many are convinced that this dynamic process must be pragmatic and fallibilistic (Fraser and Nicholson 1990). Still, many see the need for independent validation – some sort of epistemological or metaphysical guarantee. Feminist standpoint theorists argue that theorizing from the social positions occupied by subordinated groups provides the needed certification (Hartsock 1983, Jaggar 1983). Separatists argue that, by absenting themselves from their oppressors and creating woman-centered sanctuaries, women protect their self-understandings from contamination (Frye 1983). Another proposal advocates dismantling oppressive contextual structures in order to create conditions that facilitate transformative feminist experiences (Babbitt 1993). Finally, some feminists advert to objective facts or interests. No feminist theory can deny the subordination of women (Alcoff 1988). Or feminist theories should be conducive to self-respect, dignity, and human thriving (Babbitt 1993, Jaggar 1989).

Plainly, feminist philosophy encompasses a wide range of views of oppositional moral agency. On all accounts, such agency is firmly anchored in social relations. Where conceptions of oppositional moral agency differ is in regard to the constraints they impose on feminist theorizing. Some accounts introduce procedural constraints; others defend empirical or moral constraints. Moreover, different accounts of oppositional moral agency point to different arenas of feminist activism. The materialist conception supports engagement in social policy debates with the aim of ameliorating poverty and securing opportunities for women (Ferguson 1987, Fraser 1989c). The discursive account stresses the importance of subverting cultural mythologies and figurations of gender that structure perception of women and that normalize women's subordination (Irigaray 1985b, Cornell 1991, Rooney 1991, Meyers 1994). Of course, these two approaches are not mutually exclusive. On the contrary, it is arguable that they are complementary (Meyers 1994).

Feminist approaches to responsibility and autonomy

The lens of gender reframes the issue of moral agency. The dual objectives of revaluing women's traditional role and overcoming women's subordination take feminist work on the topic of moral agency in two directions – care-based moral agency and oppositional moral agency. These conceptions make two significant advances over prevailing mainstream philosophical views. In the feminist literature, the topic of responsibility is construed in a constructive way, and the issue of free will is eclipsed by more concrete, practical questions about choice and action.

Philosophical discussions of responsibility typically center on issues of control and on the propriety of praising and, especially, blaming moral agents. The topic of responsibility is auxiliary to the topic of punishment. Although feminists are not loathe to raise issues of culpability, for example, in discussions of sexual harassment, woman battering, and sexual assault, the feminist theoretical discussion of responsibility and moral agency is guided by other concerns.

One feminist approach to responsibility situates the issue in the larger context of oppression. When oppressive practices are generally deemed acceptable, and when many women have internalized oppressive norms, feminists ask whether oppressors can be held responsible for their oppressive actions and whether victims of oppression can be held responsible for resisting oppressive practices. Since one of the effects of pervasive oppression is to block moral insight into the wrongfulness of certain practices, there is no reason to suppose that those who engage in oppressive conduct are vicious individuals, and it is doubtful that they are blameworthy. Still, since moral reproach serves to educate people about systematic relations of domination and subordination, since it motivates people to stop behaving in ways that perpetuate these wrongs, and since it affirms people's moral agency, holding oppressors responsible for their actions despite their ignorance of the harm they are causing has a point and may be warranted for that reason (Calhoun 1989). Parallel issues arise from the viewpoint of the oppressed. Some victims identify with oppressive values and norms and thus are ignorant of the wrongs they suffer. Other victims are so sensitized to their victimization that they exhaust their agentic powers blaming those who are harming them and fail to appreciate their own potential for responsible oppositional agency. Still, many victims struggle to understand oppressive social relations in order to recognize the range of choices available to them, to assume an appropriate degree of responsibility for making good choices, and to judge what social changes are necessary for people to function as fully responsible agents (Wendell 1995). For feminists, the role of discourses and practices of responsibility in effecting emancipatory change is paramount.

The care-based account of moral agency shifts the discussion from issues about when people can be held responsible for their actions to issues about what responsibilities people should assume (Card 1990a). Thus, an administrative, legalistic concern is displaced by a moral concern. It is incumbent on individuals to take responsibility for self and others. Detachment from and indifference to people – failure to notice and respond to their vulnerabilities and needs – is an abrogation of responsibility. In an interesting twist on this theme, Sandra Harding situates the injunction to care in the context of relations between members of relatively privileged social groups and members of subordinated social groups, and she contends that the former must take responsibility for their social identity in order to break down the barriers between such groups and form mutually advantageous political coalitions (Harding 1991). Here, a continuity between care-based moral agency and oppositional moral agency is established.

The sidelining of questions about dispensing punishment in feminist work on moral agency presages a parallel eschewal of classic philosophical questions about free will. In view of the feminist commitment to the socially constructed self, it is to be expected that free will's importance as a topic will recede and that related concepts will be reinterpreted.

Autonomy, for example, is not equated with transcendence of social relations through free will. When feminists appropriate the concept of autonomy, they maintain that autonomy can be attained within a context of lifelong socialization and a network of personal interdependencies (Govier 1993, Nedelsky 1989, Meyers 1989). Social relationships are not seen as a threat to autonomy because autonomy is not seen as the actualization of a core self, but rather as the exercise of skills that enable people to understand themselves, redefine themselves as needed, and direct their own lives (Meyers 1989). Nurturance and education are indispensable to the development of these skills (Meyers 1989), and exercising these skills requires a conducive social context (Nedelsky 1989). Proficiently exercising these skills enables individuals to identify their needs, desires, and values and to translate them into action. Enacting one's identity in this way is associated with feelings of self-assurance, power, and exhilaration that are characteristic of autonomy. Moreover, the skills that secure autonomy facilitate creative responses to life's opportunities and constraints. Thus, feminist accounts of autonomy are anchored in the phenomenology of familiar experiences of control and satisfaction as opposed to the logic of concepts like individual self-sufficiency or personal desert.

Similarly, when feminists speak of authentically feminist values and projects, they do not suppose that these values and projects can be traced to a transhistorical, pancultural essence of womanhood, but rather that these values and projects are to be defined and redefined through an ongoing, reflexive process

381

of critical reflection and emancipatory action. Both in accounts of individual autonomy and in accounts of collective oppositional moral agency, feminists are primarily concerned with analyzing how insights into the forms and mechanisms of women's subordination can be gained, how acts of feminist resistance are possible, and how women can lead lives that are fulfilling to them as individuals. Thus, feminists focus on how oppressive conditions limit and distort women's agency and propose material, institutional, organizational, and discursive changes designed to expand the scope of women's agency.

That feminist philosophers have not settled upon a unified account of moral agency is hardly surprising, for the opportunities and demands that women's diverse and complex lives present call for different forms of moral agency. Women (and men) need to know that caregiving activities neither inevitably consign caregivers to passivity and subservience nor inherently preclude agency. They need to grasp that caregiving can and should be an affirmation of moral agency and that care-based agency need not be confined to intimate relations.

Yet, women typically confront countless situations in which care-based agency seems maladapted if not doomed. Relentless advertising and "expert" advice drive women to "perfect" their bodies through regimens of weight reduction and cosmetic beautification and, when all else fails, through surgical intervention. Employers discriminate against women – refusing them employment, paying them less, and denying them promotions. Women get shamed and humiliated for refusing to marry or have children. They get bullied on the street by catcalls and leers. They are sexually harassed by supervisors and coworkers; raped sometimes by strangers and often by acquaintances; beaten by domestic partners. Women need to understand how it is possible to discredit these practices and resist this onslaught. But there is no reason to think that the form of moral agency implicit in women's caregiving role will stand them in good stead when confronting such fierce and concerted antagonism. A politicized, collective, oppositional form of moral agency is better suited to this context.

Neither the caring self-in-relation nor the defiant oppositional self seems up to meeting all of the challenges women face. Perhaps there is a way of modeling the moral subject and moral choice and action that is adequate to all of women's agentic needs – if so, that is a project for future feminist philosophical inquiry.

38

Care

ANDREA MAIHOFER

1. Introduction

The feminist debate about an ethic of care that began during the early 1980s has become so extensive that it is difficult to provide an overview of it (Feder and Meyers 1987, Brabeck 1989, Nunner-Winkler 1991, Larrabee 1993, Nagl-Docekal and Pauer-Studer 1993). Since its beginnings, the debate has generated a series of independent models for an ethic of care, as well as a vast number of articles suggesting ways to expand critically, or to provide alternative readings of, traditional conceptions of morality. Carol Gilligan sparked the entire discussion with her book *In a Different Voice* (1982a), in which she outlines her theory of the different moral developments of women and men. According to Gilligan, the "male" conception of morality may be understood as an ethic of justice, while the "female" conception can be seen primarily as an ethic of care. This thesis ignited an often very fiercely argued discussion of its empirical correctness and the validity of its generalization (Nails 1983, Auerbach et al. 1985, Nunner-Winkler 1986, 1991a, 1991b, Flanagan and Jackson 1987, Nicholson 1983b).

But there also arose a lively exchange of suggestions for its potential uses, a discussion which reached beyond the United States. In Section 3, I shall outline some of the theories of how an ethic of care can be applied as a potential critical supplement to traditional morality or as a way of rereading classical conceptions of morality. In Section 4, I shall highlight key critics' thoughts on the usefulness of an ethic of care as an independent ethical alternative. However, since all of these attempts rely to a greater or lesser degree on Gilligan's thesis, I shall first provide an overview of her formulation of an ethic of care in some detail in Section 2, and I shall then conclude with a few critical reflections on understanding morality in Section 5.

2. Gilligan's reconstruction of the female conception of morality as an ethic of care

As the point of departure for her analysis, Carol Gilligan used her discomfort with Lawrence Kohlberg's stages model of moral development within which women are always assigned a lower moral stage (Kohlberg 1981, p. 409ff.). She held a series of interviews with men and women, asking them questions about self-image and morality, and she found that the moral development of women is not somehow deficient in relation to men's, but that it follows a different logic (cf. Nicholson 1983b).

(a) From the perspective of the "male" self, whose development is bound to the experience of separation and individuation, people are individuals who are independent of one another and who are equipped with subjective rights. He sees the other primarily as a curtailment of his own sphere of will and as a possible infringement of his personal rights; coexistence in society is then imagined as the coming together of different individuals at the borders of each one's respective domain. Thus, from the "male" perspective, society arises only subsequent to the assembling of originally independent individuals, and it maintains itself with common rules that are applicable to everyone. In the understanding of morality that accompanies this "male" view, moral dilemmas are primarily conflicts between competing demands and rights. As in mathematical equations, it is a matter of finding the balance between competing rights, a matter of applying the correct norm or hierarchy of norms to the concrete case. This means, first, that there can only be *one* morally correct solution and, two, that moral decisions are above all *applications of abstract principles* to concrete circumstances. All of this, according to Gilligan, is what characterizes the "male" conception of morality as an ethic of justice.

(b) In contrast, the "female" conception of morality is centered around the terms of care and sympathy. From the perspective of the "female" self, whose development occurs along with the experience of solidarity and identification, the individual person exists only within and on the basis of a web of social relationships. She therefore views others not primarily as restrictions, but as conditions of the possibility of her own existence. This means that society consists not of isolated people. but of relationships. and that it is held together by human connections and not through a system of rules (Gilligan 1982a, p. 42). The conception of morality that accompanies this "female" perspective is thus grounded in the experience of the sociality of people, and the awareness of these bonds between people leads to the recognition of the mutual responsibility for one another and to insight into the necessity of sympathy (p. 43). This conception of morality is not in any way "typically female," that is, solely emotionally and emphatically without distance; rather, it is based on judgment and knowledge, albeit a very different judgment and a very different knowledge of the world than that of a conception of morality based on justice. A moral dilemma in this perspective thus consists above all of competing responsibilities within a complex web of social relationships, and its solution will be one that clarifies mutual responsibilities and that also maintains social coherence.

In contrast to an ethic of justice, according to which morality is based on the abstract autonomous individual, the morality of an ethic of care foregrounds the concrete individual, and the psychological and social determinedness of human relations (p. 128). Reconstructing the concrete context of a moral problem is thus decisive for a moral judgment from the perspective of an ethic of care. Because of its reliance on context, a moral decision made for a specific situation is not simply the only possible rationally grounded option, and its morality does not lie in its possible generalizability or applicability to other situations. But the fact that the moral "truth" is always a question of both perspective and concrete context does not mean that there are no criteria for the careful consideration and foundation of a decision, and this postconventional contextualization (Gilligan and Murphy 1980, p. 83), or this relativeness of moral "truth" should not be confused with a moral relativism or nihilism. Instead, morality from the perspective of an ethic of care shows up the limitedness of each solution to its specific context. And while a particular moral decision may not be appropriate for other scenarios, this process of moral decision-making can be applied to any other moral conflict (Gilligan 1982a, p. 33).

Thus, while moral judgments within an ethic of justice are made via the deductive application of rules/universal principles to a particular situation, within an ethic of care they are formed by searching inductively for a solution that best affects all involved. In the case of the former, the morality of a decision lies primarily in the rational foundation of the applied norms and only secondarily in the concrete decision; contrastingly, in the case of the latter, the morality of a decision lies in the rational foundation of the specific concrete decision (and potentially its inapplicability to other situations) (cf. Pieper 1993, p. 181f.). And while for the former, the main criteria of morality are justice and fairness, for the latter, they are care and sympathy.

(c)   According to Gilligan, there are at least two moral orientations that, in their respective "truths," can be neither reduced to one another, nor sublated into a higher morality (1991, p. 81), but each represents a productive critique of its respective "one-sidedness." Thus, the development of the "female" conception of morality requires the integration of, for example, the idea of equal rights while maintaining the normative priority of care and sympathy. In other words, this conception of morality integrates other conceptions into itself (1984, p. 202f., 1991, p. 97ff.). To illustrate the relations of the two moralities to each other, Gilligan uses the Gestalt image as an ambiguous figure that, according to an individual's perspective, can appear to be either a duck or a rabbit. Of greatest importance to her are the facts that one individual never finds both interpretations in the Gestalt and that it is impossible to determine which interpretation of the image is the "true" one (1991, p. 84ff.).

However, the different conceptions of morality are, according to Gilligan, in no way reserved exclusively to the one sex or the other. And neither one is limited to either the public or the private sphere. Indeed, because of each conception's irreducibility, Gilligan believes it is necessary to be able to switch between both moral perspectives and to be able to assess a problem from the point of view of each, and she concludes that, in order to endure the tension that such lack of clarity means, each person requires a high degree of "tolerance for ambiguity" (1982, p. 25).

Ultimately, Gilligan's thesis of two moralities unleashed a wave of criticism, and it is in this controversy that I find what is most productive and most provocative in her thought.

3. The ethic of care as critical expansion and rereading of traditional morality

(a) Critical expansion of the discourse ethics of Habermas

Seyla Benhabib was one of the first to undertake a consideration of traditional morality in light of Gilligan's arguments toward a female conception of morality, and her essay "The generalized and the concrete other: the Kohlberg–Gilligan controversy and feminist theory" (Benhabib 1986) can thus be viewed as a classic. Her critical approach has also been groundbreaking as well.

For Benhabib, the normative potential of an ethic of care lies in its specifically context-bound character. Women tend to take the "standpoint of the 'particular other'" in their moral considerations, and this standpoint becomes the normative standard against which traditional conceptions must be measured. In most of the traditional conceptions, from Hobbes to Rawls and Kohlberg, she argues, morality is based on the "standpoint of the 'generalized other.'" Rawls's image of the "veil of ignorance" is a graphic example of this. Here, Rawls summarizes the conditions under which, ideally, moral decisions are to be made, that is, in a state in which one neither acknowledges himself nor the other, a condition in which he knows nothing about the personal characteristics or social status of any of the parties involved (Rawls 1971). To define morality in this way means, however, that morals can only be conceptualized from the perspective of the abstract autonomous individual. (This abstract image of the individual becomes particularly clear in Hobbes's comparison of people to mushrooms that seem to spring from the earth independently and with no relation to each other.) This restriction means that the moral decision has an exclusively monologic structure; in other words, a kind of play of thought of a single individual allows her or him to disregard her or his particular concrete individuality.

As Benhabib further demonstrates, traditional conceptions of morality do not fulfill their own expectations of reversibility and universalizability since they base their abstractions on the concrete other and her or his difference. Beyond this problem, such abstraction leads, from a woman's perspective, to a problematic narrowing of the realm of the moral, and in this way it leads to a strict division between questions of justice and questions of the good life, that is, between the public and the private (Benhabib 1986, pp. 405–10). It is also in this way that the experiences and interests of women are kept from the realm of the moral and are privatized.

Benhabib contends that, in contrast to these "formal–universalistic moral theories", "interactive universalism," as developed by Habermas in his ethics of discourse, regards "difference as a starting point for reflection and action." The ethics of discourse allows her to arrive at a productive union of both standpoints. Discourse ethics thus guarantees for her, first, that moral decisions are based on universal principles and are generalizable – two normative standards that she finds vital that a feminist perspective guarantee. Secondly, Benhabib presents an ethics of discourse in such a way that there can be no moral prejudgment that does not decide which aspects of a person are and are not relevant to the situation, and that does not acknowledge the specific parameters of the situation at hand. As Benhabib herself emphasizes, this interpretation of discourse ethics stands in direct opposition to what Habermas himself believes (Habermas 1986). For her, only when practical discourse has no limitations in advance can the perception of the other in her or his concrete individuality and concrete needs be guaranteed (cf. Fraser 1989a, p. 144ff.).

(b) Critical reformulation of Rawls's conception of justice

Susan Moller Okin's critique of Rawls's conception of morality represents two phases of feminist theory formation simultaneously. Initially, her emphasis is on pointing out the absence of the category of gender in his conception of justice, as well as the exclusion of women's realms of existence and experiences. She most effectively reveals these gaps in his theory in his construct, the "veil of ignorance." For Rawls, this veil conceals from the individual her or his own social status, system of values, etc., during the discovery of basic moral principles; of course, he leaves matters of gender and gender relations completely unaddressed (Okin 1989a, p. 91). This means, then, that, for Rawls, gender and family relationships do not fall into the category of matters of justice, and he thus reproduces the traditional division between public and private that has been problematic for women in innumerable ways. Additionally, Rawls's exclusion of gender proves to be a blatant paradox since he makes the family the central source of an individual's moral education (p. 9). But how, asks Moller Okin, can an individual develop a sense of justice from the family, with its patriarchal and sexist structure, when even parental love for the child – for Rawls the decisive foundation of the development of a moral personality – cannot remain untainted by its injustices?

In her later critique of Rawls, as she herself emphasizes, Moller Okin takes a somewhat different direction. Now she asks primarily to what extent presuppositions about a gender-specific structure of society affect Rawls's images of justice and how significantly they lead to argumentative inconsistencies (Okin 1989b). She thus proves that Rawls, in his unquestioning acceptance of the Kantian tradition of the separation of reason and emotion – a tradition in which emotion has no moral basis and in which morality has as its foundation rational insight into and abstraction from the concrete everyday – simply accepts uncritically the existing gender-specific division of labor. Okin finds Rawls's separation of reason and emotion incongruous with the rest of his theory since he also asserts that the development of a sense of justice is based on the experience of loving acceptance during childhood. She shows that a closer investigation of Rawls's theory reveals that his prioritization of general principles of justice – despite what he himself believes – relies on an empathetic capacity and an ability to recognize the other in her or his difference; she proves that care as well as recognition of difference are constitutive of his conception of justice. In other words, through her reading of Rawls's conception of justice, Moller Okin is able to affirm both the validity of Gilligan's assertion that it is impossible to join an ethic of justice and an ethic of care, and Benhabib's advocacy of linking universalization and recognition of difference. However, what remains open in Okin's reworking of Rawls's theory is how one can explain why the general principles of justice discovered behind the "veil of ignorance" contain in themselves no trace of a perspective of care.

(c) Rereading of Kant's moral philosophy

Herta Nagl-Docekal also uses as the starting point for her reflections the problematizing of Gilligan's assertion that justice and care follow two different logics. For Nagl-Docekal, Gilligan's theory relies on an insufficient differentiation between rights and morality, a problem which becomes particularly evident in her imprecise use of the term "universalism" (Nagl-Docekal 1993, p. 19). Thus, she argues that abstracting from the particularity of the individual (for Benhabib, the generalized other) is indeed a characteristic of Kant's doctrine of law but not for his moral philosophy. In his moral philosophy, he does not, as many claim he has, insist on disregarding the particularities of the individual; rather, he advocates focusing on those specificities (p. 25) and supports the individual in her or his pursuit of particular dreams of happiness as much as possible (p. 24) (cf. O'Neill 1993, p. 346ff.). Nagl-Docekal thus finds in Kant's moral philosophy a caring turn toward the individual in the form of a general law (p. 26), and this move then unifies the expectation of universal validity with care for the concrete individual in her or his particularity. In her conclusion, however, Nagl-Docekal leaves unaddressed whether Kant really means the particular dreams of happiness of the individual or if he means, instead, those aspects of happiness that he considers applicable to and pursuable by everyone (which in my opinion is closer to Kant's formulation).

All three of these exemplary reworkings of Gilligan presuppose that the central conceptions of morality, like those of Kant, Rawls, and Habermas, already contain central aspects of an ethic of care and that they only require proper readings to reveal these aspects. But these rereadings never actually consider the question of whether or not they themselves may actually miss the normative "kernel" of the respective moral orientations. This omission is remarkable since one of the central aspects of an ethic of care is its insistence on the possibility of different normative "truths" and the corresponding recognition of several moralities, while the traditional conception of justice allows only for one truth or rightness. The present-day hegemony of the justice perspective is evident not only in critics' apparent will to try to unite both moral orientations, but also in the fact that these attempts are based on an elaboration of the justice perspective. Marilyn Friedman thus entitles her reflections "Beyond caring." But why does she not call them "Beyond justice"?

4. Ethic of care

I shall concentrate in this section on two examples: Sara Ruddick's concept of maternal thinking and Joan C. Tronto's concept of an "ethic of care" (1993). They not only represent two of the most significant variations of independent ethics of care, but they also demonstrate the breadth of range the term "care" can cover.

(a) Maternal thinking

In her elaboration of "maternal thinking," Sara Ruddick proceeds from the assumption that moral and theoretical norms, forms of knowledge and criteria of truth all arise from specific social practices (p. 18ff.), and maternal thinking, which she reconstructs as an independent normative perspective, is thus a way of spelling out what is currently lived as "maternal praxis." She explicates both the intellectual and emotional abilities that individuals who perform this praxis must learn and develop, and the normative criteria they follow when acting and making decisions in specific situations.

"Maternal praxis," tied as it is to the existence of a child, can be performed by both men and women since it is a social and not a biological praxis; however, due to gendered division of labor, it is carried out more often by women. And, despite all its change due to historical and individual differences, it still has characteristic moments, or "demands," as Ruddick calls them: preservation, growth, and acceptability. Preservation, or protection, and fostering growth are demands that the child places on the mother. Thus, the child needs, on the one hand, "preservative love." This requires of the mothering person a primary behavior which Ruddick describes as "commitment," and here she implies a rather conservative protective attentiveness to the child. On the other hand, the mothering person needs the ability not only to perceive the changes in the growing child in order to promote the emotional and intellectual development of the child, but also the capacity to permit the child's detachment, that is, to let it go. The third demand, acceptability, comes primarily from society, or more specifically, from the concrete social environment. The mothering person must raise the child according to existing conventions so that it may develop in a way that is acceptable to general society. But, as Ruddick emphasizes, this particular requirement contains the danger of conformity and unquestioning acceptance of the values of dominant culture.

Important for Ruddick is that these demands are not simply of an emotional nature – that they are not only feelings like love or empathy – but that they also require reflection, knowledge, and the capacity for reason. She therefore speaks primarily of "maternal thinking" and characterizes "maternal praxis" as a scientific activity that can, like other scientific disciplines, draw out specific insights, truth criteria and values.

389

As understandable as this comparison to other disciplines is – striving as it does to prove that there is a knowledge dimension of maternal praxis – it is equally irritating that Ruddick does not compare maternal thinking to other normative conceptions. The goal of her critical practice is to bring maternal thinking as normative perspective in its own right into the public realm as, for instance, a critique of militarism and war. This means that, in her view, this social practice is bound to moral insights and values that can be further developed into a feminist maternal peace politics. These insights and values, however, are not primarily the property of either women or men. (For Ruddick, the peace-loving nature of women is just as much of a myth as is the violence of men.) They are, rather, abilities that are cultivated in social practice. But her presentation of maternal thinking as an independent normative alternative needs a moral-theoretical development, and by this I mean a critical analysis of existing moral problems of both feminist and traditional conceptions of morality. Without such a moral-theoretical situating, her approach remains helplessly simplistic.

(b) An ethic of care/an ethic of caring for others

In light of the inability of political theory to change the world, Joan Tronto (1993) wants, as she puts it, to enable with her book at least a glimpse of another world, a world "where the daily caring of people for each other is a valued premise of human existence" (p. x). Like Ruddick, Tronto proceeds on the assumption that forms of knowledge, insights, and values develop in concrete social praxes, and she seeks to construct an ethic of care from the everyday praxis of care for others. But unlike Ruddick, Tronto bases her thought on a very broad concept of care for others, one which, when examined closely, goes beyond "care" to a "caring for others." Compared to "care," a term of such breadth contains little danger of being misunderstood as a construction for an exclusively female morality since it covers many activities that men can also perform. "Caring for others" also makes clear that the current degradation of such activities is a problem not only of sexism, but also of racism and classism that can occur among women as well (p. 112ff.).

In developing the normative implications of the praxis of care for others, Tronto differentiates "four phases of caring" (p. 105ff.). The four elements of care are: caring about, noticing the need to care in the first place; taking care of, assuming responsibility for care; care-giving, the actual work of care that needs to be done; and care-receiving, the response of that which is cared for to the care (p. 127). Thus, for Tronto, the success of caring for others depends, firstly, upon the perception of the needs of another, as well as the readiness to take responsibility for those needs. But the action of caring is inadequate if the reaction of that other to the care is not first considered.

Further, Tronto extrapolates from this praxis of care for others "four ethical elements of care: attentiveness, responsibility, competence, and responsiveness" (p. 127). The first element of an ethic of caring for others is the attentiveness to the needs of others, or more precisely, for the concrete individuality of a person in her or his specific historical and social situation. But in order to fine-tune the capacity for such attentiveness in our society, there must be an increase in respect given to the care for others (p. 130). Additionally, Tronto argues that only those who are able not only to perceive their own needs, but also to satisfy them, are able to reach such a level of attentiveness to the needs of others.

Tronto distinguishes responsibility as a second ethical element from duty or obligation (p. 131). For her, what is important is the desire or willingness to do something for others. Acting out of a sense of duty means that one stands in an abstract relation to the situation at hand, and Tronto would rather see a "flexible notion of responsibility" in which the meaning of "responsibility" shifts according to each concrete context. She also believes that one requires a certain degree of competence to be able to carry out the work of caring successfully. She bases care-receiving, the fourth ethical element, on the insight that caring for others always occurs under conditions of vulnerability and inequality, and that it therefore requires a large capacity for attentiveness to others. And it is here that Tronto shows how closely her four elements work together, each providing the basis for the others (p. 136ff.).

Although Tronto understands her construction of an ethic of care as an independent normative conception, she simultaneously emphasizes the necessity of combining it with the perspective of justice. The latter is vital for the functioning of existing society, but the conception of justice must be transformed by its union with the ethic of care if we are to come close to realizing Tronto's vision of a "more just world that embodies good caring" (p. xii). But just exactly how this transformation is to take place remains unclear.

5. Concluding remarks

In all of these models, the primary goal is a further development of morality. Only rarely do indications that morality has anything to do with power, domination, and oppression appear. Moreover, these theories restrict themselves to only certain aspects of traditional morality. Interestingly, they primarily problematize moral norms like care and sympathy as elements of patriarchal oppression, while ignoring the inherent connection of norms like justice and equality to patriarchal domination (cf. Nagl-Docekal 1993, Rommelspacher 1992, p. 63ff.). Additionally, a fundamental critique of modern bourgeois moral discourse, or of even morality itself, never becomes a theme; therefore, critical considerations of the social origin, function and meaning of morality also never enter into this debate.

I, however, understand morality as such as a hegemonic discourse. Conceptions of morality are not merely certain sets of norms or social expectations that people do or do not follow. They are, rather, complex amalgamations of a multiplicity of ways of thinking, feeling, and acting, body praxes, forms of knowledge, social relations, and institutions. Within them, thinking, feeling, and acting are normativized, censored and disciplined, as well as constituted. This is how single individuals become autonomous moral subjects within modern bourgeois moral discourse.

Gilligan's formulation of the gender-specific, different moral orientations gives a graphic representation of the hegemonic "effect" that structures the entire personality within the dominant moral discourses of Western bourgeois–capitalist societies. Her theory shows this effect's elemental contribution not only to the constitution of gender-differentiated moral subjects, but also those very subjects and genders (Maihofer 1988, 1995). Also apparent in her theory is the structural tendency of morality – and also for the ethic of care – to individualize and personalize social relations.

I argue, however, not for an abstinence from normative discourses. I believe this would be neither politically sensible (as long as morality remains central for societies) nor practicable (as long as the individual remains foundational for the moral subject). I would instead advocate the critical analysis and transformation of essential structural elements of dominant morality (for example, the traditional notion of universalism) in order to make them available for new uses. The explosive effect of the perspective of care and empathy as formulated by Gilligan lies in my view less in individual norms or in its critique of traditional morality than it does in the proof of the existence of (at least) two moral perspectives. And it is here that I find a productive critique of traditional universalism. In contrast to the monistic conception of universalism and its belief that there can be only one morality or none at all, the insistence on at least two conceptions of morality points toward the idea of a plural universalism. In light of the increasing bumping up against each other of different cultural normative standards both within a single society and on a worldwide level, it seems to me that the idea of the coexistence of several equally valid conceptions of morality must be foregrounded. The conception of a plural universalism necessitates the discursive institutionalization of a permanent self-critical reflection on, one, the structural imperialism of traditional universalism on the basis of its inherent hegemonic expectation of the universal validity of its own norms (an expectation that even a plural universalism could only avoid through constant self-critique); two, the social relativity and limitation of its own norms; and three, the fact that conceptions of morality are always constitutive elements of existing social relations of power and domination, and that analyses of norms are always also analyses of social relations of power and domination. Additionally, it needs the development of normative rules and political praxes that are able to guarantee a mutual, nonhierarchical recognition of sociocultural differences, a goal toward which the paradoxical idea of a plural universalism could be a first step.

39

Impartiality

MARILYN FRIEDMAN

In modern Western philosophy, impartial reasoning has defined the moral point of view and determined the strategies of moral justification. Political philosophers have invoked it as well, to legitimate certain governmental and social institutions. Normative impartiality has become highly controversial in recent years, however, and feminists have contributed substantially to these debates.

Impartial reasoning is, in two senses, not partial. First, it is not incomplete, but rather involves complete. or at least adequate. consideration of all relevant interests. Second, and more importantly, it is not one-sided or biased among those relevant interests. Impartiality manifests a special sort of consistency: similar cases are to be considered similarly, regardless of the subjective commitments of the moral reasoner. Differential consideration requires some genuine difference in the cases themselves and not merely a difference in the reasoner's loyalties. In traditional discussions, human beings are assumed capable of approximating the impartial point of view to a degree significant enough to warrant its role as a definitive standard of justified normative reasoning and deliberation.

Feminists have challenged the concept of impartiality in both of its major normative uses. We have contested its employment as a definition of the moral point of view and we have disputed its capacity to legitimate political institutions. These trends in feminist philosophy parallel recent critical developments within mainstream moral philosophy against its own modern traditions. Feminist criticism, however, brings to this movement a distinctive concern for the cultural practices of gender, hierarchy, and oppression, and the role played by impartialist normative traditions in sustaining those practices. Despite expressing the notion of unbiased concern for all interests, according to many feminists, impartialist theories and their practical applications have contributed to the subordination of women.

Impartiality in moral philosophy

In ethical theory, impartiality is often expressed as the equal consideration of the interests of all persons. This general requirement is articulated differently in the two major ethical traditions of modern philosophy. In utilitarianism (Mill 1979), impartiality requires that one consider the well-being of everyone who is affected

393

by one's behavior, and that one balance the pains and pleasures of all affected parties against each other, foes and strangers as well as friends, when determining the right thing to do. In Kantian ethics (Kant 1964), impartiality requires pure rational apprehension of the moral law, a disregard of one's own subjective emotions and attachments, an equal regard for all persons as intrinsically valuable ends-in-themselves, and a sense of duty and respect for the moral law as the primary moral motivation, even in close personal relationships. Kantian ethics has probably served as the paradigm of an impartialist ethical tradition.

In at least two respects, the traditional ideal of impartiality contributes to the age-old devaluation of women's moral capacities. First, the concept of impartiality undergirds modern moral theory's emphasis on moral rationality at the expense of moral emotion. Because women have long been stereotyped as more emotional and less rational than men (e.g. Kant 1960), the ideal of impartiality defines yet another rational achievement of which women were presumed incapable.

Second, in requiring the absence of bias toward or against any subjective interests, impartiality thereby demands that the moral agent reason in detachment from her own loyalties, projects, and emotions. These forms of detachment, however, are inimical to what is required for the maintenance of close personal relationships. Personal relationships call for emotional attachment, preferential commitment, responsiveness to the particularity of the loved one, and a direct concern for her well-being as the primary moral motivation. Impartial reason thus seems on the face of it to be incapable of motivating or justifying the close personal relationships that are so important to our lives. It seems no coincidence that modern moral philosophy's emphasis on impartial reason has coincided with widespread theoretical neglect of the morality of close personal relationships.

Women's moral horizons have long been regarded as limited by their commitments to close personal relationships, especially those of family, commitments which they were presumed incapable of surmounting. By seeming to devalue the moral importance of close relationships, the traditional ideal of impartiality again diminishes esteem for women's moral capacities and concerns. Even though women do not all take up traditional female roles, nevertheless, social esteem for women in general appears to hinge importantly on the degree of societal value accorded to traditional female work. Many feminists have therefore made a point of vindicating the values embodied in that work, especially those of emotionality and attention to close personal relationships.

Around 1980, capping a decade of related work by other theorists, moral psychologist Carol Gilligan articulated what she portrayed as a distinctively female moral voice: an ethical orientation toward care (Gilligan 1982a). Gilligan's studies upheld the traditional view that emotionality and care for particular others were distinctive features of women's moral standpoint. Where traditionalists had seen these traits as moral deficits, however, Gilligan hailed care ethics as the moral equal of the contrasting, impartialist (and apparently masculinist) ethic preoccupied with matters of rights and justice.

Care ethics appears to disregard the impartialist requirements of equal concern for all involved parties and an absence of preference for any particular interests over others. The care-ethical point of view does not require such emotional detachment and disengagement. Instead, one's own concern for the interests of particular others itself defines the caring point of view. In addition, a care orientation seems to call for the moral motivation of direct emotional concern for the loved one and her well-being, rather than a Kantian, impartialist motivation of duty based on a rational respect for the moral law. Even kindness and generosity toward strangers often depart from impartialism in being oriented toward the differentiating particulars of those in need (Blum 1987, pp. 321–35). Care ethics, and especially the morality of close personal relationships, have thus seemed to require a moral orientation that is decidedly not impartial.

Defenders of impartial moral theories have responded extensively to this critique (e.g. Hill 1987, pp. 131–3; Baron 1991, pp. 838–44). They agree that close personal relationships are central to fulfilled human lives and that the partial concern we each feel for our loved ones is not something that most human beings can feel for all other persons equally. Impartialists, however, distinguish between the abstract standpoint required for justifying moral reasoning and the practical standpoint that a moral agent takes up when deciding what to do in a particular situation facing her. They argue that impartiality is a stance required for justifying moral principles and judgments, but not necessarily a stance for deliberating about what to do in everyday moral situations, in which one usually cares about some but not all others. As the particular persons we are, facing our everyday lives, we certainly do not, nor should we, think ourselves equally responsible for the well-being of all other persons indiscriminately.

If our partial loves and loyalties are morally permissible or required, however, say the impartialists, they must be justifiable from an impartial, or subjectively unbiased, standpoint. This means that they must be justifiable in accord with reasons that give no special weight to one's own interests or those of people for whom one happens to be specially concerned. If it is morally permissible or right, for example, that I, as a mother, care preferentially for my own child, then this rightness must be impartially recognizable; it does not follow from my subjective preferences alone (Hill 1987, pp. 132–3; Baron 1991, pp. 842–4).

The impartial motive of duty, argue its defenders, embodies a commitment to take the moral rightness of an action as a reason for doing it and the moral wrongness of an action as a reason for not doing it (Herman 1993b, ch. 2). It functions importantly as a "secondary motive," a limiting condition on the other aims and projects an agent will undertake; the agent is thereby committed to doing only what is morally permitted. Loves and loyalties are not intrinsically so motivating and can as easily prompt us to do wrong as good for the sake of those we love. The motive of duty is, furthermore, compatible with the simultaneous influence of a motivation to care for a particular other person. Duty, in other words, does not rule out congruent affections. The best emotions and caring attachments, however, are those guided by a commitment to be moral.

395

Impartialists, furthermore, warn of the moral dangers involved in some forms of care, commitment, and preferential concern for certain others. Some forms of partiality are morally problematic, for example, sexism and racism. Too much of an emphasis on partiality may well license parochial moral attitudes limited merely to a concern for "my own" friends, family, or kind (Friedman 1993, ch. 2). On the impartialist view, impartial moral principles remain the best basis for differentiating morally permissible from impermissible forms of partiality.

Contemporary moral impartialists thus accommodate the "personal turn" in ethics by singling out and vindicating the role played by impartiality in the process of moral justification. Conscious impartial reasoning is not necessarily required for everyday moral deliberation and responsiveness. It is, however, the requisite standpoint for justifying behavior on moral grounds. If the moral agent herself is to act in a way that manifests her own commitment to behaving morally, then she must now and then, from an impartial standpoint, consider the moral legitimacy of the rules, judgments, maxims, motivations, and responses that guide her everyday actions. For impartial moral theorists, the justificatory role for impartiality is definitive and irreducible; no partial perspective can provide adequate moral justification for moral rules, judgments, maxims, motivations, or responses. The more impartial a perspective is, the more it approximates the ideal point of view for moral justification.

This impartialist response shifts the terms of the debate. The question now is not whether impartial reason is sufficient to motivate the concern and emotionality required by close personal relationships; impartialists agree that it is not. It is still needed, however, to *justify* that concern from a moral standpoint. Impartialists thus reassert the ubiquity of impartiality as a defining criterion of the point of view required for moral justification. This requirement holds, according to impartialists, regardless of the moral matter under consideration, whether broad-scale questions of social justice or small-scale questions of domestic intimacy.

The new defense of impartiality, in general, thus consists in admitting its restricted role in moral deliberation while insisting on its preeminent role in moral justification. The contribution of impartiality to morality is thus clarified and qualified. Criticisms of impartiality, however, have not abated. In the current state of the debate, the most relevant challenges are those that question whether impartiality, and the methods lately conceptualized for attaining it, really provide either a necessary or sufficient standard for moral justification.

Few feminists today, it seems, regard the ideal of impartiality as providing an adequate or exhaustive standard for moral justification. Many feminist philosophers argue either that (1) impartiality is altogether useless as an ideal of moral justification, or (2) that it is useful, perhaps necessary, but insufficient in some way, either because it needs to be supplemented by other moral capacities and resources, or because it applies only to a limited domain of morality. Many feminists contend, in addition, that the ideal of impartiality has been deployed in a positively misleading manner in both theoretical and practical contexts, often to the detriment of women.

396

Some feminists have concluded that impartiality is useless for moral justification since it constitutes an impossible human attainment. Human thinking cannot be entirely detached from the social or historical context of its origin, nor can it be completely severed from its motivating passions and commitments (Young 1990a, pp. 103–5). We have, at any rate, no way of knowing with sufficient reliability that we have achieved impartiality by any of the major methods lately recommended by prominent philosophers, such as the "veil of ignorance" or universalizability (Friedman 1993, ch. 1).

Bypassing the question of whether impartiality is humanly possible, other feminists simply consider impartiality to be a useful but limited ideal for guiding the process of moral justification. On one view, the impartial standpoint applies mainly to the public realm of impersonal relationships and to the exercise of formal offices defined by duties of fairness. It is not capable of justifying or properly motivating all the various behaviors that we intuitively regard as morally necessary or important to personal relationships. Caring for a friend, say, will fulfill the requirements of friendship better if grounded in care for that particular person than if grounded in impartial motives. A person's very specific loyalties, loves, commitments, and caring responses are just as adequate in defining a standpoint for moral justification, for the personal realm, as is impartiality, for the public realm (Blum 1980, ch. 3; Blum 1994, ch. 2).

Other feminists urge, by contrast, that matters of care and personal relationship are just as much a part of impartialist morality as the public issues of justice that often serve as paradigmatic impartialist moral concerns. On this view, the real problem lies in traditional philosophy's misconception of impartial reason as excluding close relationships and care from its domain. Along with matters of justice, however, those concerns fall under the scope of an impartial perspective premised on the equal worth of all persons and on equal respect for the viewpoints of others (Benhabib 1992b, pp. 178–89).

Still other feminists warn that impartialist ethical reasoning might be incomplete even for public or administrative contexts. Impartiality requires that persons and situations be conceptualized in terms of generalizable categories. This approach ignores the rich contextual detail of particular situations. Comprehending particularity, however, is a crucial part of moral understanding. Where it must be neglected for the sake of bureaucratic efficiency, the resulting generality of thought is not ideal but is rather a deficient, even if necessary, compromise (Flanagan and Adler 1983; Walker 1989a, p. 23).

A related criticism of the justificatory insufficiency of impartial reason is that it cannot accommodate morally salient human differences such as sex or race. Impartiality requires that the morally relevant categories used to describe persons and circumstances be generalizable and be applied consistently across actual and possible cases. The particulars that differentiate moral subjects and situations and that cannot as such be grasped through generalizable categories are ignored, thus omitting a recognition of "difference" from moral thinking (Young 1990a, pp. 97–9).

397

In addition, the generalizable categories that we have to rely on for the purposes of impartial thinking often hide covert biases that impartial reason is powerless to extirpate. Understanding persons and their experiences is a process that is usually carried out in terms of culturally transmitted moral images and concepts. These representations tend to express the perspectives of socially dominant groups and often misrepresent the identities, experiences, and perspectives of widely devalued or marginalized groups. Understandings of gender, for example, teem with such cultural prejudices.

Culturally entrenched biases might well not be apparent to the consciousness of a moral subject and might harbor no obvious inconsistency. In the absence of noticeable inconsistency or bias, the conventionally recommended methods for thinking impartially are powerless to recognize or correct the biases in question. The well-rounded moral agent needs reflective strategies additional to those of impartial reason to correct culturally pervasive, group-based biases. On this view, impartiality is necessary for moral justification but must be supplemented by other moral capacities and resources, such as empathy with others, if moral justification is to be thoroughgoing (Meyers 1994).

The ideal of impartiality, furthermore, has been conceptualized and deployed in a manner that oversimplifies and misrepresents the complex nature of moral reasoning. The rhetoric of impartiality, for example, has presupposed the standpoint of a detached, uninvolved, judge/administrator reasoning in isolation. This portrait emphasizes resources such as full knowledge that are humanly unachievable. At the same time, it fails to illuminate the authentic capacities, such as concerned attentiveness and interpersonal dialogue, that contribute to real human moral reasoning and understanding under conditions of human finitude, uncertainty, and risk (Walker 1989a, 1991).

Also, impartiality has been traditionally explicated as a "monological" enterprise, the task of an isolated reasoner relying on her own intellectual resources without the benefit of dialogue with others. This picture conceals the socially shared nature of moral knowledge. The best, and perhaps the only genuine, moral understandings emerge from a process of real dialogue among people with differing viewpoints (Young 1990a, pp. 106–20; Benhabib 1992b, pp. 163–70).

Finally, even if impartiality is a sufficient standpoint for moral justification across all moral domains, nevertheless there is more to moral understanding than simply moral justification. The obsession with justification has led moral philosophy to neglect, for example, the developmental origin of adult capacities for moral reflection, a topic of special concern to women, whose nurturant labors have been central to those processes (Calhoun 1988, pp. 456–8). It has also distracted philosophers from exploring other capacities that are critical to moral understanding, such as the caring attentiveness to particular persons that is necessary if we are to grasp actual human needs and circumstances (Blum 1994, ch. 2).

To summarize feminist views about impartiality and moral theory: impartiality is, at best, a partial ideal of moral justification, one that needs to be supplemented by other moral capacities and resources, and, at worst, an unattainable and therefore completely misleading ideal. Those who regard it as attainable diverge over whether it is limited in scope to the moral domain of impersonal relationships and formally defined roles, or whether it extends as well to caring connections, family life, and gender relationships. Recent state-of-the-art accounts of the methods for achieving impartial reasoning, however, often call for humanly impossible reflective tasks (such as subjective detachment and full knowledge). In addition, they obscure the role of the other moral capacities and resources (such as empathy and dialogue) that finite and limited human beings require for real-world moral justification, capacities that suspiciously tend to be associated with women more than men.

Impartiality in political philosophy

Impartiality, in liberal political philosophy, has been a legitimating ideal for the "public" sphere of government, state, and civil society where (male) citizens have long met as hypothetical equals to authorize their common political life. Women's near-complete historical exclusion from the public realm until the twentieth century was rationalized at least in part by women's presumed incapacity for the impartiality demanded by the public sphere. At the same time, impartiality has decidedly not been idealized for the "private" sphere of marriage and family life. Women's presumed rational incapacity also served to legitimate men's domination of women within the private sphere (Young 1990a, pp. 107–11). Mindful of this historic role of the ideal of impartiality, feminists look with suspicion at any appeals to impartiality that are used today to justify political institutions.

Notions of impartiality have especially pervaded social contractarian defenses of liberalism. According to contract theory, a form of government is legitimate if it was, or hypothetically could be, the object of consent by each of its citizens reasoning in a certain defined manner about the political institutions that would best serve what are assumed to be her or his basic interests. By modeling commonalities of reason underlying the varied viewpoints of differently situated citizens, contractual thinking is supposed to disclose the form of political organization to which it would be rational for all citizens to consent.

John Rawls's social contract theory has dominated recent Anglo-American political philosophy as a paradigm of liberal contractarianism (Rawls 1971, 1993). Rawls's social contractor reasons behind a "veil of ignorance." She has no intrinsic interest in the well-being of other persons, and she avoids appealing to any particular self-identifying knowledge, including her actual social position and privileges (or lack of them). This contractual reasoner may appeal to the basic goods that she (and anyone) has an interest in pursuing and to general knowledge of social life. Her reasoning is thereby supposed to represent how any rational person would think about the principles of justice that should regulate her society (Rawls 1971, pp. 136–42).

399

One feminist concern about Rawlsian impartial reason is the "monological" nature that it shares with traditional moral theory in general (Benhabib 1992b, pp. 163–70). Rawls portrays contractual thinking as the isolated reflections of a lone reasoner deciding the principles of an ideally just society. This solitary portrait of normative political reasoning obscures the fundamentally interpersonal, social, communicative, or "dialogical" nature of normative political reasoning. In liberal democracy, in particular, intersubjectively shared moral understandings should constitute the legitimating standard of political institutions and practices.

Another problem in Rawls's theory lies in its conception of social contractors as rational deliberators who lack any particular interest in, or emotional concern for, each other. Given the historic association of women with emotion, any theory of moral understanding that disregards emotion is suspect. Some feminists argue, however, that Rawls's account of impartiality can be remedied to accommodate moral emotion (Okin 1989b, pp. 238–49). If a Rawlsian contractor is to represent the viewpoints of all other persons equally, as Rawls would have her do, then she must understand those others, a feat requiring empathy and concern for them.

A different problem with impartialist social contract theories is their obsessive focus on matters of distributive justice. The impartial notion of equal consideration for all persons yields a theoretical predilection for problems about the equitable distribution of social benefits and burdens. This approach is deeply individualistic, however, and excludes consideration of all those group-based oppressions, such as cultural marginalization, that do not constitute strict distributive injustices (Young 1990a, ch. 1 and pp. 112–20).

Contractarian impartialists have historically presumed a male citizen as the model contractual reasoner (Benhabib 1992b, pp. 152–8). No serious political philosopher today would limit citizenship to men only and, indeed, Rawls calls for contractual reasoners to disregard their sex identity altogether when reasoning behind the veil of ignorance (Rawls 1971, pp. 24–5). Feminists have doubted, however, that such sexless reasoning is possible (Okin 1989a, pp. 106–8). They have suspected that, under the guise of sexlessness, male bias reappears covertly, for example, in Rawls's suggestion that all social contractors be considered "heads of households," a traditionally masculine role identity (Rawls 1971, p. 128).

The apparent male bias of the head-of-household imagery is reinforced by Rawls's retention of the historic liberal split between public and private realms, a split that has confined and disadvantaged women. Rawls's 1971 social contract theory confines the family and the sphere of domestic and personal relationships to the private realm, thereby excluding them from the purview of impartial reason and public principles of justice. This approach shields domestic violence and oppression, such as woman battering, from legal intervention and permits male power to dominate family life. Given their well-known abuses, family life and gender relationships are surely proper subjects for impartial justice reasoning (Okin 1989a, ch. 5).

The Rawlsian requirement that the impartial reasoner disregard her own self-identifying knowledge has also come under attack. Feminists question whether such disengaged reasoning is even possible, particularly with regard to the social relationships and communities that constitute self-identity, and which seem to be more readily acknowledged as such by women than by men (Benhabib 1992b, pp. 155–62).

The view of contractual reasoners as devoid of self-identifying particulars furthermore turns them into "generalized others" whose differentiated identities disappear. Moral reasoning based on this conception of persons neglects the morally important particularity and concrete identity of others. Selves can no longer be individuated and the notions of respecting and taking the perspective of the other become meaningless under such forms of reasoning. The remedy for this problem consists in viewing selves as "concrete others" (Benhabib 1992b, pp. 158–66).

In general, public appeals to impartiality have been politically deceitful, again to women's detriment. In the public sphere of government and citizen participation, the rhetoric of impartiality masks the exercise of power by socially dominant groups. Lawmaking and bureaucratic administration reflect the interests of those who are powerful enough to control those processes and to influence cultural representations and understandings. The power of such groups is obscured both by the rhetoric of an idealized state transcending partial and particular interests in the name of the common good, and by the rhetoric of ideal legislators or judges supposedly transcending politics and ideology (Young 1990a, pp. 111–16). While this abuse of the concept of impartiality does not itself show the concept to be intrinsically flawed, it does show that appeals to impartiality can be oppressively misused in practice.

To summarize feminist views about impartiality in political philosophy: impartiality, as an ideal for legitimating political institutions, is historically untrustworthy in practice because it has been particularly identified with masculinity and the public sphere and used to rationalize women's confinement to and subordination within the private domestic realm. The domestic institutions of family and gender relationships have thereby been shielded from the reach of law and public policy, thus giving free reign to male dominance in family and gender life. Even if reconceptualized without those associations, current notions of impartiality are still limited in their justificatory political authority. In Rawls's social contract theory, for example, impartiality is misconceived as an undertaking of persons who do not communicate with each other and are prohibited from appealing to the particular knowledge of self or other by which alone they might genuinely comprehend and represent alternative viewpoints. Furthermore, the impartialist emphasis on fairness toward individuals has biased the focus of impartiality-based theories of justice toward matters of distributive justice, thereby ignoring matters of non-distributive, group-based oppression.

40

Lesbian ethics

SARAH LUCIA HOAGLAND

Lesbian ethics is an ethics of resistance and creation. It is not a set of rules of right behavior or injunctions of duty and obligation or delineations of good character that one may find in utilitarian, deontologic, and virtue treatises. It is a liberatory conceptual journey which emerges from recognized contexts of oppression, and as such challenges some unstated assumptions of traditional Anglo-European ethics. Lesbian ethics is an envisioning and discussion of possibilities, given lesbian lives, for a transformation of values. As such it is not a matter of moral reform, a matter of preservation of and better adherence to existing values. It is a call for another type of moral change, moral revolution.

Emerging from the women's liberation movement, lesbian ethics challenges the concept of female agency prescribed by the feminine fiction of masculine discourse, the model of the good woman. Lesbian ethics also addresses various consequences of oppression among lesbians, both as victims and as perpetrators of oppression. Its theorists consider, in one way or another, questions of liberatory value.

Much work of the early women's liberation movement exposed patriarchal lies about women's lives (for example, lesbian invisibility, myths of motherhood, and the misnaming, trivializing and/or naturalizing of male violence against women), thereby breaking silence. In 1979 Adrienne Rich raised the question of lying among women, challenging us to address ways we treat each other: "There is a danger run by all powerless people that we forget we are lying, or that lying becomes a weapon we carry over into relationships with people who do not have power over us." With "Women and honor" she calls for a new ethics for women: an honorable relationship is not possible until there can be truth between us, for the lie is "a shortcut through another's personality": often when one lies to another it is because she does not want to deal with the other's reactions (Rich 1989b).

Mary Daly (1978) began exploring feminist metaethics, gyn/ecology, revealing ways patriarchal value structures our thinking about good and evil, beginning with Eve. Patriarchal categories and myths form and limit moral values; for example, the destruction of the Western goddesses left us with the Virgin Mary, who is the only female near-deity we have access to in mainstream Christian society, and she is a paradigm rape victim. These mythic texts "legitimate institutions that degrade women's being" and stunt women's agency. Ancient goddesses were powerful forces in societies – goddesses of wisdom, of the hunt, of justice, of weaving, of revenge ... Mary Daly challenges the sense of female agency promoted through patriarchal myth – the heteropatriarchal category of "good woman" which includes neither female power (powerful women are evil) nor female bonding. She goes into the background to un/cover *possibilities* of self-creation, woman-identification, female agency, and a new ethic – helping us to re/member our selves. Gloria Anzaldúa notes Coatlicué and Tonantzin were similarly suppressed in the case of Guadalupe, the Mexican Virgin Mary (Anzaldúa 1987).

Developing what she calls materialist lesbianism, Monique Wittig (1992) argues that lesbians are not women. This is not a point about biology. Heterosexuality is a political regime resting on the submission and appropriation of women by men. She likens this to class conflict, arguing that just as the conflict between worker and employer becomes apparent when workers resist, so the conflict between men and women becomes apparent when women resist – for example, when women love women. Love between women defies the arbitrary division of man into Norm and Other. Challenging the concept of "difference," she argues the categories "man" and "woman" must be destroyed. Central to her position are the material conditions of the man/woman distinction: men arrogate women economically, sexually, and politically. "Lesbian" is a category outside the distribution of women by men much like a runaway slave is outside the regime of slavery. Thus the category "lesbian" holds the possibility of not replicating domination.

French-speaking radical lesbians (in Quebec and France) and, more generally, French feminists, focus on the concept of "difference" as key. The cliché, "Vive la différence!" appeals to an idea of "natural difference" between men and women. Following Simone de Beauvoir, Monique Wittig challenges biological essentialism. She argues that those in power construct sex difference and race difference for the purpose of masking conflicts of interest and maintaining domination. Difference is essentially dualistic and hence hierarchical. Unlike mainstream French feminists, radical lesbians refuse to romanticize or reify difference, alterity. Refusing to valorize the feminine spaces of masculinist discourse, French-speaking radical lesbians do not embrace the very characteristics men assign to women and claim to value while simultaneously citing as reasons to diminish and exclude women.

Whether we appeal to a notion of universality or to Hegelian and Marxist dialectics, the resulting concept of "difference" condemns the Other to always remain Other; agency, including the power of naming, remains with the One. Monique Wittig cites, for example, the failure of the Communist revolution – the bourgeoisie retained the power of naming, denying agency to the proletariat except through the framework of exchange. Thought based on the primacy of difference is the thought of domination. "Sexes (gender), difference between the sexes, man, woman, race, black, white, nature are at the core of [the straight mind's] set of parameters. They have shaped our concepts, our laws, our institutions, our cultures." Challenging mainstream French feminists, Monique Wittig argues that if lesbians keep the categories of wo/man, we embrace categories upheld by material conditions of appropriation and exploitation. Instead we must face the historical necessity of constituting ourselves as individual subjects of our history and conceptually revaluing the world.

In the United States we have been less broadly affected by Marxist ideology (there is no "Communist" voter category in the United States, as there is in European countries, and Marx is not regularly taught as part of our intellectual history). On the other hand, in the United States "worker" has been constructed as "white" while "black" is constructed in the dominant ideology as an economic drain. Theorists of color have created strong counter hegemonic discourses (largely tamed, appropriated, and/or ignored by white academics). And women of color have forced white women to directly consider race. So while in the United States and Canada there are strong strains of Marxist/socialist feminist theorizing, and while among lesbians there has also been significant focus on questions of difference, arguments concerning difference have developed distinct from those of many European radical lesbians and feminists.

Perhaps the most resounding retheorizing of difference began with Audre Lorde challenging white women's ignoring of racism (1984). She starts with a Marxist/Hegelian notion of difference as dialectic but takes her explorations in a direction distinct from Monique Wittig. While recognizing that in much of Western European history, difference between us has meant that one of us must be inferior, she nevertheless finds the concept of difference the source of possibility for new value. She argues, for example, that to deny difference between two of us in the name of love is to abandon the relationship.

However, she does not accept difference as constructed by white men in power. Audre Lorde's insight is to rest not with dualism, but to work toward pluralism. Lesbians and women need to look at the particulars of our different lives, how they develop in specific contexts, how conditions of oppression affect them, how racism and classism, for example, as well as sexism and heterosexism, inform them. If we do not we will not recognize or understand various ways we resist, nor will we understand various manifestations of oppression nor how we are indoctrinated in ways we have not suspected and perpetuate oppression, and we will not understand how we create alternatives.

Basically, Audre Lorde argues that the Other is created by *ignoring* difference(s). For example, when white women ignore our built-in privilege of whiteness and (re)define woman in terms of our own experience, then women of color become Other. White women erase, white out, the fact that women of other cultures have constructed means of resistance from within distinct traditions, thereby relying on Anglo-European forms of resistance and hence on Anglo-European culture for our conceptual possibilities, even when attempting to separate from that culture because of its oppressive values. And that puts white feminists in the position of making women of color Other. Thus while recognizing women are Other, actually many others, Audre Lorde does not move away from difference but rather into it. Most importantly, she does not romanticize difference or treat it as uniform, nor does she leave it in a dualistic relationship with the Norm, rather she rejects the Norm, refusing it as a standard of measure. She locates explorations of difference in the very real lives of many different and particular women in distinct contexts. This work is a source of women's and lesbians' strength and resistance.

Shortly, Cherrie Moraga and Gloria Anzaldúa's anthology, *This Bridge Called My Back* (1981), arrived. Radical women of color, many lesbian, began giving voice to radically distinct experiences, constructing theory at times through storytelling. This work complicates understanding and develops concepts not addressed by Euro-centered ethical theory. One theme concerns having learned to live with contradictions, especially the contradiction of the pressure to fit into a dominant (white) culture while realizing that success would lead to self-annihilation. Another concerns how white women use race privilege at the expense of women of color, for example using something a woman of color has said when it supports the white woman's theory, but otherwise ignoring the work of women of color as if there were nothing to learn there, nothing that could challenge her own theory. A third is that one could be both an oppressor and a victim. These developments continue the exploration of ways one could move out of the trap of being either in the conceptual framework of the Norm (in this case, whites) or of the Other as constructed by the Norm.

I consider how lesbians undermine our efforts to escape heteropatriarchal traps, particularly as we use our survival skills against each other and as we are drawn into the framework of the Norm by means of ethics. As political analyses developed complexity, feminist activists reached uncritically for traditional Anglo-European ethical concepts to quell dissent, often to ignore difference. These ethical concepts coerce "consensus" rather than enable individual agency and integrity; thus they undermine lesbian connection and community.

By looking to lesbian lives, we find values of female agency and community distinct from those promoted under heterosexualism where female agency is developed in terms of self-sacrifice, and where community is understood as hegemonic and difference a threat. For example in heteropatriarchy, self-sacrifice is contrasted with selfishness, a good woman being self-sacrificial, caring; she who chooses herself is selfish. Implicit in this dichotomy is the idea that choice involves a loss – I must choose between two things (myself or my husband/children) and sacrifice one (myself). Behind this is an imperialist idea – that everything that exists is ours or ought to be – so when we choose between two things, we lose something that is ours. Among lesbians, however, nothing that exists is ours; everything lesbian that exists has been created by lesbians – publishing houses, journals, bookstores, coffeehouses, festivals, even lesbian motherhood. So from lesbian lives we can understand that agency is creative, not sacrificial. Choice is a source of enabling power: where I focus my attention and put my energy, there I create meaning.

Community for lesbians also holds new conceptual possibilities, new value; since we come from every culture, we have possibilities of understanding difference in ways distinct from Anglo-European culture. Under white, colonial heteropatriarchy we are infused with the Hegelian understanding of difference as

405

oppositional, hence a threat: for me to be self-consciously aware I need to be reflected back by others, but if others don't reflect me as I want to be seen, I lose my self. So I try to dominate the Other as the Other tries to dominate me. If we exist in a Hegelian one-on-one antagonistic relationship it seems either the Other's values or mine must prevail and thus difference is capable of annihilating me.

However we exist as selves in community, autokoenously, as one among many. As I meet you, you can make me self-conscious of being other than I think of myself. This does not lead to annihilation. For example, a lesbian of color can mirror a white lesbian in ways that expose the white lesbian's racism which can lead the white lesbian to new knowledge, knowledge she has no access to if she simply discounts this mirroring. On the other hand, a white lesbian can racistly mirror a lesbian of color. This can't just be discounted, it must be dealt with and resisted. However, it does not follow that only one value persists. Instead, as we are multiply mirrored in community, our selves become refracted and complex (Lugones, forthcoming). And within community I can assess the mirrors, gain vital information, and consider what I will resist and what I will develop (of my own values as well as of others'). Once we understand this, we realize that difference is not only not a threat, it is, as Audre Lorde argues, a source of knowledge at the center of our survival. And community can be understood not as a state or a formal institution, but a context, a place of reference, where new meaning, lesbian meaning, can emerge (Bechdel 1986, 1988, 1990, 1992).

Pursuing a transformation of values while addressing questions of difference, Gloria Anzaldúa (1987) develops the concept of *la mestiza*, the borderdweller. Borders are dividing lines defining places safe and unsafe, distinguishing "us" from "them." She argues the "us/them" dichotomy is the root of all violence, reality split in two. People living in the borderlands, the place between cultures where reside those who inhabit both but fit nowhere, become adept at switching modes. They are the queer, the half-breed, la mestiza. Significantly Gloria Anzaldúa makes it clear that in the borderlands the Other has its own identity separate from the narcissistic consciousness of the Norm, and further that those exist who exceed dualism, who are neither Norm nor Other.

Thus la mestiza goes beyond a synthesis of two opposing powers, in fact she may even separate from them. Instead, by straddling two or more cultures and being caught where beliefs are not constructed and there are no definitions, she experiences a loss of meaning and sense of agency, she enters a state of intimate terror. Once here, by calling on Coatlicué who devours terror, and finding the strength of the resistor who refuses to accept outside authority, la mestiza can create a new consciousness and develop new abilities. But she must give up all pretense to safety; for the borders that supposedly keep undesirable ideas out are our entrenched habits and patterns of behavior. La mestiza makes herself vulnerable to foreign ways of seeing and thinking, strengthening her tolerance for ambiguity and her flexibility, because rigidity means death. The work of la mestiza is to break down the subject–object duality and create another culture, a new mythos, particularly new ways of relating to each other for, as Gloria Anzaldúa argues, our desire is relational.

Addressing our relations and desire, Marilyn Frye (1983) analyzes the concept of love as developed in heterosexual romance, connecting it to the arrogant eye that organizes the world with reference to himself – everything is either for him or against him. The arrogant perceiver's expectation creates an environment into which the Other must fit; she becomes someone interested in serving him. If she does not, something is (morally) wrong with her. In contrast, the mark of a voluntary association is that one can survive displeasing the other. The one who loves is not selfless, she knows and has her own desire. But she perceives the other without the presupposition that the other poses a constant threat or exists for her service. She pays a certain attention, acknowledging where her interests leave off and those of the other begin. The loving eye knows the independence of the other, knows her complexly.

María Lugones (forthcoming) pursues the question of arrogant perception, especially in terms of racism and ethnocentrism. However, rather than stressing the independence of the other, she focuses on failure to identify with the other, as whites fail to identify with people of color. She names this a failure of love, a failure to love cross-racially and cross-culturally. She notes how often white women ignore, ostracize, stereotype, tokenize, or render women of color invisible, even while women of color are present. She describes her failure to love her mother as similar; loving her mother requires not just that she acknowledge her mother's independence, but that she also see with her mother's eyes, that she travel to her mother's world, that she perceive both herself and her mother as constructed in her mother's world, that she see how her mother resists there, and that she witness herself from within her mother's world. Only then would she cease ignoring her, only then could they be fully subjects to each other.

María Lugones develops the notion of "playful world-travel," traveling between worlds, even though for people of color, white worlds are hostile and much of the traveling done by people of color is against people of color's wills. Playful world-traveling involves shifting from being one person to being a different person. This is distinct from men's idea of play developed in terms of winning and losing, competition, rules, and battles. Playful world-travel involves going to the world of another quite different from us without trying to destroy it or them. It involves finding oneself to be another person there, embracing ambiguity, being open to uncertainty and surprise – what Gloria Anzaldùa calls "atravesando fronteras" (crossing borders), avoiding the "seriousness" that honors only one set of meanings. It involves understanding what it is to be the other, and what it is to be ourselves in their eyes (Anzaldúa 1987, 1990). Through the attending of playful world-travel we become subjects to each other (whereas Hegelian attending makes us objects).

Focusing on attending that neither affirms independence nor crosses borders, Claudia Card (1994) explores the dynamics of a certain type of hostile and objectifying attending: not racism, but incest and lesbian battering and stalking. She suggests that communities of lesbians raised in patriarchy are time-bombs, particularly where female caretakers are often each other's instruments of tor-ture. The terrorism of intimate invasion robs one of agency, holding one captive through fear: the suddenness of violence catches you off guard, riveting you on pain and away from the agency of the batterer. The victim, focused on being trapped, can not look outward toward escape. This loss of agency from violence poses a particular problem for lesbian ethics.

Joyce Trebilcot (1993) is also concerned with resisting invasion, penetration, as well as the coercion of guilt through which we are made to conform and make others conform to dominant values. For example. a mother. feeling guilty about her own aberrations from the myth of motherhood, uses guilt to try to bring her daughter in line. As a partial solution among ourselves, Joyce Trebilcot proposes dyke methods: (1) speaking only for herself; (2) not trying to get other wimmin to accept her beliefs in place of their own; and (3) recognizing there are no givens. The principles come from anger about being controlled. She wants mainly to be left alone, having refused all her life to do what others demand of her, facing the craziness this brings. She argues that victim's/survivor's understanding must be seen as particularly lucid, not damaged. And she argues that our feelings, especially our feelings of guilt, have been constructed: we can think about them, contextualize them, and choose not to act on them, redirecting our energy.

Mary Daly (1984) dissects deadly deceptions of foreground or surface con-sciousness that diminish women's be-ing and dull women's passions, distinguish-ing real from plastic passions. Plastic passions, including anxiety, guilt, depression, hostility, resentment, resignation, and fulfillment, function to mask the agents of oppression and must be dealt with endlessly resulting in discon-nectedness. Real e-motions such as rage or lust have a clearly defined object and move women from a state of stagnation.

Claudia Card (1994) suggests some difficulties may be alleviated by friendlier background institutions supporting female friendship; in fact she suggests we institutionalize friendship, formalizing boundaries, even roles. Following Janice Raymond (1986), she argues that institutions don't simply impose restrictions, they can create forms of agency. Fostering lesbian friendship requires creating and maintaining conditions of respect. Respect, and the distance that comes with it, is a kind of friendship without intimacy or closeness. She argues what distinguishes a true friend may be character, that possibly one can ground a friendship without knowing much of the other's history or likes and dislikes. Audre Lorde (1984) would disagree. Failing to understand class or ethnic differ-ences as more than generalizations, for example, robs women of each others' energy and creative insight.

I challenge the trust in rules and institutions. Principles or rules don't tell us when to apply them, and neither they nor boundaries help when goodwill fails. Addressing those who want to change and develop liberatory value, I argue against an ethics of control. Claudia Card (1994), on the other hand, focusing on the situation of attack, argues control is necessary to self-defense (one must control access to one's self to be an agent). One must have a sense of boundaries in order to gain agency and make judgments, for example, that a particular intimacy is violation.

I focus on a complex agency, for one message of Anglo-European ethics is that either our wills are free or we are not capable of morality. However, it is not because we are free and moral agents that we make moral choices, as arguments about free will and determinism suggest; rather by making choices, acting within limits, we declare ourselves to be moral beings.

María Lugones (forthcoming) argues agency may not be always central to the transformation of value. The agency in question is agency under oppression, wherein one is forced to enact servile intentions. What counts as agency within the dominant framework will not be liberatory – the revolutionary exists outside the bounds of (dominant) sense. Further, while considering questions of hostile attention, María Lugones does not equate loss of ability to judge with loss of boundaries, as does Claudia Card. In fact moving outside the bounds of sense, of the normal, is what helps us develop resistant thinking. Rather than focusing on hostile attending, for after all, goodwill attending done in ignorance across patriarchal categories also robs one of agency, María Lugones and Gloria Anzaldúa focus on the subjectivity and strategies of she who is oppressed in more than one world. Arguing that we have plural selves in multiple structures of oppression, María Lugones proposes that as la mestiza goes between structures, where agency is not key, and comes to the Coatlicué state, she can develop resistant thinking. And if she can remember how she was in one context when she is in another, then she can begin to think complexly.

For this reason, world-travel, crossing borders, is crucial. Further, the lack of ability of world-travel means that while we may recognize resistance in our own logic, we fail to see others with resistant eyes, not understanding their logics of resistance. Instead we judge them through dominant values, the Norm. For example, how can a critical academic perceive the peripheral economy of gangs as resistance to cultural extermination? It is only in the borderlands, the place between structures, that one can begin to enact a liberatory imagination.

Thus I pursue liberatory possibility through lesbian communities, contexts not riveted on the agendas of the fathers, which lesbians of all cultures construct. Claudia Card's concern (1994) is with institutions, structures, that promote female bonding and protect victims, particularly against female violence, within heteropatriarchy. And María Lugones looks to the Coatlicué state for the possibility of liberatory imagination, the state between structures and boundaries where habitual thinking fails.

Significantly, focusing on loss of agency is not to disregard activity or abilities. For example, playful world-travel involves skills of playfulness and flexibility to undermine seriousness and rigidity. Such play is not role-playing which leads to fixed conceptions of self. To be able to play, we have to let go of our world/ reality/sense of order, while also being partly at ease with ourselves. This is the ability to suspend not belief, but disbelief, disbelief fostered by institutions and rules and boundaries of all that lies outside them.

Challenging concepts such as duty because they undermine responsiveness, I explore abilities supporting cooperative interaction rather than the coerced competitiveness of US imperial society. Audre Lorde (1984) argues, "interdependency between women is the only way to the freedom which allows the 'I' to be, not in order to be used, but in order to be creative." María Lugones argues this interdependency, this being with others, is necessary if we are to remake ourselves into active, creative selves, if we are to (re)construct our agency.

In pursuing mestiza ability, Gloria Anzaldúa discusses la facultad, the capacity to perceive in surface phenomena the meaning of deeper realities – anything that interrupts one's habitual perception, causing a break in one's defenses and resistance, causing a shift in perception. Mary Daly encourages prudish prudence that helps us discover background patterns reversed in foreground (patriarchal) phenomena. These skills deepen the way we judge, we lose our safe and easy ignorance/ignoring.

Another ability is that of the trickster. One can play the fool, playing on others' ignorance/privileges, by playing with structures. María Lugones notes that she can play the Latin American as gringos construct her – stereotypically intense, or she can play the real thing. An Angla who knows nothing of playful world-travel will not be able to notice the difference. The trickster, the clown, is crucial for dismantling the seriousness of tyranny and the power of privilege, leaving one a fool if she persists in a state of ignoring. One must become a self-conscious critical practitioner of her culture; lack of this ability is a serious hindrance to lesbian ethics.

Journals of lesbian ethics pursue transformation of value and lesbian bonding, articulating and negotiating differences while dissecting oppressor valuations. Recent themes include racism, antisemitism, and nationalism in "reunited" Germany; sexuality, desire, gender; money, class, work; lesbians on history; lesbians in men's society (Ihrsinn); abuse and surviving; class; separatism; friendship and betrayal; multiple selves; lesbians and our mothers; and community (Lesbian Ethics); and faith and community; old lesbians/dykes; allies; lesbian resistances; and the lesbian body (Sinister Wisdom).

41

Communicative ethics

JOHANNA MEEHAN

Provoked by postmodernist critiques such as those of Jean-François Lyotard and Judith Butler, Linda Nicholson and Nancy Fraser, in their essay, "Social criticism without philosophy," reject feminist essentialism and foundationalism and speculate as to how to combine "a postmodern incredulity toward metanarrative with the social-critical power of feminism" (Nicholson 1990). Lyotard had offered the sweeping argument that "grand narratives of legitimation," like the Enlightenment story of the gradual and inevitable progress of reason and its concomitant notions of human rights, were no longer credible. While such narratives once functioned to legitimate social institutions, practices, and discourses as true and just, he claimed they could no longer do so. The metaphysics in which they are grounded are no longer persuasive and thus we are forced to recognize a polytheism of competing, equally unprivileged discourses. While Fraser and Nicholson recognize that feminists have often lapsed into problematic foundationalism and essentialism because of metaphysically grounded theoretical commitments to such narratives, they argue that feminists committed to avoiding these modernist mistakes need not abandon theoretical tools of evaluation and analysis, as there is nothing inherently contradictory in the notion of postmodern *theory* (Nicholson and Fraser 1990, p. 34). Lyotard himself, they argue, paradoxically offers a normative vision of a good society made up of democratic self-managing groups while having ruled out the possibility of the normative political theorizing which would legitimate such a vision (Nicholson and Fraser 1990).

In a similar vein, Judith Butler asked, "What form of insidious cultural imperialism here legislates itself under the sign of the universal?" and warned that we must be wary of privileging the claims of normative political theory because "power pervades the very conceptual apparatus that seeks to negotiate its terms, including the subject position of the critic." No theory is benign because "the recourse to a position – hypothetical, counterfactual, or imaginary – that places itself beyond the play of power, and which seeks to establish the metapolitical basis for a negotiation of power relations, is perhaps the most insidious ruse of power (Butler 1990, p. 39).

Fraser points out that while one can appreciate Butler's deconstructive critiques of identity, her concept of liberation suffers from normative shortcomings. Viewing identity itself as inherently oppressive, Butler ultimately understands women's liberation as liberation *from* identity. Her commitment is thus to deconstructive critique and reconstructive positions are viewed with suspicion as normalizing and oppressive. But as Fraser argues, feminists "do need to make normative judgments and to offer emancipatory alternatives. We are not for anything goes." The proliferation of identities which Butler calls for is not in and of itself dereifying or emancipatory. Feminists, Fraser insists, need "both deconstruction and reconstruction, destabilization of meaning and projection of utopian hope" (Fraser 1990, p. 71).

With those needs in mind, a number of feminists, including Nancy Fraser, have turned to the normative political theory of Jürgen Habermas and found useful tools for analyzing "sexism in all its endless variety and monotonous similarity" (Nicholson and Fraser 1990, p. 34). For although Habermasian theory is an Enlightenment-inspired normative political theory of the sort Lyotard dismisses and Butler construes as yet another ruse of power, his discourse theory of ethics remains one of the most systematic and insightful current reflections on politics and moral and social norms. Consequently it is of great interest to those feminists committed to the kinds of reconstructive analyses of politics and identity Fraser calls for, despite Habermas's failure to specifically theorize gender. Because it offers a normative political framework for analyzing the structures of modern life and of assessing the emancipatory potential of modernity in view of simultaneous increases in political repression, market manipulation, and domination, Habermas's work has been of various uses to feminists engaged in the clarification of the ways in which gender functions to produce and reproduce male domination and female subordination.

Habermas's communicative theory of ethics

The ethical theory Habermas elaborates is referred to as "discourse ethics" or "communicative ethics" because it makes central a theory of communicative competence, emphasizes the intersubjective and linguistic processes of the constitution of identity, and analyzes the social grounding of norms in discourse. Though Habermas, like Kant, views the possibility of morality as rooted in human linguistic and cognitive competence, unlike Kant he views normative discourses and their social and political institutionalization as a historical achievement. Thus discourse ethics is a reformulation of Kant's idea of practical reason that retains an emphasis on universality while conceiving moral agents to be historically situated and intersubjectively constituted, and norms to be socially generated and discursively testable. Arguing against ethical relativists, he insists that there is a communicative rationality which makes normative claims analogous to objective claims insofar as they appeal to *reasons* which are accessible via a critical reflection on the socially constituted practice of moral discourse and a transcendental–pragmatic analysis of it.

Habermas's historicized ethics is based on an analysis of the historical origins of communicative rationality and its conflicting relationship to strategic rationality and the modern economic sphere. From his earliest work, *The Structural Transformation of the Public Sphere* (1989), to his most recent work, *Between Facts and Norms* (1986) Habermas has argued that modernity brings with it an increased rationalization of the life-world. Multiple spheres of discourse originally unified in mythological worldviews are separated and made the subject of reflective elaboration. Max Weber and earlier members of the Frankfurt School, including Theodor Adorno and Max Horkheimer, had viewed this "disenchantment" of the world as wholly negative, marked by the stealthy encroachments of strategic rationality. Habermas argues that restricting the analysis to the development of strategic rationality, especially in capitalist market relations, made the early Frankfurt School unable to recognize or explain either the normative character of modern institutions and behaviors, or gains in the spheres of theoretical, practical, and aesthetic rationality. From the perspective of an analysis of communicative rationality the differentiation of the world into the multiple spheres of the scientific, aesthetic, and the moral is a positive development because it makes possible the increased reflexivity of social and political norms and a decentered and reflexive moral point of view. This is expressed and embodied in institutions that demand and foster normatively regulated discourses. Thus, Habermas answers Hegel's question of how reason can be made practical by locating communicative rationality in such social and political institutions.

Like the earlier members of the Frankfurt School, Habermas identifies capitalism and the strategic rationality it demands and fosters as modernity's most characteristic and problematic moment. For Habermas, the problems and conflicts of modernity arise from the domination of instrumental rationality in conjunction with the organization of the social and political world in and through capitalistic market relations. This one-dimensional rationalization of culture and society leads to the cultural and institutional dominance of forms of instrumental rationality dictated by logics of power and money, and displaces communicative rationality and symbolic expression to the margins of social life and legitimacy. Habermas concludes that the undermining of communicative rationality, the essential coordinator of social interaction and the locus for the generation and interpretation of meaning, can only be corrected by opening more areas of life to forms of communication which allow for open, public debate about issues of public policy. Thus, he insists that it is only truly functional democratic institutions which mitigate the bureaucratization and monetarization of the "iron cage" of modernity described by Max Weber.

Habermas's reflections on ethics and morality are, therefore, inherently political and historical. For while agreeing that the encroachments of strategic rationality lead to repression, he argues that it is the increases in communicative rationality that modernity has also made possible which have allowed for "a decreasing degree of repressiveness and rigidity, increasing role distance and the flexible application of norms – socialization without repression" (Habermas 1979, 1987). However, his optimism about the moral and political gains modernity makes possible is not naive. While he argues that the media-steered mechanisms of money and power marked by strategic rationality can be distinguished from social interaction guided by communicative rationality, he is well aware that strategic rationality often disrupts communicative rationality. Thus, he believes that realizing the emancipatory potential of communicative interaction depends on effective resistance to the "colonization of the life-world," that is, the increasing domination of social, cultural, and political life by the logic of instrumental rationality. He is also aware that the potency of political resistance is undermined by the imperatives of the very systems it seeks to check. It is here that Habermas distinguishes himself from the earlier members of the Frankfurt School, as well as most contemporary deconstructionists. He embraces the Enlightenment convictions that rationality – reconceptualized as communicative rationality – is potentially liberatory and that the promises of democracy remain unfulfilled as long as the Enlightenment project remains unfinished.

Feminist appropriations of Habermasian theory

Feminists have found quite valuable normative resources in Habermasian discourse theory and have applauded the historical and political contextualization of ethics and morality. Habermas's critiques of democracy and his diagnoses of the ills of our times provide analyses of exploitation, of ideological distortion, of the invidious manipulation of public discourses. However, his understanding of individuals, social relations, and political needs and expectations remains to a great extent embedded in the conceptual schemata of liberal individualism and rights. While articulated as universally applicable, these schemata reflect a gendered world where men (at least some men) were figured as social, economic, and political agents and women (at least some women) were understood in terms of an agency defined by and exhausted within the context of marriage and family. Thus, the lines between public rights and private needs were drawn and the concepts of individual and agency delineated in a social context much different from our own, one which made those demarcations and delineations clear, if not just. Consequently, feminists such as Nancy Fraser, Jean Cohen, Marie Fleming, Seyla Benhabib, and Joan Landes, who wish to draw on the insights of Habermas's account of the historically changing relationships of the modern state, the capitalist market, and the public and private agency of the individual, have had to recast much of his thought in order to consider issues of rights, needs, citizenship, and agency from a gendered perspective. While their criticisms and the directions of their arguments differ, all agree that inasmuch as Habermas's account suffers from a gender blindness that occludes the differential social and political status of men and women, his model of modernity falls short and needs revision and reconceptualization. Nancy Fraser deepens Habermas's sophisticated analyses of the interinstitutional relations among various spheres of public and private life in classical capitalism by thematizing the gendered distribution in the historical configurations of the roles of family member, consumer/client, soldier, and citizen. Noting the advances Habermas's account makes over the standard dualistic approaches to the distinction between the public and private in capitalist economies, Fraser extends his account to remedy his failure to "thematize the gender subtext of the relations and arrangements he describes" (Fraser 1989b).

Jean Cohen shares Nancy Fraser's interest in the Habermasian analysis of the complex interplay of relations between state, economy, family, and the public sphere. She has argued that when Habermas's account is gendered, some of his prognoses about modernity can be seen to be inaccurate and incomplete. She has, for example, claimed that Habermas's failure to appreciate the fluidity between the public and the private sphere has led him to characterize most contemporary social movements (including feminism in many of its moments) as purely particularistic and defensive and thus as not furthering the universalistic emancipatory goals of modernity. She views Habermas as failing to recognize that these movements also generate new relations of solidarity, alter the nature and structure of civil society, revitalize old public spaces, and create new ones. Thus, the feminist struggle to reconfigure identity and gender relationships is an essential moment in the reconstruction of the institutions of civil and political society (Cohen 1995).

Marie Fleming (1995) and Joan Landes (1988) reassess the historical account of the emergence of the public sphere, arguing that Habermas is wrong to see the exclusion of women from the bourgeois public sphere as simply the failure of the bourgeoisie to realize its own normative ideals. They extend the Habermasian account so that the exclusion of women, and of affect and interest associated with the feminine domain, are revealed as historically constitutive of the bourgeois split between the rational and the irrational, the public and private. Therefore, the Habermasian public sphere, identified with equality and reason, favors certain abilities and interests over others and, in effect, if not in intention, ensures that male subjects will be its dominant inhabitants. However, in the contemporary world, where politics and style are entwined, there is play in politics, and, in play, lies a potential for political performance and gesture. Thus, Landes suggests the political is inextricably tied to the private sphere through the non-discursive critique and subversion made possible by action, the spectacle, the body, and style.

While some feminists have focused their analyses on the interplay of public and private, extending and correcting the Habermasian analysis of the interinstitutional relationships constitutive of modern social organizations, others have used the insights that gender analyses provided to interrogate, correct, extend, and reject Habermasian notions of subjectivity, rationality, morality, and justice. Such reflections have led to suggested reformulations and redefinitions of key Habermasian concepts while allowing discourse feminists to still employ the powerful discourse ethics framework to identify gender injustices and to conceptualize more emancipatory social and political relationships.

Habermas's intersubjective account of identity formation has proved especially fruitful in this regard. Habermas argues that we are not first individuals and then social agents who relate to each other, but rather we are individual identities only as a result of social relationships. The constitution of the self is concomitant with the establishment of social relationships, which are themselves structured

415

by norms of equality or inequality, freedom or repressiveness, authority or reason. Because we are physically, socially, and psychically vulnerable beings, however, social interaction is only possible through the *normative* maintenance and reproduction of communal life. Morality thus functions as a compensatory mechanism discoverable through analysis of the everyday intuitions and preunderstandings which structure social exchange. This opens up a theoretical space which allows feminists to consider normative ideals of self–other relationships and the implicitly and explicitly gendered discursive contexts in which they are negotiated. This creates the possibility of traversing the split between public and private, personal and political.

Many of the feminist readings of Habermas's work reflect attempts to use Habermas's discourse theory to bridge the gap that arises from significant feminist critiques of deontological ethics, ranging from the issues of the universal and the particular, to criticisms of Habermas's account of the generalized other, and to discussions of autonomy and of social and moral recognition. It is perhaps ironic that while the normative thrust of discourse ethics has appealed to feminists, at the same time it is the specifics of Habermas's account of norms and autonomous moral identity that has been identified as one of the most problematic aspects of his theory. Even otherwise sympathetic feminist readers have argued that Habermas recapitulates many of the shortcomings of deontological ethical theories from Kant's to Rawls's: subjectivity is abstract rather than particular and historical; rationality is made central and emotions marginalized; the right is thought to be easily extirpated from the good; fairness is defined in relation to an ideal of justice which excludes notions of care and underemphasizes bonds of solidarity; autonomy is extolled and dependence unrecognized or eschewed; and the gendered, raced, and class-constructed aspects of identity are considered irrelevant. Nonetheless, by conceiving of identity as radically intersubjective while at the same time offering a normative account of egalitarian relationships and discourses, some feminists have found it worth the effort to reconstruct, reanalyze, and reconceive Habermas's concepts of the subject, identity, intersubjectivity, autonomy, and justice within the discourse ethics framework.

Feminist critique is predicated on the hope, if not the vision of social relations which, because they are better, truer, or more just, can lead to more equitable human flourishing. Habermas's account of validity, justice, and the norms of equality and reciprocity is a useful resource for feminists who criticize and condemn ideologically defended inequities of power in political, social, and personal relationships because it offers a foundation for the articulation of a feminist standard against which actual political and personal relations and discourses can be measured and criticized. Specifically, Habermas claims that the force of normative claims is derived from their rationality and universality, and that normative claims assert a claim to truth analogous to scientific claims, though different from them. Discourse ethics, as Habermas views it (contrary to the view of some of both his feminist and non-feminist readers), reconstructs the moral point of view only in relation to issues of justice which can be scrutinized from an abstract and universal perspective. By preserving the deontological character of his discourse ethic, Habermas attempts to insure that it retains its universalism and impartiality. By setting up a purely formal notion of right he allows for the legitimacy and reality of the diversity and plurality of different and legitimate versions of the good.

Seyla Benhabib counters Habermas's easy distinction between evaluative concerns and issues of justice, arguing that a consideration of concrete moral actions and choices quickly reveal the degree to which these issues are inextricably entwined. Carol Gilligan, she argues, is right to see issues of relational obligation and care as genuinely moral ones, "belonging to the center and not to the margins of morality," and claims Habermas's discourse ethics is a call not just for a formal proceduralism, but for a "conversational model of enlarged mentality" that makes it possible for a universalist ethical perspective to incorporate Gilligan's insight, while retaining its desirable universalism. While acknowledging the importance of postmodernist critiques of metaphysically grounded accounts of a unitary subject and of post-Enlightenment morality, she defends a notion of the subject as a unitary narrative perspective, and of ethical norms as discursively negotiable and universalistic (Benhabib 1995).

These critiques and reflections are also reflected, though differently nuanced, in the work of Herta Nagl-Docekal, Jodi Dean, Andrea Maihofer, Georgia Warnke, Alison Weir, and Johanna Meehan. Nagl-Docekal and Maihofer have focused on the distinctions between the right and the good and the way they are confounded when a feminist perspective is introduced (Maihofer 1988, Nagl-Docekal 1994, Dean 1995, Warnke 1995, Weir 1995, Meehan 1995). Dean has argued that in Habermas's account of the formation of social and moral identity, the subject's ability to take up the "objective" stance of the other is crucial, but involves a conflation of two notions which elides a crucial distinction between the third-person observer and the structuring of the generalized Other. The significance of this elision becomes apparent when viewed from the perspective of gender. While a child's ability to adopt the observer perspective is essential to achieving a post-conventional moral consciousness and entails generalizing from particular interactions to larger, normatively defined roles, Dean argues, the neutrality that Habermas ascribes to this observer perspective fails to take into account the content entrenched in social positionality. Insofar as gender is negotiated in a world of differently valenced gender relations, the perspective of the subject, of the third person, and the structuring content of the generalized Other cannot be conceived apart from those hierarchically ordered gender relations.

Warnke argues in favor of reconceiving Habermas's notions of argumentation and his demand for arriving at a consensus about the better argument in terms of an aesthetic model of interpretation which would allow for a multiplicity of interpretive views while not viewing all interpretations as equally compelling. In addition, values and norms could be seen as rooted in a multiplicity of evaluative notions about the good about which it may be reasonable to disagree. Warnke has articulated a rereading of Habermas's discourse ethics which offers a new

417

synthesis of Gadamer's notion of interpretation with Habermas's concept of ideal discourse.

Weir and Meehan have considered the political specificities of identity constitution and the ways they complicate the Habermasian account of norms. Weir argues that seemingly intractable discussions of difference, as well as feminist critiques of notions of individuation, agency, and autonomy, point to a critical need to reconceptualize our notions of selfhood. A useful account of agency, she argues, must recognize that individual identity is embedded, embodied, localized, constituted, fragmented, fragile, and vulnerable to social, political, and linguistic forces, while at the same time retaining a vision of humans as actors who learn, change, interpret, and reinterpret the world. She contends that the most significant feature of modern identity is the capacity to reconcile often conflictual multiple identities and to understand, criticize, and to live with conflicting interpretations of identity. The ability to reconcile conflicts without excluding or repressing difference and nonidentity requires an ego with the ability to deal with difference reflexively, not through a denial of its connection to others, but through its recognition of itself as both intersubjectively constituted and autonomously capable, both dependent upon and independent of others.

Both Meehan and Weir claim that identity formation is always a psychically, socially, and symbolically mediated process of negotiating and interpreting fundamentally socially given meanings. Meehan points out that the intersubjective constitution of identity means that subjectivity formation always takes place in a nexus of power relations, including those of gender, race, class, and sexual identity. This means that issues of agency and recognition are inevitably entwined in normative discourses about rights though they are often obscured or ignored in reflections on those discourses.

Some feminists have reflected on the relation of Habermasian theory to feminist social practice. Jane Braaten argues that to a significant extent, Habermas's theory of communicative rationality converges with the ideals of feminism, and can be put to good use by that community as it formulates its political critiques and projects. At the same time, she has criticized Habermas's understanding of communicative rationality as non-substantive, and develops the thesis that feminists in the pursuit of solidarity, in effect reverse the order of the development of Habermas's argument, deriving criterion of rationality and knowledge from substantive ideals of solidarity and community, rather than deriving ideals of solidarity from notions of rationality and abstract ideals of equality. Simone Chambers (1996) has pointed out the difficulties of making ideal discourse actual, and articulated some of the conditions which must be met in order to instantiate such discourses. For instance, while Habermas argues that fully consensual discourse requires not only the right to and wherewithal to speak, he does not explore what would make exercising this right either possible or meaningful. Consensual discourse requires not only the right and wherewithal to speak, but in addition, the possibility that speech will be listened to and heard in the fullest sense possible. It requires that participants adopt attitudes and responses toward one another that create a positive environment in which the procedural norms of discourse become more than abstract and significantly unexercised rights (Braaten 1995).

It is difficult to briefly summarize the feminist responses to Habermas's normative universalism. Some have engaged in a reconstruction which embraces much of Habermas and which condemns deconstructive critiques of the Kantian thrust of Habermas's ethics as a dangerous "tarrying with the negative." Some of the more critical views of Habermas find deconstructive critiques of modernism and deconstructive analyses of the relatedness of truth and power and the production of the subject insightful and illuminating, particularly for understanding issues of gender, while at the same time wishing to mine Habermasian critical theory for its normative resources. While there is no one feminist Habermasian position, it would be fair to say that those who view a discourse ethics reconceived from a feminist perspective as valuable, believe that discursive power fairly appropriated and exercised is the only *moral* form of suasion, the only right way to change the hearts and minds of the people.

42

Health care

SUSAN SHERWIN

Introduction

As one might expect, feminist health-care ethics takes place at the intersection of feminist ethics and health-care ethics (also known as (bio)medical ethics and bioethics). It encompasses a wide range of efforts to bring feminist perspectives and tools to bear on the set of ethical issues that arise within the realm of health and health care. These efforts expand and modify debates in both fields: that is, they add the perspective of gender analysis to the apparently gender-neutral tradition of medical ethics, while also enriching the often theoretical discussions of feminist ethics through focus on the concrete reality and complexities of health-care practices.

Just as health-care ethics is, ultimately, about ethics, feminist health-care ethics is a specialized area of feminist ethics. As such, it can be distinguished from other ethical orientations by its commitment to including feminist issues and analyses in its approaches to moral questions. Where traditional thought typically excludes political questions from the sphere of ethics, feminist ethics recognizes the moral significance of questions regarding power and privilege; in particular, it perceives oppression to be a moral as well as a political wrong. Although feminists are especially concerned with gender oppression, their moral objection encompasses all forms of oppression. Most understand, also, that gender oppression is a complex phenomenon which may vary in accordance with a woman's race, class, ethnicity, age, degree of physical and mental ability, and sexuality. In contrast to traditional approaches to ethics which tend to ignore or obscure details of social location in favour of abstract universal claims, feminist ethics recognizes the importance of grounding ethical discussion in contextual details that include aspects of personal and political relationships. When investigating the moral status of particular practices or policies, feminist ethics requires us to consider its relational (and not merely its individualistic) dimensions and implications; more specifically, it requires exploration of the likely effects the practice or policy in question will have on existing patterns of oppression.

Taking this orientation to the field of health-care ethics, we can identify several levels at which feminist ethics can initiate, intervene, and transform discussions. These include: (1) investigating the standard questions in the field of bioethics from a distinctively feminist viewpoint; (2) broadening the perspectives addressed beyond those considered by the traditional orientations; (3) expanding the agenda of ethical questions pursued; and (4) revising the terms and methods used in bioethical reflection. I shall briefly review each of these areas.

Traditional questions

Perhaps the most obvious influence of feminist health-care ethics is the application of the strategies and concepts of feminist ethics to the various topics discussed within the field of biomedical ethics. Feminists seek to ensure that the potentially oppressive nature of the various health-care proposals under review is treated as a morally significant factor in these discussions. Raising questions about gender (and race, class, sexuality, age, and disability) often adds important dimensions to familiar debates. Although there is probably scope for feminist analysis on virtually every topic explored within bioethics, so far only a few areas have been subject to systematic feminist study.

The most extensive feminist engagement can be found within the set of ethical questions that surround medical intervention in procreation, especially abortion and the new reproductive technologies. Nonfeminist approaches to these questions tend to base their analyses on either an absolute principle of sanctity of human life (e.g. Brody 1975) or a general liberal commitment to personal autonomy (e.g. Robertson 1994); either way, they seek to resolve the central questions by appeal to an abstract, universal principle. Feminist discussions remain grounded in interpretations of reproductive freedom that are sensitive to the ways in which women's broader social freedom is deeply connected to women's control over their own reproduction (e.g. Petchesky 1985, Overall 1987, Callahan 1993). They approach questions about abortion or new reproductive technologies, not by isolating them from the context in which they are raised, but by examining the ways in which each practice affects different women's roles and status in society (see Article 43, PROCREATION).

Feminist perspectives can also be found in discussions about the ethics of conducting clinical research on human subjects. In the nonfeminist literature, there is wide consensus about the need for strong ethics guidelines to protect the subjects of clinical research from exploitation and abuse, especially when dealing with members of groups that are especially vulnerable, such as institutionalized populations and persons with mental disabilities (Rothman 1987). Because being a member of an oppressed and socially devalued group can also make one vulnerable to research exploitation, feminist ethics suggests that research guidelines should explicitly protect members of oppressed groups from reckless experimental abuse (Sherwin 1992). At the same time, feminists have raised objections to the historical pattern in which therapeutic research has been largely directed at the needs and responses of the most privileged members of society (usually white men) while the distinct health needs of members of other groups (e.g. women, visible minorities) are neglected; such a skewed research agenda provides reliable health data about the populations that are studied but it leaves health-care providers with insufficient data for making treatment decisions on

421

behalf of patients from neglected population groups (Dresser 1992). Feminist ethicists have shown why it is important to demand that more research money be directed toward investigating women's specific health needs (e.g. breast cancer, better contraception) and to insist on an end to research policies that systematically exclude women from the pool of subjects for clinical studies. Further, drawing on feminist work in epistemology, feminist health-care ethicists challenge the objectification of subjects that is inherent in traditional research models; they insist on the inclusion of more diverse voices in the ranks of those who set research agendas, design studies, and choose subject populations.

Feminists are also making important contributions to discussions about the nature of the relationship between health-care provider and patient. The medical model at the heart of most Western health-care systems presumes that doctors (and, to a lesser degree, other health professionals) have specialized knowledge that authorizes them to make decisions regarding the well-being of their less knowledgeable patients; this assumption is especially strong when the patients belong to groups that are widely assumed to be ignorant and irrational. Although nonfeminist bioethicists have called into question the long-standing belief that medical expertise suffices to allow physicians to make reliable decisions about their patient's well-being, they have done so on the basis that patient *values* ought to be ultimately decisive (provided the patient is rational). They have largely accepted the idea that physicians possess the *knowledge* necessary for effective decision-making (e.g. Beauchamp and Childress 1994). In contrast, feminists question the privileging of technical, professional knowledge over experiential knowledge and insist that we recognize that patients (and their home caregivers) also possess relevant knowledge that must be respected and included in the process of deciding on treatment options (e.g. Lebacqz 1985). In addition, feminists have challenged the traditional dichotomous framing of these debates as involving *either* autonomy *or* paternalism. Instead, some have suggested that we need to find a more complex third option that recognizes ways in which medical decision-making typically involves aspects of both autonomy and paternalism (Mahowald 1993).

Clearly, then, there has been important feminist input into many of the central areas of health-care ethics, but there are still several important gaps. For example, feminist perspectives have only just begun to enter into discussions of issues involving the end of life, especially euthanasia and physician-assisted suicide (Downie and Sherwin 1996, Wolf 1996). This is an area that seems to require sustained feminist engagement since women are likely to be affected in distinct ways by whatever policies emerge. This issue is especially complicated for feminists, however, because it is generally the case that when very ill patients are not permitted to choose the time and means of their death, the burden of caring for them falls disproportionately on the shoulders of female health workers and female family members. Yet, feminists need to be particularly wary about the dangers of loosening the social constraints against legalized euthanasia, since there is a very real risk that if voluntary euthanasia becomes legal and widely accepted it may eventually lead to practices of non-voluntary euthanasia; in that case, members of society who are devalued on the basis of gender, race, etc., would be especially vulnerable to such abuses. Until we reduce the prejudices against victims of oppression in our society, we must find ways to ensure that any policy that eases the restrictions against killing people whose lives are judged to be not worth preserving does not increase the very real threat that those who are devalued in our culture could become subject to immoral killing under the label of medical beneficence or cost-saving efficiency.

Other areas that await more extensive feminist analysis are those that arise in conjunction with certain sorts of illness, especially AIDS and psychiatric illness. Both conditions are sources of profound stigmatization, so diagnosis of either condition exposes patients to potentially severe social and economic hardship. Moreover, both conditions are characterized and treated differently according to the sex of the patient. In ethics discussions, as in medical research, AIDS has been viewed as a disease that primarily affects men and it is male experiences that shape most discussions to date; relatively little regard has been paid to the threat that AIDS poses to women or to the distinctive ways in which it affects them. The danger of an AIDS epidemic has been used as license for promoting and regulating norms governing sexuality that are oppressive to women and homosexuals. In a culture that traditionally blames women for sex-related problems, the fear of AIDS makes urgent the need for feminist analyses of sexuality that avoid demonization of sexually active women. Feminist approaches are also needed to explore the significance of the fact that only women can be considered potential sources of transmission of HIV to fetuses, making them the unique subjects of invasive policies aimed at reducing rates of infection among infants. Further, the relatively high rates of HIV infection among poor black, Hispanic, and aboriginal populations make it particularly important that we develop analyses that are sensitive not only to gender, but also to race, class, and cultural dimensions when evaluating policies that construct medicine's understanding of AIDS and its ways of responding to it.

In contrast to AIDS, psychiatric illness has long been viewed as a condition more commonly found among women than men. It is important to recognize the role of social expectations and oppressive norms in framing the conditions that are often characterized as forms of mental illness. Women and members of other oppressed social groups face serious double binds in the realm of mental illness where they are subjected to especially oppressive mental health standards which seem to require them to accept the subordinate positions they are assigned. Feminist history is filled with tales of women who have been diagnosed as mentally ill and prescribed horrifying forms of "treatment" when they have attempted to escape from the demands of traditional heterosexual expectations. Moreover, psychiatry typically identifies unconventional behaviors and deep forms of unhappiness as personal problems requiring medication or other efforts to change the individuals who display such "symptoms"; in contrast, feminists ask us to consider the role that is played by the intolerable conditions of many women's lives in explaining their "problems." Feminist therapists provide alternative treatment models aimed at responding to the crises of individuals in the

423

context of a political analysis of the source of their problems; they insist that clients control the direction and scope of their own therapy and encourage them to examine the relevance of social patterns to their own experience (Laidlaw and Malmo 1990).

Shifting perspectives

Feminist health-care ethics goes beyond intervention in the traditional bioethics agenda. Nonfeminist medical ethics is largely focused on ethical issues that arise from the perspective of physicians and senior health administrators (e.g. Beauchamp and Childress 1994). Here, as elsewhere, feminists see the importance of approaching issues from the perspectives of less powerful participants, such as patients. other members of the health-care team. and patients' friends and family (Warren 1992). Even though nurses and other health professionals have taken an interest in bioethics and have developed their own distinctive approaches to bioethics, these discussions tend to be viewed as specialized and confined to the margins of mainstream bioethics. Nursing ethics is the most developed of the nonmedical approaches; it highlights the ways in which nurses distinguish their work from that of physicians (Pence 1990). Typically, nursing ethics promotes a relational approach to ethics that contrasts with the principle-based strategies so common to medically oriented approaches. Two factors are especially prominent in nursing ethics: the importance of nurses' understanding of their professional activities as more oriented to caring than to curing and the fact that nursing has evolved as a primarily feminine profession (Leininger 1981). Hence, the ethics of care has been especially welcomed in nursing ethics. It is important to note, though, that not all work in nursing ethics is feminist. Much of it lacks any specific gender analysis, let alone attention to other forms of oppression. And while many accounts do recognize the distinctively feminine nature of nursing, they often uncritically perpetuate stereotypical (and oppressive) gender norms. If the version of nursing ethics in question is to be feminist, the theoretical commitments it rests on must not simply valorize women's traditional responsibility to care but rather, they should challenge oppressive gender norms while promoting a politicized (feminist) social ideal of interdependency and collective obligations to care (e.g. Nelson 1992).

Feminist health-care ethics rejects traditionally hierarchical medical structures which view health professionals as the central agents of health care, and treat patients and their home caregivers as mere objects or instruments of health services in favor of structures that help to empower patients as active participants, with significant control over the choice of services and the manner in which they are delivered (Whitbeck 1982). Hence, most feminists insist on women-centered, experientially defined approaches to women's reproductive health and they reject medical appropriation of the power to shape women's experience of reproductive events including menstruation, contraception, conception, pregnancy (and abortion), birth, lactation, and menopause. They demand new interpretations of the medically defined norms of health, illness,

424

and reproduction and assign to medicine the more modest role of supporting and promoting – but not defining – health.

Further, feminism urges us to question the unremitting tendency of medicine to define and address health problems as entirely contained within individual bodies. Disease and disability are viewed as attached to individuals and best addressed by treating the individual. While we still need to respond to the needs of individuals, we must also realize that many problems cannot be fully addressed by limiting our attention to their effects on individuals. We need to recognize and respond to practices such as domestic violence, unwanted pregnancy, and race and gender-skewed pay scales, not merely by trying to fix the damage done by each event, but by changing social attitudes and policies and by demanding an end to inequitable practices. Feminist health-care ethics reflects the truth of two important mottoes of the feminist movement: The personal is political and there are no private solutions. When women present themselves to the health-care system in need of care, we need always to ask not only what care these particular individuals need but also what larger issues their situation represents.

Medicine encourages us to see the personal but not the political dimensions of a woman's struggle with psychiatric illness, or with an unwanted pregnancy, or infertility, disability, breast cancer, or advanced old age. Typically, bioethics replicates this medical bias and asks us to find out what the patient in question wants when she seeks treatment that raises complex issues involving, for example, AIDS, contractual pregnancy, assisted suicide, or long-term care. In contrast, feminist bioethics raises questions about the context that surrounds the medical or social problems identified. For example, it urges us to examine breast cancer not only as a tragic illness that affects millions of individual women, but also as a condition that has increased dramatically in this century, perhaps because of environmental factors that have yet to be adequately explored. Cancer, like rape and poverty, is not merely a technical medical problem; it is also a social problem that is better addressed when its victims are encouraged to come together and act collectively than when they are kept isolated, made to feel embarrassed by their condition, and treated as objects for medical intervention. Feminist bioethics promotes empowering patients and ensuring that medical decision-making includes the disadvantaged and disempowered as well as the privileged and influential (Roberts 1996).

Expanding the agenda

Another feature distinctive of feminist health-care ethics is that it expands the agenda of topics to be addressed. For example, feminists have questioned the norms that guide the practice of cosmetic surgery, a risky and expensive form of "elective" surgery that is primarily conducted on women in order to help them better adapt to artificial and elusive norms of female beauty (Morgan 1991). Although there are serious medical risks attached to these procedures, cosmetic surgery is widely practiced in the absence of any explicit health need. It is by no

425

means clear how we are to identify appropriate standards of informed consent when the culture continually signals to women that signs of aging or fat are intolerable, and when some women accurately calculate that their chances of success in both work and romance will be significantly enhanced if they conform to the oppressive external standards of feminine beauty that surround us all. Yet, there has been virtually no examination of the moral problems associated with cosmetic surgery in the nonfeminist bioethics literature.

More broadly, feminism helps us to see the need to question the theories of the body that are inherent in medical ways of seeing (see Article 32, BODY POLITICS and Article 33, DISABILITY). The "scientific" or medical view of the body has become the standard in modern cultures even though it begs important questions about norms and values. It has an alienating tendency to treat the body and its parts as separable from the person who "inhabits" it. Medicine teaches us to experience our bodies as objects for surveillance: we are advised to check regularly for signs of "invasion" or "breakdown," although our own monitoring is considered a poor substitute for expert diagnosis. Because medical experts are credited with knowing our bodies better than the persons who inhabit them, we are each made to feel increasingly dependent on medical authorities. Moreover, they are the ultimate arbitrators on our eligibility for sick leave, health insurance, and other bureaucratic benefits.

There seems to be no limit to the scope of the issues that can be identified when we take up the perspective of feminist health-care ethics. Other examples of new frontiers are represented in the efforts of theorists calling for development of feminist theories of disability that address the oppression implicit in the norms that govern standards of disability (Wendell 1989). Others have shown why proper understanding of eating disorders requires a political analysis that is seldom captured in medical responses (Bordo 1993). And still others have challenged the move to "geneticization" of social problems (Lippman 1991). Also, feminism helps reveal the need to examine carefully the ethical implications of medicalizing sexuality and makes urgent an examination of the hierarchical structure of the health-care system (Sherwin 1992).

New tools

In addition, feminist health-care ethics incorporates the use of alternative methodological and conceptual tools. Methodologically, feminist health-care ethicists tend to reject traditional distinctions between fact and value, and theory and practice; they can often be seen willingly crossing artificial boundaries between academic theorizing and social activism. On the conceptual front, it is clear that many of the key concepts of health-care ethics require feminist reinterpretation. For example, feminists have been struggling to find a term to replace the unsatisfactory label "patient." Couched as it is in metaphors of passivity and dependence, its use perpetuates unacceptable assumptions about the nature of the relationship between health providers and those seeking their care. Popular alternatives, such as "consumer" or "client," carry with them their own problems for they import ideals of the marketplace which also distort relationships with health-care providers in important ways. Feminist efforts in relational ethics promises to help provide us with a richer range of models for the many sorts of relationships that exist between so-called patients and health-care providers.

The principle of justice is central to many current health-care debates and feminists have proposed alternative interpretations and applications of this principle (Nelson and Nelson 1996). In the nonfeminist literature, discussions of justice are almost universally interpreted as being about the allocation of scarce health-care resources and they are perceived as involving norms of distributive justice. Feminists have consistently challenged the limitations of standard conceptions of distributive justice, however (see Article 49, JUSTICE). Feminism reveals the need to expand our conception of justice to include attention to questions of power and privilege on the one hand and oppression and domination on the other. Treating health care as a matter of consumer choice, as many nonfeminist authors do, betrays their own privilege and fails to account for the essential and inaccessible status of health care in the lives of more disadvantaged citizens. Discussions of health-care distribution that proceed as if all patients are comparably situated obscure the ways in which other forms of injustice have made some members of society more vulnerable to illness than others and, at the same time, less able to get health care. For feminists, it is significant that women are more dependent on health-care services than are men, yet they usually have fewer resources with which to pursue treatment. When financially privileged authors propose providing those without private insurance with only a "decent minimum of health care," while reserving the right of others to choose more and better services, and when they support rationing health care to the very elderly, they speak of the people affected by these policies in terms that are gender and race neutral. Feminist analysis reminds us that poverty is largely a condition of women and children, that it is especially common to visible minorities and people with disabilities, and that most of the very elderly are single women. Gender, race, and class are central factors in the impact of such policies and they ought not to be obscured in the bioethics proposals that shape them.

Further, feminist bioethicists encourage us to expand our conception of health so that we can see that fairness requires an equitable distribution not only of beds in intensive care units (as in the traditional debates) but also of the means for promoting health in the first place (Purdy 1996). Such measures would include, for example, adequate food and shelter, safety from toxic environments and physical violence, opportunities to develop self-esteem, and access to health education. This orientation implies a shift in focus for both health services and health-care ethics away from the current concentration on invasive and highly technological interventions to more communal, less expensive sorts of strategies that focus on the primary determinants of health.

Once we get beyond the restrictions of a distributive paradigm of justice we can also explore questions of social justice and injustice that are raised by the very organization of the health-care delivery systems. The hierarchical institutions of

427

the health-care system, like others in society, depend upon the concentration of power in the hands of an elite core of mostly male, mostly white physicians and senior administrators, who are supported by the work of mostly female, mostly white nurses and middle managers, while those who belong to visible minority groups are largely relegated to the ranks of the poorly paid support staff who do much of the physical labor of cleaning and cooking but have no input into decision making within health-care institutions. Feminist discussions of health-care ethics challenge the structural systems that limit widespread access to important health resources and the power to shape health policies. They support radical transformations of our entire health-care system and provide resources for returning control over health matters to those most directly affected.

43

Procreation

LAURA SHANNER

Because women gestate pregnancies while men do not, and because reproductive decisions have an enormous impact on the health, economic security, and social status of women, it is not surprising that procreation is an early and frequent subject of feminist scholarship. In recent decades, rapidly evolving technologies in infertility treatment, prenatal diagnosis, fetal tissue use, and genetics have made woman-centered analysis of reproduction particularly urgent. Responding to evolving technology requires an interdisciplinary approach, incorporating medical technology assessment, law, health policy, sociology, and other fields in addition to more traditional philosophical methodologies of values clarification and concept analysis. Even the most basic concepts require reexamination, however; the significance of birth has been given shockingly little serious philosophical attention outside of feminist approaches (Held 1989, Warren 1989) compared to the vastly greater reflection on the legal, moral, and philosophical implications of death.

Common themes

Asking "what does this mean for women?" encourages a thorough analysis of the physical risks of contraceptives, new reproductive technologies (NRTs), prenatal tests, abortions, pregnancy, and childbirth. Feminists are the only consistent voices asking whether drugs and invasive procedures harm women's bodies, and in some cases have complied better data on outcomes than the clinicians offering the procedures (Rutnam 1991, Rowland 1992). FINRRAGE, the Feminist International Network of Resistance to Reproductive and Genetic Engineering, has been particularly influential in raising concerns about the safety and efficacy of NRTs such as in-vitro fertilization (IVF) in public dialogue and policy discussions, especially in Australia. Questions about IVF's efficacy and long-term safety, both for women and for the offspring they bear, are only now being studied systematically after fifteen years of use worldwide.

In addition to physical risks, reproductive and genetic interventions often pose substantial emotional, social, and financial costs for women and their families (Corea et al. 1987, Stanworth 1987, Overall 1987, 1993, Rothman 1989b, Sherwin 1992). The political structures that shape women's reproductive choices require analysis (Petchesky 1980, O'Brien 1981, Spallone 1989), with special attention to the effects of pronatalist attitudes for women, children, and an overpopulated planet. The social importance not just of reproducing, but of producing healthy or "high-quality" offspring, may support increasingly invasive "management" of pregnancy.

New techniques involving ovum and embryo transfer have fragmented the formerly unified process of biological motherhood: in all of human history before 1978, a pregnant woman was undoubtedly the genetic progenitor of the off-spring she carried. Pregnancy with a genetically-unrelated embryo or fetus now forces us to ask, "who is the mother of this child?" Alarm at this fragmentation is raised regarding inconsistent legal and social perceptions of the "real" mother (Rothman 1989a), the devaluation of pregnancy relative to genetic contribu-tions, the equating of eggs and sperm despite the much greater invasiveness and risk required to retrieve ova, secrecy, and discontinuities in family relationships, and the fear that women themselves will be increasingly devalued and margin-alized in reproductive decisions.

Images of women as sexual objects become, in a pronatalist lens, images of women reproductive vessels or "baby machines" (Corea et al. 1987, Scutt 1988). Women literally fall out of view in prenatal imaging techniques (Stabile 1992), while women's humanity is denigrated in agricultural metaphors of ova "harvesting," "uterine environments," and treatments originally developed for farming and "animal husbandry" (Morgan 1989).

Different voices

There are multiple feminist points of view, conclusions, and disagreements in most procreative contexts. This rich chorus of voices ably reflects the diversity of women's experiences, but also points to fundamental schisms within feminism more widely.

One foundational point of disagreement, for example, is whether reproducing itself is the source of women's powerlessness, or whether it is women's greatest strength. Simone de Beauvoir described gestation as "a fatiguing task of no individual benefit to the woman but on the contrary demanding heavy sacri-fices" (1952, p. 33). Jeffner Allen radically equates motherhood with "the annihilation of women" as women's bodies are appropriated by men "as a resource to reproduce patriarchy" (1983, p. 317).

In contrast, a "matrist" approach (Bunkle 1988) depicts childbearing as a source of women's inherent power; the male drive to subjugate this power explains the development of male social dominance (Corea 1979). Regulating contraception and abortion, moving childbirth from the home to the hospital, and developing reproductive and genetic technologies are thus seen as "an attempt by men to sublimate their envy of women's awesome creative force; to imitate it, extract it, and finally to exorcize its power over them" (Bunkle 1988, p. 96). Broader social restrictions on sexuality, marriage, divorce, and women's participation in professional and political realms are indirect but more pervasive mechanisms to control women's reproductive capacities. "Womb envy" has even been invoked to invert Freud's theories of female neurosis rooted in penis envy (Kittay 1983b).

Shulamith Firestone (1970) is rare in her optimism that genetic engineering and artificial wombs will free women from their biological constraints in reproducing. More often, the suspicion is that new technologies will not free women from the bonds of patriarchy, but instead are deceptively attractive, silken ropes that tie women down even more tightly.

Most feminists stress women's liberties and rights to make reproductive decisions free of control by men, doctors, states, or patriarchal social institutions, and frequently emphasize a right *not* to reproduce. International codes of human rights can ground important changes in social policy and health care for women (Cook 1993). Another strategy is to defend some reproductive choices (e.g. gestational contracts) not on their own merit, but because restricting some practices sets the dangerous precedent of constraining women's reproductive autonomy (Andrews 1988). This emphasis on freedom is not the same thing as a traditional *ethical liberalism*, however, which feminists rarely defend straightforwardly. The liberal ethic – emphasizing the rights of autonomous, rational agents to act freely as long as their actions do not violate the equal rights of other agents to act freely – requires minimal restrictions on abortions, high-tech infertility and pregnancy interventions, genetic diagnosis and selection, reproductive contracts, and the sale of ova, sperm, embryos, and gestational services. More radically, since men are able to father children late in their lives, postmenopausal infertility treatment would offer women an equal right to procreate over a longer part of the lifespan. Despite a desire to expand women's choices, most feminists view at least some of these practices with unease.

More fundamentally, most liberal analyses leave out serious consideration of the interests of the children produced by the exercise of reproductive liberty. As Virginia Held remarked, "It stretches credulity even further than most philosophers can tolerate to imagine babies as little rational calculators contracting with their mothers for care" (1987b, p. 120). Of particular concern is the liberal claim of a right to reproduce, which often seems to characterize children as objects to be obtained, bartered for, and created at our whim (Uniacke 1987, Mahowald 1993, Shanner 1995), and with little regard for injury that might be sustained by the resulting offspring (Purdy 1992).

Social feminists call attention to contextual constraints on liberty and prefer to restructure social and cultural institutions to suit women's reproductive lives (Rothman 1989b, Sherwin 1992, Shanner 1995). For example, IVF has been marketed to women who delayed childbearing to launch their careers; liberal feminists defend a woman's right to use IVF, but social feminists would rather restructure educational and business institutions to allow women to achieve economic security while having families when it is healthiest to do so. Social feminism also calls greater attention to the moral costs of individual choices for a whole society, and for people who are disadvantaged and unable to bargain on equal footing with others. From this perspective, gestational contracts and ovum-selling risk exploiting poor women and/or children, while genetic interventions

431

and changing definitions of "normal" are seen to be threatening to people with disabilities.

Radical feminism reaches more unequivocal conclusions than social approaches, often rejecting reproductive interventions entirely (Daly 1978, Arditti et al. 1984, Corea et al. 1987, Rowland 1992). Pregnancy itself is more likely to be characterized as oppressive, making any intervention related to procreation suspect. Radical critiques have provided some of the most vivid imagery of women as procreative objects, and give voice to the more extreme fears of technology run amok.

Several theorists observe that *labor and delivery* are usually ignored in economic discussions of *productive labor*, making childbearing another form of women's uncompensated work (Schwartzenbach 1987, Anderson 1990, Moody-Adams 1991). The image of a baby as a product is disturbing, however, and the full force of a Marxist critique of the industrial economy takes on a special poignancy in procreative contexts (Oliver 1989). The Marxist terminology of "alienation" can describe some women's feelings of distance from their babies and even their own bodies due to invasive treatments and fragmented reproductive processes; this seems especially apt when the baby is treated as a desired object with specified genetic traits, or as a product to be sold or given to someone else in gestational arrangements.

The normative ethic of care builds upon the work of Carol Gilligan (1982a), whose original studies involved women considering abortion. Reversing the liberal focus on liberty and its limits as structured by rules and abstract principles, the caring agent reaches out in response to contextual need, attempts to solidify and support relationships, and highlights the duties of the more powerful toward the less powerful. In what appears to be the first governmental adoption of an ethic of care (in a document otherwise widely perceived as nonfeminist), Canada's Royal Commission on New Reproductive Technologies (1993) identified care as a foundational moral orientation to be supplemented with eight ethical principles. The supplementary principles illustrate two key criticisms of a care ethic: principles such as justice and liberty seem to be necessary to moral reasoning, although perhaps not sufficient, and caring gives little specific guidance for behavior.

Topics in procreative ethics

Women's insights have altered the discourse on many reproductive issues by identifying new problems and introducing evocative new terms. Debates not just between feminists and nonfeminists, but also among groups of feminists, represent the cutting edge of scholarship in procreative ethics.

Abortion

The rancorous mainstream debate over abortion usually emphasizes the moral and legal status of fetuses. If fetuses are persons with a corresponding right to life,

432

then abortions are equivalent to murder. If fetuses have no compelling moral claims, then an abortion is the morally neutral removal of tissue from a woman's body. Embryos and fetuses may also be described as related to us genetically, developmentally, and through pregnancy, giving them some status above that of mere objects but still below the status of persons (English 1975). Even if the fetus is considered a person, Judith Jarvis Thomson (1971) demonstrated the limits of one's right to impose oneself on the body and life of another person. Thomson's self-defense arguments have been expanded in two generations of scholarship (Warren 1973. Kamm 1992) to protect not just a woman's life, but also her emotional, social, and economic well-being.

Unique to a feminist perspective is detailed attention to what it is like to be pregnant (E. Martin 1987, Eisenstein 1988, Sherwin 1991, Gatens-Robinson 1992, Mackenzie 1992). There simply is no such thing as a fetus without a pregnant woman sustaining it; describing pregnancy as a lived phenomenon or as part of the narrative of a woman's life refocuses our attention on this often-neglected fact. Marx's distinction between the architect and the bee – human creativity versus mindless, instinctive activity – has been invoked in competing descriptions of pregnancy as purposeful and as merely physical (O'Brien 1981, Overall 1987, Nelson 1994). Gilligan (1982a) articulated the relationships and responsibilities that women perceive to their fetuses; significantly, abortion, adoption, and keeping a child one cannot support can *all* be viewed as moral failures to maintain the mothering relationship.

Fetal tissue use

The abortion debate has largely stymied discussion on using fetal tissue for research or transplantation, especially in the United States. The benefits that might arise from fetal tissue use are often perceived to be morally "tainted" because of their origins in abortion, much like the Nazi experimental data obtained by torturing concentration camp victims. Feminists often express frustration at the impasse, however, since most defend the availability of abortions and the tissue would therefore not be "tainted."

More compelling concerns arise about coercion to donate fetal tissue, and women's safety while undergoing the abortion. Donating fetal tissue may reduce the stigma and guilt associated with abortion, but increased use of fetal tissue may create pressures to donate it or even to have an unwanted abortion. The timing or method of abortion procedures might be changed in order to procure more useful fetal tissue, perhaps at greater risk or discomfort for the woman, and perhaps without the woman's consent for a change from the standard procedure or for use of the tissue itself. Quite unclear is the role, if any, that the father of the fetus should play in the decision to donate fetal tissue. Particularly contentious is the possibility of intentionally conceiving and then aborting in order to provide tissue for a specified relative's therapy; risks of exploitation by the woman's family are weighed against the opportunity to relieve a loved one's distress through the exercise of reproductive liberties.

433

New reproductive technologies and embryo experimentation

IVF and its variants involve large doses of hormones to cause 5–15 ova to mature at one time instead of the usual one per month, surgical retrieval of the ova, fertilization outside of the body (in vitro), transfer of embryos to the uterus, and possible frozen storage of excess embryos for transfer in a later cycle. The pronatalist imperative driving IVF does not promote equal access to infertility treatments for all women, however; marital status, sexual orientation (Hanscombe 1983), and income are often barriers to assisted procreation.

A central criticism of NRTs is that the constantly evolving techniques are inadequately tested for safety and efficacy before being offered clinically. Meanwhile, well-structured research involving human embryos is controversial and has even been banned in some countries, largely due to worries about embryo status. As a result, women and their offspring are very frequently the unsuspecting subjects of ongoing experimentation, although the rigorous scientific and ethical structures of good research are usually not employed in "therapeutic" protocols (Rowland 1992). Further, research guidelines for scientific inquiry into fertilization and human embryology usually emphasize the treatment of embryos, forgetting that the source of these embryos is women seeking infertility treatment (Rowland 1987).

Recent developments in IVF, such as postmenopausal pregnancies or injecting a single sperm into an ovum to treat *healthy* women for fertility problems in their male partners, are sometimes hailed as options that expand freedom and open doors. They also tend to increase the pressure on women to continue invasive infertility treatment because they have not exhausted every possible option. Overcoming the healthy infertility of mid-life also calls into question attitudes about menopause, offering yet another link between procreative ethics and larger feminist discussions of women's social roles and personal images.

Genetics, prenatal diagnosis, and pregnancy management

While prenatal diagnosis offers some expansion of women's reproductive choices, most feminists view the burgeoning bank of tests with suspicion. It is widely feared that more extensive genetic testing will become routine and difficult to avoid, as has already happened with ultrasound and amniocentesis. The cost-cutting pressures on most health-care systems may lead to expectations of compliance to prevent expensive birth defects, if not outright coercion by insurance companies to submit to tests during pregnancy. Prenatal testing in the context of pregnancy as a lived experience creates an emotional limbo; in a "tentative pregnancy" (Rothman 1986), the pregnant woman and her partner cannot celebrate a pregnancy that might be terminated, cannot mourn a loss that has not yet occurred, and feel responsible no matter what they choose.

434

If no cure is available for an identified genetic trait, then abortion or disposal of the embryo is the only option to prevent injury to a child; as more tests are made available, women may feel increased pressure to have unwanted abortions. The ability to detect genetic flaws in embryos may also encourage fertile women to seek IVF, with its risks of ovarian stimulation and surgical egg retrieval, to avoid later prenatal diagnosis and abortion. Some fetal malformations have been corrected with intrauterine surgery before the baby is born; this, of course, entails surgery on the mother. Court-ordered Caesarean sections offer a worrisome precedent for the coercive use of fetal therapies.

Another fear is that increased testing leads us to view the baby as a product to be rejected if not satisfactory; if babies are rejected, then the women who produce them might be similarly rejected, or at least subject to greater social control. Genetic engineering in embryos, if ever available, would vastly increase our freedom to choose our children's traits; might such choice slip into custom-ordering the children we want to have? Is sex selection a terribly sexist form of genetic choice (Holmes 1985), or less worrisome than is often supposed (Warren 1985)? These concerns illustrate the tensions within feminism to promote freedom for women while challenging oppressive and objectifying social practices.

Gestational contracts

Perhaps the most divisive procreative issue facing feminists is that of gestational arrangements, or "surrogate mothering." Many writers admit to ambivalence on the issue (Andrews 1988, Tong 1990). Even the naming of the practice is contentious, as the word "surrogate" fragments motherhood, marginalizes pregnancy, and ignores the perspectives of the pregnant woman and offspring to focus on the interests of the person(s) who want a genetically-related baby to raise.

There is substantial disagreement over whether the practice is one of providing gestational services or of providing children as products; the latter is clearly more objectionable than the former. Is compensating women for their risk and effort equivalent to baby-selling, making altruistic arrangements morally preferable, or does an unpaid arrangement exploit women's labor and still treat the baby as an object? The economic and Marxist analyses of reproduction noted above have offered particularly valuable insights into contracted pregnancy.

Gestational contracts are frequently compared to prostitution, and are equally divisive: both activities may allow women to control and perhaps profit from their bodily capacities, but are also widely viewed as exploitative, dehumanizing, and alienating from intimate bodily experiences. Of particular concern is that poor and socially marginalized women are much more likely to engage in both prostitution and gestational arrangements than are women with other resources, and that men rather than women are the primary recipients of the sex or the babies.

Gestational contracts, like many other procreative options, raise many paradoxes and double binds. When motherhood is fragmented, emphasizing the

435

importance of pregnancy and the maternal–fetal relationship may reinforce unacceptable expectations of femininity and mothering, but downplaying this relationship risks characterizing women as mere fetal containers. The freedom to engage in reproductive agreements may, itself, reinforce pronatalist assumptions that limit women's freedom more broadly, but regulating this reproductive option sets a dangerous precedent. It is indeed hard to know where a feminist ought to stand.

Conclusions

Amid the diversity of feminist conclusions, there is a shared desire to maximize the authority that women exercise over their own bodies and reproductive lives. However, the researchers who develop contraceptives and fertility treatments, the geneticists who test embryos and fetuses, the fertility specialists who "create" babies, the obstetricians who "deliver" the babies, and even the doctors who perform abortions, are predominantly male. Pregnancy is a lived, bodily phenomenon for women, but not for men, and procreating is situated within families, medical institutions, social norms, and power structures that influence reproductive decisions and perceptions. When male-dominated medical professions coexist with male-dominated religious hierarchies and political structures, it is hard to see how women are really gaining greater control over these processes.

Feminist scholars are articulating the experience of pregnancy in evocative, meaningful terms that were unavailable to male observers. Unfortunately, however, such descriptions have not been fully integrated into either the popular discourse or regulatory literature, although some political progress is being observed in Canada and Australia. More work is also required in analyzing the maternal–fetal relationship; although a depiction of fetuses as free-standing rights-bearers is widely and rightly rejected, we lack fully developed terminology and a moral framework to support women's liberties while also preventing irresponsible procreation and harm to developing offspring.

Feminist analysis has excelled at challenging male privilege and control over women's bodies in reproductive contexts and in larger social constructs. Less clear is how the different reproductive roles of males and females will be reconciled to protect the interests of women along with the legitimate reproductive interests of individual men. Unlike power, money, or social status, reproductive roles cannot be redistributed or equalized between the sexes, and thus a challenge to the status quo does not provide as clear guidance for reform in procreative policies as elsewhere.

Perhaps the greatest challenge is to address and resolve an underlying theoretical schism: is feminism about placing the interests of women *above* all others, or should it *integrate* women's interests with those of men, children, and communities? This tension between freedom and interdependence forces us to strive for greater clarity and tighter argument, but also threatens to obscure larger, shared feminist insights. We risk pitting fertile against infertile women, women

436

with social or economic advantages against disadvantaged women, and women who value motherhood against those who reject it. A feminist procreative ethic must somehow make room for all of these perspectives without losing women's articulated truths in philosophical divisiveness. Above all, procreative ethics must not be viewed as merely academic: reproductive regulations, medical interventions, and social expectations are rapidly evolving and deeply important in the lives of all women, and thoughtful guidance on these matters is urgently required in the real world.

PART IX

SOCIETY

44

Education

JANE ROLAND MARTIN

The great Western political and social philosophers had no doubts about the importance of education. Feminist philosophers of the past also understood the significance for their own projects of educational theory and philosophy (Martin 1985). Today, however, there is an education gap in the feminist philosophy text. Books in the field pay little attention to the subject of education and rarely cite feminist research in this area. Widely circulated bibliographies of feminist philosophy and overviews of the field have tended, in turn, to make this whole area of feminist philosophical research invisible (e.g. Addelson 1994, Ferguson 1994). The feminist theorist/activist Charlotte Bunch once wrote that feminist theory must, among other things, hypothesize how to change what is to what there should be (1979, p. 253). She did not say – nor would I – that every feminist who puts forward an account of what there should be must also address the practical issue of how to achieve the hoped-for results. One wonders, however, if it is possible to achieve the transformations of marriage, family, reproduction, workplace, science, society, not to mention gender itself, that feminist philosophers espouse without effecting a correspondingly great transformation of this culture's educational theory and philosophy.

The education-gender system

What could be more important than education? Yet if the feminist literature on the subject demonstrates anything at all, it is that even as there is a science-gender system that places our dreams for a feminist future at risk (Keller 1985, cf. Harding 1986), there is an education-gender system that also jeopardizes our projects. Comprising this culture's dominant educational practices and ideology, this system includes institutional forms and structures, accepted pedagogies, standard approaches to curriculum and organizations of subject matter, definitions of the function of school, conceptions of an educated person, and much, much more.

Feminist scholars have quite rightly denied the descriptive adequacy of one or another version of the public/domestic dichotomy. Nevertheless, our culture's educational thinking is predicated on this split (see, e.g., J. Martin 1985, 1992, 1994a). Implicitly dividing social reality into the world of the private home and the world of work, commerce, politics, and the professions, just about all of us – parents, politicians, schoolteachers and administrators, and just plain citizens –

take it for granted that the function of education is to transform children who have heretofore lived their lives in the one place into members of the other. Assuming that the private home is a natural institution and that, accordingly, membership in it is a given rather than something one must achieve, we see no reason to prepare people to carry out the tasks and activities associated with it. Perceiving the public world as a human creation and membership in it as something at which one can succeed or fail and therefore as problematic, we make the business of education preparation for carrying out the tasks and activities associated with it.

This in itself does not make our educational system gendered. That quality is conferred on it by the fact that, culturally speaking, the public world and the world of the private home are gender-coded. Given that the one is considered men's domain and the other is considered women's, and that education's ideology and practices are predicated on this dichotomy, gender becomes a basic dimension of the whole system.

To illustrate. The assumption that becoming educated is a process of acquiring new ways of thinking, feeling, and acting might appear to be gender-neutral. Yet it is not. If the educational system is to be "rational," these new ways must be functional – or at least they must be thought to be functional – in relation to life in the public world. But this, in turn, is to say that they must be functional in a world that, historically speaking, was a male preserve and to this day reflects this fact. Furthermore, in the context of this education-gender system there is no need at all for the newly acquired ways of thinking, feeling, acting to be – or to be considered – functional in relation to the world of the private home, a world whose inhabitants are presumed to be female. On the contrary, since these two worlds are culturally represented as polar opposites, preparation for life in the one will not be expected to foster ways of thinking, feeling, and acting that are functional in the other.

Virginia Woolf, whose *Three Guineas* (1938) can be profitably read as a treatise in the philosophy of education (see, e.g., J. Martin 1994a), said that life in the world across the bridge from the private home is competitive and that the people there have to be pugnacious and possessive in order to succeed (Woolf 1938, p. 72). We in the West signify our agreement by assuming that the qualities or traits of love, nurturance, and the three Cs of care, concern, and connection that are associated with the private home – and, of course, with women – run counter to education's raison d'être. Indeed, we take these to be such obstacles to the achievement of the objective of preparing children for life in the public world that we make one of early schooling's main tasks that of casting off the attitudes and values, the patterns of thought and action associated with home, women, and domesticity (Martin 1992).

It is surely no accident that the reports on the condition of American education published in the 1980s and 1990s gave home the silent treatment. Viewing children as travelers to the public world, they saw school as the place children stop en route in order to acquire the knowledge, skill, attitudes, and values that they presumably will need when they reach their destination – a kind of wayside inn. Once children enter school they do not go home again in this unexamined scenario; not ever, not even as adults. The authors of these volumes totally forgot that life is lived in both places and almost all of education's theorists and practitioners, critics, and reformers have forgotten too.

Constituting both a cause and an effect of our education-gender system, the amnesia is not surprising. One major conclusion of Nancy Chodorow's psycho-analytic study of mothering was that women's mothering "includes the capacities for its own reproduction" (1978, p. 206). Whether or not one accepts her thesis, there can be no doubt that the education-gender system includes the capacities for *its* own reproduction. The mechanism is the hidden curriculum.

In *Deschooling Society* Ivan Illich maintained that schooling perpetuates itself through a hidden curriculum that teaches dependency on schools. Confusing process and substance, school successfully transmits the lesson that to get an education you must go to school (Illich 1972). Well, education perpetuates itself too. I do not mean that educated people become addicted to education, although this may be true. My point is that we are indoctrinated in the belief that education has a fixed, unchanging nature: so indoctrinated, indeed, that most feminist scholars find fundamental educational change practically unthinkable (J. Martin 1994a).

Marilyn Frye has described women's existence as "a background against which phallocratic reality is a foreground" (1983, p. 167), a background "unseen by the eye which is focused on foreground figures." Education is in the same position as Frye's women. Almost all of us fall into the trap of essentializing education because the hidden curriculum of traditional schooling encourages students to see education as the static backdrop against which social, political, economic, and cultural events both great and small take place. Feminist philosophers are not exempt from this process of indoctrination. Trained to interrogate the works of white men, to problematize the idea of a canon, to historicize the concepts of gender and race, and to treat the human body itself as a social construct, we too have been covertly schooled in the belief that the present conceptual framework of education – its logical geography, if you will – is one of this world's brute facts.

Add to the hidden curriculum in the essentialization of education the hidden curriculum in "domephobia" – the devaluation of and morbid anxiety about things domestic – that liberal education transmits through both its silences on the subject of home and the negative attitudes embodied in the history and literature it teaches (Martin 1992, ch. 4), and it is all too easy to overlook the genderization of education. Nevertheless, even as the educational is political, social, and cultural, the political, the social, and the cultural are inextricably tied to education. Thus, just as it requires an understanding of politics, culture, and society to change education, an understanding of education is needed to transform politics, culture, and society.

As Plato needed a theory of education for the male and female rulers of the just state he put forward in the *Republic*, feminist philosophers need a well thought-out theory of the education of the male and female citizens and family members

443

of the societies they envision. Such a theory needs to acknowledge the now highly gendered structures of educational theory and practice lest these end up being presupposed. I do not think it possible for gender-egalitarian ideals of justice or anything else to be actualized in a society whose members receive an education that is thoroughly gender-bound and gender-biased from start to finish. Be it war or peace, the workplace or the academy, violence against women or the abuse of children, racism or homophobia, poverty or teenage pregnancy, science or technology: education is implicated in the problem and must therefore be addressed in the solution.

An overview of the literature

As the foregoing discussion indicates, there is now a body of feminist literature on education. This work is by no means exclusively devoted to the explication of the education-gender system. However, even those inquiries that eschew explicit reference to gender have the potential to contribute to one's understanding of this cultural construct.

Describing feminist philosophy's struggles within the American Philosophical Association, Kathryn Pyne Addelson judged that the field "has triumphed in these internal battles and achieved subdisciplinary status" (1994b, p. 217). Although the same cannot be said for feminist philosophy of education in relation to its professional organization, the Philosophy of Education Society, this field has been an active one since the early 1980s.

Mary Leach's important review of women's writing in philosophy of education (1991) reminds us that there was some feminist activity in the official precincts of philosophy of education before the 1980s (e.g. Greene 1978, Morgan 1979). It was the decade of the 1980s, however, in which feminist philosophy of education began to come of age.

Citing the permeability of the boundaries between feminist philosophy and feminist theory, in an overview of feminist philosophy Ann Ferguson (1994) listed contributions made by poets and anthropologists, economists and psychologists, as well as by trained philosophers. In a survey of feminist philosophy of education it is equally important to cast one's net widely, for the borders dividing feminist philosophy of education from feminist theory in general and from feminist educational theory in particular are also easily crossed. Think of Adrienne Rich's lectures on women's higher education in *On Lies, Secrets and Silence* (1979a); Carol Gilligan's research on the development of girls and women and on the ethics of care (1982a, 1988, Gilligan and Brown 1992); the Belenky, Clinchy, Goldberger, and Tarule volume, *Women's Ways of Knowing* (1986); bell hooks's essays on feminist pedagogy and women's higher education (1984, 1989). In addition to these widely read works, a broadly defined feminist philosophy of education would include research such as Dale Spender's examinations of women's education (1982); Madeleine Grumet's explorations of women and teaching (1988); Patti Lather's analyses of curriculum (1991); Jo Anne Pagano's studies in feminist theory and teaching (1990); Lyn Yates's (1993) and Victoria

444

Foster's (1996) studies of gender and education in the Australian context; Patricia Thompson's work on home economics and feminism (1986); Valerie Walkerdine's research in England on schoolgirls (1990).

Many of these writers are represented in Lynda Stone's 1994 anthology, *The Education Feminism Reader*. Yet if it is unwise to employ the sort of narrow, stipulative definition of the field of philosophy of education that has for too long served to exclude works by and about women (Martin 1982), the feminist research done by those who identify themselves professionally as philosophers of education warrants particular attention. Needless to say, this body of work can be organized in a variety of ways. In writing this article, I have found it helpful to distinguish three separate research programs, all of which were launched in the early 1980s and have continued into the 1990s. Since my categories do not reflect philosophical schools, I hasten to say that the research programs I outline embrace as broad a spectrum of philosophical approaches and methodologies as feminist philosophy in general does.

One such ongoing research program has been devoted to reclaiming, reconstructing, and reinterpreting historical theories of the education of girls and women. Although philosophical conversation on women's education began centuries before the birth of Christ and continues into the present time (cf. Kersey 1981), it was ignored by the standard texts and anthologies in the history of educational thought. Not only did women's contributions to this discussion go unrecorded, but when canonical texts contained sections on women's education, the portions devoted to this topic were set aside. The historically oriented feminist philosophy of education research program has for good reason, then, had two strands. Containing reinterpretations of standard historical works, it also brings women's voices into the conversation.

In the reinterpretation category fall my own rereadings of the educational philosophies of Rousseau and Plato, which then became the point of departure for my *Reclaiming a Conversation: The Ideal of the Educated Woman* (1985). Susan Laird's important studies of Dewey's educational philosophy (1988a, 1994) also belong here. Those sections of *Reclaiming a Conversation* in which I took Mary Wollstonecraft, Catharine Beecher, and Charlotte Perkins Gilman to be the authors of bona fide philosophical treatises on women's education belong in the new voices category, as do Laird's innovative readings of the educational thought of Louisa May Alcott (1991, 1995b) and my rereading of Maria Montessori's work (Martin 1992). Although Mary Catharine Baseheart did not cite the relevant feminist philosophy of education literature in her reconstruction of Edith Stein's philosophy of women's education (Baseheart 1989), or give any indication that she was aware of that research program, her essay is obviously related to this ongoing project. So, too, is the section devoted to Mary Astell's work on women's education in Margaret Atherton's edited volume, *Women Philosophers of the Early Modern Period* (1994).

A second, very different, feminist philosophy of education research program has taken as its starting point the ethics of care. Given voice by Gilligan in *In a Different Voice* (1982a), and sustained philosophical elaboration by Nel Noddings

445

in her 1984 volume *Caring: A Feminine Approach to Ethics and Moral Education*, this theory has by now commanded so much philosophical notice that it needs no introduction here. It is not just moral philosophers who have demonstrated an interest in the ethics of care, however. Feminist philosophers of education have also articulated, criticized, and applied the care perspective to a wide range of contexts.

Thus, for example, in a long, thoughtful review of *Caring*, Ann Diller (Diller et al. 1996) surveyed the major criticisms of an ethics of care, considered its overall significance for education, and pointed to questions that still required to be answered. Barbara Houston, in an equally perceptive inquiry, critically assessed Gilligan's and Noddings's formulations of the ethic in her "Prolegomena to future caring" (1989). Noddings herself addressed the subject of moral education in the last chapter of *Caring* and she has since further developed the theory's implications for moral education (1989, 1992) and applied the care perspective to teaching (1988). In addition, Audrey Thompson has used the theory to illuminate the concept of friendship (1990); Diller has worked out an ethics of care approach to pluralism in education and has also discussed the relationship between nurturance and educational criticism (Diller et al. 1996); Barbara Thayer-Bacon has explored the relationship of caring to critical thinking (1993); and Houston has applied the theory to the area of children's rights (1993).

The third feminist research program in the philosophy of education I discern has been devoted to developing a normative philosophy of education for both sexes. This project has at least five separate, albeit closely related, strands.

There are the feminist critiques of dominant educational paradigms. Among these are my deconstructions of the governing ideal of an educated person and the accepted theory of liberal education (1985, 1992, 1994a); Noddings's criticisms of liberal education (1992); Laird's rejection of the standard philosophical analysis of teaching (1988b, 1989, 1991, 1995b; cf. Martin 1987b); and Patricia Rohrer's critique of individualism in education (1994).

A second strand consists in analyses of educational concepts and practices that explicitly relate to gender. There is, for instance, Houston's "Theorizing gender: how much of it do we need?" (Diller et al. 1996); Maryann Ayim's and Houston's conceptual analysis of sexism and education (Diller et al. 1996); Linda Nicholson's attempt to give a theoretical grounding to the felt antagonism between the women's movement and the values and goals of schooling (1980) and also her discussion of affirmative action (1983a); the Ayim, Kathryn Morgan, Houston symposium, "Should public education be gender free?" (Diller et al. 1996); Morgan's explorations of the androgynous classroom and her analysis of three myths of educational equity (Diller et al. 1996); Suzanne de Castell's and Mary Bryson's interrogation of policy initiatives intended to promote gender equity in education (1993); and Laird's critiques of coeducation (1994, 1995b; cf. Martin 1992).

In addition, there are feminist discussions of particular curriculum areas. Some of the most important are Diller's and Houston's essay on physical education (Diller et al. 1996); Morgan's philosophical inquiry into sex education (Diller et al. 1996); Deanne Bogdan's work on the teaching of literature (1982); and

446

papers on thinking and education by James Garrison and Anne Phelan (1990), Betty Sichel (1993), Thayer-Bacon (1992, 1993) and Martin (1992); as well as my essay on gender bias in science education (1991).

A fourth strand of this research program specifically addresses questions about curriculum, goals, teaching methods, and the like in relation to the education of girls: see, for instance, Laird's "Who cares about girls?" (1995b) and my "The contradiction and challenge of the educated woman" (in 1994a). And finally, a fifth strand contains two well-developed overlapping, albeit quite different, general proposals for schooling, both of them published in 1992: Noddings's *The Challenge to Care in Schools* and my *The Schoolhome: Rethinking Schools for Changing Families*.

Conclusion

It may be wondered why I have not delineated a separate research program dedicated to the deconstruction of the education-gender system. On the one hand, I see all the work that has been done to date in feminist philosophy of education as either directly or indirectly illuminating this phenomenon. Furthermore, some research in each of the three programs described here intentionally engages in the project of deconstruction. Thus, I prefer to think of the explication and critique of the education-gender system as a consequence or a by-product of feminist research in the philosophy of education rather than as a single, self-contained set of inquiries. It is by no means the case that every feminist philosopher of education deliberately studies this construct. Indeed, one major difference between *The Challenge to Care in Schools* and *The Schoolhome* is that the former does not treat gender as a factor having deep significance for education, in fact does not even list the subjects of sex or gender in its index. In contrast, the latter offers insight into the education-gender system and proposes measures for dismantling it. Yet even that feminist research which does not interrogate the workings of gender in education ultimately sheds light on the education-gender system.

As I have already intimated, the field of philosophy of education has not been as hospitable to feminist research as Addelson says philosophy in general has been. Members of the profession have clung to narrow definitions of their area's domain so as to avoid making the education of girls a legitimate subject of study. They have dismissed out of hand the claims of women educational thinkers such as Maria Montessori to be treated as bona fide philosophers of education. With few exceptions (most notably, Norris 1995), they have failed to take seriously demonstrations of gender bias in the field's controlling paradigms. They have even gone so far as to say that writing produced in a reformist spirit is not philosophy.

I leave it to others to determine the effects, if any, of the gender gap in the philosophy of education text and the education gap in the feminist philosophy text on feminist philosophy of education. There is no doubt that impressive work has been and is now being done in this area. It is my hope that when these gaps are closed, even more scholars will want to contribute to the three research programs I have outlined and that brand-new programs will be launched.

45

Work

BARBARA HILKERT ANDOLSEN

Work is purposeful human activity oriented toward a useful outcome, particularly, but not exclusively, activity directed toward the satisfaction of human needs. It is distinguished from leisure, which encompasses human activity undertaken primarily for enjoyment or relaxation. Work includes *both* wage labor *and* uncompensated activities that, nevertheless, provide human beings with useful goods and services. Nurturing labor – sustaining the lives of children and preparing them for mature participation in society – is work, too.

Human labor, as done by either men or women, has received limited attention throughout the history of philosophy. Aristotle's subordination of manual labor to the life of the mind has been a fairly typical stance among male philosophers. When Aristotle did comment on the division of labour in his society, he argued that tasks were justly allotted according to the natural distribution of specific aptitudes among particular groups of human beings. Free women and slaves performed those household duties for which they were naturally suited. A non-citizen group engaged in the trade and craft work for which nature had given them special aptitudes. This left elite, male citizens free to concentrate on the most valuable human endeavors: politics and philosophy. While there are very important exceptions – such as John Locke's regard for labor as the foundation for property rights, G.W.F. Hegel's description of the self-awareness that the slave achieves through work, and John Dewey's respect for manual labor (associated with his stress on experience as a source for understanding) – human labor has been a relatively neglected topic among philosophers.

Another important exception to the dearth of sustained philosophic thought about work is Hannah Arendt's analysis in *The Human Condition*. Her category "labor" is especially pertinent for this article. For Arendt, labor encompassed all those repetitive human activities that are necessary for bodily survival. Labor, such as cooking, results in products that are consumed almost as soon as laborers make them. Therefore, labor involves effort that "is hardly ended when it must be started over again" (1958, p. 100). Housework is a prime example of labor.

It was probably not accidental that it was a *female* philosopher who provided a cogent description of the repetitive labor necessary to sustain human life. But Arendt's analysis mirrored Aristotle's in that labour was at the bottom of her hierarchy of human activity. ("Action," that is, self-disclosing participation in

448

the public world, was at the pinnacle.) In *The Human Condition*, Arendt acknowledged neither women's limited access to the public realm nor the connection between the fact that women were expected to do most of the world's labor and the fact that women had far fewer opportunities for "action."

Marxism and feminist analysis of work

Feminist thinkers have examined the gendered aspects of labor that Arendt ignored. However, an important segment of theorists turned not to the work of Arendt, but rather, to the thought of Karl Marx as a starting point. These scholars reexamined Marx's distinction between productive and reproductive work. According to Marx, reproductive work is necessary for the survival of individuals and the species, but it offers no avenue to specifically human satisfactions. Reproductive labor includes the energy expended to sustain the lives and labor power of workers. The effort involved in producing meals for workers is one example of reproductive labor. The reproduction of children and the rearing of children to become the next generation of workers are also reproductive labor. Most reproductive labor is performed by women.

Angela Davis perpetuated a low valuation of reproductive labor when she described housework as "invisible, repetitive, exhausting, unproductive, [and] uncreative" (1981a, p. 122). Davis proposed that women should no longer do housework in individual homes. Rather, housework should be done by specialized workers using efficient, technologically sophisticated methods. Since such services would not be profitable, Davis suggested that the government should subsidize housekeeping services for families that could not otherwise afford them. (However, Ruth Schwartz Cowan (1983) documented that nineteenth-century experiments providing centralized domestic services floundered because families wanted greater personal choice and greater privacy.)

Other Marxist feminists assigned a much greater value to women's reproductive labor. Indeed, Alison Jaggar and William McBride challenged the standard Marxist distinction between production and reproduction, charging that it was "invidious and male biased" (1985, p. 185). Italian commentators, especially Mariarosa Dalla Costa (1975), declared that homemakers were exploited as a crucial stratum of workers whose activity is absolutely essential to the functioning of the capitalist system. The housewife makes it possible for her husband to devote his energies to his job, and she raises the next generation of workers. Since housewives contributed directly to the labor power of their husbands and children, some writers – particularly some in Italy and Great Britain – declared that housewives deserved wages that compensated them for this labor power. Advocates of wages for housework said that transforming housework into wage labor would make this important area of women's work economically "visible." Many proponents suggested that wages would give housewives greater economic independence, enhance their self-esteem, and enlarge their bargaining power within the family.

449

However, others warned that salaries for housewives would only trap many women in yet another low-paid, female job. Moreover, there was a practical difficulty in the wage proposal. Who would pay the wages? Husbands? Corporations? The government? Opponents of pay for housework often insisted that unpaid household labor should be redistributed more equitably between husband and wife. Sex equity in the performance of household and child rearing duties would undermine the oppressive ideology that women are naturally suited for house work (Andolsen 1985).

In response to feminist thought, Philip Kain has examined how housekeeping and child care, which potentially offer intrinsic satisfactions, become oppressive when they are demanded of women as essential feminine duties (1993, p. 128). Domestic work is particularly exploitative when it is required of wage earning women in dual income marriages as an unpaid "second shift." (For a sociological analysis of the "second shift," see Hochschild 1989.)

Giuliana Pompei (1978) asserted that, unless there is a social transformation in the sexual division of domestic work, women will continue to bear disproportionate burdens to humanize their communities during times of economic stress. Women struggle to make ends meet when wages stagnate. When politicians cut social services, women step in to help family members and neighbors. Currently, across the globe, attacks on the social welfare state make Pompei's warnings prescient.

Another breakthrough in philosophic treatments of women's reproductive labor was Sara Ruddick's insightful analysis of the *work* of mothering (1989). Ruddick insisted that child rearing is not a facile, instinctive feminine response to an infant. It is hard work that requires judgment and creativity. Indeed, she described mothering as a practice that gives rise to a particular, valuable form of practical reasoning. She also stated that mothering work can be done by males as well as females.

Emotional labor and beauty work

Philosophers, such as Sandra Lee Bartky and Susan Bordo, have recently begun to examine other forms of effort expected of women, but rarely explicitly discussed: beauty work and emotional labor. Beauty work encompasses all the tasks that women do in order to come closer to the socially constructed ideal of feminine beauty. Dieting, purchasing flattering cosmetics and clothes, and applying makeup artfully are examples of beauty work. While the effort to look beautiful is often seen as a form of self-expression or a means for a woman to attract a male sexual partner, women also have to labor to achieve the right look for a variety of jobs. Many traditionally female jobs, such as that of receptionist, involve an expectation that the employee will display an attractive appearance. Professional women are often pressured to achieve a businesslike, *but feminine*, look. Bordo draws attention to the "inequalities of privilege, money and time" that allow certain women to be more successful at beauty work, although often these women pay a high price in fragile self-esteem (1993, pp. 247–8). For

Bartky, the indignity is that the carefully constructed feminine body is a "subjected body, i.e. a body on which an inferior status has been inscribed," in part, through women's own beauty work (1990a, p. 71).

Women are also expected to do most of society's emotional labor. Cheshire Calhoun offers the following examples of such work: "soothing tempers, boosting confidence, fueling pride, preventing frictions, and mending ego wounds" (1992, p. 118). Bartky investigates the injustice that occurs when women are required to produce more emotional support for men than men produce for women (1990a, p. 100). Emotional work is an explicit or implicit job task in many female-dominated occupations. An excellent sociological study of emotional work is *The Managed Heart*, a study about flight attendants (Hochschild, 1983).

Feminist philosophers need to examine critically the element of emotional labor often intertwined with bodily labor in the work of "caring." To care for another is a multifaceted experience. Care sometimes means the mental and physical labor involved in meeting the needs of another person who cannot perform self-care activities independently. Care may also mean an attitude of attentive concern for the well-being of another. This attentiveness to the needs of the one-cared-for may be motivated by a positive emotional attachment to the other. But feminist philosophers need to be cautious lest *the bodily labor of care taking* be obscured or devalued by an emphasis on the positive emotional dimension of some caring. For example, the philosopher Nel Noddings once suggested that morally worthwhile care *must* involve positive feeling for the other. She said: "in the deep human sense that will occupy us, I cannot claim to care for [another] if my caretaking is perfunctory or grudging" (1986, p. 9). She has also been unduly suspicious of care rendered in order to earn a pay check. Theorists should explore more fully the moral dimensions of the emotional labor involved in providing "good" care. Must good caretaking involve caring feelings?

Women's welfare may be harmed by idealization of "loving care." A belief that women have a *natural* instinct for caring suggests women have corresponding duties to care. According to one view, social utility is advanced when care taking is done by "loving" women who provide better care. Currently, we are faced with a dangerous moral irony: women's ethical commitment to care could be exploited by government officials – who withdraw funding for publicly sponsored child-care and home health-care programs while uttering sanctimonious praise for the "family value" of tender, feminine care.

Social justice issues and caring labour

There are important social justice questions associated with women's caring labor. Sarah Ruddick has realized, for example, that mothers' labors are often undermined by public policies that provide inadequate social support for maternal work. She declares that a mother's "ability to determine her own and her children's lives depends on economic and social policies over which she has

451

minimal control. *Contrary to myth, mothers do not work in private.* They are always in public" (1989, p. 35, emphasis added).

Specific justice questions arise when middle- and upper-class, white families hire women of color as domestics, child-care workers, and home health aides on exploitative terms (Kittay 1995, Tronto 1993, Andolsen 1993). Marilyn Friedman has argued that cuts in welfare benefits are forcing a growing number of poor women into accepting such domestic jobs. She perceives a "significant *relocation* of patriarchal control of women's domestic labor from the family hearth and the governmental [welfare] bureaucracy to the class-structured marketplace" (1988, p. 148).

Susan Okin (1989a) has provided a thorough analysis of an associated problem. She focuses on the economic vulnerability of married women and their children in a society where divorce is prevalent. The domestic work expected of wives and mothers puts them at a serious disadvantage as economic competitors in the marketplace. Women's disadvantaged positions as workers makes them economically dependent on their husbands' wages. Justice is violated when married women who have limited economic resources in their own right suffer serious and disproportionate economic harms in a divorce.

Some thinkers would reply that divorced women's economic vulnerability is an unfortunate result of these women's prior, rational choices to devote their energies to homemaking. Ann Cudd (1994) has challenged the notion that women make fully autonomous choices to put their domestic responsibilities ahead of their career opportunities. She contends that women's choices are constrained within an interlocking system of sexual disadvantage in the home and the workplace. Economic pressures, particularly the pay gap between women and men, constrain women's choices with respect to housework. The family will have a higher standard of living if the lower-paid female worker assumes a larger share of household duties. Burdened by household chores, women are subtly pushed toward traditionally female occupations that have low pay and prestige, but some flexibility that facilitates fulfilling household responsibilities. Under such social circumstances, women's choices about family and career are not completely autonomous.

Wage-earning women, reproduction, and fair treatment

Throughout the twentieth century, a steadily growing percentage of women has joined the paid labor force. As more women bear children while also working for wages, contested social justice issues arise. In the early 1980s, feminists debated whether to demand guaranteed maternity leave for pregnant women.

Those who advocated that pregnancy and birth ought to be covered under general employee medical leave policies warned that women of childbearing age would be discriminated against if they demanded special, expensive maternity leave. H.E. Baber stipulated that if women workers chose to take extended maternity leaves, then "all other things being equal ... the employer is well within his rights to prefer more committed workers" (1990, p. 326). Others cautioned that a special focus on the bodily demands of pregnancy could perpetuate stereotypes that women are physically fragile and less reliable workers. A special focus on pregnancy obscures the fact that many workers, male as well as female, are absent from the job for health reasons. These universalist feminists argued that employers have a moral obligation to offer a reasonable medical leave to any employee with a medical need (Williams 1982).

Those who supported special maternity leave protections asserted that a normal pregnancy culminating in a normal birth is not a disease. Handling pregnancy and birth under medical leave policies risks labeling pregnant women as disabled. Fighting for mandatory maternity leave through court cases or legislation would give badly needed protection to pregnant workers whose companies do not provide adequate medical leave. Some also argued that the labor of carrying a fetus and giving birth is valuable, but unrecognized, work that women perform on behalf of society. According to this view, maternity leaves provide social recognition for women's uniquely valuable bodily work in human reproduction.

Another moral issue involves fetal protection policies. Corporations designed these policies to limit harm to children, who were at risk of serious birth defects because of prenatal exposure to toxic substances. (Their mothers worked in contaminated workplaces.) Companies with fetal protection policies were also trying to avoid legal liability for the harm suffered by a child who had been exposed in utero to workplace toxins. In several cases, companies barred all women of childbearing age from jobs in work sites where toxins were present, unless the women workers had proof of sterility. These policies usually existed in blue-collar workplaces, where women were beginning to get higher-paying, nontraditional jobs.

Mary Gibson (1983) criticized these policies because they focused on reproductive harms to women workers, but ignored the reproductive harms facing men. She argued that, given the history of discrimination against women in blue-collar workplaces, barring them from such positions was especially objectionable. She insisted fertile workers should not be excluded from hazardous work settings unless there was no other way to protect pregnant workers from exposure to proven fetotoxins and unless other legitimate interests of the workers were protected. For example, fertile workers should be offered a transfer to a position in a less toxic environment with *no loss of pay, benefits, or seniority.*

Feminist scholars who examined fetal protection policies agreed that the first emphasis should be on the employer's obligation to provide the safest possible work environment, including one where reproductive capabilities of women *and men* are safeguarded to the maximum extent feasible. Many commentators objected strenuously to employers' tendencies to view all women as potentially pregnant. They countered that women are active moral agents shaping their reproductive capacities in their own and their families' best interests. Joan Callahan (1994) warned that the Supreme Court decision (*United Autoworkers v. Johnson Controls*) that struck down fetal protection policies had drawbacks.

453

According to Callahan, the Supreme Court decision protected employers from liability for prenatal injuries to children, but did not require them to clean up the workplace. The decision also affirmed women's freedom to control their reproduction and to choose risky employment, but it created the risk that women might be scapegoated for harms suffered by children born with defects.

Social justice and the gendered division of wage labor

Few philosophers have given careful attention to the specific realities of women's wage labor. One exception is Alison Jaggar's discussion of women's wage labor contained in her analysis of socialist feminist politics (1983). Sex segregation in employment, while declining, remains a fundamental economic reality that should raise important questions concerning justice. The majority of women workers are still clustered in a variety of traditionally female occupations, such as those of sewing-machine operator, secretary and nurse. Even though women, especially European-American women, are gaining a large share of professional and managerial jobs, there still is a "glass ceiling" of discrimination that prevents women from rising to the highest echelons in these job categories.

In 1983, Janice Moulton and Francine Rainone warned that, as a result of unjust sex-role definitions, the employment options of women were constricted in unfair ways. Those jobs socially defined as fitting for women offered little pay, power, or prestige. Despite a lessening of sexual discrimination in employment, an increase in the number of women pursuing training for formerly "male" occupations, and affirmative action efforts, women continue to suffer economic disadvantages based on gender disparities in employment.

One response to persistent economic inequalities, rooted in occupational sex segregation, was a proposal called pay equity or comparable worth. Pay-equity schemes involved evaluating all job categories according to a standardized set of criteria, such as education required, supervisory responsibility, or nature of the working conditions. If female job categories paid significantly less than male job categories with similar scores for "compensable features," employers raised the salaries for the female jobs.

Pay-equity systems need careful ethical scrutiny. Barbara Bergmann has warned that evaluators may give undue weight to factors more characteristic of male jobs, such as duties involving heavy lifting, while underestimating women's skills, such as attention to detail (1986, p. 182). Evaluators should assign appropriate value to job requirements involving emotional labor. Weights assigned to educational qualifications should be scrutinized for class bias.

Pay equity was debated seriously in the early 1980s, but appears dormant in the current conservative, free-market, political climate. Indeed, some commentators contend that there is no legitimate way to assess a fair wage other than the impartial mechanism of the unimpeded labor market. Deborah Rhode counters that strong evidence of persistent underestimation of the worth of women's work, particularly work by women of color, establishes that "market forces" are "unreliable guardians of equitable compensation structures" (1988, p. 1228).

454

Scholars such as Iris Marion Young (1990a) and Deborah Rhode have insisted that achieving fairness for women in the workforce ultimately requires a social justice analysis of the basic cultural and economic structures of society. One urgent question that no one has addressed is the widening economic gap between African-American women and European-American women. In the United States in the 1970s, as a result of the civil rights movement, affirmative action programs, and growth in service jobs, African-American and European-American women achieved near-parity in pay for fulltime, year-round employment. Much of the improvement in the status of African-American women was due to their movement from domestic work into clerical and retail jobs. However, the convergence of employment opportunities for women of different racial and ethnic groups may have been a temporary phenomenon. More recently, a larger proportion of young, European-American women have moved into traditionally male, managerial, and professional jobs. Social class, often mediated through access to quality education, increasingly determines women's workplace opportunities. Technological changes are exacerbating divisions among women (Andolsen 1989). Younger women with limited education are shunted into low-paying, dead-end service jobs. Simultaneously, in the United States, women in the "knowledge worker" class command ever higher salaries. Growing wage inequalities *among women in different occupational groups* need to be examined as a justice issue. In this economic context, the insights of scholars such as Young and Rhode become particularly important. They insist that justice entails the dismantling of structures of inequality – cultural and economic barriers that keep women in disadvantaged positions relative to male peers and that perpetuate inequalities among women.

Justice for women requires more than equal access to the wage labor force as it is presently structured. Justice requires a fundamental restructuring of the so-called "workplace" to allow more humane connections between paid labor and household labor, including childbearing. Women's "invisible" work – caretaking and emotional labor – needs to be recognized and shared more equitably with men. Privileged men need to perform a greater share of essential, repetitive labor in the home and on the job – to use Arendt's distinction. Then, women and less privileged men would have greater opportunities to experience the satisfaction of work as a communal enterprise in which human beings develop their personal talents through jointly shaping a common world.

46

Privacy

ANITA ALLEN

Introduction

If feminism has taken a stance toward privacy, the stance is ambivalence. Conceptions of privacy have been central to many critiques of what feminists term the "liberal" and "patriarchical" dimensions of Western societies. Just how privacy has been central to feminism is a worthwhile subject of inquiry. Interestingly, conceptions of privacy have functioned within feminist thought both as targets and as tools of critique. Some feminists target privacy for condemnation as a barrier to female liberation, while others embrace it as a tool of female liberation.

As targets of critique, conceptions of privacy have signified problematic ideals of isolation and individualism that conflict with certain ideals of nurture and care (Williams 1991b, West 1990, Colker 1992). They have also signified unwanted conditions of female modesty and confinement to traditional domestic roles (MacKinnon 1987b). Privacy has sometimes been synonymous with the private sphere of home and family life, a context of traditional female subordination in dependent socioeconomic relationships. Harm can befall vulnerable women and children in any area of domestic or commercial life in which a community or its government abrogates responsibility to male-dominated institutions and practices tagged "private." Thus, some feminists advocating liberty, equality, and security for women have tended to look upon privacy with disfavor.

Others have not. The legal right to birth control and abortion were won in the United States under the banner of "the right of privacy." Some feminists understandably endorse conceptions of privacy as tools for expressing ideals of independent, autonomous decision-making respecting sex, reproduction, family and health (Allen 1988, Roberts 1991, McClain 1992b).

The goal of this article is to describe the competing friendly and unfriendly stances feminists have taken with respect to important conceptions of privacy. My descriptive analysis of privacy's ambivalent standing within feminism will include a basic characterization of moral principles and legal doctrines associated with privacy in the United States. Inside the United States and without, privacy has had an expansive role in morals, politics, and law.

In morals, though with significant cultural variations, daily intercourse is constrained by expectations of mutual respect for the privacy of certain dwellings, communications, and behavior (Moore 1984, Pennock and Chapman

1971). In politics, particularly in the Western-style democracies, privacy stands virtually on a par with liberty and equality as a core liberal value. But privacy as a political value is not limited to liberal regimes (Sandel 1996, pp. 92–119). People around the world consider protecting at least some privacy interests a core function of good government (Blaustein and Flanz 1994). In law, virtually every country's constitution or comparable basic law contains privacy principles limiting authorized government access to people and possessions. The civil law of individual European nations and the official directives of the European Community include standards for the disclosure of personal and commercial information. Privacy as a legal norm is especially pervasive in the United States. The First, Third, Fourth, Fifth, and Fourteenth Amendments of the US Constitution implicitly recognize rights of privacy (Allen 1996a, 1996b, Rubenfeld 1989). Statutes, common law, and state constitutions create additional rights of privacy for American victims of unwanted intrusion, publicity, and breaches of confidentiality.

A once-neglected subject

Privacy was once a neglected subject. Scholarly discussions of Roman law's *res privatae*, along with "private" property and the "private" law of property, contracts, and tort, have been commonplace for centuries. But, prior to the twentieth century, only a handful of essayists, lawyers, philosophers, and social scientists wrote about privacy. One of them was Charlotte Perkins Gilman. Gilman closely analyzed the ideal of domestic privacy in her book, *Women and Economics* ([1898] 1966). She argued that although the home is generally regarded as a haven of privacy, family life typically offers very few opportunities for solitude, particularly for women, children, and poor people.

The notion of a "right to privacy" prominently entered US common law at the close of the nineteenth century. It found its way into constitutional law in the 1960s and into the federal statutory arena in the 1970s and 1980s. Today, individuals who spy or gossip risk civil suit; state governments that enacted laws banning contraception or miscegenation face swift constitutional challenges. This is because Americans now have an array of positive privacy rights that include "individual-against-individual" common law, constitutional and statutory rights to physical seclusion and limited publicity, and "individual-against-government" constitutional rights to a limited, tolerant, neutral government that leaves people alone to make a range of decisions in peace and with relative autonomy.

Women's interests and feminist activism have played major roles in the development of privacy law and scholarship in the United States. In US law, the right to privacy is a feature of positive law as a consequence of contradictory subordinating and liberating impulses relating to women (Allen 1996a, 1996b, Allen and Mack 1990).

DeMay v. *Roberts* (1881), the earliest American case citing privacy rights as the basis of decision, held a physician liable for permitting his lay assistant to witness

457

a woman's labor and childbirth. The court's written opinion suggests a special solicitude for married women's modesty. Concerns about family seclusion and women's modesty figured importantly in the privacy tort law spawned by Louis Brandeis and Samuel Warren in a famous 1890 *Harvard Law Review* article (Allen and Mack 1990). Women's right to legal use of contraceptives was centrally at issue when the US Supreme Court first recognized a constitutional right to privacy in *Griswold* v. *Connecticut* (1965). *Roe* v. *Wade* (1973), the US case that first established women's right to abortion, held that the decision whether or not to bear a child is protected by a fundamental constitutional right of privacy.

American scholars, politicians, and the general public exhibited intense interest in privacy after the 1960s, 1970s, and 1980s. Some of this can be attributed to the impact of the *Griswold* and *Roe* cases and to subsequent health-, sex-, and family-related cases heard in the courts for which they served as precedents. But the privacy explosion stemmed also from heightened concern respecting electronic surveillance and computer databanks developed by business and government. Concerns over the implications of drug, alcohol, HIV, and genetic testing further fueled the privacy explosion. These phenomena raise concerns about "privacy" in at least three commonplace senses of the term: physical, informational, and decisional.

Physical privacy

In one pervasive sense of the word, "privacy" consists of freedom from unwanted physical observation or bodily contact. It signifies limited access to those desiring seclusion, solitude, or intimacy.

Americans, Europeans, and people around the world often associate privacy in this "physical" sense with homes and home life. As a matter of law and social practice, adults generally possess physical structures respected as realms of exclusive personal dominion. For some, homes are havens of personal privacy. However, for women with parental and other caretaking responsibilities, homes do not serve as havens of individual privacy (Allen 1988). Eschewing or delaying marriage and childbearing is a way some women contrive to lead lives of scholarly or artistic solitude.

Yet companionship and care rather than solitude is what some women are after (Allen 1988, pp. 72–5). For them, a crowded, noisy family home can be a boon rather than a bane. While such homes offer individual family members little physical privacy vis-à-vis one another, they offer family units a great deal of physical privacy vis-à-vis the rest of the world. Persons seeking to avoid relationships and children in favor of individual solitude are seeking physical privacy, but so too are those who crave exclusive intimacy with families or domestic partners. The shared, communal varieties of privacy hold great appeal. Indeed, in so far as it connotes isolation and independence from others, "privacy" may fail to resonate with some women.

Physical privacy is an expectation at home, but it can also be an expectation outside the home, in public places (Allen 1988, pp. 123–52). Whether at work, shopping, engaging in recreation, or simply walking down a public street, people expect a degree of physical separation from others. Even in crowded subways, there are standards of appropriate touching and eye contact. A woman seeking relief from sexual harassment on the public streets understands that complete privacy in the midst of a busy city is impossible; she nonetheless believes she is entitled to freedom from stalking, gratuitous crowding, groping, and similar highly offensive contact.

Physical privacy is often a grave concern when a person is in the custody of law enforcement and prison officials (Allen 1988, pp. 153–79). However legitimate and justifiable, police detention and arrest diminish privacy, as do body, body cavity, and prison-cell searches. For a man or woman in solitary confinement, prison may afford what might be aptly phrased too much physical privacy.

Physical privacy is of concern when persons who are not in detention are objects of surveillance. Physical privacy is also of concern in the contexts both of health examinations, medical treatment, and surgery, and of employer testing for substance abuse (Allen 1995a). In all of these contexts, the notion that privacy is threatened is tied to the fact of bodily encroachment, such as a touch, a needle puncture, an incision. Privacy is further threatened by the fact that physical encroachments can disclose otherwise concealed or secret personal *information*.

Informational privacy

In a second sense of the expression, "privacy" is the secrecy, confidentiality, or anonymity of information. It requires limits on the disclosure of personal information obtained from persons, tissue samples, files, records, computers, or databanks. Informational privacy concerns are often motivated by fear that discrimination will result from disclosure. Responding to discrimination for and against married women, laws enacted in the 1960s and 1970s free women who apply for credit or jobs from the need to reveal their marital status. Some bioethicists disapprove of mandatory genetic and HIV testing on the ground that testing facilitates discrimination in employment, education, and insurance (Allen, forthcoming). Advocates of legal limits on the disclosure of genetic information fear discrimination by private insurers and employers.

Today many adoptions are "open." In open adoptions a child's natural parents participate in selecting specific adoptive parents, with whom some degree of contact may be sustained throughout the child's life. But a woman planning to surrender a child for adoption anonymously must rely upon the confidentiality of adoption agency employees, lawyers, and physicians. Concerns about informational privacy have led women's reproductive health clinics to object to state record-keeping laws that would give the general public access to the names of their abortion patients. On informational privacy grounds, women's reproductive health clinics also object to abortion protesters who photograph or videotape people entering their facilities.

Computer technologies have inspired an expanded definition of privacy, whereby "privacy" designates so-called "fair information practices." These require, for example, that government, businesses, and other institutional collectors of data about identifiable individuals (1) protect personal information from public exposure; (2) take reasonable steps to verify and update information; (3) allow individuals access to records of which they are the subject; and (4) obtain consent prior to otherwise unauthorized uses of personal information. As leading consumers of health-care and retail services, data protection norms have special significance to women.

Decisional privacy

In a final sense, privacy signifies the ability to make one's own decisions and to act on those decisions, free from governmental or other unwanted interference. Philosophic rationales for decisional "privacy" often incorporate ideals of limited, tolerant, neutral government (Rubenfeld 1989, Richards 1986); moral conceptions of human beings as bearers of dignity, autonomy, or interests, by virtue of which they ought to have lives and ties of their own choosing (Feinberg 1983, Bloustein 1964); or both. The US Supreme Court ascribes individuals decisional privacy rights to the use of contraception (*Griswold* v. *Connecticut*, 1965), to medical abortions (*Roe* v. *Wade*, 1973), to interracial marriage (*Loving* v. *Virginia*, 1967), and to the consumption of pornography (*Stanley* v. *Georgia*, 1967). The Supreme Court or lower state and federal courts have refused to ascribe decisional privacy rights to the parties to surrogate mother contracts (In re *Baby M*, 1988), or to gays and lesbians seeking to be immune from the threat of criminal punishment for consensual sodomy (*Bowers* v. *Hardwick*, 1986).

The "decisional" usage of privacy has come under fire (Ely 1973). Critics of abortion law's privacy rationale have frequently asserted that abortion rights promote women's equality and liberty but have little to do with privacy (Sunstein 1992). By "privacy" these critics mean privacy in the physical and informational senses. Many argue, first, that, as an aspect of liberty, freedom, or autonomy, decisional privacy stands apart from the concepts like seclusion and confidentiality, paradigmatic forms of privacy (Parent 1983). Second, we diminish our ability to explain privacy and liberty, freedom, or autonomy as distinct concepts, if we follow the Supreme Court and speak of "decisional" privacy (Gavison 1980). Confusing uses of the concept of privacy in the Court's early reproduction rights cases lend a degree of merit to this objection.

Defenders of the decisional usage of privacy counter that "decisional" privacy is worthy of the name. They emphasize that although decisional privacy denotes aspects of liberty, freedom, and autonomy, it denotes aspects of these that pertain to deeply felt conceptions of a private life beyond legitimate social involvement (Allen 1995a, DeCew 1987, Gerety 1977). Using "privacy" to denote a domain of decision making appropriately outside of legitimate social concern is now an entrenched practice in the United States and a number of other countries.

460

The public and the private

Some decisional uses of "privacy" seem to presuppose that social life is divided into distinguishable public and private spheres, the private sphere being a realm of individual decision making about sex, reproduction, marriage, and family. So conceived, "decisional" privacy has origins in classical antiquity. The Greeks distinguished the "public" sphere of the *polis*, or city-state, from the "private" sphere of the *oikos*, or household (Habermas 1989, Arendt, 1958). The Romans similarly distinguished *res publicae*, concerns of the community, from *res privatae*, concerns of individuals and families (ibid.) The public realm was the sector in which free males, whose property and economic status conveyed citizenship, participated in collective governance. By contrast, the private realm was the mundane sector of economic and biologic survival. Wives, children, slaves, and servants populated the private sphere, living as subordinate ancillaries to male caretakers. The classical premise that social life ought to be organized into public and private spheres survives in the post-Enlightenment Western liberal tradition. So too does the premise that the private sphere consists chiefly of the home, the family, and apolitical intimate association.

There is an irony in the aspiration for legal rights of privacy conceptually dividing social life into well-bounded private and public spheres: the public sphere is ubiquitous. Law, and therefore the arms of "public" government, define and mediate the complex of individual-to-individual and individual-to-government relations that constitute "private" life. For example, a person is permitted to drive a car, adopt a child, practice a religion, marry outside of another race, expect confidentiality of physicians, belong to exclusive private clubs, and use birth-control pills, all because of legislative and constitutional provisions created and enforced by government. Moreover, government serves essential policing and adjudicative functions without which personal privacy would be impossible for most people. If someone is being harassed in ways that violate privacy, he or she can call the police. If someone harms another's privacy interests, he or she may be able to bring a lawsuit to have losses compensated.

The private sphere is permeated by government. To the extent that government is infused with patriarchal, heterosexual ideals, men and women's privacy rights are likely to reflect patriarchal, heterosexual ideals of a private sphere. As a woman, "my" legal privacy is limited by "his" and "their" conceptions of the good life. Thus a lesbian's desire to live in peace with her female lover and to rear her own or adopted children may be thwarted by others' conceptions of the good family and family values.

Responding to liberals who speak of "the public" and "the private" as if they were fixed categories constraining good government, critics sometimes argue that public and private are contingent, transformable conceptions of how power ought to be allocated among individuals, social groups, and government (Radest 1979). Feminist critics of liberalism are apt to insist that the public/private distinction is altogether an ideological tool of subordination in societies in

461

which white men with property dominate other groups (MacKinnon 1987a, Olsen 1989). "Privacy" justifies exclusive monopolies over social resources and societal indifference to the violence and poverty that characterize the "private" lives of many women and children (Schneider 1991). Liberal society thrives on open government and closed personal relations. Feminists have stressed that closed personal relations make it more likely that serious harm will go undetected. A parent–child relationship may be one in which a child is being sexually abused or an elderly parent is being neglected. A marriage may be one in which one of the partners is being beaten or raped. Government cannot protect vulnerable citizens from domestic violence if high boundaries of legally sanctioned privacy surround the family.

Feminists who do not reject the public/private dichotomy have sometimes argued that the line between public and private should be redrawn to allow women greater power over their own bodies and lives. The line between public and private has already been redrawn in the criminal law of rape where, in many jurisdictions, "marital privacy" no longer immunizes married men from prosecution for raping their wives.

Most liberals depict privacy rights limiting government regulation as negative liberties to freedom from government involvement with private decision making. The negative liberties approach supports decisions of the Supreme Court holding that the "right to privacy" does not require that the public sector pay for the abortions of poor women otherwise unable to obtain them. In an attempt to reconceive public and private, feminists have argued that privacy rights can entail the right to make welfare demands on the public sector. It is sometimes argued that the right to privacy could support, rather than defeat, the case for government payment of Medicaid-eligible poor women's abortions (Pine and Law 1992, Roberts 1991).

Definition and value

Scholars, including many feminists, now regularly debate how best to define, value, and regulate privacy (De Cew 1987, Schoeman 1992a, Inness 1992, Wacks 1989, Allen 1988). No single definition of privacy or account of its value has gained universal acceptance. Theorists disagree about how to approach defining and evaluating privacy. Disagreement persists about whether privacy should be defined as a value or as a fact; whether it should be defined as a moral claim or as a right; whether definitions of privacy should prescribe ideal uses of the term or should describe actual usage.

Scholarly definitions of privacy range from "being let alone," popularized by Samuel Warren and Louis Brandeis (1890, p. 193), to Alan F. Westin's more specific "claim of individuals, groups, or institutions to determine for themselves when, how, and to what extent information about them is communicated to others" (Westin 1967, p. 7). Many writers say privacy denotes conditions of restricted access to persons, their mental states, or information about them (Gavison 1980, Allen 1988, Bok 1983). According to Ruth Gavison (1980,

p. 428), "in perfect privacy no one has any information about X, no one pays any attention to X, and no one has physical access to X." So conceived, privacy functions as an "umbrella" concept, encompassing a family of concepts each of which denotes a form of limited access to others. Theorists disagree about the membership of the privacy family. Members plausibly include seclusion, solitude, anonymity, confidentiality, modesty, intimacy, reserve, and secrecy.

In the place of "restricted access to persons, their mental states and information about them," a number of definitions emphasize control, either control over information or avenues of observation (Parent 1983, Fried 1970, Westin 1967). Many legal and moral theorists characterize privacy as a social practice with normative functions (Post 1989). In this vein, Jeffrey Reiman (1976) links privacy to the formation of individuality and personhood: "Privacy is a social ritual by means of which an individual's moral title to his own existence is conferred" (Reiman 1976, p. 39).

Physical and informational privacy practices serve to limit observation and disclosure deemed inimical to well-being (Altman 1976). Psychologists have long emphasized the unhealthy effects of depriving individuals of opportunities for socially defined modes of privacy (Schneider 1977). Moral philosophers maintain that respecting the many forms of privacy is paramount for respect for human dignity and personhood, moral autonomy, and workable community life (Schoeman 1992a, Kupfer 1987, De Cew 1987, Feinberg 1983, Pennock and Chapman 1971). Many philosophers point to the political morality of a limited, tolerant government as the moral basis of privacy rights against government control of sexuality, reproduction, and health care (Richards 1986). Lawyers often say that the high moral value of privacy is the justification for legal rights of privacy (Allen 1988, Feinberg 1983, Gavison, 1980, Westin 1967).

Feminism against privacy

Ideals of privacy have been central to liberal feminists' assessments of the rights and responsibilities of women. Although the concept of privacy connotes female power and responsibility for reproductive decision-making, it also suggests female powerlessness and dependence in traditional private roles. Accordingly, feminist theorists have approached privacy from opposing directions. One direction is friendly, emphasizing women taking control of their own lives through conditions of privacy and rights of privacy. The other direction is unfriendly, emphasizing female powerlessness within male-dominated spheres, or conflicts between ideals of privacy and ideal ethics of care and compassion. The latter direction runs against the grain of liberal moral philosophy's endorsement of privacy as a core human value. What exactly has made privacy a target of negative feminist critique? Why have some feminists only reluctantly applauded privacy discourse as a tool of feminist activism? I will mention three criticisms feminists have leveled against privacy: the under-participation critique, the violence critique, and the conservative tilt critique, respectively.

463

For many feminists, "privacy" and "private sphere" connote problematic conditions of female seclusion and subordination in the home and in domestic caretaking roles. This seclusion and subordination has meant that women have not generally been able to participate in society up to their full capacities. Women have under-participated.

Feminists have attacked the assumption that the proper role of women is to live within the "private sphere" under the authority of men as daughters, wives, and mothers with chiefly domestic duties. Women's traditional caretaking tasks have included cooking, shopping, gardening, cleaning, and childrearing. These tasks have kept many women's lives centered in the privacy of the family home. Conventions of female chastity and modesty have shielded women in a mantle of privacy at a high cost to sexual choice and self-expression. Expectations of emotional intimacy have fostered beneficial personal ties. Gardening, cooking, and needlework have served as outlets for creativity. At the same time, women's prescribed roles have limited their opportunities for individual forms of privacy and independently chosen personal association. Maternal and social roles have kept women in the private sphere who might otherwise have distinguished themselves in the public sphere as businesswomen, scholars, government leaders, and artists. To increase women's participation in society, feminist activists have fought for the right of women to hold property, to vote, and to work outside the home in jobs of varied description for which they would be compensated as men are compensated.

The ideal of a private sphere free of government and other outside interference has currency, despite the reality that in the United States and other Western democracies virtually every aspect of nominally private life is a focus of direct or indirect government regulation. Marriage is considered a private relationship, yet governments require licenses and medical tests, impose age limits, and prohibit polygamous, incestuous, and same-sex marriages. Procreation and childrearing are considered private, but government child-abuse and neglect laws regulate, if at times inadequately, how parents, and possibly even pregnant women, must exercise their responsibilities. The ideal of a private sphere can be no more than an ideal of the ability of ordinary citizens to make choices that are relatively free of the most direct forms of governmental interference and constraint.

The worthiness of this ideal has been called to question in the United States where problems of domestic violence suggest a need for more rather than less involvement in the traditionally "private" spheres of home and family life. Although violence occurs in the home, it is no longer legally permissible for a man or woman to beat a spouse or lover; or for a parent or guardian to severely beat children in the name of anger or discipline.

Some feminists view the concept of privacy as having an inherently conservative tilt in the Western liberal societies where it has had the greatest currency. The privacy banner waves away public intervention calculated to reinvent customary standards of behavior that lead to female under-participation and male violence or harassment. Legal feminists commonly argue that the liberal ideology of "privacy" is inherently conservative and has therefore slowed the growth of the laws beneficial to vulnerable classes of women (Olsen 1989).

Conservatives have generally opposed government welfare programs, especially any that are amenable to characterization as inessential. It is perhaps not surprising, then, that they have generally opposed government funding for poor women's "elective" abortions. Many conservatives and liberals interpret the right to privacy in the context of contraception and abortion as a negative right *against* government decision-making respecting procreation, not as a positive right *to* governmental programs designed to make contraception and abortion services available to those who cannot afford to pay (Sher 1982). For some, it is self-evident as a matter of logic that a privacy right is not something the public should have to pay for. Many feminists blame the emphasis on privacy in abortion law for the failure of legal efforts to secure government funding for poor women's abortions (Olsen 1989, Mackinnon 1987b, Colker 1992).

Conclusion

Philosophers observe that privacy is a complex concept with varied applications about which there is practical and theoretical controversy. Feminists have good reason to be critical of what the "privacy" of the private sphere has signified for women in the past and what the rhetoric and jurisprudence of "the right to privacy" could signal for the future. At the same time, there is little doubt that women seeking greater control over their lives have already benefited from heightened social respect for appropriate forms of physical, informational, and decisional privacy. The insights gleaned from the examination of feminist theories of privacy ultimately suggest that one adopt a vigilant attitude toward applications of privacy.

47

Community

MARIA LUGONES

Why does one write about community? For whom? With whom? In the midst of what company? From inside which collectivity? Given what traditions? From what "location"? Given what self-understandings? While doing what? Staying put or in movement? Resting while moving? Preparing to move? To what extent is the writing one's own map for the direction of the movement? How many voices can one hear in the writing/planning?

Problematizing "One": In *Inessential Woman*, Elizabeth Spelman taught me to use "woman" as a schema to be filled out. A woman is a gendered female of the species, where gender configuration can vary very significantly from society to society and within a given society (Spelman 1988, p. 134). In this writing I want to mean the word without losing the insights gained from practicing the schema sense of "woman," but gaining in concrete plurality. I want to initiate the practice of uttering/writing and reading/hearing words like "woman" and "lesbian" concretely and specifically in their plurality and as emphatically open-ended – as if you held a multitude of interrelated subjects in your attention and you thought, felt, understood yourself as among them in your own specificity and in the problematic character of that specificity, as enmeshed in both shifting and historically threaded but also ossified relations of solidarity and exploitation, of tenderness and abuse.

As I form my words in this multitude, I hear my voices, and hear you hearing me. I/you extend myself/yourself or recoil, stand my/your ground among subjects, consider my/your concreteness. As I live and think our relations, given the history and contemporary situation, I ponder and negotiate details and larger strokes, stolen kisses and endearing embraces, entrapments and tortures and, inevitably, the identity markers and community relations, many fragmented and plural communities. As I feel my ground, it is in the midst of concrete, complex, nonreducible, cantankerous, fleshy, interrelated, positioned subjects, noncontainable within any easy, abstract, hard-edged, simple classification. It is from within this multitude that I want to consider the question of community.

I will consider three contemporary reflections on community and I will ask of them – from my complex positioning – the questions I listed at the outset: Marilyn Friedman's treatment of community in "Feminism and modern friendship: dislocating the community" (1995), Sarah Hoagland's treatment in *Lesbian Ethics* (1988), and bell hooks's in *Yearning* (1990).

466

I have taken these ideas to different "communities" in the process of reconsidering the place and meaning of community and home within a politics of resistance and liberation. I have included them as I devised theoretical workshops, exercises and dialogue to provoke reflection on "common-sense" understandings of everyday life – including institutional life – in the United States with other popular educators. We have taken these ideas to rural New Mexico, to Mexican and Puerto-Rican communities in Chicago, to women's communities and women in communities in Minnesota, New Mexico, to diverse groups focusing on lesbian life, on land and water struggles. violence against women. The process of bringing these ideas to different "communities" was highly collective and through it many different collectivities have intersected. In the process of moving geographically/conceptually these understandings have undergone critique. We have become refracted in this movement through different and interconnected universes of sense; we have become aware of our own and each other's plurality. One way of intimating the critique is to say that appreciating liberatory possibilities in seen here through a combination of movement and stasis, and that both point to disjunctures and multiplicities that make the ideal of community in urgent need of reconceptualization.

This writing is, then, part of the project of "building community/ies" as it problematizes it – a project unstably perched between the dangers lying in waiting in the apparent safety of community and home, and the promise that community and home offer of overcoming a solitude and separation that condemns us to making an angry but accommodating life within ready-made oppressive senses. Collectivity comes to be inhabited with a sense of possibility and great discomfort, sometimes to the point of self-betrayal, as a problem to be resolved rather than a solution.

It is emancipatory intent that explains the need for collectivity. Liberation is understood here as initially depending on multiple, in tension, contested cotemporaneous constructions of reality. Differently positioned subjects recognize different constructions and often exercise "multiple vision," they recognize more than one cotemporaneous construction. Though each construction is social, not all have the same power over institutional life. Some constructions constitute some subjects with the logic of oppression. In such a logic there is a fundamental lack of agency for oppressed peoples and no possibility of the dominated subject unveiling domination within it. Such unveiling would already place the subject within a logic exterior to the logic of oppression. Within a logic of oppression the subaltern cannot name the dominator/dominated asymmetries and cannot speak a liberatory sense.

Resistant subjects negotiating and contesting multiple oppressive constructions of themselves and their possibilities have an understanding of their subordinations and of other forms of oppression at some level of articulation. Sometimes the understanding is not articulated but contained in the meaning of acts of resistance whose interpretation unveils the particularities of oppression that are being resisted. Resistant constructions vie as interpretations of everyday life, but lack a degree of institutional recognition, or the institutions they constitute are

467

themselves institutions of a dominated culture. The resistor, then, moves socially in several constructions of the social world, herself included. Liberation requires both articulation and development of resistant sense. The development of sense requires sociality among resistors who share a sometimes highly inarticulate understanding of oppression and inarticulate techniques of resistance, making community/home not only appealing but necessary.

Communities are appealing as places for the creation of the process of developing alternative sense and for the development of sense itself. In particular, when we are thinking of communities resistant to intermeshed oppressions, communication is difficult, choppy, in and out of the master's tongue. There cannot be an expectation of understanding or even of the possibility of understanding. That is why methods or processes of sense-making require attention. There cannot be an expectation that sense is already made. Often communication occurs through gestural, non-verbal communication, and actions.

Communities have also been understood as relations of commonality, or grounded in commonalities, even when extant communities contain great and silenced complexity. In thinking of communities as transformative, creative, attentive to what Audre Lorde called "non-dominant differences" (Lorde, 1984, p. 111), there is always the danger of holding to what is in common or of not attending to the difficulties of overcoming silencings, fragmentation, univocal communication. Communities attentive to "nondominant differences" require the development of complex communication. Standing together in the borders, in in-between, resistant spaces, does not provide collectivity. It rather problematizes collectivity. Avoiding the possibility of dispersion, lack of communication, a repetition of fragmentation, requires the development of a distinctly contemporary radical attitude that holds a highly refracted understanding of the self in relations.

The distinction between oppressive and resistant/emancipatory constructions of reality is an abstract distinction. The distinction does not map out onto social reality in such a way that particularly located people function within or with one logic exclusive of the other. Most particular subjects work with both logics. All subjects can be understood as active contributors to, collaborators in, creators of oppressive or resistant practices even when the logics of oppression constitute some subjects as passive. That is, resistance and oppression vie as constructions of everyday life. One way of putting the point is to think of particular subjects as oppress-*ing* (or collaborat-*ing*) or be-*ing* oppressed and as resist-*ing*.

In "Feminism and modern friendship: dislocating the community" Marilyn Friedman proposes a feminist communitarianism that locates itself in the intersection between the feminist and communitarian traditions. She argues for an understanding of community that preserves one of the cornerstones of communitarian philosophy, the social construction of the self, without having to accept a definition of the communitarian self that irrevocably forms that self to social roles and structures which have been highly oppressive to women. Friedman wants an understanding of the communitarian self that allows for the recognition of oppression within and across communities.

468

The view of the self that Friedman proposes is social both in the sense of socially constituted and communitarian. The communitarian subject is constituted not just in relation to communities to which she is "involuntarily bound" – communities of place – but also in relation to communities of choice. Our communities of origin do not necessarily constitute us as selves who agree or comply with the norms which unify those communities. "Some of us are constituted as deviants and resisters by our communities of origin, and our defiance may well run to the foundational social norms which ground the most basic social roles and relationships upon which those communities rest" (Friedman 1995, p. 197). Unchosen communities are sometimes communities we should leave to discern who we really are. Identities shaped within communities of place may come to be questioned and transformed within communities of choice. Friedman does picture most lives as containing "mixtures of relationships and communities, some given/found/discovered/ and some chosen/created. Most people are, to some extent, ineradicably constituted by their communities of place" (p. 203). When she thinks of communities of place, like the "new communitarians" – in particular Michael Sandel and Alasdair MacIntyre – she has in mind the community defined by family, neighborhood, school, church, nation (pp. 188–90, 194). Communities of choice help us counter oppressive and abusive relational structures in those nonvoluntary communities by providing models of alternative social relationships as well as standpoints for critical reflection on self and community. Given her understanding of communities of place, communities of place cannot do that.

Friedman thinks of friendship and urban communities as providing models for communities of choice. She thinks of both as voluntary, that is as arising out of one's *own* needs, desires, interests, values, and attractions, in contrast and often in opposition to motivations, expectations assigned, ascribed, expected, or demanded by one's found communities (pp. 199–200). One is not assigned friends by custom or tradition. In urban settings women can join with each other in associations that develop their own values. Friedman thinks of urban relationships as characteristically modern in their greater voluntary basis.

Friedman's distinction between communities of place and communities of choice is a distinction that became part of my politics. I went to "communities" with that distinction in mind, trying it in popular education workshops. Trying it led me to see the problematic character of bringing that distinction to communities of place when folks were not about to leave them and when the point of the discussions was not to provoke them to leave them, but rather to transform them, beginning by a structured critique of them. What was crucial about the concept of a community of choice for me was the possibility of its leading to the critical turn characteristic of the popular education situation. The distinction between community of place and community of choice seemed to me to capture the distance of critique, the "place" where we became critical of institutions constitutive of communities of place and of common sense.

In Hoagland's text she is purposefully vague about the term "community." In her search for emancipatory possibilities she understands social reality as refracted. She reads social reality as constituted by several cotemporaneous, overlapping social contexts that contain different possibilities and stand in significant tension with respect to each other. Heterosexualism constitutes an oppressive context that erases female agency. Lesbian community constitutes an alternative context that not only does not make oppression credible, but is constituted by and constitutes female agency. In the context of oppression lesbians are not primarily scapegoated or characterized as inferior or as culturally backward. The oppression of lesbians is not a relationship. "The society of the fathers, rather, formally denies lesbian existence ... . The idea of women loving women is impossible, inconceivable" (Hoagland 1988, p. 4). Hoagland connects this erasure of lesbians to female agency. Lesbian community is that context in which lesbian existence and female agency are both a reality and possibility. Lesbian community is "the loose network – both imagined and existing now – of those who identify basically as lesbians. What I am calling 'lesbian community' is not a specific entity; it is a ground of our be-ing; and it exists because we are here and move on it now" (p. 3). Lesbian community is that context in which lesbians create new value.

The sense of self that Hoagland invokes is inseparable from community, but this community does not fit in the distinction between community of place and community of choice, precisely because the distinction between the given and the to-be-created is not possible in Hoagland's understanding of lesbian community. The self in community involves each lesbian making choices within a context created by community (p. 145). Since the lesbian context overlaps the context of oppression, agency here is agency under oppression. The creation of new value outside the conceptual parameters of heterosexualism and the avoidance of avoiding demoralization – the undermining of moral agency – constitute the tasks of the "autokoenonous self," the self in community.

Hoagland refuses the task of definition of either lesbian or of the lesbian context. To define would be to assume that we are not the norm and thus to recognize a norm. It would be to assume that we need to defend our borders against invasion and threats from the outside. "So I let go of the urge to define. And I begin to think of lesbian community in a different way. I think of community as a ground of possibility, in which we create lesbian meaning" (p. 9). Hoagland does not think of lesbian community in terms of safety (p. 195), but in terms of emancipatory possibility. "Our growth as lesbians is essentially related to the values that emerge in lesbian community" (p. 144). Membership in lesbian community is a voluntary act. Hoagland invokes Julia Penelope's sense that one joins a community because she finds companionship, support, and commitment to common ideals within that community and it is internally defined by its members on the basis of shared experiences and common interpretations of events in the real world (p. 146).

I took to "communities" Hoagland's profoundly empowering understanding of the grounds of emancipation, a sense that is made possible by the tense, disjunctive overlapping of oppressive and liberatory contexts. The task for the popular educator became for me the task of affirming contexts that are disjunct-ive from oppressive constructions of self, relations, practices, and locations.

In the process of having the popular education work informed by Friedman's and Hoagland's insights, I came to understand the abstraction from place, environment, relations, multiple oppressions, and resistances understood in their cultural concreteness. I also came to see the abstractions as remarkably different in a way that led me to abandon the community of place/community of choice distinction completely, but to retain Hoagland's understanding of the possibility of emancipation through a refocusing of attention, an epistemic shift.

What I found very valuable in hooks is a recognition that communities are places where people already exercise themselves in resistance and where "choice" is already an ingredient of community life. It is the distinction between communities where one is passive and others in which one is active that is problematic in Friedman's account. Hooks understands what she calls "home-place" in terms of black women's resistance by "making homes where all black people could strive to be subjects, not objects ... where we could restore to ourselves the dignity denied us on the outside in the public world" (hooks 1990, p. 42). Hooks acknowledges the sexism in delegating the task of creating home environment to women, but she honors this work in its resistant guise and emphasizes the "importance of homeplace in the midst of oppression and dom-ination" (p. 43). She decries both thinking about domesticity that obscures this "re-visioning of both woman's role and the idea of 'home' that black women consciously exercised in practice" (p. 45) and the African-American tradition of "mother worship." The latter reduces black women's creation of homeplaces to a fulfillment of natural roles or role-duties, thus erasing "choice and will" (p. 45). These racist and sexist readings collude in the erasure of resistance subjectivities. The distinction between communities of place and communities of choice obscures this resistance.

Hooks's description of "homeplace" makes a parting from it not an abstract disengagement from reified institutions, but a loss of bearing, of attachments, to sounds, smells, concrete spatial environments (pp. 41–2). Hooks is also clear about the fragility of "homeplace," "always subject to violation and destruction" (p. 47). So she calls black women to a renewal of their political commitment to homeplace.

Yet, hooks did part from the concrete spatiality of homeplace. In "Choosing the margin" the spatiality of the journey from homeplace to choosing the margin and the accompanying difficulties in finding inter-subjective spaces for her multi-ple voices is made vivid (pp. 146–7). She tells us of the silencings of home and her need both to leave and return. The return is also given a spatial description, a "going up the rough side of the mountain on my way home" (p. 148). This journey back reconfigures the very meaning of "home." "Home is that place which enables and promotes varied and ever-changing perspectives, a place where one discovers new ways of seeing reality, frontiers of difference. One confronts dispersals and fragmentation as part of the construction of a new world order that reveals more fully who we are, who we can become, an order that does not demand forgetting" (p. 148).

Hooks articulates this reconfiguration of home in spatial terms. She speaks of a reconceived margin, margin as central location for resistance, for "the production of a counter-hegemonic discourse that is not just found in words but in habits of being and the ways one lives" (p. 149). She rejects an understanding of marginality as a place of despair where one's imagination is at risk of being fully colonized. I am interpreting hooks as not giving up the call to black women to renew their commitment to homeplace, but rather as tying the commitment to homeplace with its reconfiguration. She connects the formation of a "counter-language" with remembrance of the past, "which includes recollections of broken tongues giving us ways to speak that decolonize our minds, our very beings" (p. 150).

Hooks, like Hoagland, teaches us this epistemic shift from oppression to resistance, but she cultivates a sensual acuteness for resistance as enacted in very located traditions. It is this attention to spatiality, sensuality, historicity, as well as to the fragility of resistant spaces that I took to the popular education work in "communities." Yet, though hooks's going home up the rough side of the mountain evidences great attentiveness to encounters with those who greeted her as colonizers, *she does not – and this is crucial – evidence attentiveness to the great diversity among whose who did not*. Thus there is a univocity to the traditions of resistance that bring her back to a reconfigured sense of home and consequently a stable, unproblematized sense of its possibility.

I think that part of what led Friedman to what I see as the wrong turn was beginning her task by conversing with Sandel and MacIntyre. It is this conversation that led her to an understanding of communities of place in terms of family, neighborhood, church, and nation and to a reduction of them to ossified, reified institutions conceived in a monocultural vein. Though Friedman is extremely critical of their version of communitarianism, she appears to share Sandel's and MacIntyre's view that there are communities that constitute us passively. Instead of questioning their understanding of community, she renames that understanding "communities of place" and rejects the communities themselves. The sense that history is given to us, that as children and adults we merely receive and reduplicate institutional injunctions, gives us too passive an understanding of social relationships. This account fails to explain the existence of resistance as social. It fails to explain without introducing a liberal conception of the subject, the existence of motivations arising out of "one's *own* needs, desires, interests, values, and attractions, in contrast and often in opposition to motivations, expectations assigned, ascribed, expected, or demanded by found communities." Why not think that as contradictory identities are formed within communities of place, these communities are revealed as not univocal, passing on and embodying an undisturbed common sense, but as complex and tense sites of identity formation?

I see a confusion in Friedman between "one did not choose to be in one's found community" and "one is passive in that community." It is because she is conversing with Sandel and MacIntyre that she sees passivity in community of place: ossified hierarchies and roles. She misses the ingenuity and constant creativity in relationships among neighbors, people in families, and in relations that cannot be easily placed in either. She misses the resistant creativity with which women negotiate institutionalized life. The "foundness" of neighborly and family ties does not entail the "foundness" of norms, practices, beliefs, and desires of people in them. Resistant negotiation of everyday life does not require the formation of associations that lift one from community of place, it rather constitutes life in communities of place. Why would one think that women forming patrols to deal with battery after significant strategizing places them in a community of choice, while women and men creating strategies to deal with alcoholics that bang at your door asking for money for liquor, with welfare officers coming to police one's daily living, deciding to cut enough wood for folks who can't go "a la leña," deciding how to stand against evictions, are inserted in communities of place? Certainly it isn't nonvoluntary activity, but resistant activity. Institutions do not run that monolithically and they are not external to us. Norms of everyday relating are in constant refashioning, contestation, maneuvering. Resistance has itself a social history.

As I considered Friedman's distinction, I wondered as to how does one go to and from communities of choice and communities of place? Does she mean that women intent or in need of self-transformation should give up the task of transforming their original communities? There is ambiguity in Friedman's text in this respect as the *emphasis* is on self-transformation, not on transformation of communities of place. But if there is to be a back and forth, there will be arrogance and depersonalization in the task of changing communities of place distant from an appreciation of resistant traditions of negotiation of everyday life. There won't be a conversation, an interaction that begins with granting personally conceived subjects with authority in the art of resistance. The distinction between community of place and community of choice suggests either indifference to communities of place or high and impersonal confrontation in their transformation, a confrontation that is not informed by an affection for resistant, embodied, located subjects. It is a confrontation that demands forgetting.

Another way of making the point takes me to rural New Mexico where Chicanas and Chicanos fight for control over their ancestral water rights. When the confrontation takes place in front of EID and EPA officials, one can hear the difference in the voices of native inhabitants and Anglo counterculturals who moved to the region during the 1960s. As countercultural environmentalists testify in support of the position of indigenous inhabitants, they distinctly employ the language of choice over the language of place as giving them greater authority in their understanding of the issues. They claim they know more about the value of what is to be preserved because they have chosen to be there. This position fails to understand the care that indigenous communities have exercised in their use of water, a care that is resistant to internal colonialism and the devastation of resources that ground material life in this particular cultural vein.

473

That is, the region is one in which contestation over water is part of colonization and resistance to colonization.

The more I looked at Friedman's own text the more I understood it as a modern text, containing a very abstract conception of space in its strong distinction between communities of place and communities of choice. It is as a modern text that one needs to understand Friedman's emphasis on choice. In communities of place territory is emphasized, in communities of choice there seems to be flight from territory. There is a sense that communities of choice can be just anywhere. The abstraction from territory as the place for choice helps me introduce a distrust of nomadism, of middle-class sojourners, of anthropologists, of tourists. This is a very large topic, but I want to introduce the need to reflect on geography, movement, and stasis as one thinks of communities that would develop a noncolonialist account of complex, liberatory possibilities where movement to and fro carries with it located responsibilities and commitments.

As I learned from hooks and Hoagland, I also saw the need to complicate the worlds of resistance. It is interesting in itself that they are thinking of very different resistant worlds. Like Friedman, hooks and Hoagland emphasize shared experience as a ground for resistance. In Friedman this is accomplished by the move away from communities of place to communities initiated by shared needs, interests, and experience. In Hoagland it is a move to an abstract understanding of lesbians that makes the sense of community so readily available. This is not to ignore Hoagland's attention to the diversity among lesbians, it is rather to emphasize the concrete locatedness of that diversity and the interplay between colonialism and fragmentation. It is to emphasize the journeys of lesbians of color from homeplace to lesbian community as extremely spatial, tortured, fragmenting journeys. In hooks there is a singularity of resistant locales, a not seeing, for example, the Latina lesbian as any sort of companion in her journey "home."

I suggest the need for and the difficulties in the construction of collective resistance to multiple oppressions attentive to the multiply located, historically varied, resistant negotiations of everyday life under oppression. I intimate complex reconfigurations of communities that would find us developing multiple fluencies in complex communication; highly refracted senses of selves and relations; questionings of the inside/outside distinctions to any lived sense of homeplaces; refigurations of public spaces; the developing in ourselves of the need to become special and specially resistor–residents in each other's concreted located worlds attentive to the interconnections among local struggles against intermeshed oppressions. I see this reconfiguration as crucial for the emancipation of women and lesbians conceived in their concrete plurality.

48

Racism

LINDA MARTÍN ALCOFF

Feminist philosophy has been concerned with race and racism since its inception for both historical and conceptual reasons. Historically, the struggle against sexism consistently followed in the footsteps of the struggle against slavery and racism, both in the nineteenth as well as the twentieth centuries. Women who resisted slavery and racism began to rethink common beliefs about women's role, and took inspiration from the abolitionist and civil rights struggles. Nineteenth-century transcendentalist Margaret Fuller Ossoli (1875) made a conceptual analogy between slavery as an unfair restriction on human freedom and the social and economic restrictions on white women. Simone de Beauvoir argued (1952) that slaves and white women had been infantilized in similar ways. Many early feminist accounts of sexism borrowed from analyses of slavery and racism, how these were justified through attributions of inferiority and dependence, and how these affected the subjectivity of the oppressed.

More recent feminist philosophical work, which this article will discuss, has focused on the limitations and dangers of this analogy (Stimpson 1971, Simons 1979, hooks 1984, Spelman 1988, Rothenberg 1990). A portrayal of white upper-class women as "slaves" in an undiffererentiated system of "patriarchy" obscures the dissimilar access to power white and nonwhite women experience, as well as the power white women have over nonwhite women and men. The racism/sexism analogy often took white women's experience as paradigmatic of sexism and black men's experience as paradigmatic of racism, rendering the experiences of women of color invisible as well as limiting the adequacy of the analyses of sexism. An attempt to compare racism and sexism assumes their separability and thus erroneously suggests that sexism can be described and analyzed without addressing racial differences among women. Thus, one of the tasks of feminist philosophy has been to explore the way in which feminist theory has itself maintained a conceptual legacy and a philosophical methodology rooted in racist presuppositions.

An overview

Feminist philosophy has pursued many questions in relation to race and racism, such as the following: How do racist and sexist ideologies intersect? Is racist ideology less or more fundamental than sexist ideology? How, and to what extent, can women of different races form an alliance? In particular, how should feminists articulate political agendas concerning reproductive rights and sexual violence in such a way that will represent the critical issues facing diverse communities of women, negotiating between problems of forced sterilization and racist, false accusations of rape as well as the need for accessible abortion and strong anti-rape laws? How can women of color fight sexism inside their already embattled communities? Does feminism require the eradication of traditional belief systems and ways of life that strengthen the solidarity of oppressed communities and that make possible their resistance? What political obligations do North American feminists have vis-à-vis women from formerly colonized countries, and how are these best carried out? Where are white women situated on the map of social power and privilege? Is it even possible to develop a theory of women's oppression that encompasses all races, or to represent all women in one category of analysis? Are the very categories of "woman," "women's experience," or "women's oppression" transportable in any meaningful way across racialized communities? How, and why, has mainstream feminism been racist and antisemitic?

The answers to these question will necessarily require empirical studies of women's lives and of existing social structures, and thus will involve the social sciences. But there are also conceptual, methodological, ethical, and epistemological issues involved in these questions which feminist philosophers have begun to address. For example, there are questions about how to understand the metaphysics of racial and gendered identity, questions about what race is and how it connects with gender to form social identity. And there are questions about who has the epistemic authority to make claims about racism, about whether a Marxist class analysis can explain both sexism and racism in its causal account of oppression, and about what other philosophical traditions of thought – liberalism, pragmatism, and poststructuralism – as well as Marxism, can help illuminate the way forward.

Second-wave feminist theory (from the 1960s) has generally recognized the importance of addressing racism and racial differences among women. Early anthologies included essays on feminist issues like the family from black and Latina perspectives and explored the specific forms of sexism that nonwhite women face. Enriqueta Longauex y Vásquez (1970) explained the need to develop forms of feminist practice that would not tear apart the necessary political alliances in communities of color. Black and Asian women and Latinas offered a very different political approach to the family and to men, weighing the need to resist oppressive traditional institutions and relationships against the need to maintain strong communities. Within another ten years incisive critiques of the false universalism and ethnocentrism within feminism itself were published by feminist theorists such as bell hooks (1981, 1984), revealing the ways in which the "women" in the phrase "women and minorities" were always white. The exclusive focus on white women's experience of sexism was sometimes justified on the grounds that it was not "distorted" by racism, but hooks and others pointed out that white women's experiences of sexism were affected by race privilege. The mistake lay in assuming that white women are unraced.

476

Furthermore, as Ada María Isasi-Díaz argued (1985), the very demand for equality is inappropriate in a racially hierarchical society, since it becomes an implicit demand to be equal to white men rather than to dismantle racism. What feminists should demand instead is liberation or social revolution.

However, although some good work has been done, the percentage of feminist philosophy concerned with questions of race and racism is still very small. Most of the focus has been limited to black/white relations. The early critiques showing how feminist theory often assumes a white racial context still bear repeating. But it is also evident that a concern with racism and with racial differences among women has been in the background of most of the critical debates within feminist theory since the early 1980s. The debates over essentialism and universalism have been motivated in large part by a concern with the tendency to overgeneralize from white Anglo women's lives. Monocausal explanations of women's oppression have tended to die out in the face of the variety of forms of sexism and family structures. And the development of standpoint epistemologies and postmodern forms of feminism have been motivated by the felt need to address the irreducible differences among women and to find productive rather than disenabling responses to these differences through more sophisticated feminist methodologies and theoretical approaches. Some see a feminist postmodernism as the best way to make difference intrinsic in feminist theory, by avoiding any foundational concepts that could smuggle in cultural specificity, and by refusing a universal category of "women" or "women's experience" that will necessarily be exclusivist. Others argue that postmodernism's implicit claim to have a "view from everywhere" exhibits the persistence of ethnocentric mastery and promotes a superficial, touristic attitude toward difference without attending to power and privilege. But in all of these debates, the problem of racial difference and racism operates increasingly as a crucial condition of adequacy for acceptable feminist theory.

Sexism and racism: a useful analogy?

Sexism appears to be a similar form of oppression as racism in the following ways. Both involve essentialist attributions of inferiority over whole categories of persons, and thus both are fundamentally identity-based forms of oppression. Racial or sexed identity is said to determine life aspirations, achievable skills, and intellectual abilities, among other things. The result in both cases is a kind of social segregation to appropriate spheres enforced by violence and economic blackmail. Moreover, differential treatment and decreased political and economic liberties have often been justified in both cases on a welfare utilitarian argument, that is, that the designated groups are unfit for self-governance and would fare better by beneficent oversight. Some have argued that both are the product of pseudo-rational responses to the self-protective fear of difference (Piper 1992–3). Finally, the attributions of inferiority and the need to be governed covered over a real economic exploitation of labor power, such that the designated groups can be paid less or not at all for work considered their natural lot in life.

477

However, though both sexism and racism have economic motives, most theorists emphasize that the reproduction and perpetuation of these forms of oppression require a powerful, self-sustaining ideology. As a result, theorists have paid increasing attention to cultural representations in literature and the arts and to social institutions like education and the law (see e.g. hooks 1989, 1990, Ferguson 1989, Davis 1990). "White supremacy" and "male supremacy" were parallel concepts developed to describe the structures of naturalized social hierarchies corresponding to each form of oppression as distinct and semi-autonomous from the economy.

Thus, there were good justifications to explore similarities between racism and sexism, but there were also arguments developed that emphasized their dissimilarities and, like Catherine Stimpson (1971), pointed out that the analogy appropriated the strength of the Black Liberation movement in a manner all too typical of whites. Other feminists argued that racism and sexism are dissimilar because sexism is primary. Early radical feminist work developed an integrative model that portrayed racism as an extension of sexism, thus making sexism fundamental. For example, Shulamith Firestone (1970) argued that racism feminizes nonwhite men by sexualizing them and portraying them as inferior. On Firestone's view, sexism developed first and then served as a model for all other forms of social hierarchy. The racism that exists among white women is a form of inauthenticity or false consciousness that does not represent their true interests. Mary Daly similarly argued (1978) that sexism is fundamental. On her view, charges of racism against feminists serve patriarchal ends by promoting divisiveness among women. Feminists should disengage from male-created identifications with race, nation, or ethnicity.

Other feminists criticized this view. Margaret A. Simons argued (1979) that the claim that sexism is primary trivializes racist oppression and implausibly assumes that sexism alone can provide an adequate explanation for genocide and war. And she pointed out a number of racist stereotypes in Firestone's widely read book, *The Dialectic of Sex* (1970). Simons argued that the fact that some form of sexist oppression exists in every society does not justify an absolute concept of patriarchy, or a concept that generalizes all men and all women into one undifferentiated analysis.

Gloria Joseph (1981) also criticized any integrative models that take as their object of analysis one monolithic category of "woman." She argued that white women are both tools and benefactors of racism, and that feminists must recognize and address white women's social position as both oppressors and oppressed. White women have direct power over black men in regard to rape accusations as well as other areas of social life. For these reasons, Joseph contended that white women's immediate self-interest is to maintain racism, and they are thus inconsistent allies in the struggle for black women's liberation. Moreover, given that white solidarity across gender differences is stronger than male solidarity across race differences, black women have as much reason to ally with black men as they do with white women. The claim that "Patriarchy equals male domination over women" is oversimplified and inaccurate, according to Joseph, because of men's differential political status. We need to explore the concept of "white female supremacy" as well as white male supremacy. Joseph also criticized versions of Marxism that attempt to reduce the problem of racism to a class problem; on her account, racism has its own independent dynamic and is nonreducible to other systems of oppression and exploitation.

Racism and white women

In light of these critiques, Adrienne Rich (1979) developed the concept of "white solipsism" to describe a racist perceptual practice that implicitly takes a white perspective as universal. Colorblindness, or the ideal of not perceiving people's racial identities, should be rejected because it falls into white solipsism: there is no truly accessible colorblind perspective in a racist society, and so the claim to a colorblind perspective by whites just works to conceal the partiality of their perceptions. On the other hand, white women's guilty feelings about racism only perpetuate white solipsism by continuing the preoccupation of white women with their own feelings.

Thus, Rich went further than Daly in acknowledging racism, but she continued to put sexism at the center of all women's lives and to portray white women as primarily victims of racism rather than agents who help to sustain it. Rich claimed that white women did not create racism but have been forced to serve racist institutions, and those who think that they benefit from racism are deluded. White women's racism is actually a misdirected outlet for their rage over their own powerlessness. On Rich's account, slavery is more accurately described as an institution of patriarchy rather than of white supremacist society, and to blame white women is to impede the progress of forging political and emotional connections between white and nonwhite women. Rich warns against participating in the game of ranking oppression, and she argues that white women's oppression, though different from nonwhite women's, is very significant. The apparent protection some white women get from patriarchy degrades them through enforcing childishness and helplessness. Therefore, white women's true interests are in making alliances with other women, not with men.

Marilyn Frye (1983, 1992b) has explored the implications of the fact that, despite the severity of sexism, white women do not escape race privilege entirely. It is a feature of this race privilege that white women have a choice to hear or not to hear – and to respond or not to respond to – the demands and criticisms of women of color. Thus, Frye suggests that racism distorts and limits the matrix of choices and perceptions for all involved. And it differentially distributes general epistemic authority to make judgments and determinations, such that, for example, whites often assume the right to decide the true or accurate racial identity of everyone.

On Frye's view, "whiteliness" is a socially constructed sense of entitlement and authority. Because white women understandably want to be treated as human beings, they often seek the entitlements of "whiteliness". The demand for equality has in practice meant the demand for an equality with white men; an

479

equality with Chicanos, for example, would hardly mean liberation. But the demand to be equal to white men is necessarily a demand to achieve "white-liness," a status that is dependent on racist structures of social relations for its power and autonomy. And such a strategy of empowerment is not in white women's interest because it will increase their identification with the white men who oppress them. Moreover, Frye argued, white women need to understand that racism has targeted them as well by instituting compulsory motherhood to regenerate the white population.

The philosopher Angela Davis (1981b, 1990) has contributed toward under-standing how racism has been specifically manifested in black women's lives, developing accounts of sexist forms of racism. Although she has argued that coalitions and alliances are the only way to thwart interlocking forms of oppres-sion, she has also provided an important critique of the implicit racism present in some white feminist work on the problem of rape, which ignored the problem of lynching in the United States. Thousands of black men were tortured, burned, mutilated, and killed for ostensibly defiling pure white womanhood. Given this history, strengthening anti-rape laws has a differential effect on white men and on men of color. Far from acknowledging or exploring this problem, some white feminists even perpetuated the myth that men of color are especially prone to rape. Davis's conclusion is that the anti-rape movement must make anti-racism a key component of its agenda in order to untangle these knotted relationships between sexism and racism.

Feminism in the context of racial difference

Audre Lorde (1984) argued that feminism must not be afraid to face the differ-ences among women because it is this fear that encourages an overemphasis on the similarities between forms of sexist oppression. The tendency to ignore or underemphasize differences only creates anger, alienation, and distrust from those whose experiences and perspectives are left out, and thus it reduces the chances for building solidarity. And Lorde also pointed out that it is a mistake to see our differences as simply obstacles to the feminist movement: we must learn to see difference as a resource and an enrichment rather than a problem to be minimized.

Socialist feminists like Ann Ferguson (1989, 1991b) and Alison Jaggar (1983) argued in light of these analyses that the forms of radical feminism that prioritize sexism and encourage women-only organizations can never sufficiently address problems of racism or create broad coalitions. Sexism may have been historically first and more universal but it is not always primary. Socialist feminism is a better programmatic approach because it seeks an understanding and a form of political practice that reveals the interconnections between racism, sexism, and class exploitation. Ferguson developed a tri-systems theory of class/gender/race that analyzes society as an interrelation between three forms of exploitation and differential social power: (1) relations between capital and labor; (2) relations between men and women; and (3) relations between races. This approach reveals, according to Ferguson, that simply positing the existence of "patriarchy" is not very useful for social theory. We need to understand patriarchy in its historically specific, different forms. There is the patriarchy of feudalism, or "father-right," in which fathers controlled the resources available to children; then there is "husband-right," based on a division between public and private spheres in which wage-earning husbands dominate non-wage earning wives; and finally there is a form of public patriarchy in which the state administers resources for children on the basis of rules that control women. These forms of patriarchy can then be correlated and analyzed in relation to white supremacy, to reveal the abuses against poor nonwhite women as a feature of patriarchy as well as racism. We need to develop new categories of "racial genders" to adequately analyze these complexities.

Much of the theorist bell hooks's work has advanced the analysis of these interconnections between racism, sexism, and class exploitation (1981, 1984, 1989, 1990, 1995). Like Davis, hooks argued that we need categories of racist sexism and sexist racism to comprehend the forms of oppression black women suffered under slavery and in its aftermath. Hooks also critiqued the concept of black matriarchy used widely in government reports as well as cultural representations that falsely portrayed black women as stronger, more confident, and more capable than white women because of their experiences of the double burden of racism and sexism. In reality, black women have less power, money, and freedom. On the other hand, the argument that female-headed households are pathological and that black men have been emasculated by racism involves the sexist assumption that men should protect women and be economically dominant over women. Part of the legacy of slavery, according to hooks, has been that white misogyny has permeated black culture and black liberation movements, and black women are still treated as degraded property while white women are treated as more valuable property. Black male sexist behavior is not a response to racism or a legitimate compensation for the racism they suffer. Rather, as Pauline Terrelonge has also argued (1989), sexism has its own dynamic within black communities, and is sometimes connected in important ways to racism and sometimes not.

Hooks has also denounced the view that feminism is the prerogative or invention of white women. There is a long history of struggle against sexism within the abolitionist, civil rights, and Black Liberation movements, and black women who denounce and work against sexism in their communities are not traitors but are continuing a long tradition of struggle. Moreover, Terrelonge has pointed out that some of the problems and divisions inside black communities are due to sexism, and reducing sexism would thus strengthen these communities.

What policies and programs should feminists promote to combat racism and sexism? Anita Allen (1992/3) has analyzed "role-model arguments" that promote the hiring of women of color, among others, to serve as role models for students. Allen distinguishes three different aspects of the role-model argument usually conflated, in which role models are viewed as ethical templates, symbols, or nurturers. While not rejecting the need for role models entirely, Allen argues

481

that when this consideration becomes the centerpiece of a recruitment decision, it has disadvantageous effects. It puts unreasonable burdens on nonwhite faculty to be "perfectly black" or "perfectly female," it can communicate to white male faculty that they cannot or should not mentor students of color. and it can even enhance myths of inferiority unless the appointment is "made on grounds that yield to or aggressively contest traditional notions of merit."

Another policy that has been promoted within feminist philosophy as a way to reduce racism is to confer epistemic privilege on the oppressed on the grounds that they will know better about the nature of oppression as well as other elements of reality invisible to dominant perspectives. Partially against this view, Uma Narayan (1988) has argued that, while the oppressed do know more concerning the *daily conditions* of oppression, they do not have an advantage in knowing the *causes* of oppression. However, "outsiders" should use methodological caution and have a strong sense of their own fallibility when they disagree with "insiders." And part of what constitutes the epistemic privilege of the oppressed is conferred by the emotional response to oppression, despite the fact that both white women and people of color have often been derogated on the basis of their purportedly greater emotional intensity.

Critiquing and strengthening feminist theory

Feminist philosophy has generally argued against abstract, disembodied conceptions of philosophy which would render the social identity of philosophers irrelevant to the philosophies they produce. Thus, it has argued that the overwhelming maleness of philosophy has made a substantive difference in the content of the historical canon, the kinds of questions it addressed, and the range of answers considered plausible. Feminist philosophers themselves have in consequence acknowledged that our voices are not simply the "voice of reason" but, in part, the voice of women.

However, social identity is in fact always compound, whether one is white or nonwhite. The concept of the generic "woman" is as exclusivist as the concept of the generic "man." Women in general have been silenced from participating in the discourse of philosophy, but the degree of this silencing has been differentially distributed among women by race and class. And the dictates of theoretical production endemic to dominant Anglo-European philosophy have worked to alienate nonwhites from philosophy and created a hierarchy, even within feminist philosophy, between those who write theory and those who are theorized about.

Maria Lugones and Elizabeth Spelman (1986) thus argued that feminist theory cannot presume to speak simply in "a woman's voice." In order to avoid replicating the androcentric presumptions of male-centered philosophy with Eurocentric presumptions, feminists need to develop dialogic models of theory making that will include different women's voices in a genuine reciprocity. They also argue that feminist theory should be accountable to and written for all women, not out of obligation, but out of a spirit of friendship.

482

Feminist philosophy has been deformed by taking white women as normative for all women, and Spelman (1988) has demonstrated this through the debates over Aristotle's arguments concerning "women and slaves." Moreover, on her view there is no "basic form" of gender oppression that can be characterized by leaving aside other aspects of social identity. This is because gender identity is not separable from race and class, among other things, since the form gender takes is dependent on other variables. The additive analysis that assumes a separability between race and gender presupposes a metaphysics of identity in which different social markers lie separate but alongside each other to make up a single individual. The fact that this metaphysical view of the self is inadequate also entails that feminism cannot contrast the condition of women in general from the condition of men in general, or develop a universal comparison. As Kimberle Crenshaw (1989) has pointed out, unlike the white gender stereotypes, black men are not viewed as capable and powerful, nor are black women viewed as passive and dependent. There is no essential "womanness."

What, then, of feminist philosophy's future? On Spelman's view, feminist philosophy must become more reflective about the insidiousness of its privileged position, in which it can decide when and where to include or tolerate difference, and in which the concept of "difference" itself is often put forward in such a way that the relations of power between women are made invisible within a pluralistic ontology of multiple, and equal, differences. But this does not mean the end of feminism. Gender remains a critically important concept of analysis because it is connected literally to everything, and just as we cannot study gender by itself, so too, we cannot study race or class by themselves without attending to their gender specificities.

Feminist philosophy needs to rethink the universalist aspirations of philosophical argument, and to critique the unreflective arrogance implicit in philosophy itself. Rather than the model of the Socratic midwife who brings forth knowledge, or the queen of the sciences who sits in judgment on the epistemic adequacy of all truth claims, Spelman suggests the model of the apprentice, who acknowledges her imperfection as well as her dependence on others. Lugones (1987) has also suggested models of cognition across racial difference that can be an alternative to what she calls "arrogant perception." The latter is a mode of cognition that presumes to know in a nonreciprocal manner without opening one's own framework of presuppositions to modification by the encounter. However, Lugones says that feminist critique of arrogant perception cannot simply shut off communication or avoid attempting to develop knowledge about women's lives from different races. Rather, we should engage in "world-traveling" in which we understand ourselves to be traveling to different worlds of perception, experience, and perspective. This involves viewing the other not simply as an object of knowledge but as another knower, and it will require immersion in the others' language, community, and way of being in the world. We need to cultivate a spirit of playfulness to be successful world-travelers, Lugones counsels, in the sense of risk-taking, an openness to surprise and self-reconstruction, and an attitude of delight rather than fear when we find we need to modify our previous conceptions.

Noting the intersections of racism and sexism will not debilitate feminist analyses but strengthen them. We can begin to see, for example, how white supremacy has played a crucial role in enforcing white male control over white women's sexuality and reproductive capacities, in order to regenerate a "pure" white race. We can begin to discern how liberal feminist demands for equality and inclusion aim in effect to achieve the social status of white middle- and upper-class men, rather than some abstract and generally applicable standard. We can perhaps in the future avoid mistakes like making the argument for legal abortion hinge on privacy rights that then undercut our ability to demand government funding for reproductive options. When we move beyond a single axis framework of analysis, we can also begin to overcome the limitations of the oppressor/victim binary, in which individuals are characterized monolithically as one or the other. New, more complex and sophisticated methodological approaches and conceptual frameworks are now being developed in response to the need to include racial difference in feminist theory.

PART X

POLITICS

49

Justice

ELIZABETH KISS

Feminist theory in all its diversity begins from the conviction that the social, political, and cultural arrangements that shape women's lives are unjust. Biological sex is a major determinant of people's status, power, and opportunities in all known societies, with women systematically subordinated to men. Feminists aim to understand and end these patterns of subordination. Yet, while the Romans portrayed Justice as a woman, theories of justice have tended either to justify women's subordinate status or to render it invisible. Many accounts of just social arrangements have legitimated men's rule over women by appeal to patriarchal norms. Others have either neglected to mention women entirely, or placed them in a separate domestic sphere lying beyond the scope of considerations of justice. Justice thus represents both a core project for feminism and a tradition of argument which has often been dismissive of, or resistant to, feminist concerns. Small wonder, then, that arguments over justice have raised so many theoretical and practical quandaries and produced some of contemporary feminist philosophy's liveliest debates.

Justice and gender

Justice is traditionally defined as the virtue or norm by which all receive their due. Theories of justice set out a morally appropriate distribution of social benefits and burdens, rewards and punishments, status and voice. Feminism's most basic contribution to understandings of justice has been to show that the status of women raises issues of justice in the first place. To make this point, feminists have politicized sexual difference, arguing that women's subordination is not an inevitable natural destiny but the result of an institutionalized social hierarchy called gender (Okin 1989a, p. 6). Yet this argument flies in the face of common intuitions about sex and justice. The pervasiveness and apparent biological foundation of behavioral differences between women and men, combined with Aristotle's famous dictum that justice requires treating like cases alike and different cases differently, can be invoked to undermine the claim that women's subordination is unjust. Feminists have countered these intuitions by showing how the range of gendered behavior cannot plausibly be understood as biologically ordained and inescapable but must be the product of interlocking social forces (Frye 1983). Since the forces that shape gender operate across both the traditional public spheres of politics, law, church, and economy, and the private sphere of sexual and domestic life, feminist arguments challenge the traditional boundaries of the political. Power relations permeate domestic life, diminishing women's public power and opportunities. At the same time, these domestic hierarchies are legally defined and maintained (Olsen 1995, pp. 107–42). Attention to gender thus reveals the complex interpenetration of public and private (Pateman 1989b, ch. 6). The slogan "the personal is political" summarizes a broad range of feminist arguments which redescribe sexual difference as gender hierarchy and criticize gender as unjust (Millett 1970, MacKinnon 1987a, 1989, Okin 1989a).

While all feminists agree that gender hierarchy is unjust, they offer very different analyses of its sources and main features. Some see women's subordination as arising primarily from divisions of labor, particularly domestic labor (Okin 1989a, ch. 7, Delphy 1984). Others focus on sexual domination and violence as the linchpin of gender (MacKinnon 1989). Neither of these strands of analysis seems reducible to the other, and both capture important aspects of women's subordination. Efforts to deepen such analyses and to explore their intersections with each other and with other axes of social disadvantage like class and race will be important to the future development of feminist theory. But the demand to identify a single cause of gender is misplaced, reflecting an imperative of theoretical elegance rather than attentiveness to social and cultural complexity.

Feminist theorists also disagree about which forms of sex-differentiated behavior beyond pregnancy and lactation arise from unjust gender hierarchies and which (if any) do not. And even when they agree about the injustice of a particular instance of gender hierarchy, they may have very different views about what it is permissible to do to change it. For instance, patterns of income distribution within households that favor men over women represent a pervasive form of gender hierarchy. But should the state enforce a more equal distribution? Some feminists argue that justice urgently requires state intervention (Okin 1989a), while others consider such a remedy worse than the malady it is designed to address (Elshtain 1990).

However, there is consensus among virtually all feminist theorists that, in a just society, women and men would have equal status. Thus feminism shares an "egalitarian plateau" with other modern Western understandings of justice which affirm that justice requires treating people as equals (Kymlicka 1990, p. 4). Despite this consensus around the goal of equal status and power for women, feminist efforts to identify the means and ends of gender equality continue to be torn by tensions between "the ideal of sexual equality and the apparent reality of sexual difference" (Jaggar 1990, p. 239).

The debate over means: gender and equal treatment

The debate over means centers on whether justice is best advanced through gender-neutral or gender-conscious policies and laws, and has received fullest treatment among feminist legal theorists (Weisberg 1993, Olsen 1995). Advocates of gender-neutral laws and policies argue that the differential treatment of

488

women violates gender equality and reinforces gender stereotypes (Jaggar 1974). Proponents of gender-conscious laws and policies, by contrast, point to how laws and policies formulated in gender-neutral language can systematically disadvantage women. For instance, no-fault divorce laws end up working to women's economic detriment (Weitzman 1985). And ostensibly gender-neutral employment practices and insurance policies can disadvantage women by, for example, refusing to cover pregnancy expenses, a practice the US Supreme Court upheld in *Geduldig v. Aiello* in 1974 on the grounds that, since not all women are or become pregnant, these programs did not amount to sex discrimination.

The discriminatory effects of gender-neutral laws and policies are now generally acknowledged to be a problem which feminist theory has to confront. In recent years theorists have attacked the claim that gender justice can only be pursued through adherence to gender-neutral laws on two closely related grounds. First, they have shown how gender-neutrality is all too often defined on the basis of a male norm. Gender differences come to be perceived as problems in need of special treatment only in the context of unexamined biases. Thus, for instance, changing equipment to make it suitable for use by shorter people (thereby enabling more women to perform a job from which they were previously excluded by gender-neutral minimum height rules) is better conceived, not as an example of special treatment for women to compensate for their deviance from a norm, but as a gender-inclusive practice designed to accommodate differences which are in and of themselves neutral and unrelated to job performance. Similarly, laws protecting pregnant women from workplace discrimination are better understood, not as special privileges for pregnant women, but, as the Supreme Court put it in 1987, as means to ensure that women as well as men can "have families without losing jobs" (Minow 1988, p. 57; Minow 1990, ch. 3). Second, theorists have argued that law and policy should be guided not by a formulaic insistence on gender neutrality but by a concern to foster greater gender equality and to counteract women's actual disadvantages (Rhode 1989, MacKinnon 1987a, 1993a, Cornell 1992).

These two arguments advance the debate over means by showing that the distinction between "equal" and "differential" or "special" treatment is often misleading and that it obscures what should be at stake in policies aimed at treating people as equals. Indeed, recent feminist arguments about gender and equal treatment deepen our understanding of equality under law as "lack of hierarchy, not sameness" – an insight that is applicable to many issues and contexts beyond gender (MacKinnon 1993a, p. 102, Minow 1988, p. 47).

Nevertheless, it is important to recognize that these arguments do not completely dissolve the original strategic dilemma between gender-neutral and gender-conscious means. Nor do they conclusively lay to rest the concerns raised by those who advocate gender-neutral policies. For instance, feminists remain divided over the advisability of legal norms like the "reasonable woman" standard which was articulated by the Ninth Circuit Court in *Ellison* v. *Brady* (1991) to guide courts in adjudicating charges of sexual harassment. Does the reasonable woman standard serve to counteract gender hierarchy by compelling

489

judges, lawyers, and policy makers to attend more closely to women's experiences, and hence lead to more equal treatment for women in the legal system (Abrams 1995b)? Or does it reinforce oppressive gender stereotypes of women as weak, hypersensitive creatures in need of paternalistic protection, and therefore lower women's social and legal status? There are no easy answers to such questions, which require us to make complex empirical judgments. Thus, while it is unhelpful to cast the debate over means as if it required an overarching choice between genderconscious and gender-neutral approaches, controversies over whether specific gender-conscious means help or hinder efforts to foster gender equality are likely to persist into the foreseeable future.

The debate over ends: justice and the future of gender

The relationship between gender equality and difference also raises important questions about the ends of feminist justice, and highlights tensions within feminism between impulses to abolish and to valorize gender differences. If gender is a hierarchical social institution that subordinates women, then, as Susan Okin (1989a) puts it, "a just future would be one without gender," a future in which social structures and practices would accord no more relevance to one's sex than to "eye color or the length of one's toes" (p. 171). Proponents of a genderless society may argue that gender-conscious policies are needed in the present, but their ultimate goal is to transcend gender altogether (Phillips 1991). But others have argued that one of feminism's central aims should be to valorize women's experiences and capabilities, which tend to be devalued under gender hierarchy. Many works in feminist philosophy have been devoted to this project of revaluing practices associated with women.

As James Sterba (forthcoming, ch. 4) points out, there is no contradiction between wanting to abolish gender and wanting to valorize some differences traditionally associated with women. One can, for instance, affirm the value of mothering while arguing that in a just society women and men would "mother" children in more or less equal measure. This is important common ground, and most future efforts to articulate an ideal of gender justice are likely to occupy it. Even so, some tension between the two impulses will remain. Theorists who stress the injustice of gender will be inclined to approach any virtue or practice associated with women with suspicion, wary that it represents a sexist stereotype or a historical adaptation to subordination (MacKinnon 1987a, p. 39). They will emphasize that gender corresponds to enormous disparities in power. Conversely, theorists whose work focuses on revaluing practices associated with women may become skeptical about whether the ideal of gender equality adequately expresses feminist aspirations for justice (Jaggar 1990), stressing that the issue is "not simply equality between the sexes, but the quality of life for both of them" (Rhode 1989, p. 320).

490

Is justice antifeminist?

Some feminists have concluded that doing justice to the distinctive voices and experiences of women requires abandoning the vocabulary of justice altogether, or at least displacing it from any central role within feminist theory and practice. Often drawing on Carol Gilligan's influential contrast between a masculine ethic of justice and rights and a feminine ethic of care and relationship (Gilligan 1982a), they argue that a morality of justice is gender-biased and inhospitable to feminist aspirations and concerns.

There is no question that many classical and contemporary theories of justice are antifeminist or blind to gender (Elshtain 1981, Okin 1989a, 1992). But this critique goes deeper, claiming that considerations of justice in general are morally problematic for feminists. The strongest and least persuasive version of this critique proposes a feminist or feminine ethic of care as a comprehensive alternative to considerations of justice (Noddings 1984). On this view, all we need is care – or, even if care must be supplemented by other values, justice has little or nothing to contribute (Noddings 1990). The problem, as many critics have pointed out, is that such a view offers little or no guidance in deciding what constitutes an appropriate distribution of care – in deciding who gives and receives it, who can expect or demand it, and how we should distribute it among intimates and strangers. Nor does this view address the relationship of care to other social benefits and burdens, or to status and voice. Any effort to tackle such questions brings justice back into the picture. The best feminist attempts to elaborate an ethic of care (Tronto 1993) strongly acknowledge the continuing relevance and urgency of considerations of justice.

As Hume famously argued, justice is a remedial virtue which assumes that scarcity and limited sympathy are permanent features of the human condition. Justice can be generous and merciful, but She also holds a sword, for the possibility of coercive enforcement lurks in the background of nearly all discussions of justice. Some moral and political thinkers, unhappy with this picture, have envisioned creating a world which transcends the need for justice, in which limited desires or unlimited resources, combined with universal sympathy, render hard questions of justice obsolete. Feminists, too, have occasionally been drawn to some version of this view – for instance, to the idea that, by turning our attention away from notions of justice and focusing on becoming more compassionate toward and affirming of one another, we can make injustice disappear, or that by adopting a relational ethic we can transform all conflictual relationships into cooperative ones. This is wildly unrealistic. Feminist abandonment of justice is unhelpful and irresponsible, because it ignores the practical struggles women face and avoids confronting injuries and inequalities beyond gender.

This certainly does not mean that all feminist work on care, compassion, and relationship is unhelpful. While it is a serious mistake to deny the need for justice, feminist theorists have persuasively affirmed a "need for more than justice" (Baier 1987b), arguing that prevailing approaches to justice should pay more attention to values like care, empathy, and trust, for at least two reasons. First, contemporary justice theorists tend to devote little or no attention to moral capacities and dispositions. They focus on generating correct principles, neglecting the question of what enables people to live in accordance with such principles. Yet living by just principles requires moral imagination and sensitivity, responsiveness and empathy (Blum 1994). Indeed, efforts to make the world more just depend as much or more on developing people's capacities to relate to and sympathize with others than they do on refining people's capacity to discern rational principles (Baier 1987b, 1994a). The problem, critics charge, that dominant approaches to justice appear to assume that work exploring the moral dispositions which make justice possible lacks philosophical relevance. So, for instance, moral education within families is taken for granted as something prior to the "real" subject of moral theory (Blum 1994, Okin 1989a). The claim that justice theorists need to acknowledge the importance of moral dispositions is therefore a challenge to dominant understandings of the scope and tasks of moral theory. A similar challenge is raised by some critics of the Kantian–utilitarian mainstream of contemporary moral philosophy, like Alasdair MacIntyre and Bernard Williams, who pay little or no attention to gender. But attention to women's lives and experiences has greatly assisted in identifying this lacuna within contemporary approaches to justice and ethics.

Feminist theorists have also made a strong case for taking care seriously in the construction of just principles and policies. This second strand of criticism focuses on how theories of justice neglect basic, universal human issues of childrearing and care for dependents (Kymlicka 1990, Hirschmann 1992). By taking rational, autonomous, and healthy adults as their starting point, many justice theorists overlook the facts of human neediness and dependency and the necessity and social importance of care work – work which, not coincidentally, is overwhelmingly performed by women. Dependency, vulnerability, illness, and incapacity are not exceptional conditions but basic features of human life. What is just treatment of the vulnerable and dependent, and those who care for them? While some influential theories of justice do offer theoretical resources for addressing this question – notably John Rawls's difference principle, which holds that social inequalities should be arranged to benefit the worst off (Rawls 1971) – they devote little attention to exploring the changes in domestic and economic arrangements that justice in this realm might require. In recent years feminist work on justice has increasingly focused on these issues (Fraser 1994, 1989a, chs 7–8, Okin 1989a, chs 7–8, Rhode 1989, Tronto 1993, Young 1995).

Justice is, and will remain, central to the feminist project. But, as these last two arguments show, feminists are frustrated by some aspects of prevailing theories of justice. The core frustration remains the tendency for these theories to ignore gender and domestic life as social phenomena that come under the scope of principles of justice. However, a number of feminist theorists have suggested that the problem and its remedy can be stated more generally. Making theories of justice hospitable to feminist (and other) moral concerns requires a change in the model of moral reasoning currently associated with justice. Justice is conceived too abstractly (Benhabib 1992a), is linked to unrealizable notions of impartiality and universality (Young 1990a, ch. 4), and is focused too narrowly on issues of distribution (Young 1990a, chs 1–2, Fraser 1995). Feminists should champion approaches to justice that are more contextual, that acknowledge theorizing from a particular position or perspective, and that pay more attention to issues like violence, domination, and cultural injustice.

These arguments about justice represent some of the most insightful work in feminist theory today. Unfortunately, they are also susceptible to overstatement in ways that rob them of coherence and persuasiveness. Before outlining and evaluating them, it's worth noting two features they share. First, they reflect efforts to think about justice not only through the lens of gender, but with attentiveness to other social categories like class, race, ethnicity, religion, and culture. They take seriously the criticisms directed in the last fifteen years against feminist theory for its blindness to the way gender intersects with other social differences, categories, and identities. The attempt to understand multiple, cross-cutting social differences makes this literature especially ambitious in its scope.

Second, these arguments are directed primarily against a particular kind of reasoning about justice, with roots in the liberal social contract tradition and in Kantian ethics (and to a lesser extent against socialist approaches). The primary objects of criticism are the works of theorists like John Rawls, Robert Nozick, and Jürgen Habermas, and not, for instance, natural law theories or traditional patriarchal views of justice. This context helps to explain certain tendencies toward overstatement in feminist criticisms of justice. Theorists engaged in projects of criticism and reconstruction often exaggerate the contrast between their own position and the objects of their critique. This is not altogether a bad thing: sharp phrasing can be intellectually clarifying. But it can also be misleading or inaccurate. The pointedness of some feminist objections to liberal conceptions of universalism, for instance, may give the impression that the Enlightenment was the worst thing that ever happened to women – hardly a historically defensible assessment. The differences between some feminist approaches to justice and those of mainstream contemporary liberalism are real and interesting enough without distorting exaggeration.

Abstraction versus context in approaches to justice

Feminist efforts to criticize and reconstruct reasoning about justice can be organized under three headings. The first is a critique of inappropriate abstraction. According to this critique, contemporary approaches to justice are pitched at too high a level of abstraction, and so ignore morally relevant human experiences and differences. Reasoning about justice needs to be more contextual, to take a "bottom-up" approach which builds from concrete human experiences.

Feminists have identified many examples of inappropriate abstraction in justice theory. For instance, they have shown how social contract theories that approach questions about the just distribution of social benefits and burdens through a thought experiment involving healthy adults end up ignoring universal human experiences of dependency and vulnerability, and indeed the entire realm of family life (Pateman 1988, Hirschmann 1992). What theorists abstract out obviously affects the substance of their principles. Indeed, women's invisibility within many theories of justice helps explain why so many harms and deprivations specific to women have not been perceived as unjust. And the category of gender itself can become an inappropriate abstraction if it serves to obscure harms and deprivations experienced as a result of other factors like race (Crenshaw 1989).

This insight can be reformulated in constructive fashion. Justice theorists must begin from a concrete understanding of the lives of those about whom they theorize. This requires a strong commitment to contextual analysis. Theories of justice often enjoin us to adopt the point of view of others, but they underestimate the challenges involved in doing this. Hence both Seyla Benhabib's (1992a) argument that justice requires an imaginative encounter with a "concrete other" rather than a "general" one, and Susan Okin's sympathetic reconstruction of John Rawls's original position as requiring just this kind of encounter (Okin 1989a, p. 101) are efforts to give attentiveness to concrete human experience and difference a central role within justice theory. This commitment to "bottom-up" theorizing is reflected as well in growing feminist interest in incorporating personal narratives into theoretical work. But it also shapes arguments pitched at a far more abstract level. So, for instance, the "five faces of oppression" outlined by Iris Marion Young (1990a, ch. 2) – exploitation, marginalization, powerlessness, cultural imperialism, and violence – offer a more nuanced portrait of injustice than mainstream theories because Young pays closer attention to the experiences of disadvantaged people and groups.

The critique of inappropriate abstraction does not, however, mean that feminists can or should eschew abstraction. Nor does it entail that the more contextual a theory of justice is, the better it is from a feminist perspective. All theorizing involves abstraction, and feminist theories are certainly no exception. Identifying gender hierarchy is itself a formidable act of abstraction, and the claim that all human beings need care is no less abstract than, say, the claim that all human beings pursue their self-interest. Moreover, as Okin (1989a, chs 3, 5) shows in her comparison of the work of John Rawls and Michael Walzer, a more abstract theory of justice may offer feminism greater theoretical resources than a more contextual theory, even when the latter, as is true in Walzer's case, pays more explicit attention to gender issues. Indeed, the demand to pay attention to context is empty without guidance concerning what is and is not morally relevant – and as Kymlicka points out (1990, p. 267), this guidance is provided by moral principles. So, for instance, the argument that justice requires attentiveness to the lives of disadvantaged people depends on a principled commitment to equality. Principles without moral dispositions may be worthless, and we cannot evaluate principles without a nuanced sense of what it means to apply them in many contexts. But without principles, moral dispositions are blind.

Feminists must not succumb to a sweeping (and, ironically, highly abstract) preference for "context" over "abstraction." Instead, the strength of this critique lies in the way it reveals how apparently benign processes of abstraction can lead to glaring moral omissions within theories of justice – and how correcting and avoiding such omissions requires justice theorists to pay far more attention to the concrete circumstances of others' lives.

Questioning the possibility and value of impartiality

A second feminist critique questions the emphasis placed in theories of justice on impartiality. Since Kant's formulation of the categorical imperative, theorists have often associated justice and morality with an impartial, universal point of view, and argued that we arrive at principles of justice by adopting such a point of view. Some feminists object to this approach, arguing that impartiality is impossible to attain, since all moral and political reasoning is shaped by a particular and partial perspective. Moreover, they claim, even the pursuit of an ideal of impartiality has adverse consequences, since it inevitably masks social hierarchy and serves the interests of the dominant (Young 1990a, ch. 4). Impartiality and universalism are beyond redemption; justice theories need to reject these ideals and openly embrace particularism, "heterogeneity and partial discourse" (Young 1990a, p. 112).

Though efforts to unmask false claims to impartiality have a long history, feminism has certainly contributed to heightening awareness of how ostensibly impartial reasoning can obscure and legitimate social hierarchy. Gender-neutral laws and policies, impartially applied, can still systematically disadvantage women because they are designed to apply to people who never get pregnant and who have wives at home. Feminist literature also offers insights concerning how and why theorists need to understand the partiality of their perspective. Acknowledgment of an interested perspective lies at the heart of feminism's self-definition as a project committed to understanding and ending women's subordination. Even so, in the past two decades white, Western middle-class heterosexual feminist theorists have been taught sharp and valuable lessons about the perils of universalizing one's particular experience to that of all women.

But it is one thing to say that impartiality is never fully realizable, and another to claim that aspiring to be as impartial as possible is always morally dangerous. This latter claim exaggerates the dangers of impartiality and ends up undermining the aims of feminist justice.

Do efforts to be impartial always serve dominant interests, as critics allege? For instance, do efforts to be impartial to sex or race necessarily reinforce male or white dominance? This is an implausibly sweeping claim. In some contexts attempts to be impartial are not only benign but obligatory. It is appropriate, for instance, to try to be impartial to gender when deciding how to rotate leadership positions within a group, in critiquing someone's work, such as a paper, symphony, or scientific theory, in opening a door for someone, or in evaluating someone's cruel or abusive action. Impartiality can also be a just

495

corrective to practices in which partiality unjustly favors the privileged. A judge who scrupulously ignores the defendant's gender, race, and class in sentencing drunk drivers is more just than one who gives wealthy white defendants community service and poor black defendants jail time.

Moreover, if the aim of feminist justice is "inclusion of everyone in moral and social life" (Young 1990a, p. 105), then this entails devising principles and practices that will provide justice for all regardless of their particular experiences or identities. Feminist justice does, then, aspire to construct a general point of view encompassing all members of society. This point of view is, moreover, impartial in the sense that it does not privilege some over others. It reconstructs notions of impartiality by stressing that fairness requires that we be mindful of differences. But the motivation for that mindfulness is the same as what motivates a commitment to impartiality in the face of views which defend status hierarchy. Feminists are right, then, to urge vigilance against hasty and unreflective claims of impartiality, and to stress the challenges of moral theorizing in a world of difference and hierarchy. But it is important not to overstate these points by claiming that impartiality is always dangerous or that it has no place within feminist ideals of justice.

Beyond the politics of distribution

Finally, some feminists claim that justice has become too narrowly focused on issues of distribution, obscuring other important forms of injustice. They note that most contemporary theories of justice conceive justice primarily in terms of the distribution of rights and resources, especially economic resources like property and income. This is true even in the case of theorists who identify core elements of justice which are harder to fit into such a distributive framework, like Rawls's primary good of "the social bases of self-respect" (Rawls 1971, p. 440, Fraser 1995, p. 73).

But a vision of justice focused on economic distribution has difficulty encompassing key aspects of gender injustice, from violence and harassment to demeaning cultural images and understandings of women. Attempts by feminists to transform cultural meanings associated with women are likewise hard to capture in a framework that sees the politics of justice primarily in terms of demands for legal or economic redistribution.

According to a number of feminist theorists, this points to the need for a more differentiated framework of justice. For example, Iris Marion Young identifies five forms of injustice – exploitation, marginalization, powerlessness, cultural imperialism, and violence – which she claims are not adequately captured by distributive approaches (Young 1990a, ch. 2). And Nancy Fraser (1995) distinguishes between two contemporary paradigms of justice, one focused on redistribution and the other on recognition. Redistributive justice aims to overcome social inequalities and hierarchies. What Fraser (following Charles Taylor) calls "the politics of recognition," by contrast, strives to overcome cultural domination by affirming and revaluing specificity. Demands for welfare or health-care rights are an example of redistributive claims, while efforts to win public acceptance of gay and lesbian households exemplify a politics of recognition. People subjected to both forms of injustice face a dilemma, since redistribution claims tend to undermine specificity, while recognition claims affirm and promote it (Fraser 1995, p. 74). The tension within feminism between impulses to abolish gender and to valorize some gender differences is a case in point. The challenge, Fraser argues, is to combine just claims for redistribution and recognition in ways that support rather than undermine one another.

How deep and persuasive a challenge do these arguments present to prevailing understandings of justice? Proponents of a distributive framework may object that if rights and economic resources were justly distributed the forms of injustice cited by Young and Fraser would not arise. This is at least partly true. It is important not to exaggerate the difference between these proposed approaches and the distributive frameworks they criticize. Efforts to remedy powerlessness, violence, and cultural dominance will depend at least in part on a redistribution of resources. And in a general sense feminist demands for justice *are* demands for redistribution – demands, that is, to change a gendered distribution of social benefits, status, and voice.

Nevertheless, the call to move beyond distribution opens up important new terrain in thinking about justice. Some of the forms of injustice highlighted by Young and Fraser, like violence against homosexuals, Jews, and women, are to a significant extent autonomous from questions of resource distribution. Since pervasive practices of violence and harassment are a major determinant of many people's social status and voice, and represent a source of hierarchical social control, they belong within accounts of justice. But such patterns of social violence (as distinct from official violence like war and legal punishment) have largely been ignored by theorists of justice.

Attempts to remedy cultural or symbolic injustices also appear to go beyond issues of distribution. To be sure, overcoming such injustices entails redistributing voice and status to stigmatized persons and groups – or increasing their access to what Fraser calls the means of interpretation and communication (Fraser 1989a). But ideas like cultural stigma and respect have a substantive element which is easily lost when translated into distributive terms. And even the categories that appear to be closest to purely distributive ones, like exploitation and marginalization, capture a difference between structures of economic inequality with immense repercussions for poor people's status and voice. Exploited and marginalized people may be equally poor, but their differences in social position and experience must be taken into account in attempts to diagnose and remedy the injustice of their condition. Once again, Young and Fraser demonstrate the value of attending more closely to social context in justice theory. Their work offers tools for comparing and evaluating claims of injustice without assuming either that each represents an essentially different phenomenon (like sexism, heterosexism, or racism), or that they are examples of an undifferentiated "politics of identity." Young and Fraser's work also highlights the importance of concentrations of power (such as the influence of professions

497

and the role of information and communication) all too often ignored by justice theory.

Many questions remain about these proposals for more differentiated approaches to justice. For instance, while egregious cases of stigmatization clearly raise questions of justice, the more general criteria for cultural or symbolic injustice remain vague. How do patterns of stigmatization and disrespect get changed, and to what extent is it possible or appropriate to enforce such changes? Are these changes to be accomplished through grassroots mobilization, or should state institutions be involved, and if so. how? Young and Fraser offer interesting and controversial proposals for what justice would require – for Young, groupdifferentiated forms of democratic participation (Young 1990a, p. 95), and for Fraser, "socialism in the economy and deconstruction in the culture" (Fraser 1995, p. 91). But just as feminists disagree about the scope of legitimate state intervention in family life, they will disagree about what justice requires or permits in efforts to overcome stigma and violence – and about when claims for respect and recognition deepen and enhance, and when they undermine, the core egalitarian commitments of feminist justice.

Conclusion

As Socrates discovers in Book V of the *Republic*, when theorists of justice take women's lives into account, the consequences can be unnervingly radical. Gender justice cuts "close to home" (Delphy 1984). By redefining sexual difference as gender hierarchy and proclaiming that justice requires the equal status of women and men, feminism has changed the scope of justice in ways that are just beginning to be acknowledged within moral and political theory.

In recent years, feminists have clarified the issues at stake in debates over the goal of gender justice and strategies for attaining it. While moves to reject justice or deny its relevance to feminist concerns are incoherent and counterproductive, arguments criticizing and reconstructing approaches to justice have yielded interesting insights. Feminists now play a central role within efforts to articulate just principles and practices in a world of inequality and difference.

Feminist justice remains a work in progress. In conclusion, I will mention three areas which particularly need attention. First, feminists need to settle accounts more fairly with other traditions of justice theory. Interesting arguments in this area are often marred by overstatement. Better identification of areas of overlap and disagreement would help to refine and clarify feminist arguments. Second, with some notable exceptions, such as Susan Okin's argument for extending equal legal entitlement to earnings to spouses and Anne Phillips's proposals for increasing the presence of women and other disadvantaged groups in decision-making bodies (Okin 1989a, ch. 8, Phillips 1995), few feminist discussions of justice offer specific recommendations for institutional or policy change. This reticence reflects a preference for abstract argument that all of us trained in theory can readily understand. It may also stem from a widely shared conviction that, in Western societies at least, the political possibilities for the women's movement have diminished for the moment. Nevertheless, a greater willingness to engage in debate over specific policies would strengthen feminist discussions of justice (Okin 1989a, pp. 329–37). Third, feminist theory would also benefit from more attention to both principled and pragmatic constraints on efforts to achieve gender justice. How should claims of gender injustice be balanced with other moral considerations like freedom of religion, association, or expression, or concerns about cultural respect? How much public structuring of personal choices is permissible to foster gender justice? What unintended consequences might proposed policies have in a world where most public decision-making is dominated by people who do not support feminist goals? While many feminists are aware of these issues, they need to be incorporated more fully into discussions of gender justice. This would make feminist accounts of justice more complete. But it would also enhance their contribution to the search for justice in practice – which is the heart of the feminist project.

50

Rights

VIRGINIA HELD

Feminism is sometimes equated with demands for equal rights for women. Mary Wollstonecraft in the eighteenth century argued, against Rousseau, that women should be accorded the same rights and freedoms based on rational principles that were being demanded for men (Wollstonecraft 1975). In the nineteenth century, John Stuart Mill and Harriet Taylor Mill, rejecting prevailing views of the time, called for an end to the subjection of women through an extension to women of equal rights and equal opportunities (Mill and Mill 1970). Women, they argued, should have the same rights as men to own property, to vote, to receive education, and to enter any profession. In the twentieth century, women's movements often focused their attention on winning for women the right to vote, achieved in the United States in 1920, in England in 1918 and 1928, in France in 1946, and in Switzerland only in 1971. The second wave of the women's movement in the United States, starting in the late 1960s, placed strong emphasis on achieving an Equal Rights Amendment to the US Constitution (the amendment failed to be ratified by the required number of states), and on ending discrimination against women in all its forms (Rhode 1989). Arguments for welfare rights, valid independently of feminism, were seen as particularly important to women: how could a person enjoy rights to freedom or equal protection of the laws without assurance of the means to stay alive and to feed her children? Either employment and child care must be available, or persons must have access by right to the basic necessities of life. Negative freedoms from discriminatory interferences are insufficient; positive enablements to be free and equal agents must also be assured by rights (Held 1984, Sterba 1989).

Rights can be either moral or legal, or both. Many rights are articulated as justifiable moral claims, such as rights to not be raped or murdered, which ought also to be, and often are, legal rights recognized in and protected by an actual legal system. But some rights, such as those in many legal systems giving husbands a legal right to do to their wives what would otherwise be rape, are not justifiable as moral rights and ought not to be legal ones. And some of what we may think we are morally entitled to may be claimed as rights, as when we say to a friend, "I have a right to have you tell me the truth," but such moral rights should not be subject, as legal rights are, to the intrusions and mechanisms of legal enforcement.

When women are denied such fundamental rights as the right to own property or to vote, or when women are openly discriminated against in education and employment, arguments that women are entitled to equal rights play a large role in feminist movements. But feminism has moved far beyond such demands.

Feminism has by now contributed fundamental critiques of the language and concepts of rights. Overcoming the pervasive patriarchy of traditional and existing societies is seen to require not only far more than equal rights for women but, to some feminists, a shift of focus away from rights.

Feminist critiques of rights

Criticisms of the concepts of rights and the framework of justice in which they are articulated have come from at least two major sources. First, feminists developing what has come to be called "an ethic of care" have cast doubt on traditional moral theories focused on justice and rights. Second, feminists examining actual legal systems have shown how law and rights incorporate patriarchal attitudes and uphold oppressive social structures.

Rights in moral theory

The literature developing a feminist ethic of care includes fundamental criticisms of theories and ways of thinking that interpret moral problems in terms of rights and justice. An ethic of care is seen as contrasting with the dominant moral theories and ways of thinking constituted by an ethic of justice. An ethic of care examines the moral issues, values, and problems discernible in human relationships, especially in the family and among friends, and especially as women experience and evaluate these relationships. An ethic of care values connections between persons, in contrast with what is seen as the excessive individualism of dominant moral theories. It values trust between persons and the caring concerns that can characterize relations between family members and friends. The activities of caring for actual vulnerable persons require moral considerations such as empathy, sensitivity, and attention to the particular aspects of persons and their needs become salient. By now, various feminist moral theorists have developed an ethic of care which they advocate as an improved morality for both women and men, or which they think must be incorporated, along with an ethic of justice, into any adequate morality (Baier 1994a, Held, 1993, 1995b, Tong 1993).

Advocates of an ethic of care sometimes see the morality of rights and justice as inherently masculine and not only neglectful of women's experience but actually hostile to the handling of moral problems as women interpret them. Carol Gilligan noted that "a morality of rights and noninterference may appear frightening to women in its potential justification of indifference and unconcern" (Gilligan 1982a, p. 22). Nel Noddings pointed out "the destructive role of rules and principles," of which rights are reflections, in contexts of care. She suggests that we may come to rely on rules to lighten the load of responding to everyone we encounter, but if we "come to rely almost completely on external rules (we) become detached from the very heart of morality: 'the sensibility that calls forth caring'" (Noddings 1986, p. 47). And Annette Baier writes that "the moral tradition which developed the concept of rights, autonomy, and justice is the same tradition that provided 'justifications' of the oppression of those whom the primary rights-holders (got) to do the sort of work they themselves preferred not to do. The domestic work was left to women and slaves" and the official morality ignored their contribution. "Rights have usually been for the privileged," she observes, and "the 'justice perspective' and the legal sense that goes with it are shadowed by their patriarchal past" (Baier 1994a, pp. 25–6).

Rights, whether moral or legal, are usually thought to attach to persons as individuals, though some theorists argue also for group rights (Nickel 1994, Young 1990a). In traditional moral and legal theory, rights call attention to individuals even more strongly than do other concepts, such as obligations and responsibilities. Respect for rights may presuppose a context of social trust, since without social trust there may be little respect for rights, but the traditions in which rights have been developed have done little, themselves, to contribute to that trust. As Annette Baier notes, "the language of rights pushes us ... to see the participants in the moral practice as single, clamorous" individuals (Baier 1994a, p. 237).

The emphasis of much feminist theory, especially moral theory, on caring relationships between persons rather than on individuals and their rights and possessions, seems thus to present a conflict with a morality of justice and rights. In addition, the tendency of much feminist theory and practice to value attending to actual persons and particular contexts rather than to abstract from such actual contexts in search of a purely rational and impartial point of view, presents a further contrast with moral ties of abstract rights and justice applicable only to an ideal or hypothetical world. Whether rights are seen as based on deontological principles or utilitarian rules, they may be ill-suited for dealing with many relationships between actual persons (Wolgast 1980). Many feminist moral theorists suggest that an ethic of care may be much more suitable for doing so. But they do not limit an ethic of care to personal relations; care is being developed as a political and social value as well (Held 1993, Tronto 1993).

Feminists call attention to whole domains of human experience where moral issues are pervasive, yet which have been overlooked or neglected by dominant moral theories of rules and rights: mothering children's trust, the care of the vulnerable – whether in the family or through social practices and institutions. An ethic of care may contribute far more to understanding the moral issues in such contexts than can an ethic of justice and rights. In criticizing the presuppositions of liberal conceptions of justice and rights, Eva Feder Kittay notes how "liberalism constructed an equality for heads of households ... and then counted the head of household as an *individual* who is independent and who can act on his own behalf" (Kittay 1995, p. 11). Like others, she argues that this creates the illusion that dependencies do not exist, that society is composed of independent, free, and equal individuals who come together to form associations, whereas in fact social cooperation is required as a prior condition and for those who are not independent. All of us are dependent for periods of our lives, and many of us are what Kittay calls "dependency workers," those on whom the dependent must rely to fulfill basic needs, and who are then themselves second-arily dependent on others for the resources needed to sustain cared-for and caregiver. Such dependencies are part of the vast network of interdependencies that constitute the central and essential bonds of human social life. Theories of justice and rights that omit the dependent and dependency-workers are ill suited for meeting the needs which dependency makes pressing.

It is of course not only feminists who have seen social relations as central, and interdependencies as real. Marxists see humans as social beings rather than as isolated individuals, and have criticized rights for their individualism. They have emphasized the historical development of rights as bourgeois claims protecting the capitalist accumulating his own property to the detriment of the community. Socialist feminists share many of these criticisms but go beyond them in showing how women are oppressed as women, not only as members of the working class (Ferguson 1989, Jaggar 1983). Feminist attention to relations in the family and to the values of care and connection have called attention to different kinds of interdependencies than the basically economic ones emphasized by Marxists.

Thus feminist thinking has led to different and new critiques of rights and the framework of justice. Questions about whether women's and men's rights should be the same or different are being addressed in a number of new ways (see below); many feminists suggest that to think of women's subordination primarily in terms of rights may not be the best way to do so, and feminist moral thinking often displaces justice and rights from a previously central position.

Rights in legal theory

Criticisms of rights have also come from many feminist legal scholars. Patricia Smith writes that "the rejection of patriarchy is the one point on which all feminists agree" and "feminist jurisprudence is the analysis and critique of law as a patriarchal institution" (Smith 1993, p. 3). Feminist analyses have shown how law and its scheme of rights support patriarchy. In Catharine MacKinnon's words, "In the liberal state, the rule of law – neutral, abstract, elevated, pervasive – both institutionalizes the power of men over women and institutionalizes power in its male form ... . (M)ale forms of power over women are affirmatively embodied as individual rights in law ... . Abstract rights authorize the male experience of the world" (MacKinnon 1989, pp. 238–48). Carol Smart sees a "congruence" between law and "masculine culture," and examines how law "disqualifies women's experience" and women's knowledge; she urges feminists to resist a focus on rights (Smart 1989, p. 2). Even where the law appears to accord women equal rights, police, prosecutors, and judges often apply the law in ways that uphold patriarchal power. The state has done little to prevent violence against women and children. When violent actions that would be prohibited among strangers occur within the family, the law has been reluctant to inter-vene, thus reinforcing male supremacy in the family (Smith 1993, p. 139). The

503

judicial system has been more concerned with protecting white men from unjust accusations than with protecting women, especially non-white women, from the real harm of rape (Crenshaw 1989).

Not only does the law in fact support the subordination of women, but in the view of various feminist legal scholars, so does the whole of modern legal theory, whether liberal or not. Robin West sees it all as "essentially and irretrievably masculine" in its acceptance of the thesis "that we are individuals 'first,' and ... that what separates us is epistemologically and morally prior to what connects us" (West, p. 2).

Some feminists see rights as inherently abstract and reflective of a male point of view. Some think the use of rights discourse requires a social movement to adapt its goals unduly to what an existing legal system will permit, fostering conflict within the movement and diverting its strength (Schneider 1986). And feminists allied with critical legal studies and postmodern approaches have subjected rights claims to critical analysis and have deeply questioned the significance of legal argumentation focused on rights. They often see law as an expression of power rather than of morality or reasoned argument, and they are skeptical of all claims, including any about rights, to truth or objectivity (Schneider 1986, Smart 1989, Smith 1993).

Feminist reconstructions of rights

Such fundamental critiques do not, however, constitute a rejection of rights by most feminists. Rather, they can be interpreted as (a) demands for reformulations of existing schemes of rights; (b) calls to reconstruct the concept of rights; and (c) moral recommendations for limiting the reach of law to its appropriate domain.

Reformulations of existing rights

Starting with feminist views on law, we can see very many feminist legal theorists working within the framework of law to improve the rights protected and the principles upheld by law. For instance, feminist jurisprudence is developing more satisfactory ways of interpreting equal rights than those which simply require women to be treated in the *same* ways as men where differences between women and men are significant and where similar treatment means that women must adapt to a male standard already in place. As Patricia Smith asks, "Why should equal protection of the law depend on being relevantly similar to men?" (Smith 1995a, p. 39). She concludes that the analysis of equality in feminist jurisprudence now revolves around understanding what equal treatment requires among persons who are different in important respects. This advances the interpretation of equality, she writes, "from the first half of Aristotle's formula to the second half – from the idea that like cases must be treated alike to the idea that unlike cases should be treated in proportion to their differences" (Smith 1995a; see also Smith 1993, Part I).

Christine Littleton reinterprets what is required by equal protection away from sameness of treatment to equality of disadvantage brought about by the treatment. Her argument is that difference should not lead to disadvantage, it should instead be costless (Littleton 1987). Such interpretations provide the basis for arguing that if, for example, a pension scheme that excludes part-time workers and appears to be gender-neutral has a much more adverse effect on women than on men, it is discriminatory. And it shows how equality may require support for pregnancy leave and child-care facilities. Equality that respects rather than ignores difference may well require governmental action rather than inaction to bring about substantive equality.

The potential of legal rights to bring about social change for women can be seen in the area of sexual harassment. Feminist jurisprudence turned the injuries that women had long experienced into a form of discrimination from which they could seek legal protection. Catharine MacKinnon writes that the law against sexual harassment is a test "of possibilities for social change for women through law" (MacKinnon 1987b, p. 103). The victims of sexual harassment now have a name for the harm of having sexual pressure imposed on them and not being in an economic position to refuse it. "They have been given a forum, legitimacy to speak, authority to make claims, and an avenue for possible relief ... . The legal claim for sexual harassment made the events of sexual harassment illegitimate socially, as well as legally for the first time" (MacKinnon 1987b, p. 104).

The difficulties but also the possibilities of relying on law to reduce the subordination of women are illustrated in a discussion of statutory rape laws by Frances Olsen. She finds in such laws "a concrete example of the advantages and disadvantages of rights analysis" (Olsen 1984, p. 401). Such laws "both protect and undermine women's rights, and rights arguments can be used to support, attack, or urge changes in the laws" (p. 402). Although such laws do provide young women some protection against coerced sex, they violate the privacy and sexual freedom of young women compared to young men, and they perpetuate sexist stereotypes. "[A]ny acknowledgment of the actual difference between the present situation of males and females stigmatizes females and perpetuates discrimination. But if we ignore power differences and pretend that women and men are similarly situated, we perpetuate discrimination by disempowering ourselves from instituting effective change" (p. 412). Yet reforms can and do take place and do change people's lives, and some of the proposed changes can be seen as better than others. Some recommended changes in statutory rape laws would be: allowing underage women to control the decision of whether or not to prosecute, and taking the young woman's characterization of the sexual encounter as voluntary or coerced as determinative. Although the major efforts must be beyond the law – empowering women generally, and transforming sexuality from sexualized violence and domination to eroticized mutuality – the changes law can bring about can be significant.

Feminists are demanding reform in many aspects of law. In the area of rape law, for instance, they ask why women should be expected "to fight like men" to demonstrate non-consent in potentially life-threatening circumstances where their attackers are often far stronger than they are. Feminist jurisprudence has clarified how statutes and the courts use standards about rape, consent, force, resistance, and reasonable belief that fail to take account of the perspectives of women. The law's standard "reasonable person" is one who fights back, though many women typically do not respond to threatening situations by fighting. As Susan Estrich puts it, "the reasonable woman, it seems, is not a schoolboy 'sissy'. She is a real man" (Estrich 1987a, p. 1114).

Of utmost importance to women are reproductive rights. It is generally recognized that reproductive freedom is a precondition to most other freedoms or equality for women, yet reproductive rights are continually contested and threatened. Patricia Smith argues that "it is inconceivable that any issue that comparably affected the basic individual freedom of any man would not be under his control in a free society" (Smith 1993, p. 14). But because the capacity to bear children is such an important capacity that women have and men lack, and because it has throughout history been under the control of men, the unwillingness to accord reproductive rights to women is especially deep. As feminists challenge the subordination of women in countless ways, women's rights to control their own sexuality and reproductive capacities, and to avoid commodification as sexual or reproductive objects are crucial (Smith 1993, Part IV).

There are many ways in which law itself could be more receptive to care-based values, for instance in dealing with the harms of hate speech, or devising more satisfactory ways than those previously available for handling the sexual abuse of children (Meyers 1995, Smart 1989). This would involve greater sensitivity than is often seen in the determination of which rights there are, but since rights necessarily lead to dichotomous determinations that there is or is not a given right and that it has or has not been violated, the discourse of rights may often be less suitable than that of care for many moral concerns, and society and law itself could increasingly recognize when other institutions than law should be employed for given kinds of situations.

There have also been strong voices reminding feminists of the centrality of rights arguments to movements for social justice. As the experience of many women and US minority members affirms, and as Patricia Williams shows, persons suffering domination on grounds of race, gender, or sexual orientation usefully think in terms of rights to counter the disrespect they encounter (Meyers 1989). In taking issue with a critical legal studies critique of rights, Williams writes that "although rights may not be ends in themselves, rights rhetoric has been and continues to be an effective form of discourse for blacks" (Williams 1991a, p. 149). Describing needs, she asserts, has not been politically effective for blacks; what she recommends instead is "a political mechanism that can confront the *denial* of need," and rights can do this (p. 152).

Uma Narayan also raises cautions about emphasizing care at the expense of asserting rights. She recalls the colonialist project of denying rights to the colonized in the name of paternalistic concern for their welfare. The colonized were seen as childlike and inferior, in need of guidance and control by the colonizers,

506

and a discourse of care was used to justify such domination. Rights discourse, in contrast, played a powerful role in the emancipation of colonized people. Within such movements, however, traditional and oppressive views on women were often prevalent. And here again the discourse of rights was and is useful to women contesting patriarchal views (Narayan 1985).

Rights are not fixed but are contested, and political struggles are effectively organized around the indignation widely felt over clear denials of rights and persuasive reasons to recognize new rights. Among the strongest arguments women and minorities and colonized peoples have made are that they have not been accorded even the minimums of equal respect supposedly guaranteed by law. The basis for many of the most substantial advances made by disadvantaged groups has been composed of justice, equality, and rights; of course this discourse should not be abandoned.

This does not mean, however, that rights arguments serve well for the entire spectrum of moral or political concerns or that legal discourse should be the privileged discourse of morality or politics. The framework of justice and rights should be one among others rather than dominant. And the kinds of persons conceptualized as being the bearers of rights should not be imagined to be complete conceptions of moral subjects. The law treats persons as conceptually self-contained individuals, not the relational persons of much feminist theory and of the ethic of care (West 1988).

From a feminist perspective, the individual of law and liberal political theory is an artificial and misleading abstraction, but it may be an abstraction that is useful for some legal and political purposes (Frazer and Lacey 1993). The mistake is to suppose it is adequate for morality in general.

Feminist reconceptualizations of rights

Related to the previous argument about the utility of rights for social movements is an argument that rights need to be reconceptualized as nonideal. Instead of thinking of rights as belonging to a consistent scheme of rights and liberties worked out for an ideal world of perfect justice, we should think of rights as reflecting social reality and as capable of decreasing actual oppression and injustice (Meyers 1995, Minow and Shanley 1996).

Martha Minow has been very critical of the tendency of rights rhetoric to ignore relationships. She argues that we ought never to lose sight of the social relations, often of power and privilege, within which the rights of individuals are constructed. She advocates "a conception of rights in relationships" that can counter forms of both public and private power that have been oppressive (Minow 1990, p. 14). She argues for "a shift in the paradigm we use to conceive of difference, a shift from a focus on the distinctions between people to a focus on the relationships within which we notice and draw distinctions" (p. 15). In the family, for instance, rights rhetoric has "assigned the burdens of difference to women and children" (p. 14), but merely extending existing rights from the male head to others in the family "fails to acknowledge the special situations and needs of women and children – and neglects the significance of relationships within the family" (p. 268).

Yet Minow wants to "rescue" rights, not abandon them. With many other feminists she believes that "there is something too valuable in the aspiration of rights, and something too neglectful of the power embedded in assertions of another's need, to abandon the rhetoric of rights" (p. 307).

Also needed are reconceptualizations of the ways rights are formulated with respect to given categories. Kimberle Crenshaw notes that antidiscrimination law proceeds by identifying a category such as race or sex on the basis of which wrongful discrimination has occurred, and then seeks remedies. She shows how this overlooks what she calls the "intersectionality" of categories. Black women, for instance, have been marginalized not only by the courts but also in feminist theory and antiracist politics because their experience of race and sex intersects, and they are covered by neither the paradigms of sex discrimination against white women nor of race discrimination against black men (Crenshaw 1989).

Limiting the reach of law

At the level of moral theory there has also been an appreciation of rights and justice along with the development of an ethic of care. Moralities of justice can well be interpreted as generalizations to the whole of morality of ways of thinking developed in the contexts of law and public policy. Feminists often do resist such expansions of legalistic approaches, seeing them as unsatisfactory for many contexts. But this does not imply that justice and moral rights are dispensable. Although some have thought that care should replace justice as the central moral concept, many others have argued that both care and justice must be acknowledged as essential for any adequately developed morality (Held 1995b, Tong 1993).

There has been an understanding that more than a care ethic may be needed to evaluate oppressive social arrangements and to deal with various types of problems (Card 1990a, Houston 1987). Alison Jaggar argues that the weakness of care thinking "is that its attention to situations' specificity and particularity diverts attention away from their general features such as the social institutions and groupings that give them their structure and much of their meaning" (Jaggar 1995a, p. 194). And Marilyn Friedman shows why she thinks that "traditional concepts of justice and rights may fare better than care ethics in handling problems of violence" (Friedman 1993, p. 150). Others argue that justice must be extended to the family (Okin) and reconceptualized for families (Ruddick 1995), but certainly maintained.

Further, there is an understanding that the relational self conceptualized by many feminists in place of the abstract individual of dominant moral theories must still allow the person enmeshed in relationships to change her situation: to break free of patriarchal communities and to alter oppressive social ties. Appeals to autonomy and rights need to be reformulated but not dispensed with (Friedman 1993, Meyers 1989).

How care and justice should be related is a topic being addressed by feminist moral inquiry, along with developing formulations of care and reconceptualizations of justice. It is unsatisfactory to think of justice as the value appropriate to public life and care as the value appropriate to a private sphere. Women and children clearly need greater justice in the household: protection against rape and domestic violence, a more equitable division of labor in the family, better protections against child abuse of all kinds. And care is clearly a value that should infuse the policies and programs of the welfare state and the practices of society; it should also be increasingly influential in international relations. But just how justice and care should be meshed involves many questions needing further clarification and new recommendations.

Among the questions being explored are the following: Are justice and care compatible? Are they alternative and incompatible ways of interpreting the same moral situations? Are both indispensable for adequate moral understanding? Should care supplement justice, or justice supplement care, while one or the other is the more fundamental? Do they appropriately apply to different domains or do both apply to all or most domains? Can either one be included within the other as a special case, and then which is the more comprehensive?

The criticism of rights from the perspective of care may perhaps best be seen as a criticism of the conceptually imperialistic role that law has played in moral thinking. It is not directed at overthrowing rights in the domain of law, but at limiting legal interpretations to the domain of law rather than supposing them to be suitable for all other moral problems as well. Once the framework of justice and rights is understood as a limited one rather than as the appropriate way to interpret all moral problems, other moral arguments can become salient and social and political organization can develop around other aims than those of justice, law, and rights.

These issues may be illustrated in current efforts to implement human rights at the international level. Some of these efforts benefit women in concrete ways by demanding an end to such human rights violations as denying women the vote, or forcing women to marry against their will. But the dominant discourse of human rights may also draw attention away from pressing issues not best formidable in terms of human rights, such as the needs of women for more status and consideration within their families and communities, for cooperative economic development in common with other women, or for more empowering images in the media productions that shape their society's attitudes (Grand and Newland 1991).

Choices need constantly to be made about whether to interpret various issues as primarily matters of justice and rights or primarily matters to be approached from the perspective of care. Feminists may believe that persons are not actually the individualistic, self-contained abstract entities which the law and dominant moral theories imagine them to be, and that they should not be thought to be such entities any more than is necessary for limited, legal purposes. If more

509

satisfactory conceptions of persons and human relationships and morality are adopted, as feminists urge, then other interpretations than those of justice and rights often seem more appropriate. Greater attention may come to be paid, for instance, to social arrangements for the care and education of children, and to the ways in which culture shapes society and can bring about social change. This does not imply that rights will be unimportant, but it may move them from the center of attention. Feminist morality may in time bring about a shift such that the legal system itself will be a far less central form of social organization and influence than in the past, as other ways of influencing attitudes and actions and practices play larger roles.

51

Democracy

ANNE PHILLIPS

Modern feminism is often traced back to a seventeenth-century liberalism that rejected the patriarchal basis of political power. This liberalism proved a powerful impetus to the development of modern democracy, and because it queried the presumption of "naturally" ordained hierarchies, it also gave women a new language in which to claim their equality with men. The critique of arbitrary and absolute government looked all too obviously pertinent to the relationship between husbands and wives, and the rights of man had barely been proclaimed when Mary Wollstonecraft produced her *Vindication of the Rights of Woman* [1790] (1972). Yet with all the seeming parallels, democracies were slow to acknowledge women as equal citizens; and even after their belated enfranchisement, women have continued to feel themselves second-class citizens.

Feminist theories of democracy have typically started from this conundrum. What is it about democracy – a tradition apparently defined by principles of equality and opposed to tyrannical rule – that kept it so long impervious to the claims of sexual equality? One way of answering this is to say that the practice fell short of the theory, and that while the principles of democracy always implied equality between the sexes, the vested interests of men delayed any action on this. This, essentially, is what John Stuart Mill argued in *The Subjection of Women* [1869] (1983). Mill saw the subjection of women as the largest single exception to the principles that defined the modern age, and he attributed its persistence to the benefits that all men of all classes could hope to derive from having a household "slave." What contemporary writers concentrate on is the additional *theoretical* basis for the failures of modern democracy. The bias against women is increasingly viewed, not just as a matter of inconsistency or a failure of nerve, but as something written deep into the theory itself. "For feminists," as Susan Mendus (1992, p. 208) puts this, "democracy is not something which, as a matter of unfortunate fact, has failed to deliver on its promises to women. It embodies ideals which guarantee that it never will deliver unless it embarks upon extensive critical examination of its own philosophical assumptions."

Feminists have argued that the qualities associated with democratic citizenship – "the characteristics, qualities, attributes, behavior and identity of those who are regarded as full members of political community" (Jones 1990, p. 781) – derive from a complex of values and experiences that privileges masculinity and men. Simply extending to women what used to be attached to men cannot then secure democratic equality. It may even prove incoherent. Consider the high

511

degree of political participation that was enjoyed by the citizens of Athens in the fifth century BCE. Citizenship in the ancient Greek democracies involved attendance at frequent citizen assemblies, as well as extensive responsibilities for serving on juries and executive councils; but citizens were "freed" for this activity by the labors of women, metics, and slaves. Because the rights and duties of the citizen depended on this underpinning – citizens could participate extensively in politics only because citizens were a numerical minority and citizens did not work very hard – these rights and duties could never be universalized to all. Failing a major revision of its rights and responsibilities, this kind of citizenship could not be extended to women as well.

The early examples are the most straightforward, for they refer to a period when maleness was inscribed on the citizen body. Feminists have argued that maleness was also written into the later conceptions of the seventeenth and eighteenth centuries, where seemingly innocent notions of freedom, equality, or consent still derived from a masculine experience. In her influential work on *The Sexual Contract*, for example, Carole Pateman (1988) argues that democracy has been conceived in terms of the free consent of free individuals, but that this freedom derives from a masculine paradigm, which cannot be easily extended to women. She traces this conception back to the social contract theorists whose ideas laid the groundwork for thinking of government as based on consent; she argues that the social contract was simultaneously a sexual contract, which subordinated women to men. The new theorists of government by consent overthrew the "rule of the fathers" in not just one, but two senses. They undermined the patriarchal basis for monarchical rule, but they also pushed aside the fathers in a more symbolic way, to establish direct access to women as wives. Freedom was then premised on subordination. "Civil freedom depends on patriarchal right" (Pateman 1988, p. 4).

Pateman argues that this leaves us with notions of freedom, contract, and consent that are peculiarly antagonistic to the experiences of women. The rights and freedoms of the democratic subject have been formulated within what she calls a "masculine conception of the individual as owner" (p. 216). This treats the body and its capacities almost as material possessions, and regards freedom as the ability to do what you will with your own. Such a characterization is particularly inappropriate to the kind of relationship women have to their bodies (Pateman explores and criticizes the various "body-contracts" implied in prostitution or surrogate motherhood), and it lends itself to an impoverished understanding of democracy as anything to which people have given their "free consent." The ideals of democratic equality have to be freed from these masculine origins if they are to deliver genuine equality between women and men.

One characteristic of this argument is that it attributes the problems women experience with democracy to a specifically *liberal* version of democracy; in doing so, it is typical of many of the arguments from the 1970s and 1980s. In the early years of the contemporary women's movement, liberal democracy was disparaged for its excessive individualism and its naive confidence in equal rights, and

512

feminists took particular exception to the way that liberalism had recast divisions between public and private life as determinedly separate spheres. This separation treated inequalities in the private sphere as irrelevant to the functioning of democracy, ignoring the way that sexual inequalities in the household or labor force could affect women's chances of acting as political equals (Phillips 1991, ch. 4). The strong separation between public and private spheres also made domestic power relations a matter of individual "choice" or personal negotiation, not to be included in the scope of democracy. For feminists, by contrast, democratic ideals had to be put into practice "in the kitchen, the nursery and the bedroom" (Pateman 1988, p. 216), and this more ambitious programme of democratization linked feminism to a tradition of participatory rather than liberal democracy.

Pateman's analysis of the gender subtext to political theory has been replicated across a number of different terrains, and theorists have variously called attention to the way that the "individual" of liberal democratic theory turns out to be a male head of household (Okin 1989a); the way that men were incorporated into democracy as citizen-warriors, but women as citizen-mothers (Pateman 1992); or the way that notions of equality, difference and disadvantage "assume a standard of normality which is inherently male" (Mendus 1992, p. 215). Many of these arguments, it should be noted, combine two rather different points. First, they draw attention to the way that supposedly gender-neutral categories have built in a preference for the male; left to itself, this seems to point toward a more genuine gender-neutrality that no longer distinguishes between the sexes. But this first argument is frequently combined with a second, which presents gender-neutrality itself as the culprit. In Carole Pateman's work, for example, the "individual" of liberal-democratic theory is said to be both masculine *and* disembodied, and her proposed solution is not to strip away the masculine characteristics, but to develop a democracy that can recognize us as both women and men. All democracies now present themselves as indifferent to sexual difference, and they proclaim their citizenship as equally available to both women and men. This very indifference, however, is part of what feminists have criticized. In detaching itself from what is particular, concrete, or bodily, democratic theory is said to write in one sex alone as its norm.

"To become a citizen is to trade one's particular identity for an abstract, public self" (Jones 1990, p. 784), and this trade-in has been regarded as peculiarly advantageous to men. Consider the different balances men and women have had to strike between their public and private lives, and the far greater ease with which men detach themselves (both practically and emotionally) from their private or domestic concerns. In the "male" norm of democratic politics, the boundaries between public and private worlds are relatively well policed, and those who stray across these boundaries (taking their babies to political meetings, letting their emotions "intrude" on rational debate) will be regarded as disruptive or peculiar, as failing to abide by the standards of democratic life. These standards are of course presented as neutral – the same criticisms would apply equally to a woman or a man – but since social characteristics *are*

513

gendered, what passes for neutrality turns out to be preferential treatment for men.

Gender-neutrality: the solution or part of the problem?

This points to one of the central issues in contemporary analyses of democracy, which is whether gender-neutrality should be regarded as the solution or as part of the problem. As translated into specific policy proposals, the first approach encourages us to remove any remaining disadvantages associated with sex. Thus if the laws of citizenship allow men to pass on their nationality to their wives, the same laws should allow women to pass on their nationality to their husbands; or if men are regarded as appropriate candidates for political office regardless of the age or number of their children, women should be regarded as equally appropriate candidates even when their children are of preschool age. All this can be understood as saying that sex should be made irrelevant to democracy. But when feminists also support quota mechanisms to secure a minimum number of women elected, or propose some form of guaranteed representation for women *as women*, they are saying something considerably stronger. They are building sexual difference more explicitly into democratic life.

In her theorization of this second approach, Iris Marion Young takes issue with what she perceives as the impossible ideal of impartial reason: that "transcendental 'view from nowhere' that carries the perspective, attributes, character, and interests of no particular subject or set of subjects" (Young 1990a, p. 100). This ideal, as she notes, has been particularly prevalent among radical critics of contemporary democracy, for those who query the sordid interest-group bargaining that underlies so much conventional politics are often drawn to a more generous democracy that will promote common concerns. But in a society

> where some groups are privileged while others are oppressed, insisting that as citizens persons should leave behind their particular attributes and experiences to adopt a general point of view serves only to reinforce that privilege; for the perspectives and interests of the privileged will tend to dominate this unified public, marginalising or silencing those of other groups.   (Young 1990a, p. 257)

Against this, Young argues that democracies can only approximate more just social outcomes when they allow for dialogue and contestation between different voices and perspectives, and she calls for additional mechanisms of group representation for those who are currently oppressed. Women would then be represented, not just as citizens, but as women.

The arguments in favor of specifically group representation have proved particularly controversial: partly because of the problems in establishing which are the appropriate groups; partly because of the risks of freezing what are multiple and shifting identities into a potentially essentialist category of "women"; partly because of the difficulties in establishing clear lines of accountability from a group to the people who claim to represent it (Phillips 1993, ch. 5.)

514

But even the less controversial (and more widely adopted) practice of gender quotas to guarantee a minimum number of women elected to political office has to be understood as a critique of gender-neutrality. In the conventions of liberal democracy, citizens are encouraged to choose their representatives by virtue of their policies or opinions or beliefs, and if a free and fair process of party competition throws up assemblies that are overwhelmingly composed of men, this will only be noted as an unfortunate fact. When feminists nonetheless argue that the sex of the representatives matters, they are saying that the shared experiences associated with gender are a necessary part of what makes democratic institutions representative (Phillips 1995). If gender parity in politics is to be regarded as a significant goal, this must be because sex is still relevant to democracy.

There is no consensus among feminists on this point. Some have looked to a "sexually differentiated" citizenship that recognizes "two figures; one masculine, one feminine" (Pateman 1988, p. 224). Some have presented feminism as searching "for an understanding of democracy as something to be aimed at *through* difference, not something to be attained via the *removal* of difference" (Mendus 1992, p. 218). Others, meanwhile, have argued for "a new conception of citizenship where sexual difference would become effectively irrelevant" (Mouffe 1992, p. 82). Chantal Mouffe, for example, rejects both the "sexually differentiated" version put forward by Carole Pateman and the "group differentiated" version put forward by Iris Marion Young, and argues that differential treatment is entirely inappropriate at the level of democratic citizenship. When it comes to matters of social policy, it may well be that men and women must be treated differently in order to be treated as equals. But "in the domain of politics, and as far as citizenship is concerned, sexual difference should not be a valid distinction" (1994, p. 82). In similar vein, Mary Dietz (1985, 1987) argues that politics must be seen as a very distinct kind of activity, and she sees democracy as something that transforms "the individual as teacher, trader, corporate executive, child, sibling, worker, artist, friend or mother into a special sort of political being, a citizen among other citizens" (1985, p. 14). In political activity, Dietz argues, human beings should be relating to one another "as equals who render judgement on matters of shared importance, deliberate over issues of common concern, and act in concert with one another" (1985, p. 28). They may not drop all their other identities when they engage in politics, but they should no longer regard these as definitive.

The disagreement is clearly substantial, but is perhaps best understood as a disagreement about how much difference has to be recognized in order to promote the kind of democracy where citizens can engage on "matters of shared importance." Iris Marion Young, for example, shares much of the radical distaste for interest-group bargaining; and her own formulation of the democratic ideal is premised on the transformative effect of having to engage with people who are different, and in the process modify what may be revealed as a biased or partial point of view (Young 1993a). The point she stresses is that this transformation is most likely to happen when people have been exposed to those different interests

515

or experiences or perspectives. Failing the more explicit recognition of sexual (and other kinds of) difference, democratic decision-making will continue to reflect the prejudices and preoccupations of the dominant groups. Unless sex is recognized as one of the salient differences, there will be little chance of achieving a more sexually egalitarian democracy.

Women's values: transforming democratic practice

This remains one area of continuing controversy among feminists – at both theoretical and policy levels. The second area of controversy relates to the modifications that women's experiences and culture can be expected to make to the practices and conventions of democracy. Many have argued that the experiences women have as the carers in society (those primarily responsible for looking after children, those primarily responsible for caring for parents as they grow old) provide a model for a more generous and less conflictual democracy. This has been commonly claimed as part of the case for more women in politics, and it draws on widely held beliefs about women being more at ease than men in intimate relationships, more willing to listen, less insistent on their own selfish interests, more sensitive to personal appeals. When Sara Ruddick (1980) developed her analysis of "maternal thinking," she argued that women could bring to the public world a greater degree of humility, good humor, respect for persons, and responsiveness to growth than has characterized conventional politics. When Kathy Ferguson (1984) developed her feminist case against bureaucracy, she argued that nurturance, empathy, caretaking, and connectedness were built into the very structure of women's experience, and that these provided the basis for alternative forms of organization that do not depend on domination.

None of these arguments, it should be stressed, relies on claims about women's "essential" nature. All that they require is some notion that the different kinds of experience currently associated with being a woman and a man lend themselves to different kinds of values or priorities. But there is still a danger, signalled by a number of feminist writers, that such arguments could end up reinforcing conventional notions of femininity. Kathleen Jones is broadly sympathetic to the notion that women's experiences and values will reshape the priorities and practices of democracy. But she notes that feminists "have not always been careful to disentangle these values from the context of domination that threatens to transform every alternative voice into a new song of self-sacrifice" (1990, p. 794); and that the feminist citizen model could then "validate the idealized image of an all-nurturing, all loving woman even as it rejects the patriarchal system that created that image" (p. 809). In her much stronger critique of "maternal feminism," Mary Dietz (1985) argues that what is a virtue in the private sphere is not necessarily such a virtue in the public, and that the kind of attentive care a mother may give to her vulnerable child should not be viewed as a model for citizens engaging with their political equals. The values associated with female experience may then be of limited relevance to democracy.

516

In contrast to this, Jane Mansbridge (1990, 1993) argues that feminism has a great deal to offer on the issue of democratic community, and that what it offers is grounded in the kind of empathy or connectedness that is so often claimed as a female value. No democracy, she argues, can operate without some ties that bind a community together. Even when people reach agreement on the standard (and rather minimal) formula that "each should count for one and none for more than one," they must be operating with enough sense of community to see that others are entitled to be treated as they wish to be treated themselves. And since democracies cannot consistently deliver even on this strictly procedural fairness (Mansbridge argues that no democracy can be perfectly just), the failures become more acceptable because of the ties of mutual connectedness that enable losers to see winners as part of the same community as themselves. Mainstream theorists of democracy have been slow to recognize this crucial importance of community; hampered by their perception of community or connectedness as "female," they have preferred the tougher language of self-interest or rights.

Mansbridge does not base her argument on any strong claim about the differences between women and men; indeed she notes some fascinating research which suggests that the sexes hardly differ at all in physiological measurements of empathy, like whether the heart beats faster when we hear a baby cry, or whether we sweat when others take a test (1993, pp. 347–8). But when questioned more directly on their degrees of emotional involvement or their sensitivity to others, girls and women score noticeably higher on empathy than do boys and men. What is at issue, Mansbridge suggests, is not so much the *actual* difference of behavior, and more the gender-coding of certain qualities or actions. Within the realm of democratic theory, however, this gender-coding has had a powerful effect. Because it discourages (disparages) the "softer" language of nurturance or emotion, it leaves Anglo-American theory mired in the language of self-interest instead.

Three developments in theorizing democracy

As these examples indicate, theorists differ considerably in their assessment of the specifically feminist contribution to democracy, and the broad agreement that democracies have failed to ensure political equality for women does not translate into any substantial consensus on why this should be so. Despite this, it is possible to identify three major lines of development in current thinking on feminism and democracy. The first is already apparent from Jane Mansbridge's discussion of feminism and democratic community, where she detaches female qualities or values from any strong position on the differences between women and men. Those who stress the importance and validity of sexual difference usually take pains to dissociate themselves from any claims about the "essential" female; they also take pains to dissociate themselves from any stark opposition between claiming equality and asserting sexual difference. For much of the 1980s, feminist scholarship seemed to face an unenviable choice between claiming a strict equality that treated men and women exactly the same, or asserting

517

those distinctive characteristics of women that required differential treatment. This either/or choice is now largely a thing of the past and while feminists continue to argue over the status of gender-neutrality or the precise weight to be attached to sexual difference, their arguments are more commonly along a continuum that recognizes both equality *and* difference. As Carole Pateman has stressed, "the equal political standing of citizenship is necessary for democracy and for women's autonomy," but "(t) his does not mean that all citizens must become (like) men or that all women must be treated in the same way" (1992, p. 29). Equality has been most problematic for feminism when it has been associated with treating people the same, for this tends to set up an abstract norm ("the individual," "the citizen") that disdains anything peculiar to female experience. Once detached from this notion of sameness, however, it should become possible to pursue our equality as citizens while recognizing our differences more adequately.

The second important development is that feminist theorists have positioned themselves firmly in the mainstream of democratic theory, focusing as much on what feminism has to offer the wider theorization of democracy as on how democracies have failed the women. Feminists have contributed extensively, for example, to the recent theorization of deliberative or communicative democracy (e.g. Mansbridge 1990, 1993, Young 1993a, Phillips 1995). Theorists of deliberative democracy criticize the anonymous politics of the ballot box, and highlight the crucial importance of public discussion in arriving at just decisions about common concerns. Feminists have often shared this critique of interest-driven, ballot-box politics, noting that it has never proved itself a particularly satisfactory mechanism for exploring new needs or concerns; and they have have favored a more inclusive and discussion-based democracy that will help transform the political agenda. But feminists have also raised some uncomfortable questions about the notions of the "common good" that often underlie theories of deliberative democracy. Because they "bring a vivid recognition of the capacity of a dominant group to silence or ignore voices it does not wish to hear" (Mansbridge 1990, p. 127), feminist theorists have been particularly attuned to the way that premature appeals to shared interests or common concerns can reinforce existing inequalities in the political process.

Feminists have also contributed to the theorization of democracy in multicultural or multiethnic societies, for they have seen their analysis of equality *through* difference as highly pertinent to any consideration of democracy in heterogeneous societies, and they have often drawn explicit parallels between sexual and other kinds of difference. "Difference," as Susan Mendus (1992, p. 216) notes, "is not going to go away, nor is it something for which those who are different feel disposed to apologize." When feminists have sought to revise democratic ideals to accommodate significant and sustained differences between citizens, the issues they have addressed then relate to some of the most troubled questions in contemporary debate. How are democracies to achieve equality while still respecting difference? Should citizenship be viewed as a matter of universal or differential rights? What is the relationship between the individual, the group, and the nation? Feminist philosophy provides a particularly important resource for addressing these wider questions.

Though these explorations involve substantial revisions to the understanding of liberal democracy, they coincide with a third major development, which Judith Squires (1994, p. 62) describes as a "move within feminist literature on citizenship to recuperate the liberal project." This recuperation is something that feminists share with political theorists of all persuasions, for the collapse of socialist alternatives to liberal democracy has combined with a loss of confidence in more participatory forms of democracy to reestablish liberal democracy as almost the only legitimate variant around. For many feminists, this more general trend has been reinforced by the difficulties women experienced in developing alternative forms of democracy within the framework of the women's movement. Stressing participation "almost to the point of obsession" (Jones 1990, p. 788), women had put their trust in a more direct form of face-to-face democracy; but the preference for informal and non-hierarchical modes of organization often generated exclusive friendship networks that then operated as a barrier to women outside. The subsequent fragmentation of the women's movement, amid acute criticisms of its predominantly white and middle-class membership, exposed the limits of these alternative forms. Feminists became increasingly aware "that applying the logic of intimate relations to the organization of political life is fraught with contradictions" (Jones 1990, p. 787), and many returned with somewhat chastened expectations to the traditions of liberal democracy. A number of recent contributions (e.g. James 1992, Phillips 1993 ch. 6; Mouffe 1992) have then explicitly reformulated the relationship between feminism and the liberal project.

Susan James, for example, argues that there is "more continuity between liberal and feminist conceptions of citizenship than is generally appreciated" (1992, p. 49), and she looks to the as yet unexplored potential in liberal notions of independence as a basis for female citizenship. She does not claim that liberalism has already met feminist concerns: women have been systematically denied independencies that are central to liberal theory; and liberalism has simply taken it for granted that all citizens have the self-esteem they need to speak in a voice of their own. But she sees the analysis of independence as pointing the way "towards a conception of the citizen which is sensitive both to the emotionally dependent relations traditionally associated with women, and to the male norm of impartiality so important to liberalism" (p. 63). The liberalism that was initially regarded as a problem may then provide the necessary tools for reconciling feminism with democracy.

Feminist theorization of democracy has been largely a feature of the 1980s and 1990s, and over this brief period, it has opened up a wide range for future debate. The questions covered include the nature of democratic citizenship, the role and implications of gender-neutrality, the relationship between seeking equality and recognizing difference, and the contribution that female values and experiences may make to the development of a better democracy. There is no unified voice on any of these issues, but this growing area of feminist philosophy promises to make an increasing impact on mainstream theory and practice.

519

52

Socialism

ANN FERGUSON

Definitions

Feminist philosophy is an engaged theoretical enterprise with a critical perspective on any philosophical positions which may perpetuate male dominance. It also seeks a general understanding of what needs to be changed in the social world so as to empower women. According to this general characterization, many socialist thinkers could be counted as feminist philosophers, since they assume that male domination has its roots in systems of private property and believe that empowering women requires constructing socialist alternatives to capitalism. However, for the purposes of this article I will consider only those thinkers who wrote specifically about the relation between women's situation and socialism, thus setting aside writers like Rosa Luxemburg, Simone Weil, and Hannah Arendt, important though they may be for the development of anti-capitalist thought in general.

Socialism as a feminist issue

The three leading demands of the French Revolution (liberty, equality, fraternity) were values developed in the populist religious, peasant, democratic, anti-slavery, workers', and women's rights movements of the early periods of capitalist development. But, from the beginning, "liberty" and "equality" were given different political interpretations, depending on whether the main obstacle was seen as church or aristocratic control of the state (classical liberalism) or the economic class inequalities of the capitalist economy (classical socialism). Nineteenth- and twentieth-century feminist thinkers who emphasized the latter prioritized social equality over individual liberties, since they saw the persistence of male domination as an aspect of the capitalist system. Consequently they developed various anti-capitalist positions, including Marxism, anarchism, and socialist feminism.

Eighteenth-century French anarcho-socialists Proudhon, Fourier, and Saint-Simon drew parallels between private ownership of land and productive capital and male ownership of women in patriarchal systems of marriage. Such ideas were popularized in radical circles of nineteenth-century popular movements in England, France, Germany, and the United States (for the feminist thinkers and speakers of these popular movements, see Taylor 1983, and Rowbotham 1992).

Although the eighteenth-century discussions foreshadowed questions concerning the possibility and nature of connections between feminism and socialism, it was really the development of industrial capitalism in the nineteenth and twentieth centuries, as well as the Russian and Chinese socialist revolutions, that provided the material and political conditions for a number of theoretical disagreements about these connections to surface. One disagreement was reflected in the split between Marxism and anarchism regarding the role of the state and vanguard party in the process of revolution (for a classic anarcho-feminist position, see Goldman 1972; for Rosa Luxemburg's mass strike politics, see Luxemburg 1986; for a general summary of this debate, see Albert and Hahnel 1978). Engels's critique of utopian socialism (Engels 1978) implied that the feminist focus in grassroots workers' movements was utopian thinking in the bad sense, i.e. impractical. Contemporary feminist anarcho-socialists, however, argue that a revolutionary process for social equality must be *prefigurative*, that is, radical movements must show forth egalitarian relationships in their leadership, membership, and organizational practices (cf. Rowbotham et al. 1979, Taylor 1983, Addelson, 1991b).

Another major disagreement continues on reform versus revolution. Marxists and anarchists opposed reform rather than overthrow of the capitalist system, and feminists were also divided on this issue. Reformers included, in England, the Fabian socialists, the Webbs, 1969; and in the United States, Gilman (1966) and Eastman (1978). Revolutionaries included, in Europe and Russia, Rosa Luxemburg, Clara Zetkin and Alexandra Kollontai (1927, 1971a, 1971b, 1972a, 1972b, 1975, 1977), and in the United States Emma Goldman (1972). This disagreement continues today in feminism in divisions between liberal feminists (reformers) on the one hand versus radical and socialist-feminists on the other.

A third important disagreement of continuing interest involves questions about the origins of patriarchy. Although most anticapitalist feminists reject the liberal theory that it is due to outmoded precapitalist traditions (cf. Mill and Taylor 1970), contemporary radical, anarchist, and socialist feminists disagree as to whether to support the Marxist theory that it originates in systems of private property (cf. Engels 1972, Bebel 1910, Marx et al. 1951), or whether patriarchy is a semi-autonomous or more overarching domination system that may underlie class-based systems of private property (Beauvoir 1952, Firestone 1970, Mitchell 1974, Rubin 1975, Barrett 1980, Coward 1983, Delphy 1984, Lerner 1986, Folbre 1987, 1994, Ferguson 1989, Walby 1990). Sometimes patriarchy is itself seen to be a mode of production where elder men control the labor of women and children (cf. Hartmann 1981a, Folbre 1987, Courville 1993).

A split also occurred between autonomous liberal or bourgeois women's movements who organized to demand women's suffrage, and working-class women leaders who maintained that workers' rights against capitalist owners should take priority (cf. Lenin 1934, Kraditor 1965, Flexner 1972, Rowbotham 1973a, Davis 1981b). Socialist women leaders who supported this latter position defended Engels's and Bebel's view that women's liberation required bringing women into public industry as full equals to men and the socialization of women's private unpaid housework and child care in the home, something that would not be profitable to capitalists. Other early twentieth-century anticapitalist analyses included those of Emma Goldman (1972), who claimed that prostitution was the obverse side of bourgeois marriage, and defended free love as essential to women's liberation, while she and Margaret Sanger (1920) denounced the prohibition of birth control by the capitalist state. Socialist feminists Charlotte Perkins Gilman (1966) and Crystal Eastman (1978) critiqued patriarchal marriage and unpaid housework which made women economically dependent on men, although Gilman's own solutions – socialism, communal kitchens, and paid services to eliminate housework – seemed utopian to many urban US working-class women (cf. Kraditor 1965, Hartmann 1981a, Hayden 1985). Disagreements about how much to prioritize the fight against capitalism as a means to women's liberation reemerged in the second-wave women's movements of the 1960s and 1970s in the United States and Europe (Jenness 1972).

Socialist revolutions and the "Woman Question"

The three major socialist revolutions of the twentieth century, in Russia, China, and Cuba, were Marxist-inspired. Although attention was paid to socialism as the precondition for women's liberation, and both Russian and Chinese revolutions involved massive mobilizations of women peasants and workers, many have critiqued such revolutions as being inadequate both in theory and practice to overturn entrenched male-domination relations.

Alexandra Kollontai was a brilliant socialist feminist thinker and organizer in the Russian Bolshevik party who wrote both essays and works of fiction advocating the need to challenge patriarchal marriage and sexual double standards in the process of building a socialist revolution that would eliminate male dominance (for her essays, cf. Kollontai 1971b, 1972a, 1972b, 1975, 1977; for works of fiction dealing with communal living and feminist free-love experimentation, cf. Kollontai 1927, 1971a). Although Kollontai was able to engineer many radical legal and social reforms in the initial stages of the Russian revolution – communal and factory kitchens, the legalization of abortion and homosexuality, the elimination of the concept of illegitimate children and the equalization of marriage, divorce, and alimony laws, such reforms were later scaled back by Stalin, and Kollontai lost her leadership position.

Although there was no feminist leadership as prominent as Kollontai's in the Chinese, Cuban, or East European revolutions, a similar process of initial reforms benefiting women and later backsliding occurred there. This led many theorists to speculate as to whether the persistence of patriarchy in state socialist systems was due to material or cultural backwardness, patriarchal reorganization of state economic priorities, sexual repression, or other patriarchal character traits (cf. Reich 1970, 1974, Mitchell 1990, 1974, Scott 1974, Weinbaum 1978, Croll 1978, Stacey 1983, Kruks et al. 1989). More recently, the institutionalization of socialist feminism in the academy in the United States, the collapse of the Soviet Union and the fall of East European socialist countries has led some hitherto identifying as "socialist feminists" to eschew this label and argue instead for "radical democracy" (cf. Philipson 1985, Laclau and Mouffe 1985, Eisenstein 1990).

Socialism in second-wave European and US women's movements

Rise of autonomous women's movements out of New Left movements in the 1960s

The importance of socialist ideas in recent Western feminist philosophy and theory stems from the influence of autonomous women's movements arising out of the other social movements of the 1960s in Europe and the United States, including the Vietnam antiwar movement, the black and other minority civil rights movements in the United States and the student movement. During this period, Marxist thought was revived, in part as an effort to understand French and US imperialism in Vietnam. Subsequently many antiwar activists turned Marxist theory toward understanding the structures of racism and sexism in capitalist systems as well. But the emphasis on decentralization and participatory democracy characteristic of these movements produced an impatience with the sectarian vanguard party Marxist position, which prioritizes the fight against capitalism and downplays divisions around racism and sexism in the interest of a unified front. Instead, there was an emphasis on *prefigurative politics*, that is, that participatory democratic movements must present their visions in their actions and modes of life, and egalitarian ends or goals do not justify the tolerance of inegalitarian means. Thus "unite and fight" slogans which do not prioritize the challenging of racism, sexism, class privilege, heterosexism, etc., are not acceptable.

Socialist and anarchist visions of the 1960s and 1970s

One of the most interesting intellectual developments of autonomous women's movements in the United States and Europe in the 1960s and 1970s was a proliferation of theory and visions of androgyny. Androgyny is the view that all humans have the underlying potential to develop both traits thought of as masculine and those thought of as feminine, although feminists maintain this does not typically occur because male dominance socially constructs gender-differentiated traits. Though androgyny as a vision did not necessarily connect to the need for socialism, some feminist thinkers explicitly made these connections (cf. Firestone 1970, Dworkin 1974, Ferguson 1977, Piercy 1979, Vetterling-Braggin 1982).

Although her version of socialist-feminism did not achieve popularity when first published in 1915, Gilman's utopian novel *Herland*, which described a socialist society consisting only of women, was republished in 1966 (cf. Gilman 1966) and became popular with the utopian radical and socialist-feminist thinking of the second-wave 1970s US women's movement, where a

523

form of lesbian-feminist separatism which envisaged anarcho-socialism for women only flourished (e.g. Wittig 1971, Gearhart 1979). Some radical feminists rejected the ideal concept of androgyny because they regarded it as being coopted by heterosexual liberal feminists who wanted to downplay the connections between structural sexism and heterosexism (Raymond 1979, Daly 1978).

Attempts to create economic models of socialism which emphasize participatory democracy, thus avoiding the problems of the top-down hierarchically run Soviet-style economy (sometimes called "command" socialism), began in the 1970s and have continued to the present day. Anarchist feminists critiqued the hierarchical organizing processes assumed necessary by male radical thinkers (cf. Rowbotham et al. 1979, Addelson 1994a). Some were concerned to develop models of democratic socialism which involved workers' (not vanguard party) management and participatory democracy (Pateman 1970). In my books (Ferguson 1989, 1991b) I defend Albert and Hahnel's council socialism (cf. Albert and Hahnel 1978, 1981, 1991). We express the concerns of the US New Left, black civil rights and women's movements regarding the dangers of statism which inhibits participatory democracy, sexism based in a sexual division of labor which benefits men, and racism based on racial segregation and white community control of greater economic resources. The "council" socialist model advocates a planned but decentralized economy based on participatory democracy rather than command socialism or market socialism, the model operative in the former Yugoslavia and in the city of Mondragón, Spain (for how to challenge the sexual division of labor in a council socialist model, cf. Ferguson 1989, 1991b; for a defense of market socialism, cf. Schweickart 1993).

Socialist feminists have also challenged classical liberal and socialist paradigms of the ideal society in other ways. Iris Young (1990a) proposes the reworking of the concept of justice as a democratic process value. A complementary approach is favored by Carol Gould, who develops the values of democracy and reciprocity, requiring a democratic socialism, as key to justice (Gould 1988). Joan Tronto has argued we need a public policy based not merely on securing rights but on a general ethic of care, and Nancy Fraser has suggested that we resist the power/knowledges characteristic of the capitalist welfare state by a radical democratic politics of need interpretation (cf. Fraser 1989a, Tronto 1993, and also Article 14, LANGUAGE AND POWER). Ecological feminists suggest that Western thought with its subject/object, mind/body, society/nature splits has alienated us from a more holistic relation to nature and each other, thus harking back to the early Marx (cf. Marx 1964, Mies 1986, Shiva 1989, and Article 21, THE ENVIRONMENT).

Theoretical relations between Marxism, radical feminism and socialist feminism in the 1970s and 1980s

Many women theorists who had been led to anticapitalist perspectives by their participation in social movements sought to expand the available Marxist paradigms of social domination relations with a deeper explanation of the persistence

524

of male domination, not only in capitalist countries but also in existing state socialist societies. In one way or another, such theorists sought to modify the predominant Marxist base/superstructure model which posits that mainstream economic relations are the underlying root cause of all other social relations, e.g. in the church, family, legal and political institutions (for a general comparison of the 1970s feminist theoretical tendencies, cf. Jaggar 1983, Tong 1988).

In the 1970s a dynamic relation existed between radical feminism and Marxist feminism. Radical feminism is a tendency which began in the United States as anticapitalist (cf. Firestone 1970) and increasingly developed the view that patriarchal relations were the original cause of capitalist and other relations of social domination (Myron and Bunch 1974, Daly 1978, Rich 1980, Hartsock 1985). An influential radical feminist was Mary O'Brien (1981), who argues that the differences between men and women in biological reproduction creates male alienation from life continuity, with children retained by women who find it easier to identify with children and natural processes. This reproductive difference motivates men to control women by initiating public spheres of culture, state, and economy which they dominate, thus establishing patriarchy. In the process they also set up systems of private property which they control and relegate women to the private sphere of the household and nature. O'Brien sees possibilities for change through a dialectic between the spheres of production and reproduction in which birth-control techniques, allowing more reciprocity between men and women, will also create the material conditions for the overthrow of both capitalism and patriarchy and the overcoming of human alienation from nature.

Later work by radical feminist Catharine MacKinnon does not explore the origins or historical background of patriarchy, but maintains that the contemporary social construction of gender, in compulsory heterosexuality in the family and in media construction of sexuality such as pornography, is more important than capitalist social relations as the underlying cause of all domination relations (MacKinnon 1982, 1983, 1987b, 1989).

In France an anticapitalist radical feminism initially developed as a critique of Freudian and Lévi-Straussian fatalism, although it agreed with them that women have been treated as objects of exchange between men rather than subjects in their own right (cf. Irigaray 1985b, Wittig 1992). In Germany the work of Maria Mies (1986) provides another interesting example of the tendency to make patriarchy the basic form of exploitation on which capitalism is parasitic. Like Rosa Luxemburg in *The Accumulation of Capital* (Luxemburg 1951, cf. also Dunayevskaya 1991), Mies argues that capitalism must start with capital appropriated from non-capitalist systems of exploitation, but unlike Luxemburg contends that patriarchy was the first such system. Work by Indian Vandana Shiva draws dire ecological implications from the economic "maldevelopment" she argues is a destructive effect of capitalist patriarchy (Shiva 1989). Gerda Lerner also argues that patriarchy is the first exploitative labor system, claiming that women were the first slaves, appropriated in battle by one tribe from another (cf. Lerner 1986).

525

Unlike radical feminists, Marxist feminists posit a unitary system consisting of a dominant mode of private property relations, such as capitalism, which controls all other social relations for its own purposes. Thus, patriarchy and other social domination systems such as racism and heterosexism function as means to reproduce private property relations.

There are a number of alternative Marxist feminist models. First is an Althusserian model which rejects a monocausal model of social causality. Rather, social relations occur on different social levels, each of which have their own causal effectivity not reducible to their economic function. Feminist Althusserians view patriarchy as a lived ideology perpetuated by *gender roles*, or socially constructed relations between men and women. Most would agree with the influential view of Juliet Mitchell (1972) that these are developed in the interconnecting spheres of production, reproduction, socialization, and sexuality, and many would place the family as the central site for these spheres (cf. Barrett 1980, Barrett and McIntosh 1982). Most Althusserian feminist theorists adapted a feminist interpretation of Freud's analysis of gender development (Kuhn and Wolpe 1978, Chodorow 1978, 1979, Mitchell 1972, 1974).

A second Marxist feminist model is based on Marxist "social formation" theory. On this view, the economy of any particular nation-state is not a factor of only one set of economic relationships, but can contain a number of different economic spheres or institutions in which economic exchanges operate according to different principles and which privilege certain social groups over others. On this model, Margaret Benston and Sheila Rowbotham posit that the unpaid work in the family-household assigned to women, "housework," is a feudal mode of economic production which, as a subordinate mode of production in a mainstream capitalist economic system, perpetuates women's oppression (cf. Benston 1969, Rowbotham 1973a, Dalla Costa 1974).

A third kind of Marxist feminism posits some sort of Hegelian synthesis in a social system in which all parts are equally important. One such view is that patriarchy is lodged in the reproductive relations of capitalism ignored by classic Marxism which concentrates mostly on production relations (Vogel 1983, Foreman 1977). Another version of the functional interactive system view is that early espoused by Iris Young in a critique of "dual systems" socialist feminism theory (discussed below), in which she argues that the sexual division of labor creates an integrated capitalist patriarchy (Young 1981).

Finally, an important position, not initially different from Althusserian feminism, now calls itself "materialist feminism" and has been adopted by feminists who favor Marxist-oriented discourse theory and postmodernist approaches. They posit an ideological or discursive realm, thought to have its own "material" effectivity, and seek a rapprochement between Althusser and Foucault on the connection between discourses and other disciplinary practices (cf. Barrett 1980, Barrett and McIntosh 1982, Barrett and Phillips eds., 1992, Landry and MacLean 1993, Hennessy 1993). Such positions straddle the fence between Marxist feminism and socialist feminism, as I will discuss below.

The distinction between Marxist and socialist feminism is a rather subtle one which developed in the United States in the 1970s but not so clearly in England and Europe. That this distinction was emphasized in the United States may be due to the American autonomous left feminist tendency at that time, which had appropriated elements of both radical and Marxist feminism yet was suspicious of the reductionist tendencies of both. US socialist feminism defines itself in opposition to a separatist radical feminism on the one hand and an integrationist Marxism on the other: it assumes that capitalism and patriarchy are equally basic, thus denying that one is the root or the historically moving cause of the other (cf. Chicago Women's Liberation Union 1973). Sometimes socialist feminist positions advocate a "dual systems" or "multi-systems" approach, in which they see capitalism and patriarchy, and sometimes racism, as autonomous systems of social power which sometimes support each other and sometimes come into conflict or undermine each other.

There are two types of dual systems theory. One is Juliet Mitchell's psychoanalytic Marxist feminism which assumes that forms of symbolic gender are universal in the patriarchal family structure characteristic of economic systems of private property. In other words, the foundations of patriarchy are relatively static and unchanging (Mitchell 1972, 1974). This contrasts with the historically dynamic socialist feminist dual systems theory of Gayle Rubin (1975). Rubin puts further emphasis on the relative independence of what she calls "the sex/gender system," or the social arrangements which transform biological sexuality into gender norms and practices. Succeeding socialist feminists influenced by Rubin, including myself, assume that there are historically different "modes of sex/gender" or "patriarchal sex/affective production" in which there may be conflicts between the prevalent form of material patriarchal control and economic systems of domination (cf. Ferguson 1989, 1991b). This type of historical feminist materialism posits two different material bases for patriarchy, class-based modes of economic production, on the one hand, and gender-based modes of sexual and kinship production, on the other.

Although Rubin develops the radical feminist concept of compulsory or "obligatory heterosexuality" as an analytic category of male dominant connection between gender identity, sexual identity, and sexual and kinship practices in a way that Adrienne Rich's radical feminist formulation of compulsory heterosexuality (Rich 1980) tends to foreclose, Weinbaum (1978) offers an original and historicized Freudian reading of male revolutionary leaders who initially oppose the patriarchs of the ruling classes with their revolutionary "sisters," but upon assuming state power and the position of patriarchs themselves, act to demote women's status to subordinate wives by, for example, subordinating women's organizations to vanguard party male leadership.

Heidi Hartmann gives an influential development of Rubin's position in a way that highlights the possibilities for tension between patriarchal family relations in the sex/gender system and capitalism. This tension, she argues, was resolved in the late nineteenth century by the compromise made between male trade unionists and male capitalists to institute the "family wage" which could allow a male union member to pay for the living costs of wife and children without these family members having to themselves work in wage labor, thus preserving male privilege to unpaid women's work in the family (Hartmann 1981a, 1981b). Sylvia Walby (1986, 1990) and I extend this type of historical reading of tensions between patriarchy and capital to sketch out paradigms of differently articulated patriarchal relations such as father patriarchy, husband patriarchy, and public patriarchy (cf. Brown 1981, Ferguson and Folbre 1981, Ferguson 1989, 1991b, Folbre 1994.) Another dual systems theory which is not so historically positioned is that of Christine Delphy, who argues that women's unremunerated household work perpetuates male privilege even after divorce, since mothers continue to do the bulk of the child care (Delphy 1981, 1984). Carole Pateman's theory of the sexual contract (in patriarchal marriage systems) is a type of dual systems theory. She shows that the classic liberal authors of social contract theory see marriage as analogous to a slave contract between men and women, since the former are natural superiors and the latter inferiors. Patriarchal interests create the modern theory of separation of the public or social space of contracts between equals from the private space of the household, where natural inequalities preclude contracts between free individuals (Pateman 1988).

Racism, difference and postmodernism

One of the problems of early 1980s socialist feminist theories is the failure to locate race and racism in any systematic way within their models (cf. Joseph 1981, Joseph and Lewis 1981, hooks 1984, Spelman 1988, and Article 48, RACISM). Contemporary postmodernist theories of sexuality such as queer theory have similarly faulted theories of male dominance based on binary gender structures for being essentialist (cf. Articles 31, SEXUALITY and 8, POSTMODERNISM). Many socialist feminists have responded either by becoming multi-systems theorists (hooks 1984, Ferguson 1991b, Collins 1990, Folbre 1994, Eisenstein 1994, the authors in James and Busia 1993) or by rejecting the modernist theory-making enterprise in favor of a postmodern and contextual approach (cf. Haraway 1989, 1991b, 1991d, Fraser and Nicholson 1990, and Article 8, POSTMODERNISM).

The failure of dual-systems socialist feminist theory to give equal theoretical importance to race spawned the theoretical tendency which calls itself "materialist feminism." Proponents accept aspects of the structuralism of earlier Marxist feminist theory, but subject it to a poststructuralist critique which problematizes the role of theorists themselves in the construction of binary positing power/ knowledges which also cede authors epistemic authority (Hennessy 1993, Spivak 1987a, 1990, Mohanty 1984, Barrett and Phillips 1992, Landry and MacLean 1993).

It is true that earlier formulations of dual-systems socialist feminism went so far as to claim that women constitute a sex class across race and economic class because of the patriarchal production of gender, sexuality, and parenthood (cf.

528

Eisenstein 1979, Ferguson 1989, 1991b). Clearly all such dual-systems approaches were too simplistic in their failure to theorize racism as a material form of domination on a par with patriarchy and capitalism (or other class-based modes of production). However, it could be argued that contemporary multi-systems socialist feminist theories are no longer at a disadvantage in comparision with materialist feminist positions on race, since both approaches now see it as a historically central division of women through systems of racial privilege and oppression. The difference is in theoretical strategy: materialist feminists handle race through the poststructuralist and postmodernist strategy of problematizing white theorists' power knowledge positions which ignore or trivialize race, while multi-systems theorists present a historical argument for the existence of different racial formations which provide a changing material base for racism (cf. Hennessy 1993, Landry and MacLean 1993, hooks 1990, for materialist feminism: for multi-systems theory, cf. Ferguson 1991b, Young 1990b, Collins 1990, Brewer 1993, Courville 1993, Steady 1993, Omi and Winant 1994, Folbre 1994).

The fall of Eastern European state socialist systems beginning in 1989, women's differences across race, class, sexuality, and nationality, and the postmodern critique of modernist theorizing have all weakened socialist feminism as a theoretical tendency. Many former socialist feminists have become postmodernists who argue that general concepts such as "capitalism", "socialism," or "patriarchy" obfuscate the particular relation to historical context of the thinkers who use them (Nicholson 1986, Nicholson and Fraser 1990, and cf. Article 8, POSTMODERNISM). Some, like Gayatri Spivak, Chandra Mohanty, and Rey Chow, retain the analytical categories of Marxism to explain global capitalist development but use deconstructive approaches to problematize Western feminist, as well as Third World nationalist generalizations (Spivak 1987a, 1987b, 1988, Mohanty 1984, 1991, Chow 1991, 1992). Others, such as Zillah Eisenstein and Chantal Mouffe, prefer to defend the concept of radical democracy rather than to take on the baggage associated with the word "socialism" (cf. Laclau and Mouffe 1985, Philipson 1985, Eisenstein 1990). But I and others would argue that our project should still be to defend a democratic feminist socialism as an ideal toward which we can work (Ferguson 1991b). New theoretical coalitions are emerging between old and new feminist critics of capitalism which promise to change some of the key terms of the debate in the future.

53

Anglo-American law

KATHARINE T. BARTLETT

Feminist jurisprudence is less a body of thought than a family of different perspectives or frameworks used to analyze the actual, and the desirable, relationship between law and gender. These frameworks are not mutually exclusive. Theorists work across their permeable boundaries, which cannot fully discipline the various modes of analysis in this maturing field. They provide a necessary, simplifying structure, however, for managing common themes and important points of divergence.

Formal equality

Formal equality is the familiar principle that individuals who are alike should be treated alike, according to their actual characteristics rather than stereotyped assumptions made about them. The principle can be applied either to single individuals, whose right to be treated on their own merits can be viewed as a right of individual autonomy, or to groups, whose members seek the same treatment as members of other, similarly situated groups. What makes an issue one of *formal* equality is that the claim is limited to treatment in relation to another, similarly situated individual or group and does not extend to demands for some particular, *substantive* treatment.

The explosion of legal reform on behalf of women begun in the 1970s was guided largely by the formal equality model. Landmark Supreme Court decisions, as well as legislation in the areas of employment, education, credit, and the family, presupposed the similarities between men and women and the desirability of treating them by the same rules. The approach has been as used as much against rules and practices that appear to favor women, as against those that discriminate against them, for the premise of formal equality is that even "benign" treatment for women sets them apart from men and hence perpetuates the attitudes that keep them unequal (Williams 1982, 1985). Most legal scholars continue to use empirical methods associated with formal equality, as they examine the factual assumptions of sex-based rules, expose the stereotypes on which they are based, and question the legitimacy of their purposes – all with a view toward eliminating rules that treat women differently from men. As most explicit forms of sex discrimination have been eliminated, these methods have been pushed to reveal how more subtle and apparently neutral practices, such as dress and appearance codes and personality qualifications in the workplace, interact with stereotypes and expectations about women to disadvantage their employment opportunities (Chamallas 1990, Bartlett 1994).

Formal equality faces its biggest challenge in rules and practices based on differences between men and women. Some scholars, as discussed in greater detail below, urge measures to overcome the disadvantages women experience as a result of these differences. Mandatory job security for pregnant women who leave work to bear children is one example. Formal equality adherents oppose such "special" measures, on the grounds that differences between men and women are too easily exaggerated and rarely justify the consequences – harmful or corrective – that are attached to them. They point to the similarity between arguments used to justify special accommodations for women and nineteenth-century arguments used to keep women out of certain jobs and to "protect" them from long hours, immoral influence, and damage to their reproductive capacity. To avoid the same trap, formal equality advocates urge the strategy of minimizing women's differences, rather than calling attention to them. Thus, they compare pregnancy with disabilities that men also experience, and insist it be treated no worse, or no better. Likewise, they urge that average differences in physical strength, size, and speed, as well as differences in temperament, propensity for violence, and job preferences be disregarded. Women should be treated as individuals, competing – an increasing number of them successfully – on the same terms as individual men rather than as members of a group needing special protection. Such an approach may have short-term disadvantages for women, formal advocates concede, but in the long run it has the greatest capacity to bring about enduring change (Williams 1982, 1985).

Substantive equality

While formal equality judges the form of a rule, requiring that it treat women and men on the same terms without special barriers or favors due to their sex, substantive equality looks to a rule's results or effects. Its critique of formal equality is that, as a result of current societal conditions and sex-based differences, equal treatment results in unequal outcomes. Advocates of substantive equality demand that rules take account of these conditions and differences to avoid unfair, gender-related outcomes (Becker 1988). Just what differences should be recognized and how they should be taken into account, however, is a matter of considerable debate. The different possibilities have resulted in several, overlapping versions of the theory, reflecting different substantive goals.

One version of substantive equality focuses on remedying the effects of past discrimination. Women historically have been excluded, either by law or by societal gender role expectations, from having certain jobs or earning wages comparable to those earned by men. "Affirmative action" designed to boost women into occupational fields dominated historically by men (Law 1989, Schultz 1990), overhaul of the system for compensating part-time workers to do away with structural bias against those whose worker profiles do not correspond with the full-time, working male norm (Chamallas 1986), and "comparable worth" schemes designed to restructure wage scales to eliminate the effects of past patterns of gender-based job segregation and revalue "women's work" (Rhode 1988) are examples of remedial measures designed to reverse the effects of past discrimination.

Another type of substantive equality focuses on eliminating the effects of biological differences between men and women. Several theorists accept the basic premises of formal equality but argue for narrow accommodations to women's unique childbearing functions (e.g. Law 1984, Kay 1985). Others press the substantive equality approach for accommodations to women's smaller average size and lesser average strength, such as alterations in the assembly line or lighter equipment (Littleton 1987).

As confounding for equality analysis as biological differences are differences associated with social and cultural forces, affecting such matters as women's style of interpersonal relationships and their employment, educational, and family role preferences. Some theorists emphasize measures to alter social expectations and practices that steer women into lower-paying occupational categories, encourage their economic dependence on men, and lead them to be the primary caretakers of children. Vicki Schultz (1990), for example, argues that employers should be required to undertake initiatives designed to make previously male-dominated job categories seem appealing to women. Christine Littleton (1987) takes a more radical tack, seeking to change not women, but rather the society that penalizes them for engaging in "socially female" activities. Littleton reveals the severity of the penalty when she theorizes a society dedicated to equalizing the costs of engaging in socially female and socially male activities. It is a society that would assure, for example, that mothers who raise society's children are compensated as much as the fathers who fight society's wars, or that female executives who cry at business meetings be treated the same as men who show their tempers.

Substantive equality seeks equal outcomes, but not necessarily identical or even mirror-image ones. Thus, for example, advocates seek access for women to men's athletic teams, private clubs and colleges, while at the same time arguing that women also need separate teams, clubs, and colleges to meet their special needs (e.g. Rhode 1986). In family law, substantive equality theorists support the elimination of rules that give husbands power to control the property of their wives, but favor custody standards that take special account of women's disproportionate investment in childrearing (e.g. Fineman 1989, Becker 1992), as well as standards for property division and alimony at divorce that are more likely to eliminate society-wide disadvantages faced by women than current gender-neutral rules currently do (Fineman 1991). In each instance, the argument is not that women should be entitled to whatever is most favorable to them but that, depending on the circumstances, equality sometimes requires that affirmative measures be taken to undo men's current structural advantages.

Substantive equality theorists contend that formal equality advocates mistake the ideal for the real (McCloud 1986). This charge highlights the basic strategic disagreements between the two camps: Is pretending women are the same as men a self-fulfilling prophecy, or blind naiveté? Does the correction of unequal outcomes reinforce the underlying inequalities, or eliminate them? Is equality best advanced by focusing on long-term ideals, or on current realities?

Nonsubordination

The nonsubordination perspective shifts the focus of attention from gender-based difference to the imbalance of power between women and men. This perspective, also known as dominance theory, does not focus on how to treat differences between women and men; indeed, from the nonsubordination perspective this focus is flawed in that it treats differences as inevitable givens. Instead, differences should be viewed as man-made social constructs designed to justify men's power and make women's subordination seem natural and legitimate. The focus of nonsubordination theory is on demystifying these and other constructs of male domination, so that they might be dismantled.

Nonsubordination theory bears a complex relationship to equality theory. Catharine MacKinnon, its original and most significant proponent, has strongly criticized both formal and substantive equality approaches on the grounds that each approach maintains men as the reference point – the basic norm – to which women are compared (MacKinnon 1987b, pp. 34–6). As a result, women's equality interest is limited to that which men have already defined for their own needs, and does not extend to what women require. At the same time, MacKinnon's principal work in the areas of sexual harassment and pornography demonstrates how purportedly neutral practices and legal concepts operate as forms of sexual discrimination which disadvantage, or "subordinate," women in relation to men. Thus, even as MacKinnon presents equality theory as a tool furthering women's subordination, subordination theory retains a comparative framework within which men's and women's situations are described in relation to one another.

A major contribution of nonsubordination theory to feminist method is its emphasis on women's account of their own experiences, both as a challenge to conventional understandings of objectivity and as a source of truth. According to MacKinnon, conventional understandings of objectivity disguise as point-of-view-lessness what is actually a male point of view (MacKinnon 1983, pp. 636–9). The turn to women's experience, or "consciousness-raising," to expose this disguise (MacKinnon 1982, pp. 535–7) has generated considerable interest in, and use of, narrative as a method of loosening settled understandings of what is objective and fair.

The outlines of MacKinnon's dominance theory were first established in her work on sexual harassment, in which she establishes that sexually predatory conduct, long accepted as the normal give and take between men and women in the workplace, constitutes a form of sex discrimination. According to her analysis, such conduct systematically demeans women as sexual objects, and thereby reinforces male control and power (MacKinnon 1979). The theory that sexual harassment is a form of harassment was eventually recognized by the courts, in decisions that increasingly have recognized that conduct is not acceptable merely because it has long been accepted. A number of legal scholars demonstrate, using MacKinnon's basic insights about the invisible presence of the male perspective in "objective" legal standards, how questions about whether conduct alleged to be harassment is unwelcome or sufficiently pervasive are predetermined by prevailing gender-role expectations based on male dominance and female submission. For example, women who wear short skirts and make-up are assumed to find repeated sexual propositions at work welcome, even as women considered unattractive are also thought to welcome sexual attention, or else to be incapable of attracting it and thus not credible victims. Meanwhile, those whose method of survival in a sexualized workplace is to play along with the sexual banter, or who initially shrug off harassing behavior as "not that big a deal" are viewed as conceding that the behavior was not sufficiently severe or pervasive to constitute harassment (Estrich 1991, Abrams 1989).

The most controversial application of MacKinnon's dominance theory is the contention that pornography constitutes discrimination based on sex. According to MacKinnon, pornography defines women in terms of their sexual use (and abuse) and constructs sexuality in terms of women's objectification for men's sexual pleasure. In eroticizing sexual violence against women, along with the submission, pain, and humiliation it produces, pornography systematically lowers inhibitions on aggression against women, increases the acceptance of women's sexual servitude, and silences women who might wish to define themselves, and sexuality, in terms other than male dominance and female submission. Law, as always, plays a complicit role. Laws that prohibit the most excessive or "obscene" material in fact legitimize and thus reinforce the power of the remainder. Courts have held that the First Amendment protects pornography as "free speech" and that the appropriate remedy for harmful speech is counter-speech. MacKinnon responds that this remedy is illusory because pornography silences women, defining them as sexual objects who could have nothing to say that is worth listening to. Indeed, she argues that the pretense that women are free to define themselves only strengthens the appearance of neutrality and thus, ultimately, the non-neutral way in which those in power use words and images to maintain existing hierarchies (MacKinnon 1987b, 1990).

Some theorists, while not rejecting nonsubordination theory altogether, have resisted firmly MacKinnon's position on pornography and free speech. Nan Hunter and Sylvia Law (1987/88) argue that the legal prohibition of pornography reinforces sexist stereotypes about men as "irresponsible beasts, with 'natural physiological responses' which can be triggered by sexually explicit images of women, and for which the men cannot be held accountable," and sexist stereotypes about women such as that they are incapable of consent and that "'good' women do not seek and enjoy sex" (pp. 127, 129). Mary Dunlap (1987) stresses that society needs more, not less, sexually explicit expression, in order to address issues of child and other forms of sexual abuse, AIDS and other sexually-transmitted diseases, and the improvement of all forms of consensual, intimate relationships. Jeanne Schroeder (1992) argues that MacKinnon's theory of

534

pornography, by assuming that (1) men are free subjects who use pornography to construct and impose their views of sexuality on women; and (2) women are involuntary actors who lack subjectivity, is a "constant reaffirmation" of male power and an "unending rewriting of the myth of male subjectivity" (pp. 179–80).

Nonsubordination theorists also fit rape and domestic violence into the totalizing, self-reinforcing scheme of male dominance. Just as the First Amendment protects pornographic constructions of women as sexual objects for men's pleasure, the law of rape and domestic violence shields men who physically abuse women. Susan Estrich demonstrates how various evidentiary rules reflect notions of consent, resistance, and self-defense that are more characteristic of men's responses to danger than women's (Estrich 1987b). Others stress how women's accounts of rape are often undermined at trial by stylized descriptions of the sexual encounter (Maguigan, 1991, Scheppele 1992) or interpreted as motivated by fantasy or revenge, suggesting the conclusion that women invite their own abuse (Henderson 1987, Torrey 1991). In the domestic violence context, feminist writing draws attention to the need for law to understand the responses of battered women on their own terms, including why they may stay with their batterers well beyond the point of "reason," and why when they finally act to protect themselves it may be in circumstances in which they do not appear to be immediately threatened (Mahoney 1991, Schneider 1992). It also highlights how, as a result of women's subordination to men, certain procedural reforms in the law that would appear to be woman-friendly, such as divorce mediation, reinforce the risks of standing up to abuse (Grillo 1991). By examining women's victimization through the nonsubordination theory lens, these writers frame abused women's situations not simply as individual problems, but as a part of the overall institutional oppression of women. The institutionalization of oppression is facilitated in many ways, among them the dichotomization between the public and the private, which justifies the law's protection of strangers from one another in public, while shielding "private" violence that harms mainly female victims (Taub and Schneider 1982, Schneider 1993).

While these critiques highlight the absence of a universal perspective from which the law might issue just and objective rules relating to rape and domestic violence, they also lead to concerns among scholars about the extent to which the critiques themselves universalize the experience of women, thereby undermining the accounts of women who do not fit either the law's, or law reformers', preestablished scripts. As victims who cannot control their own fates, for example, they appear in court as poor candidates for custody of their children (Mahoney 1991, Cahn 1991). Moreover, women who fit the victim profile featured in nonsubordination analysis may attain credibility at the expense of those who do not (Schneider 1992, Dowd 1992). From these concerns emerge more textured work demonstrating, on the one hand, multiple and overlapping forms of subordination and demonstrating, on the other hand, how victims of abuse may retain aspects of their agency (Mahoney 1991, Schneider 1992, Abrams 1995a).

Another application of nonsubordination theory concerns discrimination against homosexuals. Several scholars argue that laws that deny homosexuals the opportunity to marry, be parents, and enjoy other benefits available to conventional family units are a form of sex discrimination because they are an integral part of the same fixed heterosexual norms that subordinate women to men (e.g. Law 1988, Koppelman 1994). The reluctance to extend to homosexuals the protection of laws banning sexual harassment in the workplace is explained in the same way (Abrams 1994). Further work on the appropriate role of law in addressing the subordination faces profound questions about the immutability of sexual orientation and the interrelationships between sex, gender, and sexual orientation (Halley 1994, Valdes 1995, Case 1995), and the divergences in perspectives between gay men and lesbian women (Robson 1992).

Woman's "different voice"

Equality and nonsubordination theories of gender view women's differences as factually insignificant, as problems to be solved through remedial accommodations, or as excuses used by a corrupt system to subordinate women. In contrast, different voice theory, also referred to as connection theory, views women's differences as potentially valuable resources that might serve as a better model of social organization and law than existing "male" characteristics and values. Within different voice theory, women are said to have a greater sense of interconnectedness than men and to value relationships more than individual rights. Women are said to favor an "ethic of care" over "justice" or "rights" models of morality, and to use less abstract, more contextual forms of reasoning than men (DuBois 1985, Sherry 1986, West 1988, Bender 1990b). Different voice theorists argue that as to each of these distinctions, women's values have the potential to improve existing law.

Scholarship that uses different voice theory to promote legal reform has extended to so many fields of law that it is possible to speak of the "mainstreaming" of this theory (Menkel-Meadow 1992). Leslie Bender uses different voice theory to justify a "duty to rescue" in tort law (Bender 1988) and obligations of corporate officers with mass tort liability to provide personal caretaking services to their victims (Bender 1990a). Other scholars use different voice theory to urge workplace policies that allow workers to better integrate responsibilities to their families and employers (Finley 1986), union policies that better acknowledge the values of connection and community (Crain 1991, 1992), and corporate strategies that better reflect the ethics of care, responsibility, connection, and sharing (Lahey and Salter 1985). Proposals to reform the tax system (Kornhauser 1987), bankruptcy law (Gross 1990), and international human rights law (Engle 1992a, 1992b), also incorporate the notions of responsibility and care promoted by connection theory.

In addition to proposals for substantive law change, theorists have also called for process and method reforms that cut deeply into conventional notions of legal practice. Carrie Menkel-Meadow (1984) proposes techniques and ethical standards for negotiation that challenge the adversarial models of adjudication that form the backbone of the American legal system. Some theorists have called for more contextualized methods of legal reasoning and decision making, not only because these methods better correspond to women's "different voice," but also because they illuminate the "maleness" of abstract legal principles, encourage a greater respect for difference, and foster a more critical awareness of the importance of the reasoner's own particular perspective (Minow 1987, Bartlett 1990, Radin 1993). Some have also called for methods of judging that emphasize not only greater contextualization, but also collaborative decision making and empathy (Resnik 1988, Sherry 1986).

A central challenge for different voice theory is avoiding the subordination historically associated with the assertion of women's differences. Although some conclude that this association undermines the capacity of different voice theory to provide a positive model for feminist legal reforms (DuBois 1985, MacKinnon 1987b, J. Williams 1991a), the most recent analyses of different voice theory attempt to integrate a concern for relationships and responsibility within a framework that protects women's autonomy and independence (Nedelsky 1989, 1991, McClain 1992a, Karlan and Ortiz 1993). This renewed attention to women's autonomy has been sparked, in part, by the challenges of postmodern feminism, explored below.

Postmodern feminism

The perspectives described thus far share common assumptions about the rationality of law, the possibility of objective truth on which the law can be based, and the coherence and stability of the individual subject on whom the law acts. Postmodern feminism launches a set of critiques of these assumptions. Postmodern feminism made its entry into the law first by way of the critical legal studies movement (CLS), a loose coalition of left-leaning academic scholars who, beginning in the 1970s, argued that law is indeterminate, non-objective, hierarchical, selflegitimating, overly-individualistic, and morally impoverished (Taub and Schneider 1982, Olsen 1983, Dalton 1985, Rhode 1990b). While the CLS movement faced heavy fire for its failure to develop a positive program that could survive its own critique, feminist scholars have absorbed the insights of this movement and attempted to transform them into the basis of a constructive feminist practice (Schneider 1986, Menkel-Meadow 1988, Rhode 1990b). Starting from the proposition that no social arrangements or legal rules are inevitable or natural, they have defined this practice in terms of support for those arrangements and rules which, under existing, nonideal social conditions, seem most just (Minow 1987, J. Williams 1991a).

Autonomy

An important target of the postmodern challenge is the law's assumption that individuals are capable of having "intent," of exercising "choice" or "consent," and of acting and thinking like "reasonable" people. The postmodern view of the individual or the "legal subject" opposes the Enlightenment view of the stable, coherent, and rational self with a more complicated view of the individual as "constituted" from multiple institutional and ideological forces that, in various ways, overlap, intersect, and even contradict each other. Although these forces join to produce a reality that the individual subject experiences as real or true, it is in fact a reality or truth that is "constructed." Under the postmodern view, the individual's experience of reality is more a function of fluctuating, constructed possibilities than a representation of what is real, rational, or in some transcendent sense, true (Bartlett 1990, pp. 877–87, Cornell 1991, 1993).

Feminist theorists join the postmodern view of the constituted subject with analyses of how concepts of consent, intent, and reasonableness in law have been constructed in gendered ways. Thus, for example, whether women in particular circumstances have consented to sexual intercourse (Henderson 1987, Scheppele 1987, Torrey 1991) or to give up their child at birth (Radin 1987, Ashe 1988) or whether they intended to form a contract (Dalton 1985) or to abuse drugs while pregnant (Roberts 1991), have all been analyzed from the perspective of the institutional and ideological forces that constrain and construct those choices. While recognizing and defining the often invisible constraints which make autonomy a legal fiction, however, these theorists contend that meaningful distinctions nevertheless can be made between "more" and "less" autonomy and that autonomy remains a positive goal for women (Nedelsky 1989, J. Williams 1991b, Abrams 1990, 1995a, McClain 1992a).

Some feminist theorists who bring postmodern insights about the individual subject to bear on the law focus on how the law constricts and defines the female body. Building on insights of French feminists, Marie Ashe demonstrates how a woman's physical body is constructed by the management and control of her reproductive functions (Ashe 1988). Other theorists, such as Mary Joe Frug (1991) and Drucilla Cornell (1991, 1993), stress concrete physical and sensual aspects of women's bodies as sources of imaginative experiences that might emancipate women from the reality – and seductions – of gender oppression.

Antiessentialism

The critical edge of postmodern feminism has been directed not only outward, against conventional legal doctrine, but also inward, against feminist theory itself. Much of this internal criticism has been articulated as a charge of "essentialism."

There are at least three phenomena to which the charge of essentialism refers. One is a critique of false generalizations or universalisms. Much of feminist jurisprudence, as discussed above, has been directed toward exposing the extent to which the law's supposedly objective norms in fact reflect male interests and male points of view. The charge of feminist essentialism is that in speaking about women and women's identity and interests, feminists, too, often presuppose a particular privileged norm – that of the white, middle-class, heterosexual woman

– and thereby deny or ignore differences based on race, class, sexual identity, and other characteristics that inform a woman's identity. Essentialism, in this context, refers to the exclusion that follows from such unstated norms (Minow 1987, Harris 1990). A related claim, made by critical race theorists, is that race and sex are often bifurcated in legal claims of discrimination brought by black women, thus ignoring exclusions, often unrecognized as discrimination, based on the intersection of race and gender (Crenshaw 1989, Kline 1989, Caldwell 1991). These criticisms have led feminist scholars to be increasingly careful of their own unstated assumptions, despite the difficulties of doing so (Nedelsky 1991).

A second form of essentialism is what might be called the "naturalist" error. Again, this form of essentialism is the mirror image of a critique feminists have made against conventional legal theory – namely, the charge that legal principles are falsely assumed to be inherent, transcendent, universal, or natural, instead of socially constructed. As applied to feminist jurisprudence itself, this critique cautions that treating "woman" as a self-explanatory, natural category and assuming that once certain "man-made" or false forms of oppression are removed women will find their "true" identities accepts the mistaken view of truth as absolute, findable, and final. The critique has special force against the charge that women who do not accept a particular feminist program or agenda are the victims of "false consciousness" (Bartlett 1987, Abrams 1990, Cornell 1993). In response to this charge, scholars increasingly are moving away from the notion that the central feminist project consists in finding woman's true consciousness, toward a view of women's liberation that recognizes both social constraints and the creative possibilities women have to participate in their own construction (J. Williams 1991b, Frug 1991, Cornell 1991, 1993, Bartlett 1992).

A more recent version of the naturalist error critique questions the conventional division between sex, which has been understood to be biological and fixed, and gender, which has been understood as cultural and fluid. Both halves of the sex/gender dichotomy are under fire, as the line between male and female is ever more in play (Case 1995, Franke 1995, Valdes 1995), and cultural differences between men and women are increasingly explained as the efficient product of natural selection processes (Browne 1995). The implications for the collapse of these categories for the law are only beginning to be explored.

The third essentialist critique of feminist jurisprudence is one of gender imperialism. This critique is that feminists give too much primacy to sex as a basis of discrimination and too little to other forms of oppression, such as those based on race, class, and sexual orientation. On this ground, Angela Harris (1990) criticizes Catharine MacKinnon's analysis of a Santa Clara Pueblo tribal ordinance that denies Pueblo membership to the children of female, but not male, members of the Pueblo who marry nonmembers of the tribe, arguing that MacKinnon's analysis wrongly assumes that a Pueblo member's gender-based identity is more important than her tribal identity. More recently, the imperialism criticism is used to caution feminists who condemn practices in Muslim societies that subjugate women to men, especially the practice of female genital mutilation, on the

grounds that this condemnation disrespects the cultural and religious significance of these practices and accepts white, Christian, American women as the
standard for all (Engle 1992a, Gunning 1992). This debate is just one example of
the struggle in feminist jurisprudence to define how much room the critique of
objectivity and universal norms leaves to claim some basic feminist truths
(Bartlett 1990, 1992, Cornell 1991, 1993, West 1987).

To combat all these forms of essentialism, many scholars have urged greater
use of the narrative method. Individual and group narratives offer alternatives to
the dominant stories or universal narratives on which the law is based and give
voice to the actual, otherwise submerged, experiences of the dominated (West
1987, Austin 1989, White 1990, Mahoney 1991, J. Williams 1991b). Insofar as
these alternatives help individuals to reveal their own, unstated assumptions and
the experiences of others who do not share these assumptions, they also facilitate
empathic understanding (Henderson 1987, Massaro 1989). Paradoxically, at the
same time that they reveal differences in perspective, narratives also help to
create coherent identities by identifying, stabilizing, and integrating common
bonds among women (Abrams 1991, Dailey 1993). Recent writing on narrative
attends to criticisms of feminist narratives, including criticisms that narratives
merely substitute one universal narrative for another, that they are too subjective, that they exclude others who have not had the same experiences, or that
they sometimes are simply not "true" (Abrams 1991, Cahn 1993).

Conclusion

The determination of feminist legal scholars to move from the safety of critique to
the vulnerable ground of positive reconstruction of law, and to turn the lens of
feminist method inward, upon itself, demonstrate both the confidence and the
fluidity of feminist jurisprudence. Its self-conscious status as ongoing rather than
complete, questioning rather than declarative, and self-critical rather than com-
placent, makes it difficult to predict what lies ahead. But these same characteristics make it likely that it will occupy an ever-increasing presence in legal theory
and practice.

Note

This article first appeared under the title "Gender law," in *Duke Journal of Gender Law and
Policy*, 1 (1994), 1–18.

54

Islamic law

AZIZAH Y. AL-HIBRI

An overview of the concerns of Muslim women

The NGO Forum, held in Houairou, China, in the fall of 1995, was a defining moment in the global dialogue among women on issues relating to Islam. Prior to that event, discussions of Islamic *shari'ah* law (law based on religious foundations), in particular, and Islam, in general, had been escalating both in the West and in Muslim countries. In the regional conferences held in preparation for the United Nations Fourth World Conference on Women, held concurrently with the NGO Forum, the intellectual fault-lines surrounding these issues became pronounced between two radically different schools of thought. The first school of thought argued that *shari'ah* law was outmoded and should be discarded in favor of a modern Western secular model. The second school of thought denied any problems under existing *shari'ah* laws. Each group felt very strongly about its point of view. The battle was joined in Houairou.

The resulting polarization was so disturbing that it prompted several Muslim women's organizations and individuals to write a letter to the NGO Forum publication, stating in part the following:

> Two dominant and opposing views on Islam which have emerged in the NGO Forum have been challenged by a group of women activists ... The first view reflects an ultraconservative position, focusing on comparing the ideals of Islam with the reality and ills of the Western world. A second view rejects religion as a reaction against Islamic conservatism and abuses committed in the name of Islam. For many of us, both views are unrealistic and untenable. Islam recognizes equality between men and women ... Islam has been used to justify laws and practices which oppress women ... This group advocates a reconstruction of Islamic principles, procedures and practices in light of the basic Qur'anic principles of equality and justice. (Sisters in Islam et al. 1995, p. 3)

It is important to understand that the differences between the two opposing schools of thought are political as much as they are religious. The first school of thought wants to emulate the West in its recent legal and social transformations relating to gender issues. The second school rejects all things Western because it rejects Western political/cultural hegemony. The emerging third school of thought wants to discover its own authentic dialectic of transformation, based on its indigenous historical context and the world of the twenty-first century.

The differences among all three schools are rendered, in certain cases, quite severe by the after-effects of colonialist policies in the Muslim world. One major aspect of such policies was educational/cultural.

In Algeria, for example, in an attempt to permanently transform Algerian culture along Western lines, French language and culture were emphasized in the educational system to the detriment of local ones. Consequently, many Algerians belonging to the colonized generations were often more familiar with the French culture and language than with their own (Lazreg 1994, especially pp. 59–67). This state of affairs severely hampered them from the outset in developing a social and political critique rooted in the area's heritage.

Other factors appear to play an indirect role in shaping the line of thought some women ultimately adopt. They include the economic and social class of these women, their particular relation to the power structure, if any, and the general nature of the power structure and its relative degree of misogyny.

This article will focus exclusively on womanist Islamic thought. (For more on the use of the term "womanist," see the press release issued in Beijing in September 1996 by "Karamah: Muslim Women Lawyers for Human Rights" (Karamah), a Virginia-based organization which I co-founded.) The importance of such thought stems, in my opinion, from the nature of the population, both male and female, in Islamic societies. The population is predominantly committed to spirituality (whether Islamic or otherwise), which has often been unfortunately confused with patriarchal interpretations of religious heritage. Consequently, any profound changes in these societies will have a better chance of success if approached from within a spiritual framework. For this reason, the development of a womanist Islamic jurisprudence is of paramount importance.

We start with a quick overview of the Muslim world. There are over one billion Muslims, and they live all over the globe. It is therefore expected that the problems facing the Pakistani woman will turn out to be quite different from those facing her Egyptian, Lebanese, South African, Malaysian, or American Muslim sister. More interestingly, the personal status codes (family laws) in Muslim countries differ significantly, despite the claim of each country that its code is based at least partially on Islamic principles (al-Hibri 1992, *passim*). As a result, women in different countries have different agendas.

Also, the cultures in these countries vary dramatically. For example, genital mutilation is a concern for Egyptian, Sudanese, Somali, and Nigerian women, but not for Syrian, Jordanian, Kuwaiti, Tunisian, Moroccan, or Lebanese women, whose cultures do not have that custom (Tubia 1995, p. 54). Because countries where genital mutilation is practiced have used religious arguments to justify it, it became necessary to refute these religious claims on their own grounds. In Nigeria, for example, which has a Christian majority with a sizeable Muslim minority, patriarchal authorities have attempted to legitimize the cultural practice of genital mutilation by utilizing arguments supposedly based on Christian and Islamic foundations. For this reason, Christian as well as Muslim women have had to refute these arguments from within their own religious tradition (Ras-Work 1992, vol. 2, pp. 62–3). This approach is quite important to allay the fears of religious women who are averse to the custom, yet fear divine retribution if they were to reject it.

Women activists in Egypt have been concerned about the Egyptian personal status code and its limitations on women's freedoms. Recently, some of them developed a model marriage contract that better protects the rights of the woman within the marriage (National Committee of NGOs, 1995, pp. 53–9). This model was based upon straightforward traditional Islamic jurisprudence which recognizes the contractual nature of marriage. Many Muslims, Egyptian as well as non-Egyptian, responded negatively to the model marriage contract branding it immediately as Western and contrary to Islam. These attacks continued even after the *Mufti* of Egypt, one of its two highest religious authorities, found the proposed model religiously acceptable.

Pakistani women suffer from a different kind of oppression, deriving in part from the historical attitudes toward women in the Indian subcontinent, compounded by lack of direct knowledge of traditional Islamic jurisprudence. A major concern of these women is the handling of rape cases under present law. In some cases, this law punishes the raped woman for adultery while leaving the rapist free. This result is produced by a fundamental misconstrual of Islamic laws on adultery and by analogizing rape to adultery. This is done despite clear traditional Islamic jurisprudence that classifies rape either as a crime or a tort. Under the former classification, rape is viewed as a violent taking or forced assault, similar to armed robbery, and may even be punishable by the death of the rapist. Under the latter classification rape is viewed as a type of compensable bodily harm. Womanist Islamic thought is being developed to reveal fundamental flaws in the religious arguments on which the present law and its application rest (see, e.g., Quraishi, forthcoming).

In Malaysia, *hudud* laws, which were adopted by the Kelantan State in 1993, appear to be a major issue for Muslim women. *Hudud* laws involve severe bodily punishments or death for the commission of certain crimes. The crimes include rape, adultery, and theft. Sisters In Islam ("SIS"), a Malaysian womanist organization, published a collection of articles critiquing Malaysian *hudud* laws (Ismail 1995). One contributor, Salbiah Ahmad, argues that the law of adultery and rape was based on an opinion in the Maliki school of thought which "lacks authenticity as it is not the view arrived at by consensus ... nor held by the majority ... of jurists" (Ismail 1995, p. 19). In another article, Nourani Othman argues that such laws have become outdated and must no longer be practiced. She notes that "There is no doubt that the *shari'ah* principles which are explicitly contained in the Qur'an are divinely-sanctioned but it is another thing to claim that the interpretation of those *shari'ah* principles by the Committee which was appointed by the state government ... is divine" (Ismail 1995, p. 35).

North African countries also have their distinctive set of problems. For example, Moroccan women are very concerned about the right of a woman to work outside the home without her husband's permission. The Moroccan personal status law contains a provision, borrowed from French law and supported by some traditional Islamic jurisprudence, which prohibits the woman from working outside the home without the consent of her husband (Bennani 1992, p. 149). This issue will be addressed below in greater detail.

"Collectif 95 Maghreb Egalité" (Algeria, Morocco, and Tunisia), which was very active in Beijing, published a proposed personal status code which provides for gender equality, including specifically women's right to work, free travel and equal inheritance by siblings (Collectif 95 Maghreb Egalité 1995, pp. 17, 25–6). Some Muslim women have regarded this and other similar organizations as primarily secular in their approach. They regard the organization's occasional use of religious arguments as an attempt to make their proposals more palatable to a Muslim population.

This quick geographical overview is selective and thus, by necessity, incomplete. Therefore, the reader should not conclude that there are no additional areas of interest for Muslim women in these countries or around the world. This geographical survey highlights only those issues that tend to illustrate the rich diversity of concerns in various parts of the Muslim world. A case in point is Sisters in Islam, which has not only addressed *hudud* laws, but also such other fundamental topics as gender equality, the Islamic position on violence against women, and the relationship of *shari'ah* law and the modern nation-state (Othman 1994, Sisters in Islam 1991a, 1991b).

Despite the diversity of issues and problems facing Muslim women around the world, it is possible to discern some emerging general outlines of womanist Muslim thought. Broadly speaking, three major approaches are utilized and sometimes combined. The first argues that existing problems are not the result of Islam itself, but of patriarchal interpretations of the religion and use of fabricated or questionable *hadith*, i.e. statements attributed to the Prophet. This line of thought leads to a critical reexamination of existing religion-based laws which exposes their patriarchal underpinnings. The second line of thought argues that certain Islamic laws have become obsolete and that we need simply to suspend or discard them, while adhering to basic Qur'anic and jurisprudential principles. The third sees no problem with the laws themselves, but only with their modern formulation and application.

Arguments against genital mutilation and Pakistani rape laws usually fall into the first category. Arguments by Sisters in Islam on *hudud* laws appear to fall in the second category. I believe, however, that more compelling arguments could be developed by simply relying on straightforward early traditional jurisprudence which has often been distorted and misapplied. These proposed arguments would then fall into the third category, as does the attempt at formulating a model marriage contract.

We have already seen examples of these three lines of thought, but will now focus on them in a more thorough fashion by singling out two major issues of general concern to Muslim women. They are: (1) gender equality; and (2) women's right to work.

Gender equality

Muslim women agree that Islam gave women their full rights. They disagree, however, over the definition of these rights. In particular, Muslim women are in the midst of a debate as to whether Islam provides them with "gender equality" or "gender equity". The former concept is viewed by its detractors as coming dangerously close to the Western concept of mechanical equality, based on an individualistic view of society. The latter concept is viewed by its detractors as leaving the door wide open for misuse by patriarchal adversaries. The debate became very intense in Houairou and was resolved by adopting the compromise slogan "Equality with Equity."

To frame the debate, we turn to selections from a forthcoming booklet by Karamah, a forthcoming grassroots book by the Muslim Women's League (the "League"), a California-based organization, works of other authors, and a position statement issued by the Muslim Women's Georgetown Project (the "Project"), a Washington DC-based organization, in connection with the Beijing meetings.

Karamah and the League both adopt the "equality" point of view. In its forthcoming booklet on Islam and women's rights, which relies heavily on traditional Islamic sources, Karamah states:

> *Tawhid* [the belief in a single God] is the core principle of Islamic jurisprudence. From it flow many secondary principles, including the one that asserts that God is the supreme being, and that all human beings are only creatures of God. This latter principle in turn leads to the conclusion that all human beings, regardless of gender, class or race, are equal in the eyes of God. Consequently, no man is superior to a woman, by virtue of his gender alone.

In a recent paper, I have further bolstered the above position by arguing that the Qur'an articulates a clear and basic principle of gender equality (al-Hibri 1996). The argument is based on such well-known verses as "O people! reverence God who created you from a single *nafs* (soul) and created from her (the *nafs*) her mate and spread from them many men and women" (Qur'an 4: 1). The Muslim Women's League book states that "[s]piritual equality and accountability for both men and women is a well-developed theme in the Qur'an ... [and] is the basis for equality in all temporal aspects of human endeavor" (Muslim Women's League, n.d.). The book continues:

> The concept of gender equality is best exemplified in the Qur'anic rendition of Adam and Eve .... . [T]he Qur'an states that both sexes were deliberate and independent and there is no mention of Eve being created out of Adam's rib .... . Even the issue of which sex was created first is not specified, implying that for our purposes it may not matter. (Muslim Women's League, n.d.)

The book then launches into a discussion of the various roles Muslim women have played throughout history, from rulers to religious leaders and even warriors. The arguments of Karamah and the League in support of their positions tend to fall in the first and third categories discussed earlier.

The title of the paper by the Muslim Women's Georgetown Project, "Islam: a system of reciprocal partnership" (1995). signals its "equity" approach to social relations and to the rights issue. It argues in the introduction that "[t]he Islamic social system integrates family, community, society, politics and economics in a mutually dependent system which becomes *self-preserving*" (1995, p. 1). By placing its emphasis on the responsibilities of the parents toward the child, the paper cites approvingly the traditional Islamic law requiring the nearest male to provide sustenance for the woman. It argues that:

> [t]he reason for such discrimination is that at some point in her life, the woman might find herself pregnant and in the process of caring for another life. She should never in this condition shoulder alone that responsibility for her partner has a duty to share in this task. Society as well has a vested interest in the new generation and should provide help if the family of the woman is incapable or not available.   (1995, p. 1)

It is important to note that the Project's views reflect the preferences of a significant group of Muslim American women who are tired of working outside the home, while raising their children in a single-parent household. This position is also supported by other Muslim women, such as a leading Saudi women's rights advocate, Fatima Nasif (Nasif 1992, especially pp. 239–40), and tends to rely on arguments that fall in the third category mentioned earlier.

The Project's position, however, is still being developed and may turn out to be more complex than the above quote suggests. In fact, as the first draft of this paper was being written, the Project came under attack by a conservative American Muslim woman for subscribing to the "equality" position (*AMC Report* 1996, p. 11).

In stating the Islamic position on gender equality, Amina Wadud-Muhsin, an American Muslim scholar who spent some time working with Sisters in Islam in Malaysia, exhibits sensitivity to the concerns of various Muslim women groups. She notes that:

> [t]he Qur'an does not attempt to annihilate the differences between men and women or to erase the significance of functional gender distinctions ... . In fact. compatible mutually supportive functional relationships between men and women can be seen as part of the Qur'an with respect to society. However, the Qur'an does not propose or support a singular role or single definition of a set of roles, exclusively, for each gender across every culture.   (Wadud-Muhsin 1992, p. 8)

Patriarchal men have rejected such statements by pointing to a particular verse in the Qur'an which they interpret as saying that men are superior to women (Qur'an, 4: 34). From this one verse a host of consequences flow, affecting the legal rights of the Muslim woman in the family and society. Therefore, no discussion of gender equality is complete without attention to this verse.

The first part of the verse states that "men are *qawwamun* over women." The controversial word is "*qawwamun*," which has been interpreted to mean "superior." In an earlier work, I have contested the validity of this interpretation on linguistic, grammatical, and other grounds (al-Hibri 1982, pp. 217–18). In a later work, I rejected it altogether as contradictory to the fundamental principle of equality clearly and repeatedly expressed in the Qur'an (al-Hibri 1996, *passim*). More importantly, all previous discussion has centered on the meaning of this one word, ignoring the structure of the Qur'anic verse itself. I have argued that, properly read, the verse places restrictions on men, rather than endowing them with privileges (al-Hibri 1996).

Put simply, the verse carefully circumscribes the conditions under which a man may provide advice or guidance to a woman (which, incidentally, she is free to ignore). There are two clearly articulated conditions. First, the man may offer such advice or guidance only to women who are financially dependent on him. Second, he may do so only with respect to matters about which this particular man is more informed or experienced than the particular woman he is advising. In other words, the verse limits the ability of a man to interfere in the affairs of a woman simply because she is a woman or is at a stage in her life where she is financially dependent on him. It also reduces that interference to an advisory function.

This interpretation falls squarely within the first category of approaches mentioned earlier. Significantly, it is not only consistent with the primary principle of gender equality in the Qur'an, but also with the clear Islamic position, undisputed by a majority of traditional scholars, that a woman is entitled to full financial independence, even within a marriage (Abu Zahrah 1957, p. 128, al-Jaziri 1969, vol. 4, p. 46). Her spouse may not touch her money, and she may engage in business on her own account (Abu Zahrah 1957, p. 128; al-Jaziri 1969, vol. 4, p. 46). Traditional jurists, without denying that right, rendered it moot by relying on the superiority interpretation of the above-mentioned verse to require wives to "obey" their husbands. This obedience condition is included (directly or indirectly) even today in many personal status codes in Muslim countries. Consequences of this view, many of which have been codified, range from the claim that women are required to secure the consent of their husbands to work outside the home, to the claim that men are heads of the household and that women may never hold a position of authority over men.

The right to work

In a book entitled *Spousal Division of Labor* (Arabic), Farida Bennani (Morocco) contests the views of traditional jurists who focused on gender differences to justify a traditional division of labor within the family (Bennani 1992, passim). She flatly states that Islam is innocent of such views and of related views, such as those declaring the husband as head of the household (Bennani 1992, p. 40). She also notes that the stereotypes of husband and wife necessitated by such views do not exist in her society (Bennani 1992, p. 78). Consequently, her

547

approach falls within the first and third categories of the approaches discussed earlier.

Bennani notes that the Maliki school of thought, followed in Morocco, recognizes that in Islam the wife is not required to perform any housework (Bennani 1992, p. 147). Therefore, scholars of that school formulated their views by reference to custom instead. They stated that women are not obligated to perform such household duties, "*unless* required by local custom" (Bennani 1992, p. 147). Since local custom is patriarchal, the end result required the woman not only to do housework, but even help the husband in the field. This led to an even more patriarchal conclusion, prohibiting the wife from selling outside the home her residual capacity for work, if any, without her husband's consent (Bennani 1992, p. 147).

Some personal status codes, however, do permit women to work outside the home without their husband's permission, *so long as the job (or hours, in some statutes) is morally acceptable and does not contradict the interest of the family* (Egyptian Code, Law No. 25 (1920), as amended, Bk 1, Ch. 1, Art. 1; Kuwaiti Code, Part 1, Bk 1, Title 3, Art. 89). These types of laws reflect different patriarchal customs and, in many cases, economic necessity.

It is important to note that the general Islamic principle of equality, referred to earlier, which establishes equality regardless of gender or race, together with a Qur'anic verse which celebrates diversity (Qur'an, 49:13), led jurists to permit the inclusion of local custom in the law of the land, *so long as that custom did not contradict Qur'anic principles*. But the application of this juristic rule fell short of the ideal when patriarchal customs were codified along with religious laws.

It is also important to note that, in an attempt to shift the burden of housework from the husband, some male jurists stated that since the wife is not obligated to perform any housework, she is entitled to a servant. In fact, the Prophet Muhammad himself, the ideal role-model for Muslim men, participated in housework. Historians have even reported the nature of some household chores he performed. These included cutting meat, sewing, and helping with the children (al-Ghazali 1939, vol. 2, p. 354, al-Nadawi 1977, p. 370). However, the farthest distance Muslim jurists have travelled down this road is to observe that fairness required that men help their wives in performing housework, *when the wives are working outside the home*.

Clearly then, *ijtihad* (jurisprudential interpretation) in this area is in flux. Missing in our discussion is a report on the contributions of Iranian women on the subject, since most of these contributions are in Persian, a language I unfortunately cannot read. However, reports abound that new womanist jurisprudence is being accepted and codified in Iran in such areas as housework and divorce. The two subjects are not unconnected, since recognition of the fact that the woman is not required to perform housework and that housework has economic value, lead to the conclusion that upon divorce this contributed value must be taken into consideration in settling marital property or alimony.

Conclusion

This article focuses on two basic issues relating to Muslim womanist thought. It is my belief that other issues can also be properly addressed from within such a line of thought. The fundamentals for the liberation of Muslim women are all contained in the Qur'an, the example of the Prophet and the women leaders surrounding him, and often even in early traditional *ijtihad*. The Muslim women's interest today in developing a womanist jurisprudence will drastically accelerate the process of their liberation. But as Nourani Othman, of Sisters in Islam, observes, "[t]he modernization of Islam must take place from the inside and be carried out by Muslims themselves" (Ismail 1995, p. 39). Consequently, Muslim womanist thought offers the only real hope for the transformation of Muslim societies.

55

International justice

NATALIE DANDEKAR

International inequities disproportionately burden women

Consider the following well-attested observations: (1) Forty years of international development policies have increased rural poverty in a gender-disproportionate manner. During the last twenty years, even as USAID policies mandated concern for women, "the number of rural women living in absolute poverty rose by about 50 per cent ... as against an increase of about 30 per cent for rural men" (Jazairy et al. 1992, p. xix). Against this, international justice would require that women's development be secured as a part of international development.

(2) Approximately 75 percent of the world's 18 million refugees are women and girls, at risk of "endemic sexual violence against refugee women" (Zalewski 1995, p. 342). International justice would require that women's rights to be secure in owning her own body, and thus to be secure against rape, be recognized as human rights. But even at the level of ordinary living, in cities, suburbs and rural districts, sexual violence is endemic, while the state has too frequently proven a poor or indifferent protector.

(3) Environmental degradation disproportionately increases the difficulty women face in carrying out responsibilities socially adherent to gender. For example, where women must collect the biomass necessary to food preparation, loss of biodiversity adds hours to the unpaid domestic burdens of the poorest women. Where food is insufficient, social patterns of intrafamily distribution ensure that women and young girls eat least and bear the burdens of malnourishment. Where women bear primary responsibility for nursing the sick, environmentally produced illnesses require that the poorest women accept the burden of nursing those suffering from these environmentally induced diseases. International justice would require that the wrongs of environmental degradation be remedied in ways that do not require women to suffer inequitably.

Policies of "structural adjustment" imposed on national governments by lending agencies of last resort (such as the World Bank) exploit the coping skills of women as resources of last resort. "Efficiencies" required by structural adjustment policies increase the normal burden of women's domestic work so that a sixteen-hour working day becomes normal. Cash-strapped states encourage the exploitation of women's femininity as a resource for earning cash through sex tourism (Enloe 1989). "Mail-order brides" (Narayan 1993) and "mail-order domestic servants" (Enloe 1989) have fewer legal protections than other categories of economic migrant, so women migrating from poor countries risk more serious harms than male migrants. At a still more general level, women "find that their social agency is frequently undercut by inappropriate forms of sexual recognition which displace the specific forms of social recognition and reward their actions deserved and would have received if they had been performed by men" (Mann 1994, p. 11).

Women's relative political disenfranchisement and disempowerment within almost all existing states raise serious methodological questions. As Kate Young (1993) points out, women who are politically disenfranchised and disempowered will have difficulty getting their demands placed on the agenda. But more importantly, women socialized to lack any sense of having rights or needs except in relation to others will typically see themselves "as conduits for the well-being of others" (Young 1993, p. 148). Unless they are informed by feminist awareness, planners, too, tend to focus on women in terms of mothering and other family-centered responsibilities. Thus even data collection is skewed toward topics which reflect assumptions that women are properly subsumed within a family unit and properly focused on the nurturance of that unit, rather than recognizing women as having interests independent of gender-specific cultural responsibilities. International justice would require the remedy of all such gender inequities. An adequate concept of international justice requires an adequate awareness of gender.

State-centered positions

Contemporary "state-centered" theories of international justice, be they Utilitarian, Kantian, or Communitarian, are inadequate to the challenge of international inequities on two closely related grounds. First, these theories uncritically adhere to a "gender-blind" approach. In refusing to consider gender central, this approach becomes blind to the way men are privileged in existing (apparently neutral) theories, policies, and institutions. Where the norm that is accepted as neutral puts "the man of reason" at its center, the normatively autonomous agents whose consent constitutes state sovereignty are themselves abstract, disembodied males. To be blind to gender under these circumstances is to be blind to the systemic supports that relegate women to a private realm in which they are held to be naturally subordinate to and dependent upon a male head of household. Such gender blindness is far from neutral, for it fails to see the extent to which, as Carole Pateman (1988) has shown, even the most democratic liberal state retains a patriarchal aspect. Second, these theorists necessarily hold international justice hostage to national sovereignty in ways that fail to institute gender equity as a central concern.

Goodin (1995) argues for Utilitarianism, "the moral theory that judges the goodness of outcomes – and therefore the rightness of actions insofar as they affect outcomes – by the degree to which they secure the greatest benefit to all concerned" (p. 3), as our best guide to public policy decisions. Goodin holds that a utilitarian resolution of global environmental and human rights problems does best to rely on the model of a "family of nations." In (Western, middle-class, nuclear) families "each parent is responsible for assuming complete responsibility for catering to the basic needs of the couple's children, should the other partner prove unable or unwilling to shoulder his or her share of the burden" (Goodin 1995, p. 314). Each nation would be responsible for making up shortfalls, when other nations fail to do their part. Moreover, "as in the example of family relations it is thought to be perfectly proper to use the force of law to extract child support payments" (p. 314), so in the international arena each nation can properly press others to do their part toward shared ends.

Goodin's utilitarian "family" model suffers from both the failures described above. First, it presumes that the situation of a post-divorce North American single mother struggling to raise children is a (gender-blind) model of justice. Second, nations motivated by national commitments to international justice can do no more than pressure less committed nations. Women disenfranchised in most nations remain marginalized as international agents.

National sovereignty is equally central to Nagel's (1991) Kantian (hypothetical social contract) model, where justice consists in finding principles "no one could reasonably reject, given the aim of finding principles which could be the bases of general agreement among persons similarly motivated" (Nagel 1991, p. 36). His sense that the contemporary situation is one of "spiritually sickening economic and social inequality" (Nagel 1991, p. 5) leads him to advocate "a minimally decent level of international assistance" (p. 174). Nevertheless, as a practical man, Nagel accepts that a "world legal order must content itself with expressing those values and protecting those interests which are shared by most of the existing states, many of which are morally abominable" (p. 176).

Walzer's (1983) influential communitarian account differs radically. First, he postulates that social justice means the elimination of institutionalized domination. But, then, he equates the absence of domination with complex equality in the distribution of socially meaningful benefits and burdens. According to him, this requires a radical respect for the particular ways in which particular political communities have constructed criteria of distribution, in accordance with the social meanings constructed through the social interactions internal to this particular political community at this particular time.

Acknowledging that three minimal prohibitions (on murder, deception, and gross cruelty) run across all cultures (Walzer 1988, p. 22), Walzer nevertheless holds that questions of justice belong wholly within a politically organized community and maintains a strong doctrine of non-interventionism. Barry (1995) points out "an immediate implication of Walzer's particularism ... there can be no such thing as international distributive justice. For there is manifestly no international community in Walzer's sense of a set of people with shared understandings of the meaning of social goods" (p. 79). More pointedly still, Onora O'Neill (1993) notes that socially accepted meanings of established communities commonly relegate "women's lives to a 'private' sphere, within which the political virtue of justice has no place ... [and] endorse institutions that exclude women from the 'public' sphere, where justice is properly an issue" (p. 303).

Despite their manifest differences, Goodin, Nagel, and Walzer share a conception of the international as limited to the actions of states. But the assumption that the sovereign acts of states fully define the international arena is descriptively false to the world in which we live. Multinational monetary lending agencies, transnational corporations, humanitarian agencies like the Red Cross or "Doctors without Borders," and nongovernmental interest groups like Greenpeace all function across international boundaries, often in ways which contravene the fiction of national sovereignty. State-based theories also fail to capture the reality of imploding or failed states.

Recognizing the prescriptive falsity of this skewed gender blindness is even more important for the project of discovering a concept of international justice which does not fail women. Classical formulations of the social contract postulate a prepolitical realm in which abstractly conceived freely consenting individuals come together to form a nation-state. Criticism reveals the manifold extent to which these disembodied individuals are male. Women who enter public life must do so either as if they too are men or "as beings whose sexual embodiment prevents them enjoying the same political standing as men" (Pateman 1989b, p. 4; cf. also Pateman 1988, Okin 1979, 1989a). Justice as the constitutive principle freely agreed to by such abstract individuals (disembodied men of reason) not surprisingly tends to privilege males who conform to the disembodied standards set by the appeal to the reasonable man. Such systems disregard (are blind to) the specificities of the subjection and oppression of women (cf. Pateman 1989b, p. 35).

By accepting patriarchal states as the only units of international activity, international relations professionals uncritically perpetuate a wide range of flawed presumptions. States likened to autonomous individuals must maintain crucial parameters of difference in order to secure national legitimacy. When foreigners must remain foreign or the society will have lost its unique identity as a state, justice too frequently remains the shared property of citizens, a position that promotes injustice toward aliens. At the same time this definition of a state privileges the public (male) world as the realm of justice and productive desert. Women's contributions are devalued, exploited, trivialized, or overlooked and relegated to a private realm of caring, where justice lacks dominion. This promotes injustice toward women since, as Virginia Held (1995a) maintains, "Justice is badly needed in the family ... in a more equitable division of labor between women and men in the household, in the protection of vulnerable family members from domestic violence and abuse, in recognizing the rights of family members" (p. 129). A theory of international justice must answer such injustices, repairing classical theories of states which are built upon gender injustices.

Theories of international justice which stress finding neutral universals may, like Barry's (1993) second-order impartiality, help us visualize a world in which human rights have normative force everywhere. However, assumptions of male privilege are so pervasive that unless theorists deliberately focus on questions reflecting feminist concern, they are very likely to continue to perpetuate the fallacy that privileging the rights important to independent (male) moral agents is consistent with impartiality.

Making women central to theories of international justice

Three theoretical approaches to international justice make women central: Kantianism promulgated by Onora O'Neill, the capabilities approach of Amartya Sen and Martha Nussbaum, and ecofeminists like Vandana Shiva each in different ways make women's subjection and oppression central to theories of international justice. For O'Neill, "Justice is ... a matter of keeping to principles that can be adopted by any plurality of potentially interacting beings" (1993, p. 314). Focus on gender provides the critical balance necessary to develop a standard for international justice which could be adopted by agents who are numerous and diverse but neither ideally rational nor ideally independent of one another (p. 313). "(A)t the least action and institutions should not be based on principles of deception and victimization" (p. 315). In operation, this demand requires that we ask "to what extent the arrangements that structure vulnerable lives are ones *that could have been refused or renegotiated by those whom they actually constrain*" (original emphasis, p. 318). O'Neill argues that perceivable connections of gender, vulnerability, and systems of oppression require that an impartial principle is not simply neutral among agents described as equals. In a just principle, "more will be demanded when others are vulnerable than when they are secure" (p. 318). O'Neill shows how this abstract realization applies to institutions, i.e. family and property, that influence the capacities and opportunities of poor women.

Nussbaum and Sen also focus on poor women as a central concern in a theory of international justice. Their approach urges parties "to ask themselves what aspects of living comprise ... the good life for a human being" (p. 327). The goal of the capacities approach is to discover objective standards for assessing the extent to which persons realize the various capacities that enable living a good human life, although quality of life assessments postulate there will be a plurality of incommensurable components.

The capabilities approach promoted by Nussbaum differs from O'Neill's Kantianism in at least two ways. First, not all good human lives will accord with a single universalizable principle. Second, unlike O'Neill's insistence on generating ethical content by way of consistency and universalizability, Nussbaum emphasizes the important moral work to be done by emotion and imagination.

Sen (1993) distinguishes the capabilities approach from rival theories in other ways. He distinguishes four objective categories of assessment, "namely, well-being achievement, well-being freedom, agency achievement, and agency freedom" (p. 49). As Sen (1985) documents, women may not be the best judge of their own status in these categories. Women socialized to eat less than others of their households report that their nutritional status and physical health are good even when suffering from ailments associated with malnutrition. The capabilities approach thus provides alternative objective standards for assessing the impact of (gender) socialization upon quality of life.

Discovering objective standards of international justice by focusing on inequities is, as Nussbaum says, "a human problem .... But right now it is in most societies particularly a women's problem" (1991b, p. 334). However, the capabilities theory is open to criticism, especially with respect to the potential conflict among the various objective standards interrelated as aspects of a good human life. In one essay, Sen (1985) seems to prefer China's pattern of enhanced educational and nutritional capabilities despite human rights abuses. But neither Sen nor Nussbaum offer guidance about an internationally appropriate standard by which to weigh conflicts between different capabilities.

Again, Nussbaum's Aristotelianism is deeply rooted in established traditions of Western philosophy. To what extent should this be seen as a liability? How appropriate is a standpoint promoted by Western theorizing to the demands of formulating a theory of international justice? To what extent are such theories prey to the charge of cultural imperialism? (cf. Lugones and Spelman 1986). Nussbaum and Sen both accept the theoretician as providing objective expertise, though they ask that this expertise be put at the service of women. Women matter in these theories of international justice, but it is the expert who determines what counts as a capability, and which rights of women count.

Ecofeminists like Vandana Shiva (1988) adopt a different mode of making women central in that the women made central are seen as agents who, by working together, determine what matters. Ecofeminism presents a theoretical stance which consciously combines insights gained through feminist critique of human relationships with an ecologically oriented analysis. This theory began in grassroots political activism (Lahar 1991). Confronting issues of obviously practical import, ecologically motivated feminist activists began to explicate a consistent realization that: (1) the practice of ecology demands feminist understanding of transformative consciousness; (2) the feminist understanding of oppression and technical exploitation of nature are intrinsically linked; and (3) both are forms of hierarchic commodification which must be transformed into more respectful relationships. For ecofeminists the same mistaken presumptions of alienation and hierarchical superiority underlie treating an other (whether woman or nature) as resource and means to be used (up). The wrongnesses that distort human life chances and ultimately threaten to destroy us are linked because exploitation and oppression are rooted in a falsely narrowed view of who counts (Dandekar 1990). To belong to a culturally exploited group by virtue of ethnic identity, religion, or gender is to be forced to consider oneself as less than fully human, as "exploitable," rather than one to whom respect is due.

"Development" policies, which Vandana Shiva (1988) aptly renamed "maldevelopment", seek to alleviate the miseries produced by historically prior exploitations by promoting quantitative remedies – more food, wages, Gross National Product. These require further exploitation of resources. Alternative

555

practices and concepts developed, e.g., by rural Indian women struggling to conserve native forests, land, and water critical to their own survival provide oppositional categories. Simultaneously ecological and feminist these categories offer models of transformative action and promote development of a non-violent, humanly inclusive alternative development paradigm (Dandekar 1990).

Directions for further development of a theory of international justice

Inclusion of "care ethics" as an element of international justice and greater attention to eliminating the five forms of oppression described by Iris Marion Young (1990a) provide two directions for deepening theories of international justice. Tronto (1993) already specifically connects her understanding of care-ethics with Martha Nussbaum's notion of human capacity and flourishing. Moreover, as Tronto (1995) holds, care can guide thinking about global issues in terms of substantive notions of justice because the "care ethic posits a very different set of standards for desert: people are entitled to what they need because they need it; people are entitled to care because they are part of ongoing relations of care" (p. 146). Possibly, the substantive meaning of international justice might combine the care perspective which takes needs as central, with a rights orientation that includes women's rights as human rights. As Seyla Benhabib (1987) points out, feminist efforts to join justice and care suggest a model of communicative need interpretations, that moves from understanding judgment as imposition of rules from outside to a dialogic inquiry that permits "moral and political agents to define their own concrete identities on the basis of recognizing each other's dignity as generalized others" (Benhabib in Benhabib and Cornell 1987, pp. 89–93; cf. Jones 1993). But the full work of developing an internationally focused understanding of the meaning of needs (what counts as a real need rather than a mere want?) and the limits of care (when is one unjustly manipulated by one's caring?) still awaits its author.

A second direction in which theorizing may prove fruitful for further developing the concept of international justice begins with Young's (1990b) premise that social justice requires "institutions that promote reproduction of and respect for group differences without oppression" (Young 1990b, p. 47). Young distinguishes five types of oppression. Only one, exploitation, the "[institutionalized] social processes that bring about a transfer of energies from one group to another to ... enable a few to accumulate while they constrain many more" (p. 53) is already a central category of ecofeminist critique. Analyzing the international occurrences of the remaining types of oppression Young describes offers potentially fruitful approaches to developing a more comprehensive theory of international justice.

For example, marginalization is the form of oppression which deprives one "of cultural, practical and institutionalized conditions for exercising capacities in a context of recognition and interaction" (p. 55) and powerlessness reflects a social division of labor inhibiting "development of one's capacities. lack of decisionmaking power in one's working life, and exposure to disrespectful treatment because of the status one occupies" (p. 58). The capacities focus of exploitation, marginalization, and powerlessness provide substance for further analysis. For example, enabling women to earn resources may merely help them fulfill gender-specific responsibilities without affecting larger strategic issues of gender equality. However, if women earn resources in ways that develop their capacities to engage in forms of organization which promote greater self-worth, agency, and common purpose, cash earned for family needs also increases women's equality. Exploring how the capacities which combat marginalization and powerlessness map onto the capabilities Sen and Nussbaum theorize in discussing international justice, may offer a way to answer the questions of what capabilities count and why, by providing theoretical grounds connected with the meaning of social justice.

The remaining categories of oppression discussed by Young (1990) are cultural imperialism and violence. As Young notes, systemic violence characteristic of oppression intersects with cultural imperialism along a number of parameters (Young 1990b, pp. 62–3). However, with respect to deepening our concept of international justice, a nexus of great interest is the dimension of women's rights as human rights. This is especially riveting because the arguments for human rights are frequently dismissed as a legacy of the cultural imperialism which has been adherent to Western humanism.

Cultural imperialism is defined as the universalization of a dominant group's experience and culture as the norm, so that the perspective of a (non-dominant) group becomes "invisible, stereotyped by its Otherness from the norm" (Young 1990b, pp. 58–9). This form of oppression must be overcome if international justice is to be fully conceived. Monica Lazreg (1990) is not alone in indicting Westernized women for practicing cultural imperialism, reproducing the power of men over women in the power of women over women adopting stereotypes of Otherness in respect to the foreign, Arab, Muslim, or Algerian women in place of attending respectfully to particular lived realities (Lazreg 1990, pp. 338, 341; also Mohanty 1984, Ong 1988). But Lazreg's argument, complex in that she holds respect for a particular culture, must be recognized as respect for a complex social organization that is actively responding to cross-cultural contacts. Where the empowering aspect of rights results in a cross-cultural contact spurring culturally viable development, it need not be avoided for fear that women's rights represent a victory for Western humanism as a form of cultural imperialism.

A superb example of the educative effect of raising awareness of women's human rights as challenging distinct cultures to develop through cross-cultural contacts is furnished by Georgina Ashworth's (1995) description of the way her own efforts inspired others and came full circle. Her book *Of Violence and Violation: Women and Human Rights* was published in 1986, to educate the human rights organizations to recognize the need to protect women's human rights. Drawing upon other work linking culture and prostitution, the economy and the abuse of women's human rights in Thailand, Ashworth describes linking the indifferent protection states provide to women as a ground for the human rights organizations to take up the challenge. She sent copies to a range of persons, including members of the UN Human Rights subcommission and then watched as *Of Violence and Violation* "reached round the world … " and became a teaching text that inspired campaigns to take violence against women to the Human Rights Commission (Ashworth 1995, pp. 232–3). By seeing that a culture develops through cross-cultural contacts, we become capable of transforming avoidance of cultural imperialism in ways compatible with working to protect women's rights as human rights. When a person is beaten or allowed to die because she is female, this cannot be dismissed as cultural tradition (cf. Zalewski 1995).

Conclusion

When gendered inequities become visible, injustice shows global as well as local patterns. One global pattern is revealed in international development policies that work to the disadvantage of women. Attending to gender as a central category enables recognition that the global patterns of environmental degradation impose differential burdens as they are filtered through gendered assignment of social responsibilities. Where women bear the great responsibility for food preparation, food distribution, and nursing care, the hardships imposed by environmental degradation have a distinctly gendered impact. The risk of violence and violation which darken the lives of refugee women are a stark expression of the more widespread pattern by which most state governments fail to protect women against threats of violence and sexual violation. Women's relative disenfranchisement and disempowerment in almost every nation around the world promote continued inequities, frequently rendered invisible by traditional perspectives on justice as a property of states and on the international as the realm within which sovereign states act as independent agents.

Once theorists make gender central to conceptions of international justice they can recognize and document the persistent oppressions suffered by women, but they can also work out bases and principles in accordance with which action to institute a more comprehensively just system can be undertaken. Theories of international justice which make gender central can be, as Onora O'Neill demonstrates, more balanced fulfillments of the promise offered by universalistic (Kantian) reasoning. They can also be, as Sen and Nussbaum show, extensions of the communitarian vision supplemented by objective standards designed to measure quality of life. As ecofeminists demonstrate, the practical implications of feminist grassroots organizing can lead to a theory of international justice premised upon the undoing of exploitation.

Each of these approaches represents a major development of understanding, but each is susceptible to important criticism. Important as the undoing of exploitation is, oppression has, as Young (1990b) demonstrates, four other dimensions as well. A fully worked-out approach to international justice would explore and utilize efforts to oppose each of these forms of oppression. Moreover, future developments of the theory of international justice which makes gender central may also require a critical working-out of the relative place of an ethics of care for our understanding of international justice.

558

56

Equal opportunity

LAURIE SHRAGE

Contemporary debates about equal opportunity

In the post-civil rights era in the United States, it is common to see included in a job announcement a declaration of the following sort: "we are an equal opportunity/affirmative action employer." The ideal of equal opportunity has a complex relationship to the idea and practice of affirmative action, which is taken for granted in a typical job ad. I will explore the notion of equal opportunity insofar as it has figured in feminist philosophical writings about practical agendas and programs for change, such as affirmative action, pregnancy and maternity leave, and comparable worth. As the concept of equal opportunity has gained moral and legal authority, social theorists have concentrated on what is practically required to guarantee equal opportunity. Identifying and articulating the practical requirements depends upon some conception of the obstacles to equal opportunity, such as discrimination based on race and sex, poverty, unequal needs and abilities, and so on. I will especially concentrate on how feminist philosophers have grappled with sex-based discrimination and needs in proposing or advocating programs intended to broaden women's opportunities.

On a classical liberal model of equality, women have achieved equality when they have the same citizenship rights as men and when the justice system is neutral with regard to differences of gender. On a socialist model of equality, women have achieved equality when the class differences between women and men are removed – i.e. differences of education, wealth, and control over the state and the means of production. The ideal of equality of opportunity falls somewhere between these two models: achieving equality of opportunity requires more than removing the formal and legal barriers to equality, yet less than eradicating all class differences between men and women. In contemporary debates, achieving equality of opportunity implies that, in addition to achieving equality under the law, social goods and benefits are distributed fairly among competing parties. A fair distribution of goods and benefits – especially well-paying jobs and seats in high-quality educational programs – to competing parties does not require that these benefits are distributed equally among them, but only that each party is not hindered by society in its pursuit of particular goods, so that those persons who genuinely earn or merit them receive them. In short, achieving equality of opportunity is about "leveling the playing field," so to speak, or making the competition for resources fair, rather than achieving

559

more equal outcomes. In this way, the notion of equal opportunity is tied more to liberal principles of distributive justice than to radical egalitarian ideals (see Eisenstein 1984, Rawls 1971, pp. 83–90). Unfortunately, debates about equal opportunity often foreclose more fundamental and probing questions about the structures that limit the supply of employment and educational opportunities. How do particular economic and political forces create an environment that is intensely competitive and conflictual – one in which employment or educational success must be justified or explained in terms of individual merit or desert (see Young 1990a)?

Assuming opportunities will be distributed in our society through a competition based on skills, credentials, and qualifications, how do we determine whether women are unfairly blocked by society in their pursuit of particular goals? Feminists concerned with this question are interested in a host of issues, but primarily: the ways in which girls and women are socialized in our society to withdraw from the competition for certain jobs or educational programs, the ways in which women's qualifications and skills are undervalued, and the ways in which women's reproductive physiology and assigned family responsibilities handicap women's efforts to pursue degrees and jobs. What are the subtle and not-so-subtle ways in which girls are discouraged from aspiring to positions of status and influence in our society? Does low self-esteem and lack of ambition in girls result from lower abilities or lower expectations? Are the norms of femininity in our culture disempowering and disabling? Are women expected to make greater career sacrifices to support families and partnerships than men? Are the standards by which individuals are measured for jobs inflected by male norms, in terms of size, strength, expectations, and experience? Does the current under-representation of women in high-level management positions and political office, the persistent wage gap, and the increasing impoverishment of female-headed households reflect unequal accomplishment or unequal reward for the same accomplishment? Do women require different treatment than men in regard to employment leave and other parental benefits in order to have an equal chance of success, mainly because of their unique capacity to give birth? Feminist social scientists and theorists have addressed many of these questions, but below I will focus on how these questions have been taken up by feminist philosophers.

Barriers to equal opportunity

After several decades of empirical feminist research, no one disputes that within virtually all professions and industries, the higher one looks in the hierarchy of prestige, authority, and compensation, the smaller the proportion of women one sees. What is disputed are the reasons for this situation. Anti-feminists argue that women are by nature less ambitious, less willing to compete for, or are less suited for positions of authority and power. Feminists have countered that, if women are less ambitious and competitive, or are less prepared to assume high-profile roles, this is not due to nature but to the way women are socialized and stereotyped in our society (O'Neill 1977, Richards 1980). The British philosopher John Stuart Mill engaged this issue in his book *The Subjection of Women* (1869):

> I deny that any one knows, or can know, the nature of the two sexes, as long as they have only been seen in their present relation to one another ... . What is now called the nature of women is an eminently artificial thing – the result of forced repression in some directions, unnatural stimulation in others.   (1978, p. 22)

Here Mill warns us of the pitfalls in appealing to underlying "natural" causes for present states of affairs, given that invisible social forces may be at work shaping what we think of as natural. Indeed, attributing current and past patterns of accomplishment and behavior to natural forces leads to a kind of blame-the-victim approach to social problems, whereby we blame the failure of a group to achieve parity in some respect on some characteristic that members of the group supposedly share. Those who take this "essentialist" approach in order to defend the status quo demonstrate how difficult it is to effect social change. For their speculations show how current states of affairs can reinforce cultural stereotypes and prejudices about the nature of female adults that then serve to deprive women of opportunities, thus perpetuating the same outcomes.

Feminist philosophers have been concerned, not so much with resolving what has come to be known as the "nature/nurture" debate but, first, with exposing the ways that the playing field tilts when women enter and, second, justifying proposals that aim to give women a better shot at their fair share of goods and benefits. Below I will outline some of the ways that educational systems, family arrangements, and the workplace can limit women's opportunities, and then I will consider some proposals for change that feminist philosophers have defended by appealing to the standard of equal opportunity.

Many have observed that, in formal schooling, students are channeled in particular directions based on their gender (see J. Martin 1994a). In particular, elementary and secondary-school teachers and counselors often direct girls away from pursuing high-level math and science study because they assume that girls are not good at these subjects. In high-school and university classrooms, the lack of female instructor role-models often confirms existing student and faculty prejudices. Since mastering these subjects is required in order to enter particular fields – such as engineering, medicine, or computer programming and design – girls who have been directed away from these subjects will not gain the qualifications they need in order to consider opportunities in these fields. Unfortunately, there are often more subtle ways in which girls are discouraged from studying these subjects: the books and materials used to teach these subjects may fail to reflect the contributions of women to these fields; the examples and cases used to teach these subjects may draw on the cultural knowledge that boys are more likely to possess (e.g. the use of baseball or military examples); the language in which course texts are written may use only male pronouns when referring to "scientists" and "mathematicians"; and the low numbers of girls taking classes in these fields may make female students feel like outsiders.

561

Our formal educational system may treat girls differently in other ways. Authoritarian models of instruction practiced in the context of a society that socializes girls relative to boys to be submissive and passive may result in a situation where girls, on average, participate less actively in the classroom and thus get less attention than boys for their work and ideas. An educational system that requires students to compete for grades and rewards, in a society in which girls are socialized to be less competitive than boys, may result in girls showing lower achievement. Girls more than boys receive unwanted sexual attention, which can create an environment in school not conducive to their success. Schools may distribute resources, such as equipment and facilities, in ways that favor the activities of boys. And finally, colleges and universities may use criteria to admit students that favor boys over girls, such as participation in sports, or scores on "objective" tests that have been shown to underpredict women's chances of success (Sadker and Sadker 1994).

The family or domestic environment also contributes to narrowing women's opportunities. Susan Okin writes,

> The family is a crucial determinant of our opportunities in life, of what we "become." It has frequently been acknowledged by those concerned with real equality of opportunity that the family presents a problem ... . They have seen that the disparity among families in terms of the physical and emotional environment, motivation, and material advantages they can give their children has a tremendous effect upon children's opportunities in life ... .
>
> But even if all these disparities were somehow eliminated, we would still not attain equal opportunity for all. This is because what has not been recognized as an equal opportunity problem, except in feminist literature and circles, is the disparity *within* the family, the fact that its gender structure is itself a major obstacle to equality of opportunity ... . The opportunities of girls and women are centrally affected by the structure and practices of family life, particularly by the fact that women are almost invariably primary parents. (p. 16)

Okin and others have pointed out that the unequal distribution of child-care and household responsibilities to women limits their opportunities to seek and succeed in paid employment (see also Held 1982, 1993, Moulton and Rainone 1983b). This leaves women especially vulnerable when marriages and partnerships break up or partners die (Rhode 1989, p. 150). Also, the lack of child-care options, publicly or otherwise supported, has a different impact on women's lives than on men's. Furthermore, unequal amounts of moral and emotional support in the family for women's and girls' educational and employment interests, and unequal amounts of family resources allocated to women's and girls' pursuits, also affect women's opportunities. Moreover, for many women in our society, the family is the site of their physical and sexual abuse, which has a devastating impact on a woman's life chances.

Because women are expected to make a greater contribution to child care and housework than men, and then typically receive less tangible and nontangible support from families to pursue their nonfamily activities, control over family size is crucially relevant to the issue of equal opportunity for women. To exert some control over family size, women need to have access both to adequate birth control and to affordable and medically safe abortions. In this way, having control over one's fertility has become an equal opportunity issue for women. In a society where child responsibilities were more equally shared between women and men, and between private households and the larger community, this would not be so (Jaggar 1980a).

Women's opportunities for work outside the home are also limited by workplace structures that are not responsive to women's family responsibilities. such as excessively long work hours or work hours that extend into evenings and weekends, when employees may have less access to child care. Lack of flexibility in work schedules, so that women can compensate for lost work time when children are sick or out of school, often forces women to exhaust their sick pay. Employment that requires workers to travel frequently, with no special accommodations for children, impacts women differently than men, as does employment that requires workers to relocate. Women are less likely to have partners who are prepared to move with them. Employment that does not allow children to be present on the worksite when it is occasionally needed also impacts women, as primary parents, more severely. Employment where workers are penalized for taking pregnancy leave, and other child care-related leaves of absence, is more problematic for women than men.

Women's opportunities for paid employment are unfairly limited in other ways. Numerous studies indicate that gender affects how the qualifications and abilities of job applicants are judged. A resumé with a woman's name on it may be judged more negatively than the identical resumé with a man's name on it (Rhode 1989, p. 170) Employers' decisions are often influenced by myths that women are less committed or are not primary breadwinners (Warren 1977), or by some discomfort with placing women in nontraditional, nonfeminine roles. Even if employers believe themselves to be unbiased in terms of gender, they often respond to projections of their customers' or male employees' biases. Women often do not have access to informal social channels that can assist prospective job applicants. Women frequently internalize negative attitudes toward them which can undermine their confidence and performance. Women, many believe, are more frequently judged by irrelevant characteristics such as their looks or clothes. And finally, because women in our society are more likely to be victims of sexual assault, employment that requires women to forego many precautions, such as working alone late at night in areas with little security, is less likely to be acceptable to women and their employers.

By having less access to family resources and employment opportunities, women on average own less property and have fewer financial assets than men. This in turn makes it difficult for women to gain access to other financial resources and services, such as loans and credit. Without these resources, women are less able than men to start businesses or purchase real estate, acquisitions that can provide for long-term material security.

Achieving equality of opportunity

Given the variety and stubbornness of the barriers women face, feminist activists and theorists are among those who see the value of and need for "affirmative action." Some have argued that affirmative action programs are necessary to insure that women have equal opportunity with men for jobs and promotions (Fried 1976, Harris and Narayan 1994). Their argument is essentially that because social forces at present work to give men, on average, an advantage over women in the competition for desirable jobs, the establishment of goals that, at a minimum, aim at hiring women in proportion to the percentage of qualified female applicants is necessary to insure that women have an equal chance. Stated somewhat differently: because gender often affects an employer's perception of different candidates, in many hiring decisions a woman's qualifications will be underrated or overlooked, and thus affirmative action is necessary to insure that those with the best qualifications, without regard to gender, are hired. While we must ultimately work to alter the social forces that place women at a disadvantage for jobs and other benefits, until we do, affirmative action offers a temporary measure to insure that women get more equal treatment. It also provides a policy whose primary effect – placing competent women in nontraditionally female jobs – can serve to dislodge some of the entrenched social attitudes that limit their opportunities. Unfortunately, affirmative action of this kind will not help those women who are unable to acquire qualifications due to discrimination they faced in the home or school, or those who are unable to compete for paid employment because of family responsibilities.

A more simple argument for affirmative action based on the idea of equal opportunity is this. If opportunities for men and women in our society were genuinely equal, then women's and men's rates of success in employment (measured in terms of representation in high-status, high-income jobs) would not differ significantly. Women's and men's rates of success in employment differ significantly. Therefore, opportunities for men and women in our society are not genuinely equal. And consequently, until opportunities are equal, affirmative action is necessary to insure that women achieve parity with men. This argument places the burden on opponents to explain how different patterns and rates of success in employment can be consistent with the achievement of equal opportunity for women and men. Some economists believe that women characteristically have different preferences than men for jobs, and that these preferences express themselves in choices women make, which then lead to different patterns of employment for women. Women presumably prefer jobs and careers that interfere less with their familial roles and these often tend to be lower-status and lower-paying jobs. Of course, this response does not question why women allegedly prefer such jobs and careers or why men do not, or it assumes that the reasons for this are unproblematic – e.g. nature or nonpernicious sex-role conditioning.

564

Onora O'Neill (1977) offers a "reduction"-style argument for affirmative action based on the standard of equal opportunity. She states that to achieve equality of opportunity without policies like affirmative action,

> children from each major social group would have to be given a distribution of health care, diet, socialization, consideration and respect, as well as of schooling, which would ensure the same distribution of competencies ... . [S]hort of such measures it is difficult to see how equality of opportunity can ever be more than formal and from one standpoint a sham: a pretense that certain goods are equally accessible to persons of all backgrounds when in fact they are far more easily available to persons from some groups than others. (p. 185)

Since the equal distribution of goods and benefits to children would involve significant redistributions of personal wealth, something likely to be opposed by many, O'Neill argues that we should accept efforts like affirmative action in order to have some hope of making opportunities more equal between those adults who have been privileged and those who have not. O'Neill defends an aggressive affirmative action strategy, which she calls "preferential treatment," where jobs are given to women who are competent but who are not necessarily the best qualified. By using this strategy, employers would be penalizing women less for the social discrimination they have faced in competing for qualifications.

O'Neill points out that reducing the differential rates of success between different social groups through social policies such as affirmative action, and thus creating what we think of as "equal opportunity," is not tantamount to eliminating social inequality or achieving a just distribution of societal resources. A society could be pyramidal in terms of the distribution of education and wealth while "each segment of the pyramid ... contain[ed] the same proportion of persons from each major social group" (p. 189). O'Neill questions whether a society committed to equality should accept substantial inequalities within groups but not between them. Since the ideal of equal opportunity seems to be consistent with a "winner take all" mentality, this ideal is not useful in the service of more robust egalitarian aims.

For many women, discrimination based on race, sexual orientation, disability, and age seriously constrains their employment options. While women and men often face unequal treatment, white women and women of color, heterosexual and lesbian women, able-bodied and disabled women, middle-class and working-class women, and young and old women are often treated unequally. A young, white, middle-class, able-bodied heterosexual woman may fare quite differently in the competition for desirable jobs than an elderly, black, working-class, disabled lesbian. Indeed, when we focus on a single variable that limits a person's opportunity, we fail to see how the presence of two or more stigmatizing categories compounds the social obstacles a person faces in competing for opportunities (Crenshaw 1989). Perhaps, instead of merely adopting affirmative action for women and members of other stigmatized groups, we need to frame specific policies of affirmative action to help those who fall into two or more oppressed

565

groups. Otherwise, the most privileged members of each underprivileged group will be most likely to benefit from affirmative action.

In addition to supporting affirmative action, feminist philosophers have argued for other reforms in the name of equality of opportunity. For example, feminist philosophers have argued vigorously for improved pregnancy and infant-care employment leave policies, so that women who had jobs would not lose them when especially demanding family responsibilities occasionally intervened in their lives. In the mid-1970s, a number of cases involving employers' pregnancy and maternity leave policies were under review by the US judicial system. Within a few years, the Pregnancy Discrimination Act (PDA) was passed in a successful effort to connect the differential or unfavorable treatment of pregnancy and childbirth in employment practices and medical policies with sex discrimination (Williams 1991a). The feminist legal, scholarly, and activist community split on whether guaranteed pregnancy leave would bring about greater equality of opportunity for women, and whether the PDA should be interpreted to support such leave policies. Some feared that, by increasing women's rights for pregnancy and related leaves, employers would be more hesitant to hire female workers out of fear that women would exercise these rights. In the next decades, feminist theorists debated proposed employment policies relating to pregnancy, as well as different conceptions of equal opportunity that would support or go against such policies. Feminist philosophers took up these debates in volume 2, number 1 of *Hypatia* (Winter 1987), which contains five articles that directly or indirectly deal with pregnancy leave.

In her essay "Wrong rights" (1987), Elizabeth Wolgast claimed, "The common argument that a right to a maternity leave is a special and unfair right of women unless it is somehow extended to men ... puts men in the position of jealous siblings ... *competing* with pregnant women for favorable treatment, one in which they disregard the reality of childbirth" (pp. 34–5). Wolgast argued for a conception of equality that involved treating agents with different needs and situations nonidentically. She emphasized that, in gaining a right to pregnancy leave, women were not being given special treatment or rights that should earn them the justified resentment or envy of others.

According to Linda Krieger (1987), an employment law attorney writing in the same issue of *Hypatia*, the work of scholars like Wolgast and Carol Gilligan (1982a) led to a paradigm shift in feminist jurisprudence. This shift involved a move from an equal treatment paradigm to a "reasonable accommodation" one. Under the latter paradigm, policies that mandate such things as employment leave for non-Christian religious observances or wheelchair ramps are regarded as just or fair, and the absence of such policies is seen as discrimination on the basis of religious affiliation or physical ability. The argument is that, without such policies, people are not really equal in their ability to practice their religion if their religion is not that of the dominant group, nor are people equal in their ability to compete for jobs or enjoy public services if the places which provide them are not physically accessible to all. Reasoning in a similar fashion, feminists argued that "men and women are not interchangeable with respect to physical conditions which may affect their need to be absent from work" (Krieger 1987, p. 57) and, without policies that recognize this, women cannot equally compete with men for jobs and promotions. For many feminists, guaranteed pregnancy leave of significant duration (e.g. six weeks to four months) represents a reasonable accommodation to the different needs and situations of female workers, and thus is fair and just, and the absence of such permitted leave constitutes sex discrimination (see also Tong 1989).

In her article "Pregnancy leave, comparable worth, and concepts of equality" (1987), Marjorie Weinzweig critiques the work of feminist legal scholar Christine Littleton. Littleton has argued that institutions and social practices ought to be structured in ways that make gender, racial, and other such differences between individuals – whether they are culturally or biologically based – costless or insignificant in terms of material punishments and rewards. Littleton's view differs from the equal (identical) treatment model of equality and the nonidentical treatment for unequal biologically-based needs model of Wolgast. Littleton questions whether we can distinguish those differences between men and women that are biological from those that are cultural, as approaches like Wolgast's assume. Weinzweig agrees with Littleton that we cannot be sure what differences between men and women will persist as our society changes, and thus our institutions should not attempt to enforce sameness (equal treatment approach) or difference (special needs and accommodation approaches). However, Weinzweig does not share Littleton's ideal of "costless difference" because she is skeptical that an appropriate method can be found for identifying which differences should be costless. Also, she believes that an equal distribution of rewards across identified differences (equality of effect) is neither a plausible goal nor a necessary concept for justifying the policies of guaranteed pregnancy leave. Indeed, Littleton's model of equality reaches beyond equal opportunity and toward more equal outcomes.

Instead, Weinzweig argues that we should aim for equal participation in the political community, and economic and social spheres (p. 95). Weinzweig links equality opportunity with the end of the segregation of women into a private sphere centered around unpaid caregiving work, the elevation of the status of caregiving work, and a more equal distribution of this work between women and men. On her view, the maintenance of separate public and private spheres, with separate reward and opportunity systems and responsibilities, serves to maintain the social, economic, and political inequality of those assigned to distinct spheres. This model of equal opportunity incorporates women into the public world, not as honorary men, but as androgynous beings with the needs and talents traditionally assigned to both men and women, and it sees the traditional male breadwinning role as limiting for both men and women.

Weinzweig argues that her notion of equal opportunity supports pregnancy leave, since such benefits facilitate the balancing of caregiving work with paid work, and thus furthers the integration of the private and public spheres. This model also supports comparable worth policies – policies that adjust salary levels in accordance with internal criteria of "job worth" – as a means of reducing wage discrepancies correlated with the sex or race of the workers who predominantly fill particular job categories. Comparable worth entails appreciating the skills possessed and work performed by workers in sex-segregated, female-dominated occupations (perhaps even in traditional unwaged work), and not overvaluing the work performed by workers in male-dominated occupations, so that women and men can receive more equal amounts of social recognition and material compensation for their skills, efforts, and achievements. Weinzweig suggests that comparable worth contributes to realizing the social conditions that maximize people's opportunities for self-development, empowers them in their relationships with others, and allows for their fuller participation in all spheres of life.

In "Some implications of comparable worth" (Shrage 1987), I too argue that comparable worth is an important component of any feminist agenda to end women's political, social, and economic subordination. Numerous studies indicate that jobs performed predominantly by persons of color and white women pay significantly less than those primarily occupied by white men, even when the jobs compare favorably in terms of the level of skill, responsibility, experience, effort, and formal training they demand. Such a pervasive pattern of salary differentials that correlate closely with the race and gender of the traditional job holders reflects the existence of cultural ideologies and principles that devalue the skills and abilities of women and men of color. The adoption of comparable worth standards of pay by employers will serve to reduce the wage inequities that have evolved due to historical and ongoing race and gender prejudice. Instead of setting salaries internally in accordance with the social status of the worker, employers would devise procedures for setting salaries in accordance with some agreed-upon criteria of job worth. Without such procedures, women and men of color are likely to find that their efforts do not really "pay." which serves as a disincentive to compete for desirable positions.

Striving for equality of opportunity is an important but incomplete agenda for social and political change, for it will not fundamentally increase the opportunities there are. Equality of opportunity can be used to argue for broad social change, such as the distribution of goods and benefits to those traditionally denied them, the abolition of separate private and public spheres, and the reorganization of worker compensation systems, but it needs to be supplemented by other moral and political ideals.

57

Social policy

EVA FEDER KITTAY

Introduction

Defining social policy

Social policy, broadly understood, is an intervention by government or other public institution designed to promote the well-being of its members or intended to rectify perceived social problems. Governmental policy can issue from legislative, executive, or judicial actions. Regulations and rules governing major public establishments, such as universities or medical institutions, and directed at promoting the aims of the larger social body can also be considered instruments of social policy. Social policy is sometimes understood more narrowly as interventions of the state in the domain of distribution or redistribution, when action has been thought necessary to correct for the instability inherent in a given social structure or created by pressures for social change (Ferge 1993). In this sense, it pertains to welfare policies aimed at the poor. In this article, we will deal primarily with social policy in the broad sense, reserving a brief discussion at the end on social policy in the narrow sense, as welfare policy.

Feminist philosophy engages social policy – policy and context

Feminist philosophers have engaged policy both as its critics and as its proponents, making use of feminist empirical and legal scholarship. (For examples of case material see Winston and Bane 1993, and for feminist legal studies see P. Smith 1993; also see Article 53, ANGLO-AMERICAN LAW.) While some argue that philosophers should steer clear of concrete policy, others have argued that such engagement is crucial to good political and social philosophy (Brison 1995).

The contextual nature of policy issues poses special challenges for the theory. Overarching theories can be of limited value in analyzing and proposing policy without a familiarity with the local political terrain. For instance, women's health, violence against women, and reproductive control are issues women face across the globe, but policies addressing these concerns may be geographically precise. So while women's control over their own bodies raises questions about the appropriate response to addicted pregnant women in the United States, Pynne (1995), writing in the Burmese context, looks for policy that will address the sexual enslavement and consequent spread of AIDS among victimized Burmese women. In this article, I survey the application of theory to policy issues, especially as they emerge in the local terrain of US politics, but whenever appropriate, I have included reference to international dimensions of the issues discussed.

The political context also constrains what can be accomplished even with social policy that aims at transforming (or subverting) that context. Radical political alterations, such as the abolition of capitalism or the state, advanced in socialist, Marxist, radical (Jaggar 1983) or anarchist feminisms (see Addelson et al. 1991, K. Ferguson 1983) therefore sit uncomfortably with the reformist nature of social policy. Still, many who identify with one of these positions argue that feminists, whatever their political outlook, should join forces in working toward reform and look for common criteria to evaluate these reforms. (See Wendell 1987, Harding 1973–4. See Bunch (1981) for a proposed set of criteria by which to evaluate policies.)

Evolving/alternative social policy strategies

Since the field of feminist philosophy was first mapped in the late 1960s and early 1970s, writings on policy have evolved and have been shaped by a response to historical, social, economic, and political developments, by progress in feminist theory, and by the changing nature and scope of feminist demands. The trajectory of feminist public policy begins with nondiscrimination, moves to debates on fostering the inclusion of women in traditionally male domains, and then progresses to efforts to transform the institutions and norms that have served as the baseline for nondiscrimination and inclusion.

This trajectory differs as it applies to different issues. Some institutions are especially resistant to feminist analyses or demands, others yield more quickly. Furthermore, it is sometimes more appropriate to speak of nondiscrimination, inclusion, and transformation not as different historical phases but as alternate strategies, driven, at least in part, by different political visions. In either case, we can organize the preoccupation with, and treatment of, much policy in terms of these concepts.

Nondiscrimination

Nondiscrimination is continuous with the liberal goals of freedom and equality as realizable by the removal of constraints and impediments. Wollstonecraft (1792) captured this Enlightenment ideal in her appeal to Tallyrand as he was about to revise France's Constitution. "Let there be no coercion *established* in society," she wrote, "and the common law of gravity prevailing, the sexes will fall into their proper places" (1993, pp. 71–2, emphasis author's). To demand nondiscrimination is not only (1) to insist on the removal of laws that overtly discriminate against women; and (2) to demand the presence of laws that make such discrimination unlawful; it is also (3) to direct attention to the presence of policies and institutional structures that *implicitly* discriminate against women.

Feminist philosophers, in this first phase of the new wave of feminism, demanded policy change with respect to rape (Griffin 1977, Shafer and Frye

1977, Foa 1977, Peterson 1977, Curley 1976), abortion (Jaggar 1980a, Thompson 1971, English 1975), marriage law (Ketchum 1977) and argued for equal opportunity in education and employment (O'Neill 1977, Ezorsky 1974). Socialist democracies such as Sweden approached the question of women's equality by shoring up antidiscrimination law begun in the earlier part of the twentieth century and developing social policy instruments such as government-subsidized child care, paid parental leave, and separate taxation of husbands' and wives' earnings (resulting in a better payoff for equalizing distribution of paid work in a household). In the United States, although progressive traditions other than liberalism urged pay for housework and affordable or free child care, the dominant concerns of liberal policy were to expand opportunities for women in spheres dominated by men through the establishment of antidiscrimination and equal opportunity legislation. (See Schmid and Weitzel 1984 for a comparative study of antidiscrimination policies and equal opportunity legislation in Sweden, the United Kingdom, the United States and West Germany.)

The radical feminist slogan "the private is political" was important in turning issues of rape, abortion, domestic abuse, and domestic work into public and *political* concerns, especially in North America and Europe – though a deeper theoretical development had yet to take place. However, in the arena of international human rights, the struggle to expose "private" concerns such as genital mutilation, rape in war, domestic violence, and reproductive abuses as "public" human rights violations continues. To correct such practices calls upon more than arguments based on nondiscrimination. It demands a transformation of the very concept of "human rights". (See Peters and Wolper 1995 for articles representing a wide array of issues from different global perspectives that revision women's rights as human rights.)

Inclusion

When progress removing formal constraints is not found to significantly alter distributions in wealth, power, or position, the demand becomes one for policies that *foster* inclusion. Again policies promoting women's participation within paid employment have figured prominently, but now affirmative action and preferential treatment are highlighted. (See Thompson 1971, Thalberg 1973–4, Fried 1976, Vetterling-Braggin 1973–4, Newton 1973, Hawkesworth 1990, Kaminer 1990, Ezorsky 1991. Also see Outshoorn 1991, criticizing the Netherlands' affirmative action push as crowding out other concerns.) Once women are in the workplace, their ability to participate fully also requires protection against sexual harassment (MacKinnon 1979b, Superson 1993, Altman 1996); equal pay through policies of pay equity and comparable worth (Weinzweig 1987, Steinberg and Haignere 1991, Kaminer 1990); maternal leave (Weinzweig 1987, Baker 1987, Kaminer 1990, Vogel 1985, Bacchi 1991); and adequate child care (Midgley and Hughes 1983, Kaminer 1990).

Theorists have developed better tools with which to demand – or interrogate – inclusion as a strategy and as a goal. For example, psychoanalytic feminism has

571

provided compelling arguments for the need to include men in the rearing of even young children – an insight missing in eighteenth-, nineteenth-, and early twentieth-century feminist writings – thereby adding weight to policy demands for expansive parental leave for both men and women, for educational efforts directed at men's parenting, and for joint custody. (See, for example, Okin 1989a, Held 1982; although see essays in Trebilcot 1983a for a more critical perspective by US feminists. On parental arrangements, joint custody and "father's rights," etc., in Canada, Britain, Australia, the Netherlands, Ireland, Norway, France, and the USA see the essays in Smart and Sevenhuijsen 1989.)

Some of the most important theoretical developments have come from newly systematic questionings of the historic divides between private/domestic and political/public domains, dichotomies that structure both liberal and Marxist political theory (Elshtain 1981, Pateman 1989c). When private concerns have precluded women's full accommodation into "public" domains, women have demanded state intervention into the private domain. "Intimate" violence, e.g. wife battering and violent and degrading pornographic images, join sexual harassment and need for maternity leave and child care as ways in which private domain domination precludes women's full inclusion as citizens. The dialectical relation between full participation in the social, political, and economic spheres and women's well-being in the private domain has a different dimension in many developing nations. Sen (1989) demonstrates that women's access to public domains of paid employment in developing countries is an important prophylaxis against women suffering often lethal abuse in the domestic sphere.

The nature and basis for state intervention into presumed private domains have not always found feminists in accord. The question of when such state intervention is called for is sometimes a point dividing liberal and radical feminists. Pornography and hate speech is a case in point. (See *Hudnut* v. *American Booksellers* 1985; see Carse 1995 for a recent discussion. For an overview see Tong 1989; on the relevance of social science research, see Kittay 1988a. On hate speech, see Brison, forthcoming; Meyers 1995.)

Feminists have also pointed to the complex nature of the public/private divide in countries where demands of women are inflected with conflicts between either historic, religious, or tribal differences and the nation-state. Pathak and Rajan (1992) give a fascinating account of how one divorced Muslim woman's suit to be maintained at the equivalent of $14 a month from her husband "created a furor unequaled ... since 'the upheaval of 1857'"(p. 257).

Full inclusion in military service, deemed necessary by some, has others concerned that such equality would condemn women to a Procrustean bed formed according to men's measure. Should women heed Woolf's (1938/1966) insistence on a pacifist, anti-nationalist feminism, or is the willingness to participate in military service, including combat duty, a *sine qua non* for full citizenship (Ruddick 1983, 1989, Swerdlow 1989, Stiehm 1989, Held 1993, De Cew 1995, Card 1995c)?

The goal of inclusion not only touts the ideal of equality, it also affirms women's full autonomy (Midgley and Hughes 1983): If we are to be included as full citizens, should we not eschew constraints on consent and contract? Still, under patriarchy, does false consciousness wrest false consent from women; does their disadvantaged position subject women to exploitative contracts?

These questions have been discussed with respect to a very wide array of issues. Debates arise with respect to prostitution (Danielle 1982, Jaggar 1980b, Pateman 1983, Shrage 1990b), cosmetic surgery (Morgan 1991, Parker 1995), sexual desire (Hart 1990, Bar On 1994), legal responses to women who kill batterers (Hasse 1987), and "date rape" (Francis 1996). Consent, autonomy, and the implications of the increased choices and possibilities become explosive matters in the arena of reproductive technology. Among the issues of concern are the impact of such technologies on low-income women and women of color (Nsiah-Jefferson 1989) and long-term contraception and its impact on social policies affecting poor women (Moskowitz et al. 1995, Nelson and Nelson 1995). A spate of books and articles deal with surrogacy (among which are Macklin 1988, Radin 1988, Anderson 1990, Feldman 1992, Kymlicka 1991, Holmes and Purdy 1992, Allen 1991, Baker 1996, Michaels 1996, Shanley 1993, and other reproductive technologies, such as in-vitro fertilization, fetal monitoring and fetal surgery, fertilization techniques (Corea 1983, Overall 1987, Singer and Wells 1984, Lasker and Borg 1987, Spallone and Steinberg 1987, Stanworth 1987), genetic testing and prenatal testing for gender, paternity, and disability (Warren 1985, Cohen and Taub 1989, especially Asch 1989, Baruch et al. 1988, Wertz and Fletcher 1993). Among the concerns raised in these debates is the question of which women benefit from these technologies and whether they do so at the expense of other women.

Transformation

When policies of inclusion either fail to benefit women, benefit them differentially, or reveal deeper social problems that inclusion policies do not address, women's demands turn to policies that will *transform* culpable institutions – gender and sexual identity, marriage, the family, the workplace, nationhood, and a human's relation to the nonhuman world. Looking beyond the liberal and Marxist traditions to critical theory, Foucauldian poststructuralism, psychoanalysis, postmodernism, postcolonial studies and ecology, feminist philosophers have not merely applied these notions to women's concerns, but have developed some distinctively feminist conceptual tools. They have searched for policies that will degender and refigure traditional gender roles, not so much by androgynizing men and women, as by reconstituting roles and institutions.

But the project of transformation runs headlong into the question of *what* women's needs are and *which* women's needs they are. Can we speak of women as a group, and how can we grapple with differences among women in formulating social policies? Concerns with differences among women challenge us to look at a context broader than one defined strictly by gender.

573

The seeds of transformative possibilities in social policy affecting women may in fact be found by looking beyond gender as such. The effort to have women's rights recognized as human rights depends not only on the transformation of the concept of human rights, but also expands feminist concerns to conditions prevailing in postcolonial developing nations (Bahar 1996, Nussbaum 1993, Peters and Wolper 1995). The new question of gay and lesbian marriage has a potential to transform that prime example of patriarchy, the traditional marriage (Kaplan 1993). While most of the welfare states of central Europe and Scandinavia had already well-established paid parental and family sick-leave policies, US feminists work to expand the demand for leave for maternity alone to leave to care for dependents – irrespective of the gender of the "dependency worker." (See Kittay 1995, on the US Family and Medical Leave Act of 1993.) This expansion provides an opening for transforming the workplace into one in which workers' needs to be caretakers are recognized (Young 1995). In the process, we glean the possibility of finding inroads to a real transformation of what constitutes a worker, what sorts of social contributions deserve the title of "work," and what constitutes "family."

Most all of these questions have important racial dimensions. and even which issues receive scholarly attention are inflected with race, especially in the United States. Williams (1995) and Spillers (1987) write of the racial dimension of gender with respect to family and welfare policies. Furthermore, we find that feminist philosophers have seized on public policy issues as a way of transforming the institution of race, as, for example, when they examine policies pertaining to the category of "mixed race" (Zack 1995b) and interracial adoption (A. Allen 1990, Smith 1996). Perhaps most significant are issues such as poverty and racism, which affect not only women, but also the men, children, and community which form the context of women's lives (Malveaux 1990, Young 1990a).

Radical reconceptions of fundamental institutions and categories, such as race and gender identity, are similarly evident in the interrogation of policies aimed at children whose gender expression is judged deviant (Feder 1997). (Also see Singer 1993, on public policy as regulating marginalized sexualities.)

In the case of earlier issues such as abortion and reproductive rights, feminists increasingly have moved from contesting the personhood of the fetus to focusing on social and political issues that drive reproductive debates. These, claims Petchesky (1981), go to the core of the transformations feminists have effected. She writes, "[T]he meanings resonating from abortion politics have more to do with compulsory heterosexuality, family structure, the relationship between men and women and parents and children, and women's employment than they do with the fetus" (p. 228).

Today, in the United States, many antiabortion forces have conceded for now the legal right to abortion, but have successfully put in place legislation that inhibits access to abortion to many poor and young women. Stroud (1996) argues such regulations (e.g. a mandatory twenty-four-hour waiting period, parental or judicial consent for minors, the demand that those seeking abortions be provided with certain information) amount to the imposition of one religious interpretation *by the state* of the sanctity of human life. Therefore they constitute the establishment of a state religion with respect to abortion. As feminists transform the social landscape, opponents will respond with new efforts to effectively vitiate the advances. Feminists must look to both new resources of feminist theory, as well as older resources, as does Stroud when she invokes the constitutional prohibition against state establishment of religion, to fight the transformed battles.

The current terms of debate

Differences over policy issues have often been aligned with different classical political traditions (see Jaggar 1983), yet current thinking is more often formed by new feminist theory and current social developments. Three axes of debate, which I identify as equality versus difference, universality versus diversity, and justice versus care, have been important in sharpening discussion concerning the strategies of nondiscrimination, inclusion, and transformation.

Equality versus difference

The debate between equality and difference is "the site where feminist theory meets feminist practice" (Boehm 1992, p. 203). "Equality feminists" largely depend on nondiscrimination and inclusion strategies, while "difference feminists" favor transformative strategies. The question debated is as simple as the response is complicated: If, as Aristotle tells us, justice requires that we treat those who are alike similarly and those who are unalike differently, then, for the sake of justice, should we say that women and men are alike and so require the same treatment or that they are different and so require different treatment? Minow (1991a) points to "a dilemma of difference": to insist on women's difference is to dangerously court the stigma and disadvantage associated with difference. But to insist on women's and men's sameness disregards men's and women's different situations and how that difference, if ignored, can perpetuate or even worsen women's condition.

Whether social policy should be guided by difference or equality is not a new question for feminism. (See Pateman 1992, Rhode 1992, Katzenstein and Laitin 1987 for some brief historical accounts.) Lesbian separatists, for example, have long asked if sex equality is not itself a patriarchal institution (Frye 1983, Card 1990b). The critiques of equality come not only from the claim that women are different from men in certain crucial respects, but also that this difference is structured as dominance (MacKinnon 1990, Pateman 1992). Women's traditional care of dependents may be understood either in terms of difference or dominance. Some feminists instead offer dependency and disadvantage as the concepts we need in order to question strategies of equality (Baier 1987b, Elshtain 1990, Kittay 1995, Young 1995, Rhode 1992). Still others hold fast to the claim that strategies of equality, properly understood, or of an equality properly transformed, offer the best hope for progress toward a feminist future. (See Okin 1994, Kaminer 1990, Littleton 1987; and legal theorists' work sampled in Smith 1995b. Also see Bussemaker 1991 for a defense of equality based on Dutch policy claiming that equality can incorporate plurality.)

Pateman (1992), pointing to the experience of women in the United States, Great Britain, Australia, and New Zealand, argues that more egalitarian changes already indicate that if we are to go beyond the equality/difference debate, we need to break the tie between employment (figured on the model of the male worker) and citizenship. This suggestion emphasizes the dialectic between theory and practice. A similar dialectic is Jaggar's (1980a) "dynamic" approach, emphasizing the context framing any policy debate. A difference policy, such as affirmative action, may one day justifiably give way to gender-blind policies in education and hiring, while an equality approach to parenting and custody may be unfeasible as long as women remain disadvantaged in a market economy and high-quality child care remains unavailable.

Such pragmatic approaches suggest that while feminists need to attend to difference, they should work toward an equality that transforms the very categories and practices from which difference emerges. For example, women must have pregnancy leave and more support to fulfill responsibilities to dependents. But such policies have to transform the interpretation of that need from one that *women* have to one that *society as a whole* has. This means having gender-neutral policies, but ones fashioned on the model of women's lives.

Universality versus diversity: differences among women

The title of Bethel's (1979) essay "What chou mean 'we' white girl?" and hooks's (1987) query "When feminists demand equality to men, what men are they asking to be equal to?" smartly capture the vexing problem of universal gender claims. The supposition that women speak with one voice has been challenged both by postmodernists and feminists inspired by women's concrete differences – difference with respect to color and ethnicity, sexuality, ability. (On women and disability see Wendell 1989, Fine and Asch 1988a, 1988b, Silvers 1995.)

Minow's dilemma of difference has its correlate in the question of whether we can (or should) posit a singular category "women." If we grant such a unitary category, then we are in danger of universalizing the concerns of only some women – those best situated to voice their own concerns. In so doing we consolidate the interests of women who already are among the most privileged. But if we deny that women form a unified category, then to whom are policies directed at "women" aimed at? (For a defense of women as a category see Okin 1996, Nussbaum 1993a. Also see Yeatman 1993, discussing an Australian case of a white anthropologist who defended her right and responsibility to write about rape in Aboriginal culture.)

Postmodern feminism has helped articulate a language of difference and to caution feminists against lapsing into discredited foundationalist and essentialist presumptions in thinking about policy. (See Riley 1988, Scott 1988, Alcoff 1988,

Nicholson 1990, especially Fraser and Nicholson 1990, Yeatman and Gunew 1993, Yeatman 1994.)

African-American women and women of color point to the history of racism and colonialism that make universal claims of white women suspect. Davis (1990) provides a history of racial divisions among American feminists, one reflected in recent history by Lorde's (1984) famous open letter to Mary Daly.

A way out of the dilemma of difference urged by many has been to form coalitions and so forge a unity which is not already given. As such theorists as Lugones and Spelman (1986), Lugones (1990, 1991), Spelman (1988), Malveaux (1990), and hooks (1984), among others, have pointed out, this will mean paying special heed to those issues that affect subjected communities and understanding the intersectionality (Crenshaw 1989) of non-gender- and gender-based oppression. Of pressing concern, then, are questions of how to build secure coalitions. (See Fraser 1986, Young 1990a, Jakobsen 1995, Malveaux 1990, Kittay, forthcoming.) The concern to build a broad-based feminism that will endure in the face of reaction and backlash provides rife ground for philosophical reflection concerning issues of solidarity and difference, and will constitute feminism's ultimate test both as a theoretical outlook and as a social movement.

Care versus justice

Social policy has been dominated by distributive paradigms whose legitimation rests with notions of justice, whether contractarian or utilitarian. Policies are framed with respect to risk/benefit assessments and demands articulated as rights. Feminist theorists have developed an ethic of care, based in part on women's traditional role as caretakers. They have asked whether and how caring, an activity and moral stance significantly associated with women, can or should be brought into the public arena of social policy and law, and have challenged rights as the appropriate or *only* appropriate vehicle by which to address needs and concerns women share. (See Article 40, LESBIAN ETHICS.)

A first attempt to locate the importance of a care ethic in the "public domain" is Ruddick's maternal-based peace politics (Ruddick 1983, 1987, 1989). Tronto (1993) proposes that a model of care offers a better guide to social welfare policies because of its attention to the context of actions, the particularity of persons, and the evaluation of sentiment. Furthermore, according to Tronto, care is more inclusive than justice, involving as political actors those who do most of society's caring work, that is, men and women of color and white women. Therefore, she contends, a care ethics is better equipped to deal with otherness, providing, as it does, a strategy of learning to respond to others' need. (Narayan 1995 is more critical of care as responsive to "otherness." For additional critical evaluations of care as generally applicable social policy see Brooks 1991, Dietz 1985, Katzenstein and Laitin 1987, Bassham 1992, MacKinnon 1990.)

Medical policies are an especially ripe area for the engagement of a feminist care ethic, as Sevenhuijsen (1996) points out in discussing proposed changes in the Netherlands' health-care system. Health policies concern both the provision

577

of care and its providers, who are largely women. Nonetheless, care-related concepts are rarely employed in considering how to allocate medical resources, as Sichel (1989) points out in studying medical institutional ethics committees. (See also Holmes and Purdy 1992. Mahowald 1987, 1993. See Silvers 1995 on care as an approach to the dilemma of difference in dealing with disability.)

A number of reproductive issues have also been importantly reshaped by a consideration of care ethics, especially as notions of responsibility, context, and the relationality of the self are juxtaposed to notions such as rights, principles, and autonomy. The latter, it can be argued, poorly suit the situation of women contemplating or encountering a pregnancy. Gilligan (1982a) is the point of departure for a care ethic applied to abortion. (Also see Wolf-Devine 1989, Gatens-Robinson 1992, Colker 1995. See Thompson 1990 for an argument cautioning against using care as a basis for the permissibility of abortion.) Some feminists have thought to deploy a care ethics for the vexing problems of reproductive technologies (Weiss 1995, Michaels 1996).

A number of other issues pertaining to public policy have made use of an ethic of care. By evoking a "feminine ethic of care" as the rationale for the woman who remains in an abusive domestic situation, Hartline (1996) proposes a new defense for the woman who subsequently kills an abusive spouse (cf. Hasse 1987). As feminist philosophers continue to explore the resources of a feminist ethic of care and offer it as a challenge to the paradigms which dominate public policy discussions, we can expect to see an ever-widening range of issues yielding to this approach, and a richer debate concerning the relative usefulness of care and justice applied to policy.

Welfare and women

Central to the notion of public policy and feminism is the idea of citizenship. What right does the state have in controlling the behavior of its citizens; and what obligations does it have to provide for its members? This question takes on special importance in the case of welfare policies.

As of this writing, the "welfare wars," which are largely wars "about, even against, women" (Fraser 1987, p. 103), have been fought and lost in the United States, as it ends its sixty-year entitlement to cash assistance for needy families with dependent children. Central Europe, Scandinavia, Australia, and New Zealand are all facing a "restructuring" of the welfare state that threatens to cut back on the breadth and scope of welfare provisions. With reference to the United States Piven and Cloward (1971) argued that welfare provisions expand and contract in response to the need for labor and the control of social unrest. As such, social policy serves as an instrument of control, particularly affecting the lives of the poor, who are more subject to governmental regulation since they are more directly dependent on the state for subsistence.

In the United States, the welfare wars have been fought by conservative forces under the triple banner of "saving marriage and the family" (understood implicitly as the white, heterosexual, patriarchal family), "saving taxpayers' money," and "encouraging independence." Those welfare programs of which *women* are almost the exclusive adult beneficiaries are means-tested, stigmatized, under-funded, and despised by the taxpaying public and beneficiaries alike. Although the welfare participant is as likely to be white as a person of color, the image most often projected is the face of an African-American woman. In contrast, the welfare programs from which men benefit in large numbers (e.g. unemployment insurance, old-age social security) are "contributory programs," not means-tested but universal in scope, well funded, and highly popular. The face of the stereotypical beneficiary of these programs is that of a white male. (On the two-tiered, gendered nature of the welfare state in the United States and other English-speaking nations, see Fraser 1987, Fraser and Gordon 1994, Pearce 1979, and Pateman 1989c, 1992. See also Duran 1988 on the gendered nature of social work.)

The two-tiered system of benefits raises questions concerning the appropriate terms in which to couch the kind of provisions women, especially poor women, require to function as equal citizens: rights? entitlements? needs? The two-tiered system also raises significant questions about the meaning of the touted values "independence," "work," and "family," and the place of care in a just social order. While Fraser provides an overarching framework of needs interpretation which is to take place on the contested ground of the "social," others have examined specific provisions of the welfare state in light of feminist concerns and frameworks.

Young (1994b) makes concrete policy proposals, with regard both to drug-addicted pregnant women (see also Bordo 1993) and to welfare "reform" policies such as "workfare," and warns against ones that use rhetoric of "empower-ment" to reprivatize rather than politicize individuals. She shifts the discourse away from "welfare" for the neediest to universal provisions of full employment and a guaranteed income. As Gordon (1994), among others, has argued, fem-inists must work for universal provisions: for child care, for cash assistance for children, for flexible work hours at public and private jobs, for medical care, and care support for elderly or sick or disabled persons, and for greater flexibility in living arrangements to accommodate single-parent households.

It is also important to note, with Friedman (1988), the rise of a new form of class-based market patriarchy. Cuts in welfare benefits favor middle-class women, providing a cheap source of labor for domestic work, services which middle-class women increasingly pay for to lighten their own "double load" of domestic and non-domestic labor. Such developments work against a feminist-based solidarity.

Feminists have in fact changed much of public discourse and contributed to changes in the behavior of women and men alike. Most people no longer presume that a mother will stay at home and devote her exclusive attention to children and home; nor do we presume that pregnancy just befalls women – having a child is increasingly viewed as a choice for which a woman is respons-ible. These positive changes have unfortunately also been misappropriated by those who attack women too poor or too poorly equipped to enter the job market

579

and earn a living wage, and by those who vilify poor women as being "irresponsible" if they have children and must turn to public assistance. That is to say, the very substantial gains feminists have made are also used as cudgels against women, especially the most vulnerable. Zack (1995b), in a different context, writes that "Tigers have to be dismounted with great care." The enthusiasm with which some of us have dismounted the tiger patriarchy may well have left others all the more vulnerable to its formidable jaws. Feminists have again to engage the dialectic of practice and theory, and demand public policies that will address that vulnerability.

58

War and peace

SARA RUDDICK

Feminists have long hoped to intervene in the practice of war. Many have thought of war as a masculine endeavor which endangers women in distinctive ways and reflects and contributes to men's violence against women in civil society. Some have also believed that women have distinct capacities for making peace. In recent decades, feminists have elaborated these insights, offering a more precise understanding of war's masculinity, war's victimization of women and feminine peacefulness. Despite the vitalizing presence of many military feminists, the cumulative effect of feminist intervention has been to question the practice of warmaking itself and to challenge the cultures which prepare, justify, and suffer from war.

War's masculinity

Feminists begin by insisting that militaries and their wars are "masculine." They attend especially to a predatory, misogynist, heterosexually bigoted soldier who experiences a "naked, hideous male gratification" (Wolf 1984, p. 73) in injuring and killing, and sometimes in rape and sexual torture. More casually misogynist masculinity is expressed in training rituals, graffiti, gestures and boasts of soldiers returning from battle, and sexy, tough talk of commanders and strategists (Hartsock 1985, 1989, Theweleit 1987, 1990, 1993, Woolf 1938, 1984, Cohn 1987, 1989, 1993, Ruddick 1993).

Predatory rapaciousness is only one, particularly repellent, expression of war's masculinity. Soldiers are also seen and encouraged to see themselves as comradely brothers, team players, conquering heroes in the nation's service, adventurous rescuers, and just warriors who protect women and other vulnerable people (Hartsock 1989, Lloyd 1987, 1989). These masculine identities are collectively expressed for participants and spectators in the sexualization of weapons and fantasized attack. In many cultures, the penis is transformed into a phallus which is then represented in sword, gun, or missile. The ubiquitous "asshole" becomes the organ through which the rapist–soldier renders his enemy female (Held 1993, Cohn 1993, Keller 1990).

Feminists force into focus war's masculinity but rarely accept it as "nature." Rather, they offer accounts of warmaking which specify and explain its masculinity while also allowing for change. It seems plausible to begin by tracing war's masculinity to men's aggression. Men are not all aggressive, nor is aggression exclusively male. But there is evidence, and certainly widespread belief, that men, especially in adolescence and early adulthood, act aggressively, and take pleasure in their aggression, to a degree that women do not. In addition to the desire and ability to injure, warmaking also depends upon capacities only indirectly related to aggression: the ability to separate one's ordinary affection and tenderness from newly ordinary willingness to kill; indifference to the pain of others; toleration of boredom; the ability to see the other as enemy and the enemy as killable other (Griffin 1992, Ruddick 1993, Peach, 1996). Some theorists have claimed that capacities of abstraction and disassociation are, to a degree, "masculine" (e.g. Theweleit 1987, 1990, Keller 1985, Ruddick 1993). Combat also requires collective bonding and obedience to commanders, characteristics which militarists often attribute to masculinist training and exclusively male groups.

In order to explain men's many distinctive capacities for warmaking, some feminists have invoked a version of psychoanalytic theory known as object relations (e.g. Theweleit 1987, 1990, Hartsock 1989, Ruddick 1989). To put matters simply: in masculinist social groups where men hold the principal governing posts and are responsible for hunting, war, or other "legitimate" aggression, and where women are responsible for childtending and other care-taking activities, masculinity is both highly valued and imperious. Boys in these societies are encouraged to define themselves as not-female and to devalue whatever characteristics are associated with females in their particular culture. To this end, they submit to male authority with which they ambivalently identify and bond with other males to exclude females. They deny their envy of female birthgiving, their longing for mothering women, and their fear of female retaliation for male privilege. Because these defenses are rigid and fragile, boy-men have to reject and conquer the (m)other again and again.

Object relations theory makes sense of a number of tendencies expressed in collective violence: fear of the Other; aggression against women and whatever is labeled feminine; denial and abstraction; obedience to male authority; passions of brotherly love. It also explains why war might disturb combat soldiers' "normal" adaptive restraint. In combat men are away from the women and "home" whose seductions they have learned to manage. They are usually frightened, typically physically miserable, and often under attack. In these circumstances they are subjected to male authority, dependent upon their "brothers," and encouraged to hate and injure. It is not surprising. then. if adaptive "normal" restraint gives way to misogynous and xenophobic hatred and sexual desire (Ruddick 1993).

Because object relations theory relates "masculine" tendencies to particular kinds of masculinist social groups, the "masculinity" it accounts for is subject to change. Moreover, within any society, individual men's (and women's) acquisition of "masculinity" depends on the sexual make-up of their families, the social status of their family group, familial power relations, school experience, and many other factors. Thus object relations theory can account for "normal masculinity" as well as for individual and social exception and variation.

A second conceptual innovation of recent feminist theory directs attention away from gendered individuals to "gender discourse." A "gender discourse" is a symbolic system which dichotomizes human characteristics such as thought and feeling, mind and body, confrontation and accommodation, and systematically associates the first and valued set of characteristics with masculinity, the second, and opposite set with femininity (Lloyd 1987, Cohn 1993). In a series of influential works, Carol Cohn (1987, 1989, 1990, 1993) has described the effect of gender discourse on the discourse of defense analysts and strategists. Within the largely white and middle-class community of defense intellectuals, a general cultural devaluation of the feminine is intensified by a specific professional identification with "masculinity" and an "objective," abstract style of thinking. The entrenched superior status of masculinity and the pervasiveness of abstract denial make it "extremely difficult for anyone, female or *male*, to express concerns or ideas marked as 'feminine' and still maintain his or her legitimacy" (Cohn 1993, p. 238). Since empathy, the desire to accommodate, horror of concrete suffering, interest in the enemy, and a range of other attitudes are discursively marked "feminine," they cannot enter into "reasonable" discussion.

The concept of "gendered discourse" and the psychoanalytic theory of objections relations can be seen as complementary. Like object relations theory, the concept of gender discourse construes identities as many-faceted intersections of gender, race, class, and other social characteristics. As in object relations, these identities are not fixed but mobilized, evoked, enforced, and defended in particular circumstances.

> There are many specific discourses of gender, which vary by race, class, ethnicity, locale, sexuality, and other factors. The masculinity idealized in the gender discourse of new Haitian immigrants is in some ways different from that of sixth generation white Anglo-Saxon protestant business executives, and both differ somewhat from that of white-male defense intellectuals and security analysts. One version of masculinity is *mobilized* and *enforced* in the armed forces in order to enable men to fight wars, while a somewhat different version of masculinity is *drawn upon* and expressed by abstract theoreticians of wars. (Cohn 1993, p. 230, emphasis added)

"Gendered discourse" shows how males, females, ideas, and emotions, are positioned as masculine and legitimate, or feminine and despised, and how, therefore, men and women are limited by a *system* which makes it difficult to think in a "voice" that is both "different" and credible. Object relations theory explains why men may be drawn more, and drawn differently, than women to masculine positions and to the attitudes and cognitive styles they require and legitimate.

Four figures of femininity

War's masculinity is partnered by a myth of loyal femininity. Feminine loyalists are mothers of the nation who weep for the fallen and pray for the absent soldier's return. Sometimes, too, they galvanize patriotic sentiments, including hatred for the enemy, and excoriate "cowards" who refuse to fight. More prosaically, they take up "feminine" war work – social services or nursing, for example. In film and legend, at least, military women, in direct contrast to misogynist soldiers, are androphiliac. They eroticize "our" heroes, memorialize "our" just warriors, and matronizingly cheer "our" boyish adventurers. Masking or denying the predatory behavior and attitudes of "our troops," they ascribe assaultive, predatory rapaciousness only to enemy men (e.g. Elshtain 1987, Ruddick 1993).

Feminists have a complex attitude toward "feminine" loyalists. They document women's contributions to war efforts, the real advantages war offers women – employment, new kinds of knowledge, adventure – and the real harms war does them. They are particularly concerned to challenge the idea – common in countries that fight wars "abroad" – that women are safe while soldiers are endangered. On the other hand, insofar as military femininity does make war more acceptable, antimilitarists deplore it. Moreover, feminists criticize women who enact their gender roles in patriotic scripts.

By contrast, even antimilitarist feminists tend to admire a second (anti)"feminine" figure: military women who participate in war but challenge its gender divisions. In revolutionary and anticolonial wars women have fought and commanded fighters. In established states, like the USA, women defy discriminatory policies throughout the services, most importantly asserting their right and capacity to engage in combat (Segal 1982, Enloe 1988, Stiehm 1989). Some lesbian military women are also coming forward to challenge the heterosexist bigotry and superstition which marks the US military and which reinforces gender fears and defensiveness (Cammermeyer 1994).

A contrasting, familiar figure of war's femininity is the woman war victim who symbolizes war's suffering. War routinely includes the rape and enslavement of conquered or enemy women. Prewar and postwar women "serve" occupying armies with their labor and bodies and predominate in the always increasing, already numerous refugee "camps" where they attempt to keep people alive. All of "women's work" – mothering, feeding, sheltering, tending the ill and elderly, maintaining kin connections – is endangered by war; therefore through women's eyes and lives anyone can see the ravages war wrecks on relationships and on bodies of both sexes of all ages (e.g. Ruddick 1989).

A fourth figure of femininity, a woman of "peace," haunts feminist hopes and history. Recently, feminist ethicists have offered a thick(er) description of a "peacefulness" which is positioned as "feminine" and may be somewhat more characteristic of women than men. "Feminine peacefulness" is expressed in a style of reasoning which, for example, attends to actual rather than hypothetical relationships, trusts emotion as a source and test of insight, and is more concerned with effective dialogue than proof (see, e.g., Held 1993, Walker 1992, Ruddick 1993). This way of reasoning, however its particulars are described by different philosophers, contrasts with tendencies of just war theorists and realist strategists to reason abstractly, argue competitively, suspect emotion, and value sharp definition and individual proof (Peach 1996).

584

These ways of reasoning are intertwined with related moral capacities. One such capacity is the ability and willingness to maintain friendship, a relationship which, in contrast to collective bonding or individualist self-interest, is committed to preserving both self and other (Bar On 1996). Another is "respect for embodied willfulness," which, in defining contrast to militarism, is unwilling to control others by threatening to inflict or actually inflicting painful injuries upon them (Ruddick 1993).

In addition to offering a more nuanced description of "feminine" peacefulness, feminists also account for ways in which norms of femininity undermine women's capacity for effective political peacefulness. Some disabilities are psychological. Norms of femininity often create in the women governed by them a pervasive sense of shame, excessive trust, self-loss, and other tendencies which undermine their ability to withstand the collective will. These "defects" are intertwined with "virtues" of peacefulness. Subordinated women learn to "manage feelings" of resentment, a learned restraint which is useful in negotiation and nonviolent protest but which sabotages the ability to express principled anger. Women often experience their anger as a sign of impotence and loss of control (especially Campbell 1993). This contrasts with men's alleged tendency to experience anger and aggression as a means and expression of mastery which leads in turn to overvaluing the effectiveness of violence. On the other hand, nonviolent protest requires *fighting* to get what one needs and to protect what one loves without damaging others or being damaged oneself. And this requires distinguishing anger and aggression from hate and violence. Finally, and more generally, it is difficult to translate the virtues and epistemologies of private care into public and political form. Capacities for empathy, for example, may promote blindness to those outside the gaze while commitment to caring for one's own may heighten fears of threatening "outsiders." Habits of concern for one's intimates may be extended, with imperialist arrogance, to intrusive concern for different or needy strangers.

By articulating difficulties and dilemmas within the virtues of "feminine" peacefulness, feminists identify opportunities for intervention. Feminist consciousness and politics are themselves agents of change. The critical, resistant spirit of feminism can have a transformative effect on women who do not trust their own judgment and have not yet risked disobedience to familial or patriotic norms. Equally transformative are women's movements which creatively and courageously resist destructive policies of their governments. The "feminine" voice of peace has almost always spoken in opposition to official policies; peaceful women have typically met with ridicule and ostracism. Argentinean Madres and Chilean Women for Life, the Greenbelt movement in Kenya, Greenham Common Women in England, Women's Strike for Peace in the United States, and Women in Black in Israel are only a few of the collectives of angry, disobedient women who, in recent decades, have expressed a robust feminine peacefulness (see Harris and King 1989, Jetter et al. 1997).

585

Questioning war

Feminists have been slow to address the question that traditionally preoccupies philosophers: How can war – deliberate, collective efforts to injure and kill – be justified? Feminists' writings can, however, usually be placed on a continuum (Cady 1989) from realism to pacifism, with the notable difference that feminists' "realism" – the refusal to entertain moral questions about war – is, unlike its philosophical counterpart, antimilitarist (see, e.g., Tickner 1992).

Commonly, feminists have given increasingly precise accounts of the horror of war and terror (e.g. Bar-On 1991) but, like conventional realists, have refused to distinguish between more or less justifiable wars or just ways of fighting. There are both historical explanations and quasi-conceptual grounds for this refusal.

From the end of World War II until at least 1989, Euro-American feminist thinking about war and peace was largely motivated by terror of nuclear war and abhorrence of the "military–industrial–intellectual" complex. Given the prospect of a "war" which endangered all life, a "feminine" voice of peace could be introduced as a counter to nuclear thinking, images of the suffering of women intensified protest, and revelations of the "masculinity" of nuclear weapons and nuclear analysis contributed to a suspicion of a war establishment which was not only dangerous but also ecologically, economically, and socially disastrous. Literary feminists, especially, supplemented a focus on nuclear war with attention to "senseless" wars, particularly the 1914–18 European wars, which do not raise questions of just cause.

Euro-American feminists have also focused on the gendered aspects of wars which appeared to them and many others to be so clearly unjust as not to require argument, especially the US war against Vietnam. Like nuclear war and senseless wars, clearly unjust wars allow an easy critique of war itself. To be sure, many women participated in revolutionary and anticolonial armies whose cause they considered just. Many Euro-American feminists applauded them and their cause. But feminists did not much discuss the relative merits of violent military action as opposed to nonviolent resistance and revolution. Nor did they distinguish just from unjust ways of fighting except for publicizing enemy atrocities and, crucially, declaring rape and other abuses against women to be war crimes.

There are two conceptions of war which might underlie feminist refusal of moral questions about war. One, a central, nearly constituent tenet of much feminist writing, is that war is not episodic – a matter of threat, invasion, battle, and ceasefire – but a systematic expression of the culture from which it arises, particularly, but not only, its patriarchal ideologies. To paraphrase Virginia Woolf, military and civil worlds are inseparably connected; the tyrannies, servilities, conquests, and humiliations of the one reflect the structure and experience of the other. People are taught not to hate force but to use it in order to acquire possessions and defend power through economic, racial, and sexual violence (e.g. Woolf 1938, Cock 1991).

586

The concept of a war culture directs attention away from battle to civil assaults which fuel the desire for violence in assaulter and assaulted. It identifies "war zones" where the weapons and ravages of battle – injury, hunger, homelessness, chaos, despair – exist in the midst of "peace." It ferrets out violences concealed within order, including the global order in which military and economic force inextricably, though often invisibly, combine to exploit the bodies and labor of millions of women while adorning and enriching some (Enloe 1989, 1993). The concept of a war culture is also a hopeful one; if war is within and among us, rather than visited upon us, we can begin to prevent war by changing our societies and ourselves.

Feminist writing also tacitly expresses an understanding, familiar from anti-militarist fiction and poetry, of war as somehow unreal, of the language of war as a fiction in need of unmasking. In Elaine Scarry's influential formulation of this view (1985) the constitutive business of war is to impose one's will by "out-injuring" opponents. The activities of injuring inevitably evoke blood lust, cruelty, and a drive for revenge that overshadow virtues of loyalty and courage (Weil 1977a). More generally, a collective's ability to out-injure is neither conceptually nor morally anchored in justice or any other moral superiority; only amoral capacities to arm and strategize determine winners or losers; only chance separates the good from the bad army or soldier, the comrade from the enemy (Weil 1977b). Winning itself is an illusion which discounts the sufferings and impermanence of victory (see especially Scarry 1985, Weil 1977a, 1977b).

In the face of determined armed aggression or even of sharp moral "asymmetry" (Sharoni 1995) between violently contending opponents, evenhanded rejection of violence may appear cynical. When wars no longer appear universally annhiliating or senseless, but instead a military conflict is highly moralized – e.g. Israel and Palestine – or brutal aggression or massacre seems to call for "humanitarian intervention" – e.g. in Rwanda, Burundi, Haiti, and Bosnia – more feminists may turn to just war theory, in order to justify military action. Briefly, just war theorists believe that collective violence is intrinsically evil but nonetheless sometimes justified as a "last resort" when non-violent negotiation has failed to stop aggression or prevent massacre. The task in particular instances is to assess morally the justice of the cause, of the ways in which it is fought, and the likelihood that benefit will be "proportionate" to suffering endured (Cady 1989, Elshtain 1992, Peach 1996).

Feminists have attended rarely, and for the most part critically, to just war theory (Elshtain 1985, 1987, Segers 1985, Ruddick 1993, see Peach 1996). Consonant with the cognitive tendencies and attitudes of "feminine" peacefulness, feminists have criticized just war theorists' preoccupation with boundaries, questioned their allegiance to existing states, and suspected an array of abstractions – war/peace; soldier/civilian; killable enemy/object of mercy – at the heart of the theory. Instead they attend to the cultures in which war arises, offer more holistic, concrete, and accurate assessments of the benefits and costs of violence occurring both before and after its official battles, and of the particular kinds of moral as well as psychological and social damage wrought by terror and its

587

threat. More appreciative of war's costs, more skeptical of its causes, they are slower to relinquish possibilities of nonviolence or to accept the warrior diplomat's judgment of "last resort" (Peach 1996, Ruddick 1993). Despite these and other criticisms, some feminists have endorsed a radically revised theory of just war (e.g. Elshtain 1992, Peach 1996).

From the Cold War to the present, some feminists have counted themselves as pacifists who believe that war is in principle unjustifiable (see Deming 1984, Brock-Utne 1985, Reardon 1985). Many others refuse ever to justify war, though they will not condemn it on principle in advance of particular circumstances (Bell 1993, Noddings 1989, Ruddick 1989). Feminist pacifism tends to be distinguished from many of its mainstream counterparts in two ways. Like antimilitarist realists, feminist pacifists tend to think of peace and war as connected and systemic expressions of a culture. They therefore try to imagine "nonviolence as a way of life" (Kirk 1993a, 1993b) and undermine general systems of race, class, and sex domination as well as domination of non-human animals and, especially, of nature and its resources (e.g. Warren 1994, Warren and Cady 1996). Secondly, even committed pacifists like Barbara Deming are not so much concerned to condemn war abstractly, or to defend an abstract pacifism, as to insist on the possibilities of effective nonviolence and to develop practices of nonviolent resistance and negotiation.

Women, many of whom are feminists, have developed dramatic, spectacular, nonviolent protests. These women's protests reveal distinctive features (Harris and King 1989, Ruddick 1997, Jetter et al. 1997). Consistent with a general feminist refusal of the distinction between private and public, women protesters, symbolically and literally, bring women's bodies and the artifacts of women's caregiving into public spaces where they were never meant to be. Thus women of Greenham Common pinned diapers and children's drawings to a missile fence (Kirk 1993a, 1993b); the Madres of Argentina processed in the most public square in front of the most central public building wearing around their necks the photographs of their disappeared children (Ruddick 1989, Elshtain and Tobias 1990). Women's protests typically have a ritualistic and sometimes a carnivalesque aspect; the women of Greenham Common covered themselves with honey before climbing the missile fence so that arresting soldiers with sticky hands found themselves at a "teddy bears' picnic"; women in Kenya marched naked through the streets, sexually taunting arresting soldiers; while Aba women challenged authority by using their own bodies – their nakedness, menstrual blood, and sexuality – to ridicule and provoke (Ruddick 1997).

Feminist theorists have also focused on "undramatic," daily expressions of nonviolence. Some offer accounts of human nature which, while not denying brutality, claim that connectedness is equally primary and violence not inevitable (e.g. Noddings 1989, Held 1993, Ruddick 1989). Others identify resources for nonviolence in particular kinds of relationship – friendship (Bar-On 1996), caregiving (Gilligan 1982a, Noddings 1989, Ruddick 1993), or maternal practices of nonviolence (Ruddick 1989). These theorists of ordinary nonviolence draw upon and contribute to a feminist ethics of care.

Coda: future feminist thinking about war

Feminist inquiry into the gender relations of war has not been outdated by history. Feminists attuned to the many forms of war's masculinity are poised to notice the ways in which concerns for hanging tough, and for honor and heroic rescue, distort the consideration of military response even to intolerable aggression. In the justest of wars, they would highlight the masculinity of the protected and protector relation, replacing it with less masculinist notions of just rescue and defense (see Cock 1991). Although ideas of gender identity are giving way to conceptions of identity as fluid, mobile, and multiple, many movements still draw upon women's ways of knowing and symbols of femininity to imagine peace.

Understandings of war and peace as connected and systematic expressions of a culture are likely to remain nearly defining of feminist inquiry and increasingly of peace research. Feminists can elaborate these connections in ways particularly attentive to, though not obsessed with, gender. To cite one example, poststructuralist and feminist psychoanalytic studies of complex, multiple, and yet gendered identities are drawing new connections between cultural fantasies of war, nation, and gender. These studies contribute to an understanding of the racialism and racism which fuels organized violence and also sustains the exploitation of vulnerable peoples or at least a lethal indifference to their minimal flourishing.

A second tactic for elaborating the workings of a war culture is to reflect upon the stories of war's armaments. To cite only one example, some feminists might follow the trail of "light arms" – weapons "light" enough to be "packed over a mountain on a mule" – for example, stingray missiles, AK47s, machine guns, grenades, assault rifles, or small explosives. These weapons are easily bought and sold, instruments of states' greed but barely susceptible to state control. They have a long shelf life, travel easily, and therefore can, in the course of time, be turned against the enemy or one's own people, can be traded or brought home. Through travel and trade they tend to make their way predominantly into countries and neighborhoods of people of color. Women can carry them, as can "child soldiers," but they tend to remain the property of men, reflecting and shaping gender relationships of power. Thus their stories, as feminists would tell them, can symbolize connections feminists insist upon between military violence, economic greed, and racial exploitation; between private and public violence; the terrors of battle and of home.

Finally, the women and men who fight wars also come from, and sometimes return, home. They are figures of peace shaped and changed by the wars they make. As some feminists countenance justified wars, and as women in many countries are increasingly included in combat troops, it seems likely that feminists, familiar with many forms of coercion, will think more seriously about conscription, conscientious objection, the meaning of heterosexually bigoted codes for the soldiers subject to them, the class and race injustices of deploying an All Volunteer Force in combat, and the increased recruitment of "child soldiers" whose identities are shaped in a milieu of violence. Anyone who supports any military actions should also become committed to achieving the physically safest and least psychologically and morally risky conditions of combat. For the success of this endeavor, it will be crucial to vanquish lethal expressions of war's predatory "masculinity" and, more generally, to create a gender and sexually inclusive military.

In each of the examples I cite – exploring war's identities, trailing its arms, caring for its troops – feminists are moving from an antimilitarist realism to an alternative moral language for "rethinking ethics in the midst of violence" (Bell 1993). This language may sometimes draw upon just war or pacifist theory, more often on feminists' ethics of justice and care. Whatever its personal and philosophical sources, it will be a language less constrained by the gender identities and "gender discourses" (Cohn 1993) that keep us entrained in fantasies of combat and habits of abstraction, unable to "feel with sharp regret what violence kills and will kill again" (Weil 1977b, p. 177), unable to imagine with pleasure the accommodations and cooperations of "peace."

Bibliography

Abrams, K.: "Gender discrimination and the transformation of workplace norms," *Vanderbilt Law Review*, 42 (1989), 1183–1248.

——: "Ideology and women's choices," *Georgia Law Review*, 24 (1990), 761–801.

——: "Hearing the call of stories," *California Law Review*, 79 (1991), 971–1052.

——: "Title VII and the complex female subject," *Michigan Law Review*, 92 (1994), 2479–540.

——: "Sex wars redux: agency and coercion in feminist legal theory," *Columbia Law Review*, 95 (1995a), 304–76.

——: "The reasonable woman: sense and sensibility in sexual harassment law," *Dissent*, 42: 1 (1995b), 48–54.

Abu Zahrah, M.: *Al-Ahwal al-Shakhsiyah* (Cairo: Dar al-Fikr al-Arabi, 1957).

Adams, C. J.: *The Sexual Politics of Meat: A Feminist Vegetarian Critical Theory* (New York: Continuum, 1990).

——: "Ecofeminism and the eating of animals," *Hypatia*, 6: 1 (1991), 125–45.

——: *Ecofeminism and the Sacred* (New York: Continuum, 1993a).

——: "The feminist traffic in animals," *Ecofeminism: Women, Animals, and Nature*, ed. G. Gaard (Philadelphia, PA: Temple University Press, 1993b), pp. 195–218.

——: "Comment on George's 'Should feminists be vegetarians?'," *Signs* (Autumn 1995), 221–9.

Addams, J.: *Democracy and Social Ethics* [1902] (Cambridge, MA: Belknap Press of Harvard University Press, 1964).

——: *Twenty Years at Hull House* [1938] (New York: Macmillan, 1981).

Addelson, K. P.: "The man of professional wisdom," *Discovering Reality: Feminist Perspectives on Epistemology, Metaphysics, Methodology, and Philosophy of Science*, ed. S. Harding and M. Hintikka (Boston: D. Reidel, 1983).

——: *Impure Thoughts: Essays on Philosophy, Feminism, and Ethics* (Philadelphia: Temple University Press, 1991b).

——: "Knowers/doers and their moral problems," *Feminist Epistemologies*, ed. L. Alcoff and E. Potter (New York: Routledge, 1993).

——: *Moral Passages* (New York: Routledge, 1994a).

——: "Feminist philosophy and the women's movement," *Hypatia*, 9: 3 (1994b), 216–24.

——, Ackelsberg, M., and Pyne, S.: "Anarchism and feminism," *Impure Thoughts: Essays on Philosophy, Feminism, and Ethics*, ed. K.P. Addelson (Philadelphia, PA: Temple University Press, 1991).

——, and Potter, E.: "Making knowledge," *(En) Gendering Knowledge: Feminists in Academe*, ed. J. E. Harman and E. Messer-Davidow (Knoxville: University of Tennessee Press, 1991a).

Adelman, P.: *Miriam's Well: Rituals for Jewish Women Around the Year* (Fresh Meadows, NY: Biblio Press, 1986).

Adler, R.: "The Jew who wasn't there: Halakah and the Jewish woman," *Davka* (Summer 1971).

——: "Tum'ah and Tahara: ends and beginnings," *The Jewish Catalog*, ed. M. Strassfeld, S. Strassfeld, and R. Siegal (Philadelphia, PA: Temple University Press, 1973).

——: "Feminist folktales of justice: Robert Cover as a resource for the renewal of Halakah," *Conservative Judaism*, 45 (1993).

——: *Engendering Judaism: Inclusive Ethics and Theology* (Philadelphia, PA: Jewish Publication Society, 1997).

Agarwal, B.: "Gender and the environment: lessons from India," *Proceedings of the International Conference on Women and Biodiversity*, ed. L. Borkenhagen and J. Abramovitz, 1992.

Ahmad, A.: *Islam Main Aurat Ka Maqaam* (Pakistan: Markazi Anjuman Khaddam al Quran, 1984).

Akerkar, S.: "Theory and practice of women's movement in India," *Economic and Political Weekly* (April 29, 1995).

Albert, M., and Hahnel, R.: *UnOrthodox Marxism: An Essay on Capitalism, Socialism and Revolution* (Boston: South End Press, 1978).

——: *Socialism Today and Tomorrow* (Boston: South End Press, 1981).

——: *Looking Forward: Participatory Democracy in the Year 2000* (Boston: South End Press, 1991).

Alcoff, L.: "Cultural feminism versus post-structuralism: the identity crisis in feminist theory," *Signs*, 13: 3 (1988), 405–36.

——: "Justifying feminism social science," *Feminism and Science*, ed. N. Tuana (Bloomington: Indiana University Press, 1989).

——, and Potter, E., eds.: *Feminist Epistemologies* (New York: Routledge, 1993).

Alexander, W. M.: "Philosophers have avoided sex," *The Philosophy of Sex: Contemporary Readings*, ed. A. Soble (Savage, MD: Rowan and Littlefield, 1991), pp. 3–20.

Allen, A.: "Privacy, private choice and social contract theory," *Cincinnati Law Review*, 56: 401 (1987).

——: *Uneasy Access: Privacy for Women in a Free Society* (Totowa, NJ: Rowman and Littlefield, 1988).

——: "Surrogacy, slavery and the ownership of life," *Harvard Law Journal*, 13 (1990), 139–49.

——: "The black surrogate mother," *Harvard Blackletter Journal*, 8 (1991), 17–31.

——: "The role model argument and faculty diversity', *Philosophical Forum*, XXIV: 1–3 (1992/3), 267–81.

——: "Privacy in health care," *Encyclopedia of Bioethics*, ed. W. Reich (New York: Macmillan, 1995a), pp. 2064–73.

——: "The proposed equal protection fix for abortion law: reflections on citizenship, gender, and the Constitution," *Harvard Journal of Law and Public Policy*, 18 (1995b), 419– 55.

——: "Constitutional privacy," *A Companion to Philosophy of Law and Legal Theory*, ed. D. Patterson (Oxford: Blackwell, 1996a), pp. 139–55.

——: "The jurispolitics of privacy," *Reconstructing Political Theory*, ed. U. Narayan and M. Shanley (Cambridge: Polity Press, 1996b).

——: "Genetic privacy: emerging concepts and values," *Genetic Secrets*, ed. M. Rothstein (New Haven, CT: Yale University Press, forthcoming).

——, and Mack, E.: "How privacy got its gender," *Northern Illinois University Law Review*, 10 (1990), 441–78.

Allen, J.: "Motherhood: the annihilation of women," *Mothering: Essays in Feminist Theory*, ed. J. Trebilcot (Savage, MD: Rowman and Littlefield, 1983).

——: *Lesbian Philosophy: Explorations* (Palo Alto, CA: Institute for Lesbian Studies, 1986).

—— ed.: *Lesbian Philosophies and Cultures* (Albany: State University of New York Press, 1990).

Allen, P.: *The concept of woman: The Aristotelian Revolution 750 BC – AD 1250* (London: Eden Press, 1985).

Almond, B.: "Philosophy and the cult of irrationalism," *The Impulse to Philosophise*, ed. A. P. Griffiths (Royal Institute of Philosophy Supplement 33) (Cambridge: Cambridge University Press, 1992), pp. 201–17.

Altman, A.: "Making sense of sexual harassment law," *Philosophy and Public Affairs*, 25: 1 (1996), 36–65.

Altman, I.: "Privacy: a conceptual analysis," *Environment and Behavior*, 8 (1976), 7–30.

AMC Report: Letter to the Editor (Washington, DC: American Muslim Council, January 1996, p. 11.

Amorós, C.: *Hacia una Crítica de la Razón Patriarcal* (Madrid: Anthropos, 1985).

——: *Feminismo: Igualdad y Diferencia* (Mexico City: UNAM PUEG, 1994).

Anderson, E. S.: "Is women's labor a commodity?," *Philosophy and Public Affairs*, 19: 1 (1990), 71–92.

Andolsen, B.: "A woman's work is never done," *Women's Consciousness, Women's Conscience*, ed. B. H. Andolsen, C. E. Gudorf, and M. D. Pellauer (San Francisco, CA: Harper and Row, 1985), pp. 3–18.

——: *Good Work at the Video Display Terminal: A Feminist Ethical Analysis of Changes in Clerical Work* (Knoxville: University of Tennessee Press, 1989).

——: "Justice, gender and the frail elderly: reexamining the ethics of care," *Journal of Feminist Studies in Religion*, 9 (1993), 127–45.

Andrews, L.: "Surrogate motherhood: the challenge for feminists," *Law, Medicine and Health Care*, 16 (1988), 72–80.

Annas, J.: *An Introduction to Plato's Republic* (Oxford: Clarendon Press, 1981).

Antony, L.: "Quine as feminist: the radical import of naturalized epistemology," *A Mind of One's Own: Feminist Essays on Reason and Objectivity*, ed. L. Antony and C. Witt (Boulder, CO: Westview Press, 1993).

——, and Witt, C., eds.: *A Mind of One's Own: Feminist Essays on Reason and Objectivity* (Boulder, CO: Westview Press, 1993).

Anzaldúa, G.: *Borderlands/La Frontera* (San Francisco, CA: Spinsters/Aunt Lute, 1987).

——: *Making Face, Making Soul – Haciendo Caras: Creative and Critical Perspectives of Women of Color* (San Francisco: Aunt Lute Foundation Books, 1990).

Appiah, K. A.: "Soyinka and the philosophy of culture," *Philosophy in Africa: Trends and Perspectives*, ed. P. O. Bodunrin (Ile-Ife: University of Ife Press, 1985), pp. 25–263.

——: " 'But would that still be me?' Notes on gender, 'race', ethnicity, as sources of 'identity,' " *Journal of Philosophy*, LXXXVII:10 (1990), 493–9.

——: *In My Father's House: Africa in the Philosophy of Culture* (London: Oxford University Press, 1992).

Arditti, R., Klein, R. D., and Minden, S., eds.: *Test-Tube Women: What Future for Motherhood?* (Boston: Pandora, 1984).

Arendt, H.: *The Human Condition* (Chicago, IL: University of Chicago Press, 1958).

Arsic, B.: "Mislim, dakle nisam zena," *Filozofski godisnjak*, 6 (1993), 60–102.

——: Recnik/*Dictionary* (Belgrade: Dental, 1995).

Asch, A., and Fine, M., eds.: *Women with Disabilities: Essays in Psychology, Culture, and Politics* (Philadelphia, PA: Temple University Press, 1988a).

——: "Beyond pedestals," *Women with Disabilities: Essays in Psychology, Culture, and Politics*, ed. A. Asch and M. Fine (Philadelphia, PA: Temple University Press, 1988b).

——: "Shared dreams," *Women with Disabilities: Essays in Psychology, Culture, and Politics*, ed. A. Asch and M. Fine (Philadelphia, PA: Temple University Press, 1988c).

——: "Reproductive technology and disability," *Reproductive Laws for the 1990's*, ed. S. Cohen and N. Taub (Clifton, NJ: Humana Press, 1989), pp. 69–129.

Ashe, M.: "Law-language of maternity: discourse holding nature in contempt," *New England Law Review*, 22 (1988), 521–59.

Ashworth, G.: "Piercing the eye: taking feminism into mainstream political processes," *A Diplomacy of the Oppressed*, ed. G. Ashworth (London: Zed Books, 1995).

Assiter, A.: *Enlightened Women* (New York: Columbia University Press, 1996).

Atherton, M.: "Cartesian reason and gendered reason," *A Mind of One's Own: Feminist Essays on Reason and Objectivity*, ed. L. Antony and C. Witt (Boulder, CO: Westview Press, 1993).

——ed.: *Women Philosophers of the Early Modern Period* (Indianapolis, IN: Hackett, 1994).

Auerbach, J., Blum, L., Smith, V., and Williams, C.: "Commentary on Gilligan's *In a Different Voice*," *Feminist Studies*, 11: 1 (1985), 149–61.

Austin, R.: "Sapphire bound?," *Wisconsin Law Review* (1989), pp. 539–78.

Awe, B.: "The Iyalode in the traditional Yoruba political system," *Sexual Stratification: A Cross-Cultural View*, ed. A. Schlegel (New York: Columbia University Press, 1977), pp. 144–95.

Babbitt, S.: "Feminism and objective interests," *Feminist Epistemologies*, ed. L. Alcoff and E. Potter (New York: Routledge, 1993).

Baber, H. E.: "Two models of preferential treatment for working mothers," *Public Affairs Quarterly*, 4 (1990), 323–34.

——: "How bad is rape?," *The Philosophy of Sex: Contemporary Readings*, ed. A. Soble (Savage, MD: Rowan and Littlefield, 1991), pp. 243–58.

Bacchi, C.: "Pregnancy, the law and the meaning of equality," *Equality, Politics, and Gender*, ed. E. Meehan and S. Sevenhuijsen (Beverly Hills, CA: Sage, 1991), pp. 71–87.

Bacon, F.: *Advancement of Learning*, ed. A. Wright [1963] (Oxford: Clarendon Press, 1968).

Bagchi, J.: "Representing nationalism: ideology of motherhood in colonial Bengal," *Economic and Political Weekly* (October 20–27, 1990).

Bahar, S.: "Human rights are women's rights: Amnesty International and the family," *Hypatia*, 11: 2 (1996), 105–34.

Baier, A.: "Cartesian persons," *Postures of the Mind: Essays on Mind and Morals*, ed. A. Baier (Minneapolis: University of Minnesota Press, 1985), pp. 74–92.

——: "Trust and anti-trust," *Ethics*, 96 (1986), 231–60.

——: "Hume: the women's moral theorist?," *Women and Moral Theory*, ed. E. Kittay and D. Meyers (Totowa, NJ: Rowman and Littlefield, 1987a), pp. 37–55.

——: "The need for more than justice," *Science, Morality, and Feminist Theory*, ed. M. Hanen and K. Nielsen (Calgary: University of Calgary Press, 1987b), 41–56.

——: "How can individualists share responsibility?," *Political Theory*, 25: 2 (1993a), 228–48.

——: "Hume: the reflective women's epistemologist?," *A Mind of One's Own: Feminist Essays on Reason and Objectivity*, ed. L. Antony and C. Witt (Boulder, CO: Westview Press, 1993b), pp. 35–49.

——: *Moral Prejudices: Essays on Ethics* (Cambridge, MA: Harvard University Press, 1994a).

——: "What do women want in a moral theory?," *Moral Prejudices: Essays on Ethics*, ed. A. Baier (Cambridge, MA: Harvard University Press, 1994b), pp. 1–17.

Baker, B. M.: "A case for permitting altruistic surrogacy," *Hypatia*, 11: 2 (1996), 34–48.

Baker, G. S.: "Is equality enough?," *Hypatia*, 2: 1 (1987), 63–5.

Balint, A.: "Love for the mother and mother-love," *Primary Love and Psychoanalytic Technique*, ed. M. Balint (New York: Liveright, 1965).

Balint, M.: *The Basic Fault: Therapeutic Aspects of Regression* (London: Tavistock, 1968).

Bammer, A.: *Partial Visions: Feminism and Utopianism in the 1970s* (New York: Routledge, 1991).

Barnes, H. E.: "Sartre and sexism," *Philosophy and Literature*, 14 (1990), 340–7.

Bar-On, B.: "Feminism and sadomasochism: self-critical notes," *Against Sadomasochism: A Radical Feminist Analysis*, ed. R. Lindon *et al.* (Palo Alto, CA: Frog in the Well, 1982), pp. 72–82.

——: "On terrorism," *Feminist Ethics*, ed. C. Card (Lawrence: University of Kansas Press, 1991), 45–58.

——: "The feminist sexuality debates and the transformation of the political," *Hypatia*, 7: 4 (1992).

—— ed.: *Engendering Origins: Critical Feminist Readings in Plato and Aristotle* (Albany: State University of New York Press, 1994).

——: "Reflections on national identity," *Bringing Peace Home*, ed. K. J. Warren and D. Cady (Bloomington: Indiana University Press, 1996)

Baron, M.: "Impartiality and friendship," *Ethics*, 101: 4 (1991), 836–57.

——: "Kantian ethics and claims of detachment," *Feminist Interpretations of Kant*, ed. R. Schott (University Park: Pennsylvania State University Press, 1997).

Barrett, M.: *Women's Oppression Today: Problems in Marxist and Feminist Analysis* (London: Verso, 1980).

——: *The Anti-Social Family* (London: Verso, 1982).

——: and McIntosh, M.: "Towards a materialist feminism?," *Feminist Review*, 1 (1979), 95–106.

——: "Words and things: materialism and method in contemporary feminist analysis," *Destabilizing Theory: Contemporary Feminist Debates*, ed. M. Barrett and A. Phillips (Stanford, CA: Stanford University Press, 1992).

Barrett, M., and Phillips, A., eds.: *Destabilizing Theory: Contemporary Feminist Debates* (Stanford, CA: Stanford University Press, 1992).

Barry, B.: *Justice and Impartiality* (Oxford: Clarendon, 1993).

——: "Spherical justice and global injustice," *Pluralism, Justice and Equality*, ed. D. Miller and M. Walzer (Oxford: Oxford University Press, 1995).

Barry, K.: *Female Sexual Slavery* (Englewood Cliffs, NJ: Prentice-Hall, 1979).

Barthes, R.: "Inaugural lecture, Collège de France," *A Barthes Reader*, ed. S. Sontag (New York: Hill and Wang, 1982).

Bartky, S.: "Feminine masochism and the politics of personal transformation," *Women's Studies International Forum*, 7: 5 (1984), 323–34.

——: *Femininity and Domination: Studies in the Phenomenology of Oppression* (New York: Routledge, 1990a).

——: "Shame and gender," *Femininity and Domination* (New York: Routledge, 1990b).

Bartlett, K. T.: "MacKinnon's feminism: power on whose terms?," *California Law Review*, 75 (1987), 1559–70.

——: "Feminist legal methods," *Harvard Law Review*, 103 (1990), 829–88.

——: "Minow's social-relations approach to difference: unanswering the unasked," *Law and Social Inquiry*, 17 (1992), 437–70.

——: "Only girls wear barrettes: dress and appearance standards, community norms, and workplace equality," *Michigan Law Review*, 92 (1994), 2541–82.

——, and Kennedy, R., eds.: *Feminist Legal Theory: Readings in Law and Gender* (Boulder, CO: Westview Press. 1991).

Baruch, E. H., D'Amado, A., Jr, and Seager, J., eds.: *Embryos, Ethics, and Women's Rights* (New York: Harrington Park Press, 1988).

Barwell, I.: "Towards a defense of objectivity," *Knowing the Difference: Feminist Perspectives in Epistemology*, ed. K. Lennon and M. Whitford (New York: Routledge, 1994).

Baseheart, M. C.: "Edith Stein's philosophy of woman and of women's education," *Hypatia*, 4: 1 (1989), 120–31.

Bassham, G.: "Feminist legal theory: a liberal response," *Notre Dame Journal of Law Ethics*, 6: 2 (1992), 293–319.

Battersby, C.: *Gender and Genius: Towards a New Feminist Aesthetics* (London: The Women's Press, 1989).

Beardsley, E.: "Referential genderization," *Women and Philosophy: Toward a Theory of Liberation*, ed. C. Gould and M.W. Wartofsky (New York: G. P. Putnam's Sons, 1976), pp. 285–93.

——: "Traits and genderization," *Feminism and Philosophy*, ed. M. Vetterling-Braggin, F. Elliston, and J. English (Totowa, NJ: Littlefield, Adams, 1977), pp. 117–23.

——: "Degenderization," *Sexist Language: A Modern Philosophical Analysis*, ed. M. Vetterling-Braggin (Totowa, NJ: Littlefield, Adams, 1981), pp. 155–60.

Beauchamp, T. L., and Childress, J. F.: *Principles of Biomedical Ethics* (New York: Oxford University Press, 1994).

Bebel, A.: *Women and Socialism*, trans. M. Stern (New York: Socialist Literature Co., 1910).

Bechdel, A.: *Dykes to Watch Out For* (Ithaca, NY: Firebrand Books, 1986).

——: *More Dykes to Watch Out For* (Ithaca, NY: Firebrand Books, 1988).

——: *New Improved Dykes to Watch Out For* (Ithaca, NY: Firebrand Books, 1990).

——: *Dykes to Watch Out for: The Sequel* (Ithaca, NY: Firebrand Books, 1992).

Beck, E. T., ed.: *Nice Jewish Girls: A Lesbian Anthology* (Boston: Beacon Press, 1989).

Becker, M.: "Prince Charming: abstract equality," *Supreme Court Review* (1988), 201–47.

——: "Maternal feelings: myth, taboo, and child custody," *Southern California Review of Law and Women's Studies*, 1 (1992), 133–224.

Becker-Schmidt, R.: "Identitätslogik und Gewalt. Zum Verhältnis von Kritischer Theorie und Feminismus," *Beiträge zur Feministischen Theorie und Praxis*, 24 (1989), 31–64.

Bedecarre, C.: "Swear by the moon," *Hypatia*, 12: 3 (1997).

Bedregal Sáex, X.: "¿Hacia dónde va el movimiento feminista?," *La Correa Feminista* [Mexico], 12 (1995), 10–16.

Beitz, C.: *Political Theory and International Relations* (Princeton, NJ: Princeton University Press, 1979).

Belenky, M. Field, Clinchy, B. M., Goldberger, N. R., and Tarule, J. M.: *Women's Ways of Knowing* (New York: Basic Books, 1986).

Bell, L.: *Rethinking Ethics in the Midst of Violence* (Lanham, MD: Rowman and Littlefield, 1993).

Bell, V.: *Interrogating Incest: Feminism, Foucault, and the Law* (New York: Routledge, 1993).

Bender, L.: "A lawyer's primer on feminist theory and tort," *Journal of Legal Education*, 38 (1988), 3–37.

——: "Feminist (re)torts: thoughts on the liability crisis, mass torts, and responsibilities," *Duke Law Journal* (1990a), 848–912.

——: "From gender differences to feminist solidarity," *Vermont Law Review*, 15 (1990b), 1–48.

Benhabib, S.: *Critique, Norm, and Utopia* (New York: Columbia University Press, 1986).

——: "The generalized and the concrete other," *Women and Moral Theory*, ed. E. Kittay and D. Meyers (Totowa, NJ: Rowman and Littlefield, 1987), pp. 154–77.

——: "Die Debatte über Frauen und Moraltheorie – eine Retrospektive," *Zielicht der Vernunft: Die Dialektik der Aufklärung aus der Sicht von Frauen*, ed. C. Kulke and E. Scheich (Pfaffenwieler: Centaurus, 1992a), pp. 139–48.

——: *Situating the Self: Gender, Community and Postmodernism in Contemporary Ethics* (New York: Routledge, 1992b).

——: "The debate over women and moral theory revisited," *Feminists Read Habermas: Gendering the Subject of Discourse*, ed. J. Meehan (New York: Routledge, 1995), pp. 181–204.

——, and Cornell, D.: *Feminism as Critique: On the Politics of Gender* (Minneapolis: University of Minnesota Press, 1987).

——, and Nicholson, L.: "Politische Philosophie und die Frauenfrage, *Pipers Handbuch der Politischen Ideen*, ed. I. Fetscher and H. Muenkler (Munich: Piper, 1985–88), Vol. 5, 513–62.

Benjamin, J.: *The Bonds of Love: Psychoanalysis, Feminism and the Problem of Domination* (London: Virago, 1988).

Benn, S. I.: *A Theory of Freedom* (Cambridge: Cambridge University Press, 1988).

Bennani, F.: *Taqsim al-'Amal Bayn al-Zawjayn* (*Division of Labor Between Spouses*) (Marrakesh: School of Legal, Economic and Social Studies Series, 1992).

Bennent, H.: *Galanterie und Verachtung. Eine philosophiegeschichtliche Untersuchung zur Stellung der Frau in Gesellschaft und Kultur* (Frankfurt/Main: Campus, 1985).

Bennett, J., and Chaloupka, W., eds.: *In the Nature of Things: Language, Politics and the Environment* (Minneapolis: University of Minnesota Press, 1993).

Bennent-Vahle, J.: "Moraltheoretische Fragen und Geschlechterproblematik," *Aspekte feministischer Wissenschaft und Wissenschaftskritik*, eds. W. Herzog and E. Violi (Chur/Zürich, 1991), pp. 45–69.

Bensinger, T.: "Lesbian pornography: the re/making of (a) community," *Discourse*, 15: 1 (1992), 69–93.

598

Benston, M.: "The political economy of women's liberation," *Monthly Review*, 21: 4 (1969).

Bergmann, B. R.: *The Economic Emergence of Women* (New York: Basic Books, 1986).

Berkeley, G.: *The Works of George Berkeley* (Oxford: Clarendon Press, 1871).

Berleant, A.: "The historicity of aesthetics," *British Journal of Aesthetics*, 26: 2–3 (1986), 101–11, 195–203.

Berman, R.: "From Aristotle's dualism to materialist dialectics," *Gender/Body/Knowledge*, ed. A. M. Jaggar and S. Bordo (New Brunswick: Rutgers University Press, 1989).

Bernstein, R.: *The Restructuring of Social and Political Theory* (Philadelphia: University of Pennsylvania Press, 1976).

——: *Beyond Objectivism and Relativism: Science, Hermeneutics and Praxis* (Philadelphia: University of Pennsylvania Press, 1983).

Betcher, S.: unpublished dissertation on feminist pneumatology (Drew University Graduate School, n.d.).

Bethel, L.: "What chou mean 'we' white girl?," *Conditions Five*, 11: 2 (1979), 86–92.

Bhattacharya, S.: "Motherhood in ancient India," *Economic and Political Weekly* (October 20–27, 1990).

Biehl, J.: *Rethinking Ecofeminist Politics* (Boston: Southend Press, 1991).

Bigwood, C.: "Renaturalizing the body (with a little help from Merleau-Ponty)," *Hypatia*, 6: 3 (1991), 54–73.

Birke, L.: *Women, Feminism and Biology: The Feminist Challenge* (New York: Methuen, 1986).

——: *Feminism, Animals and Science: The Naming of the Shrew* (Buckingham: Open University Press, 1994).

Birkeland, J.: "Ecofeminism: linking theory and practice," *Ecofeminism: Women, Animals and Nature*, ed. G. Gaard (Philadelphia: Temple University Press, 1993), pp. 13–59.

——: "Comment: disengendering ecofeminism," *Environmental Ethics*, 9 (1995), 443–4.

Blaustein, A. and Flanz, G. H.: *Constitutions of the Countries of the World* (Dobbs Ferry, NY: Oceana Publications, Inc., 1994).

Bleier, R.: "Social and political bias in science," *Genes and Gender*, ed. E. Tobach and B. Rosoff (New York: Gordian Press, 1979).

——: *Science and Gender: A Critique of Biology and Its Theories on Women* (New York: Pergamon, 1984).

——: *Feminist Approaches to Science* (New York: Pergamon, 1988).

Blok, J., and Mason, P., eds.: *Sexual Asymmetry: Studies in Ancient Society* (Amsterdam: J. C. Gieben, 1987).

Bloustein, E.: "Privacy as an aspect of human dignity: an answer to Dean Prosser," *New York University Law Review*, 39 (1964), 962–1007.

Bluestone, N. H.: *Women and the Ideal Society: Plato's Republic and Modern Myths of Gender* (Amherst: University of Massachusetts Press, 1987).

Blum, L. A.: *Friendship, Altruism and Morality* (London: Routledge and Kegan Paul, 1980).

——: "Particularity and responsiveness," *The Emergence of Morality in Young Children*, ed. J. Kagan and S. Lamb (Chicago, IL: University of Chicago Press, 1987), 306–37.

——: *Moral Perception and Particularity* (Cambridge: Cambridge University Press, 1994.

Bock, G., and James, S., eds.: *Beyond Equality and Difference* (London: Routledge, 1992).

Bodunrin, P. O.: "The question of African philosophy," *Philosophy*, 56 (1981), 161–79.

Boehm, B.: "Feminist histories: theory meets practice," *Hypatia*, 7: 2 (1992), 202–14.

Bogdan, D.: *Re-educating the Imagination: Toward a Poetics, Politics, and Pedagogy of Literary Engagement* (Toronto: Irwin, 1992).

Bok, S.: *Secrets: On the Ethics of Concealment and Revelation* (New York: Pantheon, 1983).

Boone, C. K.: "Privacy and community," *Social Theory and Practice*, 9 (1983), 1–30.

Bordo, S.: *The Flight to Objectivity: Essays on Cartesianism and Culture* (Albany: State University of New York Press, 1987).

——: "Feminism, postmodernism, and gender-skepticism," *Feminism/Postmodernism*, ed. L. Nicholson (New York: Routledge, 1990), pp. 133–56.

——: *Unbearable Weight: Feminism, Western Culture and the Body* (Berkeley: University of California Press, 1993).

Bordwell, D., and Carroll, N.: *Post-Theory: Reconstructing Film Studies* (Madison: University of Wisconsin Press, 1996).

Bortei-Doku, E.: "A note on theoretical directions in gender relations and the status of women in Africa," *Gender Analysis Workshop Report* (Legon: University of Legon, 1992).

Bowers v. *Hardwick*, 478 U.S. 186 (1986).

Braaten, J.: "From communicative rationality to communicative thinking: a basis for feminist theory and practice," *Feminists Read Habermas: Gendering the Subject of Discourse*, ed. J. Meehan (New York: Routledge, 1995), pp. 139–62.

Brabeck, M., ed.: *Who Cares?: Theory, Research, and Educational Implications of the Ethic of Care* (New York: Praeger, 1989).

Braidotti, R.: *Patterns of Dissonance: A Study of Women in Contemporary Philosophy* (Cambridge: Polity Press, 1991).

——: *Nomadic Subjects: Embodiment and Sexual Difference in Contemporary Feminist Theory* (New York: Columbia University Press, 1994).

——, Charkiewocz, E., Hauster, S., and Wierinza, S.: *Women, the Environment and Sustainable Development: Towards a Theoretical Synthesis* (New York: Zed Books, 1994).

Brand, P. Z., and Korsmeyer, C.: *Feminism and Tradition in Aesthetics* (University Park: Pennsylvania State University Press, 1995).

Brandom, R.: *Making it Explicit* (Cambridge, MA: Harvard University Press, 1994).

Breitling, G.: *Die Spuren des Schiffs in den Wellen: Eine autobiographishe Suche name den Frauen in der Kunstgeschichte* (Berlin: Oberbaum Verlag, 1980).

Brennan, T.: *Between Feminism and Psychoanalysis* (New York: Routledge, 1989).

Brewer, R.: "Theorizing race, class and gender: the new scholarship of Black feminist intellectuals and Black women's labor," *Theorizing Black Feminisms: The Visionary Pragmatism of Black Women*, ed. S. James and A. P.A. Busia (London: Routledge, 1993), pp. 13–30.

Brison, S.: "The theoretical importance of practice," *Theory and Practice*, ed. I. Shapiro and J. Wagner DeCew (New York: New York University Press, 1995), pp. 216–38.

——: *Speech, Harm, and Conflicts of Rights* (Princeton, NJ: Princeton University Press, forthcoming).

Brock-Utne, B.: *Educating for Peace: A Feminist Perspective* (New York: Pergamon Press, 1985).

Brody, B.: *Abortion and the Sanctity of Human Life* (Cambridge, MA:MIT Press, 1975).

Broner, E. M.: *The Telling* (San Francisco, CA: Harper, 1993).

Brooks, C. Whitman: "Feminist jurisprudence," *Feminist Studies* (1991), 493–507.

Broude, N., and Gerraard, M. D., eds.: *Feminism and Art History: Questioning the Litany* (New York: Icon Editions, Harper Collins Publishers, 1982).

——: *The Power of Feminist Art: The American Movement of the 1970's, History and Impact* (New York: H.N. Abrams, 1994).

Brown, C.: "Mothers, fathers and children: from private to public patriarchy," *Women and Revolution*, ed. L. Sargent (Boston: South End Press, 1981), pp. 239–68.

Brown, V. B.: "Jane Addams, progressivism, and woman suffrage: an introduction to 'Why women should vote,'" *One Woman, One Vote*, ed. M.S. Wheeler (Troutdale, OR: New Sage Press, 1995), pp. 179–203.

Browne, K.: "Sex and temperament in modern society: a Darwinian view of the glass ceiling and the gender gap," *Arizona Law Review*, 37 (1995), 971–1106.

Buikema, R. and Smelik, A.: *Women's Studies and Culture: A Feminist Introduction* (London: Zed Books, 1995).

Bunch, C.: "Not by degrees: feminist theory and education," *Quest*, 5: 1 (1979), 248–60.

——: "The reform tool kit," *Building Feminist Theory*, ed. The Quest Staff (New York: Longman, 1981).

Bunkle, P.: *Second Opinion: The Politics of Women's Health in New Zealand* (Auckland: Oxford University Press, 1988).

Bunster, X., and Rodríguez, R., eds.: *La Mujer Ausente: Derechos Humanos en el Mundo* (Santiago, Chile: Isis Internacional, 1991).

Bureau of the Census: *Survey of Income and Program Participants* (SIPP84–R3, Washington, DC: Bureau of Commerce, 1984).

Burchard, M.: *Returning to the Body: A Philosophical Reconceptualization of Violence* (Minneapolis: University of Minnesota, 1996a).

——: "The myths of bisexuality," Midwest Society for Women in Philosophy (Minneapolis: University of Minnesota, March 30, 1996b).

Burke, C., Schor, N., and Whitford, M., eds.: *Engaging With Irigaray* (New York: Columbia University Press, 1994).

Bussemaker, J.: "Equality, autonomy and feminist politics," *Equality, Politics, and Gender*, ed. E. Meehan and S. Sevenhuijsen (Beverly Hills, CA: Sage, 1991), pp. 52–70.

Butler, J.: "Embodied identity in de Beauvoir's *The Second Sex*," paper presented to the American Philosophical Association, Pacific Division (March 22, 1985).

——: "Sexual ideology and phenomenological description: a feminist critique of Merleau-Ponty's *Phenomenology of Perception*," *The Thinking Muse*, ed. J. Allen and I. M. Young (Bloomington: Indiana University Press, 1989), pp. 85–100.

——: *Gender Trouble: Feminism and the Subversion of Identity* (New York: Routledge, 1990).

——: "Imitation and gender insubordination," *Inside/Outside: Lesbian Theories, Gay Theories*, ed. D. Fuss (New York: Routledge, 1991), pp. 13–31.

——: "The lesbian phallus and the morphological imaginary," *differences*, 4: 1 (1992a), 133–71.

——: "Sexual inversions," *Discourses on Sexuality: From Aristotle to AIDS*, ed. D. Stanton (Ann Arbor: University of Michigan Press, 1992b), pp. 344–61.

——: *Bodies That Matter: On the Discursive Limits of "Sex"* (New York: Routledge, 1993).

——: "Contingent foundations: feminism and the question of postmodernism," *Feminist Contentions: A Philosophical Exchange*, ed. S. Benhabib, J. Butler, D. Cornell, and N. Fraser (New York: Routledge, 1995), pp. 35–57.

——, and Scott, J. W., eds.: *Feminists Theorize the Political* (New York: Routledge, 1992).

——: "Feminist contentions: a philosophical exchange," *Feminist Contentions: A Philosophical Exchange*, Benhabib, S., Butler, J., Cornell, D., and Fraser, N. (New York: Routledge, 1995).

Cady, D.: *From Warism to Pacifism: A Moral Continuum* (Philadelphia: Temple University Press, 1989).

Cahn, N. R.: "Civil images of battered women: the impact of domestic violence on child custody decisions," *Vanderbilt Law Review*, 44 (1991), 1041–97.

——: "Inconsistent stories," *Georgetown Law Journal*, 81 (1993), 2475–531.

Caldwell, P. A.: "A hair piece: perspectives on the intersection of race and gender," *Duke Law Journal*, (1991), 365–96.

Calhoun, C.: "Justice, care, gender bias," *Journal of Philosophy*, 85: 9 (1988), 451–63.

——: "Responsibility and reproach," *Ethics*, 99 (1989), 389–406.

———: "Emotional work," *Explorations in Feminist Ethics: Theory and Practice*, ed. E. Browning Cole and S. Coultrap-McQuinn (Bloomington: Indiana University Press, 1992).

Califia, P.: "Feminism and sadomasochism: self-critical notes," *Heresies*, 3: 4 (1981), 30–4.

Callahan, J.: "Surrogate motherhood: politics and privacy," *Journal of Clinical Ethics*, 4: 10 (1993), 82–91.

———: "Let's get the lead out: or why Johnson controls is not an unequivocal victory for women," *Journal of Social Philosophy*, 25 (1994), 65–75.

Cameron, D.: "Pornography: what is the problem?," *Critical Quarterly*, 34: 2 (1992), 3–11.

———: "Discourses of desire: Liberals, feminists, and the politics of pornography," *American Literary History*, 2: 4 (1994), 784–98.

Cammermeyer, M.: *Serving in Silence* (New York: Viking Penguin, 1994).

Campbell, A.: *Men, Women and Aggression* (New York: Basic Books, 1993).

Campbell, R.: "The virtues of feminist empiricism," *Hypatia*, 9: 1 (1994).

Card, C.: "Review essay: sadomasochism and sexual preference," *Journal of Social Philosophy*, 15: 2 (1984), 42–52.

———: "Lesbian attitudes and *The Second Sex*," *Women's Studies International Forum*, 8: 3 (1985), 209–14.

———: "Women's voices and ethical ideals," *Ethics* (October 1988), 125–35.

———: "Gender and moral luck," *Identity, Character and Morality: Essays in Moral Psychology*, ed. O. Flanagan and A. Oksenberg Rorty (Cambridge, MA: MIT Press, 1990a).

———: "Pluralist lesbian separatism," *Lesbian Philosophies and Cultures*, ed. J. Allen (Albany: State University of New York Press, 1990b), pp. 125–43.

———ed.: *Feminist Ethics* (Lawrence: University Press of Kansas, 1991a).

———: "Intimacy and responsibility: what lesbians do," *At the Boundaries of Law: Feminism and Legal Theory*, ed. M. Albertson Fineman and N. Sweet Thomadsen (New York: Routledge, 1991b), pp. 72–90.

———: "Lesbianism and choice," *Journal of Homosexuality*, 23: 3 (1992), 39–51.

———ed.: *Adventures in Lesbian Philosophy* (Bloomington: Indiana University Press, 1994).

———: "Female incest and adult lesbian crises," *Lesbian Choices*, ed. C. Card (New York: Columbia University Press, 1995a), pp. 131–47.

———: "Horizontal violence: partner battering and lesbian stalking," *Lesbian Choices*, ed. C. Card (New York: Columbia University Press, 1995b), pp. 106–30.

———: *Lesbian Choices* (New York: Columbia University Press, 1995c).

———: "Sadomasochism: charting the issue," *Lesbian Choices*, ed. C. Card (New York: Columbia University Press, 1995d), pp. 218–37.

———: *The Unnatural Lottery: Character and Moral Luck* (Philadelphia, PA: Temple University Press, 1996).

Carlson, A. C.: "Aspasia of Miletus; how one woman disappeared from the history of rhetoric," *Women's Studies in Communication*, 17: 1 (1994), 19–45.

Carroll, N.: *Mystifying Movies: Fads and Fallacies in Contemporary Film Theory* (New York: Columbia University Press, 1988).

——: "The image of women in film: a defense of a paradigm," *Journal of Aesthetics and Art Criticism*, 48 (1990); 349–60.

Carse, A.: "Pornography: An uncivil liberty," *Hypatia*, 10: 1 (1995), 155–82.

Case, M. A.: "Disaggregating gender from sex and sexual orientation," *Yale Law Journal*, 105 (1995), 1–105.

Cavell, S.: *Pursuits of Happiness: The Hollywood Comedy of Remarriage* (Cambridge, MA: Harvard University Press, 1981).

——: "Psychoanalysis and cinema: the melodrama of the unknown woman," *Images in our Souls: Cavell, Psychoanalysis, and Cinema, Psychiatry and the Humanities*, ed. J. H. Smith and W. Kerrigan, Vol. 10 (Baltimore, MD: Johns Hopkins University Press, 1987).

Chakravarti, U.: "Whatever happened to the Vedic Dasi?," *Recasting Women: Essays in Colonial History*, ed. K. Sangari and S. Vaid (New Delhi: Kali for Women, 1989).

Chamallas, M.: "Women and part-time work: the case for pay equity and equal access," *North Carolina Law Review*, 64 (1986), 709–75.

Chambers, S.: *Reasonable Democracy* (Ithaca, NY: Cornell University Press, 1996).

——: "Listening to Dr Fiske: the easy case of *Price Waterhouse* v. *Hopkins*," *Vermont Law Review*, 15 (1990), 89–124.

Chatterjee, P.: "The Nationalist resolution of the Women's Question," *Recasting Women: Essays in Colonial History*, ed. K. Sangari and S. Vaid (New Delhi: Kali for Women, 1989).

Cheney, J.: "Ecofeminism and deep ecology," *Environmental Ethics*, 9 (1987), 115–45.

——: "The neo-stoicism of radical environmentalism," *Environmental Ethics*, 11 (1989a), 293–325.

——: "Postmodern environmental ethics: ethics as bioregional narrative," *Environmental Ethics*, 11: 2 (1989b), 117–34.

Chicago, J. and Schapiro, M.: "Female imagery," *Womanspace Journal*, 1 (1973).

Chicago Women's Liberation Union (CWLU). "Socialist feminist," Chicago, mimeograph, 1973.

Chodorow, N.: *The Reproduction of Mothering* (Berkeley: University of California Press, 1978).

——: "Mothering, male dominance and capitalism," *Capitalist Patriarchy and the Case for Socialist Feminism*, ed. Z. Eisenstein (New York: Monthly Review Press, 1979), pp. 83–106.

Chopp, R.: *The Power to Speak: Feminism, Language, and God* (New York: Crossroad, 1989).

Chow, R.: "Violence in the other country: China as crisis, spectacle and woman," *Third World Women and the Politics of Feminism*, ed. C. Mohanty, A. Russo, and L. Torres (Bloomington: Indiana University Press, 1991), pp. 81–100.

——: "Postmodern automatons," *Feminists Theorize the Political*, ed. J. Butler and J. W. Scott (New York: Routledge, 1992), pp. 101–20.

Cixous, H: "The laugh of the Medusa," trans. K. Cohen and P. Cohen, *Signs*, 1: 4 (1979), 875–93.

——, and Clément, C. (1975), trans. C. Porter, *The Newly Born Woman* (Minneapolis: University of Minnesota Press, 1986)

Clark, G.: *Women in the Ancient World* (Oxford: Oxford University Press, 1989).

Clark, M. G., and Lange, L. eds.: *The Sexism of Social and Political Theory* (Toronto: University of Toronto Press, 1979).

Clausen, J.: "My interesting condition," *Out/Look*, 2: 3 (1990), 11–21.

Clement of Alexandria.: *The Instructor* (Pedagogus) in *The Ante-Nicene Fathers*, ed. A. Roberts and J. Donaldson, vol. II (Grand Rapids, MI: Eardmans, 1983).

Clifford, J.: "Traveling cultures," *Cultural Studies*, ed. L. Grossberg, C. Nelson, and P. Treichler (New York: Routledge, 1992).

Cocks, J.: *Colonels and Cadres: War and Gender in South Africa* (Cape Town: Oxford University Press, 1991).

Code, L.: *Epistemic Responsibility* (Hanover, NH: University Press of New England, 1987a).

——: "Second persons," *Science, Morality, and Feminist Theory*, ed. M. Hanen and K. Nielsen (Calgary: University of Calgary Press, 1987b), pp. 357–82.

——: *What Can She Know?: Feminist Theory and the Construction of Knowledge* (Ithaca, NY: Cornell University Press, 1991).

——: "Taking subjectivity into account," *Feminist Epistemologies*, ed. L. Alcoff and E. Potter (New York: Routledge, 1993).

——: "Who cares? The poverty of objectivism for a moral epistemology," *Rethinking Objectivity*, ed. A. Megill (Durham, NC: Duke University Press, 1994).

——: *Rhetorical Spaces: Essays on (Gendered) Locations* (New York: Routledge, 1995).

——: "What is natural about epistemology naturalized?," *American Philosophical Quarterly*, 33: 1 (1996).

Cohen, J.: "The public and private sphere: a feminist reconsideration," *Feminists Read Habermas: Gendering the Subject of Discourse*, ed. J. Meehan (New York: Routledge, 1995), pp. 57–90.

Cohen, S., and Taub, N., eds.: *Reproductive Law for the 1990s* (Clifton, NJ: Humana Press, 1989).

Cohn, C.: "The feminist sexuality debate: ethics and politics," *Hypatia*, 1: 2 (1986), 71–86.

——: "Sex and death in the rational world of defense intellectuals', *Signs*, 12: 4 (1987).

——: "Emasculating America's linguistic deterrent," *Rocking the Ship of State*, ed. A. Harris and Y. King (Boulder, CO: Westview Press, 1989).

——: "Clean bombs and clean language," *Women, Militarism, and War*, ed. J. B. Elshtain and S. Tobias (Totowa, NJ: Rowman and Littlefield, 1990).

——: "War, wimps, and women," *Gendering War Talk*, ed. M. Cooke and A. Woollacott (Princeton, NJ: Princeton University Press, 1993).

Cole, E. Browning, and Coultrap-McQuinn, S., eds: *Explorations in Feminist Ethics: Theory and Practice* (Bloomington: Indiana University Press, 1992).

Colker, R.: "Feminism, theology, and abortion: toward love, compassion and wisdom," *California Law Review*, 77 (1989), 1011–75.

——: *Abortion and Dialogue: Pro-Choice, Pro-Life, and American Law* (Bloomington: Indiana University Press, 1992).

——: "Disembodiment: abortion and gay rights." *Radical Philosophy of Law*, ed. D. Caudill and S.J. Gold (Atlantic Highlands, NJ: Humanities Press, 1995), pp. 234–54.

Collard, A. et al: *Rape of the Wild: Man's Violence Against Animals and the Earth* (Bloomington: Indiana University Press, 1988).

Collectif '95 Maghreb Egalité: *One Hundred Measures and Provisions* (Germany: Friedrich Ebert Stiftung, 1995).

Collins, P. H.: *Black Feminist Thought* (New York: Routledge, 1990).

Collins, M., and Pierce, C.: "Holes and slime: sexism in Sartre's psychoanalysis," *Philosophical Forum*, 5 (1973), 112–27.

Combahee River Collective: "A black feminist statement," *Capitalist Patriarchy and the Case for Socialist Feminism*, ed. Z. Eisenstein (New York: Monthly Review Press, 1979).

Cook, R.: "International human rights and women's reproductive health," *Studies in Family Planning*, 24 (1993), 73–86.

Cooke, M., and Woollacott, A., eds.: *Gendering War Talk* (Princeton NJ: Princeton University Press, 1993).

Corea, G.: *The Mother Machine* (New York: Harper & Row, 1983).

Corea, G., Onelli Klein, R., Hanmer, J., Holmes, H. B., Hoskins, B., Kishwar, M. Raymond, J., Rowland, R. and Steinbacher, R.: *Man-Made Women: How New Reproductive Technologies Affect Women* (Bloomington: Indiana University Press, 1987).

Cornell, D.: *Beyond Accommodation: Ethical Feminism, Deconstruction, and the Law* (New York: Routledge, 1991).

——: "Gender, sex, and equivalent rights," *Feminists Theorize the Political*, ed. J. Butler and J. W. Scott (New York: Routledge, 1992), pp. 280–96.

——: *Transformations: Recollective Imagination and Sexual Difference* (New York: Routledge, 1993).

Courville, C.: "Re-examining patriarchy as a mode of production: the case of Zimbabwe," *Theorizing Black Feminisms: The Visionary Pragmatism of Black Women*, ed. S. James and A. P. A. Busia (London: Routledge, 1993), pp. 31–43.

Cowan, R. S.: *More Work for Mother: The Ironies of Household Technology from the Open Hearth to the Microwave* (New York: Basic Books, 1983).

Coward, R.: "Sexual liberation and the family," *m/f*, 1 (1978), 7–24.

——: *Patriarchal Precedents: Sexuality and Social Relations* (London: Routledge, 1983).

——, and Ellis, J.: *Language and Materialism: Developments in Seminology and the Theory of the Subject* (London: Routledge, 1977).

Crahay, F.: "Le Décollage conceptual: conditions d'une philosophie bantue ("conceptual take-off conditions for a Bantu philosophy")," *Diogène*, 52 (1965), 61–84.

Crain, M.: "Feminizing unions: challenging the gendered structure of wage labor," *Michigan Law Review*, 89 (1991), 1155–221.

——: Images of power in labor law: a feminist deconstruction," *Boston College Law Review*, 33 (1992), 481– 537.

Creet, J.: "Daughter of the movement: the psychodynamics of lesbian S/M fantasy," *differences*, 3: 2 (1991), 135–59.

Crenshaw, K. W.: "Demarginalizing the intersection of race and sex," *University of Chicago Legal Forum* (1989), pp. 139–67.

——: "Beyond racism and misogyny," *Words that Wound*, ed. M. Matsuda et al. (Boulder, Co: Westview Press, 1993).

Croll, E.: *Feminism and Socialism in China* (Boston: Routledge, 1978).

Cudd, A. E.: "Oppression by choice," *Journal of Social Philosophy*, 25 (1994), 22–44.

Cunningham, F.: *Objectivity in Social Science* (Toronto: University of Toronto Press, 1973).

Cuomo, C.: "Unraveling problems in ecofeminism," *Environmental Ethics*, 14: 4 (1992), 351–63.

Curley, E. M.: "Excusing rape," *Philosophy and Public Affairs*, 5: 4 (1976), 325–60.

Dailey, A.: "Feminism's return to liberalism," *Yale Law Journal*, 102 (1993), 1265–86.

Dalla Costa, M.: *The Power of Women and the Subversion of the Community* (Bristol: Falling Wall Press, 1974).

Dalmiya, V., and Alcoff, L.: "Are 'old wives' tales' justified?," *Feminist Epistemologies*, ed. L. Alcoff and E. Potter (New York: Routledge, 1993).

Dalton, C.: "An essay in the deconstruction of contract doctrine," *Yale Law Journal*, 94 (1985), 997–1114.

Daly, M.: *Beyond God the Father: Toward a Theory of Women's Liberation* (Boston: Beacon Press, 1973).

——: *Gyn/Ecology: The Metaethics of Radical Feminism* (Boston: Beacon Press, 1978).

——: *Pure Lust* (Boston: Beacon Press, 1984).

——, and Caputi, J.: *Webster's First Intergalactic* Wickedary *of the English Language* (Boston: Beacon Press, 1987).

Dandekar, N.: "Ecofeminism," *American Nature Writer* (Fall/Winter 1990).

"Danielle": "Prostitution," *Freedom, Feminism and the State*, ed. W. McElroy (Washington, DC Cato Institute, 1982).

Danmer, E.: "Queer ethics: or the challenge of bisexuality to lesbian ethics," *Hypatia*, 7: 4 (1992), 91–105.

Danto, A.: *The Philosophical Disenfranchisement of Art* (New York: Columbia University Press, 1986).

607

Das, V.: *Critical Events* (New Delhi: Oxford University Press, 1995).

David-Ménard, M.: "Kant, the law, and desire," *Feminist Interpretations of Kant*, ed. R. Schott (University Park: Pennsylvania State University Press, 1997).

Davion, V.: "Is ecofeminism feminist?," *Ecological Feminism*, ed. K. Warren (London: Routledge, 1994), pp. 8–29.

Davis, A.: "The approaching obsolescence of housework: a working class perspective," *Women, Race and Class*, A. Davis (New York: Random House, 1981a).

——: *Women, Race and Class* (New York: Random House, 1981b).

——: *Women, Culture and Politics* (New York: Random House, 1990).

Davis, F. J.: *Who is Black?* (University Park: Pennsylvania State University Press, 1991).

Davis, K.: "Die Rhetorik des Feminismus. Ein neuer Blick auf die Gilligan debatte," *Feministische Studien*, 2 (1991), 79–97.

——: *Reshaping the Female Body: The Dilemma of Cosmetic Surgery* (New York: Routledge, 1995).

Dean, J.: "Discourses in different voices," *Feminists Read Habermas: Gendering the Subject of Discourse*, ed. J. Meehan (New York: Routledge, 1995), pp. 205–30.

D'Eaubonne, F.: *Le Féminisme ou la Mort* (Paris: Pierre Horay, 1974).

de Beauvoir, S.: *The Second Sex*, trans. and ed. H. M. Parshley (New York: Bantam Books, 1973).

de Castell, S. and Bryson, M.: "En/gendering equity: emancipatory programs," *Philosophy of Education 1992* (Champaign, IL: Philosophy of Education Society, 1993), pp. 357–71.

De Cew, J.: "Violent pornography," *Journal of Applied Philosophy*, 1: 1 (1984), 79–84.

——: "Defending the 'private' in constitutional privacy," *Journal of Value Inquiry*, 21 (1987), 171–84.

——: "The combat exclusion and the role of women in the military," *Hypatia*, 10: 1 (1995), 56–73.

de Lauretis, T.: "The female body and heterosexual presumption', *Semiotica*, 67: 3 (1987a), 259–79.

——: *Technologies of Gender: Essays in Theory, Film and Fiction* (London: Macmillan, 1987b).

——: "Sexual indifference and lesbian representation," *Theatre Journal*, 40 (1988), 155–77.

——: "Perverse desires: the lure of the mannish lesbian," *Australian Feminist Studies*, 13 (1991a), 15–26.

——: "Queer theory: lesbian and gay sexualities," *differences*, 3 (1991b), iii-xviii.

——: *The Practice of Love: Lesbian Sexuality and Perverse Desire* (Bloomington: Indiana University Press, 1994).

Deegan, M. J.: *Jane Addams and the Men of the Chicago School, 1892–1918* (New Brunswick, NJ: Transaction Books, 1988).

——, and Brooks, N.: *Women and Disability: The Double Handicap* (Oxford: Transaction Books, 1985).

Delphy, C.: "For a materialist feminism," *Feminist Issues*, 1: 2 (1981), 69–76.

——: *Close to Home: A Materialist Analysis of Women's Oppression* (Amherst: University of Massachusetts Press, 1984).

DeMay v. *Roberts*, 46 Mich. 160, 9 N.W. 146 (1881).

Deming, B.: *We Are All Part of One Another* (Philadelphia, PA: New Society Press, 1984).

Derrida, J.: *Of Grammatology*, trans. Gayatri Chakravorty Spivak (Baltimore, MD: Johns Hopkins University Press, 1974).

——: "Structure, sign and play in the discourse of the human sciences," *Writing and Difference*, trans. A. Bass (Chicago, IL: University of Chicago Press, 1978), pp. 278–93.

Despot, B.: *Zensko pitanje i socialisticko samoupravljanje* (Zagreb: CEKADE, 1987).

Dewey, J.: *Philosophy and Civilization* (New York: Peter Smith Edition, 1968).

——: *Reconstruction in Philosophy, the Middle Works: Vol. 12: 1920* (Carbondale: Southern Illinois University Press, 1982).

——: *Democracy and Education, the Middle Works: Vol. 9* (Carbondale: Southern Illinois University Press, 1980).

Dialectics of Biology Group, eds.: *Against Biological Determinism* (London: Allison and Busby, 1982a).

——: *Towards a Liberatory Biology* (London: Allison and Busby, 1982b).

Diamond, I.: "Pornography and repression: a reconsideration," *Women: Sex and Sexuality*, ed. C. Stimpson and E. Spector Person (Chicago, IL: University of Chicago Press, 1980).

——, and Quinby, L.: "American feminism in the age of body," *Signs*, 10: 1 (1984), 119–25.

Dieterlen, G: *Les Ames des Dogons* (Paris: Institut d'ethnologie, 1941).

Dietrich, G.: *Reflections on the Women's Movement in India: Religion, Ecology, Development* (New Delhi: Horizon India Books, 1992).

Dietz, M.: "Citizenship with a feminist face: the problem with maternal thinking," *Political Theory*, 13: 1 (1985), 19–37.

——: "Context is all: feminism and theories of citizenship," *Daedalus*, 116: 4 (1987), 1–24.

differences: "More gender trouble: feminism meets queer theory," 6: 2–3 (1994).

Diller, A., Houston, B., Morgan, K., and Ayim, M.: *The Gender Question in Education: Philosophical Dialogues* (Boulder, Co: Westview Press, 1996).

Dinnerstein, D.: *The Mermaid and the Minotaur* (New York: Harper and Row, 1976).

Di Stefano, C.: "Dilemmas of difference: feminism, modernity and postmodernism," *Feminism/Postmodernism*, ed. L. Nicholson (New York: Routledge, 1990), pp. 63–82.

——: *Configurations of Masculinity: A Feminist Perspective on Modern Political Theory* (Ithaca, NY: Cornell University Press, 1991).

Doan, L.: *The Lesbian Postmodern* (New York: Columbia University Press, 1994).

Dodson, G.: *Why the Green Nigger? Remything Genesis* (Wellesley, MA: Roundtable Press, 1979).

Dolan, J.: "The dynamics of desire: sexuality and gender in pornography perform-ance," *Theatre Journal*, 39: 2 (1987), 156–74.

——: "Lesbian subjectivity in realism," *Performing Feminisms*, ed. S. Case (Balti-more, MD: Johns Hopkins University Press, 1990), pp. 59–66.

——: *Presence and Desire: Essays on Gender, Sexuality, and Performance* (Ann Arbor: University of Michigan Press, 1993).

Donovan, J.: "Animal rights and feminist theory," *Ecofeminism: Women, Animals, and Nature*, ed. G. Gaard (Philadelphia, PA: Temple University Press, 1993), pp. 167–94.

Doubiago, S.: "Mama Coyote talks to the boys," *Healing the Wounds: The Promise of Ecofeminism*, ed. J. Plant (Philadelphia, PA: New Society Publishers, 1989), pp. 140–4.

Dowd, M.: "Dispelling the myths about the 'Battered woman's defense,'" *Ford-ham Urban Law Journal*, 19 (1992), 567–83.

Downie, J., and Sherwin, S.: "A feminist exploration of issues around assisted death," *St Louis Law Review* (1996).

Dresser, R.: "Wanted: single, white male for medical research," *Hastings Center Report*, 22 (1992), 24–9.

Dubinin, N. P.: "Race and contemporary genetics," *Race, Science and Society*, ed. L. Kuper (New York: Columbia University Press, 1965), pp. 31–67.

DuBois, E., Dunlap, M., Gilligan, C., MacKinnon, C., and Menkel-Meadows, C.: "Feminist discourse, moral values, and the law," *Buffalo Law Review*, 34 (1985), 11–87.

duBois, P.: *Sourcing the Body: Psychoanalysis and Ancient Representations of Women* (Chicago: University of Chicago Press, 1988).

DuBois, W. E. B.: *Darkwater: Voices from within the Veil* (New York: Harcourt, Brace, and Howe, 1920).

Duden, B.: *The Woman Beneath the Skin* (Cambridge, MA: Harvard University Press, 1991).

Duerst-Lahti, G., and Kelly, R., eds.: *Gender, Power, Leadership and Governance* (Ann Arbor: University of Michigan Press, 1995).

Du Fangqin, ed.: *Chinese Women and Development: Position, Health, and Employ-ment* (Zengzhou: Henan People's Publishing House, 1993a).

——: "Developing new perspectives and methods in women's studies in China with the aid of Sino-Western exchanges," *Chinese Women and Development: Position, Health and Employment* (Zengzhou: Henan People's Publishing House, 1993b).

Duggan, L.: "Making it perfectly queer," *Socialist Review*, 22: 1 (1992), 11–31.

Duhacek, D.: "Women's time in former Yugoslavia," *Gender Politics and Post-Communism*, ed. N. Funk and M. Mueller (New York: Routledge, 1993).

Dunayevskaya, R.: *Rosa Luxemburg, Women's Liberation, and Marx's Philosophy of Revolution* (Chicago: University of Illinois Press, 1991).

Dunlap, M.: "Sexual speech and the state: putting pornography in its place," *Golden Gate University Law Review*, 17 (1987), 359–78.

Dunn, L. C.: "Race and biology," *Race, Science and Society*, ed. L. Kuper (New York: Columbia University Press, 1965), pp. 68– 94.

Duran, J.: "The feminization of social work: a philosophical analysis," *International Journal of Applied Philosophy*, 4 (1988), 85–90.

——: *Toward a Feminist Epistemology* (Savage, MD: Rowman and Littlefield, 1991).

Dworkin, A.: *Womanhating: A Radical Look at Sexuality* (New York: Dutton, 1974).

——: *Pornography: Men Possessing Women* (New York: G.P. Putnam's Sons, 1981).

——: *Letters From a War Zone: Writings 1976–1987* (London: Secker and Warburg, 1988a).

——: *Intercourse* (New York: Free Press, 1988b).

Dworkin, R.: *Taking Rights Seriously* (Cambridge, MA: Harvard University Press, 1977).

Eastman, C.: *On Women and Revolution*, ed. B. Weisen Cook (New York: Oxford University Press, 1978).

Ebert, T.: *Ludic Feminism and After: Postmodernism, Desire, and Labor in Late Capitalism* (Ann Arbor: University of Michigan Press, 1996).

Eboh, P. M.: "The woman question: African and Women perspectives," *Postkoloniales Philosophieren Afrika*, ed. H. Nagl-Docekal and M. Wimmer (Vienna Munich: Oldenbourg, 1992), pp. 206–14.

Echols, A.: *Daring to be Bad: Radical Feminism in America, 1967–1975* (Minneapolis: University of Minnesota Press, 1989).

Ecker, G., ed.: *Feminist Aesthetics* (Boston: Beacon Press, 1985).

Ehrenreich, B.: "The challenge for the Left," *Democratic Left* (July/August 1992), 3–4.

Eichler, M.: *The Double Standard: A Feminist Critique of Social Science* (New York: St Martin's Press, 1980).

Eisenstadt v. *Baird*, 405 U.S. 438 (1972).

Eisenstein, Z., ed.: *Capitalist Patriarchy and the Case for Socialist Feminism* (New York: Monthly Review Press, 1979).

——: *Feminism and Sexual Equality: Crisis in Liberal America* (New York: Monthly Review Press, 1984).

——: *The Female Body and the Law* (Berkeley: University of California Press, 1988).

——: "Specifying US feminism in the nineties: the problem of naming," *Socialist Review*, 20: 2 (1990), pp. 45– 56.

——: *The Color of Gender: Re-Imaging Democracy* (Berkeley: University of California Press, 1994).

Elshtain, J. B.: *Public Man, Private Woman* (Princeton, NJ: Princeton University Press, 1981).

——: "Reflections on war and political discourse," *Political Theory*, 13 (1985).

——: *Women and War* (New York: Basic Books, 1987).

——: *Power Trips and Other Journeys* (Madison: University of Wisconsin Press, 1990).

——: *But Was It Just: Reflections on the Gulf War* (New York: Doubleday Press, 1992).

——, and Tobias, S.: *Women, Militarism and War* (Savage, MD: Rowman and Littlefield, 1990).

Ely, J. H.: "The wages of crying wolf: a comment on *Roe* v. *Wade*," *Yale Jaw Journal*, 82 (1973), 920–49.

Engels, F.: *The Origin of the Family, Private Property and the State*, ed. E. Leacock (New York: International Publishers, 1972).

——: "Socialism, utopian and scientific," *The Marx–Engels Reader*, ed. R. Tucker (New York: W.W. Norton, 1978).

Engle. K.: "Female subjects and public international law: human rights and the exotic other female," *New England Law Review*, 26 (1992a), 1509–26.

——: "International human rights and feminism: when discourses meet," *Michigan Journal of International Law*, 13 (1992b), 517–610.

Englehardt, T.: *Foundations of Bioethics* (New York: Oxford University Press, 1989).

English, J.: "Abortion and the concept of a person," *Canadian Journal of Philosophy*, 5 (1975), 233–43.

Enloe, C.: *Does Khaki Become You?* (London: Pandora/Harper Collins, 1988).

——: *Bananas, Beaches and Bases: Making Feminist Sense of International Politics* (Berkeley: University of California Press, 1989).

——: "Bananas, Bases, and Patriarchy," *Women, Militarism, and War*, ed. J. B. Elshtain and S. Tobias (Savage, MD: Rowman and Littlefield, 1990).

——: *The Morning After: Sexual Politics at the End of the Cold War* (Berkeley: University of California Press, 1993).

Erens, P., ed.: *Issues in Feminist Film Criticism* (Bloomington: Indiana University Press, 1990).

Estrich, S.: "Rape," *The Yale Law Journal*, 95 (1987a), 1087–1184.

——: *Real Rape* (Cambridge, MA: Harvard University Press, 1987b).

——: "Sex at work," *Stanford Law Review*, 43 (1991), 813–61.

Ezeigbo, T. A.: "Traditional women's institutions in Igbo society: implications for the Igbo female writer," *African Languages*, 32 (1990) 149–65.

Ezorsky, G.: "The fight over university women," *The New York Review of Books*, 16 (1974), 32–9.

——: *Racism and Justice: The Case for Affirmative Action* (Ithaca, NY: Cornell University Press, 1991).

Falk, M.: "Notes on composing new blessings," *Weaving the Visions: New Patterns in Feminist Spirituality*, ed. J. Plaskow and C. P. Christ (San Francisco, CA: Harper and Row, 1989).

——: *Book of Blessings* (San Francisco, CA: Harper and Row, 1996).

Fantham, E., Foley, H. P. Karapen, N. B. Pomeroy, S .B., and Shapiro, H. A.: *Women in the Classical World* (Oxford: Oxford University Press, 1994).

Farid, A.: *Muslim Woman In World Religions' Perspective* (Pakistan: University of Karachi, 1994).

Farnham, C., ed.: *The Impact of Feminist Research in the Academy* (Bloomington: Indiana University Press, 1987).

Farwell, M.: "Towards a definition of the lesbian literary imagination," *Signs*, 14: 1 (1988), 100–18.

Fausto-Sterling, A.: "Life in the XY corral," *Women's Studies International Forum*, 1989.

——: *Myths of Gender: Biological Theories about Women and Men* (New York: Basic Books, 1992).

Feder. E.: "Disciplining the family: The case of gender identity disorder," *Philosophical Studies*, forthcoming.

Fee, E.: "Women's nature and scientific objectivity," *Women's Nature*, ed. M. Lowe and R. Hubbard (New York: Pergamon Press, 1983).

Feinberg, J.: "Autonomy, sovereignty and privacy: moral ideals in the constitution?," *Notre Dame Law Review*, 58 (1983), 445–92.

Feinberg, L.: *Stone Butch Blues* (New York: Firebrand, 1993).

Feldman, S.: "Multiple biological mothers: The case for gestation," *Journal of Social Philosophy*, 23: 1 (1992), 98–104.

Felski, R.: "Why feminism doesn't need an aesthetic (and why it can't ignore aesthetics)," *Feminism and Tradition in Aesthetics*, ed. P. Z. Brand and C. Korsmeyer (University Park: Pennsylvania State University Press, 1995).

Femenías, M. L.: "Women and natural hierarchy in Aristotle," *Hypatia*, 9 (1994), 164–72.

Ferge, Z.: "Social policy," *Blackwell Dictionary of Twentieth-Century Social Thought*, ed. W. Outhwaite and T. Bottomore (Cambridge: Blackwell, 1993), pp. 603–5.

Ferguson, A.: "Androgyny as an ideal for human development," *Feminism and Philosophy*, ed. M. Vetterling-Braggin, F. Elliston, and J. English (Totowa, NJ: Littlefield, Adams, 1977), pp. 45–69.

——, and Folbre, N.: "The unhappy marriage of capitalism and patriarchy', *Women and Revolution*, ed. L. Sargent (Boston: South End Press, 1981), pp. 313–38.

——: "The sex debate within the women's movement," *Against the Current* (September/October 1983a), 10–16.

——: "On conceiving motherhood and sexuality," *Mothering: Essays in Feminist Theory*, ed. J. Trebilcot (Totowa, NJ: Rowman and Allanheld, 1983b).

——: "Sex war: the debate between radical and libertarian feminists," *Signs*, 10: 1 (1984), 106–35.

——: "Lesbian identity: Beauvoir and history," *Women's Studies International Forum*, 8: 3 (1985), 203–8.

——: "A feminist aspect theory of the self," *Science, Morality, and Feminist Theory*, ed. M. Hanen and K. Nielsen (Calgary: University of Calgary Press, 1987).

——: *Blood at the Root: Motherhood, Sexuality and Male Domination* (London: Pandora, 1989).

——: "Patriarchy, sexual identity, and the sexual revolution," *Sexual Democracy: Women, Oppression, and Revolution* (Boulder, CO: Westview Press, 1991a), pp. 52–65.

——: *Sexual Democracy: Women, Oppression and Revolution* (Boulder, CO: Westview Press, 1991b).

——: "Twenty years of feminist philosophy," *Hypatia*, 9: 3 (1994), 197–215.

——, Philipson, I., Diamond, I., Quinby, L., Vance, C. S., and Snitow, A. B.: "Forum: the feminist sexuality debates", *Signs*, 10: 1 (1984), 106–35.

Ferguson, K.: "Bureaucracy and public life: The feminization of the polity," *Administration and Society*, 15: 3 (1983), 295–322.

——: *The Feminist Case Against Bureaucracy* (Philadelphia, PA: Temple University Press, 1984).

Fernández, A. M., ed.: *Las Mujeres en la Imaginaci ón Colectiva: Una Historia de Discriminación y Resistencias* (Buenos Aires: Paidos, 1992).

Fernandez, C. A.: "Testimony of the Association of Multi-Ethnic Americans," *American Mixed Race: Exploring Microdiversity*, ed. N. Zack (Lanham, MD: Rowman and Littlefield, 1995), pp. 191–210.

Feyerabend, P.: *Against Method* (London: Verso. 1975).

Finch, J.: "Community care: developing non-sexist alternatives," *Critical Social Policy*, 9 (1984).

Findlay, H.: "Freud's 'fetishism' and the lesbian dildo debates," *Feminist Studies*, 18: 3 (1992), 563–80.

Fine, M., and Asch, A.: "The question of disability: no easy answers for the women's movement," *The Reproductive Rights Newsletter*, 4: 3 (1982).

——: "Disability beyond stigma: social interaction, discrimination, and activism," *Journal of Social Issues*, 44: 1 (1988a).

——, eds.: *Women with Disabilities: Essays in Psychology, Culture and Politics* (Philadelphia, PA: Temple University Press, 1988b).

Fineman, M. Albertson: "The politics of custody and the transformation of American custody decision making," *University of California at Davis Law Review*, 22 (1989), 829–64.

——: *The Illusion of Equality: The Rhetoric and Reality of Divorce Reform* (Chicago: University of Chicago Press, 1991).

Finley, L.: "Transcending equality theory: a way out of the maternity and the workplace debate," *Columbia Law Review*, 86 (1986), 1118–82.

Firestone, S.: *The Dialectic of Sex* (New York: William Morrow, 1970).

Fisher, L.: "Towards a phenomenology of gendered consciousness," *Feminism and Phenomenology*, ed. L. Fisher and L. Embree (Amsterdam: Kluwer, 1996).

Fitzsimons, A.: "Women, power, and technology," *Knowing the Difference: Feminist Perspectives in Epistemology*, ed. K. Lennon and M. Whitford (New York: Routledge, 1994).

Flanagan, O. J., Jr, and Adler, J. E.: "Impartiality and particularity," *Social Research*, 50: 3 (1983), 576–96.

Flanagan, O. J., and Jackson, K.: "Justice, care, and gender: the Kohlberg-Gilligan debate revisited," *Ethics*, 97 (1987), 622–37.

Flax, J.: "Political philosophy and the patriarchal unconscious," *Discovering Reality: Feminist Perspectives on Epistemology, Metaphysics, Methodology, and Philosophy of Science*, ed. S. Harding and M. Hintikka (Dordrecht, Holland: D. Reidel Publishing Co., 1983).

——: "Re-membering the selves: is the repressed gendered?," *Michigan Quarterly Review*, 26 (1987), 92–110.

——: "Postmodernism and gender relations," *Feminism/Postmodernism*, ed. L. Nicholson (New York: Routledge, 1990), pp. 39–62.

——: "'Beyond equality: gender, justice and difference," *Beyond Equality and Difference*, ed. G. Bock and S. Jones (London: Routledge, 1992), 193–210.

——: "Race/gender and the ethics of difference," *Political Theory*, 23: 3 (1995), 500–10.

Fleming, M.: "Women and the 'public use of reason,'" *Feminists Read Habermas*, ed. J. Meehan (New York: Routledge, 1995).

Flexner, E.: *Centuries of Struggle* (New York: Atheneum, 1972).

Foa, P.: "What's wrong with rape," *Feminism and Philosophy*, ed. M. Vetterling-Braggin, F. Elliston, and J. English (Totowa, NJ: Littlefield, Adams, 1977), pp. 347–59.

Folbre, N.: "Exploitation comes home: A critique of the Marxian theory of family labor," *Cambridge Journal of Economics*, 6 (1982), 317–29.

——: "Patriarchy as a mode of production," *Alternatives to Economic Orthodoxy*, ed. R. Albelda, C. Gunn, and W. Walker (New York: M.E. Sharpe, 1987), pp. 323–38.

——: *Who Pays for the Kids? Gender and the Structures of Constraint* (New York: Routledge, 1994).

Foreman, A.: *Femininity and Alienation* (London: Pluto, 1977).

Fortenbaugh, W.: *Aristotle on Emotion* (London, 1975).

Foster, V.: *Making Women the Subject of Educational Change* (Allen and Unwin, 1996).

Foucault, M.: *Discipline and Punish* (New York: Vintage Books, 1973).

——: *The History of Sexuality* (New York: Pantheon Books, 1978).

Francis, L., ed.: *Date Rape: Feminism, Philosophy, and the Law* (University Park: University of Pennsylvania Press, 1996).

Frank, F. and Anshen, F.: *Language and the Sexes* (Albany: State University of New York Press, 1983).

Franke, K.: "The central mistake of sex discrimination law: the disaggregation of sex from gender," *University of Pennsylvania Law Review*, 144 (1995), 1–99.

Frankenberg, R.: *White Women, Race Matters: The Social Construction of Whiteness* (Minneapolis: University of Minnesota Press, 1993).

Fraser, N.: "Toward a discourse ethic of solidarity," *Praxis International*, 5: 4 (1986), 425–9.

——: "Women, welfare and the politics of need interpretation," *Hypatia*, 2: 1 (1987), 103–21.

——: "Talking about needs: interpretive contests as political conflicts in welfare-state societies," *Ethics*, 99 (1989c), 291–313.

615

——: *Unruly Practices: Power, Discourse and Gender in Contemporary Social Theory* (Minneapolis: University of Minnesota Press, 1989a).

——: "What's critical about critical theory? The case of Habermas and gender," *Unruly Practices: Power, Discourse and Gender in Contemporary Social Theory*, ed. N. Fraser (Minneapolis: University of Minnesota Press, 1989b).

——: "After the family wage," *Social Justice* (Spring 1994).

——: "From redistribution to recognition? Dilemmas of justice in a 'post-socialist' age," *New Left Review*, 212 (1995), 68–83.

——, and Gordon, L.: "A genealogy of dependency: tracing a keyword of the U.S. welfare state," *Pitied but Not Entitled: Single Mothers and the History of Welfare* (New York: The Free Press, 1994).

——, and Nicholson, L.: "Social criticism without philosophy: an encounter between feminism and postmodernism," *Feminism/Postmodernism*, ed. L. Nicholson (New York: Routledge, 1990), pp. 19–38.

Frazer, E., and Lacey, N.: *The Politics of Community. A Feminist Critique of the Liberal-Communitarian Debate* (Toronto: University of Toronto Press, 1993).

Freeland, C. A.: "Nourishing Speculation," *Engendering Origins: Critical Feminist Readings in Plato and Aristotle*, ed. B. Bar-On (Albany:State University of New York Press, 1994).

——: "Feminist frameworks for horror films," *Post-Theory*, ed. D. Bordwell and N. Carroll (Madison: University of Wisconsin Press, 1996), pp. 195–218.

——, and Wartenberg, T. E.: *Philosophy and Film* (New York: Routledge, 1995).

Freeman, E. and Thorne, B.: "Introduction to 'the feminist sexuality debate'," *Signs*, 10: 1 (1984).

Freud, S.: *The Interpretation of Dreams* [1900], *Standard Edition of the Complete Psychological Works of Sigmund Freud (SE)*, ed. and trans. J. Strachey [1917], Vols 4–5 (New York: Basic Books, 1955).

——: *Three Essays on the Theory of Sexuality* [1905], *SE*, Vol. 7.

——: "Mourning and melancholia," *SE* [1917], Vol. 14, pp. 243–58.

——: *The Ego and the Id* [1927], *SE*, Vol. 19.

Fried, C.: *An Anatomy of Values: Problems of Personal and Social Change* (Cambridge, MA: Harvard University Press, 1970).

Fried, M. G.: "In defense of preferential hiring," *Women and Philosophy: Toward a Theory of Liberation*, ed. C. Gould and M. Wartofsky (New York: G. P. Putnam's Sons, 1976).

Friedman, M.: "Beyond caring: the demoralization of gender," *Science, Morality, and Feminist Theory*, ed. M. Hanen and K. Nielsen (Calgary: University of Calgary Press, 1987), pp. 87–100.

——: "Welfare cuts and the ascendance of market patriarchy," *Hypatia*, 3 (1988), 145–9.

——: *What Are Friends For? Feminist Perspectives on Relationships and Moral Theory* (Ithaca, NY: Cornell University Press, 1993).

——: "Feminism and modern friendship: dislocating the community," *Feminism and Community*, ed. M. Friedman and P. Weiss (Philadelphia, PA: Temple Press, 1995a).

——, and Weiss, P., eds.: *Feminism and Community* (Philadelphia, PA: Temple Press, 1995b).

Friedman, R. E.: *Who Wrote the Bible?* (New York: Summit Books, 1987).

Frug, M. J.: *Postmodern Legal Feminism* (New York: Routledge, 1991).

Frye, M.: "Male chauvinism: a conceptual analysis," *Philosophy and Sex*, ed. R. Baker and F. Elliston (Buffalo, NY: Prometheus Books, 1975).

——: "Some reflections on separatism and power," *The Politics of Reality: Essays in Feminist Theory*, ed. M. Frye (Trumansburg, NY: The Crossing Press, 1983a), pp. 95–109.

——: *The Politics of Reality*: Essays in Feminist Theory (Trumansburg, NY: The Crossing Press, 1983b).

——: "To be and be seen: The politics of reality," *The Politics of Reality: Essays in Feminist Theory*, ed. M. Frye (Trumansburg, NY: The Crossing Press, 1983c), pp. 152–74.

——: " 'Lesbian 'sex,' " *Sinister Wisdom*, 35 (1988), 46–54.

——: "A Response to *Lesbian Ethics*," *Hypatia* 5 (1990), 132–7.

——: "Do you have to be a lesbian to be a feminist?," *Willful Virgin: Essays in Feminism 1976–1992* (Freedom, CA: The Crossing Press, 1992a).

——: *Willful Virgin: Essays in Feminism 1976–1992* (Freedom, CA: The Crossing Press, 1992b).

——: "The necessity of differences: constructing a positive category of women," *Signs* (Summer 1996).

Fuss, D.: *Essentially Speaking: Feminism, Nature, and Difference* (New York: Routledge, 1989).

——: "Fashion and the homospectatorial look," *Critical Inquiry*, 18 (1992), 713–37.

Fuszara, M.: "Legal regulation of abortion in Poland," *Signs*, 17: 1 (1991), 117–28.

Gaard, G., and Gruen, L.: "Comment on George's 'Should Feminists be Vegetarians?'," *Signs* (Autumn 1995), 230–20.

Galler, R.: "The myth of the perfect body," *Pleasure and Danger: Exploring Female Sexuality* (London: Pandora Press, 1984).

Gallop, J.: *Thinking Through the Body* (New York: Columbia University Press, 1988).

Gariaule, M.: *Conversations with Ogotemmeli* (London: Oxford University Press, 1965).

Garland, R.: *The Eye of the Beholder: Deformity and Disability in Graeco-Roman World* (Ithaca, NY: Cornell University Press, 1995).

Garrett, R.: "The nature of privacy," *Philosophy Today*, 18 (1974), 263–84.

Garrison, J. W., and Phelan, A.: "Toward a feminist poetic of critical thinking," *Philosophy of Education 1989* (Champaign, IL: Philosophy of Education Society, 1990), pp. 304–14.

Garry, A.: "Pornography and respect for women," *Social Theory and Practice*, 4: 4 (1976), 395–421.

——: "The philosopher as teacher: why are love and sex philosophically interesting?," *Metaphilosphy*, 11: 2 (1980), 165–77.

Gatens, M.: "Towards a feminist philosophy of the body," *Crossing Boundaries: Feminisms and the Critique of Knowledges*, ed. B. Caine, E. Grosz, and M. de Lepervanche (Sydney: Allen and Unwin, 1988).

——: "Rousseau and Wollstonecraft: nature vs. reason," *Australasian Journal of Philosophy*, 64 supplement (1991), 1–15.

——: "A critique of the sex/gender distinction," *Imaginary Bodies: Ethics, Power and Corporeality* (London: Routledge, 1996a), pp. 3–20.

——: *Imaginary Bodies: Ethics, Power and Corporeality* (London: Routledge, 1996b).

——: "Power, ethics and sexual imaginings," *Imaginary Bodies: Ethics, Power and Corporeality* (London: Routledge, 1996c).

Gatens-Robinson, E.: "Dewey and the feminist successor science project," *Transactions of the Charles S. Peirce Society*, 27 (1991), 417–33.

——: "A defense of women's choice: abortion and the ethics of care," *Southern Journal of Philosophy*, 30: 3 (1992), 39–66.

Gavison, R.: "Privacy and the limits of law," *Yale Law Journal*, 89 (1980), 421–39.

Gearhart, S.: *The Wanderground* (Boston: Alyson, 1979).

Gerety, T.: "Redefining privacy," *Harvard Civil Rights–Civil Liberties Law Review*, 12 (1977), 233–96.

al-Ghazali, A. H.: *Ihya' 'Ulum al-Din* (*Reviving Religious Sciences*), 4 vols (Cairo: Dar Mustafa Babi Halabi li al-Nashr, 11th century reprint, 1939).

Gibson, M.: *Workers' Rights* (Totowa, NJ: Rowman and Allanheld, 1983).

Gill, C., Kirschner, K., and Reis, J. P.: "Health services for women with disabilities: barriers and portals," *Reframing Women's Health*, ed. A.J. Dan (Thousand Oaks, CA: Sage Publications, 1994).

Gilligan, C.: *In A Different Voice: Psychological Theory and Woman's Development* (Cambridge, MA: Harvard University Press, 1982a).

——: "Is there a feminine morality?," *Psychology Today*, 10 (1982b), 21–34.

——: "Die andere Stimme," *Lebenskonflikte und Moral der Frau* (Munich, 1984).

——: "Moral orientation and moral development," *Women and Moral Theory*, eds. E. Kittay and D. Meyers (Totowa, NJ: Rowman and Littlefield, 1987).

——: *Mapping the Moral Domain* (Cambridge, MA: Harvard University Press, 1988).

——: "Moralische Orientierung und moralische Entwicklung," *Die Kontroverse um eine geschlechtsspezifische Ethik*, ed. G. Nunner-Winkler (Frankfurt/Main, 1991), pp. 79–100.

——, and Brown, L.: *Meeting at the Crossroads* (Cambridge, MA: Harvard University Press, 1992).

——, and Murphy, J. M.: "Moral development in late adolescence and adulthood," *Human Development*, 23 (1980), 7–104.

Gilman, C. P.: *Women and Economics: A Study of the Economic Relation Between Men and Women as a Factor in Social Evolution* [1898] (New York: Harper and Row, 1966).

——: *The Man-made World or, our Androcentric Culture* (Minneapolis: University of Minnesota Series in American Studies, 1971).

——: *Herland* (New York: Pantheon Books, 1979).

Goitein, S. D.: "Women as creators of Biblical genres," *Prooftexts*, 8: 1 (1988), 1–34.

Goldenberg, N.: *Returning Words to Flesh: Feminism, Psychoanalysis, and the Resurrection of the Body* (Boston: Beacon Press, 1990).

Goldman, E.: *Red Emma Speaks: Selected Writings and Speeches by Emma Goldman*, ed. A.K. Shulman (New York: Random House, 1972).

Goldmann, L.: *Immanuel Kant*, trans. R. Black (London: New Left Books, 1971).

Goodin, R.: *Utilitarianism as a Public Philosophy* (Cambridge: Cambridge University Press, 1995).

Goodwin, B.: *How the Leopard Changed its Spots* (London: Weidenfeld and Nicolson, 1994).

Gordon, L.: *Pitied but Not Entitled: Single Mothers and the History of Welfare* (New York: The Free Press, 1994).

——: *Badfaith and Antiblack Racism* (Atlantic Highlands, NJ: Humanities Press, 1995).

——, and DuBois, E.: "Seeking ecstasy on the battlefield," *Feminist Studies*, 9: 1 (1983), 7–25.

Gottlieb, L.: *She Who Dwells Within* (San Francisco, CA: Harper, 1995).

Gottner-Abendroth, H.: *Die tanzende Gottin. Prizipien einer matriarchalen Asthetik* (Munich, 1982).

Gould, C.: *Re-thinking Democracy: Freedom and Social Cooperation in Politics, Economy and Society* (Cambridge: Cambridge University Press, 1988).

——, and Wartofsky, M., eds.: *Women and Philosophy: Toward a Theory of Liberation* (New York: G.P. Putnam's Sons, 1976).

Gould, S. J.: *The Mismeasure of Man* (New York: W.W. Norton, 1981).

Govier, T.: "Self-trust, autonomy, and self-esteem," *Hypatia*, 8 (1993), 99–120.

Graham, A.: "The making of a nonsexist dictionary," *Ms*, 2 (1973), 12–16.

Grant, J.: *Fundamental Feminism: Contesting the Core Concepts of Feminist Theory* (New York: Routledge, 1993).

Grant, R., and Newland, K., eds.: *Gender and International Relations* (Bloomington: Indiana University Press, 1991).

Graybeal, J.: *Language and "the feminine" in Nietzsche and Heidegger* (Bloomington: Indiana University Press, 1990).

Green, K.: "Prostitution, exploitation, and taboo," *Philosophy*, 64 (1989), 525–34.

——: "Reason and feeling: resisting the dichotomy," *Australasian Journal of Philosophy*, 71: 4 (1993), 385–99.

Greenberg, B.: *On Women and Judaism* (Philadelphia, PA: Jewish Publication Society of America, 1981).

Greene, M.: *Landscapes of Learning* (New York: Teachers' College Press, 1978).

Greenson, R.: "Disidentifying from mother: the special importance for the boy," *Explorations in Psychoanalysis* (New York: International Universities Press, 1978).

Greer, G.: *The Obstacle Race: The Fortunes of Women Painters and Their Work* (London: Secker and Warburg, 1979).

Griffin, S.: "Rape: The all-American crime," *Feminism and Philosophy*, ed. M. Vetterling-Braggin, F. Elliston, and J. English (Totowa, NJ: Littlefield, Adams, 1977), pp. 313–32.

——: *Woman and Nature: The Roaring Inside Her* (New York: Harper and Row, 1978).

——: *Pornography and Silence: Culture's Revolt Against Nature* (New York: Harper and Row, 1981).

——: *A Chorus of Stones* (New York: Doubleday, 1992).

Griggers, C.: "Lesbian bodies in the age of (post)mechanical production," *Fear of a Queer Planet*, ed. M. Warner (Minneapolis: University of Minnesota Press, 1993), pp. 178–92.

Grillo, T.: "The mediation alternative: process dangers for women," *Yale Law Journal*, 100 (1991), 1545–1610.

Grimshaw, J.: *Philosophy and Feminist Thinking* (Minneapolis: University of Minnesota Press, 1986).

Griscom, J. L.: "On healing the nature/history split in feminist thought," *Heresies*, 13: 4 (1981), 4–9.

Griswold v. *Connecticut*, 381 U.S. 479 (1965).

Gross, K.: "Re-vision of the bankruptcy system: new images of individual debtors," *Michigan Law Review*, 88 (1990), 1506–56.

——: "'Steps toward feminine imagery of deity in Jewish theology," *On Being a Jewish Feminist*, ed. S. Heschel (New York: Schocken Books, 1983).

Gross, M., and Averill, M.: "Evolution and patriarchal myths of scarcity and competition," *Discovering Reality: Feminist Perspectives on Epistemology, Metaphysics, Methodology, and Philosophy of Science*, ed. S. Harding and M. Hintikka (Dordrecht, Holland: D. Reidel Publishing Co., 1983).

Gross, R.: "Public and private in the Third Amendment," *Valparaiso University Law Review*, 26 (1991), 215–21.

Grosz, E.: "Interview with Gayatri Spivak," *Thesis Eleven*, 10: 11 (1984/5), 175–87.

——: *Sexual Subversions* (Sydney: Allen and Unwin, 1989).

——: "Contemporary theories of power and objectivity," *Feminist Knowledge; Critique and Construct*, ed. S. Gunew (London: Routledge, 1990), pp. 59–120.

——: "Lesbian fetishism?," *differences*, 3: 2 (1991), 39–54.

——: "Feminist theory and the politics of art," *Dissonance: Feminism and the Arts, 1970–1990*, ed. C. Moore (St Leonards: Artspace/Allen and Unwin, 1994a).

——: "Re-figuring lesbian desire," *The Lesbian Postmodern*, ed. L. Doan (New York: Columbia University Press, 1994b), pp. 67–84.

——: *Space, Time and Perversion* (New York: Routledge, 1995a).

——: *Volatile Bodies: Toward a Corporeal Feminism* (Bloomington: Indiana University Press, 1994c).

——: "Sexual difference and the problem of essentialism," *Space, Time, and Perversion: Essays on the Politics of Bodies* (New York: Routledge, 1995b), pp. 45–57.

Gruen, I.: "Towards an ecofeminist moral epistemology," *Ecological Feminism*, ed. K. Warren (London: Routledge, 1994), pp. 120–39.

Grumet, M. R.: *Bitter Milk* (Amherst: University of Massachusetts Press, 1988).

Guan Tao: "Taking economic construction as the key to promote women's liberation," *Selected Writings in Women's Studies*, 1 (Beijing, 1993).

Guerra, L.: *La Mujer Fragmentada: Historias de un Signo* (Havana, Cuba: Casa de las Américas and Instituto Colombiano de Cultura, 1994).

Gunning, I.: "Arrogant perception, world-traveling and multicultural feminism: the case of female genital surgeries," *Columbia Human Rights Law Review*, 23 (1992), 189–248.

Gutiérrez Castañeda, G.: "Feminist movements and their constitution as political subjects," *Hypatia*, 9 (1994), 184–92.

Guy, M. E., ed.: *Men and Women of the States* (Armonk, NY: M.E. Sharpe, 1992).

Haack, S.: "On the moral relevance of sex," *Philosophy*, 49 (1974), 90–5.

Haber, B.: "Is personal life still a political issue?," *Feminist Studies*, 5: 3 (1979), 417–30.

Haber, H. F.: "Muscles and politics: shaping the feminist revolt," *Exercising Power: The Making and Remaking of the Body*, ed. C. Cole and M. Mezner (Albany: State University of New York Press, forthcoming).

Habermas, J.: *Communication and the Evolution of Society* (Boston: Beacon Press, 1979).

——: "Gerechtigkeit und Solidarität," *Zur Bestimmung der Moral*, ed. W. Edelstein and G. Nunner-Winkler (Frankfurt/Main, 1986), pp. 291–316.

——: *The Theory of Communicative Action*, trans. T. McCarthy (Boston: Beacon Press, 1987).

——: *The Structural Transformation of the Public Sphere: An Inquiry into a Category of Bourgeois Society*, trans. T. Burger and F. Lawrence (Cambridge: MIT Press, 1989), pp. 3–4.

——: *Between Facts and Nouns*, trans. W. Rehg (Cambridge, MA: MIT Press, 1996).

Hacking, I.: *Representing and Intervening* (Cambridge: Cambridge University Press, 1983).

Hale, J.: "Are lesbians women?," *Hypatia* (Spring 1996).

Hall, K.: "*Sensus communis* and violence: A feminist reading of Kant's *Critique of Judgment*," *Feminist Interpretations of Kant*, ed. R. Schott (University Park: Pennsylvania State Press, 1997).

Halley, J.: "Sexual orientation and the politics of biology," *Stanford Law Review*, 46 (1994), 503–68.

Halperin, D. M.: *One Hundred Years of Homosexuality and Other Essays on Greek Love* (New York: Routledge, 1990).

Hamblin, A.: "Is a feminist heterosexuality possible?," *Sex and Love: New Thoughts on Old Contradictions*, ed. S. Cartledge and J. Ryan (London: The Women's Press, 1983), pp. 105–23.

Hanen, M. and Nielsen, K., eds.: *Science, Morality, and Feminist Theory* (Calgary: University of Calgary Press, 1987).

Hanna, W. J. and Rogovsky, E.: "Women with disabilities: two handicaps plus," *Disability, Handicap & Society*, 6: 1 (1991).

——: "On the situation of African-American women," *Journal of Applied Rehabilitation Counseling*, 23: 4 (1992).

Hanscombe, G.: "The right to lesbian parenthood," *Journal of Medical Ethics*, 9 (1983), 133–5.

Hansen, K.: "A manifesto for cyborgs: science, technology and socialist feminism for the 1980s," *Socialist Review*, 15: 80 (1985), 65–107.

——, and Philipson, I., eds.: *Women, Class and the Feminist Imagination* (Philadelphia, PA: Temple University Press, 1990).

Hanson, K.: "Provocations and justifications of film," *Philosophy and Film*, ed. C. A. Freeland and T. E. Wartenberg (New York: Routledge, 1995), pp. 33–48.

Haraway, D.: *Primate Visions: Gender, Race and Nature in the World of Modern Science* (London: Routledge, 1989).

——: "Cyborgs at large: interview with Donna Haraway," *Technoculture*, ed. C. Penley and A. Ross (Minneapolis: University of Minnesota Press, 1991a).

——: *Simians, Cyborgs, and Women: The Reinvention of Nature* (New York: Routledge, 1991b).

——: "The politics of postmodern bodies," *Simians, Cyborgs, and Women: The Reinvention of Nature*, ed. D. Haraway (New York: Routledge, 1991c).

——: "A manifesto for cyborgs: science, technology and socialist feminism for the 1980s," *Simians, Cyborgs, and Women: The Reinvention of Nature*, ed. D. Haraway (New York: Routledge, 1991d).

Harding, S.: "Feminism: reform or revolution," *The Philosophical Forum*, V: 1–2 (1973–4), 271–84.

——: "Why has the sex/gender system become visible only now?," *Discovering Reality: Feminist Perspectives on Epistemology, Metaphysics, Methodology, and Philosophy of Science*, ed. S. Harding and M. Hintikka (Dordrecht, Holland: D. Reidel, 1983b).

——: *The Science Question in Feminism* (Ithaca, NY: Cornell University Press, 1986).

—— ed.: *Feminism and Methodology* (Bloomington: Indiana University Press, 1987a).

——: "Introduction: is there a feminist method?," *Feminism and Methodology*, ed. S. Harding (Bloomington: Indiana University Press, 1987b).

——: *Whose Science? Whose Knowledge? Thinking From Women's Lives* (Ithaca, NY: Cornell University Press, 1991).

——: *The "Racial" Economy of Science: Toward a Democratic Future* (Bloomington: Indiana University Press, 1993a).

——: "Rethinking standpoint epistemology: what is strong objectivity?," *Feminist Epistemologies*, ed. L. Alcoff and E. Potter (New York: Routledge, 1993b).

622

——, and Hintikka, M., eds.: *Discovering Reality: Feminist Perspectives on Epistemology, Metaphysics, Methodology, and Philosophy of Science* (Dordrecht, Holland: D. Reidel Publishing Co., 1983a).

Harre, R.: *Varieties of Realism* (Oxford: Basil Blackwell, 1986).

Harris, A.: "Race and essentialism in feminist legal theory," *Stanford Law Review*, 42 (1990), 581–616.

——, and King, Y., eds.: *Rocking the Ship of State* (Boulder, CO: Westview Press, 1989).

Harris, L. C. and Narayan, U.: "Affirmative action and the myth of preferential treatment," *Harvard Blackletter Law Journal*, 11 (1994).

Harrison, B.: *Our Right to Choose* (Boston: Beacon Press, 1983).

——: *Making the Connections: Essays in Feminist Social Ethics*, ed. C. Robb (Boston: Beacon Press, 1985).

Hart, C. G.: "Power in the service of love, Dewey's logic and the dream of a common language," *Hypatia*, 8: 2 (1993), 190–214.

Hart, L.: *Between the Body and the Flesh: Performing Lesbian S/M* (New York: Columbia University Press, 1994a).

——: *Fatal Women: Lesbian Sexuality and the Mark of Aggression* (Princeton, NJ: Princeton University Press, 1994b).

Hart, N.: "Lesbian desire as social action," *Lesbian Philosophies and Cultures*, ed. J. Allen (New York: State University of New York Press, 1990), pp. 295–304.

Hartline, S.: "Intimate danger: the case for preemptive self-defense," *Feminist Ethics and Social Policy*, ed. P. DiQuinzio and I. M. Young (Bloomington: Indiana University Press, 1996).

Hartmann, H.: "The family as the locus of gender, class and political struggle," *Signs*, 6: 3 (1981a), 366–94.

——: "The unhappy marriage of Marxism and feminism," *Women and Revolution*, ed. L. Sargent (Boston: South End Press, 1981b), 1–42.

Hartsock, N.: "The feminist standpoint: developing a ground for a specifically feminist historical materialism," *Discovering Reality: Feminist Perspectives on Epistemology, Metaphysics, Methodology, and Philosophy of Science*, ed. S. Harding and M. Hintikka (Dordrecht, Holland: D. Reidel Publishing Co., 1983).

——: *Money, Sex, and Power* (Boston: Northeastern University Press, 1985).

——: "Masculinity, heroism and the making of war," *Rocking the Ship of State*, ed. A. Harris and Y. King (Boulder, CO: Westview Press, 1989).

——: "Foucault on power: a theory for women?," *Feminism/Postmodernism*, ed. L. Nicholson (New York: Routledge, 1990), pp. 157–75.

Hasan, Z., ed.: *Forging Identities: Gender, Communities and the State* (New Delhi: Kali for Women, 1994).

Haskell, M.: *From Reverence to Rape* (New York: Holt, Rinehart, and Winston, 1974).

Haslanger, S.: "On being objective and being objectified," *A Mind of One's Own: Feminist Essays on Reason and Objectivity*, ed. L. Antony and C. Witt (Boulder, CO: Westview Press, 1993), 85–125.

Hasse, L.: "Legalizing gender-specific values," *Women and Moral Theory*, ed. E. Kittay and D. Meyers (Totowa, NJ: Rowman and Littlefield, 1987), pp. 282–95.

Haug, F.: "Die Moral ist zweigeschlechtlich wie der Mensch," *Weiblichkleit oder Feminismus?*, ed. C. Opitz (Weingarten, 1984), pp. 95–121.

——: "Ethik und Feminismus – eine problematische Beziehung," *Sei wie das Veilchen im Moose*, ed. N. Kramer, B. Menzel, B. Möller, and A. Standhartinger (Frankfurt/Main, 1994).

Havelkova, H. "A few prefeminist thoughts," *Gender Politics and Post-Communism*, ed. N. Funk and M. Mueller (New York: Routledge, 1993a).

——: "'Patriarchy' in Czech society," *Hypatia*, 8: 4 (1993b), pp. 89–96.

Hawkesworth, M.: *Theoretical Issues in Policy Analysis* (Albany: State University of New York Press, 1988a).

——: "The politics of knowledge," *Academic Freedom and Responsibility* (London: Open University Press, 1988b).

——: "Knowers, knowing, known: feminist theory and claims of truth," *Signs*, 14: 3 (1989), 533–57.

——: "The affirmative action debate and conflicting conceptions of individuality," *Hypatia Reborn: Essays in Feminist Philosophy*, ed. A. al-Hibri and M. Simons (Bloomington: Indiana University Press, 1990), pp. 135–55.

——: "From objectivity to objectification: feminist objections," *Annals of Scholarship*, 8: 3–4 (1991), 451–77.

Hawley, J. S., and Wulff, D. M., eds.: *The Divine Consort: Radha and the Goddesses of India* (Boston, MA: Beacon Press, 1986).

Hay, M. J., and Sticher, S., eds.: *African Women South of the Sahara* (New York: Longman, 1984).

Hayden, D.: *The Grand Domestic Revolution* (Cambridge, MA: MIT Press, 1985).

Hegel, G. W. F.: *Vorlesungen über die Asthetik*, Bd. II, Werke in Zwanzig Bänden (Frankfurt/Main: Suhrkamp, 1970).

Hein, H.: "The role of feminist aesthetics in feminist theory," *Journal of Aesthetics and Art Criticism*, 48 (1990), 281–91.

——, and Korsmeyer, C.: *Aesthetics in Feminist Perspective* (Bloomington: Indiana University Press, 1993).

Heise, H.: "Eyeshadow, aesthetics and morality," *Women's Studies International Forum*, 7: 5 (1984), 365–73.

Hekman, S.: *Gender and Knowledge: Elements of a Postmodern Feminism* (Boston, MA: Northeastern University Press, 1990).

——: "Reconstructing the subject: feminism, modernism, and postmodernism," *Hypatia*, 6 (1991), 44–63.

——: "A method for difference: feminist methodology and the challenge of difference," paper presented at the Annual Meeting of the American Political Science Association, (Chicago: 1995).

Held, V.: "The obligations of mothers and fathers," *"Femininity", "Masculinity", and "Androgyny"*, ed. M. Vetterling-Braggin (Totowa, NJ: Littlefield, Adams, 1982).

——: *Rights and Goods: Justifying Social Action* (New York: The Free Press, 1984).

——: "Feminism and moral theory," *Woman and Moral Theory*, ed. E. Kittay and D. Meyers (Totowa, NJ: Rowman and Littlefield, 1987a).

——: "Non-contractual society," *Science, Morality, and Feminist Theory*, ed. M. Hanen and K. Nielsen (Calgary: University of Calgary Press, 1987b).

——: "Birth and death," *Ethics*, 99 (1989), 362–88.

——: *Feminist Morality: Transforming Culture, Society and Politics* (Chicago, IL: University of Chicago Press, 1993).

——: "The meshing of care and justice," *Hypatia*, 10: 2 (1995a).

——: *Justice and Care: Essential Readings in Feminist Ethics* (Boulder, CO: Westview Press, 1995b).

Heldke, L.: "In praise of unreliability," *Hypatia*, 12: 3 (1997).

Heller, A.: "The emotional division of labor between the sexes: perspectives on feminism and socialism," *Feministische Philosophie*, ed. H. Nagl-Docekal (Vienna: Oldenbourg, 1990), 229–43.

Henderson, L.: "Legality and empathy," *Michigan Law Review*, 85 (1987), 1574–1653.

——: "Review essay: what makes rape a crime," *Berkeley Women's Law Journal*, 3 (1987/88), 193–229.

——: "Lesbian pornography: cultural transgression and sexual demystification," *New Lesbian Criticism: Literary and Cultural Readings*, ed. S. Munt (New York: Columbia University Press, 1992), pp. 173–91.

Hennessy, R.: *Materialist Feminism and the Politics of Discourse* (New York: Routledge, 1993).

——: "Incorporating queer theory on the Left," *Marxism in the Postmodern Age: Confronting the New World Order*, ed. A. Callari, S. Cullenberg, and C. Biewener (New York: Guilford Press, 1995), pp. 266–75.

Herman, B.: "Could it be worth thinking about Kant on sex and marriage?," *A Mind of One's Own: Feminist Essays on Reason and Objectivity*, ed. L. Antony and C. Witt (Boulder, CO: Westview Press, 1993a), pp. 49–67.

——: *The Practice of Moral Judgment* (Cambridge, MA: Harvard University Press, 1993b).

Hershey, L.: "Choosing disability," *Ms.* (July/August 1994), pp. 26–32.

Herton, C.: "The sexual mountain and black women writers," *Black Scholar*, 15: 4 (1984), 2–11.

Heschel, S., ed.: "Introduction," *On Being a Jewish Feminist* (New York: Shocken Books, 1983).

Hesse, M.: *Revolutions and Reconstructions in the Philosophy of Science* (Bloomington: Indiana University Press, 1980).

Heyward, I. Carter: *The Redemption of God* (Washington, DC: University Presses of America, 1982).

——: *Our Passion for Justice* (New York: Pilgrim Press, 1984).

al-Hibri, A.: "A study of Islamic herstory: or how did we get into this mess?," *Women in Islam* (Oxford: Pergamon Press, 1982).

625

——: "Marriage laws in Muslim countries," *International Review of Comparative Public Policy*, 4 (1992), 227–44.

——: *A Critique of Personal Status Codes in Select Arab Countries*. Arab Regional Preparatory Meeting for the Fourth World Conference on Women, Beijing, 1995. ESCWA, United Nations (Arabic Draft), September 1994 (final English version forthcoming).

Hierro, G.: *Etica y Feminismo* (Mexico City: UNAM, 1985).

Hill, J.: "Pornography and degradation," *Hypatia*, 2: 2 (1987), 39–54.

Hill, T. E., Jr: "The importance of autonomy," *Women and Moral Theory*, ed. E. F. Kittay and D. T. Meyers (Totowa, NJ: Rowman and Littlefield, 1987), pp. 129–38.

Hillyer, B.: *Feminism and Disability* (Norman, OK: University of Oklahoma Press, 1993).

Hine, D. C.: *Black Women in America: An Historical Encyclopedia* (New York: Carleson, 1993).

Hintikka, M., and Hintikka, J.: "How can language be sexist?," *Discovering Reality: Feminist Perspectives on Epistemology, Metaphysics, Methodology, and Philosophy of Science*, ed. S. Harding and M. Hintikka (Dordrecht, Holland: D. Reidel Publishing Co., 1983).

Hirsch, K.: "Raising our voices: perspectives on the book *Feminism and Disability*. *Resourceful Woman*" (Health Resource Center for Women with Disabilities, Rehabilitation Institute of Chicago, Winter 1994, 3: 1).

Hirschmann, N.: *Rethinking Obligation* (Ithaca, NY: Cornell University Press, 1992).

Hoagland, S.: "Sadism, masochism, and lesbian-feminism," *Against Sadomasochism: A Radical Feminist Analysis*, ed. R. Lindon et al. (Palo Alto, CA: Frog in the Well, 1982a).

——: *Lesbian Ethics: Toward New Value* (Palo Alto, CA: Institute for Lesbian Studies, 1988).

——: "Some thoughts about 'caring,'" *Feminist Ethics*, ed. C. Card (Lawrence: University of Kansas Press, 1991).

Hochschild, A. R.: *The Managed Heart: Commercialization of Human Feeling* (Berkeley: University of California Press, 1983).

——: *The Second Shift: Working Parents and the Revolution at Home* (New York: Viking Press, 1989).

Hodge, J.: "Subject, body, and the exclusion of women from philosophy," *Feminist Perspectives in Philosophy*, ed. M. Griffiths and M. Whitford (Bloomington: Indiana University Press, 1988).

Hollibaugh, A., and Moraga, C.: "What we're rollin' around in bed with: sexual silences in feminism," *Powers of Desire*, ed. A. Snitow, C. Stansell, and S. Thompson (New York: Monthly Review Press, 1983), pp. 394–405.

Hollway, W.: "Gender difference and the production of subjectivity," *Changing the Subject: Psychology, Social Regulation, and Subjectivity*, ed. J. Henriques, W. Hollway, C. Urwin, C. Venn, and V. Walkerdine (New York: Methuen, 1984), pp. 227–63.

Holmes, H. Bequaert: "Sex preselection: eugenics for everyone?," *Biomedical Ethics Reviews–1985*, ed. J. Humber and R. Almeder (Clifton, NJ: Humana Press, 1985), pp. 38–71.

——: and Purdy, L., eds.: *Feminist Perspectives in Medical Ethics* (Bloomington: Indiana University Press, 1992).

Holmstrom, N.: "Do women have a distinct nature?," *Philosophical Forum*, XIV: 1 (1982), 25–42.

——: "A Marxist theory of human nature," *Ethics*, 94 (1984), 456–73.

——: "Humankind(s)," *Canadian Journal of Philosophy*, 20 (1994), 69–105.

The Holy Quran: trans. A. Yousuf Ali (Savage, MD: Amana Corp., 1983).

Homiak, M.: "Feminism and Aristotle's rational ideal," *A Mind of One's Own: Feminist Essays on Reason and Objectivity*, ed. L. Antony and C. Witt (Boulder, CO: Westview Press, 1993).

hooks, b.: *Ain't I a Woman: Black Women and Feminism* (Boston: South End Press, 1981).

——: *Feminist Theory: From Margin To Center* (Boston: South End Press, 1984).

——: "Feminism: A movement to end sexist oppression," *Equality and Feminism*, ed. A. Phillips (New York: New York University Press. 1987), pp. 62–76.

——: *Talking Back: Thinking Feminist, Thinking Black* (Boston: South End Press, 1989).

——: *Yearning: Race, Gender and Cultural Politics* (Boston: South End Press, 1991).

——: *Black Looks: Race and Representation* (Boston: South End Press, 1992a).

——: "The oppositional gaze: black female spectators," *Black Looks: Race and Representation*, ed. b. hooks (Boston: South End Press, 1992b), pp. 115–31.

——: *Outlaw Culture* (New York: Routledge, 1994).

——: *Killing Rage/Ending Racism* (New York: Henry Hold & Co., 1995).

Hornsby. J.: "Speech acts and pornography," *The Problem of Pornography*, ed. S. Dwyer (Belmont, CA: Wadsworth, 1995), p. 220ff.

Hountondji, P.: *Sur la Philosophie africaine* (Paris: Maspéro, 1977) [*African Philosophy: Myth and Reality*, trans. H. Evans and J. Ree (London: Hutchinson University Press for Africa, 1983)].

Houston, B.: "Rescuing womanly virtues: some dangers of moral reclamation," *Science, Morality and Feminist Theory*, ed. M. Hanen and K. Nielsen (Calgary: University of Calgary Press, 1987).

——: "Prolegomena to future caring," *Who Cares? Theory, Research, and Educational Implications of the Ethic of Care*, ed. M. Brabeck (New York: Praeger, 1989), pp. 84–100.

——: "Are children's rights wrongs?," *Philosophy of Education 1992* (Champaign, IL: Philosophy of Education Society, 1993), pp. 145–55.

Howe, L. A.: "Kierkegaard and the feminine self," *Hypatia*, 9: 4 (1994), 131–57.

Huang Qizao: "Emancipating and developing productive forces and women's liberation', *Chinese Women's Daily* (June 20, 1992).

Hubbard, R.: *The Politics of Women's Biology* (New Brunswick: Rutgers University Press, 1990).

——, Hennifin, M. S., and Fried, B., eds.: *Biological Woman: The Convenient Myth* (Cambridge: Schenkman, 1982).

——, and Lowe, M., eds.: *Genes and Gender* (New York: Gordian Press, 1979).

——: and Wald, E.: *Exploding the Gene Myth* (Boston: Beacon Press, 1993).

Hudnut v. American Booksellers, Federal 2d 771: 323. 7th Circuit (1985).

Hudson-Weems, C.: *African Womanism: Reclaiming Ourselves* (London: Bedford Publications, 1996).

Hull, D. L.: *Science as a Process: An Evolutionary Account of the Social and Conceptual Development of Science* (Chicago, IL: Chicago University Press, 1988).

Human Rights Watch Global Report on Women's Human Rights, New York, 1995.

Hume, D.: *A Treatise of Human Nature*, ed. L. A. Selby-Bigge [1739] (Oxford: Clarendon Press, 1955a).

——: *Enquiry Concerning Human Understanding* [1748] (Indianapolis, IN: Bobbs-Merrill, 1955b).

Hunter, N., and Law, S.: "Brief *Amici Curiae* of Feminist Anti-Censorship Task-force, et al. in *American Booksellers Association v. Hudnut*," *University of Michigan Journal of Law Reform*, 21 (1987/8), 69–136.

Hussain, F., ed.: *Muslim Women* (London: Croom Helm, 1984).

Illich, I.: *Deschooling Society* (New York: Harper and Row, 1972).

In re *Baby M*, 109 N.J. 396, 537 A.2d 1227 (1988).

Inness, J.: *Privacy, Intimacy, and Isolation* (New York: Oxford University Press, 1992).

Irigaray, L.: "When the goods get together," *New French Feminisms*, ed. E. Marks and I. de Courtivron (New York: Schocken Books, 1981).

——: *The Speculum of the Other Woman* (Ithaca: Cornell University Press, 1985a) trans. G. Gill from *Speculum de l'autre femme* (Paris: Minuit, 1974).

——: *The Sex Which is Not One*, trans. C. Porter and C. Burke (Ithaca, NY: Cornell University Press, 1985b).

——: "Egales à qui?," *Critique*, 480 (1987), 420–37; trans. as "Equal to Whom?," *differences*, 21 (1988), 59–76.

——: "'Is the subject of science sexed?," *Feminism and Science*, ed. N. Tuana (Bloomington: Indiana University Press: 1989).

——: *An Ethics of Sexual Difference*, trans. C. Burke and G. Gill (Ithaca, NY: Cornell University Press, 1993a).

——: "The invisible of the flesh," trans. C. Burke and G. Gill, *An Ethics of Sexual Difference* (Ithaca, NY: Cornell University Press, 1993b), pp. 151–84.

——: et al.: "Sorcerer love: a reading of Plato, *Symposium*, 'Diotina's speech,'" *An Ethics of Sexual Difference*, trans. C. Burke and G. Gill (Ithaca, NY: Cornell University Press, 1993c).

Isasi-Díaz, A. M.: "Toward an understanding of *Feminismo Hispano* in the U.S.A.," *Women's Consciousness, Women's Conscience*, ed. B. H. Andolsen, C. E. Gudorf, and M.D. Pellauer (San Francisco, CA: Harper and Row, 1985).

Isherwood, C.: *Ramakrishna and His Disciples* (Hollywood, CA: Vedanta Press, 1965).

Ismail, R., ed. *Hudud in Malaysia: The Issues at Stake* (Kuala Lumpur: SIS Forum, Malaysia, 1995).

Ivekovic, R.: "Prazno mjesto drugog/druge u postmodernoj misli," *Posmoderna - Nova epoha ili zabluda* (Zagreb: Naprijed, 1988).

——: "Remember Yugoslavia?," *And Then*, 5 (1993a), p. 63.

——: "'Women, nationalism, and war: 'make love not war,'" *Hypatia*, 8: 4 (1993b), 113.

Iversen, M.: "The deflationary impulse: postmodernism, feminism and the anti-aesthetic," *Thinking Art: Beyond Traditional Aesthetics*, ed. A. Benjamin and P. Osborne (London, 1991).

Jackson, C.: "Gender analysis and environmentalisms," *Social Theory and the Global Environment*, ed. T. Benton and M. Redclift (London: Routledge, 1994), 113–49.

Jaggar, A. M.: "On sexual equality," *Ethics*, 84 (1974), pp. 275–91.

——: "Abortion and a woman's right to decide," *Women and Philosophy*, ed. C. C. Gould and M. W. Wartofsky (New York: G. P. Putnam's Sons, 1980a), pp. 347–64.

——: "Prostitution," *The Philosophy of Sex: Contemporary Readings*, ed. A. Soble (Savage, MD: Rowman and Littlefield, 1980b), pp. 353–8.

——: *Feminist Politics and Human Nature* (Totowa, NJ: Rowman and Allanheld: Harvester, 1983).

——: "Love and knowledge: emotion in feminist epistemology," *Gender/Body/ Knowledge*, ed. A. M. Jaggar and S. Bordo (New Brunswick: Rutgers University Press, 1989).

——: "Feminist ethics: projects, problems, prospects," *Feminist Ethics*, ed. C. Card (Lawrence: University of Kansas Press, 1991).

——: "'Sexual difference and sexual equality," *Theoretical Perspectives on Sexual Difference*, ed. D. Rhode (New Haven, CT: Yale University Press, 1990), reprinted in *Living with Contradictions*, ed. A. M. Jaggar (Boulder, CO: Westview Press, 1995a).

——: "Caring as a feminist practice of moral reason," *Justice and Care: Essential Readings in Feminist Ethics*, ed. V. Held (Boulder, CO: Westview Press, 1995a).

——: "Toward a feminist conception of moral reasoning," *Morality and Social Justice: Point/CounterPoint*, ed. J. Sterba et al. (Lanham, MD: Rowman and Littlefield, 1995b).

—— and McBride, W. L.: "'Reproduction' as male ideology," *Women's Studies International Forum*, 8 (1985), 185–96.

Jahangir, A. and Jilali, H.: *Hudood Ordinances: A Divine Sanction?* (Pakistan: Photas Books, 1990).

Jakobsen, J.: "Agency and alliance in public discourse about sexualities," *Hypatia*, 10: 1 (1995).

Jameelah, M.: *Islam and The Muslim Woman Today* (Pakistan: Mohammad Yousuf Khan and Sons, 1988).

James, S.: "The good-enough citizen: female citizenship and independence," *Beyond Equality and Difference*, ed. G. Bock and S. James (London: Routledge, 1992), pp. 48–65.

——, and Busia, A. P. A., eds.: *Theorizing Black Feminisms: The Visionary Pragmatism of Black Women* (London: Routledge, 1993).

Jardine, A.: *Gynesis: Configurations of Woman and Modernity* (Ithaca: Cornell University Press, 1985).

——: "Notes for analysis," *Between Psychoanalysis and Feminism*, ed. T. Brennan (London: Routledge, 1989).

Jauch, U. P.: *Immanuel Kant zur Geschlechterdifferenz. Aufklärerische Vorurteilskritik und bürgerliche Geschlechtsvormundschaft* (Vienna: Passagen, 1988).

Jay, K., ed.: *Lesbian Erotics* (New York: New York University Press, 1995).

Jaywardena, K.: *Feminism and Nationalism in the Third World* (Sri Lanka: University of Colombo, 1986).

Jazairy, I., Alamgir, M., and Panuccio, T.: *The State of World Rural Poverty* (New York: New York University Press, 1992).

al-Jaziri, A. R.: *Kitab al-Figh 'ala al-Mathahib al-Arba'ah* (*Islamic Jurisprudence According to the Four Main Schools of Thought*), 5 vols (Beirut: Dar Ihya'al-Turath al-Arabi, 1969).

Jeffreys, S.: *The Lesbian Heresy: A Feminist Perspective on the Lesbian Sexual Revolution* (North Melbourne, Australia: Pinifex Press, 1993).

Jelín, E., ed. (1987): *Women and Social Change in Latin America*, trans. J.A. Zammit and M. Thomson (London: Zed, 1990).

Jenness, L., ed.: *Feminism and Socialism* (New York: Pathfinder Press, 1972).

Jetter, A., Orleck, A., Taylor, D., eds.: *The Politics of Motherhood* (Hanover: New England University Press, forthcoming).

Jiang Zemin: "The Marxist conception of women must be established among the entire Party and society," *People's Daily* (March 8, 1990).

Jo, B., Strega, L., and Ruston (*sic*): *Dykes-Loving-Dykes: Dyke Separatist Politics for Lesbians Only* (Oakland, CA: Battleaxe, 1990).

Johnson, C.: "Gender analysis and ecofeminism," *Social Theory and the Global Environment*, ed. M. Redclift and T. Benton (London: Routledge, 1994).

Johnson, E.: *She Who Is* (New York: Crossroad, 1992).

Jones, K.: "Citizenship in a woman-friendly polity," *Signs*, 15 (1990), 781–812.

——: *Compassionate Authority, Democracy and the Representation of Women* (New York: Routledge, 1993).

Jordanova, L.: *Sexual Visions: Images of Gender in Science and Medicine between the Eighteenth and Twentieth Centuries* (Madison: University of Wisconsin Press, 1989).

Joseph, G.: "The incompatible ménage à trois: Marxism, feminism, and racism," *Women and Revolution*, ed. L. Sargent (Boston: South End Press, 1981), pp. 91–108.

——, and Lewis, J.: *Common Differences: Conflicts in Black and White Perspectives* (New York: Doubleday/Anchor, 1981).

Kagame, A.: *La Philosophie bantu-rwandaise de l'etre* (Brussels: Académie Royale des Sciences Coloniales, 1956).

Kain, P. J.: "Marx, housework, and alienation," *Hypatia*, 8 (1993), 121–44.

Kaminer, W.: *A Fearful Freedom: Women's Flight from Equality* (Reading, MA: Addison-Wesley, 1990).

Kamm, F.: *Creation and Abortion* (New York: Oxford, 1992).

Kant, I.: *Critique of Judgment*, trans. J. C. Meredith (Oxford: Clarendon Press, 1957).

——: *Foundations of the Metaphysics of Morals*, trans. L. White Beck (Indianapolis, IN: Bobbs-Merrill Co., 1959).

——: *Observations on the Feeling of the Beautiful and Sublime*, trans. J. T. Goldthwait (Berkeley: University of California Press, 1960).

——: "What is enlightenment?," *Kant on History*, trans. L. White Beck (New York: Macmillan Publishing Co., 1963).

——: *Anthropology from a Pragmatic Point of View*, trans. V. Lyle Dowdell (Carbondale: Southern Illinois Press, 1978).

Kaplan, C.: "The politics of location as transnational feminist critical practice," *Scattered Hegemonies: Postmodernity and Transnational Feminist Practices*, ed. I. Grewal and C. Kaplan (Minneapolis: University of Minnesota Press, 1994).

Kaplan, D.: "Disability rights perspectives in reproductive technologies and public policy," *Reproductive Laws for the 1990s*, ed. S. Cohen and N. Taub (Clifton, NJ: Humana Press, 1989).

Kaplan, M.: "Intimacy and equality: The question of lesbian and gay marriage," Stony Brook Philosophy Colloquium Series (Stony Brook, NY: March 4, 1993)

Kappeler, S.: *The Pornography of Representation* (Minneapolis: University of Minnesota Press, 1986).

Karlan, P., and Ortiz, D.: "In a different voice: relational feminism, abortion rights, and the feminist legal agenda," *Northwestern Law Review*, 87 (1993), 858–96.

Katzenstein, M. F., and Laitin, D.: "Politics, feminism and the ethics of care," *Women and Moral Theory*, ed. E. Kittay and D. Meyers (Totowa, NJ: Rowman and Littlefield, 1987), pp. 261–81.

Kaufman-Osborn, T.: "Teasing feminist sense from experience," *Hypatia*, 8: 2 (1993), 124–44.

Kay, H.: "Equality and difference: the case of pregnancy," *Berkeley Women's Law Journal*, 1 (1985), 1–38.

Keith, L., ed.: *What Happened to You?: Writing by Disabled Women* (London: The Women's Press, 1994).

Keller, C.: *From a Broken Web* (Boston: Beacon Press, 1986).

——: *Apocalypse Now and Then* (Boston: Beacon Press, 1996).

Keller, E. Fox: *A Feeling for the Organism: The Life and Work of Barbara McClintock* (New York: W. H. Freeman & Co., 1983).

——: *Reflections on Gender and Science* (New Haven, CT: Yale University Press, 1985).

631

——: "From secrets of life to secrets of death," *Body/Politics*, ed. M. Jacobus, E. Fox Keller, and S. Shuttlesworth (New York: Routledge, 1990).

——: *Secrets of Life, Secrets of Death: Essays on Language, Gender and Science* (New York: Routledge, 1993).

——, and Longino, H., eds.: *Feminism and Science* (Oxford: Oxford University Press, 1996).

Kennedy, E., and Mendus, S., eds.: *Women in Western Political Philosophy* (Brighton, Sussex: Wheatsheaf Books, 1987).

Kent, D.: "In search of liberation," *Disabled USA*, 1: 3 (1977).

Kersey, S.: *Classics in the Education of Girls and Women* (Metuchen, NJ: Scarecrow Press, 1981).

Kessler, S., and McKenna, W.: *Gender: An Ethnomethodological Approach* (New York: John Wiley, 1978).

Ketchum, S.: "Liberalism and marriage law," *Feminism and Philosophy*, ed. M. Vetterling-Braggin, F. Elliston, and J. English (Totowa, NJ: Littlefield, Adams, 1977), pp. 264–76.

Kheel, M: "The liberation of nature: a circular affair," *Environmental Ethics*, 7 (1985), 135–49.

Kiczkova, Z., and Farkasova, E.: "The emancipation of women: a concept that failed," *Gender Politics and Postcommunism*, ed. N. Funk and M. Mueller (New York: Routledge, 1993).

Kim, C. W., St Ville, S., and Simonaitis, S., eds.: *Transfigurations: Theology and the French Feminists* (Minneapolis: Fortress Press, 1993).

King, K.: "The situation of lesbianism as feminism's magical sign," *Communication*, 9: 1 (1986), 65–91.

King, D. K.: "Multiple jeopardy, multiple consciousness," *Signs*, 14 (1988), 42–72.

King, R.: "Caring about nature: feminist ethics and the environment," *Hypatia*, 6: 1 (1991), 75–89.

King, Y.: "The ecology of feminism and the feminism of ecology," *Healing the Wounds*, ed. J. Plant (Philadelphia, PA: New Society Publishers, 1989), pp. 18–28.

——: "Healing the wounds: feminism, ecology, and the nature/culture dualism," *Reweaving the World*, ed. I. Diamond and G. Orenstein (San Francisco, CA: Sierra Club Books, 1990), pp. 106–21.

Kinsley, D.: *Hindu Goddesses: Visions of the Divine Feminine in the Hindu Religious Tradition* (Berkeley: University of California Press, 1988).

Kirk, G.: "Our Greenham Common: feminism and non-violence," *Rocking the Ship of State*, ed. A. Harris and Y. King (Boulder, Co: Westview Press, 1993a).

——: "Our Greenham Common: not just a place but a movement," *Rocking the Ship of State*, ed. A. Harris and Y. King (Boulder, CO: Westview Press, 1993b).

Kishwar, M.: *Gandhi and Women* (Delhi: Manushi Prakashan, 1986).

——: "Why do I not call myself a feminist?," *Manushi*, 61 (1990).

——, and Vanita, R.: "Poison to nectar: the life and work of Mirabai," *Manushi* (1989), 50–2.

Kittay, E.: "Pornography and the erotics of domination," *Beyond Domination: New Perspectives on Women and Philosophy*, ed. C. Gould (Totowa, NJ: Rowman and Allanheld, 1983a), pp. 145–74.

——: "Womb envy: an explanatory concept," *Mothering: Essays in Feminist Theory*, ed. J. Trebilcot (Savage, MD: Rowman and Littlefield, 1983b), pp. 94–128.

——: "The greater danger: pornography, social science and women's rights," *Social Epistemology*, 1988a.

——: "Woman as metaphor," *Hypatia*, 3: 1 (1988b), 63–86.

——: "Taking dependency seriously: the family and medical leave act considered in light of the social organization of dependency work and gender equality," *Hypatia*, 10 (1995), 8–29.

——: "Dependency work, political discourse and a new basis for a coalition amongst women," *Women, Children and Poverty*, ed. T. Perry, M. Fineman, and J. Hanigsberg (New York: Routledge, forthcoming).

——, and Meyers, D., eds.: *Women and Moral Theory* (Totowa, NJ: Roman and Littlefield, 1987).

Klawiter, M.: "Using Arendt and Heidegger to consider feminist thinking on women and reproductive/infertility technologies," *Hypatia*, 5: 3 (1990), 65–89.

Klein, B. S.: "We are who you are: feminism and disability," *Ms.* (November/December 1992).

Klimenkova, T.: "What does our new democracy offer society?," *Women in Russia – A New Era in Russian Feminism*, ed. A. Posadskaya (London: Verso, 1994).

Kline, M.: "Race, racism, and feminist legal theory," *Harvard Women's Law Journal*, 12 (1989), 115–50.

Klinger, C.: "Frau – Landschaft – Kunstwerk. Gegenwelten oder Reservoire des Patriarchats?," *Feministische Philosophie*, ed. H. Nagl-Docekal (Vienna/Munich: Oldenbourg, 1990).

——: "The concepts of the sublime and the beautiful in Kant and Lyotard," *Constellations*, 2: 2 (1995), 207–24.

Kneller, J.: "The ascetic dimension of Kantian autonomy," *Feminist Interpretations of Kant*, ed. R. Schott (University Park: Pennsylvania State Press, 1997).

Koedt, A.: "The myth of the vaginal orgasm," *Radical Feminism*, ed. A. Koedt, E. Levine, and A. Rapone (New York: Quadrangle Press, 1973).

Koestler, A., and Smythies, J. R., eds.: *Beyond Reductionism: New Perspectives in the Life Sciences* (London: Hutchinson, 1968).

Kofman, S.: "The economy of respect: Kant and respect for women," *Le Respect des femmes* (Paris: Galilée, 1982).

Kohlberg, L.: *The Philosophy of Moral Development, Vol. I* (San Francisco, CA: Harper and Row, 1981).

Kollontai, A.: *Red Love* (New York: Seven Arts, 1927).

——: *Love of Worker Bees* (London: Virago, 1971a).

——: *Women Workers Struggle for Their Rights*, trans. C. Britton (Bristol: Falling Wall Press, 1971b).

——: *Love and the New Morality*, trans. A. Holt (Bristol: Falling Wall Press, 1972a).

——: *Sexual Relations and the Class Struggle*, trans. A. Holt (Bristol: Falling Wall Press, 1972b).

——: *The Autobiography of a Sexually Emancipated Communist Woman*, trans. S. Attanasio (New York: Schocken, 1975).

——: *Selected Writings of Alexandra Kollontai*, ed. and trans. A. Holt (Westport, CT: Lawrence Hill, 1977).

Konvitz, M.: "Privacy and the law: a philosophical prelude," *Law and Contemporary Problems*, 31 (1966), 272–80.

Koppelman, A.: "Why discrimination against lesbians and gay men is sex discrimination," *New York University Law Review*, 69 (1994), 197–287.

Kornhauser, M.: "The rhetoric of the anti-progressive income tax movement: a typical male reaction," *Michigan Law Review*, 86 (1987), 465–523.

Korsgaard, C.: "Scepticism about practical reason," *Journal of Philosophy*, 83 (1986), 5–25.

Korsmeyer, C.: "The hidden joke: generic uses of masculine terminology," *Feminism and Philosophy*, ed. M. Vetterling-Braggin, F.A. Elliston, and J. English (Totowa, NJ: Littlefield, Adams, 1977).

——: "Gendered concepts and Hume's standard of taste," *Feminism and Tradition in Aesthetics*, ed. P.Z. Brand and C. Korsmeyer (University Park: Pennsylvania State University Press, 1995).

Kraditor, A.: *The Ideas of the Women's Suffrage Movement 1890–1920* (New York: Columbia University Press, 1965).

Kramarae, C.: *Women and Men Speaking* (Rowley, MA: Newbury House, 1981).

——and Treichler, P. A.: *Amazons, Bluestockings and Crones: A Feminist Dictionary* (London: Harper Collins, 1985).

Krasner, B.: "Impossible virgin or why I choose not to be a heterosexual," paper presented to Midwest Society for Women in Philosophy (St Louis, MI: April 1993).

Krieger, L.: "Through a glass darkly," *Hypatia*, 2: 1 (1987).

Kristeva, J.: "Woman can never be defined," *New French Feminisms*, ed. E. Marks and I. de Courtivron (Brighton, Sussex: Harvester Press, 1981), pp. 137–41.

——: *Desire in Language, A Semiotic Approach to Literature and Art* [1977], trans. T. Gora, A. Jardine, and L. S. Roudiez (Oxford: Blackwell, 1982).

——: *Powers of Horror*, trans. L. S. Roudiez (New York: Columbia University Press, 1982).

——: *La Révolution du langage poétique* (Paris: Seuil, 1974): trans. M. Walker as *Revolution in Poetic Language* (New York: Columbia University Press, 1984).

——: *The Kristeva Reader*, ed. T. Moi (Oxford: Blackwell, 1986).

——: *Black Sun: Depression and Melancholia*, trans. L. S. Roudiez (New York: Columbia University Press, 1989).

——: *Strangers to Ourselves*, trans. L. S. Roudiez (New York: Columbia University Press, 1991).

Kruks, S.: "Gender and subjectivity: Simone de Beauvoir and contemporary feminism', *Signs*, 18: 1 (1992), 89–110.

——: "Identity politics and dialectical reason: beyond an epistemology of provenance," *Hypatia*, 10: 2 (1995), 1–22.

——, Rapp, R., and Young, M., eds.: *Promissory Notes: Women in the Transition to Socialism* (New York: Monthly Review Press, 1989).

Kuhn, A., and Wolpe, A. M., eds.: *Feminism and Materialism* (London: Verso, 1978).

Kuhn, T.: *The Structure of Scientific Revolutions* (Chicago, IL: University of Chicago Press, 1962).

Kulke. C.. and Scheich. E., eds.: *Zwielicht der Vernunft. Die Dialektik der Aufklärung aus der Sicht von Frauen* (Pfaffenweiler: Centaurus, 1992).

Kumar, R.: *The History of Doing* (New Delhi: Kali for Women, 1993).

Kupfer, J.: "Privacy, autonomy, and self-concept," *American Philosophical Quarterly*, 24 (1987), 81–9.

Kuykendall, E.: "Feminist linguistics in philosophy," *Sexist Language: A Modern Philosophical Analysis*, ed. M. Vetterling-Braggin (Totowa, NJ: Littlefield, Adams, 1981).

Kymlicka, W.: *Contemporary Political Philosophy: An Introduction* (Oxford: Clarendon Press, 1990).

——: "Rethinking the family," *Philosophy and Public Affairs* (Winter 1991), 77–97.

Lacan, J.: *Ecrits* (London: Tavistock, 1977).

——: "God and the *Jouissance* of the woman. A love letter," *Feminine Sexuality: Jacques Lacan and the Ecole Freudienne*, ed. J. Mitchell and J. Rose (New York: W. W. Norton & Co., 1983), pp. 137–48.

Laclau, E., and Mouffe, C.: *Hegemony and Socialist Strategy: Towards a Radical Democratic Politics*, trans. W. Moore and P. Cammack (London: Verso, 1985).

Lahar, S.: "Ecofeminist theory and grassroots politics," *Hypatia*, 6: 1 (1991).

Lahey, K., and Salter, S.: "Corporate law in legal theory and legal scholarship: from classicism to feminism," *Osgoode Hall Law Journal*, 23 (1985), 543–72.

Laidlaw, T. A., and Malmo, C., eds.: *Healing Voices: Feminist Approaches to Therapy with Women* (San Francisco, CA: Jossey-Bass, 1990).

Laird, S.: "Women and gender in John Dewey's philosophy of education," *Educational Theory*, 38: 1 (1988b), 111–30.

——: "Reforming 'Woman's True Profession', A Case for 'Feminist Pedagogy' in Teacher Education?," *Harvard Educational Review*, 58: 4 (1988a), 449–63.

——: "The concept of teaching; Betsy Brown vs. philosophy of education?," *Philosophy of Education 1988* (Champaign, IL: Philosophy of Education Society, 1989), pp. 32–45.

——: "The ideal of the educated teacher – 'reclaiming a conversation' with Louisa May Alcott," *Curriculum Inquiry*, 21: 3 (1991).

——: "'Rethinking 'Coeducation'," *Studies in Philosophy and Education*, 13 (1994), 361–78.

——: "Curriculum and the maternal," *Journal for a Just and Caring Education*, 1: 1 (1995a), 45–75.

——: "Who cares about girls? Rethinking the meaning of teaching," *Peabody Journal of Education*, (1995b).

Lakoff, R.: *Language and Women's Place* (New York: Harper and Row, 1975).

Lamas, M.: "Cuerpo: diferencia social y género," *Debate feminista* [Mexico], 10 (1994), 3–31.

Lambert, S.: "Disability and violence," *Sinister Wisdom*, 39 (1989).

Landes, J.: *Women and the Public Sphere in the Age of the French Revolution* (Ithaca, NY: Cornell University Press, 1988).

Landry, D., and MacLean, G.: *Materialist Feminists* (Oxford: Blackwell, 1993).

Lange, L.: "The function of equal education in Plato's *Republic* and *Laws*," *The Sexism of Social and Political Theory* (Toronto: University of Toronto Press, 1979).

——: "Woman is not a rational animal: on Aristotle's biology of reproduction," *Discovering Reality: Feminist Perspectives on Epistemology, Metaphysics, Methodology, and Philosophy of Science*, ed. S. Harding and M. Hintikka (Dordrecht, Holland: D. Reidel Publishing, 1983).

Langton, R.: "Beyond a pragmatic critique of reason," *Australasian Journal of Philosophy*, 71 (1993a), 364–84.

——: "Speech acts and unspeakable acts," *Philosophy and Public Affairs*, 22: 4 (1993b), 293–330.

Laqueur, T.: "Orgasm, generation, and the politics of reproductive biology," *The Making of the Modern Body*, ed. C. Gallagher and T. Laqueur (Berkeley: University of California Press, 1987), pp. 1–41.

——: *Making Sex: Body and Gender from the Greeks to Freud* (Cambridge, MA: Harvard University Press, 1990).

Larrabee, M. J., ed.: *An Ethic of Care* (New York: Routledge, 1993).

Lasker, J., and Borg, S.: *In Search of Parenthood* (Boston: Beacon Press, 1987).

Lather, P.: *Getting Smart: Feminist Research and Pedagogy With/in the Postmodern* (New York: Routledge, 1991).

Laudan, L.: *Progress and Its Problems* (Berkeley: University of California Press, 1977).

Lauter, E.: "Reenfranchising art: feminist interventions in the theory of art," *Aesthetics in Feminist Perspective*, ed. H. Hein and C. Korsmeyer (Bloomington: Indiana University Press, 1993).

Law, S.: "Rethinking sex and the constitution," *University of Pennsylvania Law Review*, 132 (1984), 955–1040.

——: "Homosexuality and the social meaning of gender," *Wisconsin Law Review* (1988), 187–235.

——: "'Girls can't be plumbers' – affirmative action for women in construction: beyond goals and quotas," *Harvard Civil Rights–Civil Liberties Law Review*, 24 (1989), 45–77.

Lazreg, M.: "Feminism and difference: The perils of writing as a woman on women in Algeria," *Conflicts in Feminism*, ed. M. Hirsch and E. Fox Keller (New York: Routledge, 1990).

——: *The Eloquence of Silence* (New York: Routledge, 1994).

Leach, M.: "Mothers of In(ter)vention: women's writing in philosophy of education," *Educational Theory*, 41: 3 (1991), 287–300.

Lebacqz, K.: *Professional Ethics: Power and Paradox* (Nashville, TN: Abington Press, 1985).

Le Doeuff, M.: *The Philosophical Imaginary*, trans. C. Gordon (Stanford, CA: Stanford University Press, 1990a).

——: "Women, reason, etc.," *differences*, 2: 3 (1990b), 1–13.

——: *Hipparchia's Choice*, trans. T. Selous (Oxford: Blackwell Press, 1991).

Lefevre, H.: *The Production of Space* (Oxford: Blackwell Publishers, 1991).

Leibowitz, F.: "Apt feelings, or why 'women's films' aren't trivial," *Post-Theory: Reconstructing Film Studies*, ed. D. Bordwell and N. Carroll (Madison: University of Wisconsin Press, 1996), pp. 219–29.

Leininger, M.: *Care: The Essence of Nursing and Health* (Thorofare, NJ: Slack, 1984).

Leiris, M.: "Race and culture," *Race, Science and Society*, ed. L. Kuper (New York: Columbia University Press, 1965), pp. 135–72.

LeMoncheck, L.: *Dehumanizing Women: Treating Persons as Sex Objects* (Totowa, NJ: Rowman and Allenheld, 1985).

Lenin, V. I.: *The Emancipation of Women* (New York: International Publishers, 1934).

Lennon, K., and Whitford, M., eds.: *Knowing the Difference: Feminist Perspectives in Epistemology* (New York: Routledge, 1994).

——: "Gender and knowledge." *Journal of Gender Studies*, 4: 2 (1995), 133–45.

Lerner, G.: *The Creation of Patriarchy* (New York: Oxford University Press, 1986).

Lévi-Strauss, C.: "Race and History," *Race, Science and Society*, ed. L. Kuper (New York: Columbia University Press, 1965), pp. 95–134.

Levine, E. R., ed.: *A Ceremonies Sampler: New Rites, Celebrations, and Observances of Jewish Women* (San Diego, CA: Women's Institute for Continuing Jewish Education 1991).

Levy-Bruhl, L.: *Primitive Mentality* (New York: AM Press, 1978).

Lewontin, R., Rose, S., and Kamin, L.: *Not in Our Genes: Biology, Ideology and Human Nature* (New York: Penguin, 1984).

Li Jingzhi, Zhang Xinxu and Ding Juan: *The Marxist Concept of Women* (Beijing: People's University Press, 1992).

Li, Xiao Jiang: *Gender Gap* (Beijing: Sanlian Publishing House, 1989).

——: "My view on women's studies and movements in the new era," *Chinese Women and Development; Position, Health and Employment*, ed. D. Fangqin (Zhengzhou: Henan People's Publishing House, 1993).

——: *Toward the Woman* (Zhengzhou: Henan People's Publishing House, 1995).

Lindon, R., Pagano, D., Russell, D., and Star Leigh, S.: *Against Sadomasochism: A Radical Feminist Analysis* (Palo Alto, CA: Frog in the Well, 1982).

637

Lippard, L.: *From the Center: Feminist Essays on Women's Art* (New York: Dutton, 1976).

Lippman, A.: "Parental genetic testing and screening: constructing needs and reinforcing inequities," *American Journal of Law Medicine*, XVII (1991), 15–50.

Littleton, C.: "Reconstructing sexual equality," *California Law Review*, 75: 4 (1987), 1279–1337.

Lloyd, G.: "Rousseau on reason, nature and women," *Metaphilosophy*, 14: 3–4 (1983), 308–26.

——: *The Man of Reason: "Male" and "Female" in Western Philosophy* (Minneapolis: University of Minnesota Press, 1984).

——: *Polarity and Analogy: Two Types of Argumentation in Early Greek Thought* (Cambridge: Cambridge University Press, 1986).

——: "Selfhood, war and masculinity," *Feminist Challenges*, ed. E. Gross and C. Pateman (London: Allen and Unwin, 1987).

——: "Woman as other: sex, gender and subjectivity," *Australian Feminist Studies*, 10 (1989).

——: *Methods and Problems in Greek Science* (Cambridge: Cambridge University Press, 1991).

——: "Maleness, metaphor and the crisis of reason," *A Mind of One's Own: Feminist Essays on Reason and Objectivity*, ed. L. Antony and C. Witt (Boulder, CO: Westview Press, 1993), pp. 69–83.

——: *Part of Nature: Self-Knowledge in Spinoza's Ethics* (Ithaca, NY: Cornell University Press, 1994).

Locke, J.: *An Essay Concerning Human Understanding* (London: 1694).

Longauex y Vásquez, E.: "The Mexican-American woman," *Sisterhood is Powerful*, ed. R. Morgan (New York: Random House, 1970).

Longino, H.: "Can there be a feminist science?," *Feminism and Science*, ed. N. Tuana (Bloomington: Indiana University Press, 1989).

——: *Science as Social Knowledge: Values and Objectivity in Scientific Inquiry* (Princeton, NJ: Princeton University Press, 1990).

——: "Essential Tensions," *A Mind of One's Own: Feminist Essays on Reason and Objectivity*, ed. L. Antony and C. Witt (Boulder, CO: Westview Press, 1993a).

——: "Subjects, power and knowledge," *Feminist Epistemologies*, ed. L. Alcoff and E. Potter (New York: Routledge, 1993b).

Lopate, C.: "Women and pay for housework," *Feminist Frameworks*, ed. A. M. Jaggar and P. S. Rothenberg (New York: McGraw-Hill, 1978), pp. 211–17.

Lorde, A.: *Sister Outsider* (Trumansburg, NY: The Crossing Press, 1984).

Lovenduski, J.: *Women and European Politics: Contemporary Feminism and Public Policy* (Amherst: University of Massachusetts Press, 1986).

Loving v. *Virginia*, 388 U.S. 1 (1967).

Lowenberg, B. J., and Bogin, R., eds.: *Black Women in Nineteenth Century American Life* (University Park: Pennsylvania State University Press, 1976).

Lugones, M.: "Playfulness, 'world'-traveling, and loving perception," *Hypatia*, 2 (1987), 3–19.

——: "Hispaneando y lesbiando: on Sara Hoagland's *Lesbian Ethics*," *Hypatia*, 5 (1990), 138–46.

——: "On the logic of pluralist feminism," *Feminist Ethics*, ed. C. Card (Lawrence: University Press of Kansas, 1991), pp. 35–44.

——: *Pilgrimages/Peregrinajes: Essays in Pluralist Feminism* (Albany: State University of New York Press, forthcoming).

——, and Spelman, E.: "Have we got a theory for you!," *Women and Values*, ed. M. Pearsall (Belmont, CA: Wadsworth, 1986), pp. 19–31.

Lukic, J.: "Women-centered narratives in Serbian and Croat literatures," *Engendered Slavic Literatures*, ed. P. Shester and S. Forrester (Bloomington: Indiana University Press, 1996).

Lundgren-Gothlin, E.: *Sex and Existence: Simone de Beauvoir's* The Second Sex (London: Athlone Press, 1996).

Luo Qiong: *Basic Knowledges about the Question of Women's Liberation* (Beijing: People's Publishing House, 1986).

Luxemburg, R.: *The Accumulation of Capital*, trans. A. Schwarzschild (New Haven, CT: Yale University Press, 1951).

——: *The Mass Strike* (London: Bookmarks, 1986).

Lyotard, J-F.: "The sublime and the avant-garde," *The Lyotard Reader*, ed. A. Benjamin (Oxford: Blackwell, 1989).

MacCormack, C., and Strathern, M., eds.: *Nature, Culture, and Gender* (Cambridge: Cambridge University Press, 1980).

MacIntyre, A.: *After Virtue* (Notre Dame, IN: University of Notre Dame Press, 1981).

Mackenzie, C.: "Abortion and embodiment," *Australian Journal of Philosophy*, 70: 2 (1992), 136–55.

——: "Reason and sensibility: the ideal of women's self-governance in the writings of Mary Wollstonecraft," *Hypatia*, 8: 4 (1993), 35–55.

MacKinnon, C.: *The Sexual Harassment of Working Women* (New Haven, CT: Yale University Press, 1979).

——: "Feminism, Marxism, method, and the state: an agenda for theory," *Signs*, 7 (1982), 515–44.

——: "Feminism, Marxism, method and the state: toward feminist jurisprudence," *Signs*, 8 (1983), 635–58.

——: "Difference and dominance: on sex discrimination," *Feminism Unmodified: Discourses on Life and Law* (Cambridge, MA: Harvard University Press, 1987a), pp. 32–45.

——: *Feminism Unmodified: Discourses on Life and Law* (Cambridge, MA: Harvard University Press, 1987b).

——: *Toward a Feminist Theory of the State* (Cambridge, MA: Harvard University Press, 1989).

——: "Legal perspectives on sexual difference," *Theoretical Perspectives on Sexual Difference*, ed. D. Rhode (New Haven, CT: Yale University Press, 1990).

——: "Crimes of war, crimes of peace," *On Human Rights*, ed. S. Shute and S. Hurley (New York: Basic Books, 1993a), pp. 83–109.

——: *Only Words* (Cambridge, MA: Harvard University Press, 1993b).

Macklin, R.: "Is there anything wrong with surrogate motherhood?: An ethical analysis," *Law, Medical and Health Care*, 16 (1988).

Maffia, D. H.: "De los derechos humanos a los derechos de las humanas," *Capacitación Politica para Mujeres: Género y Cambio Social en la Argentina Actual*, ed. D. H. Maffia and C. Kuschnir (Buenos Aires: Feminaria Editora, 1994), pp. 63–75.

Maguigan, H.: "Battered women and self-defense: myths and misconceptions in current reform proposals," *University of Pennsylvania Law Review*, 140 (1991), 379–486.

Mahasweta Devi: "Sanjh Sakaler Ma," *Mahasweta Devir Chhotogalpo Sankolan (Bengali)* (New Delhi: National Book Trust, 1993).

Mahoney, M.: "Legal images of battered women: redefining the issue of separation," *Michigan Law Review*, 90 (1991), 1–94.

Mahowald, M. B.: *Philosophy and Women* (Indianapolis, IN: Hackett Publishing Co., 1983).

——: "Sex-role stereotypes in medicine," *Hypatia*, 2: 2 (1987), 21–38.

——: *Women and Children in Health Care: An Unequal Majority* (New York: Oxford University Press, 1993).

Maihofer, A.: "Ansatze zur Kritik des moralischen Universalismus," *Feministische Studien*, 1 (1988), 32–52.

——: *Geschlecht als Existenzweise. Macht, Moral, Recht und Geschlechterdifferenz* (Frankfurt/Main, 1995).

Malveaux, J.: "Gender difference and beyond: An economic perspective on diversity and commonality among women," *Theoretical Perspectives on Sexual Difference*, ed. D. Rhode (New Haven, CT: Yale University Press, 1990), pp. 226–38.

Mann, P.: *Micro-Politics: Agency in a Postfeminist Era* (Minneapolis: University of Minnesota Press, 1994).

Mannheim, K.: *Ideology and Utopia* (London: Routledge and Kegan Paul, 1960).

Manning, R.: *Speaking From the Heart* (Lanham, MD: Rowman and Littlefield, 1992).

Mansbridge, J.: "Feminism and democracy," *The American Prospect*, 1 (1990), 126–39.

——: "Feminism and democratic community," *Democratic Community*, ed. J. Chapman and I. Shapiro (New York: New York University Press, 1993), pp. 339–95.

Manuh, T.: "Methodologies for gender analysis – an African perspective," *Legon Gender Analysis Report* (Legon: University of Legon, 1992).

Manushi, Tenth Anniversary Special Issue on Women Bhakta Poets, 50–2 (1989).

Marks, E.: "Lesbian intertextuality," *Homosexualities and French Literature*, ed. E. Marks and G. Stambolian (Ithaca, NY: Cornell University Press, 1979).

Marshall, B.: *Engendering Modernity: Feminism, Social Theory and Change* (Boston: Northeastern University Press, 1994).

Martin, B.: "Sexualities without gender and other queer utopias," *Diacritics*, 24: 2–3 (1994), 104–21.

Martin, E.: *The Woman in the Body: A Cultural Analysis of Reproduction* (Boston: Beacon Press, 1987).

——: "The egg and the sperm," *Signs*, 16: 3 (1991), 485–501.

——: *Flexible Bodies* (Boston: Beacon Press, 1994).

Martin, J.: "Sex equality and education," *"Femininity," "Masculinity," and "Androgyny: A Modern Philosophical Discussion"*, ed. M. Vetterling-Braggin (Totowa, NJ: Littlefield Adams, 1982).

——: "Bringing women into educational thought," *Educational Theory*, 34: 4 (1984), 341–53.

——: *Reclaiming A Conversation: The Ideal of the Educated Woman* (New Haven, CT: Yale University Press, 1985).

——: "Martial virtues or capital vices?," *Journal of Thought*, 22: 3 (1987a), 32–44.

——: "Reforming teacher education, rethinking liberal education," *Teachers' College Record*, 88: 3 (1987b), 406–10.

——: "What should science educators do about the gender bias in science?," *History, Philosophy, and Science Teaching*, ed. M.R. Matthews (Toronto: OISE Press, 1991), pp. 151–67.

——: *The Schoolhome: Rethinking Schools for Changing Families* (Cambridge, MA: Harvard University Press, 1992).

——: *Changing the Educational Landscape* (New York: Routledge, 1994a).

——: "Methodological essentialism, false difference, and other dangerous traps," *Signs* 19 (1994b), 630–57.

Marx, K.: *The Economic and Philosophic Manuscripts of 1844*, ed. D.J. Struik (New York: International Publishers, 1964).

——: *Capital* (New York: International Publishers, 1967).

——, and Engels, F.: *German Ideology* (New York: International Publishers, 1970).

——, Engels, F., Lenin, V. I., and Stalin, J.: *The Woman Question* (New York: International Publishers, 1951).

Mascia-Lees, F., Sharpe, P., and Ballerino-Cohen, C.: "The postmodern turn in anthropology: cautions from a feminist perspective," *Signs*, 15: 1 (1989), 7–33.

Masolo, F. D. A.: "History and the modernization of African philosophy: a reading of Kwasi Wiredu," *Postkoloniales Philosophieren Afrika*, ed. H. Nagl-Docekal and M. Wimmer (Vienna/Munich: Oldenbourg, 1992), pp. 67–97.

Massaro, T.: "Empathy, legal storytelling and the rule of law: new words, old wounds?," *Michigan Law Review*, 87 (1989), 2099–127.

Masters, J.: "Revolutionary theory: reinventing our origin myths," *Reinventing Biology*, ed. L. Birke and R. Hubbard (Bloomington: Indiana University Press, 1995).

Mathews, F.: *The Ecological Self* (London: Routledge, 1991).

Mattick, P.: "Beautiful and sublime: 'Gender tokenism' in the constitution of art," *Feminism and Tradition in Aesthetics*, ed. P. Z. Brand and C. Korsmeyer (University Park: Pennsylvania State University Press, 1995).

Maududi, S. A. A.: *Purdah and the Status of Woman in Islam*, 6th edn (Pakistan: Islamic Publications Ltd, 1981).

Mbiliyi, M.: "Research priorities in women studies in East Africa," *Women Studies International Forum*, 7: 4 (1984), 289–300.

McBride, W., and Raynova, I.: "Visions from the ashes: philosophical life in Bulgaria from 1945 to 1992," *Philosophy and Political Change in Eastern Europe*, ed. B. Smith (La Salle, IL: Hegler Institute, 1993).

McClain, L.: " 'Atomistic man' revisited: liberalism, connection, and feminist jurisprudence," *Southern California Law Review*, 65 (1992a), 1171–264.

——: "The poverty of privacy?," *Columbia Journal of Gender and Law*, 3 (1992b), 119–74.

McCloud, S. G.: "Feminism's idealist error," *New York University Review of Law & Social Change*, 14 (1986), 277–321.

McClure, K.: "The issues of foundations," *Feminists Theorize the Political*, ed. J. Butler and J. W. Scott (New York: Routledge, 1992).

McCormack, C.P.,: "If pornography is the theory, is inequality the practice?," *Philosophy of Social Theory*, 23: 3 (September 1993), 298–326.

—— and Strathern, M., eds.: *Nature, Culture and Gender* (Cambridge: Cambridge University Press, 1980).

McFague, S.: *Models of God* (Philadelphia, PA: Fortress Press, 1987).

——: *The Body of God* (Minneapolis: Fortress Press, 1993).

McFall, L.: "What's wrong with bitterness?," *Feminist Ethics*, ed. C. Card (Lawrence: University of Kansas Press, 1991).

McNeil, M.: *Gender and Expertise* (London: Free Association Books, 1987).

Meehan, J.: "Autonomy, recognition, and respect: Habermas, Benjamin, and Honneth," *Feminists Read Habermas: Gendering the Subject of Discourse*, ed. J. Meehan (New York: Routledge, 1995), pp. 231–46.

Mellor, M.: *Breaking the Boundaries* (London: Virago, 1992).

Ménage, G.: *The History of Women Philosophers* [1690], trans. B. Zedler (Latham, MD: University Press of America, 1984).

Mendus, S.: "Losing the faith: feminism and democracy," *Democracy: The Unfinished Journey*, ed. J. Dunn (Oxford: Oxford University Press, 1992), 207–19.

Menkel-Meadow, C.: "Toward another view of legal negotiation: the structure of problem solving," *University of California Law Review*, 31 (1984), 754–842.

——: "Feminist legal theory, critical legal studies, and legal education," *Journal of Legal Education*, 38 (1988), 61–85.

——: "Mainstreaming feminist legal theory," *Pacific Law Journal*, 23 (1992), 1493–1542.

Merchant, C.: *The Death of Nature: Women, Ecology and the Scientific Revolution* (San Francisco, CA: Harper and Row, 1980).

——: *Radical Ecology* (London: Routledge, 1994).

——: *Earthcare: Women and the Environment* (London: Routledge, 1996).

Merleau-Ponty, M.: (1945), trans. C. Smith, *The Phenomenology of Perception* (London: Routledge and Kegan Paul, 1962).

Mernissi, F.: *Beyond the Veil: Male/Female Dynamics in Modern Muslim Society* (London: Al Saqi Books, 1985).

Merriam, E.: "Sex and semantics: some notes on BOMFOG," *New York University Education Quarterly*, 5: 4 (1974), 22–4.

Meyers, D.: "The socialized individual and individual autonomy," *Women and Moral Theory*, ed. E. Kittay and D. Meyers (Savage, MD: Rowman and Little-field, 1987), pp. 139–53.

——: *Self, Society, and Personal Choice* (New York: Columbia University Press, 1989).

——: *Subjection and Subjectivity: Psychoanalytic Feminism and Moral Philosophy* (New York: Routledge, 1994).

——: "Rights in collision: A non-punitive, compensatory remedy for abusive speech," *Law and Philosophy*, 14 (1995) 203–43.

Meznaric, S.: "Gender as an ethno-marker: rape, war, and identity politics in the former Yugoslavia," *Identity Politics and Women*, ed. V. Moghadan (Boulder, CO: Westview Press, 1994).

Michaels, M.: "Other mothers: Toward an ethic of postmaternal practice," *Hypatia*, 11: 2 (1996), 49–70.

Midgley, M.: *Beast and Man* (London: Methuen, 1980).

——: "On not being afraid of natural differences?," *Feminist Perspectives in Philosophy*, ed. M. Griffiths and M. Whitford (Basingstoke: Macmillan. 1988).

——, and Hughes, J.: *Women's Choices: Philosophical Problems Facing Feminism* (New York: St. Martin's Press, 1983).

Mies, M.: *Patriarchy and Accumulation on a World Scale* (London: Zed, 1986).

—— and Shiva, V.: *Ecofeminism* (New Delhi: Kali for Women, 1993).

Milan Women's Bookstore Collective: *Sexual Difference. A Theory of Socio-Symbolic Practice* (Bloomington: Indiana University Press, 1990).

Mill, J. S., and Taylor, H.: "The Subjection of Women," *Essays on Sex Equality*, ed. A. Rossi (Chicago, IL: University of Chicago Press, 1970).

——: *Utilitarianism* [1861] (Indianapolis, IN: Hackett, 1979).

——: *The Subjection of Women* [1869] (London: Virago, 1983, also Cambridge, MA: MIT Press, 1978).

Miller, C., and Swift, K.: *Words and Women: New Language in New Times* (New York: Harper Collins, 1991).

Miller, M. C.: "Feminism and pragmatism: or the arrival of a 'Ministry of Disturbance, A Regulated Source of Annoyance; A Destroyer of Rhetoric; An Undermining of Complacency,'" *Monist*, 15: 4 (1992), 445–57.

Millett, K.: *Sexual Politics* (Garden City, NY: Doubleday Press, 1970).

Min Jiayin: *Variations of Masculine Strength and Feminine Grace* (Beijing: Social Science Publishers, 1995).

Minow, M.: "The Supreme Court, 1986 term – foreword: justice engendered," *Harvard Law Review*, 101 (1987), 10–95.

——: *Making All the Difference: Inclusion, Exclusion, and American Law* (Ithaca, NY: Cornell University Press, 1990).

——: "Equalities," *Journal of Philosophy* (November 1991a), 633–44.

——: "Feminist reason: getting it and losing it," *Feminist Legal Theory: Readings in Law and Gender*, ed. K. T. Bartlett and R. Kennedy (Boulder, CO: Westview Press, 1991b),. pp. 357–69.

——, and Shanley, M. L.: "Relational rights and responsibilities: revisioning the family in liberal political theory and law," *Hypatia*, 11: 1 (1996), 3–29.

Miroiu, M.: "The vicious circle of anonymity, or pseudo-feminism and totalitarism," *Thinking*, 11: 3–4 (1994), 54.

——: *Convenio: On Nature, Women and Morals* (Bucharest: Alternative Publishing House, 1996).

Mitchell, J.: *Women's Estate* (New York: Random House, 1972).

——: *Psychoanalysis and Feminism* (New York: Pantheon, 1974).

——: "The longest revolution," *Women, Class and the Feminist Imagination*, ed. K. Hansen and I. Philipson (Philadelphia, PA: Temple University Press, 1990), pp. 43–73.

Mladjenovic, L.: "Universal soldier. Rape in war," *Women for Peace* (Belgrade: Women in Black, 1995), pp. 93–7.

Moen, M.: "Feminist themes in unlikely places," *Feminist Interpretations of Kant*, ed. R. Schott (University Park: Pennsylvania State University Press, 1997).

Mohanty, C. T.: "Under Western eyes: feminist scholarship and colonial discourse," *Boundary*, 2 (1984), 337–8.

——: "Feminist encounters: locating the politics of experience," *Destabilizing Theory: Contemporary Feminist Debates*, ed. M. Barrett and A. Phillips (Cambridge: Polity Press, 1992), pp. 74–92.

——, Russo, A., and Torres, L., eds.: *Third World Women and the Politics of Feminism* (Bloomington: Indiana University Press, 1991).

Moi, T.: *Simone de Beauvoir: The Making of an Intellectual Woman* (Oxford: Blackwell, 1994).

Molyneaux, M.: "Mobilization without emancipation? Women's interests, state and revolution in Nicaragua," *Feminist Studies*, 11 (1985), 227–54.

Montrelay, M.: *L'Ombre et le nom* (Paris: Minuit, 1977).

——: "An enquiry into femininity," *M/F*, 1 (1978), pp. 83–102.

Moody-Adams, M.: "On surrogacy: morality, markets and motherhood," *Public Affairs Quarterly*, 5: 2 (1991), 175–90.

—— "Feminist inquiry and the transformation of the 'public' sphere in Held's *Feminist Morality*," *Hypatia* 1:1 (1996), 155–67.

——: *Morality, Culture, and Philosophy* (Cambridge, MA: Harvard University Press, forthcoming).

Moore, B.: *Privacy: Studies in Social and Cultural History* (Armonk, NY: M. E. Sharpe, 1984).

Moraga, C., and Anzaldúa, G., eds.: *This Bridge Called My Back: Writings by Radical Women of Color* (New York: Kitchen Table, Women of Color, 1981).

Morgan, K.: "Amazons, spinsters, and women: a career of one's own," *Philosophy of Education 1978* (Champaign, IL: Philosophy of Education Society, 1979), pp. 11–19.

——: "Romantic love, altruism, and self-respect: An analysis of Simone de Beauvoir," *Hypatia*, 1: 1 (1986), 117–48.

——: "Women and moral madness," *Science, Morality, and Feminist Theory*, ed. M. Hanen and K. Nielsen (Calgary: University of Calgary Press, 1987).

——: "Of woman born? How old fashioned!," *The Future of Human Reproduction*, ed. C. Overall (Toronto: The Women's Press. 1989). pp. 62–79.

——: "Women and the knife: cosmetic surgery and the colonization of women's bodies," *Hypatia*, 6 (1991), 25–53.

Morris, J.: *Pride Against Prejudice* (Philadelphia: New Society Publishers, 1991).

Morrison, T.: *The Bluest Eye* (New York: Pocket Books, 1970).

Morton, N.: "Beloved image!," paper presented to The American Academy of Religion (San Francisco, CA: December 28, 1977).

——: *The Journey is Home* (Boston: Beacon Press, 1985).

Morton, P.: *Disfigured Images: The Historical Assault on African American Women* (Westport, CT: Greenwood Press, 1991).

Moser, C.: "Gender planning in the Third World," *Gender and International Relations*, ed. R. Newland and K. Newland (Bloomington: Indiana University Press, 1991).

Moskowitz, E., Jennings, B., and Callahan, D.: "Feminism, social policy, and long-acting contraception," *Hasting Center Report*, 25: 1 (1995), 30–2.

Mouffe, C.: "Feminism, citizenship, and radical politics," *Feminists Theorize the Political*, ed. J. Butler and J. W. Scott (New York: Routledge, 1992).

——: "Feminism, citizenship and radical democratic politics," *The Return of the Political*, ed. C. Mouffe (London: Verso, 1994), pp. 74–89.

Moulton, J.: "The myth of the neutral 'man,'" *Sexist Language: A Modern Philosophical Analysis*, ed. M. Vetterling-Braggin (Totowa, NJ: Littlefield, Adams, 1981).

——: "A paradigm of philosophy: the adversary method," *Discovering Reality: Feminist Perspectives on Epistemology, Metaphysics, Methodology, and Philosophy of Science*, ed. S. Harding and M. Hintikka (Dordrecht, Holland: D. Reidel Publishing, 1983a).

——: "Sexual behavior: another position," *The Philosophy of Sex: Contemporary Readings*, ed. A. Soble (Savage, MD: Rowan and Littlefield, 1991), pp. 63–72.

—— and Rainone, F.: "Women's work and sex roles," *Beyond Domination*, ed. C. C. Gould (Totowa, NJ: Rowman and Allanheld, 1983b), pp. 189–203.

Mudimbe, V. Y.: *The Invention of Africa Gnosis: Philosophy and the Order of Knowledge* (Bloomington: Indiana University Press, 1988).

Mulvey, L.: "Visual pleasure and narrative cinema," *Screen*, 16 (1975), 6–18.

——: *Visual and Other Pleasures* (Bloomington: Indiana University Press, 1990).

Murphy, J. S.: "The look in Sartre and Rich," *The Thinking Muse*, ed. J. Allen and I. M. Young (Bloomington: Indiana University Press, 1989).

Musheerul Haq: *Aurat ki Hukmarani Jaez Hai* (Aik Islami Nuqta-e-Nazar: Rawalpindi, 1989).

Muslim Women's Georgetown Project: Position Paper, "Islam: A System of Reciprocal Partnership" (Washington, DC: September 27, 1995).

Muslim Women's League: Position Paper, *The Spiritual Role of Women*, n.d.

Myron, N., and Bunch, C., eds.: *Lesbianism and the Women's Movement* (Baltimore, MD: Diana Press, 1974).

al-Nadawi, A. H.: *al-Sirah al-Nabawiyah (The Prophetic Biography)* (Jeddah: Dar al-Shurouq, 1977).

Nagel, T.: *Equality and Partiality* (New York: Oxford University Press, 1991).

——, ed.: *Feministische Philosophie* (Vienna/Munich: Oldenbourg, 1990).

Nagl-Docekal, H.: "Jenseits der Geschlechtemoral," *Jeseits der Geschlechtermoral: Beiträge zur feministischen Ethik*, eds. H. Nagl-Docekal and H. Pauer-Studer (Frankfurt/Main, 1993), pp. 7–32.

——: "Ist Fursorglichkeit mit Gleichbehandlung unvereinbar?," *Duet Z Phil*, 42: 6 (1994), 1045–50.

——: "Philosophy of history as a theory of gender difference: the case of Rousseau," *Re-Reading the Philosophical Canon. Feminist Critique in German*. ed. H. Nagl-Docekal and C. Klinger (University Park: Pennsylvania State Press, forthcoming, a).

——: "Feminist ethics: How it could benefit from Kant's moral philosophy," *Feminist Interpretations of Kant*, ed. R. Schott (University Park: Pennsylvania State Press, forthcoming, b).

——, and Pauer-Studer, H., eds.: *Jenseits der Geschlechtermoral. Beiträge zur feministischen Ethik* (Frankfurt/Main, 1993).

Nails, D.: "Social-scientific sexism: Gilligan's mismeasure of man," *Social Research*. 50: 3 (1983). 643–64.

Nakashima Brock, R.: *Journeys by Heart: A Christology of Erotic Power* (New York: Crossroad, 1988).

Nanda, S: "The Hijras of India: cultural and individual dimensions of an institutionalized third gender role," *Journal of Homosexuality*, II: 3–4 (1986), 35–54.

Nandy, A.: *At the Edge of Psychology: Essays in Politics and Culture* (Delhi: Oxford University Press, 1980).

Narayan, U.: "Working together across difference," *Hypatia*, 3: 2 (1988), 31–48.

——: "Mail order brides: protecting women in international marriages," paper presented at the International Conference on Feminist Ethics and Social Policy (University of Pittsburgh, PA: Graduate School of Public and International Affairs, 1993).

——: "Colonialism and its others: considerations on rights and care discourses," *Hypatia*, 10: 2 (1995), 133–40.

Nash, M.: "The man without a penis: libidinal economies that (re)cognize the hypernature of gender," *Philosophy and Social Criticism*, 18: 2 (1992), 125–34.

Nasif, F.: *Huquq al-Mar'ah wa Wajibatiha fi Daw' al-Kitab wa la-Sunnah* (*The Rights and Duties of Woman in Light of the Qur'an and the Tradition of the Prophet*) (Jeddah: Tihamah, 1992).

National Committee of NGOs for Population and Development, Branch Committee for Women: *Al-Tariq min al-Qahira ila Pikin* (*The Road from Cairo to Beijing*) (Cairo: 1995).

Nedelsky, J.: "Reconceiving autonomy: sources, thoughts and possibilities," *Yale Journal of Law & Feminism*, 1 (1989), 7–36.

——: "The challenges of multiplicity," *Michigan Law Review*, 89 (1991), 1591–1609.

Nelkin, D., and Lindee, S.: *The DNA Mystique: The Gene as Icon* (New York: Freeman Press, 1995).

Nelson, C., and Grossberg, L., eds.: *Marxism and the Interpretation of Culture* (Chicago: University of Illinois Press, 1988).

Nelson, H. L.: "Against caring," *Journal of Clinical Ethics*, 3: 1 (1992), 8–15.

——: "The architect and the bee: some reflections on postmodern pregnancy," *Bioethics*, 8: 3 (1994), 247–67.

——: "Resistance and insubordination," *Hypatia*, 10 (1995), 23–40.

—— and Nelson, J. L.: "Feminism, social policy and long-acting contraception," *Hastings Center Report*, 25: 1 (1995), 30–32.

——: "Justice in the allocation of health care resources: a feminist account," *Feminism & Bioethics: Beyond Reproduction*, ed. S. Wolf (New York: Oxford University Press, 1996).

Nelson, L. H.: *Who Knows: From Quine to a Feminist Empiricism* (Philadelphia: Temple University Press, 1990).

——: "Epistemological communities," *Feminist Epistemologies*, ed. L. Alcoff and E. Potter (New York: Routledge, 1993a).

——: "A question of evidence," *Hypatia*, 8: 2 (1993b).

——: "A feminist naturalized philosophy of science," *Synthèse*, 104: 3 (1995).

Nestle, J.: "The femme question," *Pleasure and Danger: Exploring Female Sexuality*, ed. C. Vance (Boston: Routledge and Kegan Paul, 1984), pp. 232–41.

——: *A Restricted Country* (Ithaca, NY: Firebrand Books, 1987).

——, ed.: *The Persistent Desire: A Femme-Butch Reader* (Boston: Alyson Publications, 1992).

Newton, E.: "The mythic mannish lesbian: Radclyffe Hall and the new woman," *Signs*, 9: 4 (1984), 557–75.

Newton, L.: "Reverse discrimination as unjustified," *Ethics*, 83: 4 (1973), 308–12.

Nickel, J. W.: "Ethnocide and the indigenous peoples," *Journal of Social Philosophy*, 25 (1994), 84–98.

Nicholson, L.: "Women and schooling," *Educational Theory*, 30: 3 (1980), 225–34.

——: "'The personal is political': an analysis in retrospect," *Social Theory and Practice*, 7: 1 (1981), 85–98.

——: "Affirmative action, education, and social class," *Philosophy of Education 1982* (Norman, IL: Philosophy of Education Society, 1983a).

——: "Women, morality, and history," *Social Research*, 50: 3 (1983b), 514–36.

——: "Feminist theory: the private and the public," *Beyond Domination: New Perspectives on Women and Philosophy* (Totowa, NJ: Rowman and Allanheld, 1983c), pp. 221–30.

——: *Gender and History* (New York: Columbia University Press, 1986).

—— ed: *Feminism/Postmodernism* (New York: Routledge, 1990).

——, and Fraser, N.: "Social criticism without philosophy: an encounter between feminism and postmodernism," *Feminism/Postmodernism* (New York: Routledge, 1990), pp. 19–38.

——: "Interpreting gender," *Signs*, 20 (1994), 79–105.

Nietzsche, F.: *The Gay Science*, trans. W. Kauffmann (New York: Vintage Books, 1974).

Nochlin, L.: *Woman as Sex Object* (New York: Harper and Row, 1972).

——: *Women, Art, and Power, and Other Essays* (New York: Harper and Row, 1988).

Noddings, N.: *Caring: A Feminine Approach to Ethics and Moral Education* (Berkeley: University of California Press, 1986).

——: "An ethic of caring and its implications for instructional arrangements," *American Journal of Education*, 96: 2 (1988), 215–30.

——: *Women and Evil* (Berkeley: University of California Press, 1989).

——: "A response," *Hypatia*, 5: 1 (1990), 120–6.

——: *The Challenge to Care in Schools* (New York: Teachers' College Press, 1992).

Norris, S.: "Sustaining and responding to charges of bias in critical thinking," *Educational Theory*, 45: 2 (1995) 199–211.

Nsiah-Jefferson, L.: "Reproductive laws, women of color, and low-income women," *Reproductive Laws for the 1990's*, ed. S. Cohen and N. Taub (Clifton, NJ: Humana Press, 1989), pp. 23–67.

Nunner-Winkler, G.: "Ein Plädoyer für einen eingeschränkten Universalismus," *Zur Bestimmung der Moral*, ed. W. Edelstein and G. Nunner-Winkler (Frankfurt, 1986), pp. 126–44.

——"Gibt es eine Weibliche Moral," *Weibliche Moral. Die Kontroverse un eine geschlechtsspezifische Ethik*, ed. G. Nunner-Winkler (Frankfurt, 1991a), pp. 147–61.

——, ed.: *Weibliche Moral. Die Kontroverse um eine geschlechtsspezifische Ethik* (Frankfurt: Campus, 1991b).

Nussbaum, M.: "Nature, function and capability: Aristotle on political distribution," *Oxford Studies in Ancient Philosophy: Supplementary Volume*, ed. J. C. Kagge and N.D. Smith (Oxford: Clarendon Press, 1992).

——: "Non-relative virtues: An Aristotelian approach," *The Quality of Life,*, ed. M. Nussbaum and A. Sen (Oxford: Clarendon Press, 1993a), pp. 242–69.

——: "Onora O'Neill: Justice, gender and international boundaries," *The Quality of Life*, ed. M. Nussbaum and A. Sen (Oxford: Clarendon Press, 1993b).

——: "Human capabilities, female human beings," *Women, Culture, and Development*, ed. M. Nussbaum and J. Glover (New York: Oxford University Press, 1995).

Nye, A.: "The unity of language," *Hypatia*, 2: 2 (1987).

——: *Feminist Theory and the Philosophies of Man* (London, 1988).

——: *Words of Power: A Feminist Reading of the History of Logic* (New York: Routledge, Chapman, Hall, 1990).

——: "Frege's metaphors," *Hypatia*, 7: 2 (1992), 18–39.

——: "Semantics in a new key," *Philosophy in a Different Voice*, ed. J. Kourany (forthcoming).

O'Brien, M.: *The Politics of Reproduction* (Boston: Routledge and Kegan Paul, 1981).

O'Conner, P.: "Warning! Contents under heterosexual pressure," *Hypatia* 12: 3 (1997).

O'Flaherty, W. D.: *Sexual Metaphors and Animal Symbols in Indian Mythology* (Delhi: Motilal Banarsidas, 1980).

Okely, J.: *Simone de Beauvoir: A Re-reading* (London: Virago, 1986).

Okin, S. M.: *Justice, Gender, and the Family* (New York: Basic Books, 1989a).

——: "Reason and feeling in thinking about justice," *Ethics*, 99: 2 (1989b), 229–49.

——: *Women in Western Political Thought* (Princeton, NJ: Princeton University Press, 2nd edn 1992).

——: "Gender inequality and cultural differences," *Political Theory*, 22: 1 (1994), 5–24.

——: "Sexual orientation, gender and families: dichotomizing differences," *Hypatia*, 11: 2 (1996), 30–48.

——: "Inequalities between the sexes in different cultural contexts," *Women, Culture and Development*, ed. M. Nussbaum and S. Glover (Oxford: Clarendon Press, 1995), 274–97.

Oliver, K.: "Marxism and surrogacy," *Hypatia*, 4: 3 (1989), 95–115.

——: "The politics of interpretation: the case of Bergman's *Persona*," *Philosophy and Film*, ed. C. Freeland and T. Wartenberg (New York: Routledge, 1995), pp. 233–49.

Olsen, F.: "The family and the market: a study of ideology and legal reform," *Harvard Law Review*, 96 (1983), 1497–1578.

——: "Statutory rape: a feminist critique of rights analysis," *Texas Law Review*, 63 (1984) 387–432.

——: "Unraveling compromise," *Harvard Law Review*, 103 (1989), 105–35.

——: *Feminist Legal Theory* (New York: New York University Press, 1995).

Oluwole, S. B.: "Madonna and the whore in African traditional thought," *Journal of Philosophy and Development*, I: 1&2 (1995), pp. 18–26.

——: "Women empowerment: a demand not for equality but for equity," *Imodoye*. 3: 3 (1996).

Omi, M., and Winant, H.: *Racial Formation in the United States* (New York: Routledge, 1994).

649

Omvedt, G.: *Violence Against Women: New Movements and New Theories in India* (New Delhi: Kali for Women, 1990).

O'Neill, O.: "How do we know when opportunities are equal?," *Feminism and Philosophy*, ed. M. Vetterling-Braggin, F. Elliston, and J. English (Totowa, NJ: Littlefield, Adams, 1977).

——: *Constructions of Reason – Explorations of Kant's Practical Philosophy* (Cambridge: Cambridge University Press, 1989).

——: "Justice, gender, and international boundaries," *The Quality of Life*, ed. M. Nussbaum and A. Sen (New York: Oxford University Press, 1993).

Ong, A.: "Colonialism and modernity: feminist representations of women in non-western societies," *Inscriptions*, 3: 4 (1988).

Orenstein, D., ed.: *Lifecycles: Jewish Women on Life Passages and Personal Milestones* (Woodstock, VT: Jewish Lights, vol. 1, 1994, vol. 2, 1997).

Ortner, S.: "Is female to male as nature is to culture?," *Woman, Culture and Society*, ed. M. Z. Rosaldo and L. Lamphere (Stanford, CA: Stanford University Press, 1974), 67–87.

Oruka, H. O.: "Mythologies as African philosophy," *East African Journal*, 9: 10 (1972).

——: "Fundamental principles in the question of African philosophy," *Second Order*, 5: 2 (1976).

Ossoli, M. Fuller: *Woman in the Nineteenth Century, and Kindred Papers Relating to the Sphere, Condition, and Duties of Woman* (Boston, MA: Roberts Brothers, 1875).

Othman, N., ed.: *Shari'ah Law and the Modern Nation State* (Kuala Lumpur: Sisters in Islam, 1994).

Oudshoorn, N.: *Beyond the Natural Body: An Archeology of Sex Hormones* (London: Routledge, 1994).

Outlaw, L.: "African philosophy: deconstructive and reconstructive challenges," *Contemporary Philosophy: A New Survey, Vol. 5: African Philosophy*, ed. G. Floistad (Dordrecht, Holland: D. Reidel Publishing Co., 1987) pp. 8–44.

Outshoorn, J.: "Is this what we wanted? Positive action as issue perversion," *Equality, Politics, and Gender*, ed. E. Meehan and S. Sevenhuijsen (Beverly Hills, CA: Sage, 1991), pp. 104–21.

Overall, C.: *Ethics and Human Reproduction: A Feminist Analysis* (Boston: Allen and Unwin, 1987).

——, ed.: *The Future of Human Reproduction* (Toronto: The Women's Press, 1989).

——: *Human Reproduction: Principles, Practices, Policies* (Toronto: Oxford, 1993).

Oyama, S.: *The Ontogeny of Information* (Cambridge: Cambridge University Press, 1985).

Ozick, C.: "Notes toward finding the right question," *On Being a Jewish Feminist*, ed. S. Heschel (New York: Schocken Books, 1983).

Pagano, J.: *Exiles and Communities: Teaching in the Patriarchal Wilderness* (Albany: State University of New York Press, 1990).

Pan, Suiming: *Love: A Casual Discussion of the Psychology of Marriage and Family* (Beijing: Urban Econo-social Publisher, 1989).

650

Pandey, G., ed.: *Hindus and Others* (New Delhi: Viking Press, 1993).

Papic, Z.: "Telo kao 'proces u toku,'" *Sociologija*, 34: 2 (1992), 153.

Pappas, N.: "Failures of marriage in *Sea of Love*: the love of men, the respect of women," *Philosophy and Film*, ed. C. Freeland and T. Wartenberg (New York: Routledge, 1995), pp. 109–25.

Parent, W. A.: "A new definition of privacy for the law," *Law and Philosophy*, 2 (1983), 305–38.

Parker, L.: "Beauty and breast implantation," *Hypatia*, 10: 1 (1995), 183–201.

Patai, D., and Koertge, N.: *Professing Feminism: Cautionary Tales from the Strange World of Women's Studies* (New York: Basic Books, 1994).

Patel, K.: "Women, earth, and the Goddess," *Hypatia*, 9: 4 (1994), 69–87.

Patel, R.: *Islamicisation of Laws in Pakistan* (Pakistan: Faiza Publishers Pakistan, n.d.).

Pateman, C.: *Participation and Democratic Theory* (Cambridge: Cambridge University Press, 1970).

——: "Defending prostitution: charges against Ericson," *Ethics*, 93 (1983), 561–5.

——: *The Sexual Contract* (Cambridge: Polity Press, 1988).

——: "Feminism and democracy," *The Disorder of Women: Democracy, Feminism and Political Theory*, ed. C. Pateman (Cambridge: Polity Press, 1989a), pp. 210–25.

—— ed.: *The Disorder of Women: Democracy, Feminism and Political Theory* (Stanford, CA: Stanford University Press, 1989b).

——: "Feminist critiques of the public/private dichotomy," *The Disorder of Women: Democracy, Feminism and Political Theory*, ed. C. Pateman (Stanford, CA: Stanford University Press, 1989c), pp. 118–41.

——: "Equality, difference, subordination: the politics of motherhood and woman's citizenship," *Beyond Equality and Difference*, ed. G. Bock and S. James (London: Routledge, 1992), pp. 17–31.

Pathak, Z. and Rajan, R.: "Shahbano," *Feminists Theorize the Political*, ed. J. Butler and J. W. Scott (New York: Routledge, 1992), pp. 257–80.

Pauer-Studer, H.: "Prinzipien und Verantwortung," *Normen*, 19 (1987), 59–17.

——: "Moraltheorie und Geschlechterdifferenz," *Jenseits der Geschlechtermoral*, ed. H. Nagl-Docekal and H. Pauer-Studer (Frankfurt/Main, 1993), pp. 33–68.

——: "Kant – Vorläufer einer Care-ethik?," *Und drinnen waltet die züchtige Hausfrau*, ed. H. Kuhlmann (Gütersloh, 1995), pp. 83–93.

Peach, L.: "An alternative to pacifism? Feminism and just war theory," *Bringing Peace Home*, ed. K.J. Warren and D. Cady (Bloomington: Indiana University Press, 1996).

Pearce, D.: "Women, work and welfare," *Working Women and Families*, ed. K. Wolk Feinstein (Beverly Hills, CA: Sage Publications, 1979).

Pearsall, M., ed.: *Women and Values* (Belmont, CA: Wadsworth, 1986).

Pellikaan-Engle, M.: "Socrates' blind spots," *Against Patriarchal Thinking: Proceedings of the Fifth Symposium of the International Association of Women Philosophers* (Amsterdam, Netherlands: VU University Press, 1992).

Pence, T.: *Ethics in Nursing: An Anthology* (New York: National League Nursing, 1990).

Penelope, J.: *Speaking Freely: Unlearning the Lies of the Father's Tongues* (Elmsford, NY: Pergamon Press, 1990).

——: *Call Me Lesbian: Lesbian Lives, Lesbian Theory* (Freedom, CA: The Crossing Press, 1992).

Pennock, J. R., and Chapman, J.: *Privacy* (New York: Atherton Press, 1971).

Pérez, E.: "Sexuality and discourse: notes from a Chicana survivor," *Chicana Lesbians: The Girls Our Mothers Warned Us About*, ed. C. Trujillo (Berkeley, CA: Third Woman Press, 1991), pp. 159–84.

Person, E.: "Sexuality as the mainstay of identity: psychoanalytical perspectives," *Signs*, 4: 5 (1980), 605–30.

Petchesky, R. P.: "Reproductive freedom – beyond a woman's right to choose," *Signs*, 5 (1980), 661–85.

——: "Antiabortion, antifeminism, and the rise of the new right," *Feminist Studies*, 7 (1981), 206–46.

——: *Abortion and Women's Choice: The State, Sexuality, and Reproductive Freedom* (Boston, MA: Northeastern University Press, 1985).

Peters, J., and Wolper, A., eds.: *Women's Rights, Human Rights: Internationalist Feminist Perspectives* (New York: Routledge, 1995).

Peterson, S. R.: "Coercion and rape: The state as a male protection racket," *Feminism and Philosophy*, ed. M. Vetterling-Braggin, F. Elliston, and J. English (Totowa, NJ: Littlefield, Adams, 1977), pp. 360–71.

Petrova, D.: "The winding road to emancipation in Bulgaria," *Gender Politics and Post-Communism*, ed. N. Funk and M. Mueller (New York: Routledge, 1993).

Phelan, S.: *Identity Politics: Lesbian Feminism and the Limits of Community* (Philadelphia, PA: Temple University Press, 1989).

——: "Specificity: Beyond equality and difference," *differences*, 3: 1 (1991), 128–43.

Phelps, L.: "Female sexual alienation," *Women: A Feminist Perspective*, ed. J. Freeman (Palo Alto, CA: Mayfield, 1979).

Philipson, I.: "The impasse of socialist-feminism," *Socialist Review*, 79 (1985), pp. 93–110.

Phillips, A.: *Engendering Democracy* (Cambridge: Polity, 1991).

——: *Democracy and Difference* (Cambridge: Polity, 1993).

——: *The Politics of Presence* (Oxford: Oxford University Press, 1995).

Pieper, A.: *Aufstand des stillgelegten Geschlechts: Einführung in die feministische Ethik* (Freiburg, 1993).

Piercy, M.: *Woman on the Edge of Time* (New York: Fawcett Crest, 1979).

Pilardi, J. A.: "The changing critical fortunes of *The Second Sex*," *History and Theory*, 30: 1 (1993), 51–73.

Pine, R. and Law, S.: "Envisioning a future for reproductive liberty: strategies for making the rights real," *Harvard Civil Rights–Civil Liberties Law Review*, 27 (1992), 407–63.

Piper, A.: "Higher order discrimination," *Identity, Character, and Morality*, ed. O. Flanagan and A. O. Rorty (Cambridge, MA: MIT Press, 1990).

——: "Xenophobia and Kantian rationalism," *Philosophical Forum*, XXIV:1–3, (1992–3), 188–232.

Piven, F. Fox, and Cloward, R.: *Regulating the Poor* (New York: Pantheon Books, 1971).

Planned Parenthood v. *Casey*, 505 U.S. 833 (1992).

Plantinga, C.: "Film theory and aesthetics: notes on a schism," *Journal of Aesthetics and Art Criticism*, 51 (1993), 445–54.

Plaskow, J.: "The Jewish feminist: conflict in identities," *The Jewish Woman: New Perspectives*, ed. E. Koltum (New York: Schocken Books, 1976).

——: "The right question is theological," *On Being a Jewish Feminist*, ed. S. Heschel (New York: Schocken Books, 1983).

——: *Standing Again at Sinai* (San Francisco, CA: Harper, 1990).

——: "Jewish theology in feminist perspectives," *Feminist Perspectives on Jewish Studies*, ed. L. Davidman and S. Terrerbaum (New Haven, CT: Yale University Press, 1994).

Plumwood, V.: "Ecofeminism: an overview and discussion of positions and arguments," *Australasian Journal of Philosophy*, 64 (1986), 120–38.

——: "Women, humanity and nature," *Radical Philosophy*, 48 (1988), 16–24.

——: "Nature, self and gender: feminism, environmental philosophy, and the critique of rationalism," *Hypatia*, 6: 1 (1991), 3–27.

——: *Feminism and the Mastery of Nature* (London: Routledge, 1993).

——: "Androcentrism and anthropocentrism: parallels and politics," *Ecofeminist Perspectives*, ed. K. Warren (Bloomington: Indiana University Press, forthcoming, a).

——: "Ecofeminism and the master subject," *Environmental Ethics*, forthcoming, b.

Pollock, G.: "Degas/images/women: women/Degas/images', *Dealing with Degas: Representations of Women and the Politics of Vision*, ed. R. Kendall and G. Pollock (New York: State University of New York Press, 1987).

Pomeroy, S. B.: *Goddesses, Whores, Wives, and Slaves: Women In Classical Antiquity* (New York: Schocken Books, 1975).

Pompei, G.: "Wages for housework," trans. J. Hall, *Feminist Frameworks*, ed. A.M. Jaggar and P.R. Struhl (New York: McGraw-Hill, 1978), pp. 208–11.

Post, R.: "The social foundations of privacy: community and self in the common law tort," *California Law Review*, 77 (1989), 957–1010.

Potter, E.: "Gender and epistemic negotiation," *Feminist Epistemologies*, ed. L. Alcoff and E. Potter (New York: Routledge, 1993).

Prell, R.: "The vision of woman in classical reform Judaism," *Journal of the American Academy of Religion*, 50 (1983), 575–89.

Prosser, W.: "Privacy," *California Law Review*, 48 (1960), 383–423.

Purdy, L. M.: "Genetic diseases: can having children be immoral?," *Intervention and Reflection: Basic Issues in Medical Ethics*, ed. R. Munson, 4th edn (Belmont, CA: Wadsworth Press, 1992), pp. 429–35.

——: "A feminist view of health," *Feminism & Bioethics: Beyond Reproduction*, ed. S. Wolf (New York: Oxford University Press, 1996).

Pynne, H. H.: "AIDS and gender violence: the enslavement of Burmese women in the Thai sex industry," *Women's Rights, Human Rights: Internationalist Feminist Perspectives*, ed. J. Peters and A. Wolper (New York: Routledge, 1995).

Quine, W. V.: "Two dogmas of empiricism," *From a Logical Point of View* (New York: Harper and Row, 1963).

——: "Epistemology naturalized," *Ontological Relativity and Other Essays* (New York: Columbia University Press, 1969).

——: "On the nature of moral values," *Theories and Things* (Cambridge, MA: Harvard University Press, 1981).

Quraishi, A.: "Her honor: a Muslim gender-egalitarian critique of the rape laws of Pakistan," *Muslim Women's Scholarship-Activism in the United States*, ed. G. Webb, forthcoming.

Rachels, J.: "Why privacy is important," *Philosophy and Public Affairs*, 4 (1975), 323–33.

Radest, H.: "The public and the private: an American fairy tale," *Ethics*, 89 (1979), 280–91.

Radin, M. J.: "Market-inalienability," *Harvard Law Review*, 100 (1988), 1849–1937.

——: "The pragmatist and the feminist," *Readings in the Philosophy of Law*, ed. J. Arthur and W.H. Shaw (Englewood Cliffs, NJ: Prentice Hall, 1993).

Ramanujan, A. K.: *Speaking of Shiva* (Harmondsworth, 1985).

Ramazanoglu, C.: *Feminism and the Contradictions of Oppression* (New York: Routledge, 1989).

——: "Women's sexuality and men's appropriation of desire," *Up Against Foucault: Explorations of some Tensions Between Foucault and Feminism*, ed. C. Ramazanoglu (London: Routledge, 1993), pp. 239–64.

Ras-Work, B.: "Reclaiming religious freedom," *1992 Global Forum of Women*, 2 vols (Dublin: 1992).

Rawls, J.: *A Theory of Justice* (Cambridge, MA: Harvard University Press, 1971).

——: *Political Liberalism* (New York: Columbia University Press, 1993).

Raymond, J.: *The Transsexual Empire: The Making of the She-Male* (Boston: Beacon Press, 1979).

——: *A Passion For Friends: A Philosophy of Female Affection* (Boston: Beacon Press, 1986).

Reardon, B.: *Women and the War System* (New York: Teachers' College Press, 1985).

Reich, J.: "Genderfuck: The law of the dildo," *Discourse*, 15: 1 (1992), 112–27.

Reich, W.: *Mass Psychology of Fascism* (New York: Farrar, Straus and Giroux, 1970).

——: *The Sexual Revolution* (New York: Farrar, Straus and Giroux, 1974).

Reiman, J.: "Privacy, intimacy, and personhood," *Philosophy and Public Affairs*, 6 (1976), 26–44.

Reinelt, C., and Fried, M.: "'I am this child's mother.' A feminist perspective on mothering with a disability," paper presented at the Society for Disability Studies Meeting, Oakland, California, 1991.

Reinharz, S.: *Feminist Methods in Social Research* (Oxford: Oxford University Press, 1992).

Resnik, J.: "On the bias: feminist reconsiderations of the aspirations for our judges," *Southern California Law Review*, 61 (1988), 1877–1944.

Reti, I.: *Unleashing Feminism* (Santa Cruz, CA: Herbooks, 1992).

Rhode, D.: "Association and assimilation," *Northwestern Law Review*, 81 (1986), 106–45.

——: "Occupational inequality," *Duke Law Journal* (December 1988), 1207–41.

——: *Justice and Gender: Sex Discrimination and the Law* (Cambridge, MA: Harvard University Press, 1989).

——: "Definitions of difference," *Theoretical Perspectives on Sexual Difference*, ed. D. Rhode (New Haven, CT: Yale University Press, 1990a), pp. 197–212.

——: "Feminist critical theories," *Stanford Law Review*, 42 (1990b), 617–38.

——: "The politics of paradigms: gender difference and gender disadvantage," *Beyond Equality and Difference*, ed. G. Bock and S. James (New York: Routledge, 1992), pp. 149–63.

Rich, A.: *Of Woman Born: Motherhood as Experience and Institution* (New York: Harper and Row, 1976).

——: *On Lies, Secrets, and Silence* (New York: W. W. Norton & Co., 1979a).

——: "Women and honor: notes on lying," *On Lies, Secrets, and Silence* (New York: W.W. Norton & Co., 1979b).

——: "Compulsory heterosexuality and lesbian existence," *Signs*, 5: 4 (1980), 631–60.

Rich, B.R.: "Feminism and sexuality in the 1980s," *Feminist Studies*, 12 (1986), 525–61.

Richard, N.: "¿Tiene sexo la escritura?," *Debate feminista* [Mexico], 9 (1994), 127–39.

Richards, D.: *Toleration and the Constitution* (New York: Oxford University Press, 1986).

Richards, J. R.: *The Skeptical Feminist: A Philosophical Enquiry* (London: Routledge and Kegan Paul, 1980).

Riley, D.: *"Am I That Name?" Feminism and the Category of "Woman"* (Minneapolis: University of Minnesota Press, 1988).

Roberts, D. E.: "Punishing drug addicts who have babies," *Harvard Law Review*, 104 (1991), 1419–82.

——: "Reconstructing the patient: starting with women of color," *Feminism & Bioethics: Beyond Reproduction*, ed. S. Wolf (New York: Oxford University Press, 1996).

Robertson, J. A.: *Children of Choice: Freedom and the New Reproductive Technologies* (Princeton, NJ: Princeton University Press, 1994).

Robson, R.: *Lesbian (Out)law: Survival Under the Rule of Law* (Ithaca, NY: Firebrand Books, 1992).

Rockefeller, S. C.: *John Dewey: Religious Faith and Democratic Humanism* (New York: Columbia University Press, 1991).

Roe v. Wade, 401 U.S. 113 (1973).

Rohrer, P.: "At what price individualism? The education of Isabel Archer," *Philosophy of Education 1993* (Champaign, IL: Philosophy of Education Society, 1994), pp. 315–24.

Romano, C.: "Between the motion and the act," *The Nation* (November 15, 1993), 563–70.

Rommelspacher, B.: *Mitmenshlichkeit und Unterwerfung: Zur Ambivalenz der weiblichen Moral* (Frankfurt/Main: Campus, 1992).

Roof, J.: *A Lure of Knowledge: Lesbian Sexuality and Theory* (New York: Columbia University Press, 1993).

——: "Lesbians and Lyotard: legitimation and the politics of the name," *The Lesbian Postmodern*, ed. L. Doan (New York: Columbia University Press, 1994), pp. 47–66.

Rooney, P.: "Gendered reason: sex metaphor and conceptions of reason," *Hypatia*, 6 (1991), 77–103.

——: "Recent work in feminist discussions of reason," *American Philosophical Quarterly*, 31: 1 (1994), 1–16.

Root, M. P. P, ed.: *Racially Mixed People in America* (Newbury Park, NY: Sage Publications, 1992).

Rorty, R.: *Consequences of Pragmatism* (Minneapolis: University of Minnesota Press, 1982).

——: "Feminism and pragmatism," *Michigan Quarterly Review*, 30 (1991), 231–58.

——: "Feminism, ideology, and deconstruction: a pragmatist view," *Hypatia*, 8 (1993), 96–103.

Rose, H.: "Hand, brain and heart: a feminist epistemology for the natural sciences," *Signs*, 9: 1 (1983).

——: *Love, Power and Knowledge: Towards a Feminist Transformation of the Sciences* (Cambridge: Polity, 1994).

Rose, J., and Mitchell, J., eds.: *Feminine Sexuality: Jacques Lacan and Ecole Freudienne*, trans. J. Rose (London: Macmillan, 1982).

Rose, S.: "Introduction II," *Feminine Sexuality: Jacques Lacan and Ecole Freudienne*, trans. S. Rose (London: Macmillan, 1982).

Rosenberg, R.: *Beyond Separate Spheres: Intellectual Roots of Modern Feminism* (New Haven, CT: Yale University Press, 1982).

Rosenblatt, L. M.: *The Reader the Text the Poem: The Transactional Theory of the Literary Work* (Carbondale: Southern Illinois University Press, 1994).

Rothenberg, P.: "The construction, deconstruction, and reconstruction of difference," *Hypatia*, 5: 1 (1990), 42–57.

Rothman, B. K.: *The Tentative Pregnancy: Prenatal Diagnosis and the Future of Motherhood* (New York: Viking Press, 1986).

——: "Motherhood: beyond patriarchy," *Nova Law Review*, 13 (1989a), 481–6.

——: *Recreating Motherhood* (New York: W. W. Norton & Co. 1989b).

Rothman, D. J.: "Ethics and human experimentation," *New England Journal of Medicine*, 317: 19 (November 5, 1987), 1195–9.

Rousseau, J.: *Emile: or, On Education*, trans. A. Bloom (New York: Basic Books, 1979).

Rowbotham, S.: *Woman, Resistance and Revolution* (New York: Random House, 1972).

——: *Hidden from History* (London: Pluto, 1973a).

——: *Woman's Consciousness, Man's World* (Baltimore: Penguin, 1973b).

——: *Women in Movement: Feminism and Social Action* (London: Routledge, 1992).

——, Segal, L., and Wainwright, H.: *Beyond the Fragments: Feminism and the Making of Socialism* (London: Merlin Press, 1979).

Rowland, R.: "Making women visible in the embryo experimentation debate," *Bioethics*, 1: 2 (1987), 179–88.

——: *Living Laboratories: Women and Reproductive Technologies* (Bloomington: Indiana University Press, 1992).

Royal Commission on New Reproductive Technologies: *Proceed with Care: Final Report* (Ottawa, Canada: Minister of Government Services, 1993).

Rubenfeld, J.: "The right of privacy," *Harvard Law Review*, 102 (1989), 737–807.

Rubin, G.: "The traffic in women," *Toward an Anthropology of Women*, ed. R. Reiter (New York: Monthly Review Press, 1975), pp. 157–210.

——: "Sexual politics, the new right and the sexual fringe," *The Age Taboo: Gay Male Sexuality, Power and Consent*, ed. D. Tsang (Boston: Alyson Publications, 1981).

——: "Thinking sex: notes for a radical theory on the politics of sexuality," *Pleasure and Danger: Exploring Female Sexuality*, ed. C. Vance (Boston: Routledge and Kegan Paul, 1984), pp. 267–319.

——, English, D., and Hollibaugh, A.: "Talking sex: a conversation on sexuality and feminism," *Socialist Review*, 11: 4 (1981), 43–62.

Rubio Castro, A.: "El feminismo de la diferencial: los argumentos de una igualdad compleja," *Revista de Estudios Politicos* (Nueva Epoca) [Spain], 70 (1990), 185–207.

Ruch, E. A., and Anyanwu, K. C.: *African Philosophy* (Rome: Catholic Book Agency, 1981).

Ruddick, S.: "Maternal thinking," *Feminist Studies*, 6 (1980), 342–67.

——: "Preservative love and military destruction," *Mothering: Essays in Feminist Theory*, ed. J. Trebilcot (Totowa, NJ: Rowman and Allanheld, 1983), pp. 231–63.

——: "Remarks on the sexual politics of reason," *Women and Moral Theory*, ed. E. Kittay and D. Meyers (Savage, MD: Rowman and Littlefield, 1987), pp. 237–61.

——: *Maternal Thinking: Toward a Politics of Peace* (New York: Basic Books, 1989).

——: "Notes on a feminist peace politics," *Gendering War Talk*, ed. M. Cooke and A. Woollacott (Princeton, NJ: Princeton University Press, 1993).

——: "Injustice in families: assault and domination," *Justice and Care: Essential Readings in Feminist Ethics*, ed. V. Held (Boulder, CO: Westview Press, 1995).

——: "Rethinking 'Maternal' Politics," *The Politics of Motherhood*, ed. A. Jetter, A. Orleck, and D. Taylor (Hanover: New England University Press, forthcoming).

Ruether, R. R.: *New Woman/New Earth: Sexist Ideologies and Human Liberation* (New York: Seabury, 1975).

——: *Sexism and God-Talk: Toward a Feminist Theology* (Boston: Beacon Press, 1983).

——: *Gaia and God: An Ecofeminist Theology of Earth Healing* (San Francisco, CA: Harper, 1992).

Rumf, M.: "'Mystical aura': imagination and reality of the 'maternal' in Horkheimer's writings," *Max Horkheimer: New Perspectives* (Cambridge: MIT Press, 1993), pp. 309–34.

Rumsey, J.: "Re-vision of agency in Kant's moral theory," *Feminist Interpretations of Kant*, ed. R. Schott (University Park: Pennsylvania State University Press, 1997).

Russell, D.: *The Politics of Rape: The Victim's Perspective* (New York: Stein and Day, 1975).

Rust, P.: *Bisexuality and the Challenge to Lesbian Politics* (New York; New York University Press, 1995).

Ruth, S.: "Methodocracy, misogyny and bad faith," *Men's Studies Modified: The Impact of Feminism on the Academic Disciplines*, ed. D. Spencer (Oxford: Pergamon Press, 1981).

Rutnam, R.: "IVF in Australia: towards a feminist technology assessment," *Issues in Reproductive and Genetic Engineering*, 4: 2 (1991), 143–54.

Sadker, M., and Sadker, D.: *Failing At Fairness: How America's Schools Cheat Girls* (New York: Charles Scribner's Sons, 1994).

Sahih Al-Bukhari, I.: *Abu'Abd Allah Muhammad Ibn Ismail Al Bukhari*, trans. M Asad (Lahore: Ashraf Publications, 1938).

Salecl, R.: *The Spoils of Freedom: Psychoanalysis and Feminism after the Fall of Socialism* (New York: Routledge, 1994).

Salleh, A.: "Deeper than deep ecology," *Environmental Ethics*, 6: 1 (1984), 339–45.

——: "The ecofeminism/deep ecology debate," *Environmental Ethics*, 14: 3 (1992), 195–216.

Salmon, N.: "The art historical canon: sins of omission," *EnGendering Knowledge*, ed. J. Hackman and E. Messer-Davidow (Knoxville: University of Tennessee Press, 1991), pp. 222–36.

Sandel, M.: *Liberalism and the Limits of Justice* (Cambridge: Cambridge University Press, 1982).

——: *Democracy's Discontent: America in Search of a Public Philosophy* (Cambridge, MA: Harvard University Press, 1996).

Sands, K.: *Escape from Paradise: Evil Tragedy in Feminist Theology* (Minneapolis: Fortress Press, 1994).

Sangari, K.: "Mirabai and the Spiritual Economy of Bhakti," *Economic and Political Weekly* (July 7–14, 1990).

——, and Vaid, S., ed.: *Recasting Women: Essays in Colonial History* (New Delhi: Kali for Women, 1989).

Sanger, M.: *Woman and the New Race* (New York: Brentano's Press, 1920).

Santa Cruz, M. I., Bach, A. M., Femenías, M. L., Gianella, A., and Roulet, M.: *Mujeres y Filosofia (I): Teoría filosófica de Género* (Buenos Aires: Centro Editor de América Latina, 1994).

Sargent, L, ed.: *Women and Revolution* (Boston: South End Press, 1981).

Sarkar, T.: "Women's agency within authoritarian communalism: the Rashtra-sevika Smitiand Ramjanmabhoomi," *Hindus and Others*, ed. G. Pandey New Delhi: (Viking Press, 1993).

Sartre, J.-P.: *Being and Nothingness*, trans. H.E. Barnes [1943] (New York: Philosophical Library, 1953).

——: *Critique of Dialectical Reason*, trans. A. Sheridan-Smith [1960] (London: New Left Books, 1976).

Sawicki, J.: "Foucault, feminism, and questions of identity," *The Cambridge Companion to Foucault*, ed. G. Gutting (Cambridge: Cambridge University Press, 1994), pp. 286–313.

Saxe, L. L.: "Sadomasochism and exclusion," *Adventures in Lesbian Philosophy*, ed. C. Card (Bloomington: Indiana University Press, 1994), pp. 64–77.

Saxonhouse, A. W.: *Fear of Diversity: The Birth of Political Science in Ancient Greek Thought* (Chicago, IL: University of Chicago Press, 1992).

Saxton, M. and Howe, F., eds.: *With Wings: An Anthology of Literature By and About Women With Disabilities* (New York: The Feminist Press at the City University of New York, 1987.)

Sayers, J.: "Science, sexual difference and feminism," *Analyzing Gender*, ed. B. B. Hess and M. Marx (Newbury Park, NY: Sage Publications, 1987), pp. 68.

Scaltas, P. W.: "Virtue without gender in Socrates," *Hypatia*, 7: 3 (1992), 126–37.

Scarry, E.: *The Body in Pain* (Oxford: Oxford University Press, 1985).

Scheman, N.: "Individualism and the objects of psychology," *Discovering Reality: Feminist Perspectives on Epistemology Metaphysics, Methodology, and Philosophy of Science*, ed. S. Harding and M. Hintikka (Dordrecht, Holland: D. Reidel Publishing Co., 1983).

——: "Missing mothers/desiring daughters: framing the sight of women," *Critical Inquiry* 15 (1988), 62–89.

——: "Though this be method, yet there's madness in it," *A Mind of One's Own: Feminist Essays on Reason and Objectivity*, ed. L. Antony and C. Witt (Boulder, CO: Westview Press, 1993a), pp. 145–70.

——: *Engenderings: Constructions of Knowledge, Authority, and Privilege* (New York: Routledge, 1993b).

——: "Queering the center by centering the queer," *Feminists Rethink the Self*, ed. D. Meyers (Boulder, CO: Westview Press, 1996).

Scheppele, K. L.: "The re-vision of rape law," *University of Chicago Law Review*, 54 (1987), 1095–116.

——: "Just the facts, Ma'am: sexualized violence, evidentiary habits, and the revision of truth," *New York Law School Law Review*, 37 (1992), 123–72.

Schiebinger, L.: "Skeletons in the closet," *The Making of the Modern Body*, ed. C. Gallagher and T. Laqueur (Berkeley: University of California Press, 1987), pp. 42–82.

Schmid, G., and Weitzel, R., eds.: *Sex Discrimination and Equal Opportunity: the Labor Market and Employment Policy* (New York: St Martin's Press, 1984).

Schneider, C.: *Shame, Exposure, and Privacy* (Boston: Beacon Press, 1977).

Schneider, E.: "The dialectic of rights and politics: perspectives from the women's movement," *New York University Law Review*, 61 (1986), 593–652.

——: "The violence of privacy," *Connecticut Law Review*, 23 (1991), 973–99.

——: "Particularity and generality: challenges of feminist theory and practice in work on woman-abuse," *New York University Law Review*, 67 (1992), 520–68.

Schoeman, F.: *Philosophical Dimensions of Privacy* (Cambridge: Cambridge University Press, 1992a).

——: *Privacy and Social Freedom* (Cambridge: Cambridge University Press, 1992b).

Schor, N., and Weed, E.: *The Essential Difference* (Bloomington: Indiana University Press, 1994).

Schott, R.: *Cognition and Eros: A Critique of the Kantian Paradigm* (Boston: Beacon Press, 1988).

——: "The gender of enlightenment," *What is Enlightenment?*, ed. J. Schmidt (Berkeley: University of California Press, 1996).

Schrage, L.: "Should feminists oppose prostitution?," *Ethics*, 99 (1989), 347–61.

Schroder, H.: "Kant's patriarchal order," *Feminist Interpretations of Kant*, ed. R. Schott (University Park: Pennsylvania State University Press, 1997).

Schroeder, J.: "The taming of the shrew: the liberal attempt to tame feminist radical theory." *Yale Journal of Law and Feminism.* 5 (1992). 123–80.

Schultz, V.: "Telling stories about women and work," *Harvard Law Review*, 103 (1990), 1749–1843.

Schüssler Fiorenza, E.: *In Memory of Her: A Feminist Theological Reconstruction of Christian Origins* (New York: Crossroad, 1983).

——: *Bread Not Stone: The Challenge of Feminist Biblical Interpretation* (Boston: Beacon Press, 1985).

——: *Jesus: Miriam's Child, Sophia's Prophet* (New York: Continuum, 1994).

Schutte, O.: *Cultural Identity and Social Liberation in Latin American Thought* (Albany: State University of New York Press, 1993).

——: "Spanish and Latin American feminist philosophy," *Hypatia*, 9 (1994), 142–94.

Schwartzenbach, S.: "Rawls and ownership: the forgotten category of reproductive labor," *Canadian Journal of Philosophy*, 13 (1987), 139–66.

Schweickart, D.: *Against Capitalism* (New York: Cambridge University Press, 1993).

Scott, H.: *Does Socialism Liberate Women?* (Boston: Beacon Press, 1974).

Scott, J.: "Gender: a useful category for historical analysis?," *American Historical Review*, 91: 5 (1986), 1053–75.

——: *Gender and the Politics of History* (New York: Columbia, 1988).

——: "Deconstructing equality-versus-difference," *Conflicts in Feminism*, ed. M. Hirsch and E. F. Keller (New York: Routledge, 1990).

——: "The evidence of experience," *Critical Inquiry*, 17: 4 (1991), 773–97.

——: "Experience," *Feminists Theorize the Political*, ed. J. Butler and J. W. Scott (New York: Routledge, 1992).

Scott, R.: *The Making of Blind Men: a Study of Adult Socialization* (New York: Russel Sage Foundation, 1969).

Scutt, J., ed.: *The Baby Machine: Commercialization of Motherhood* (Carlton, Victoria: McCulloch, 1988).

Sedgwick, E.: "Can Kant's ethics survive the feminist critique?," *Pacific Philosophical Quarterly*, 71 (1990a), 60–79.

——: *Epistemology of the Closet* (Berkeley: University of California Press, 1990b).

——: *Tendencies* (Durham: Duke University Press, 1993).

Segal, L.: *Sex Exposed: Sexuality and the Pornography Debate* (New Jersey: Rutgers University Press, 1993).

Segal, M.: "The argument for female combatants," *Female Soldiers: Combatants or Non-Combatants?*, ed. N. Loring Goldman (Westport: Greenwood Press, 1982).

Segers, M.: "The Catholic Bishop's letter on war and peace: a feminist perspective," *Feminist Studies*, 11: 3 (1985).

Seigfried, C. H.: *William James's Radical Reconstruction of Philosophy* (Albany: State University of New York Press, 1990).

—— ed.: "Feminism and Pragmatism Special Issue," *Hypatia*, 8 (1993a).

——: "Shared communities of interest: feminism and pragmatism," *Hypatia*, 8: 2 (1993b).

——: *Pragmatism and Feminism: The Constant Reweaving of the Social Fabric* (Chicago, IL: University of Chicago Press, 1996).

Sen, A.: *Commodities and Capabilities* (Amsterdam: North Holland, 1985).

——: "Gender and cooperative conflict," *Persistent Inequalities*, ed. I. Trinker (New York: Oxford University Press, 1989), pp. 123–49.

——: "Capability and well-being," *The Quality of Life*, ed. M. Nussbaum and A. Sen (Oxford: Clarendon Press, 1993).

Sevenhuijsen, S.: "Feminist ethics and public health care policies," *Feminist Ethics and Social Policy*, ed. P. DiQuinzio and I. M. Young (Bloomington: Indiana University Press, 1996).

Shafer, C. and Frye, M.: "Rape and respect," *Feminism and Philosophy*, ed. M. Vetterling-Braggin, F. Elliston, and J. English (Totowa, NJ: Littlefield, Adams, 1977), pp. 333–46.

Shanley, M. L.: "'Surrogate mothering' and women's freedom: A critique of contracts for human reproduction," *Signs*, 18: 3 (1993), 618–39.

661

Shanner, L.: "The right to procreate: when rights claims have gone wrong," *McGill Law Journal*, 40: 4 (1995), 823–74.

Shariati, A.: *Fatima Is Fatima*, trans. L. Bakhtiar (Iran: The Shariati Foundation, n.d.).

Sharoni, S.: *Gender and the Israeli-Palestinian Conflict* (Syracuse: University of Syracuse Press, 1995).

Sher, G.: "Our preferences, ourselves," *Philosophy and Public Affairs*, 12 (1982), 34–50.

Sherry, S.: "Civic virtue and the feminine voice in constitutional adjudication," *Virginia Law Review*, 72 (1986), 543–616.

Sherwin, S.: "Feminist ethics and in vitro fertilization," *Canadian Journal of Philosophy*, 13 (1987), 265–84.

——: "Abortion through a feminist lens." *Dialogue: Canadian Philosophical Review*, 30: 3 (1991), 327–42.

——: *No Longer Patient: Feminist Ethics and Health Care* (Philadelphia, PA: Temple University Press, 1992).

Shiva, V.: *Staying Alive, Women, Ecology and Development* (New Delhi: Kali for Women, 1989).

——: *The Violence of the Green Revolution* (Goa: The Other India Press, 1992).

Shrage, L.: "Some implications of comparable worth," *Social Theory and Practice*, 13: 1 (1987).

——: "Feminist film aesthetics: a contextual approach," *Hypatia*, 5: 2 (1990a), 137–48.

——: "Should feminists oppose prostitution?," *Feminism and Political Theory*, ed. C. Sunstein (Chicago, IL: University of Chicago Press, 1990b), pp. 185–200.

——: *Moral Dilemmas of Feminism* (New York: Routledge, 1994).

——: "Transgressions: confessions of an assimilated Jew," *American Mixed Race: Exploring Microdiversity*, ed. N. Zack (Lanham, MD: Rowman and Littlefield, 1995), pp. 387–96.

Shulz, M.: "The semantic derogation of woman," *Language and Sex: Difference and Dominance*, ed. B. Thorne and N. Henley (Rowley, MA: Newbury House Publishers, 1975).

Schusterman, R.: *Analytic Aesthetics* (New York: Blackwell, 1989).

Sichel, B.: "Ethics of caring and the institutional ethics committee," *Hypatia*, 4: 2 (1989), 45–56.

——: "Education and Thought in Virginia Woolf's 'To the Lighthouse,'" *Philosophy of Education 1992*, (Champaign, IL: Philosophy of Education Society, 1993), pp. 191–200.

Sichtermann, B.: "Gibt es eine weibliche Asthetic?," *Wer ist Wie? Uber den Unterschield der Geschlechter* (Berlin: Wagenbach, 1987).

Silverman, K.: *Male Subjectivity at the Margins* (New York: Routledge, 1992).

Silvers, A.: "'Defective' agents: equality, difference and the tyranny of the normal," *Journal of Social Philosophy*, 25 (June 1994).

——: "Reconciling equality to difference: caring (f)or justice for people with disabilities," *Hypatia*, 10 (1995), 31–55.

Simons, M. A.: "Racism and feminism: a schism in the sisterhood," *Feminist Studies*, 5: 2 (1979), 384–401.

——: *Re-Reading the Canon: Feminist Interpretations of Simone de Beauvoir* (University Park: Pennsylvania State University Press. 1995).

Singer, L.: *Erotic Welfare: Sexual Theory and Politics in the Age of Epidemic* (New York: Routledge, 1993).

Singer, P., and Wells, D.: *The Reproductive Revolution: New Ways of Making Babies* (Oxford: Oxford University Press, 1984).

Sisters in Islam: *Are Muslim Men Allowed to Beat Their Wives?* (Kuala Lumpur: United Selangor Press Sdn Bhd, 1991a).

——: *Are Women and Men Equal Before Allah?* (Kuala Lumpur: United Selangor Press Sdn Bhd, 1991b).

Sisters in Islam, Muslim Women's League et al. "Letter to the Editor," *Forum '95*, September 7, 1995.

Sklar, K. K.: "Hull House in the 1890s: A community of women reformers', *Signs*, 10 (1985), 658–77.

Slapsak, S.: *Ogledi o bezbriznosti* (Belgrade: Radio B92, 1994).

Slicer, D.: "Your daughter or your dog?," *Hypatia*, 6: 1 (1991), 108–24.

——: "Wrongs of passage: the challenges to the maturing of ecofeminism," *Ecological Feminism*, ed. K. Warren (London: Routledge, 1994).

Smart, C.: *Feminism and the Power of Law* (London: Routledge, 1989).

——: *Law, Crime, and Sexuality: Essays in Feminism* (London: Sage Publications, 1995).

——, and Sevenhuijsen, eds.: *Child Custody and the Politics of Gender* (New York: Routledge, 1989).

Smith, B.: "The new European philosophy," *Philosophy and Political Change in Eastern Europe*, ed. B. Smith (La Salle, IL: Hegler Institute, 1993).

Smith, D.: *The Everyday World as Problematic* (Toronto: University of Toronto Press, 1987).

Smith, J.: "Analyzing ethical conflict in the transracial adoption debate," *Hypatia*, 11: 2 (1996), 1–33.

Smith, P.: "Feminist jurisprudence: social change and conceptual evolution," *American Philosophical Association Newsletter* (Spring 1995a).

——: "Feminist legal critics: The reluctant radicals," *Radical Philosophy of Law*, ed. D. Caudill and S. J. Gold (Atlantic Highlands, NJ: Humanities Press, 1995b), pp. 73–87.

—— ed.: *Feminist Jurisprudence* (New York: Oxford University Press, 1993).

Smith, S.: "Paradigm dominance in international relations: the development of international relations as a social science," *The Study of International Relations: The State of the Art*, ed. H.C. Dyer and L. Mangasarian (New York: St Martin's Press, 1989).

Sober, E.: *Philosophy of Biology* (Oxford: Oxford University Press, 1993).

Soble, A.: *Pornography: Marxism, Feminism and the Future of Sexuality* (New Haven, CT: Yale University Press, 1986).

——: *The Philosophy of Sex: Contemporary Readings* (Savage, MD: Rowan and Littlefield, 1991).

Sodipo, J. O., and Hallen, B.: *Knowledge, Belief and Witchcraft: Analytic Experiences in African Philosophy* (London: Ethnographica, 1986).

Sommers, C. Hoff: *Who Stole Feminism?: How Women have Betrayed Women* (New York: Simon and Schuster, 1994).

——: and Steinberg, D., eds.: *Made to Order: The Myth of Reproductive and Genetic Progress* (New York: Pergamon Press, 1987).

Spallone, P.: *Beyond Conception: The New Politics of Reproduction* (Granby, MA: Bergin and Garvey, 1989).

Spelman, E.: "Aristotle and the politicization of the soul," *Discovering Reality: Feminist Perspectives on Epistemology, Metaphysics, Methodology, and Philosophy of Science*, ed. S. Harding and M. Hintikka (Dordrecht, Holland: D. Reidel Publishing Co., 1983).

——: *Inessential Woman: Problems of Exclusion in Feminist Thought* (Boston: Beacon Press, 1988).

——: "Anger and insubordination," *Women, Knowledge, and Reality: Explorations in Feminist Philosophy*, ed. A. Garry and M. Pearsall (Boston: Unwin Hyman, 1989).

——: "The virtue of feeling the feeling of virtue," *Feminist Ethics*, ed. C. Card (Kansas: University Press of Kansas, 1991), pp. 213–32.

Spender, D.: *Man Made Language* (New York: Harper Collins, 1980).

——: *Men's Studies Modified: The Impact of Feminism on the Academic Disciplines* (Oxford: Pergamon Press, 1981).

——: *Invisible Women: The Schooling Scandal* (London: Writers and Readers Publishing Cooperative, 1982).

——: *The Writing or the Sex? Or Why You Don't Have to Read Women's Writing to Know it's Not Good* (New York: Pergamon Press, 1989).

Spillers, H.: "Mama's baby, Papa's maybe: an American grammar book," *Diacritics*, 17: 2 (1987), 64–81.

Spivak, G.: *In Other Worlds: Essays in Cultural Politics* (New York: Methuen, 1987a).

——: "French feminism in an international frame," *In Other Worlds: Essays in Cultural Politics*, ed. G. Spivak (New York: Methuen, 1987b), pp. 134–53.

——: "Can the subaltern speak?," *Marxism and the Interpretation of Culture*, ed. C. Nelson and L. Grossberg (Urbana: University of Illinois Press, 1988).

——: *The Post-colonial Critic: Interviews, Strategies, Dialogues*, ed. S. Harasym (New York: Routledge, 1990).

——, and Rooney, E.: "In a word, interview," *differences*, 19 (1994), 713–38.

Spretnak, C.: "Toward an ecofeminist spirituality," *Healing the Wounds*, ed. J. Plant (Philadelphia: New Society Publishers, 1989), pp. 127–32.

——: "Ecofeminism: our roots and flowering," *Reweaving the World*, ed. I. Diamond and G. Orenstein (San Francisco, CA: Sierra Club Books, 1990), pp. 3–14.

Springer, C.: "Sex, memories, and angry women," *Flame Wars: The Discourse of Cyberculture*, ed. M. Dery (Durham: Duke University Press, 1994), pp. 157–77.

Squires, J.: "Citizenship: androgynous or engendered participation," *Schweizerishes Jahrbuch für Politische Wissenschaft*, 34 (1994), 51–62.

Stabile, C.: "Shooting the mother: fetal photography and the politics of disappearance," *Camera Obscura*, 28 (1992), 179–205.

Stacey, J.: *Patriarchy and Socialist Revolution in China* (Berkeley: University of California Press, 1983).

Stanley v. Georgia, 394 U.S. 557 (1967).

Stanley, J.: "Paradigmatic women: the prostitute," *Papers in Language Variation*, ed. D. L. Shores and C. P. Hines (Birmingham: University of Alabama Press, 1977).

Stanley, L., and Wise, S.: *Breaking Out: Feminist Consciousness and Feminist Research* (London: Routledge and Kegan Paul, 1983).

Stanton, D.: "Language and revolution," *The Future of Difference*, ed. H. Eisenstein and A. Jardin (Boston: G. K. Hall & Co., 1980), pp. 73–87.

——: "Difference on trial," *Feminism and Modern French Philosophy*, ed. J. Allen and I. Young (Bloomington: Indiana University Press, 1989), pp. 156–79.

Stanworth, M., ed.: *Reproductive Technologies: Gender, Motherhood and Medicine* (Minneapolis: University of Minnesota Press, 1987).

Steady, F. C.: "Women and collective action: Female models in transition," *Theorizing Black Feminisms: The Visionary Pragmatism of Black Women*, ed. S. James and A. P. A. Busia (New York: Routledge, 1993), pp. 90–101.

Stein, A.: "Sisters and queers," *Socialist Review*, 22: 1 (1992), 33–55.

——: *Sisters, Sexperts, Queers: Beyond the Lesbian Nation* (New York: A Plume Book/Penguin, 1993).

Steinberg, R., and Haignere, L.: "Separate but equivalent: equal pay for work of comparable worth," *Beyond Methodology: Feminist Scholarship as Lived Research*, ed. M. Fonow and J. Cook (Bloomington: Indiana University Press, 1991), pp. 154–70.

Steinbock, B.: "Adultery," *The Philosophy of Sex*, ed. A. Soble (Savage, MD: Rowan and Littlefield, 1991), pp. 187–92.

Stepan, N. L.: "Race and gender: the role of analogy in science," *Anatomy of Racism*, ed. D. T. Goldberg (Minneapolis: University of Minnesota Press, 1990), pp. 38–57.

Stephen, J. F.: *Liberty, Equality, and Fraternity* (Cambridge: Cambridge University Press, 1967).

Sterba, J.: *How To Make People Just* (Lanham, MD: Rowman and Littlefield, 1989).

——: *Justice for Here and Now* (forthcoming).

Stiehm, J.: "The unit of political analysis: our Aristotelian hangover," *Discovering Reality: Feminist Perspectives on Epistemology, Metaphysics, Methodology, and Philosophy of Science*, ed. S. Harding and M. Hintikka (Dordrecht, Holland: D. Reidel Publishing, 1983).

——: *Arms and the Enlisted Woman* (Philadelphia: Temple University Press, 1989).

Stimpson, C.: "Thy neighbor's wife, thy neighbor's servants," *Woman in Sexist Society: Studies in Power and Powerlessness*, ed. V. Gornick and B. Moran (New York: Basic Books, 1971), pp. 622–57.

Stone, L., ed.: *The Education Feminism Reader* (New York: Routledge, 1994).

Straumanis, J.: "Generic 'man' and mortal woman," *The Structure of Knowledge: A Feminist Perspective*, ed. B. Reid, Proceedings of the 4th Annual GLCA Women's Studies Association, November 1978, pp. 25–32.

Stroud, S.: "Dworkin and *Casey* on abortion," *Philosophy and Public Affairs*, 25: 2 (1996), 140–70.

Sunder Rajan, R.: *Real and Imagined Women: Gender, Culture and Postcolonialism* (London: Routledge, 1993).

Sunstein, C.: "Neutrality in Constitutional law," *Columbia Law Review*, 92 (1992), 1–52.

Superson, A.: "A feminist definition of sexual harassment," *Journal of Social Philosophy*, 24: 1 (1993), 46–64.

Swerdlow, A.: "Pure milk, not poison: Women strike for peace and the test ban treaty of 1963," *Rocking the Ship of State*, ed. A. Harris and Y. King (Boulder, CO: Westview Press, 1989).

Swiderski, E.: "The crisis of continuity in post-Soviet Russian philosophy," *Philosophy and Political Change in Eastern Europe*, ed. B. Smith (La Salle: The Monist Institute Library of Philosophy, 1993).

Synthèse: special issue on feminism and science, 104: 3 (1995).

Szalai, J.: "Some aspects of the changing situation of women in Hungary," *Signs*, 17: 1 (1991), 152–70.

Taft, J.: *The Woman Movement from the Point of View of Social Consciousness* (Menasha, WI: Collegiate Press, 1915).

Tagg, J.: "Postmodernism and the born-again avant-garde," *The Cultural Politics of "Postmodernism,"* ed. J. Tagg (Binghamton: State University of New York Press, 1989).

Tao Chunfang, Jiang Rongru, Zhu Mingmei, eds.: *An Outline of the Marxist Connection of Women* (Beijing: Women's Press, 1991).

Tao, J.: "Feminism and justice," paper presented at the International Symposium on Chinese Women and Feminist Thought (Beijing: June 1995).

Taub, N. and Schneider, E.: "Women's subordination and the role of law," *The Politics of Law: A Progressive Critique*, ed. D. Kairys (New York: Pantheon Books, 1982), pp. 117–39.

Taylor, B.: *Eve and the New Jerusalem: Socialism and Feminism in the Nineteenth Century* (New York: Pantheon, 1983).

Taylor, C.: "Cross purposes: the liberal-communitarian debate," *Liberalism and the Moral Life*, ed. N.L. Rosenblum (Cambridge, 1989).

Teachout, T.: "The pornography report that never was," *Commentary*, 84: 2 (1987), 51–7.

Tempels, P.: *Bantu Philosophy* (Paris: Présence Africaine, 1959).

Terrelonge, P.: "Feminist consciousness and black women," *Women: A Feminist Perspective*, ed. J. Freeman (Mountain View, CA: Mayfield Publishers, 1989).

Thalberg, I.: "Reverse discrimination and the future," *Philosophical Forum*, V: 1–2 (1973–4), 294–308.

Thanwi, Ashraf Ali: *Heavenly Ornaments* (Pakistan: Dural-Ishaat, 1987).

Tharu, S., and Lalita, K., eds.: *Women Writing in India*, 2 vols (Delhi: Oxford University Press, 1991, 1993).

Thayer-Bacon, B.: "Is modern critical thinking sexist?," *Inquiry: Critical Thinking Across the Disciplines*, 8 (1992), 323–40.

——: "Caring and its relationship to critical thinking," *Educational Theory*, 43: 3 (1993) 323–40.

Theweleit, K.: *Male Fantasies*, 2 vols (Minneapolis: University of Minnesota Press, 1987, 1990).

——: "The bomb's womb," *Gendering War Talk*, ed. M. Cooke and A. Woollacott (Princeton, NJ: Princeton University Press, 1993).

Thistlewaite, S. B.: *Sex, Race and God: Christian Feminism in Black and White* (New York: Crossroad, 1989).

Thomson, J.: "The right to privacy," *Philosophy and Public Affairs*, 4 (1975), 295–314.

Thompson, A.: "Friendship and moral character," *Philosophy of Education 1989* (Champaign, IL: Philosophy of Education Society, 1990), pp. 61–75.

Thompson, J. J.: "A defense of abortion," *Philosophy and Public Affairs*, 1: 1 (1971), 47–66.

——: "Women and the high priests of reason," *Radical Philosophy*, 34 (1983).

——: *The Realm of Rights* (Cambridge, MA: Harvard University Press, 1990).

Thompson, P.: "Beyond gender: equity issues for home economics education," *Theory Into Practice*, 25: 4 (1986), 272–83.

Thornburgh v. *American College*, 476 U.S. 747 (1986).

Thorne, B., and Henley, N., eds.: *Language and Sex: Difference and Dominance* (Rowley, MA: Newbury House Publishers, 1975).

Three Rivers, A.: *Cultural Etiquette* (Indian Valley, VA: Market Wimmin, 1990).

Tickner, J.: *Gender and International Relations: Feminist Perspectives on Achieving Global Security* (New York: Columbia University Press, 1992).

Tirrell, L.: "Storytelling and moral agency," *Journal of Aesthetics and Art Criticism*, 48: 2 (1990), 115–26.

——: "Definition and power," *Hypatia*, 8: 4 (1993), 1–34.

Tong, R.: "Feminism, pornography, and censorship," *Social Theory and Practice*, 8: 1 (1982), 1–17.

——: *Feminist Thought* (Boulder, CO: Westview Press, 1988).

——: "The overdue death of a feminist chameleon: taking a stand on surrogacy arrangements," *Journal of Social Philosophy*, 21 (1990), 40–56.

——: "Women, pornography, and the law," *The Philosophy of Sex: Contemporary Readings*, ed. A. Soble (Savage, MD: Rowan and Littlefield, 1991), pp. 301–16.

——: *Feminine and Feminist Ethics* (Belmont, CA: Wadsworth, 1993).

Torrey, M.: "When will we be believed? rape myths and the idea of a fair trial in rape prosecutions," *University of California at Davis Law Review*, 24 (1991), 1013–71.

Trebilcot, J.: "Taking responsibility for sexuality," *Women and Mental Health: Conference Proceedings*, ed. E. Barton, K. Watts-Penny, and B. Hillyer (Norman, OK: University of Oklahoma Women's Studies Program, 1982).

——, ed.: *Mothering: Essays in Feminist Theory* (Totowa, NJ: Rowman and Allanheld, 1983a).

——: *Taking Responsibility for Sexuality* (Berkeley: Acacia Books, 1983b).

——: "Ethics of method," *Feminist Ethics*, ed. C. Card (Lawrence: University of Kansas Press, 1991), p. 50.

——: "Decentering sex," *Les Talk*, 2: 4 (December 1992).

——: *Dyke Ideas: Process, Politics, and Daily Life* (Albany: State University of New York Press, 1993).

Trinh T. Minh-ha: *Woman, Native, Other* (Bloomington: Indiana University Press, 1989).

Tronto, J.: "Beyond gender difference," *Signs*, 12 (1987).

——: *Moral Boundaries: A Political Argument for an Ethic of Care* (New York: Routledge, 1993).

——: "Care as a basis for radical political judgments," *Hypatia*, 10: 3 (1995).

Trujillo, C., ed.: *Chicana Lesbians: The Girls Our Mothers Warned Us About* (Berkeley: Third Woman Press, 1991).

Tuana, N., ed.: *Feminism and Science* (Bloomington: Indiana University Press, 1989).

——: *Woman and the History of Philosophy* (New York: Paragon House, 1992).

——: *The Less Noble Sex: Scientific, Religious, and Philosophical Conceptions of Woman's Nature* (Bloomington: Indiana University Press, 1993).

——, ed.: *Feminist Interpretations of Plato* (University Park: Pennsylvania State University Press, 1994).

Tubia, Nahid, et al.: *Al-Mar'ah al-Arabia: Lamha 'an al-Tanawwu' wa al-Taghyir* (*The Arab Woman: A Glance at Variety and Change*) (Cairo: International Population Council, 1995).

Turley, D.: "The feminist debate on pornography: an unorthodox interpretation," *Socialist Review*, 16:3–4 (1986), 81–96.

Udis-Kessler, A.: "Bisexuality in an essentialist world," *Bisexuality: A Reader and Sourcebook*, ed. T. Geller (Ojai, CA: Times Change Press, 1990).

Umansky, E. and Ashton, D., eds.: *Four Centuries of Jewish Women's Spirituality* (Boston: Beacon Press, 1992).

Uniacke, S.: "*In Vitro* fertilization and the right to reproduce," *Bioethics*, 1: 3 (1987), 241–54.

Vadas, M.: "A first look at the pornography/civil rights ordinance," *Journal of Philosophy*, 84: 9 (1987), 487–511.

Valdes, F.: "Queers, sissies, dykes and tomboys: deconstructing the conflation of "sex", "gender", and "sexual orientation" in Euro-American law and society," *California Law Review*, 83 (1995), 1–377.

Valverde, M.: "Beyond gender dangers and private pleasures: theory and ethics in the sex debates," *Feminist Studies*, 15: 2 (1989), 237–54.

Vance, C.: *Pleasure and Danger: Exploring Female Sexuality* (London: Routledge and Kegan Paul, 1984).

——: "Negotiating sex and gender in the Attorney General's Commission on Pornography," *Uncertain terms: Negotiating Gender in American Culture*, ed. F. Ginsberg and A. Lowenhaupt Tsing (Boston: Beacon Press, 1990), pp. 118–34.

Vaz, K. M., ed.: *Black Women in America* (Thousand Oaks, CA: Sage, 1995).

Veatch, R. M.: *Medical Ethics: An Introduction* (Boston: Jones and Bartlett Publishers, 1989).

Verma, R. R.: "Development and gender equality," *Women, Culture, and Development*, ed. M. Nussbaum and J. Glover (New York: Oxford University Press, 1995).

Vetterling-Braggin, M.: "Some common sense notes on preferential hiring," *Philosophical Forum*, V: 1–2 (1973–4), 320–5.

——: ed.: *Sexist Language: A Modern Philosophical Analysis* (Totowa, NJ: Littlefield, Adams, 1981).

——, ed.: *"Femininity", "Masculinity", and "Androgyny": A Modern Philosophical Discussion* (Totowa, NJ: Littlefield, Adams, 1982).

——, Elliston, F., English, J., eds.: *Feminism and Philosophy* (Totowa, NJ: Littlefield, Adams, 1977).

Vianello, M., Siemienska, R., Darmian, N., Lupri, E., D'Arcangelo, E., and Bolasco, S.: *Gender Inequality: A Comparative Study of Discrimination and Participation* (Newberry Park, CA: Sage Publishing Company, 1990).

Vogel, L.: *Marxism and the Oppression of Women: Toward a Unitary Theory* (New Brunswick, NJ: Rutgers University Press, 1983).

——: "Debating difference: feminism, pregnancy, and the workplace," *Feminist Studies*, 16: 1 (1985), 9–32.

Voronina, O.: "Soviet patriarchy: past and present," *Hypatia*, 8: 4 (1993), 97.

——: "The mythology of women's emancipation in the USSR as the foundation for a policy of discrimination," *Women in Russia*, ed. A. Posadskaya (London: Verso, 1994).

Wacker, R. F.: *Ethnicity, Pluralism and Race* (Westport, CT: Greenwood, 1983).

Wacks, R.: *Personal Information: Privacy and the Law* (Oxford: Clarendon Press, 1989).

Wadud-Muhsin, A.: *Qur'an and Woman* (Kuala Lumpur: Penerbit Fajar Baki Sdn Bhd, 1992).

Wagner, S. R.: "Pornography and the sexual revolution: The backlash of sadomasochism," *Against Sadomasochism*, ed. R.R. Lindon, D. Pagano, D. Russell, and S. Star Leigh (Palo Alto, CA: Frog in the Well, 1982).

Waite, M. E., ed.: *A History of Women Philosophers* (Boston: Martinus Nijhoff, 1987).

Wajcman, J.: *Feminism Confronts Technology* (Oxford: Polity Press, 1991).

Walby, S.: *Patriarchy at Work: Patriarchal and Capitalist Relations in Employment* (Cambridge: Polity Press, 1986).

——: *Theorizing Patriarchy* (Oxford: Blackwell, 1990).

Walker, A.: *In Search of Our Mothers' Gardens* (New York: Harcourt Brace Jova-novich, 1983).

Walker, M. U.: "Moral particularity," *Metaphilosophy*, 18 (1987), 171–85.

——: "Moral understandings: alternative 'epistemology' for a feminist ethics," *Hypatia*, 4: 2 (1989a), 15–28.

——: "What does the different voice say?," *Journal of Value Inquiry*, 23 (1989b), 123–34.

——: "Partial consideration," *Ethics*, 101: 4 (1991), 758–74.

——: "Feminism, ethics, and the question of theory," *Hypatia*, 7 (1992), 23–38.

——: "Feminist skepticism, authority, and transparency," *Moral Knowledge? New Readings in Moral Epistemology*, ed. W. Sinnot-Armstrong and M. Timmons (New York: Oxford University Press, 1996a).

——: "Picking up pieces: lives, stories, and integrity," *Feminists Rethink The Self*, ed. D. Meyers (Boulder, CO: Westview Press, 1996b).

——: *Moral Understandings* (New York: Routledge, forthcoming).

Walkerdine, V.: *Schoolgirl Fictions* (London: Verso, 1990).

Walsh, S. I.: "On 'feminine' and 'masculine' forms of despair," *International Kierkegaard Commentary*, ed. R.L. Perkins (Macon, GA: Mercer University Press, 1987).

Walzer, M.: *Spheres of Justice* (New York: Basic Books, 1983).

——: "Interpretation and social criticism," *The Tanner Lectures on Human Values*, ed. S.M. McMurrin (Salt Lake City: University of Utah Press, 1988).

Ward, J.: "Harmonia and *Koinonia*: moral values for Pythagorean women," *Explorations in Feminist Ethics*, ed. E. Browning Cole and S. Coultrap-McQuinn (Bloomington: Indiana University Press, 1992).

——: ed.: *Feminism and Ancient Philosophy* (New York: Routledge, 1996).

Warnke, G.: "Discourse ethics and feminist dilemmas of difference," *Feminists Read Habermas: Gendering the Subject of Discourse*, ed. J. Meehan (New York: Routledge, 1995), pp. 247–62.

Warren, K. J.: "Feminism and ecology: making connections," *Environmental Ethics*, 9 (1987), 17–18.

——: "The power and promise of ecological feminism," *Environmental Ethics*, 12: 2 (1990), 121–46.

——: "Toward an ecofeminist peace politics," *Ecological Feminist Philosophies*, ed. K. Warren (London: Routledge, 1994).

——, and Cady, D., eds.: *Bringing Peace Home* (Bloomington: Indiana University Press, 1996).

——, and Cheney, J.: "Ecological feminism and ecosystem ecology," *Hypatia*, 6: 1 (1991), 179–97.

Warren, M. A.: "On the moral and legal status of abortion," *Monist*, 57: 1 (1973).

——: "Secondary sexism and quota hiring," *Philosophy and Public Affairs*, 6: 3 (1977).

——: *Gendercide: The Implications of Sex Selection* (Totowa, NJ: Rowman and Allenheld, 1985).

——: "The moral significance of birth," *Hypatia*, 4: 3 (1989), 46–65.

Warren, S. D., and Brandeis, L. D.: "The right to privacy," *Harvard Law Review*, 4 (1890), 193–220.

Warren, V. L.: "Feminist directions in medical ethics," *Feminist Perspectives in Medical Ethics*, ed. H. Bequaert Holmes and L. Purdy (Bloomington: Indiana University Press, 1992).

Wartenberg, T. E.: "An unlikely couple: the significance of difference in *White Palace*," *Philosophy and Film*, ed. C. Freeland and T. Wartenberg (New York: Routledge, 1995), pp. 161–79.

Waugh, J. B.: "Analytic aesthetics and feminist aesthetics: neither/nor?," *Feminism and Tradition in Aesthetics*, ed. P. Z. Brand and C. Korsmeyer (University Park: Pennsylvania State University Press, 1995).

Webb, B., and Webb, S.: *The Decay of Capitalist Civilization* (New York: Greenwood, 1969).

Weil, S.: "The *Illiad*: or, The Poem of Force," *Simone Weil Reader*, ed. G. Panichas (New York: McKay, 1977a).

——: "Letter to Georges Bernanos," *Simone Weil Reader*, ed. G. Panichas (New York: McKay, 1977b).

Weinbaum, B.: "Women in transition to socialism: perspectives on the Chinese case," *Review of Radical Political Economics*, 8: 1 (1976), 34–58.

——: *The Curious Courtship of Women's Liberation and Socialism* (Boston: South End Press, 1978).

——: *Pictures of Patriarchy* (Boston: South End Press, 1983).

Weinzweig, M.: "Pregnancy leave, comparable worth, and concepts of equality," *Hypatia*, 2: 1 (1987), 71–101.

Weir, A.: "Toward a model of self-identity: Habermas and Kristeva," *Feminists Read Habermas: Gendering the Subject of Discourse*, ed. J. Meehan (New York: Routledge, 1995), pp. 263–82.

Weisberg, D. K., ed.: *Feminist Legal Theory: Foundations* (Philadelphia: Temple University Press, 1993).

Weiss, G.: "Sex-selective abortion: A relational approach," *Hypatia*, 10: 1 (1995), 201–17.

Weisstein, N.: "'Kinder, Kuche, Kirche' as scientific law: Psychology constructs the female," *Sisterhood is Powerful*, ed. R. Morgan (New York: Random House, 1970).

Weitzman, L.: *The Divorce Revolution: The Unexpected Social and Economic Consequences for Women and Children in America* (New York: The Free Press, 1985).

Welch, S.: *A Feminist Ethic of Risk* (Minneapolis: Fortress Press, 1990).

——: "Sporting power: American feminism, French feminism and an ethic of conflict," *Transfigurations: Theology and the French Feminists*, ed. C.W. Kim, S. St Ville, and S. Simonaitis (Minneapolis: Fortress Press, 1993).

Welsch, W.: *Unsere postmoderne Moderne* (Weinheim: VCH acta humanoria, 1987).

Wendell, S.: "A (qualified) defense of liberalism," *Hypatia*, 2 (1987), 65–93.

——: "Toward a feminist theory of disability," *Hypatia*, 4: 2 (1989), 104–24.

——: "Oppression and victimization: choice and responsibility," "Nagging" Questions, ed. D. E. Bushnell (Lanham, MD: Rowman and Littlefield, 1995).

——: The Rejected Body: Feminist Philosophical Reflections on Disability (New York: Routledge, 1996).

Wender, D.: "Plato: misogynist, paedophile, and feminist," Women in the Ancient World, ed. J. Peradotto and J. Sullivan (Albany: State University of New York Press, 1984).

Wertz, D. and Fletcher, J.: "A critique of some feminist challenges to prenatal diagnosis," Journal of Women's Health, 1: 1 (1993), 173–88.

West, C.: The American Evasion of Philosophy: A Genealogy of Pragmatism (Madison: University of Wisconsin, 1989).

West, R.: "The difference in women's hedonic lives: a phenomenological critique of feminist legal theory," Wisconsin Women's Law Journal, 3 (1987), 81–145.

——: "Jurisprudence and gender," University of Chicago Law Review, 55 (1988), 1–72.

——: "Forward: taking freedom seriously," Harvard Law Review, 104 (1990), 43–106.

Westcott, M.: "Feminist criticism of the social sciences," Harvard Educational Review, 49 (1979), 422–30.

Westin, A.: Privacy and Freedom (New York: Atheneum, 1967).

Wheeler, D. L.: "A growing number," Chronicle of Higher Education (February 17, 1995). A9–A10. A15.

Whitbeck, C.: "Women and medicine: an introduction," Journal of Medicine and Philosophy, 7 (1982), 119–33.

——: "A different reality: feminist ontology," Beyond Domination, ed. C. Gould (Totowa, NJ: Rowman and Allanheld, 1983), pp. 64–88.

White, L.: "Subordination, rhetorical survival skills, and Sunday shoes: notes on the hearing of Mrs. G.," Buffalo Law Review, 38 (1990), 1–58.

Whitford, M.: "Luce Irigaray's critique of rationality," Feminist Perspective in Philosophy, ed. M. Griffiths and M. Whitford (Bloomington: Indiana University Press, 1983).

——: Luce Irigaray, Philosophy in the Feminine (New York: Routledge, 1991).

Wider, K.: "Women philosophers in the ancient Greek world: donning the mantle," Hypatia, 1 (1986), 21–62.

Wilkerson, A.: "Desire(s) unlimited!, or Do you have to be a cyborg to be bisexual?," Hypatia, 12: 3 (1997).

Williams, D.: "Sin, nature and black women's bodies," Ecofeminism and the Sacred, ed. C. Adams (New York: Continuum, 1993a).

——: Sisters in the Wilderness: The Challenge of Womanist God-Talk (Maryknoll, NY: Orbis Books, 1993b).

Williams, J.: "Deconstructing gender," Feminist Legal Theory: Readings in Law and Gender, ed. K. T. Bartlett and R. Kennedy (Boulder, CO: Westview Press, 1991a).

——: "Gender wars: selfless women in the republic of choice," New York University Law Review, 66 (1991b), 1559–1634.

Williams, L.: *Hard Core: Power, Pleasure, and the "Frenzy of the Visible"* (Berkeley: University of California Press, 1989).

Williams, P. J.: *The Alchemy of Race and Rights* (Cambridge, MA: Harvard University Press, 1991a).

——: "On being the object of property," *Feminist Legal Theory: Readings in Law and Gender*, ed. K. T. Bartlett and R. Kennedy (Boulder, CO: Westview Press, 1991b), pp. 165–80.

——: "Scarlet, the sequel," *The Rooster's Egg*, ed. P. J. Williams (Cambridge, MA: Harvard University Press, 1995).

Williams, W.: "The equality crisis: some reflections on culture, courts, and feminism," *Women's Rights Law Reporter*, 7 (1982), 175–200.

——: "Equality's riddle: pregnancy and the equal treatment/special treatment debate," *New York University Review of Law and Social Change*, 13 (1985), 325–80.

Williamson, J.: *New People: Mulattos and Miscegenation in the United States* (New York: New York University Press, 1984).

Willis, E.: "Toward a feminist sexual revolution," *Social Text*, 6 (1982), 3–21.

Wilson, H.: "Rethinking Kant from the perspective of ecofeminism," *Feminist Interpretations of Kant*, ed. R. Schott (University Park: Pennsylvania State University Press, 1997).

Wilson, T. P.: "Blood quantum: Native American mixed bloods," *Racially Mixed People in America*, ed. M. P. P. Root (Newbury Park, NY: Sage Publications, 1992), pp. 108–25.

Winnicott, D. W.: *The Maturational Process and the Facilitating Environment* (London: Hogarth, 1965).

Winston, K., and Bane, M. J., eds.: *Gender and Public Policy: Cases and Comments* (Boulder, CO: Westview Press, 1993).

Wire, A.: *The Corinthian Women Prophets* (Minneapolis: Fortress Press, 1990).

Wiredu, K.: *Philosophy and African Culture* (Cambridge: Cambridge University Press, 1980).

Wittig, M.: *Les Guerrillères*, trans. D. LeVay (Boston: Beacon Press, 1971).

——: "One is not born a woman," *Feminist Issues*, 1: 2 (1981).

——: "On the social contract," *Feminist Issues*, 9: 1 (1989).

——: *The Straight Mind* (Boston: Beacon Press, 1992).

Wolf, C.: *Cassandra* (New York: Farrar, Straus, and Giroux, 1984).

Wolf, N.: *The Beauty Myth: How Images of Beauty are Used Against Women* (New York: Anchor Books, 1991).

Wolf, S.: "Gender, feminism, and death: physician-assisted suicide and euthanasia," *Feminism & Bioethics: Beyond Reproduction*, ed. S. Wolf (New York: Oxford University Press, 1996).

Wolf-Devine, C.: "Abortion and the feminine voice," *Public Affairs Quarterly*, 3 (1989), 81–97.

Wolff, J: "On the road again: metaphors of travel in cultural criticism," *Cultural Studies*, 7: 2 (1993).

Wolgast, E.: *Equality and the Rights of Women* (Ithaca, NY: Cornell University Press, 1980).

——: "Wrong rights," *Hypatia*, 2: 1 (1987).

Wollstonecraft, M.: *A Vindication of the Rights of Woman* [1790] (London: Penguin, 1975).

Woolf, V.: *Three Guineas* (London: Hogarth Press, 1938).

Wright, E.: *Feminism and Psychoanalysis. A Critical Dictionary* (London: Blackwell, 1992).

Wylie, A.: "Feminist critiques and archaeological challenges," *The Archaeology of Gender*, ed. D. Wald and N. Willows (Calgary: Archaeological Association of the University of Calgary, 1991a).

——: "Gender theory and the archaeological record," *Engendering Archaeology: Women and Prehistory*. ed. J. M. Gero and M. W. Conkey (Oxford: Basil Blackwell, 1991b).

——: "Reasoning about ourselves," *Women and Reason*, ed. E. Harvey and K. Okruhlik (Ann Arbor: University of Michigan Press, 1991c).

——: "The interplay of evidential constraints and political interests," *American Antiquity*, 57 (1992), 15–35.

Yarbro-Bejarano, Y.: "Cherrié Moraga's 'Giving Up the Ghost': the representation of female desire," *Third Woman*, 3: 1–2 (1986), 113–20.

Yates, L.: *The Education of Girls* (Hawthorn, Victoria: Australian Council for Educational Research, 1993).

Yeatman, A.: "A feminist theory of social differentiation," *Feminism/Postmodernism*, ed. L. Nicholson (New York: Routledge, 1990).

——: "Voice and representation in the politics of difference," *Feminism and the Politics of Difference*, ed. A. Yeatman and S. Gunew (Boulder, CO: Westview Press, 1993).

——: *Postmodern Revisionings of the Political* (New York: Routledge, 1994).

——, and Gunew, S., eds.: *Feminism and the Politics of Difference* (Boulder, CO: Westview Press, 1993).

Young, I.: "Beyond the unhappy marriage: A critique of the dual systems theory," *Women and Revolution*, ed. L. Sargent (Boston: South End Press, 1981), pp. 43–70.

——: "Humanism, gynocentrism and feminist politics," *Women's Studies International Quarterly*, 3 (1985), 173–83.

——: "Impartiality and the civic public," *Praxis International*, 5: 4 (1986), 381–401.

——: *Justice and the Politics of Difference* (Princeton, NJ: Princeton University Press, 1990a).

——: *Throwing Like a Girl and Other Essays in Feminist Philosophy and Social Theory* (Bloomington: Indiana University Press, 1990b).

——: "Throwing like a girl," *Throwing Like a Girl and Other Essays in Feminist Philosophy and Social Theory* (Bloomington: Indiana University Press, 1990c).

——: "Justice and communicative democracy," *Radical Philosophy: Tradition, Counter-Tradition, Politics,* ed. R. Gottlieb (Philadelphia, PA: Temple University Press, 1993a), pp. 123–43.

——: "Sexual ethics in the age of epidemic," *Hypatia,* 8: 3 (1993b), 184–93.

——: "Gender as seriality: thinking about women as a social collective," *Signs,* 19: 3 (1994a), 713–38.

——: "Punishment, treatment, empowerment: Three approaches to policy for pregnant addicts," *Feminist Studies,* 20: 1 (1994b), 33–57.

——: "Mothers, citizenship and independence: a critique of pure family values," *Ethics,* 105: 3 (1995), 535–6.

Young, K.: *Planning Development with Women: Making a World of Difference* (New York: St Martin's Press, 1993).

Yusuf Ali, A., trans.: *The Holy Qur'an: Text, Translation and Commentary* (Brentwood, MD: Amana Corp., 1983).

Zack, N.: *Race and Mixed Race* (Philadelphia, PA: Temple University Press, 1993).

——: "Race and philosophic meaning," *American Philosophical Association Newsletter on Philosophy and the Black Experience,* 93: 2 (1994).

—— ed.: *American Mixed Race: Exploring Microdiversity* (Lanham, MD: Rowman and Littlefield, 1995a).

——: "Mixed black and white race and public policy," *Hypatia,* 10: 1 (1995b), 120–32.

Zalewski. M.: "Well, what is the feminist perspective on Bosnia?," *International Affairs,* 71: 2 (1995), 339–56.

Zerilli, L.: "A process without a subject: Simone de Beauvoir and Julia Kristeva on maternity," *Signs,* 13: 1 (1992), 111–35.

Zhou Yi: "A tentative analysis of several shifts in women's studies in China," *Jianghai Academic Journal,* 1 (1996).

Zielinska, E.: "Recent trends in abortion legislation in Eastern Europe, with particular reference to Poland," *Criminal Law Forum,* 4: 1 (1993), 47.

Zinn, M. B.: "The costs of exclusionary practices in women's studies," *Signs,* 11: 2 (1986), 290–303.

Zita, J.: "Lesbian body journeys: desire making difference," *Lesbian Philosophies and Cultures,* ed. J. Allen (New York: State University of New York Press, 1982), pp. 327–42.

——: "The future of feminist sex inquiry," *The Knowledge Explosion: Generations of Feminist Scholarship,* ed. C. Kramarae and D. Spender (New York: Teachers' College Press, 1992a), pp. 480–94.

——: "Male lesbians and the postmodernist body," *Hypatia,* 7: 4 (1992b), 106–27.

——: "Gay and lesbian studies: yet another unhappy marriage," *Tilting the Tower: Lesbian Studies in the Queer Nineties.* ed. L. Garber (New York: Routledge, 1994), pp. 258–78.

——: *Body Talk: Reflections on Sex, Gender and Racism* (New York: Columbia University Press, 1997).

Zones, J., ed.: *Taking the Fruit: Modern Women's Tales of the Bible* (San Diego, CA: Women's Institute for Continuing Jewish Education, 1981).

Index

676

681

687

689

691

703